INSIDE

3D STUDIO
MAX

VOLUME I

STEVEN ELLIOTT
PHILLIP MILLER

CONTRIBUTING AUTHORS:

JEREMY HUBBELL
JOHN N. JORDAN
DOUG KING
LARRY MINTON
GENE RUDA
ANDREW VERNON

CD-ROM textures created by Tim Forcade
Cover art by Frank DeLise

New Riders Publishing, Indianapolis, Indiana

Contributions from KINETIX

A Division of Autodesk

Inside 3D Studio MAX Volume I

By Steven Elliott, Phillip Miller, Jeremy Hubbell, John N. Jordan, Doug King, Larry Minton, Gene Ruda, and Andrew Vernon

Published by:
New Riders Publishing
201 West 103rd Street
Indianapolis, IN 46290 USA

Printed in the United States of America   2 3 4 5 6 7 8 9 0

Library of Congress Cataloging-in-Publication Data

    CIP data available upon request

Warning and Disclaimer

This book is designed to provide information about the 3D Studio MAX computer program. Every effort has been made to make this book as complete and as accurate as possible, but no warranty or fitness is implied.

The information is provided on an "as is" basis. The author(s) and New Riders Publishing shall have neither liability nor responsibility to any person or entity with respect to any loss or damages arising from the information contained in this book or from the use of the disks or programs that may accompany it.

PUBLISHER	Don Fowley
PUBLISHING MANAGER	David Dwyer
MARKETING MANAGER	Mary Foote
ASSOCIATE MARKETING MANAGER	Tamara Apple
SOFTWARE SPECIALIST	Steve Flatt
MANAGING EDITOR	Carla Hall

PRODUCT DIRECTOR
Alicia Buckley

SENIOR EDITOR
Sarah Kearns

DEVELOPMENT EDITORS
Laura Frey, John Kane, Laurie McGuire

PROJECT EDITOR
Jennifer Eberhardt

COPY EDITORS
Carol Bowers, Larry Frey, Charles Gose, Howard Jones, Molly Warnes, Phil Worthington

TECHNICAL EDITORS
Larry Minton, Jon Parker, Todd Peterson, Mark Gerhard

ACQUISITIONS COORDINATOR
Stacey Beheler

ADMINISTRATIVE COORDINATOR
Karen Opal

COVER DESIGNER
Karen Ruggles

COVER PRODUCTION
Aren Howell

BOOK DESIGNER
Anne Jones

PRODUCTION MANAGER
Kelly Dobbs

PRODUCTION TEAM SUPERVISOR
Laurie Casey

GRAPHICS IMAGE SPECIALISTS
Steve Adams, Kevin Cliburn, Brad Dixon, Dan Harris, Jason Meyer

PRODUCTION ANALYSTS
Jason Hand, Bobbi Satterfield

PRODUCTION TEAM
Dan Caparo, Kim Cofer, Tricia Flodder, Aleata Howard, Laure Robinson, Elizabeth San Miguel, Scott Tullis

INDEXER
Erika Millen

About the Authors

Steven Elliott is Lead Technical Writer for 3D Studio MAX documentation in the Technical Publications group of Kinetix. He is a registered architect. Prior to joining Kinetix, Steven was an independent consultant who specialized in computer graphics training and production. He was also an instructor of AutoCAD and 3D Studio for the Autodesk Authorized Training Center network. Steven graduated from the University of Illinois with masters degrees in architecture and computer science.

Steven is the co-author of *Inside 3D Studio Release 3, Inside 3D Studio Release 4* and a contributor to *3D Studio Special Effects*, both by New Riders.

Phillip Miller is the Product Manager for 3D Studio MAX at Kinetix. He is responsible for coordinating support for 3D Studio MAX from the Kinetix side, while working closely with the Yost Group to ensure the best possible tool is created for the artists that use it. He previously managed Autodesk Multimedia's Developer Relations Program and has also led Autodesk's 3D Studio training program. Phillip is a registered architect, who before joining Autodesk, was a project architect in the Midwest. He graduated from the University of Illinois with a masters degree in architecture.

Phillip is the co-author of *Inside 3D Studio Release 3, Inside 3D Studio Release 4* and a contributor to *3D Studio Special Effects*, both by New Riders.

Jeremy Hubbell is a senior technical instructor for Kinetix. His primary responsibilities range from developing multimedia course curriculum to worldwide training and product development. His current project is the development of all training for 3D Studio MAX and the implementation of that training within the U.S., Canada, and Latin America. Since joining Autodesk in 1994, Jeremy has been involved in many projects—from the complete re-engineering of Kinetix training materials and curriculum to the development and publishing of all Autodesk training materials on an interactive CD.

John N. Jordan is a graduate in broadcast communications/video production from Asbury College. He has worked with such firms as Toyota, Super America, Lexmark, Bank One, the U.S. Department of Transportation, the City of Cincinnati, Kentucky Utilities, and many local and regional corporations. A member of the Computer Game Developers Association, John is co-author of *Cutting-Edge 3D Game Programming with C++*. John has also created artwork for *Vigilance on Talos V*.

Douglas King has been a writer/producer for the entertainment industry for six years. He is also a contributing editor for *Computer Graphics World* and *RePlay* magazines, writing columns about computer animation and the out-of-home entertainment industry. Douglas is also a computer animator who uses 3D Studio and Studio MAX exclusively, running on the Intergraph TDZ 400 workstation.

Larry Minton is owner of Avguard Animations, located near Columbus, Ohio. He has been a 3D Studio hobbyist since 1991 but recently decided to turn his hobby into a career. Larry was a 3D Studio MAX beta tester and was a technical editor for New Riders' *3D Studio MAX Fundamentals*. Larry is an active participant in CompuServe's KINETIX and AMMEDIA forums.

Gene Ruda is a writer, educator, and multimedia enthusiast who resides in the San Francisco Bay area. He provided consulting services to Kinetix as a Quality Assurance Analyst and Product Support specialist during the development and initial release of 3D Studio MAX. His experience combines film and television production with developing business, educational, and entertainment applications. He has most recently focused his efforts in the area of graphics tools and educational applications for children, providing creative and technical services for companies such as Broderbund, Mindscape, Autodesk, and Premavision (Gumby). Gene holds a degree in film from San Francisco State University and a Lecturer's position at Golden Gate University in San Francisco.

Andrew Vernon Andrew Vernon is an animator who specializes in Character Studio. He operates Moving Figure Animation & Multimedia in San Rafael, CA. Andrew worked in Kinetix Technical Publications and was the online Help System writer for both 3D Studio MAX and Character Studio. He frequently writes articles on 3D graphics, animation, and multimedia for magazines such as *3D Design*. For information about Moving Figure, see http://www.movingfigure.com.

About the Cover Art: Frank DeLise is a 3D artist and animator. He's a member of Autodesk's 3D Studio Max demonstration team. This image is a still frame from an 800-frame animation called "Render Engine." It is Frank's visual representation of what goes on inside the 3DS Max renderer.

Trademark Acknowledgments

Acknowledgments

Steven Elliott wishes to thank his wife, Jean, daughter, Mary, and son, Cameron. Their love, support, and—most of all—patience made this book possible. Thanks are also due to his colleagues at Kinetix who offered valuable insight and support. Lastly, Steven thanks J.C. Malitzke and Don McIntyre of Moraine Valley Community College for their professional support and encouragement over the years.

Mr. Miller thanks his wife, Karen, for her incredible understanding, support, and toleration during the writing of this book and the creation of this program.

New Riders would like to acknowledge all of the long hours, sleepless nights, worked weekends, gray hairs, headaches and backaches, and endless dedication that went into making this book the best it can be. Special thanks go to: Jennifer Eberhardt and Alicia Buckley who fought long and hard to keep quality high under a ruthless schedule; Stacey Beheler for always lending a helping hand and keeping the team organized; John Kane, Laura Frey, and Laurie McGuire for being a great team of developers; David Dwyer, Carla Hall, and Don Fowley for constant support and understanding; Larry Minton for great tech edits and bravely entering the world of authoring; Mark Gerhard, Todd Peterson, and Jon Parker for their eleventh-hour tech reviews; Frank DeLise for coming to the rescue with his fabulous artwork; our incredible production and art/illustration teams for pulling off the unthinkable; our outstanding design team for always enduring our last-second changes and creating a beautiful package; all the artists who contributed images to make this book fun to look at; Kinetix for always being so helpful and supportive; the contributing authors who did great work under the gun; and last, but definitely not least, Steve Elliott and Phil Miller whose commitment to bringing the best to the industry at the sacrifice of a personal life is truly amazing. Again, thanks to all!

Contents at a Glance

Contents

Introduction

When 3D Studio appeared in 1990, it was a breakthrough product. Until then, the few rendering or animation programs available for the PC were either extremely limited, very expensive, or both. 3D Studio opened the door to affordable, professional, and productive desktop rendering and animation on the PC and made computer animation a career possibility for many who would not have been able to do so otherwise.

The latest incarnation of 3D Studio is 3D Studio MAX. You should not think of 3DS MAX as an upgrade or even closely related to previous versions of 3D Studio. 3DS MAX is an entirely new program that shares the heritage and the name of 3D Studio and little else. But like 3D Studio, 3DS MAX is another breakthrough product. Until now, 32-bit workstation class animation and rendering was available only on expensive hardware platforms running equally expensive software. 3DS MAX again opens the door to professional quality animation and rendering, workstation class performance of Window NT, and a modern Windows interface at a price that is affordable to the desktop animator. *Inside 3D Studio MAX* is a companion to the excellent *User's Guide* and *Tutorials* that ship with 3DS MAX. This book adds greater detail to the new and sophisticated concepts that you must master. *Inside 3D Studio MAX* also demonstrates techniques and strategies for accomplishing effects that will help you to produce more and better results.

Inside 3D Studio MAX will help you get more out of the program, regardless of your current experience level. If you are new to using 3DS MAX, you will find this book to be a valuable next step on the learning curve—after you work through the documentation included with the software. If you are an intermediate or advanced user of 3DS MAX, you will find that this book provides many fresh insights and tips that you can add to your professional toolkit. If you are a veteran 3D Studio DOS user, you will find that many correlations are made between 3DS MAX and its predecessor.

3D Studio MAX Background

It is rare that a program and its creators evolve to a point where an entire rewrite of the code base is ventured upon. 3D Studio MAX is such a program. The Yost Group, the creative programming team behind 3D Studio, had the courage and vision in 1993 to leave behind the code it had created and optimized for MSDOS and embark on an entirely new operating system (from DOS to Windows NT), programming language (from C to Visual C++), and architecture (from specific to object-oriented). In all, 3DS MAX is the Yost Group's fifth modeling program, with its earliest roots reaching back to CAD-3D, Cyber Studio, and Cyber Sculpt on the Atari. Members of the Yost Group were also responsible for Animator, Animator Pro, and Deluxe Paint—the definitive programs for 8-bit paint and animation.

As always, the direction for 3D Studio MAX came from its users. The wishes from thousands of loyal 3D Studio users made it clear that an upgrade to the existing product would not do and that an entirely new product was needed to grant what was wished for. 3D Studio had reached its maturity and its core team was intact, growing, and ready to take on the challenge. Several lessons learned from 3D Studio R1-4 that were instrumental in forging 3DS MAX were the need for extensibility, constant feedback, flexibility, total animation, and designing for the future.

3D Studio was first made extensible in Release 2 with IPAS plug-ins. IPAS was enormously popular, with hundreds of routines being created that allowed 3D Studio to be customized for professional needs. But IPAS was modal. Every plug-in was unique in operation, required a tremendous amount of user interface programming, and could not interact dynamically with the scene. For true extensibility, a program needs to be specifically built for expansion. With 3D Studio MAX, nearly every function, even the Renderer, is a plug-in component that can be replaced and modified. Plug-ins created by developers or yourself integrate seamlessly into the interface. There is no difference in a core function and a third-party plug-in because nearly everything in 3DS MAX is actually a plug-in to begin with. In design, 3DS MAX is more of a platform for modeling, animation, and rendering than it is a tool for doing such.

3DS MAX achieves constant feedback through the modeless nature of plug-in components and their dynamic link to its fast 3D graphics. The days of blindly adjusting values in a dialog box and having to click on OK to see the result are gone. In 3DS MAX, adjustments you make are immediately shown in the viewports as you adjust them in the scene. Flexibility is achieved through the concept of an edit history, where every modeling action is recorded for future modification. You can always experiment and change your mind. Animation permeates the system, where nearly every parameter you adjust can be animated over time. The edit history extends this concept by making it possible to animate the very modeling decisions used to form the model.

Finally, 3DS MAX is designed for the future. 3D Studio was bold in being designed for hardware that was not yet available. 3D Studio debuted with the Intel 386 and the capability to use extended memory and never looked back. 3DS MAX came into being along side the Intel Pentium Pro and is similarly thinking progressively by being designed specifically for Windows NT, multiple processors, graphics acceleration, rendering across the Internet, and being a platform for every 3D developer. 3D Studio MAX is clearly a broad, solid foundation that you can build a modeling and animation career upon.

Getting the Most from *Inside 3D Studio MAX*

As previously stated, *Inside 3D Studio MAX* is a companion to the documentation that ships with the 3DS MAX program, not a replacement. The best approach to getting the most out of 3DS MAX is to make sure that you have at least lightly read the *User's Guide* volumes and performed the *Tutorials*. The 3DS MAX documentation provides the foundation on which *Inside 3D Studio MAX* is built.

Two approaches are available for using *Inside 3D Studio MAX*. One is to just sit down and read it. Several figures are included to illustrate techniques and discussions in the book. In addition, you will find figures for the major steps in the examples so that you can simply read the examples and pick up the important concepts.

A better method for using *Inside 3D Studio MAX*, however, is to try working through the examples at your computer. To expect you to sit at your computer while reading the sections between the examples is unrealistic. Therefore, here is one possible strategy. Read one or two chapters at your leisure, away from the computer. While reading, mark the examples or techniques that you have trouble visualizing. After completing one or two chapters, go to your computer and try the examples for those chapters. Refer to the marks you made while reading and manually work through those techniques. By using this method, you can maximize your comfort while reading in your favorite chair and maximize your productivity at the computer.

Using the 3D Studio MAX Documentation with This Book

To save time and maximize the value you receive from this book, a strong effort was made to avoid repeating information that you could get from the 3DS MAX documentation. Although it was not possible to avoid repetition completely, you will find that the majority of the information *Inside 3D Studio MAX* presents is either a completely new strategy for using 3DS MAX or information that builds upon concepts and functions that were only introduced or lightly covered in the documentation.

This approach assumes you are partially familiar with the information in the 3D Studio MAX documentation. Sometimes you will encounter a reference to a description or tutorial in the 3D Studio MAX documentation while reading this book. You need not be familiar with the referenced information to proceed, but it will help. You can use references from *Inside 3D Studio MAX* to help identify portions of the documentation that you missed or forgot about and then return to the 3DS MAX documentation and review the appropriate sections.

Organization of the Book

Inside 3D Studio MAX is organized around four sections:

I   "An Introduction to 3D Studio MAX and Windows NT," Chapters 1 through 6

II   "Building 3D Scenes," Chapters 7 through 22

III   "Animating Your Scenes," Chapters 23 through 25

IV   "Output Techniques," Chapters 26 through 29

Part I covers issues of setting up and configuring 3D Studio MAX, file management techniques, concepts of perspective, color, motion, and some universal techniques that are common to most tasks that you perform with 3DS MAX. The chapters in this section provide a framework for using 3DS MAX and later sections depend on your understanding of the basics presented here. Think of it as setting up your workshop—by the end of this section, you will have arranged all of your tools and prepared them for use. The remaining chapters provide information on how to use these tools.

Part II is relatively large because it contains the detail for creating models, constructing hierarchies, lighting and viewing your scene, and defining the materials for surfaces. This section is the core to this book and relies on your understanding of what was presented in Part I.

Part III relates specifically to animation. This section may appear to be small in size because animation within 3DS MAX can be summed up as "if you can adjust it, you can animate it." So rather than describe what can be animated, this section explores how to control animation.

Part IV concludes by detailing the methods for getting the incredible images created in 3DS MAX to print, video, or film.

How to Read the Examples

Unlike most tutorials that you read, the *Inside 3D Studio MAX* examples do not rigidly dictate every step you perform to achieve the desired result. These examples are designed to be flexible and to work with a wide range of situations. The benefits you receive from this approach include

- A better understanding of the concepts because you must think through the example rather than blindly follow the minutiae of many steps.

- A stronger ability to apply the examples to your own work.

Most exercises begin with some explanatory text as shown in the following sample exercise. The text tells you what the exercise should accomplish and sets the context for the exercise.

SAMPLE EXAMPLE FORMAT

You may encounter text such as this at the beginning of or in the middle of an exercise when one or more actions require an extended explanation.

1. Numbered steps identify your actions to complete the exercise.

   Indented text adds extra explanation about the previous step when it is needed.

The word *choose* in an example always indicates a menu selection. If the selection involves a pull-down menu, you will be told explicitly where to find the menu item. If the selection is from another part of the user interface, you will be told which component to click and the location of the interface. Setting the Hemisphere option for a Sphere object, for example, requires clicking the Hemisphere check box in the Creation Parameters rollout (you would have been told previously whether you were accessing the rollout from the Create panel or the Modify panel). The word *select* always refers to selecting one or more objects, elements, faces, or vertices. Select never refers to menus or other user interface components.

Because this book is designed for people who already have some experience with 3D Studio, some exercise steps are implied rather than explicitly stated. You may, for example, find yourself instructed to "Create a smooth, 20-segment Sphere with a radius of 100 units," rather than reading all of the steps required to create the sphere.

Exercises and the CD-ROM

Some of the examples and exercises use files that are either included on the *Inside 3D Studio MAX* CD-ROM or shipped with 3D Studio, or they show you how to create the necessary geometry. Example files are located in the projects folder and are organized by chapter on the CD-ROM. Instructions on how to use the CD-ROM files or how to install them on your hard drive are described in the following section.

Using the *Inside 3D Studio MAX* CD-ROM

Inside 3D Studio MAX comes with a CD-ROM packed with many megabytes of texture maps, demos, plug-ins, and other sample software. The files can be used directly from the *Inside 3D Studio MAX* CD-ROM, or you may want to copy files from the CD-ROM to your hard drive or another storage device. In that case, you can use the CD-ROM install routine or copy the files directly to a directory on your hard disk. A number of sample scenes and several megabytes of texture maps are provided on the CD-ROM for your use. These scenes and texture maps are licensed free for use in your animations. You cannot, however, resell or otherwise distribute the files.

Installing the Example Files

Example files not included with 3D Studio MAX are contained in a single subdirectory on the *Inside 3D Studio MAX* CD-ROM: projects. You can access these files directly from the CD-ROM when you execute the examples, or you can run the install routine by double-clicking setup.exe. Some of the example files require maps from the CD-ROM that ships with 3D Studio MAX. You will need to copy these files to a subdirectory that is referenced in the 3DS MAX Map-Paths parameter. See Chapter 5, "Planning Your Projects," for details on setting your map paths.

3DS MAX automatically looks for map files in the directory from which a scene file was loaded. If you copy the example files to your hard drive, make sure you keep the mesh files and map files together or at least put the map files in a directory where 3D Studio can find them at rendering time. Details about organizing and managing map files are also presented in Chapter 5.

Using CompuServe and the Web

The CompuServe Information Service is an online, interactive network that you can access with a modem and special access software. The most important feature of this service (at least as far as this book is concerned) is the KINETIX forum.

The KINETIX forum is an area of CompuServe that is maintained by Kinetix for the direct support of 3D Studio MAX and other Kinetix software. Hundreds of people from all over the world visit this forum daily to share ideas, ask and answer questions, and generally promote the use of 3D Studio MAX. If you ask a question on the forum, you are as likely to receive an answer from one of the original programmers as you are to receive an answer from any number of other 3D Studio MAX artists. And every question, from the most basic to the most mind-bending puzzler, receives the same quick and courteous treatment.

Kinetix also maintains a site on the World Wide Web where you can get the latest information about 3DS MAX, future software releases, and plug-in development. You can also send questions and feedback direct to Kinetix and download software. The Kinetix web site is www.ktx.com.

New Riders Publishing

The staff of New Riders Publishing is committed to bringing you the very best in computer reference material. Each New Riders book is the result of months of work by authors and staff who research and refine the information contained within its covers.

As part of this commitment to you, the reader, New Riders invites your input. Please let us know if you enjoy this book, if you have trouble with the information and examples presented, or if you have a suggestion for the next edition.

Please note, however, that New Riders staff cannot serve as a technical resource for 3D Studio MAX or for questions about software- or hardware-related problems. Please refer to the documentation that accompanies 3D Studio MAX or to the application's Help systems.

If you have a question or comment about any New Riders book, there are several ways to contact New Riders Publishing. We will respond to as many readers as we can. Your name, address, or phone number will never become part of a mailing list or be used for any purpose other than to help us continue to bring you the best books possible. You can write us at the following address:

New Riders Publishing
Attn: 3DS MAX Product Director
201 W. 103rd Street
Indianapolis, IN 46290

If you prefer, you can fax New Riders Publishing at 317-817-7448.

New Riders' 3D Studio MAX Web Site

New Riders has devoted an entire Web site at www.mcp.com/newriders/MAX to the 3DS MAX community. At this site you will find demos and reviews of many plug-ins, 3DS MAX-related hardware and software reviews, a shareware bank, image and animation galleries, a bug list, tips and techniques, and New Riders 3DS MAX book announcements. This list is updated regularly to bring you the most current information.

At the site you will also find updates to *Inside 3D Studio MAX*. Although the book is already published, the authors are committed to further updating the material. Appendices, updated chapters, new exercise files, and more will be posted to give all *Inside 3D Studio MAX* readers the highest quality and most current information available. Be sure to check the site often for updates.

The Three-Volume Set

Inside 3D Studio MAX is actually the first of a three-volume set. Due to the robust nature of 3DS MAX, New Riders is dedicated to bringing users detailed, top-quality information on all the features and functions of the software. Although *Inside 3D Studio MAX* is a complete tutorial and reference, we are publishing two more volumes to provide in-depth, advanced information on modeling, Material Editor, and animation not available anywhere else. These volumes will be presented in the favorite *Inside* style, packed full of detailed tutorials and valuable tips and techniques from industry experts to take you to the next level after mastering *Inside 3D Studio MAX*. *Volume II: Advanced Modeling and Material Editor* and *Volume III: Animation and Character Studio* will be published in early 1997.

Part I

AN INTRODUCTION TO 3D STUDIO MAX AND WINDOWS NT

Created by Robert Cobb
Advanced Video Communications, Inc.
Ft. Lauderdale, FL

Chapter 1

CORE CONCEPTS OF 3D STUDIO MAX

3D Studio MAX is a radically new approach to 3D modeling and rendering. The underlying concepts and methods of how 3DS MAX manages objects and data in your scene are radically different from earlier versions of 3DS and other 3D modeling and rendering programs. You need to understand these concepts if you are to be productive with 3DS MAX.

Concepts covered in this chapter include the following:

- Object-oriented behavior and the basic 3D Studio MAX object types

- Definition of sub-objects and how to access them

- Object Dataflow and how it affects your modeling process

- Using transforms and modifiers, and how they differ

- Copies, instances, and references, and how they behave

- How 3D Studio MAX uses hierarchical organization

- How 3D Studio MAX defines and controls animation

- Description of plug-ins and how to organize them

Concepts of 3DS MAX Objects

The term *object* is used repeatedly throughout 3DS MAX; it is an object-oriented program. Looking at 3DS MAX in programming terms, everything you create is an object. The geometry, cameras, and lights in your scene are objects. Modifiers are also objects, as are animation controllers, bitmaps, and material definitions. You can manipulate many objects, such as meshes, splines, and modifiers, at a sub-object level.

For the purposes of this book, the term *object* refers to anything you can select and manipulate in 3DS MAX. When extra clarity is needed, the term *scene object* is used to differentiate geometry and anything created using the Create panel from other object types. Scene objects include lights, cameras, space warps, and helper objects. Other objects are referred to by specific type, such as modifiers, maps, keys, and controllers. The following sections explain object-oriented behavior in 3DS MAX.

Object-Oriented Behavior

What is meant when it is said that 3DS MAX is an object-oriented program? *Object-Oriented Programming* (OOP) is a sophisticated approach to writing software that is currently becoming widely adopted in the design of commercial software. From your point of view as a 3DS MAX user, the most important aspect of object-oriented programming is how it affects the user interface.

When you create objects in 3DS MAX, those items carry with them information about what functions can be performed on them and what is considered valid behavior for each object. This information affects what you see in the 3DS MAX interface. Only operations that are valid for the selected object are active; other operations become inactive or are hidden in the interface.

Consider the following examples of object-oriented behavior:

- Select a sphere in your scene and click the Modify panel to apply a modifier to the sphere. Notice that the Extrude and Lathe modifiers are inactive. This occurs because Extrude and Lathe are invalid operations for a sphere. Only Shape objects can use the Extrude or Lathe modifiers. Figure 1.1 shows how the Modify panel changes when a sphere primitive is selected as compared to when a shape is selected.

FIGURE 1.1

The Modify panel for a selected sphere primitive and for a circle shape.

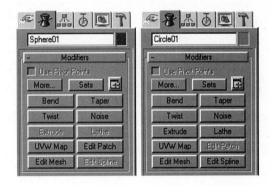

- For example, let's say you are creating a loft object and want to select a loft shape. After you click the Get Shape button, the cursor changes as you move over objects in your scene to indicate which objects are valid choices for the loft shape. Only shape objects meeting certain requirements are valid choices for the Get Shape operation. Figure 1.2 shows the appearance of the Get Shape cursor when it is over a valid path shape.

In both of the previous examples, 3DS MAX queries the objects to determine which choices and operations are valid based on the current program state. 3DS MAX then presents only those valid choices.

This seemingly simple concept enhances productivity and saves a considerable amount of time. Compare the behavior of 3DS MAX to older programs in which you select objects or execute commands and are confronted by an error message stating that the selected object or operation is invalid.

FIGURE 1.2
*The Get Shape cursor
as it appears when
placed over a valid
path shape.*

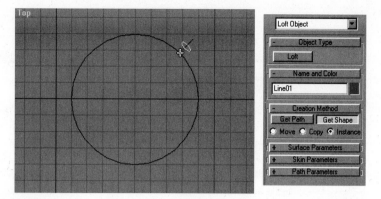

Parametric Objects

Most objects in 3DS MAX are a form of parametric object. A *parametric object* is defined by a collection of settings, or parameters, rather than by an explicit description of its form. For example, examine two methods to define a sphere—one non-parametric and the other parametric.

- **Non-parametric sphere**   Takes a radius and a number of segments and uses that information to create an explicit surface out of vertices and faces. The definition of the sphere only exists as a collection of faces. The radius and segment information are not retained. If you want to change the radius, or the number of segments, you must delete the sphere and create a new one.

- **Parametric sphere**   Preserves the parameters of the radius, and the number of segments, and displays a representation of the sphere based on the current value of the parameters. The parametric definition of the sphere is stored as the radius and number of segments. You can change and even animate these parameters at any time.

Figure 1.3 shows the base parameters for a parametric sphere and for a sphere imported as an explicit mesh.

Parametric objects provide considerable modeling and animation options. In general, you want to preserve the parametric definition of an object as long as possible. Some 3DS MAX operations convert parametric objects to non-parametric, sometimes called *explicit*, objects.

FIGURE 1.3

Base parameters for a parametric sphere and a mesh sphere.

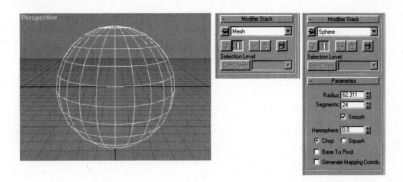

Fortunately, many operations do not discard an object's parametric properties. Examples of operations that discard parameters include the following:

- Attaching objects to each other using one of the Edit modifiers.

- Collapsing an object's Modifier Stack.

- Exporting objects to a different file format. In this case, only objects in the exported file lose their parametric properties. The original objects in the 3DS MAX scene are unaffected.

Perform these operations only when reasonably sure that you no longer need to adjust the parameters of the affected objects.

Compound Objects

In the Create panel, you can combine two or more objects to create a new parametric object, called a *compound object*. The important concept to keep in mind about compound objects is that you can still modify and change the parameters of the objects that make up the compound object. A compound object is a type of parametric object in which the parameters include the objects being combined and the description of how the objects are combined.

Examine a Boolean operation, for example, in which you subtract a sphere from the corner of a box (see fig. 1.4). When using many 3D programs, the result of this operation is an explicit mesh that represents the Boolean solution. If you want to change the position of the box or the radius of the sphere, you must create a new box and sphere, and perform the Boolean operation again.

FIGURE 1.4
*A box and sphere, and
the result of a simple
Boolean subtraction.*

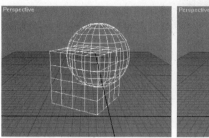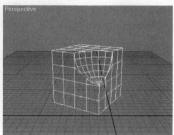

The box and the sphere are preserved as part of the parametric compound Boolean object. You can still access and animate the parameters of the box and the sphere, as well as animate their relative positions. Figure 1.5 shows the result of changing the length of the box and the radius of the sphere for the compound Boolean object shown in figure 1.4.

FIGURE 1.5
*The result of changing
the length of the box
and the radius of the
sphere for a compound
Boolean object.*

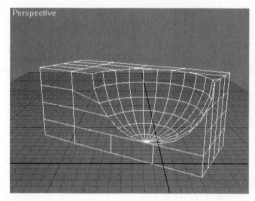

3DS MAX ships with three standard compound objects:

- Boolean objects
- Morph objects
- Loft objects

Sub-Objects

The term *sub-object* refers to any component of something that can be selected and manipulated. A common example of a sub-object is one of the faces that make up a mesh. By using the Edit Mesh modifier, you can select a sub-object, such as a face, and then move it, rotate it, collapse it, or delete it.

It is easy to think of sub-objects as vertices or faces, but the concept extends to many other things beyond scene objects. Examples of sub-objects you can manipulate in 3DS MAX include the following:

- Vertices, segments, and splines of shape objects

- Vertices, edges, and faces of mesh objects

- Vertices, edges, and patches of patch objects

- Shapes and paths of loft objects

- Operands of Boolean objects

- Targets of morph objects

- Gizmos and centers of modifiers

- Keys of motion trajectories

In turn, many of the preceding sub-objects have their own sub-objects, thus creating situations in which multiple layers of sub-object editing can be performed. For example, imagine applying a modifier to a sub-object selection of vertices from a mesh object, which itself is a sub-object operand of a Boolean object. The depth of 3DS MAX is limited only by your imagination.

In all of the previous examples, you access sub-objects by clicking a Sub-Object button in a command panel. Clicking this button puts you into a sub-object mode, restricted to working with a specific type of sub-object until you turn off the mode. Figure 1.6 shows two examples of sub-object selections and the corresponding sub-object button in the related command panel.

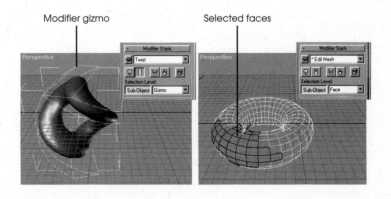

FIGURE 1.6
Sub-object selections of a modifier gizmo and selected mesh faces.

Concepts of Scene Object Creation

Your first actions with 3D Studio MAX will be the creation of scene objects that you later animate and render. When you create a scene object, you are creating a process that defines how the parameters of a basic object are modified, transformed, warped, assigned properties, and finally displayed in your scene. This process is called the *dataflow,* and understanding the dataflow is critical to understanding how 3DS MAX behaves.

The following sections describe each of the components of the dataflow individually—master object, modifiers, transforms, space warps, and properties—with the "Object Dataflow" section explaining how all of the components come together to place an object in your scene.

Master Object

Master object is the term that refers to the parameters of an original object you create using functions from the Create panel. You can think of this master object as an abstract definition of an object that does not yet exist in your scene. The object does not exist until the entire dataflow flow has been evaluated. The master object is just the first step.

The master object provides the following information about an object:

- The object type, such as a sphere, camera, loft, or patch. The object type is what you see at the bottom of the Modifier Stack or next to the Object container in Track View.

- The object parameters, such as the length, width, and height of a box. The object parameters are visible when the master object is selected in the Modifier Stack and when you expand the object container in Track View.

- The origin and orientation of the object's local coordinate system. The local coordinate system defines the origin of the object, the orientation of the object, and the coordinate space used to locate the sub-objects within the object. This definition of origin, orientation, and space is referred to as the *object space.*

Figure 1.7 shows an object with its master object properties identified. As you will learn in the section "Creating Instances," later in this chapter, more than one object in your scene can use the same master object.

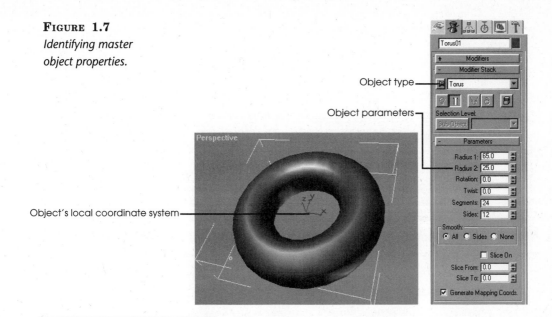

FIGURE 1.7
Identifying master object properties.

Object type

Object parameters

Object's local coordinate system

Object Modifiers

After you create a master object, you can apply any number of Object Modifiers, such as Bend or Stretch. Modifiers manipulate sub-objects, such as vertices, with respect to the object's local origin and coordinate system. In other words, modifiers change the structure of an object in object space.

Because modifiers operate on sub-objects in object space, they have the following characteristics:

- They are independent of the object's location and orientation in the scene. The top pair of objects in figure 1.8 show that a Bend is not affected if the object is moved or rotated. Both objects have the same form and same amount of bend regardless of where they are in the scene.

- They are dependent on the order of other modifiers and the structure of the object at the time they are applied. The middle pair of objects in figure 1.8 show the result of changing modifier order. Both objects have Bend and Stretch modifiers applied but the order of application is reversed.

- They can be applied to the entire object or to a partial selection of sub-objects. The bottom pair of objects in figure 1.8 show a Twist applied to the full object on the left and to a sub-object selection of only the upper-half of the object on the right.

FIGURE 1.8
*Characteristics of
Object Modifiers.*

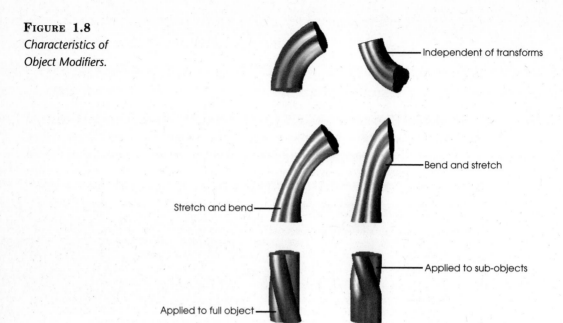

Independent of transforms

Bend and stretch

Stretch and bend

Applied to sub-objects

Applied to full object

Think of modifiers as your primary modeling tool because you have control over the order in which modifiers are applied. Also, the effect of a modifier on an object is consistent regardless of where the object is located.

Object Transforms

You position and orient objects using transforms. When you *transform* an object, you are changing its position, orientation, and size with respect to the scene. The coordinate system that describes the entire scene is called *world space*. The world space coordinate system defines the global origin of the scene and a set of global coordinate axes that never change.

Object Transforms define the following information:

- **Position** Defines the distance of an object's local origin from the world space origin. For example, position might define that an object's origin is 40 units to the right (X=40), 25 units above (Z=25), and 15 units behind (Y=15) the world origin.

- **Rotation** Defines the orientation between an object's local coordinate axes and the world coordinate axes. For example, rotation might define that an object's local coordinate axes are rotated 45 degrees about the world Y axis, 0 degrees about the world X axis, and 15 degrees about the world Z axis.

- **Scale** Defines the relative size between an object's local axes and the world axes. For example, scale might define an object's local space measurements are scaled by 200 percent in world space. Therefore, a cube might have parameters that specify a size of 40 units to a side, but because the cube was scaled 200 percent, it measures 80 units to a side in the scene.

The combination of position, rotation, and scale is called the object's *transformation matrix*. Notice that it is this matrix that you are changing when you directly transform an object and that you are working with the complete object. Figure 1.9 shows how transforms define an object's location in world space. The teapot in figure 1.9 has been moved, rotated, and non-uniformly scaled 125 percent along the Z axis and 75 percent along the Y axis.

FIGURE 1.9
Transforms define an object's location in world space.

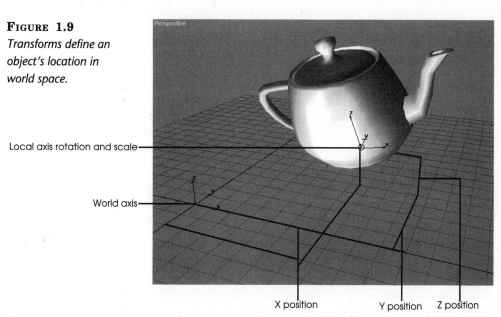

Object transforms have the following characteristics:

■ They define an object's location and orientation in the scene.

■ They affect the entire object.

■ They are calculated after all modifiers have been calculated.

This last point is particularly important. It does not matter whether you apply modifiers first and then transform the object or transform the object first and then apply modifiers. The transforms are always calculated after the modifiers.

Space Warps

A *space warp* is an object that can affect other objects based on their location in world space. You might think of space warps as combining the effects of modifiers and transforms. Like modifiers, space warps can change the internal structure of an object, but the effect of a space warp is determined by how you transform the affected object around the scene.

Quite often you will find identical effects implemented as both modifiers and as space warps. For example, look at the Ripple modifier compared to the Ripple space warp. Figure 1.10 shows a Ripple modifier and a Ripple space warp applied to identical objects. The parameters for both the modifier version and the space warp version are similar. The main difference is the way in which the two versions of Ripple act on an object. The Ripple modifier is directly applied to the object on the left and does not change as the object moves around the scene. The Ripple space warp exists as an independent object and the object on the right is bound to it. The effect of the Ripple space warp changes as the bound object moves through the scene. Notice that moving the object has no effect on the Ripple modifier but moving the object bound to the Ripple space warp has a great effect.

Use a modifier when you want to apply an effect that is local to an object and the effect is dependent on other modifiers in the dataflow. You usually use modifiers for modeling operations. Use a space warp when you want to use an effect that can be global to many objects and the effect is dependent on the objects' locations in the scene. Use space warps to simulate environmental effects and external forces.

FIGURE 1.10

Comparing modifiers to space warps.

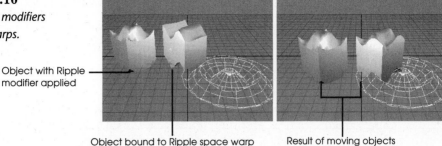

Object with Ripple
modifier applied

Object bound to Ripple space warp   Result of moving objects

Object Properties

All objects have unique properties that are neither base object parameters nor the result of modifiers or transforms. These properties include such things as the object's name, wireframe color, assigned material, and shadow casting capability. Most of an object's properties can be displayed or set using the Object Properties dialog. To display the Object Properties dialog, select an object and then right-click on it.

FIGURE 1.11

The Object Properties dialog.

The Object Dataflow

Modifiers, transforms, space warps, and object properties come together in the object dataflow to define and display an object in your scene. The object dataflow works like a set of assembly instructions. Each step is completed in the proper order before the next step is begun. The object dataflow steps are as follows:

1. The master object defines the object type and holds the values you set in the object parameters.

2. Modifiers alter the object in Object Space and are evaluated according to the order in which you applied them.

3. Transforms locate the object in the scene.

4. Space warps alter the object based on the result of the transforms.

5. Object properties identify the object name and other characteristics.

6. The object appears in your scene.

Figure 1.12 illustrates this sequence of object dataflow steps and its effect on a sphere.

FIGURE 1.12
The object dataflow.

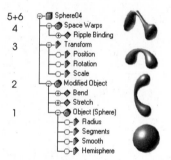

Concepts of Changing Objects

As you've read in the previous sections, there is a well-defined progression from the object parameters, through the modifiers, then the transforms, and finally the space warps and object properties. Often, you can achieve similar results by changing an object's parameters, applying modifiers, transforming the object, or even by using a space warp. Which method should you choose? Does it matter?

The answer is, "Yes, it does matter." The appropriate method for changing an object depends on the object dataflow, how the object was built, and what you plan to do with the object later. The knowledge to successfully make such a choice comes with practice and experience. The following sections provide general guidelines for determining the optimal method of changing your objects.

Changing Base Parameters Versus Transforming

The earlier in the dataflow you make a change to an object, the greater the influence that change will have on the final appearance of the object. The very first chunk of information in the object dataflow is the set of object parameters. If you want to make a fundamental change to the basic size, shape, or surface characteristics of an object, you should look at the object parameters.

For example, consider the difference between changing the height parameter for a cylinder and applying a non-uniform scale along the cylinder's local Z axis. Imagine you have a cylinder that is 40 units tall and you want it to be 80 units tall. If you're not familiar with parametric modeling, you first might think of using non-uniform scale.

If you scale the cylinder 200 percent along its length, you get a cylinder that is 80 units tall. Right? Well, not quite. If you examine the object parameters for the scaled cylinder, you see that the reported height is 40 units. What you really have is a cylinder that is 40 units tall with a 200 percent local Z axis scale. If you want a cylinder that is 80 units tall, you should change the height parameter rather than scaling the cylinder.

This change might seem like a subtle distinction, but it has a profound effect when you begin applying modifiers to the cylinder. Remember: In the object dataflow, transforms, such as scale, are calculated after the modifiers. Figure 1.13 illustrates the difference. The cylinder on the left had its height parameter changed from 40 units to 80 units and was then bent along the Z axis 180 degrees. The cylinder on the right was scaled 200 percent to reach a height of 80 units and then bent along the Z axis 180 degrees. Note that even though the scaling was performed before applying the bend, it is calculated in the dataflow after the bend—causing a non-uniform scale of the bent cylinder.

When changing an object parameter produces results similar to the results of transforming an object, use the following guides to determine which method to use:

- Change object parameters whenever you want to make a modeling change or a change that will be picked up by any modifiers.

- Transform an object when the transform effect is the last change you want to apply or when the change is being used to affect the location of the object in your scene.

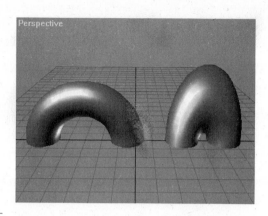

Modifying Objects

Use modifiers when you want to explicitly change the structure of an object and have the maximum amount of control over that change. Much of the modeling and animation capability of 3DS MAX is accessed through modifiers and their organization in the modifier stack.

Object parameters and object transforms affect the entire object only at the beginning or end of the dataflow. You can use modifiers to affect any portion of an object and apply changes that are dependent on their relationship to other modifiers in the stack.

For example, compare two arrangements for applying Bend and Taper modifiers to a cylinder, as shown in figure 1.14. If you taper the cylinder first and then apply a bend, as for the object on the left, you get a much different result than if you bend the cylinder first and then apply a taper, as for the object on the right.

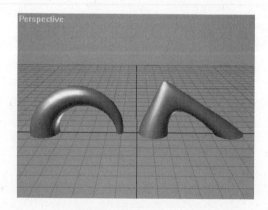

Because modifiers are so dependent on order, it is important that you plan your modeling strategy. Think about how you will approach a modeling job and the best way to combine modifiers. Your modeling plan does not need to be perfect, because 3DS MAX makes it easy to go back and change things if you change your mind. However, developing a plan can save you considerable time by avoiding the need to frequently backtrack as a result of trial and error.

Applying Transforms with Modifiers

Sometimes you need to apply a transform at a specific point in the modifier stack. For example, you may need to scale a non-parametric object along a single axis before applying a Bend. Other times you may need to move or rotate just a part of an object.

You can apply a transform at a specific point in the modifier stack, or to just a portion of an object, by using a modifier to apply the transform. The following are three ways to apply transforms with modifiers:

- **Use one of the Edit modifiers to transform sub-objects.** Edit modifiers provide access to the vertices, edges, and faces that make up various object types. Transforms that are applied with an Edit modifier cannot be animated. Figure 1.15 shows the result of scaling faces selected with an Edit Mesh modifier.

- **Transform the Gizmo or Center of a modifier.** Modifiers contain their own sub-objects, called *gizmos,* and a center that can also be transformed. Transform modifier sub-objects to rotate the orientation of a twist or move the center of a bend. Figure 1.16 shows the result of moving the center of a Bend modifier.

- **Use a special XForm modifier.** This modifier has no effect other than to supply a gizmo that you can use to transform objects and sub-objects within the modifier stack. Use an XForm modifier whenever you want a transform to occur at a specific point in the stack or when you want to animate the transforms of sub-objects selected with an Edit modifier. Figure 1.17 shows the result of moving the vertices of a spline with an XForm modifier.

FIGURE 1.15

Transforms: scaling sub-objects with an Edit Mesh modifier.

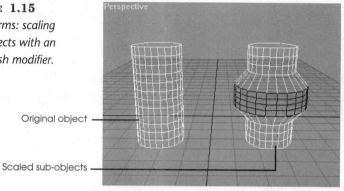

Original object

Scaled sub-objects

FIGURE 1.16

Transforms: moving the center of a Bend.

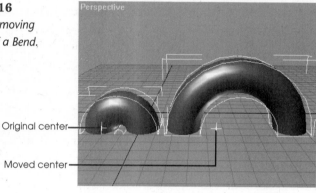

Original center

Moved center

FIGURE 1.17

Transforms: moving vertices with an XForm modifier.

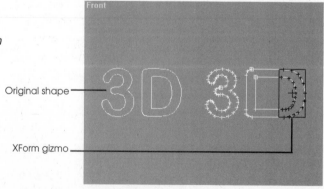

Original shape

XForm gizmo

Concepts of Cloning

You can clone just about everything in 3DS MAX. *Clone* is a general purpose term used to describe the action of creating a copy, instance, or reference. Most objects, such as geometry, modifiers, and controllers, can be copied and instanced. Scene objects such as cameras, lights, and geometry also can be referenced.

The following list defines copies, instances, and references:

- **Copies** Easy to understand. Everything that defines an object is duplicated elsewhere in 3DS MAX. Once you copy something, the original object and its copy are independent.

- **Instances** Describes the technique of using a single object definition in more than one place. Almost any thing can be instanced in 3DS MAX. A single object, modifier, or controller may be used for many purposes in your scene.

- **References** Available only for scene objects. A reference looks at the parameters of a master object and a selected number of modifiers before the dataflow splits, forming two objects that each contain its own set of unique modifiers. You can use references to build a family of similar objects that share the same basic definition, but each has its own unique characteristics.

You can choose from several methods to make clones. The method you choose to use will vary according to the type of object with which you are working. These methods include the following:

- **Press the Shift key while transforming an object.**   Depending on the object, either a copy is made or a dialog appears where you choose to make a copy, instance, or reference. For example, pressing Shift while moving animation keys copies the keys; pressing Shift while scaling a sphere displays the Clone Options dialog, where you choose to copy, instance, or reference the sphere.

- **Choose Clone from the Edit menu.**   Use this method to clone scene objects without transforming them.

- **Use Copy and Paste in Track View.**   When you paste a controller in Track View, you can choose to make a copy or instance of that controller.

- **Use Drag and Drop.** You can drag material and map definitions from one slot to another in the Material Editor. When you drop the material or map into a slot, the map is copied. You also can choose to make a copy or instance of the map.

Creating Copies

Create copies whenever you want to duplicate an object of which the duplicates are unique and have no relationship to the source object. Some examples of useful copy techniques include the following:

- Copy keys when you want to duplicate an action from one time of the animation to another time.

  For example, you might animate an object that quickly bends over and back again. To repeat that action at irregular times throughout an animation, you copy the original keys to different times.

- Copy controllers when you want the animated behavior of one object duplicated by another.

  For example, you want many objects to follow the same path, but you plan to adjust each path controller so each object is in a slightly different location. To accomplish this, assign and set up a path controller for one object and then copy the controller to all of the remaining objects. You can then change the location of each object on the path, having saved yourself the task of assigning and setting up the controller for each object.

- Copy scene objects when you want to begin with a group of similar objects and then individually modify each one.

  For example, you create a single flower and copy it repeatedly as part of a bouquet. You then change and modify the copies to give them each a unique "personality."

  When you copy a scene object, an entirely new dataflow is created for the copied object (see fig. 1.18).

FIGURE 1.18

*Dataflow after copying
a scene object.*

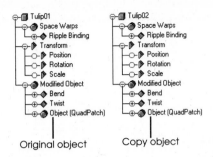

Original object   Copy object

Creating Instances

Create instances when you want to use a single object in more than one place. Because all of the instances are really the same object, changing one instance causes all of the instances to change. Instances can save considerable effort when used properly. Some examples of useful instance techniques include the following:

■ Instance modifiers when you want to apply the same effect to a selection of different objects.

For example, you create a scene where you want a selection of objects to stretch in unison. Select all of the objects and click on Stretch in the Modify panel to apply an instance of the same modifier to all the objects. Changing the Stretch parameters for any object changes them all. Figure 1.19 shows the result of an instanced stretch modifier.

FIGURE 1.19

*Using an instanced
Stretch modifier.*

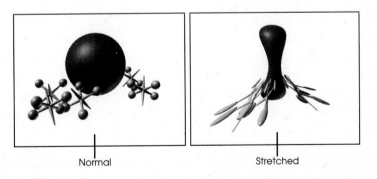

Normal   Stretched

■ Instance controllers when you want a selection of objects to behave in exactly the same way.

For example, you might model a set of window blinds and want to animate the slats tilting. You animate the rotation of one slat and use

Copy and Paste in Track View to assign an instance of the slat's rotation controller to all of the other slats. Then, when you rotate one slat, all the others rotate the same amount. Figure 1.20 shows the result of using an instanced Rotation controller to open and close blinds.

FIGURE 1.20
Results of using an instanced Rotation controller.

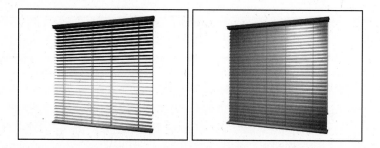

- Instance maps in the Material Editor when you want to use the same map in multiple map slots and maintain a precise registration.

  For example, you want to design a ceramic tile material. You can use instances of a map to control the diffuse texture, shininess, and bump of the material. Changing the parameters for any instance of the map changes the parameters of all the maps and maintains registration. Figure 1.21 shows the result of using an instanced map to build a material. First, the map is applied as a diffuse mask and then an instance of the map is applied as a bump map. Finally, another instance of the map is applied as a shininess map, and its tiling parameters are changed to create smaller tiles. Because diffuse, bump, and shininess are all instances of the same map, changing tiling for shininess also changes tiling for the other two.

- Instance scene objects when you want to place the same object in multiple locations in your scene. Modifying or changing the parameters of any instance changes all of the instances.

  For example, you want to show a row of bottles on a grocery shelf. Model one bottle and fill the shelf with instances. When you change the design of one bottle, the other bottles also change. Figure 1.22 shows the result of using instance objects.

  When you instance a scene object, all instances share the same dataflow from the master object through all of the modifiers. The dataflow branches after the modifiers, so each instance has its own set of transforms, space warps, and object properties. Figure 1.23 shows the dataflow for multiple instances.

FIGURE 1.21

Using instanced maps.

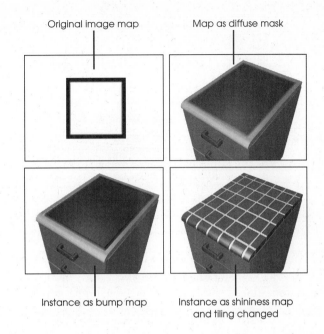

Original image map   Map as diffuse mask

Instance as bump map   Instance as shininess map
and tiling changed

FIGURE 1.22

Using instanced scene objects.

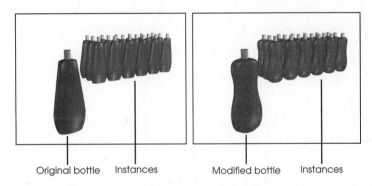

Original bottle   Instances   Modified bottle   Instances

FIGURE 1.23

Dataflow after instancing an object.

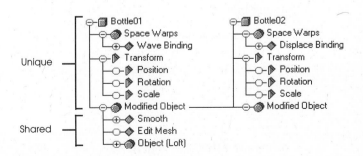

Creating References

Only scene objects can have references. Create references when you want multiple objects to share the same root parameters and modifiers, but also maintain the capability to further modify each object independently. Think of references as being a cross between copies and instances.

For example, you want to animate a line of chess pawns. Each pawn must share the same root design but also must bend or stretch on its own. First, model the basic pawn, and then make references. You can then modify each pawn independently or return to the basic model to change all of the references. Figure 1.24 shows the result of using references.

When you reference a scene object, all references share the same master object and an initial set of modifiers. When the reference is made, the dataflow branches after the last modifier, but you can still apply new modifiers that are unique to each branch. Each reference has its own set of transforms, space warps, and object properties. Whether a modifier affects one reference, some references, or all references depends on where in the dataflow the modifier is applied. A modifier affects all references that branch from the dataflow after the point in the modifier stack where the modifier is applied. Figure 1.25 shows the dataflow for multiple references.

FIGURE 1.24
Using referenced scene objects.

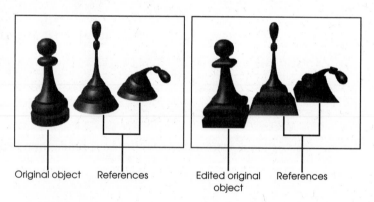

Original object   References   Edited original   References
object

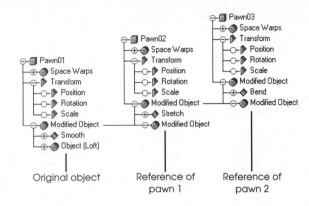

FIGURE 1.25
Dataflow after referencing an object.

Original object   Reference of pawn 1   Reference of pawn 2

Making Instances and References Unique

Anytime you are cloning an object, carefully consider whether the best choice is a copy, instance, or reference. If you are not sure, you should err on the side of instances or references. If you decide to make something an instance and later decide that you want independent copies, you can make the instances unique. Making an instance unique duplicates all of the information shared with other instances and converts the selected instance to an independent copy.

Unfortunately, 3DS MAX isn't very consistent in its methods for making instances unique. Different instances use different methods:

- Map instances are made unique by pasting a copy of the instance back into the map slot.

- Modifier instances are made unique by clicking on the Make Unique button in the Modify panel.

- Scene objects and controllers are made unique by clicking on the Make Unique button in Track View.

Concepts of Hierarchies

Almost everything in 3DS MAX is organized into a hierarchy. The concept of a hierarchy is quite easy to understand. If you've ever written a report using an outline to organize your thoughts, you've used a hierarchy.

All hierarchies in 3DS MAX follow the same principles. Higher levels in the hierarchy represent general information, or levels of greatest influence. Lower levels represent detailed information, or levels of lesser influence.

Scene Hierarchy

Track View displays the hierarchy of your entire scene, as seen in figure 1.26.

- The top level is the World. You can make certain global changes to everything in your scene by changing the World track in Track View.

- The level just below the world holds five categories that organize all of the objects in your scene. These categories are Sound, Environment, Material Editor, Scene Materials, and Objects.

- The many levels below the five categories hold the details for everything else in your scene.

FIGURE 1.26

Displaying the scene hierarchy in Track View.

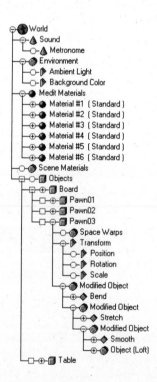

Material and Map Hierarchies

Material and map definitions are also organized in a multilevel hierarchy. Simpler programs use single materials and might allow only a single map as a texture. Others might allow one map for each channel, such as bumpiness or opacity. Using 3DS MAX, you can build hierarchical material and map definitions.

Material definitions can be multilevel hierarchies:

■ The top level holds the basic material name and material type.

■ Depending on the material type, you can have multiple levels of submaterials. These submaterials can also consist of multiple submaterials.

■ A material type of Standard is the lowest level of a material hierarchy. It contains material details such as color and mapping channels.

The mapping channels for a standard material can also be multilevel hierarchies:

■ Depending on the map type, such as Mask or Checker, you can have multiple levels of submaps. These submaps can also consist of multiple submaps.

■ A simple bitmap is the lowest level of a map hierarchy and provides details for map output and coordinates.

FIGURE 1.27

Displaying material and map hierarchies in the Material Editor.

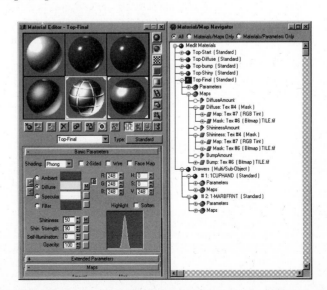

Figure 1.27 shows some materials with their hierarchies displayed. The material Top–Final shows a map hierarchy where Diffuse and Shininess use submaps combined with a mask, and Bump uses a simple bitmap. The material shows a Multi/Sub-object hierarchy with two submaterials (1CUPHAND and 1–MARBFRNT).

Object Hierarchies

Object hierarchies are probably the most familiar to anyone who has used a computer animation program. Using tools to link objects, you can build a hierarchy where transforms applied to one object are inherited by the objects linked below it. Link objects and build object hierarchies to model and animate jointed structures.

The terminology used for object hierarchies is as follows:

- The top level of the hierarchy is called the *root*. Technically, the root is always the World, but most people refer to the root as the highest level object in the hierarchy.

- An object that has other objects linked below it is called a *parent object*. All of the objects below a parent are its *descendants*.

- An object that is linked to an object above it is called a *child object*. All of the objects that can be traced from the child object back to the root are called *ancestors*.

Figure 1.28 shows an example of an object hierarchy.

FIGURE 1.28

Displaying object hierarchies.

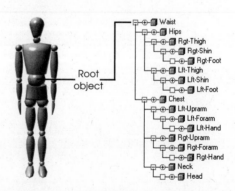

Video Post Hierarchies

Use video post to composite multiple camera views, animation segments, and images into a single animation. The way you build up the source material for Video Post is also organized as a special kind of hierarchy.

The Video Post hierarchy is organized as follows:

- Components of the Video Post hierarchy are called *events*.

- The top level of the Video Post hierarchy is called the queue. Unlike the other hierarchies, the queue can have multiple events at the top level. Each event is processed sequentially according to its order in the queue.

- Each event in the queue can represent a hierarchy of layering, filter, image, and scene events.

- The lowest level in a Video Post event hierarchy is the Image Input or Scene event.

- The last event in the queue is usually an Image Output event.

Figure 1.29 shows an example of a Video Post hierarchy and identifies its components.

FIGURE 1.29
Displaying a Video Post hierarchy.

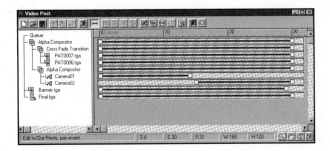

Concepts of Animation

The traditional definition of animation is the process of producing many images, showing an object changing over time, and then playing back those images so rapidly that they appear to be smooth motion. Oddly, even live action footage falls under this definition of animation. A movie or video camera captures images of live action at high speed for playback at high speed.

What differentiates animation from live action is the process of how the image is produced. Live action uses cameras to capture the images for play-back. Traditional animation requires that each image is drawn and then photographed as a single frame for playback.

This difference in process is why discussions of animation time are so heavily frame based. Each image, or frame of film, has to be drawn, inked, and colored by hand. This process led animators to think in frames:

"This action takes this number of frames."

"This should happen during that frame."

Imagine the response a director would get from an actor if the director said, "Now run to the porch in about 90 frames, pause for 20 frames, and fling open the door." Thinking in frames is an unnatural skill, forced on us by the limitations of animation technology. It would be so much easier if you could animate in real time:

"I want this to last for four seconds and then half a second later I want that to happen."

At the heart of 3DS MAX, your animation does occur in real time. You design a virtual world where actions are defined and take place in real time. It is not until you get ready to render that you must decide how you want time divided into frames.

Defining Time

3DS MAX is based on a time measurement system of ticks. Each tick is 1/4800th of a second. Everything you animate in 3DS MAX is stored in real time at a precision of 1/4800th of a second. As the animator, you choose how you want time displayed while you work and how you want it divided into frames when you render.

Specify the time display method and the rendering frame rate using the Time Configuration dialog. Using the Time Configuration dialog shown in figure 1.30, choose time display methods conforming to traditional anima-tion and video standards, or choose to work in real minutes and seconds. You can also set frame rates based on various standards or specify any custom rate that fits your needs.

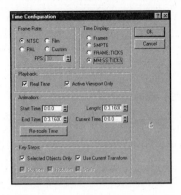

Defining Keys

Traditional animation relies heavily on a technique called keyframing. *Keyframing* is what a master animator is doing when he draws the most important frames of an animated sequence, the keys, and then passes on the work to an assistant animator to finish the frames between the keys. Depending on how difficult the animation was, the master animator might have to draw many closely spaced keys or maybe only a few keys.

3DS MAX works in much the same way. You are the master animator. You specify exactly what you want to happen and when it should happen by creating animation keys at specific times. 3DS MAX is your assistant animator and takes care of the animation that occurs in the time between the keys.

Create animation keys by doing the following:

1. Turn on the Animate button in the lower right corner of the 3DS MAX window (see fig. 1.31).

2. Drag the Time Slider, at the bottom of the 3DS MAX window, to the time when you want something to happen (see figure 1.31).

3. Move, rotate, or scale an object, or change virtually any parameter for anything in your scene. You can animate the vast majority of parameters in 3DS MAX. Only a few parameters cannot be animated.

FIGURE 1.31

Setting animation keys with the Animate button and Time Slider.

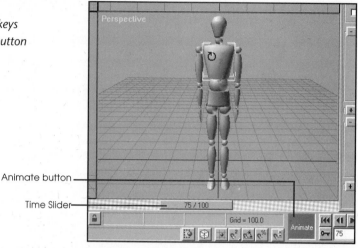

Animate button

Time Slider

Defining Parametric Animation

Another type of animation supported by 3DS MAX is parametric animation. You don't need to set keys with parametric animation because it is a preset animation effect. Specify the start and stop times for the effect and set its parameters—3DS MAX takes care of the rest. 3DS MAX ships with just a few parametric animation effects, but it is conceivable that developers will soon produce plug-ins for many more effects.

A good example of parametric animation is Noise, as shown in figure 1.32. You can assign Noise as an effect for almost any animated parameter:

- Noise assigned to an object's position makes it jump around randomly.

- Noise assigned to an object's scale makes it quiver like gelatin struck with a spoon.

- Noise assigned to a single parameter, such as a cylinder's height, makes that parameter fluctuate.

FIGURE 1.32

Parameters for Noise animation.

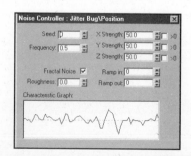

Animation Controllers

All animation in 3DS MAX, whether key-based animation or parametric animation, is managed by animation controllers. How an animation is stored, whether it uses keys or parameters, and how animation values are interpolated from one time to the next are all handled by an animation controller (or just controller for short).

3DS MAX automatically assigns a controller to any parameter that you animate using the Animate button and Time Slider technique mentioned previously. If you want to use a parametric controller, such as Noise, you must assign it yourself by using tools in Track View or the Motion panel. You can tell whether a parameter can be animated, or whether it has already been assigned an animation controller, by looking for the parameter in Track View.

■ Any item in Track View with a green triangle icon can be animated. Figure 1.33 shows cylinder parameters displayed in Track View that can be animated.

■ Parameters that cannot be animated do not appear in Track View. Figure 1.33 also compares cylinder parameters that can be animated with all of the cylinder's parameters in the Create panel. Note that only the Generate Mapping Coordinates check box cannot be animated.

■ Use filters in Track View to display the name of any controllers assigned to parameters. Controller names are appended after the name of the parameter. If a parameter does not have a controller name next to it, the parameter has not yet been animated. In figure 1.33, only the radius and height of the cylinder have been animated.

FIGURE 1.33
Animated parameters and controllers in Track View.

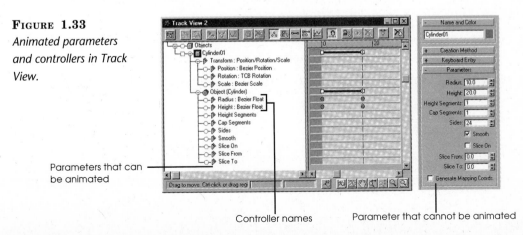

Parameters that can be animated

Controller names

Parameter that cannot be animated

Concepts of Plug-In Extensibility

Many programs support the concept of plug-ins to extend the functionality of the core application. The ease of use and value of plug-ins vary depending on the design of the core application and how well plug-in development is supported. Fortunately, 3DS MAX has a tightly integrated, robust plug-in architecture.

3DS MAX As a Plug-In System

The 3DS MAX plug-in architecture is so central to the overall design of the application, you could consider 3DS MAX to be a graphics plug-in operating system rather than a graphics application. In fact, most of the features that ship in the box with 3DS MAX are implemented as plug-ins.

You realize the following benefits from the 3DS MAX plug-in architecture:

- The core functionality of the program can be upgraded quickly and easily with new plug-ins.

- Plug-ins load automatically and are ready for use when you start 3DS MAX.

- 3DS MAX can be customized and extended as easily as dropping new plug-ins into the 3dsmax\plugins directory.

- Developers can integrate their new plug-ins so well that you may be hard pressed to tell where 3DS MAX leaves off and a plug-in begins.

Using Plug-Ins

If plug-ins are so well integrated, why have a topic about using them? Yes, you can just drop a plug-in into a directory and start using it. However, there are a few techniques that you might find helpful.

Installing Plug-Ins

If you install all of your plug-ins into the default\plugins directory, you could quickly end up with a mess of cryptic files lumped together in one place. Most major plug-in developers will write setup programs that place their plug-ins in special custom directories and register those directories with 3DS MAX. You might want to consider setting up specialized directories for other plug-ins that you collect as well.

3DS MAX makes identifying alternate plug-in directories quite easy. The Configure Paths dialog contains a panel in which you can identify as many plug-in directories as you need, as shown in figure 1.34. Any plug-ins in a directory identified in the Configure Paths dialog load whenever you start 3DS MAX.

FIGURE 1.34

The Plug-ins panel of the Configure Paths dialog.

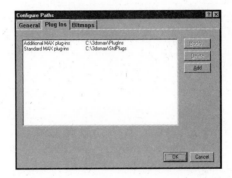

To configuring alternate plug-in directories, complete the following steps:

1. Create any new directories and place your plug-ins there.

2. Start 3DS MAX.

3. Choose Configure Paths from the File menu.

4. Click the Plug-ins tab in the Configure Paths dialog.

5. Click Add.

6. Choose one of your new directories from the directory browser, type a description in the Description field, and click OK.

Repeat steps 5 and 6 for each new plug-in directory created.

Finding Plug-Ins

After you install a new plug-in, where do you find it? That depends on what type of plug-in it is. In general, use the following four methods to access plug-ins:

- Object creators usually show up as a new sub-category under one of the seven creation categories of the Create panel.

- It is also possible for creation plug-ins to show up as a new button in the Object Type rollout of one of the existing sub-categories.

- Modifiers show up in the Modifiers dialog after you click the More button in the Modify panel.

- Other command panel plug-ins, such as in the Utilities or Motion panels, appear as either a new rollout or an entry in the category list.

- Most other plug-ins appear in option lists. Examples of these types of plug-ins include material and map plug-ins in the Material/Map Browser, controller plug-ins in the Replace Controller dialog, and atmosphere plug-ins in the Add Atmospheric Effect dialog.

Working with Missing Plug-Ins

One of the most important aspects of the 3DS MAX plug-in architecture is what happens when you load a file that uses a plug-in that is not installed on your system. It would not be too surprising if the file simply failed to load.

When 3DS MAX detects that a required plug-in is missing, it displays the Missing DLLs dialog, as shown in figure 1.35. This dialog lists the missing DLLs, provides information about their file names and usage, and provides the option to proceed loading the file or cancel.

FIGURE 1.35
The Missing DLLs dialog.

If you proceed, placeholders are created for the missing DLLs, the DLL data is saved, and everything else in the file is displayed. For example, a simple cube replaces geometry generated by an object creation plug-in. You can work with the file as you normally would, with the exception that you cannot make any changes to parts of the scene controlled by the missing DLL. Later, if you install the missing plug-in and reload the file, all of the information displays properly.

In Practice: Using 3D Studio MAX's Core Concepts

- **Object-oriented behavior** As a result of 3DS MAX being an object-oriented program, only operations that are valid for the selected object are active. Other operations become inactive or are hidden in the interface.

- **Parametric objects** Because parametric objects provide considerable modeling and animation options, you want to preserve an object's parametric definition as long as possible. Operations that discard parameters include attaching objects using one of the Edit modifiers, collapsing an object's Modifier Stack, and exporting objects to a different file format.

- **Modifiers versus space warps** Identical effects can be implemented as both modifiers and space warps. Remember, however, that modifiers are directly applied to the object and do not change as the object moves around the scene. Space warps, on the other hand, exist as independent objects to which other objects are bound. The effect of a space warp changes as a bound object moves through a scene. Use modifiers to apply an effect directly to an object. Use space warps to simulate environmental effects or external forces.

- **Changing object parameters versus transforming objects** Change object parameters whenever you want to make a modeling change or a change that will be picked up by any modifiers. Transform an object when the transform effect is the last change you want to apply, or when the change is being used to affect the location of the object in your scene.

- **Installing plug-ins** To reduce the number of plug-in files loaded into the default\plugins directory, you can set up specialized directories for plug-ins by using the Configure Paths dialog. Any plug-ins in a directory identified in the Configure Paths dialog load whenever you start 3DS MAX.

Image by Westwood Studios
Provided courtesy of Kinetix™

Chapter 2

MIXING COLOR AND LIGHT

Many skills must come together before you can create successful renderings and animations with 3D Studio MAX. When creating scenes within 3DS MAX you will realize that many disciplines are represented in the program. The arts of modeling, lighting, photography, theater, painting, and storytelling are all important skills for the professional animator. Perhaps one of the most important skills, however, is understanding how to work with color and light.

Color affects everything you see and do. Seeing the color red can make you stop, and even the color of a room affects your mood. You make important purchasing decisions based upon an object's color. Understanding the effects of color and how to exploit color to produce a desired effect are valuable tools. In this chapter, you explore various concepts of color and light and how they relate to computer graphics and 3D Studio MAX. In particular, this chapter discusses the following topics:

- Pigment color models

- Color as reflected light

- Mixing color in 3D Studio MAX

- Color composition

- Influences of natural light color

- Influences of artificial light color

- Influence of colored lamps

Color is usually the most referred to characteristic of a surface. When a stop sign appears red to your eye, you make the conclusion that the stop sign is "red." You accept this as a tangible fact and describe it as a red sign or that it is painted red. In reality, it is not the surface that is red, but the light reflected from it. The pigment with which the sign is painted absorbs all the light spectrum except for red, so it is the red part of the spectrum that reflects back to your eye. Your eye senses the reflected red light, and your brain concludes that the sign is indeed red. Figure 2.1 diagrams how white light reflects off such a sign.

Daily life and conditioning betray the effect that color is actually reflected light to most people. This should not be surprising because, as a rule, you do not interact with colors of light. You do not specify it, you rarely mix or play with it, and you are in few situations where the majority of the spectrum is not present. You are accustomed to the effects of white, or near-white, light during most of your life. For the most part, you interact with color by dealing with substances that reflect light predictably. These substances are called pigments. Even if you do not use traditional artistic pigments, such as paints or ink, you experience the color mixing of pigments whenever you cook, mix drinks, spill liquids, or even have laundry disasters. Color is an important component of your life—you coordinate and match colors whenever you design, decorate, or dress.

FIGURE 2.1
Light striking a stop sign and reflecting back red and white light.

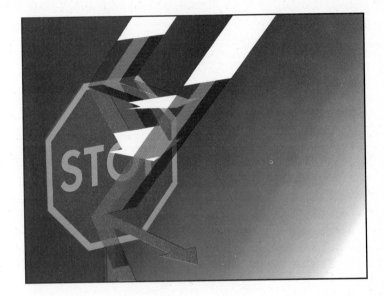

But computer rendering and painting on a computer screen are quite different from what you have been taught your whole life about color. You are now using a device that communicates with light (your computer monitor) and tools to create and manipulate light (3DS MAX and perhaps other paint programs). The important realization to make is that the color of light, which pigments reflect, is actually the "color" that your eyes see. This may be a leap in perception and your eye might take a while to become fully comfortable with the color. By first understanding the colors of pigment, learning about the intricacies and effects of light becomes much easier.

Pigment Color Models

The color model you learned as a child, and probably used since, is based on pigment. Yellow paint mixed with blue paint forms swirls of green paint. These are the color rules that pigments, paints, and even crayons follow. You were probably taught that there are three primary colors: red, yellow, and blue. As primaries, you may have been told these colors are pure—they are not mixed from any others, and they are used to mix all other colors. When these primary colors are mixed in equal strength, the secondary colors—orange, green, and purple—are formed. The infinite number of gradations possible between these primary and secondary colors is often referred to as being harmonious, or analogous. Because color models are based on their primaries, this model is often referred to as the Red-Yellow-Blue (RYB) color model. Although intuitive, this model is not completely correct because every color cannot be mixed from the three primaries.

The RYB Color Model

The color wheel is the traditional tool for demonstrating the RYB model, as shown in figure 2.2. The primaries are placed on an equilateral triangle that has the secondary colors forming an inverse triangle. Colors proceed around the circle in the order of the light spectrum, or rainbow. Many artists organize their palettes as a color wheel so that color mixing is quick and predictable. (It is somewhat ironic that although the palette is organized according to the light spectrum, it is primarily used to discuss the mixing of pigments.)

FIGURE 2.2
The RYB Color Wheel and overlapping paint circles. This figure refers to color plate 1.

Blending Pigment Color

Three overlapping circles of primary colored "paint" serve to show the basics of pigment blending (see the first color plate). In the plate, the three circles mix to form the secondaries. Brown is formed as the three blend together in the middle, which is also the result of mixing complementary colors. Because these are across from each other on the RYB color wheel, they contain all three primaries. White is represented by the absence of color because it's actually the canvas or paper on which pigment is applied.

The color missing from the color wheel is black. As a child, you were perhaps taught to create black by mixing all the other colors, but that usually results in creating "mud," not black. Because of this difficulty, many people regard black as a primary and purchase it as a separate pigment. As the properties of color are further understood, however, it is apparent that the absence of black is actually a weakness in the RYB color model. Although the RYB model is intuitive in relation to the world's common colors, it is actually incomplete.

The CYM Color Model

Although the RYB model is extremely old and was used by most of the masters, it is not an accurate color model. Obtaining the true, intense colors of violet, magenta, and cyan by mixing the RYB primaries is as impossible as mixing a true black. Confronted with this dilemma, many art students are told that these colors are simply difficult to mix and that it is best to purchase them in tube form. This is actually a misunderstanding of color because the colors mentioned previously can never be mixed from red, yellow, and blue— they are *true* primaries. This is not to say that traditional artists do not know what they are doing; they are using a color model that they can relate to the world around them.

Pigment Primaries

The three pigment primaries of cyan, yellow, and magenta are actually the complementary colors of white light, whose primaries are red, green, and blue. Both of these models are shown in figure 2.3. All pigments (or subtractive substances) are formed from these three colors. The use of these primary colors make this the CYM color model. In the CYM model, red is a mixture of magenta and yellow, blue is a blend of cyan and magenta, and what most people regard as yellow tends to be yellow with a tint of magenta. One reason the CYM color model is not extensively taught is that these intense, primary colors are unnatural and difficult to find and relate to in the real world. A true primary in nature is rare, as is its day-to-day use.

FIGURE 2.3
*Three intersecting
circles of RGB light and
CYM ink (refer also to
color plate 1).*

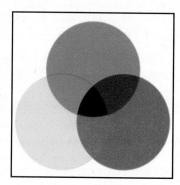

NOTE

If nature abhors a vacuum, it at least hates a pigment primary. This difficulty of creating true cyan, magenta, and yellow pigments is one strong reason why the RYB model has been used for so long and persists today. Pure yellows weren't actually available until the 1800s, and a true magenta wasn't developed until the 1850s. Artists through the ages have been forced to use pigments whose colors have already been subtracted, or mixed. A good example is to look at old color plates that use RYB as their mixing model. They often look flat and muddy because they rely heavily on black for darkening. This lack of intense primaries also is one reason that the old masters' paintings have a certain mood and color theme common to them—the intense primaries simply weren't available. You should consider this a testament to the skill and observations of earlier artists, rather than a reflection of their unfamiliarity with the CYM or RGB model.

Four-Color Printing and CYMK

An important difference with CYM is that mixing the primaries together results in black and not the familiar brown result of mixing red, yellow, and blue.

NOTE

When you create colors with the CYM model, and thus mix pigments, the ingredients often are expressed in terms of percentages of the mix (for example, 50 percent yellow, 45 percent cyan, and 5 percent magenta make a certain shade of green). These form the recipes for a painter's sundries. Using ratios to describe color is quite analogous to the color amounts you specify in 3DS MAX.

Color printing is a pigment-based media that requires black and uses the CYM model globally. Because of this, CYM often is referred to as an *ink color model*, in which cyan, yellow, and magenta are the primaries and black is created by mixing them. Three overlapping circles of "ink" serve to show this basic model. In reality, the mixed black is a very deep and intense blue or purple, but is perceived as black. Although you can mix all printed black after this fashion, the printing industry uses black ink in addition to CYM to prevent the alignment nightmare of requiring all three primaries to produce the black you see in most text and graphics. Printing is referred to as a four-color process, in which black is an added color—the K in CYMK.

Color as Reflected Light

Pigment color actually is the light reflected from an object. Colored light, the light reflected off objects, is what makes up our visible world. An object is red because it absorbs the blue and green spectrum and reflects the remaining red light. Figure 2.4 demonstrates this process by showing the illumination of two red stop signs with white lettering. The first sign is illuminated with white light, which reflects red off the field, and red, green, and blue off the lettering. The second sign is illuminated with only cyan light. Because there is no red to reflect back, the field remains black and absorbs all the green and blue light. The white lettering reflects back the green and blue light and now reads as being cyan.

Each pigment absorbs a particular portion of the spectrum and reflects the light with which it is associated. Mixed pigments actually subtract the various colors of the spectrum from the blend to form the new "color." Blue (which does not reflect red or yellow) mixed with yellow (which does not reflect red or blue) forms green by completely subtracting the capability of the blend to reflect red. Pigments are subtractive and are what 3DS MAX refers to when it talks about a transparent material in the Materials Editor being "subtractive."

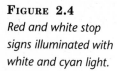

FIGURE 2.4
Red and white stop signs illuminated with white and cyan light.

The RGB Model

When white light refracts through a prism, its color components separate to create a rainbow. This rainbow is the spectrum particular to white light and the color range that the human eye can perceive. The colors proceed across the spectrum in the order red, orange, yellow, green, blue, indigo, and violet to form the acronym ROYGBIV (indigo is included primarily to make the abbreviation pronounceable). Of these spectral colors, the primaries are red, green, and blue, and the color model for light is referred to as the RGB model.

NOTE

Non-white lights refract their own spectrum because part of the total (white) spectrum must be missing for them to be "colored."

Whereas white is the absence of pigment in the CYM model (represented by the white of the canvas), black is the absence of light in the RGB model (and can be thought of as true darkness). The three primaries of light blend to form white light. As they blend with each other, they form the secondaries of cyan, yellow, and magenta, the primaries of the CYM pigment model.

The dichotomy between light and pigment is an important concept to grasp to fully understand how materials appear in varying lighting conditions. Light and pigment are opposites, yet complements to one another. One model's primaries are the other model's complements. RGB emits light; CYM reflects it. An object's pigment cannot be seen without light striking it, whereas colored light needs an opaque surface to strike to be seen. Combining all light colors results in white, whereas combining all pigment colors results in black. RGB mixes its colors by adding them, and CYM by subtracting them.

Mixing Colors of Light

Three overlapping "spotlights" of light demonstrate this basic model (refer once again to the first color plate). Here, black is represented by the absence of color, and white is created by the mixing of the three primaries red, green, and blue. As the pools of light mix, they form the secondaries cyan, magenta, and yellow. Viewing the two models side-by-side, it is suddenly obvious that the RGB model is truly the inverse of the CYM model, as each one's primaries are the other's secondaries.

The example model lightrgb.max uses three spotlights to demonstrate the additive RGB light color model. The model is made up of three spotlights shining down on a matte white square. The spotlights represent pure colored light on a white surface with no other light or pigment affecting them.

The scene in figure 2.5 shows three primary colored spotlights of red, green, and blue in two shaded viewports. These circles represent the light primaries. Where only two of the circles overlap, you see the pigment primaries of yellow, cyan, and magenta. Where all three circles overlap, you see the mixture of all light (white), which is equal to the absence of all pigment.

NOTE

The circles of light appear "jagged" around their edges in the shaded viewports because the 3DS MAX interactive renderer uses Gouraud shading for its display. This method calculates lighting effects by shading the vertices in the model. The effect of lighting will appear only as accurate as the displayed mesh is dense. To see the true effect of the light, you will need to perform a production rendering.

FIGURE 2.5
*The three
spotlights of
primary color in
lightrgb.max*

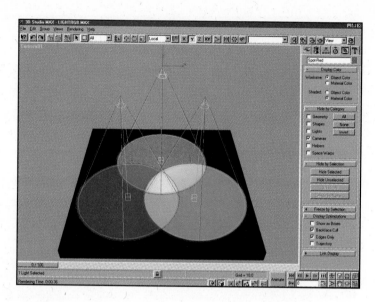

USING SPOTLIGHTS TO EXAMINE RGB COLOR

The following exercise demonstrates the additive RGB color model.

1. Load the lightrgb.max scene from the accompanying CD.

2. Activate the Top viewport and press the Quick Render button. The pools of light render as perfectly round circles.

3. Select the red spotlight, Spot-Red, and click the Modify panel to see the light's current settings.

4. Spot-Red has the RGB amounts 255,0,0—meaning that it is pure red light without green or blue components. The other spotlights are similarly saturated.

5. You can experiment with the effect of light by adjusting the color of the spotlights and repositioning them.

What you have to get used to is that light color is additive and pigments are subtractive. With additive colors, the more color you add, the whiter the hue; with pigments, the more color you add, the darker the hue. This concept is understandably foreign because most people outside the theater or lighting industry have little to no experience (or even the opportunity) mixing colors of light. But in reality, you are in the presence of the RGB model every day because every color television and computer monitor displays color through separate red, green, and blue channels.

EXPLORING RGB COLOR

A thorough understanding of the RGB model is worth mastering because nearly all computer-based color applications are based on the model. Happily, 3DS MAX's Color Selector (see fig. 2.6) provides an excellent method for mastering the concept of mixing RGB color amounts.

FIGURE 2.6

The Material Editor and 3DS MAX Color Selector.

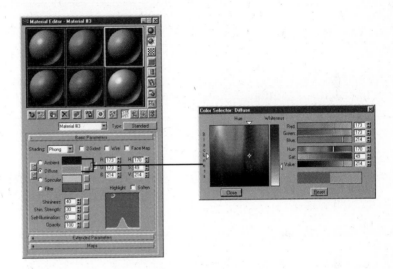

1. Enter the Materials Editor by clicking on the Toolbar's Materials Editor button.

2. Double-click on the Diffuse color swatch to bring up the Color Selector (it does not matter what material is active because you will be changing the color).

   The Color Selector simultaneously adjusts the color in its sliders and color swatch as well as the Materials Editor amounts, colors, and rendered sample sphere.

3. Click on a color in the Hue gradient or Hue slider and make sure that the Whiteness slider is not at the bottom of its range.

4. Move the Sat (Saturation) slider to 255 (all the way to the right) and ensure that the Value slider is not at an extreme.

   This creates a fully saturated color with at least one of the RGB amounts maximized to the current level of the Value slider while at least one of the others is minimized to zero.

5. Move the Hue slider back and forth while watching the RGB sliders.

As you move the slider across the Hue spectrum you notice that only one channel of the RGB sliders moves at a time. As you cycle through the spectrum, you are exploring the maximums and minimums of each red, green, and blue light component.

6. Drag the Saturation slider to 0 (all the way to the left).

As you decrease the color's saturation, notice that the RGB components slide toward one another until they align. Because the RGB amounts now are in balance, the light has no color and the swatch is gray. Remember this as a shortcut to create gray. Notice that the hue and luminance amounts are still intact, and if you increase the saturation, the original color is restored.

7. Manipulate all three RGB sliders so that they are not aligned and are not at either end of the slider and then drag any one of the RGB sliders to 0.

The Saturation slider moves to the right and the color swatch becomes fully saturated.

8. Drag the same RGB slider back to the right and you notice the Saturation slider moves to the right and the color swatch "grays."

Any color that has one or two of the RGB sliders at 0 is always a fully saturated color. This is evident as you drag one of the RGB sliders to the left. As you do this, the saturation slider moves to the right and reaches full saturation at the same time that the color slider reaches 0.

9. Set the Saturation amount to 255 and then drag the Value slider to the right and then back to the left.

All three RGB sliders move to the right and then back to the left simultaneously. As you increase the color's value, all three of the RGB channels increase to the right until the pure spectrum (hue) color is created. Decreasing the value slides the RGB sliders to the left until black is formed; no light is being reflected. You can create the same effect by sliding the RGB channels all the way to the right or left, with one important difference; the hue amount is constantly changing and is effectively eliminated at the extremes because there is no color.

FIGURE 2.7

The three negative spotlights of primary "ink."

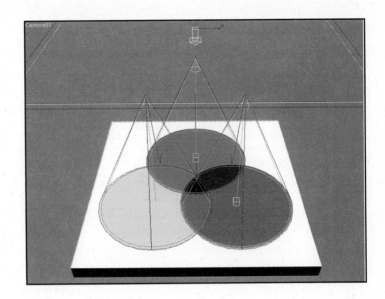

USING LIGHT TO EXPLAIN CYM PIGMENT

An interesting exercise that illustrates the CYM model can be done with light sources in 3DS MAX. Unlike the world around us, spotlights in 3DS MAX can be given negative multipliers to subtract light from the scene rather than adding it. Figure 2.7 illustrates how negative lights act much like pigments, as they strike surfaces and subtract the illumination of other (positive) light sources.

1. Load the lightrgb.max scene from the accompanying CD.

2. Click the Create tab to view the Create Command panel and click on the Lights button at the top of the Create Command Panel.

3. Click on the Directional button and place the new directional light in the center of the Top viewport.

4. Move the Directional light up to about the same height as the existing three spotlights.

5. Click on the Modifier tab and increase the V: setting to 255 to create a pure white light. You will probably notice light is restricted to a central area.

6. Check the light's overshoot box.

    This unrestricts the extents of the light source and allows it to illuminate all areas with the same intensity. The illumination of the other lights should be completely washed out because the surface is reflecting the white light back; there is nothing more for the red, green, and blue lights to contribute. The box surface should now be bright white.

7. Press the H Key and select Spot-Red and change its multiplier amount from 1.0 to –1.0. The once-red spotlight is now subtracting red from the white directional light and appears to be cyan.

8. Adjust the multiplier amounts for the remaining two spotlights to –1.0 as well.

    The result will be three circles of "ink" light—cyan, yellow, and magenta—that overlap to form the primaries of light—red, green, and blue. As all three circles overlap in the center, they form black because they are removing all positive light from the scene.

9. The resulting file can be found as lightcym.max on the accompanying CD.

Mixing Color in 3D Studio MAX

3D Studio MAX provides a unique color selector that gives you an intuitive method to select and manipulate color. Although all colors are stored within the system as raw RGB (Red, Green, Blue) values, the Color Selector (see fig. 2.8) enables you to pick and explore colors with a variety of methods.

Describing Color with HSV

Color can be elusive. "What type of green was that green awning?" "It was a deep, teal-green, but I'm not sure how blue of a teal, or really how dark it was." Recalling colors from memory accurately is difficult for anyone. Even when you concentrate on understanding an object's color, it changes as the character of the light that illuminates it shifts position and tone. "Oh, but that awning looked greener later in the day." For clarity, the color of a pigment is often described by three of its properties. Although most agree on the basis for these descriptions, there are several schools of thought as to what these terms are actually called.

FIGURE 2.8

*The standard
3DS MAX Color
Selector.*

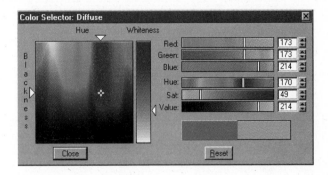

The part of the color wheel that a color is based upon is known as *hue*. If you were to take the Color Selector's Hue Slider and bend it into a circle, you'd have the color wheel. When people refer to the color of an object, they are actually referring to its hue. The term hue has fairly universal acceptance among color description systems. In the case of the awning described previously, the hue is blue-green.

The purity of a color is referred to as its chroma, intensity, strength, or *saturation* (as in 3DS MAX). You also can think of saturation as the degree to which a color has been mixed with other colors. A pure color is fully saturated because it has not been mixed with any other, in contrast to a gray color that has been mixed substantially and thus has a low or zero saturation. To continue using the awning reference, the color was teal, so it could not have been mixed with much red; it had fairly high saturation.

Each hue can range from very dark to very light and is often referred to as the color's luminance, depth, or as in 3DS MAX, its *value*. As a color deepens and approaches black, it has a low value; as it brightens its amount increases. A monochrome painting is a good example of one hue being used through all of its values. To finish with the awning, the fabric was deep in color, and so had a lower value.

Together, these descriptions of color are known as the HSV model—hue, saturation, and value—and can be used together to describe all colors. For traditional artists, these correspond directly to the Munsell System's hue, chroma, and value scales. 3DS MAX provides HSV color sliders as an option whenever you choose colors with its standard Color Selector.

Adjusting Color with Whiteness and Blackness

3DS MAX gives further control over color with the Color Selector's Whiteness and Blackness sliders. A color whitens and blackens by manipulating its saturation and amount simultaneously. The effect is very similar to adding black or white pigment to an existing paint color and is quite easy to identify with.

In practice, sliding the Whiteness slider from top to bottom adjusts Saturation from 255 to 0, while adjusting the Value from a starting amount to 255. Sliding the Blackness slider from top to bottom adjusts Saturation from a starting point to 0, while adjusting the Value from 255 to an ending amount. The Whiteness and Blackness controls do not influence each other or the Hue—their effect is to manipulate only the Saturation and Value amounts.

EXPLORING THE COLOR SELECTOR

3DS MAX's Color Selector is a great environment to learn color mixing. This exercise helps you explore the meaning of the HSV color sliders and how they affect each other. Figure 2.9 shows how the Color Selector is also available from the Object Color dialog.

1. Click the Object Color swatch in the Command Panel to access the Object Color dialog and then double-click on the Active Color: color swatch to bring up the Color Selector (this Color Selector is identical to that of the Materials Editor).

2. Click on any color in the Hue slider and increase the Saturation and Value sliders to 255.

   You now have a pure spectral, or color-wheel-based, color hue displayed in the sample color swatch.

3. Drag the Hue slider left and right and notice the color changes in the color swatch.

   As you increase and decrease the Hue amount with the slider, the color shifts smoothly across the spectrum within the swatch. You are traversing the entire spectrum for pure color.

4. Drag the Whiteness slider down to the bottom and the sample swatch increases in brightness until it is pure white.

    As you increase the Whiteness, the Saturation amount decreases because additional RGB must be added to achieve whiter colors and thus desaturated the original color, and the Value must increase to lighten the color.

5. Drag the Blackness slider down to the bottom and the sample swatch decreases in brightness until it is a gray (the lower your Whiteness slider, the brighter the gray).

    As you increase the Blackness, the Saturation amount decreases because additional RGB must be subtracted to achieve grayer colors, and the Value must decrease to darken the color.

6. Drag the Saturation slider to the right and both the Whiteness and Blackness sliders rise.

7. Drag the Value slider left and right and you will notice that as the Value increases, the Blackness rises and the Whiteness lowers; the reverse is true when the Value is decreased.

FIGURE 2.9

The 3DS MAX Color Selector from the Object Color dialogs.

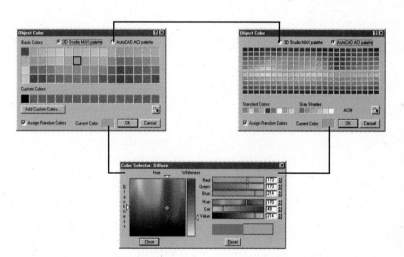

This exercise points out an important concept when mixing color in 3DS MAX. When you adjust either the Saturation or Value slider, or adjust both with Whiteness and Blackness, you are exploring the range of a given hue. Although there are similarities in creating color ramps between the two methods, the results of each are quite different. If you are creating a range of colors intended to share a chromatic range, you should stick to one method. Ramps of adjacent colors should be made by either adjusting the Value or Saturation independently or by only adjusting the Whiteness and Blackness controls. If the methods are mixed, the resulting colors will not be part of a consistent ramp.

The other fact to remember is that all color values in 3DS MAX are stored in RGB values only. This means that while HSV is displayed, it is the corresponding RGB values that are stored. Whiteness and Blackness never display values because they manipulate Saturation and Value simultaneously and are color mixing assistants only. Although you can refer to and record a given HSV value, the Whiteness and Blackness values are merely visual indicators.

Color Composition

Color is individual and personal—we all have our favorite colors and preferences for combining them. Yet there are rules or guidelines by which colors are coordinated, matched, and mixed in most things we see. An understanding of these considerations is important even when you are creating entirely imaginative worlds. These worlds are often based upon this understanding because it is our base reference for most things we create. Color composition influences us significantly whether we are painting textures with pigment or illuminating our world with light. Good color choices can set a mood and lend a sense of unity to a scene. Bad color choices make a scene look unrealistic, garish, dull, or cartoonish. This section discusses various subjective properties of color and how to use them.

You are simulating pigment in 3DS MAX when you define materials, backgrounds, and atmospheres. In all cases these are, or represent, surfaces. A surface reflects light and the light it reflects back to your viewpoint is its color. The color of this reflected light is influenced by what colors the surface absorbs (the surface's color) and the color of light that is illuminating it. When discussing pigment colors, it is assumed that the majority of the spectrum is present with near white light.

Many terms are used to describe color, and the art world has standardized many of these terms and descriptions. Although you may not consider yourself an artist or artistic at this time, it is important to develop an understanding of these concepts because your work with 3DS MAX will undoubtedly bring you into contact with artists and their writings. These terms will be used throughout the rest of this book when describing color.

Complementary Colors

Colors opposite one another on the color wheel represent each other's complementary color. For the basic RYB model, the primary color complements are red and green, yellow and purple, and blue and orange. Complementary colors can be derived from any location on the wheel, as a reddish-orange would complement a greenish-blue.

Complementary colors have several important features. Used side-by-side, a complementary color brings out the intensity in its associated color and creates the maximum visual contrast to it. This also creates the most visual strain because the complements compete for one another's color—that which is missing from themselves. This can create an undesirable "jumping" or "buzzing" effect when stared at by the human eye. Blended together, complements create shades of brown and gray, acting to neutralize the intensity of the parent's hue and are usually avoided in traditional color mixing. When a colored object casts a shadow, it is shifted toward the object's complementary color. This effect extends to colored light sources that have the effect of casting shadows with a complementary color shift.

Warm Versus Cool Colors

The type and extent of hue present is commonly referred to as the color's temperature. Warm colors contain more red, orange, and yellow, whereas cool colors contain more blue. Warm violets are red-based and cool greens are blue-based. Neutral browns and grays also are distinguished by temperature.

Temperature is an important concept when assigning colors to share across an object or a scene. You should decide if an object is "cool" or "warm," then maintain consistency with your color assignments. Animals, for example, tend to share families of warm colors, whereas plants tend to be cool. A forbidding scene would tend to be quite cool in nature, whereas a pleasant scene would usually have a warm palette.

Advancing and Receding Colors

Warm and cool colors have the psychological effect of advancing or receding, an effect of the human eye's interpretation of the spectrum order (where red is first and violet last). Warm colors, especially red, appear to advance and come closer, whereas cool colors appear to recede and move away—one reason the majority of store signage is red.

Your experience with distance serves to reinforce this perception because the atmosphere cools colors by reflecting blue onto them as they extend into the horizon. Distant objects lose their color intensity and approach gray while their hues shift toward the blue spectrum. Keep this in mind when you create and edit background images. As the scene recedes into the horizon, it should lose intensity and become cooler. Doing this manually by using a paint program, or in 3DS MAX with a Mix or RGB Tint material, should be regarded as a subtle but essential step in creating realistic backgrounds. An appropriately colored fog environment can be used to obtain the same result for both the background and the entire scene.

Restrictions on the Use of Black and Gray

Many artists never use true black, but prefer to mix their own very dark, deep color blends. When mixed in full saturation, some adjacent colors on the RYB color wheel (Indigo and Crimson or Ultramarine and Hooker's Green are common combinations) can produce deep colors that approach black. The reason for this mixing choice is that black pigment ("out-of-the-tube") gives a flat, unnatural appearance. The dark, rich colors created from mixing are preferred because they appear to the eye to have more depth, and actually appear darker than colors mixed with pure black. Artists have learned to reserve black for creating burnt and stained effects because it tends to neutralize hues and create "dirty" colors.

Black also is reserved for mixing extremely cold and unnatural true grays. Very little in the real world is actually absent of color or truly gray, let alone black. Nearly all of the colors that you see around you have some red, yellow, or blue. Because this reflects human perception, it is an important concept to remember when you assign and mix colors in 3DS MAX. Although true gray is easily attained by sliding the Saturation to zero, it isn't in the world around you.

Because it is very rare for a gray to be absent of color, you should use true grays carefully. Objects based on true grays and lit with "gray" lights look unnatural and computer-generated. The reason is simple—creating this effect in the real world is very difficult. In general, a slight warm or cool color shift in lights, as well as materials, appears much more realistic.

The Impact of Lighting's Color

A scene may be full of surfaces with vibrant and well-designed materials but still look incredibly flat and pale. This is quite possible because a surface is merely a reflection of the scene's lighting. The color, placement, and intensity of your scene's lighting has the greatest impact on the resulting images. The following sections discuss color considerations for light. Chapter 19, "Lighting and Atmosphere" explores techniques for placement and intensity.

A perceived correlation exists between the color of a light source and the level of illumination. Bright illumination usually is associated with a bright blue sky and cool colors, whereas low illumination is associated with candlelight, fire, dimmed lights, and warm colors. Keep this in mind when you select the color of a primary light source.

Influences of Natural Light Color

The light that nature provides during the day is primarily white. Experience teaches you that bright sunlight is true white light, and it is natural to believe that the colors of an object are truest when viewed under direct sunlight. In actuality, the color of sunlight varies considerably in relation to the time, season, and weather.

You might be most aware of sunlight's color rendering capabilities when it is absent. Think of the number of times you have been in a store and been unconvinced of a material's color. The man-made light that illuminates the store doesn't provide the entire visible spectrum to correctly see the color. Your eye knows it and is trying to compensate for the lost color. You might even have taken the item near a window, or out the door, to view it in natural light and confirm the "true" color.

Sunlight

Sunlight is not easy to quantify because it expresses itself in many flavors, tones, and hues. Early morning sun can be a warm gray light on a clear day or a cool gray light on a foggy day. Late afternoon sun can produce a very warm, yellow tone, whereas a sunset might range from brilliant red to a mauve-purple. High-noon sun can easily be near white, while the ambient light casting through a north facing skylight at the same time might just as easily be cool. There are no formulas to calculate all the qualities of sunlight. You must learn to observe the world around you and apply your observations to the scene you create. Learn to look deeply into a photograph or a horizon and analyze the quality of light. When animating the sun, perhaps for a shadow study, you should also take into account how the sun changes color during the course of the day.

Atmosphere

The earth's atmosphere has much to do with the quality and color of sunlight. The more atmosphere, the more color effect. That is why we have spectacular sunrises and sunsets. When the sun is perpendicular at midday, it penetrates the smallest amount of atmosphere and is at its whitest. Sunlight also has varying properties according to longitude and time of year. The sun is directly overhead at the equator, low in the sky at the poles, high in the summer, and low in the winter. The sunlight found in the equatorial desert is some of the whitest that strikes the earth.

The atmosphere also has a magnifying effect on the sun and moon when they are close to the horizon. The bodies are visually larger during this time and their color influence is magnified as well. You need to consider the condition of the atmosphere because it also affects the light quality. An industrial, polluted sky creates a warm brown light, whereas the water-laden air of fog, rain, or snow creates a cool light. An overcast sky causes most light to be of a reflective nature and notably grayer.

Light in Outer Space

If you observe a scene that has no atmosphere, there is no filtering of the light, and there is very little, if any, reflected or ambient light to illuminate other portions of the environment. Scenes on the moon or in space should have extremely white light and nearly no ambient light, resulting in very crisp, black shadows characteristic of NASA photographs. Only areas of an object that can trace a line of sight to the sun are visible. The rest of the object is as black as the surrounding void. The shadow the earth casts on the moon is such an example. The dim outline of the new moon is all that can be seen from the ambient light of space.

Moonlight

Moonlight is nature's other contribution that illuminates the world. Most of us tend to think of it as a yellow-based "light," but doing so is too simple. The moon is just reflecting light from the sun. As the sun's light filters through the atmosphere, so does the moon's. The moon changes color as it moves in the night sky, much as the sun does. The moon's light is a characteristically warm yellow as it sits low in the sky and becomes whiter as it climbs higher. Because the moon is such a weak light source, the illumination available is low and the amount of light reflected off surfaces is minimized. The ambient light of a scene that portrays moonlight should be quite low and have a strong color shift to the moon's complementary color.

Influences of Artificial Light Color

Much of your time is spent indoors within environments illuminated primarily by artificial light. If you are to render and animate interior scenes correctly, you must understand the various colors of artificial light and how your eye perceives them. The lighting industry has many terms for its trade and this book tries to respect standard terminology when appropriate. When describing real world lighting, a lamp is a light source (most often referred to as a "bulb"); a fixture or luminaire is the housing for the lamp; light is the energy from the light source before it strikes a surface; and illumination is light reflecting off surfaces. Thus, a lighting fixture contains a lamp that emits light and illuminates the scene. With 3DS MAX, a light object is equivalent to a lamp and fixtures are strictly optional, so it is appropriate to say a spotlight illuminates the scene with warm colored light.

Lamp Temperature

Man has created many forms of light. Their color characteristics are often described in terms of Kelvin temperature (not to be confused with warm and cool colors). This term is analogous to a piece of metal being heated; it begins with a deep red glow, warms to a brilliant red, heats to orange, then yellow, and on through the spectrum until it becomes "white hot." As a guideline, a sunrise is about 2,000 degrees Kelvin, the noon sun 5,000 degrees, an overcast sky 7,000 degrees, and a blue sky 10,000 degrees.

This book does not go into the specifics of each light source temperature. They are presented here primarily as a comparative tool and as a bit of background information for readers new to the subject.

Kelvin temperature is somewhat equivalent to the hue and saturation, while the brightness or intensity of a light is really a function of the light color's value. Light fixtures that are intended to be of the same type in a scene can be given different intensities, but should share close to the same hue and saturation values. In such a case, the light's color value acts much like a "dimming switch."

Incandescent Lamps

The oldest and most common artificial lamp is the incandescent light bulb. Incandescent lamps are point sources and their intensity is limited only to how many watts you provide at that point. The color cast from an incandescent lamp is warm and orange-based with a color temperatures close to that of a sunrise. The extent to which incandescent lamps vary by wattage is evident with dimmer switches where at very low levels the light is quite orange. Halogen lamps also are of the incandescent family but have a much higher temperature. They produce significantly brighter illumination and cast a far whiter, yet warm light. Halogen lamps still turn orange when dimmed.

Fluorescent Lamps

Fluorescent lamps cast a much whiter, blue-to-green-based colored light than incandescent lamps. The higher-temperature fluorescent lamps are probably at fault if you can't tell the color of an item in a store. Even though these lamps are "whiter," their light causes many colors—especially the complementary colors of red, orange, and skin tones—to wash out. The amount of light a fluorescent lamp produces is a fixed quantity. If you need more illumination, you increase the linear footage of the lamp. Although fluorescent lamps are linear light sources, they are most commonly grouped together or are folded back onto themselves to create sufficient illumination levels. In daily use, they act more as a "point" source than a linear one. This observation is important because 3DS MAX does not yet support true linear light sources.

Influence of Colored Lamps

Some artificial lamps are worse at color rendition than fluorescent ones. Sodium-based lamps often are found in use as street lights and in factories. These lamps are some of the brightest and most energy efficient available, but they cast a very saturated orange-to-yellow light. Mercury lamps are an older lamp type, common to street lamps, that cast a saturated blue-green light.

Light fixtures sometime add color to that of their lamps. Incandescent lamps are available with a wide range of tinted coatings and translucent colored lenses can be added to cast any imaginable color. Stoplights are an example of colored lenses that you see every day. 3DS MAX's spotlights and directional lights reproduce the effects of colored lenses when they are casting ray-traced shadows and the lens material is using Filter opacity with an appropriate color.

The most dramatic colored lights you experience daily are neon. These emit very saturated colors and can illuminate a scene in a fascinating way. Re-creating their effects in 3DS MAX can be tricky, but can be well worth the effort. Chapter 19 explores creating neon effects in-depth.

Although the color quality of artificial lamps varies greatly, you should be aware that this variation is not generally considered favorable. Lighting manufacturers do their best to produce lamps that come the closest to creating white light. Understanding how artificial light affects the overall quality of a scene is important when you analyze the world around you. As an artist and animator, your goal is to portray moods, not to perfectly simulate a lighting condition.

Using Colored Light

Having read about artificial light, you probably don't need to use much of it directly. Your primary goal in 3DS MAX is to create a believable scene, artistic expression, or simply a pleasing image. The way you manipulate light to achieve your results is completely up to you. You are probably best off using the information about particular lamps as a mental reference while you analyze the world around you.

What you see in your 3DS MAX world depends upon how you illuminate it—what you see is entirely dependent upon your light objects' color and position. The colors you choose for light sources have a dramatic effect on the scene's mood and the color rendition of your objects.

Highly saturated lights should be used with caution when you illuminate entire scenes because they can completely skew the perception of your world. Reproducing the characteristics of yellow/orange sodium lamps, for instance, does not illuminate blue-to-purple-based objects and makes white objects appear the same as orange objects. An example is searching for a bright blue car in a parking lot illuminated with such lights. Because there is no blue in the orange light to reflect, the car appears pure black.

Re-creating the color of poor, man-made lights can portray your scene as sterile or color-washed. This might be exactly what you want if you are demonstrating the effects of different lighting choices. For the most part, however, you want to make a scene as alive with color as possible.

NOTE

Photographers who are forced to take pictures under poor artificial lighting conditions commonly use colored filters to correct, or at least minimize, the effect that colored lights have on the scene.

Intensely colored lights can have fantastic effects if they are used with care. If you look at theater lighting from the stage's point of view, you don't see white light but entire batteries of vibrant, colored light. Theaters commonly use pure red, green, blue, yellow, magenta, and cyan lights in various combinations. These pure colors of light mix on stage, giving some areas and many shadows more richness and vibrancy than could ever be achieved from even, white illumination. Colored lights can have impressive effects when used on completely white objects as well as monochromatic scenes. The white surfaces reflect all the light spectrum and display the mixing hues and intensity of the various lights cast on them.

Complementary Colors in Light

If you are in an environment illuminated with colored light, your eye adapts to the environment by becoming very sensitive to the complementary color of the light source—the color required to restore white light. This phenomenon is known as *color constancy* and has the effect of placing the complementary color in the nonilluminated or shadowed areas in the mind's eye. The most common day-to-day example of this is the purple-to-blue based shadows evident in a scene lit by the yellow-to-orange based light of an incandescent light. The more color-intense the light source, the more shift is perceived in the shadows.

Artists, scene painters, and set designers recognize this effect and maximize the perceived depth of their shadows by color shifting them toward the complementary color of the light. Examine a theater's stage set under house lights and you will probably find an abundance of purple and deep blue being used in many of the painted shadows. Most light, whether natural or manmade, has at least a slight yellow-to-orange hue that produces complements of violet to deep blue. Because this is closer to human perception of light than actual pigment, "helping" 3DS MAX make this slight color shift is important because viewers look at an image rather than participate in the scene.

3DS MAX uses Ambient Light (located in the Environment dialog) to simulate the total accumulated reflected light present in a scene. It contributes light to all objects uniformly, regardless of additional light sources, and is the light present in nonilluminated objects and shadows. For added realism, a color shift in the ambient light to the complement of the dominant light source produces the effect of color constancy and deeper, richer darks and shadows throughout the scene.

Reflected Light and Radiosity

Light that strikes an object is absorbed or reflected. Red objects absorb green and blue light, reflecting the red light back to our eyes. This is why these objects are perceived as being "red." Besides reflecting to our eyes, the reflected light affects nearby objects with reflected, or bounced light. Placing a matte red object against a matte white wall and illuminating the scene with a white light source creates a red tint on areas of the "white" wall. The wall is said to have inherited the bounced color. A more common example is a typical room illuminated by recessed lighting fixtures. The room is being illuminated entirely from above, yet the details and color of the ceiling are distinguishable. This is because the ceiling is being illuminated from light reflected off the floor, walls, and furnishings. This effect of bounced, inherited, and reflected light is known in computer graphics as *radiosity* and is only available from renderers that specialize in that type of simulation.

Ray-traced rendering traces rays from a source to a surface, continually reflecting off surfaces and striking others until they are no longer within the scene.

Although the 3DS MAX production renderer uses ray-tracing techniques to calculate ray-traced shadows, it is a scan-line renderer (as is Pixar's famed RenderMan renderer). The traditional use of ray-tracing is for calculating reflections from shiny, specular surfaces. Full ray-traced renderers trace vectors from your viewing position to every surface. If the surface is specular, an additional ray is reflected to capture what is visible in the reflection. If another shiny surface is encountered by the ray, it is reflected again until the ray bounces out of the scene or lands on a non-specular surface. This is how the recursive reflections typical of ray-traced imagery are created and is also the reason why ray-traced rendering is slow.

Radiosity renderers differ from ray-traced renderers by calculating diffuse rather than specular reflections. The light energy from each light source is traced to each surface, calculating the absorption and then reflecting the remaining energy to other surfaces in the scene. This energy bounces in relation to diffuse surface color, rather than shine or specularity. In doing so, radiosity renders the effect of reflected light but not specular reflections. The lighting is perfect, but everything in the scene is flat.

The rendered effects of radiosity rendering are stunning, but the calculations and computer time are extremely intense. While ray-traced rendering takes an order of magnitude longer than scan-line rendering, radiosity adds yet another order of magnitude to the equation. This is because ray-traced reflections pertain to just one viewing position and the reflected rays will eventually find a conclusion, while the rays of reflected energy in the radiosity model bounce within the scene forever constantly becoming weaker. Radiosity renderings are termed solutions because they have been stopped at a certain point to produce the given image. Radiosity renderings that exhibit specular reflections are actually a combination—the radiosity solution being combined with the reflections of a ray-traced rendering.

Although 3DS MAX provides several methods to isolate or approximate ray-tracing with shadow techniques and reflection maps, the effects of radiosity are not directly built-in. This does not mean that you should disregard or give up on this effect because you can simulate much of its effects within 3DS MAX by the careful placement of lights and material definitions. Radiosity is a perceivable, real-world phenomenon and, if your goal involves photo-realism, some effort should be expended to approximate its effects. This is especially true if the final product is to be a still image where the eye has time to evaluate the scene. See Chapter 19 for more information about radiosity.

In Practice: Mixing Color and Light

- **Primary Colors** The primary colors of pigment are cyan, yellow, and magenta. These are complements to light's primary colors of red, green, and blue.

- **Mixing colors** Mixing light color is additive, where mixing more approaches white. Mixing pigment color is subtractive, where mixing more approaches black.

- **Blacks and grays** True blacks and grays should be used with caution because nearly every light source or pigment surface is either warm or cool by nature. Although true grays are all too easy to define within computer graphics, they rarely exist in daily life.

- **Colored surfaces** Surface color is actually reflected light. For a colored surface to be seen, there must be corresponding color components within the light source to be reflected. This is important to remember as you define the colors of your light sources.

Image by Westwood Studios
Provided courtesy of Kinetix™

Chapter 3

VIEWING, PERSPECTIVE, AND COMPOSITION

3D Studio MAX has many tools you can use to organize your modeling, control perspective, and view composition in your scenes. If you don't explore and try to understand the various options available, you are like a photographer trying to get by with one stock 50 mm lens. Your choices of camera lens, positioning, and composition go a long way in making the difference between a snapshot of a model and a truly professional image composition. This chapter adresses many of these fundamental aspects:

- Methods of 3D viewing, both traditionally and in 3DS MAX

- Orthographic projections and axonometrics

- Traditional perspective terminology as compared to 3D Studio MAX and the standard classifications of perspective

- Comparing human vision to 3D Studio MAX usage of cameras

- Parallax and perspective correction

- Image composition

3D Viewing Methods

Everything in our world occupies three dimensions, yet we usually need to represent them in two. Whether the medium is a drawing, photograph, or computer screen, three dimensions are being abstracted onto a two-dimensional plane. Working within this restriction, many conventions have evolved for describing and designing objects to be built or displayed. In computer modeling, you are performing the same analysis that draftsmen, designers, and artists have performed for centuries; but unlike them, you have a dynamic choice as to how to view your information at any given time because the information within a three-dimensional model can be viewed from any vantage point at any time. In this way, computer modeling is most similar to sculpture, yet you have to abstract the sculpture to the screen's two dimensions when constructing it. As a result, you will tend to use traditional and perspective views interchangeably and simultaneously as you change from drafting methods to sculptural ones.

Most everything that was or is manufactured began as drawing. Some drawings went no further than a napkin sketch whereas others involved the work of hundreds of engineers. Whether a simple gear or a highly complex aircraft, somewhere a drawing or, most likely, a series of drawings exists to define its construction. Much of what you create in 3DS MAX will come directly or indirectly from drawings. Sketches from an art director may need to be interpreted, blueprints and measured drawings may need to be translated, or drawings in digital form (from other CAD programs) may be provided that become natural templates for creating 3D models in 3DS MAX. Either way, an understanding of drawing terms and how they are used is valuable so that you can relate the world's traditionally created information to that of computer graphics. You will see that the majority of standard drawing conventions can be related to working in 3DS MAX viewports, which enables you to use established methods of construction while viewing the whole in a more natural perspective.

Orthographic Viewing

The vast majority of drawings of items to be made are orthogonal—they are drawings that represent views at exact 90-degree angles to the subject without any perspective. Orthographic views are important because they show the exact relationships of height and width. All portions of the subject are displayed parallel to the viewing plane and are free of the distortion and foreshortening found when viewing in perspective. Everything in an orthogonal view is at the same scale, unlike in a perspective view where closer subjects are larger and distant ones are smaller. The perpendicular views that characterize orthogonal viewing form a "cube" around the subject in a manner similar to figure 3.1.

FIGURE 3.1
Mechanical terminology for orthographic projections (of the orthocar.max scene).

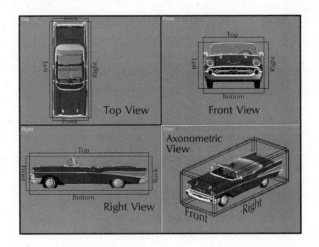

Many professions (manufacturing, for example) draw their parts with three views and perhaps an additional axonometric view. Other professions (architecture, for example) tend to show all views—even if they are redundant—and include sectional views as well as show relationships and structural details.

Projection Views

3D Studio MAX has six orthographic projections: Top, Bottom, Front, Back, Right, and Left (with standard keyboard shortcuts of T,B,F,K,R,L) which relate orthogonally to the World X,Y,Z axes. These terms are similar to those used in manufacturing where it makes the most sense to describe views in relation to the object. The architectural industry uses different terms for similar views because buildings have a universal frame of reference. In architectural terms, the Top and Bottom views are *plans* and the Front, Back, Left, and Right side views are *elevations*. This terminology is shown in figure 3.2 in relationship to 3D Studio MAX views. The term plan is usually accompanied by what it is a plan of (floor plan, ceiling plan, site plan, roof plan, and so on), whereas elevation names are paired with the direction they face on the compass (North, South, Southwest, and so on).

FIGURE 3.2

Architectural terminology for orthographic projections (of the orthouse.max scene).

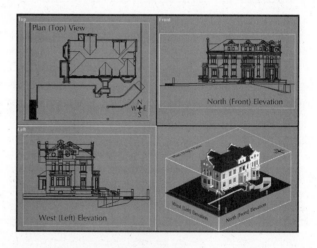

When a side view, or elevation, is taken within the space of the subject it is called an *interior elevation* and shows only what you would see if you were to stand in the space. If the view also shows the width (and perhaps structure) of the surrounding walls, it's termed a *section*. A section is basically an elevation at a given slice of the subject, as shown later in this chapter. Sections are used extensively to describe structure and interior relationships. Although often difficult to conceptualize, sectional drawings are valuable to the 3D Studio MAX modeler because they are the perfect shapes for lofting (see Chapter 10, "Building Loft Objects," for more information on modeling lofted objects). You can create a dynamic sectional view of your model in 3DS MAX by adjusting a camera's clipping planes.

Axonometric Views

When views depart from being perpendicular, they begin to display more than one side at the same time, and the view becomes skewed. Views of this type are termed *axonometric* and are what 3DS MAX terms *User views*.

NOTE

Many users refer to User views as being isometric or oblique. Isometric actually refers to a very specific type of axonometric where the angles of rotation are all the same (typically 30 degrees). Oblique drawings keep one plane undistorted (either the plan or elevation) and angle the corresponding projections. This type of projection cannot be represented in 3DS MAX with its User view.

User axonometric views are valuable references because they maintain the relationship of parallel lines. Lines do not diminish to vanishing points as they do in our daily vision; they remain parallel. Relationships are easy to identify because the location of any detail can be projected back to any other area of the view. The scale of the subject is consistent for details that lie on any given angle. In examining figure 3.3, you notice that the features of each cube remain parallel, whereas the relative scale of the features changes according to the rotation.

FIGURE 3.3
User axonometric views
of toyblock.max.

You may find User views preferable to Perspective views because the elements in the scene are in proportion to one another, relationships can be easily identified, and the viewing controls are the same as orthogonal views.

Although working in perspective can be quite natural at times, distance is often difficult to estimate and the Zoom Window option is not available.

Perspective Viewing and Cameras

In an everyday sense, perspective refers to the appearance of objects in depth as perceived by normal human vision. We view everything around us in perspective. Cameras, television, and film display the world they capture in perspective on the 2D planes of film, glass, or screen. While these devices place their images automatically, artists have traditionally needed to construct their perspectives by hand, translating the three-dimensional world they see to the two-dimensional plane of paper or canvas. The manner in which artists have come to represent perspective is important to learn so its compositional impact is understood and terminology can be exchanged with those not in computer graphics.

Within the context of drawing, *perspective* refers to the various techniques that artists have developed for representing three-dimensional objects and depth relationships on a two-dimensional surface. Several empirical, mechanical, and construction-based methods for drawing perspectives are in use daily. These methods employ very specific steps and procedures for creating a hand-drawn perspective. Luckily, 3DS MAX does all this for you within its Camera viewport with greater accuracy than most delineators even come close to achieving. The following discussion relates the perspective terms that artists traditionally use to 3DS MAX's camera analogy.

Traditional perspective theory places the observer's eye at a station point and looks at a point in the distance, termed the *center of vision*. This is equivalent to the placement of the camera and the camera's target in 3DS MAX. A correlation between the two models can be seen in figure 3.4.

A line struck between your eye and your center of vision is often termed the *line of sight*. 3DS MAX draws this line visually to connect the camera and target. This vector traces your eye's center of vision and in so doing shows what your eye is capable of seeing. If an object is blocking this line, you cannot see past it. You can use this line of sight for reference when viewing the scene from above to position your cameras and targets with the knowledge of what can be seen.

Lines of sight can be traced between your eye and each object in the scene. These lines are plotted on a theoretical plane suspended between you and the scene and is termed the *picture plane*. For an artist, this is equivalent to the piece of paper on which a scene is drawn. For 3DS MAX, it's the frame of the final image and so is actually the Camera viewport.

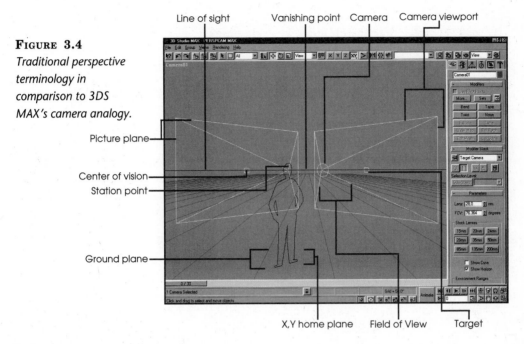

FIGURE 3.4

Traditional perspective terminology in comparison to 3DS MAX's camera analogy.

NOTE

The concept of a picture plane is actually how perspective technique was first formalized. A sheet of glass was used to frame a scene with the lines of sight between the artist and objects "traced" onto the glass.

The plane upon which the observer stands while regarding a scene is described as the *ground plane*—the floor or land on which the majority of objects in the scene are resting. The ground plane is located at your eye height's distance below you—that is, the height of the horizon between five and six feet for most people. In 3DS MAX the ground plane is the plane of the X,Y home grid displayed in User and Perspective views.

The height of your eye (station point), or camera location, is also the height of the scene's horizon. The horizon line is drawn through the station point, or camera, parallel to the ground plane. All lines parallel to the ground converge to points on the horizon. You can think of the horizon as an infinitely large plane extending into the distance that always maintains a constant height from the ground plane. As items recede into the distance, they come closer to appearing to lie on the horizon.

T I P

You can display the horizon line of 3DS MAX cameras to guide compositions and properly position camera views to match displayed background images.

The horizon is important because all horizontal lines (lines that lie on planes parallel to the ground plane) visually converge to vanishing points located on it. Lines on planes below your eye converge upward to the line of the horizon, whereas lines above your eye converge downward. Lines in the scene directly at eye level are coincidental with the horizon and read as one "line." 3DS MAX has no term for vanishing points because it doesn't require their use. By understanding the existence of vanishing points, you can better place objects within a scene and determine the best point from which to view them. Vanishing points also have a tendency to pull the observer's eye and become a natural point of interest. The location(s) will have an impact on your composition's strength.

An angle you can view from side to side is termed the *cone of vision* or *angle of view*, equivalent to 3DS MAX's Field of View (FOV), as shown in figure 3.5. When constructing traditional perspectives, the angle of view is often considered to be 30 degrees to either side of the line of sight. This is actually more from the convenience of using a 30–60 degree triangle than physical truth. The angle upon which the human eye can focus is closer to 45 degrees—the Field of View provided by 3DS MAX's default 51.944 mm lens.

FIGURE 3.5
The default Field of View from default 3DS MAX cameras.

FOV

Default FOV

Camera   FOV

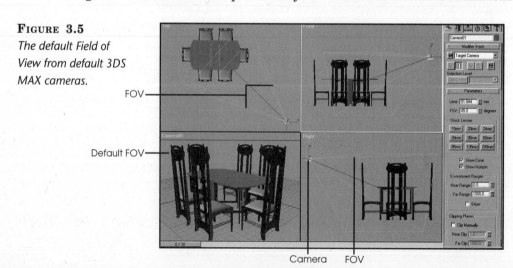

One-Point Perspective

Perspective is conventionally described according to the number of primary vanishing points occurring in the scene. The world in which we live is based primarily on right angles. You write on rectangular paper, create objects composed of square corners, and build most buildings perpendicular to the ground and place them "square to the world" on an orthogonal grid of streets and blocks. Perspective has the most impact on parallel lines and right angles. As a result, it is common to talk of perspective in relation to a simple cube (see fig. 3.6).

FIGURE 3.6

The toy block model viewed in one-point perspective.

Parallel lines

Horizon line

Diminishing lines   Vanishing point

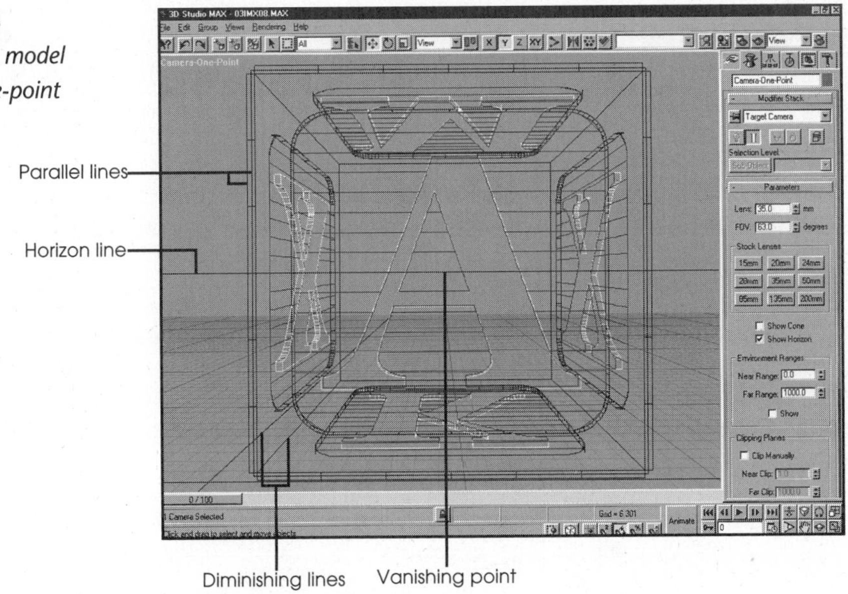

Viewing in One-Point Perspective

The following examples refer to figures of a toy block that demonstrate various principles of perspective. You can load the toyblock.max scene from the accompanying CD-ROM into 3DS MAX if you want to experiment with the views yourself.

1. Choose File, Open and then choose toyblock.max from the accompanying CD-ROM.

   When you are "square" to the side of the cube, only the lines perpendicular to you converge on the horizon. You can see the effect in the Camera01 viewport, as shown in figure 3.6. The vanishing point of the cube's sides lies on the horizon line and coincides with the center of vision. The block's other lines have a vanishing point of infinite distance to either side — thus no vanishing point at all. These lines do not converge and are parallel to you and your horizon. Such a view is termed a *one-point perspective* because there is only one vanishing point.

2. Minimize the current view by pressing W or clicking on the Min/Max icon in the lower right corner.

3. Click on the Move icon and then select both the camera and its target in the Top view.

4. While in the Top view, move the camera in the X,Y plane and notice the results in the Camera01 viewport.

   The camera view remains in one-point perspective as you move the camera because the camera and target are level and the line of sight remains perpendicular to the face of the cube. A one-point perspective is maintained as long as these conditions are met.

5. Press the spacebar to lock your selection and then move the camera and target about in the Front view.

The camera's line of sight is still perpendicular to the cube so the resulting view remains in one-point perspective.

Two-Point Perspective

If you are not square to the block, there is a vanishing point for each of the two visible sides. These vanishing points are located off camera, on the horizon line, to the left and right. You can see the result in the 2-Point Camera viewport shown in figure 3.7. Such a view is called a two-point perspective because there are now two vanishing points. Where a one-point view must be perpendicular to one of the block's faces, a two-point view can be from anywhere. Keep in mind that you must maintain a level line of sight (the target and camera must be level with the ground plane) to ensure that vertical lines remain vertical. It is quite easy for delineators to determine distances using two-point perspective because these vertical planes remain constant—one reason two-point perspective is the most common hand-drawn perspective model.

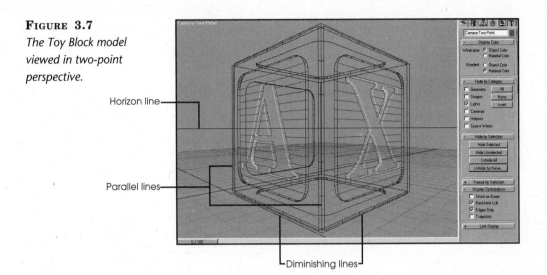

FIGURE 3.7
The Toy Block model viewed in two-point perspective.

Horizon line

Parallel lines

Diminishing lines

Changing to a Two-Point Perspective

The effect of two-point perspective can be seen by adjusting the camera in the preceding scene.

1. Unlock your selection by pressing the spacebar; select only the camera in the Top viewport.

2. Move just the camera in the X,Y plane of the Top view and examine the results in the Camera01 viewport.

    The sides of the block that were parallel are now diminishing in perspective. Two vanishing points for the scene can now be seen—one for each side of the block. Also, notice that the vertical sides of the block remain parallel because the camera and target remain level as you move just the camera.

Three-Point Perspective

When you are no longer looking at the block along a level line of sight—that is, you are looking up or down—vertical lines also converge to a vanishing point. You can see this result in the 3-Point Camera viewport, as shown in figure 3.8. All three of the block's planes now have vanishing points, and such a view is predictably termed a three-point perspective. The cube's vertical lines visually converge to a vanishing point on a line drawn vertically from the center of vision. If you are looking down at a point below the horizon, the block's vertical lines converge downward. These lines converge upward if you're looking at a point above the horizon. If you are looking level with the horizon, you have a two-point perspective.

FIGURE 3.8
The Toy Block model viewed in three-point perspective.

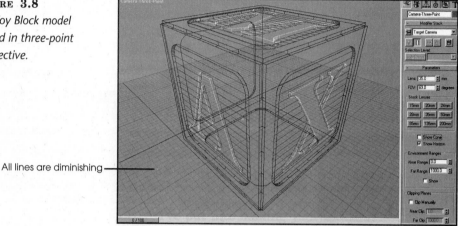

All lines are diminishing

Changing to a Three-Point Perspective

A three-point perspective is easily seen in the current scene, as follows. With just the camera selected, move the camera vertically in the Front viewport. The sides of the block that were previously parallel now begin to slant and converge to a vanishing point. A three-point perspective has been created because the camera no longer has a level line of sight to its target.

All lines have vanishing points. The block shown in figure 3.9 has only three sets of vanishing points, one for each of its groups of parallel planes. In a scene that you construct, the geometry may be at numerous angles and there may be hundreds of vanishing points. When drawing such complex scenes, delineators and artists usually concern themselves with the basic three and make approximations as to the rest. Each line that is parallel with the ground plane, or resting evenly on the floor, has a vanishing point on the horizon. If lines are vertically skewed, slanted, or leaning from the ground plane, they converge to vanishing points located directly above or below the horizon. As you can see, a full three-point perspective can be a complex ordeal. This complexity is one reason that artists prefer to avoid them. That said, don't worry about it—3DS MAX takes care of the calculations and enables you to spend your time in composition.

Understanding Horizons

A basic concept to remember is that your eye level determines the horizon. Because most people are within a foot of being the same height, their eyes share the same horizon as yours if they stand on the same ground plane as you. The eyes of a crowd are thus co-linear and align with the horizon, as illustrated in figure 3.9. If you see a head above the horizon, you know the person is taller than you are or is standing on higher ground. If a head is below the horizon, the person is either shorter than you or on lower ground.

FIGURE 3.9
The eyes of a crowd aligning on the horizon.

Eye level = horizon line

When your eye level is parallel to the ground plane, the horizon is perfectly centered in the view. As you tilt your head and move your center of vision or camera target, the horizon moves up and down in the view. Whereas the horizon moves in the composition, its height from the ground does not change; it is always at the same height as your eye.

Obviously, a horizon line exists in the computer scene only if sufficient objects exist in the distance to define it. Most models do not have geometry extensive enough to diminish to a natural horizon. An exterior scene commonly uses a background to create depth and establish a horizon. Pay careful attention to the true horizon line (the height of your camera) and the background's illustrated horizon line. If the horizons are not close, the corresponding scene looks as if it has either been sunk in a valley or perched on a hill. If neither of these effects is desirable, you should move your camera to the background's horizon level or adjust the background image. Figure 3.10 demonstrates how tilting the head up and down moves the horizon but does not change its relationship to the ground plane—as opposed to moving the camera up to higher ground.

High horizon line   Low horizon

FIGURE 3.10
The horizon positions resulting from tilting the camera and moving the camera vertically.

Camera—low

Camera—high ground

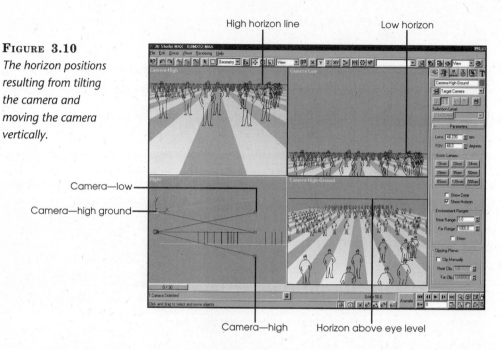

Camera—high   Horizon above eye level

It is all too easy to place a stock image as a background only to find that it does not align with the height of the camera—the true definition of where a horizon line is. Objects and lines in the scene diminish in perspective correctly, but the vanishing points do not fall on the horizon. This may seem somewhat trivial, and sometimes subtle, but most people will realize that something is not quite right with the image.

Understanding Human Vision and Cameras

You are probably familiar with the example of straight railroad tracks extending on flat ground to the horizon. The tracks appear to converge in the distance at a single point (see fig. 3.11). The convergence of these lines is a basic trait of perspective. The tracks are an extreme example because few observations are so distinct and separable. This example does not reflect the true complexity of the visual data you experience at almost any given moment.

FIGURE 3.11

Train tracks converging to a vanishing point on the horizon.

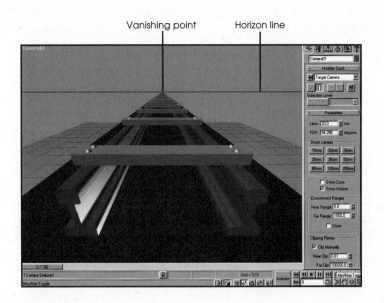

Your eye takes in many images—very rapidly—that your mind then composes to form an overall picture of the scene from which it makes conclusions. The brain organizes shapes and forms according to spatial relationships. If you analyze a snapshot of a scene, you see that all lines are "slanting" or converging. But the mind's eye tends to correct the real-world view and understands these lines as being parallel rather than converging. This is an interpretation of reality—after all, the objects really are parallel. It is also much easier to navigate through a world that your mind spatially understands. Imagine a world where you would need to constantly judge the effects of perspective before walking across the room to pick up a glass! The ability to not see the world in perspective is quite useful and by far the norm. Your mind does this spatial transformation automatically.

To truly understand perspective, you must learn how to see the world not as it appears in your mind's spatially transformed images, but rather as it appears in the snapshots taken by a camera. Perspective is learned; it is not readily apparent. Artists learn to find converging lines and vanishing points when they draw a scene and keep these rules in the back of their minds when they sketch objects. It was not until the Renaissance that a full understanding of perspective was made, so don't feel bad if it isn't immediately obvious to you.

Although your mind may not interpret what it sees according to the rules of perspective, it does know them. A drawing or illustration that has perspective flaws looks "off" to anyone. You may not be able to identify what is wrong, but you know intuitively that something is not right.

Perspective also has a great influence on the perceived mood and action of an image. A scene portrayed with flat perspective appears to be stable and at a distance. By contrast, an extremely flared perspective, makes the scene appear in motion, very close, and possibly unstable. Perspective is an important contribution to composition. Learning the basic rules of perspective helps you compose scenes to get the desired effects. Figure 3.12 shows two similar views of a city—one with a flat perspective and one with a flared perspective. Both views are along the same line of sight (through different sized lenses and at different distances) but deliver very different impressions of the same scene.

Camera—telephoto   Camera—wide angle

FIGURE 3.12
Different views of a city with very different perspective.

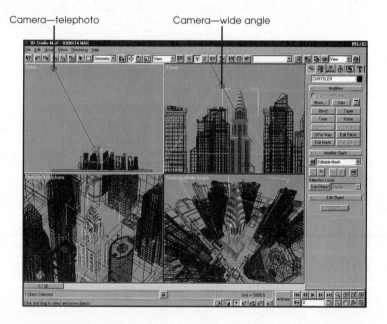

You can much more readily understand the rules and effects of perspective by analyzing photographs. These frozen images, made from a stationary vantage point, prevent you from assembling a mind's eye view of them. Each perspective view that 3DS MAX gives you is, in essence, such a photograph.

The 3D Studio MAX Camera Analogy

Excellent perspective capabilities are built into the 3D Studio MAX environment through its cameras, Perspective viewport, and even Spotlight viewports. You can use these to learn quite a bit about how perspective affects the perception and drama of a view as you experiment with them in your scenes.

3D Studio MAX relates the rules of perspective in photographic terms. The basis for descriptions is the 35 mm single-lens-reflex (SLR) camera, by far the most common camera available with interchangeable lenses. All the lens terminology that 3DS MAX uses corresponds directly to the 35 mm camera (note that the 35 mm designation refers to the size of the film and not the size of the lens).

The camera is a good analogy because you can pick up any 35 mm camera and reproduce the effects that 3DS MAX creates. Of course, using 3D Studio MAX enables you to "photograph" scenes that are impossible to capture with a camera. The compositional effects, however, are the same. If you can view it through a 35 mm camera, you can re-create it in a Camera viewport.

35 mm Camera Lens Types

You should become familiar with how the lens sizes of a 35 mm camera affect vision because it is the analogy 3DS MAX uses to describe field of view in its Camera viewports (see fig. 3.13). Note that this relationship is valid only for as long as you are referring to the same camera type. Other film dimension standards (for example, 4"×5" or 70 mm motion picture) have different ranges of lens sizes to associate with field of view. 3DS MAX's default lens is 43.46 mm, which delivers a field of view equivalent to your natural eyesight—45 degrees.

Changing Lens Sizes

The smaller your camera's lens size, the wider the field of view and the more pronounced the perspective becomes. Try this yourself by adjusting one of the cameras in the Toy Block model. As you select smaller lens sizes, the field of view increases. Manipulating the lens size makes this relationship obvious.

FIGURE 3.13

*The stock lenses for
3D Studio MAX
cameras.*

1. Load toyblock3.max from the accompanying CD-ROM.

2. Press H to access the Select Objects dialog. Choose Camera-Three-Point
    and then click on Select to select the camera.

3. Click the Modify panel to view the parameters for Camera-Three-Point.

    The camera is currently a moderately wide, 35 mm lens.

4. Click the 15 mm button.

    The camera view seems to "zoom out" while the camera itself does not
    move (as seen in the Top viewport). The camera's FOV has grown
    substantially, and the perspective of the cube in the camera view is
    extremely flared.

5. Now try larger lenses, such as 85 mm and 135 m.

    The camera does not move but the FOV indication continues to shrink
    as the camera view "zooms in" and the perspective flare lessens.

6. Click on 35 mm to restore the original FOV and activate the Camera-
    Three-Point viewport.

7. Click the Perspective icon and drag the mouse up and down.

    This performs a simultaneous dolly and FOV change that demonstrates
    exactly how much the perspective flare is changing as the lens size
    changes. (This effect is described further in Chapter 20, "Cameras and
    Setting the Shot.")

Wide-Angle Lenses

Lens sizes below 50 mm (or more appropriately, below 48.24 mm) take in
more of a field of view than is normally possible by the human cone of vision.

These lenses are considered to be wide-angle lenses, and their views often are referred to as wide-angle views. The effects of perspective viewed through such lenses are exaggerated. The stock lenses provided by Camera/Adjust correspond to stock lenses in a camera store.

Selecting a lens below the standard 35 mm and 28 mm wide-angle lenses can cause excessive perspective distortion, which can produce dramatic effects or confusing ones, depending on how you compose the final scene. The very small lenses, 10–15 mm are often called fish-eye lenses because the actual lens begins to appear spherical. Geometry viewed through fish-eye lenses' corners appear "bent" as you look from side to side. 3D Studio MAX's smallest lens, a 9.8 mm fish-eye, delivers a 178 degree field of view, which has the effect of almost seeing behind yourself! You should reserve such lenses for extremely special effects.

NOTE

The curvature of the camera lens has an impact on your photographs—the wider the lens, the more pronounced the effect. (Fish-eye lenses, for example, distort scenes dramatically.) This distortion is not an effect directly supported by computer graphics in general because diminishing lines are always straight vectors regardless of the FOV. This effect can be reproduced, however, through a post process.

An important human perception concerning three-point perspective is that the more an object flares, the larger the object (or the smaller the observer) appears to be. This effect stems from daily observations. If a building is quite tall and you are near, it is obvious that the building's vertical lines converge upward and away from you. The closer you are, the more the building fills the scene. As you strain your neck to see it, the more distorted the view becomes. The flaring of a three-point perspective (see fig. 3.14) can reinforce these effects—a simple block appears quite large.

Telephoto Lenses

Camera lenses that are more than 50 mm in length are known as *telephoto lenses*. These lenses can zoom in to the scene closer than your eye can, acting similar to a telescope. Large telephoto lenses, which you can often see in the hands of sports photographers, actually are the size of small telescopes. The amount of the scene these lenses can take in is proportionally smaller, and their effect is to flatten perspective. The perspective flare is minimized because only a small angle of the scene is viewed. You can simulate this effect on a photograph by cropping a small region and analyzing the lack of converging lines — the larger the lens, the smaller this cropped view becomes and the flatter the perspective appears. Sometimes you may prefer a flattened perspective.

FIGURE 3.14

Flaring perspective with a wide-angle lens.

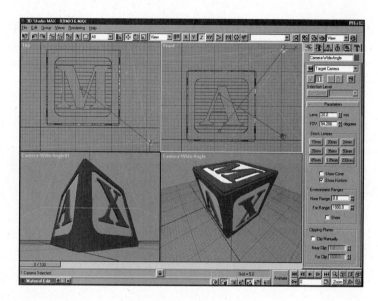

The 85 mm lens is nicknamed a *portrait lens* because it slightly flattens the features of the subject and results in a more flattering image. If you use a wide-angle lens for a portrait, it distorts your subject's features, and you might lose your commission.

You should never run out of the high range in camera lens selections. 3DS MAX has an unbelievably high 100,000 mm lens limit (with a corresponding FOV of 0.025). Such a lens is the equivalent of a large observatory telescope or highly powerful electron microscope. A lens of this size effectively eliminates perspective and makes the view appear as a planer projection or a true elevation.

Understanding Parallax

Many artists and delineators prefer to confine their illustrations to a two-point perspective because of human perception and ease of use. Human perception tends to "correct" the splaying of a scene's vertical lines. Seeing an image in three-point perspective makes many people question its correctness, which is typical in interior views where wide-angle lenses are required to get enough of the view. The vertical lines near the edge of the view begin to splay in a way that makes the viewer uncomfortable; everyone knows that walls are straight up and down.

The convergence of vertical lines in photography is termed *parallax*. Whenever you aim your camera up or down so that it is not level with the ground plane, your view becomes a three-point perspective and begins to show signs of parallax. These effects are most apparent at the edges of a view, and they exaggerate more and more as the field of view widens. Figure 3.15 shows an interior view with parallax.

FIGURE 3.15
Interior exhibiting parallax due to a tilted camera.

Perspective Correction

In traditional illustration, especially architectural and interior photography, parallax should be avoided and photographers go to great lengths to correct it. You can avoid this effect completely by always keeping your camera level to the ground. This can lead to less than exciting compositions, however, and is likely to force you to crop a scene or move your camera to an unreasonable height.

View finder cameras, also known as large format, variable plane, or 45s, enable a photographer to correct the effects of parallax by manipulating the internal mirrors. The same capability is available with 35 mm cameras that have special perspective control (PC) lenses. 3DS MAX provides much of the same capability with the Renderer's Blowup option (see fig. 3.16).

FIGURE 3.16

Same interior from identical vantage point with perspective correction.

Note

See Chapter 20, "Cameras and Setting the Shot," for more details on perspective correction using the Renderer's Blowup option.

Scene Composition

The arrangement of objects in a scene, the relationship to their surroundings, and the way they are viewed combine to form what is commonly referred to as *composition*, or the final picture. Composition can be extremely subjective and thus very confusing for those trying to learn it. Few artists agree on its definition, yet the majority agree on whether a particular piece of art has or lacks good composition. Recognizing effective composition is a feel, or intuition, developed over time and based in part on some objective guidelines.

Underlying principles exist that many people regard as rules of thumb, or at least items for consideration, when organizing a composition. Consider the following principles when you create compositions, but remember they are just guidelines and not hard and fast rules. Employing one well will often diminish the importance of the others. With experience you develop a sense of when to follow these rules and when to ignore them in the interest of good composition:

- **Center of interest**   Scenes should be organized around a center of interest. The center does not have to be the geographic center of the images, but rather the thematic focus of the scene. Scenes that lack a center of interest look cluttered, noneventful, or just plain boring. A center of interest need not be an object; it could be a vanishing point in a one-point perspective, for example.

- **Symmetry**   Scenes should not be perfectly symmetrical about either axis. Scenes that are perfectly centered on a symmetrical axis look stagnant, pat, and extremely formal. When the horizon is centered, the scene appears to be split, and it can be difficult to create a center of interest.

- **Balance**   Scenes should have balance. *Balance* refers to the overall visual "weight" that compositional pieces have. This can refer to the color, darkness, or visual complexity, as well as the size of the objects.

- **Overlap of form**   Without some overlap of form, elements within compositions may appear to float and may not seem firmly rooted to the scene. Overlapping objects within a scene provide a greater definition of depth.

- **Nongeometrical issues**   Compositional issues are not limited to an object's geometry. Textures assigned to objects, the shadows they cast, reflections of other objects, and the use of background images are all compositional elements to be considered.

As with all rules, these are made to be broken. It's possible to create a good composition that betrays the basic "rules." It is not uncommon for artists to see another's work, scratch their heads, and say, "I can't believe it works!"

Figure Ground

Artists sometimes reduce a scene's components to their silhouettes as an aid to develop and confirm their compositions. This technique makes all the objects in a scene entirely black against a white background, which has the effect of viewing the scene with a powerful white light cast from behind. Only the total, overall form is present. The internal edges and overlaps of objects are obscured. The scene reads as one quick gesture. This technique is referred to as *figure ground*.

You can analyze your image's figure ground in 3DS MAX with each rendering you do. Figure 3.17 shows how the Display Alpha Channel button displays the alpha channel for every rendering you perform in MAX. This is not an option you need to set because 3DS MAX always renders the alpha channel, and you can always view it whether you intend to save it or not.

FIGURE 3.17

Comparing the RGB rendering with the alpha channel to analyze figure ground.

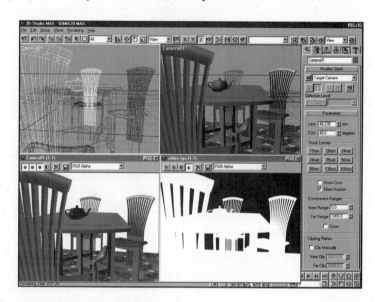

Thumbnail Sketches

Artists and filmmakers often use small, quick thumbnail sketches to develop and refine compositions. These sketches do not need to be detailed or even very accurate. The term thumbnail refers to size. A thumbnail sketch should only be big enough to capture the overall composition of a scene—a figure ground study, stick figures, overlapping box "stand-ins," or whatever best represents the elements in the composition. Many who use thumbnail sketches do them quickly and often. It is not uncommon to do five or six sketches per minute, trying different combinations. The advantage is that these thumbnail sketches give you a reference of what you've tried and where you are going.

Cloning Cameras

3DS MAX's cameras are extremely powerful compositional tools. They enable you to analyze unlimited viewing angles and proportions from any point. Specifically, one useful technique for experimenting with composition is to clone the working camera by pressing Shift as you transform it. Keep the other Camera viewport active for comparison and experiment with the new clone. After you arrive at a satisfactory view, clone again and again until you are convinced of your final composition. You may want to save some of your preliminary ideas, especially if they entail the complexity of animation. So at this point, you can keep the other cameras for reference, save them to their own MAX file for future use, or keep the original and inherit the tracks of the keeper in the Keyframer. If you're sure you won't need the ideas again, you can delete the cloned cameras.

In Practice: Viewing, Perspective, and Composition

- **Viewport options** The 3D Studio MAX viewport options relate directly to traditional methods of creating orthogonal construction documents, explanatory axonometric views, and illustrative perspectives.

- **One- and two-point perspectives** These perspectives rely on keeping the camera level to the ground plane. When level, all vertical lines perpendicular to the ground plane will be parallel in the resulting view.

- **Three-point perspective** Three-point perspectives are formed when the camera is tilted from the ground plane. The convergence to the third vanishing point produces an effect termed parallax, which is undesirable for many applications. Parallax can be overcome by keeping the camera level and using the Renderer's Blowup feature.

- **Horizon line** The horizon line is always equal to your eye level with the horizon's location in the composition being dependent on your viewing angle. If you look up, the horizon lowers, and if you tilt/roll the camera, the horizon rotates.

- **35 mm camera analogy** 3D Studio MAX's camera analogy places normal human vision at a lens size of approximately 50 mm. Lenses below this allow in more of the scene, flare the perspective, and are often called wide-angle lenses. Lenses above 50 mm zoom in on the scene, flatten the perspective, and are commonly termed telephoto lenses.

Image by Guillermo Leal Llaguna
Diseno y Animacion
Provided courtesy of Kinetix™

Chapter 4

ANIMATION AND STORY BOARDING

You are probably comfortable with the idea of planning your modeling process. We are told from an early age, "Haste makes waste" and "Measure twice, cut once." It is no surprise that we habitually think through, plan, and measure our work when we build an object. Such behavior is a habit, and we easily carry that habit into the process of building models in 3D Studio MAX and other 3D design programs.

What is not as familiar to us is the process of planning and designing animation. Unless you have studied cinematography, direction, play writing, or other motion-based arts, you may not have developed the skills for effectively planning and executing animation projects. This chapter discusses how to plan and lay out an animation project by using story boards and introduces some of the basic concepts behind effective animation.

Animation concepts covered in this chapter include:

- Use of story boards to plan your animation

- Motion design for animation

- Use of traditional animation techniques, such as squash and stretch

- Studies of natural motion for character animation

Using Story Boards

What is a story board? Many people imagine story boards as the slick pictures advertising executives create on TV. Unfortunately, this leaves the impression that story boards are used only to sell ideas. In reality, story boards are an important part of designing any presentation.

Story boards were developed in the 1930s as directors and animators came to realize that the traditional written script did not quite work for describing how to shoot an animated film. Live-action drama relies heavily on dialogue and little on complex action. Animation, on the other hand, tries to minimize dialogue and tell the story through the action. In some ways, animation has more in common with pantomime than it does with live-action drama. The result of recognizing the inherent weakness of the written script for animation was the development of the story board.

Originally, story writers sketched each major scene or important action and tacked these images to a board for review. The sketches contained a minimum amount of text to describe dialogue or camera effects. If the scene didn't work graphically, it was discarded. This technique proved so beneficial that today nearly all films and professional presentations rely on story boards during the design phase.

NOTE

One final, but very important, side benefit of using story boards involves their use as a contract document. You should create the story board for an animation and get the client to approve it before any work on building models and scenes begins. Both you and the client should sign the story board or a letter confirming its approval. Then if a dispute arises over changes to the animation, you can refer to the story board as the original source of the agreement.

The Process

So what is the process for creating story boards? Before you can create a story board, you must have a story to tell. Too many animators jump into the program and expect the story and sequence of actions to reveal themselves as the animation develops. Nothing could be further from reality. You must have three things in hand before you sit down in front of your computer:

- A story to tell
- A story board of the important scenes
- A script for the action and any sound effects

These three items are not always separate physical documents. Often the story board and the script are combined; maybe the story is only in your head. Regardless of the form that the components take, you must fully plan and develop all three before you begin animating.

Storytelling

What story are you going to tell with this animation? How will you hold the audience's attention? How will the story start? How will it end? How much time will the story take to tell? You must consider all of these things. Sometimes you have the complete story handed to you for animation; more often you receive the seed of a story idea and a requirement for a certain amount of running time.

A client may say, "Produce an animation of our proposed new building to help attract tenants." That is a story idea, but it is not detailed enough to move into the story board phase. Issues you need to consider for this story begin with questions such as, "What are the main selling features of the building?"

or "Is proximity to transportation hubs being promoted?" If transportation access is important, maybe you should consider a bird's-eye view that points out major transportation centers.

How do you show the entry sequence leading to the lobby and public reception area? How do you show the office suites? How do you get to the office suites? Computer graphics and demo tapes are littered with lifeless, boring, architectural walk-throughs that seem to be filmed by real estate zombies wandering through the building. As the animator, your job is to come up with an interesting way to tell even the most boring story and do it within the time constraints set by the client.

Story Board

Now you have a story to tell, and hopefully you've written it down and read it a few times. Make sure you're comfortable with it. How do you know whether this story will translate well into an animation? That is the job of the story board.

Take the story and break it down into the major scenes, important sequences of action, and transitions between scenes. If you are not sure a scene or action is important enough, include it anyway. You'll find it easier to weed out and discard scenes than to begin animation and discover you left an important issue unresolved.

After the story is broken down, draw quick, conceptual sketches of each scene or action. This is when many of you are saying, "Wait! I got into computer graphics because I don't like drawing by hand!" Remember that these sketches are for no eyes but your own. The story board sketches should be quick and rough, and if they look a little childish, so much the better. If you spend any time trying to make the story board sketches look good, you'll lose the flow of the action and miss the purpose of creating the story board.

With all the sketches complete, tack them on a board or spread them out on a table and review the story. Does the action flow from one scene to the next? Is there any awkwardness in the way the story unfolds? Does anything seem to be missing? Can all of these scenes be animated in the alloted time frame? These questions are much easier to answer with the sketches laid out in front of you than when the story is just written down. Analyze the story board and change any of the sketches as needed. If you have to read the notes next to a sketch to figure out what is happening at that point of the story, you have a problem. The scene or action in question is too weak. You either need to give the scene more emphasis or discard it. The text next to a sketch exists only for detail information and to describe how the scene is put together. Don't expect the text to make up for weak action or poorly planned scenes.

Script

With the story board approved, it is now time to write the script. In live action film, the script tells the actors what to say, what to do, and when to say and do it. The typical 3DS MAX animation script doesn't need to be quite so elaborate. Your script will focus on identifying animation keys and defining what happens at those keys. If you plan to include sound effects, you must indicate when sounds occur and how they relate to the animation keys as well.

One useful approach to the script is to take a copy of the story board and begin adding time references or frame numbers next to the sketches. This also provides a convenient place to note what sound effects belong with each scene. At this point your assumptions about timing and the overall length of the animation will be put to the test. Anticipate working through the story board and script many times until you find the right timing for the animation.

Types of Story Boards

You can use a couple of different types of story boards in the course of creating an animation. The first type follows closely what was described earlier—that is, a quick, rough sketch of the relevant scenes with notations to the side for timing, camera effects, and sound. This sketch is by far the most important version of the story board and is the one from which you work while creating the animation.

The other type of story board is as a presentation device. Remember the advice that both the animator and the client sign off on the final story board as part of the contract requirements? Many times you may not be comfortable presenting the rough, working version of the story board for client signature. In that case, you can buy commercially available story board forms that include small blank screens with lined blocks for your notes. A sample story board sheet is shown in figure 4.1. Redraw the story board cleanly on these forms for presentation and client approval.

You should create this type of story board only after you have completed the working story board and are satisfied with its contents. Trying to draw a presentation story board and working out the animation at the same time just doesn't work.

FIGURE 4.1

A typical preprinted story board sheet.

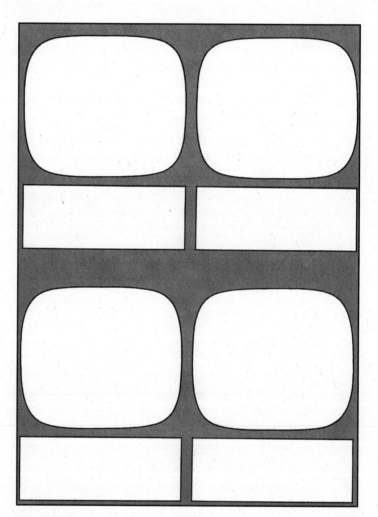

Drawing a Story Board

The process of creating a story board has been described in the preceding section. A few technical issues, however, must be addressed here. First, the drawing technique used should be fast and rough—anything that slows the flow of ideas will kill the creative process. Many people make the mistake of using the preprinted story board forms that contain multiple scenes on a single large sheet. Many problems are associated with that approach. The preprinted frames have a tendency to inhibit the drawing process; you try too hard to keep things in the lines, and the sharp edges of the frames are not compatible with a fast drawing technique. Also, if multiple frames are on a single sheet, it is difficult to discard or replace frames as you make changes. Every scene should be on a separate sheet of paper, and if that scene does not work out, discard it and try a new approach.

A second technique concerns the size of the story board. The drawings of each scene should be kept small to promote fast, conceptual drawing. If the paper is too big, you will have the uncontrollable urge to fill in unnecessary detail and background to make the drawing more "finished." The small, gummed-back sketch pads or even cheap notepads make great story board sheets. They are cheap, the pages are easy to tear out, and they are available in small sizes. After all of the scenes are drawn, the individual sketches are easy to lay out on a board and can be torn off, replaced, or rearranged with minimal effort.

After the client has signed off on the story board and you begin the animation, continue referring to the story board to guide your work. If multiple people are working on the project, give each of them a copy of the story board for reference. A Hollywood director does not go on location to shoot without taking the script along, and you should not sit in front of the workstation without having the story board close at hand.

Creating the Big Bounce Story Board

The following example gives you a chance to create a quick story board for a simple animation. Remember that the sketches for a story board should be very loose and rough. You also should keep the sketches small and use a separate page for each scene or action that you sketch.

If you do not have a small sketch book, make your own sketch sheets by tearing a standard $8^{1}/_{2}"\times11"$ page into four quarters so that each quarter is $4^{1}/_{4}"\times5^{1}/_{2}"$.

The Story

You will create a story board for the story titled "The Big Bounce." The final animation runs about 20 seconds.

You are looking at a beautiful landscape at the edge of a cliff when a red ball rolls up to the edge of the cliff and stops. The ball seems to look over the edge, and then after a brief pause, it bounces twice and jumps over the edge.

You follow the ball down, gaining speed as you go—just inches away from the face of the cliff. Suddenly, the ball strikes the ground with great force and rebounds out of view.

You are left standing at the base of the cliff, wondering what just happened, when you notice three more balls in the background. Slowly, the balls rotate, one by one, revealing scores of 9.5, 9.6, and 9.4. A near-perfect bounce.

Drawing the Story Board

The first step is to divide the story into its major scenes and action sequences. Consider the following scenes:

1. Opening shot. Cliff with landscape.
2. Ball rolls out to edge of the cliff.
3. Ball looks over edge.
4. Ball bounces.
5. Ball goes over the edge.
6. Falling.
7. Ball hits the ground.
8. Ball bounces out of view.
9. Shot of balls in the background.
10. Balls roll over revealing numbers.
11. Zoom in on middle ball.
12. Ball fades to black with just numbers on the screen.

You may have ideas for a slightly different division of scenes. If so, feel free to draw them. Figure 4.2 shows an example of what part of the story board might look like.

FIGURE 4.2
Sample story board frames.

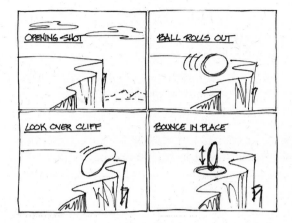

Adding Frame Numbers

Now that you have a story board, you must consider when each action occurs. Add time references and camera descriptions to each story board sketch. The following list shows a suggestion of how the timing could work out, assuming you have set a frame rate of 15 frames per second in the Time Configuration dialog:

1. Opening shot. Pause on scene of the cliff.
   (From 0.0 to 3.0 seconds, frames 1–45)

2. Ball rolls out to edge of the cliff.
   (From 3.0 to 5.0 seconds, frames 46–75)

3. Ball pauses and looks over edge.
   (From 5.0 to 7.0 seconds, frames 76–105)

4. Ball bounces two times, quickly, in place.
   (From 7.0 to 10.0 seconds, frames 106–150)

5. Ball goes over the edge.
   (From 10.0 to 10.5 seconds, frames 151–158)

6. Falling. See cliff flashing by. Ball stretches during fall.
   (From 10.5 to 13.0 seconds, frames 159–195)

7. Ball hits the ground. Squashes flat. Ground shakes.
    (From 13.0 to 13.5 seconds, frames 196–203)

8. Ball bounces out of view.
    (From 13.5 to 14.0 seconds, frames 204–210)

9. Shot of balls in the background. Pan and zoom in on balls.
    (From 14.0 to 15.0 seconds, frames 211–225)

10. Balls roll over, one at a time, revealing numbers. Pause.
    (15.0 to 18.0 seconds, frames 226–270)

11. Zoom in on middle ball.
    (18.0 to 19.0 seconds, frame 271–285)

12. Ball fades to black with just numbers on the screen.
    (From 19.0 to 20.0 second, frames 286–300)

You have just worked through the process of devising a story, drawing a story board, and producing a script for a simple animation. Even for a simple animation such as this, working out the timing and the key frames for all the scenes is quite involved. Imagine trying to create a sophisticated animation without first working out the story board and the script.

Animation Techniques

Many people approach computer animation solely from the standpoint of building the model. They assume that if you build a sufficiently good-looking model, it will come to life by itself. Unfortunately, they assume wrong. Demo tapes and even some critically acclaimed animation suffers from objects that move in an awkward and unrealistic manner. You can avoid this trap by realizing that in any animation, motion is an important part of the overall product. You must design your motion with as much care as you give to building the model and applying materials. In fact, motion is such an integral part of 3DS MAX that it is difficult to properly design materials, or model an object, without considering how they will be animated.

Understanding how objects move and how to simulate their movement in computer animation requires becoming familiar with the concepts of motion theory.

Design of Motion

Effective motion is as important to the success of your animation as any other element of the design. You readily accept animation of unreal or fantastic objects such as talking animals and battling spacecraft because those objects move in a lifelike manner. You also have seen animation where the subject is modeled in great detail and painstakingly rendered, but for some reason it just does not hold your attention. An analysis of unsuccessful animation usually reveals too little motion or motion that is not lifelike. In other words, your imagination often quietly fills in the missing detail in a model, but it does not forgive crude and unrealistic motion.

So how does motion become part of your overall design? Planning for motion must begin immediately—even before you begin to build the model. Examine your story board. How are objects moving, and where are they going?

The Physics of Motion

You understand the importance of believable motion and the need to design that motion. It is now time to study physics. You have heard the theory that states "Every action causes an equal and opposite reaction," but do you really understand how it translates into believable motion?

Imagine a standing figure about to perform a broad jump. Does the figure just suddenly pop across space? Of course not! First, the figure crouches down as the hips move back, and the torso leans forward to maintain balance. As the crouch begins, the arms swing backward until everything comes to a stop with the body in a full crouch, leaning forward, and arms extended fully back. After the most brief pause, the figure raises up on its toes, and the arms begin to swing forward. Next, the legs drive the body forward as the arms swing out, and the figure leaves the ground. Finally, as the figure flies across space, the arms reach fully forward, and the legs start to swing forward to prepare to land. Figure 4.3 illustrates this sequence.

The previous jumping sequence uses nearly all the important elements of animating believable motion:

- Anticipation
- Squash and stretch

- Overlapping action
- Follow-through
- Exaggeration
- Secondary action

These elements are covered in more detail later in this chapter. Try to imagine the landing sequence of the jumping figure. Sketch the actions of a broad jump as a story board, and then play the animation jump.avi from the CD-ROM to compare it with your sequence.

FIGURE 4.3
The motion of a broad jump.

Anticipation

Anticipation is a preliminary action that sets up a primary action. This setup action serves many useful purposes in animation. One use of anticipation is to simulate real motion. If an object is at rest, some preliminary action that transfers energy to the object must occur so that it can use that energy to execute the primary action. Use the previous broad jump sequence as an example once again. Before the figure can jump, it has to crouch down and swing its arms for counterbalance. (Just try to jump without bending your knees or swinging your arms.) Figure 4.4 identifies the anticipation portion of the broad jump motion.

Anticipation is used to prepare the audience for what is about to happen or directs audience attention to where the action is going to happen. Imagine a rope snapping under a heavy load. You have experienced this when a shoelace breaks or an overloaded clothesline snaps. The action is abrupt and without warning. If you animated such a sequence true to life, the audience would miss the actual breaking of the rope and would probably miss other important points of the animation while trying to figure out what had happened. The traditional solution to this scenario uses an extreme case of anticipation to prepare for the primary action. A close-up of the rope shows it stretching; a few strands snap; and then suddenly, POW! the rope breaks, and you accept that the heavy safe is about to land on Porky's head. The anticipation of the close-up prepares you for the breaking of the rope. You have seen this sequence a hundred times, and yet you probably never stopped to think, "Gee, ropes really don't break that way!"

FIGURE 4.4
Anticipation precedes an action.

Start pose

Anticipation pose

One final example of using anticipation to direct audience attention involves camera movement. Imagine an architectural walk-through of a house. You are in the family room, and you slowly pan around the space. Next, you want to see the kitchen on the right; turning and walking to the kitchen is boring, but a sudden jump to the kitchen in a quick cut is too abrupt and confusing. You employ anticipation by finishing the pan of the family room with the camera facing an open passage into the kitchen. A brief pause on the still image of the kitchen anticipates the cut (technically, a transition effect rather than an actual motion, but the same principle), and the audience makes the mental jump to the kitchen before the animation actually cuts to that scene.

Squash and Stretch

A property of living tissue and many other common materials is that these materials are soft and deform under the stress of motion. Think of the last time you watched the slow-motion replay of a hard-hitting football tackle. The body of the ball carrier probably stretched and deformed in ways that didn't seem humanly possible (or at least not survivable), and then suddenly the player was whole again and getting up off the field. This is an example of squash and stretch. All objects, unless they are very dense and very hard, exhibit some form of squash and stretch.

Remember the story board of the bouncing ball? The elongation of the ball as it fell and the flattening of the ball when it hit the ground also demonstrated the principle of squash and stretch. Imagine how a bowling ball and a rubber ball bounce. The bowling ball, being heavy and hard, bounces very little and does not deform at all when it hits the ground, as shown in figure 4.5—you might even consider making the ground deform when the bowling ball lands. A rubber ball, however, is much softer and lighter, so it deforms more than the bowling ball and bounces higher, as shown in figure 4.6.

FIGURE 4.5
A bowling ball bouncing on the ground.

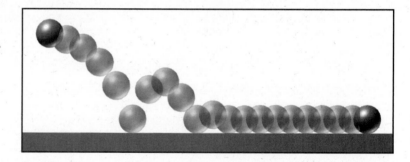

FIGURE 4.6
A rubber ball bouncing on the ground.

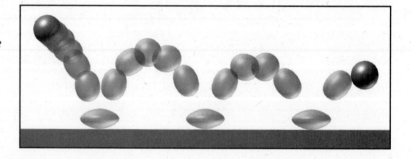

Another approach to squash and stretch applies to jointed figures. Rather than deforming the geometry of the figure, you indicate squash and stretch in the positioning of the figure's joints. You can see this by looking again at the broad jump. Anticipation often involves a squash or stretch. Quick motion almost always employs a stretch, and a sudden stop always employs a squash (sometimes a violent squash). Figure 4.7 identifies these effects in the broad jump sequence.

FIGURE 4.7
Squash and stretch in a broad jump.

Finally, you must never violate the law that states, "No matter how much an object deforms, it must always maintain the same apparent volume." Even in stylized cartoon animation, where squashing and stretching is highly exaggerated, there is an attempt to preserve a sense of constant volume. Consider a water balloon that deforms as you handle it. You aren't adding or removing any water as it deforms, so the volume remains constant. The Squash scale transformer and the Stretch modifier both employ this technique. When an object squashes along one axis, it automatically expands along the other two. However, these commands are too simple for sophisticated animation. It is up to you, the animator, to ensure that any deformation along one axis is offset by an opposite deformation along other axes, thereby maintaining a constant volume.

Overlapping Action

Another important element of believable motion is the concept of overlapping action. Not everything happens all at the same time. Overlapping action is seen in safety films that show crash dummies in a car that slams into a wall. A novice animator might position the car model at the point of impact and start adjusting the positions of all the objects in the car. When you look closely at the film, you see what really happens. In the first few frames after impact, the front of the car crumples and crushes all the way back to the front wheels, but the car's interior and the dummies haven't moved. They have yet to experience the impact. The situation rapidly changes in the next few frames as the dummies lunge forward against their safety belts, the windshield explodes, and so on. All this action is the result of a single event—the crash—yet each action begins at a different time. If you watch the rest of the crash, you notice that everything stops at different times as well.

You employ this same technique for other motion effects in your animation. Take the example of moving a figure's arm from a position of rest to pick up a glass on a table. A common mistake is to advance a few frames from the at-rest position, and then move all the arm objects to the final position. This mistake results in a very lifeless motion because everything starts and stops moving at the same time. The proper sequence requires that the upper arm begins to rise first, and then the forearm pivots out, followed by the wrist bending back. Finally, the fingers curl around the glass. Each of these motions begins before the preceding motion is complete, providing the realistic overlap that your audience subconsciously expects. Traditional animators often refer to this technique as "The Successive Breaking of Joints," because the motion is visualized by the joints breaking free from the at-rest position in a successive order. The motion begins at the shoulder and works its way down to the knuckles in the fingers.

Follow-Through

Follow-through is a companion to overlapping action and it means the same thing for animation as it does for throwing a ball or swinging a bat. An action almost never comes to a complete and sudden stop. Instead, inertia carries the object beyond the termination point, often causing the object to slowly reverse direction and settle back to the intended stop location.

3D Studio MAX includes Bézier and tension, continuity, and bias (TCB) animation controllers to help you create natural motion and follow-through. Although these controllers are useful, you must not rely on them too much. Most of the time, you need to manually specify the appropriate follow-through, and then fine-tune the motion in Track View.

NOTE

For more information about the animation controllers, see Chapter 23, "Animation Control Tools."

Staging

Staging actually has more to do with composition than motion. The idea behind staging is that objects in motion should be positioned in a way so that the motion is quickly detected and clearly understood. A common mistake involves placing an action where it cannot be noticed, such as in front of a more interesting object that divides the audience's attention. If your audience cannot detect an action, why use it?

Try to visualize the primary objects in your scene as silhouettes. If an action occurs within the silhouette of another object, that action is hard to detect. If you move the action to one side, where it is not masked by another object, the action stands out. As an example, look at figure 4.8. The rendered view of the robot arm shows it picking up a box. When you view the scene in silhouette, you cannot easily discern what is happening. Compare figure 4.8 with figure 4.9. The scene in the second figure is easier to understand in both the rendered and silhouette views. The only difference is that the action is staged to the side of the robot arm.

FIGURE 4.8
View of a robot arm with poor staging.

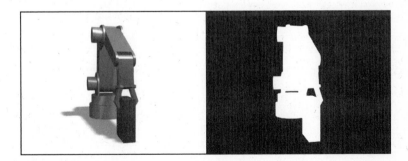

TIP

This tip provides a good test for proper staging. Turn off all the lights in the scene and hide any unimportant or distant background objects; keep only the primary object in the scene, along with any nearby secondary or background objects. Set your background color to

continues

something other than black and render a preview .avi. The result is an .avi of the main objects in your scene, rendered as black silhouettes against your viewport background color. If the motion that you want to convey is visible in silhouette, then it is easy to recognize in the final animation.

FIGURE 4.9
View of a robot arm with better staging.

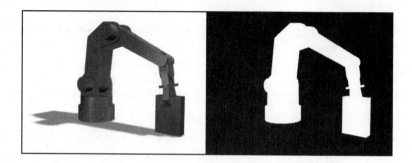

Exaggerated Motion

After all the effort you've put into making your animation "realistic," it seems counterproductive to speak of exaggerating anything. You must often exaggerate a motion or effect, however, to ensure that the audience catches it. In no way does the proper use of exaggeration invalidate or harm the believability of an animation. The possible exception is animation produced for courtroom presentations, in which strict adherence to precise motion is more important than good presentation.

Exaggeration works in conjunction with anticipation and staging to direct the audience's attention to the action that you want the audience to see. Anticipation sets up the action, staging ensures that the action occurs where it can be seen, and exaggeration makes sure that the action is not so subtle that the audience fails to notice.

You can see good examples of exaggeration while watching a TV sitcom and then a drama show. Sitcoms are full of gross exaggeration—the double takes, stumbles, and sweeping motions used to accomplish mundane tasks. Those exaggerations are employed for comedic effect. Now watch a drama with the same critical eye. The exaggeration is still there, just toned down. Notice the extra flourishes that occur when an actor reaches for the phone or pulls out some keys. Notice how facial expressions are more pronounced than in real life. Such exaggeration does not detract from the reality of the scene, rather it enhances reality by making sure the audience catches what is happening. Employ these same techniques in your animation.

Secondary Action

Secondary action happens as a result of another action. It is easy to forget about secondary action, because in real life you take such side effects for granted. Even though you might not consciously notice secondary action in real life, you need to include it if your animation is to be interesting and realistic.

A common error of omission regarding secondary motion involves bouncing balls. Consider an animation that shows a basketball bouncing off the rim of the goal. Some animators might fail to show the rim deflecting from the force of the bounce. The deflection of the rim is a secondary motion, and its absence makes the animation look fake and mechanical. Figure 4.10 shows the sequence of a rim deflecting from the bounce of a ball.

Load and play the file rim.avi from the accompanying CD-ROM to see the result of applying secondary action to the rim of a basketball hoop. Notice that the rim of the goal deflects downward as the ball strikes, and springs up when the ball leaves.

FIGURE 4.10
Rim deflection as a secondary action.

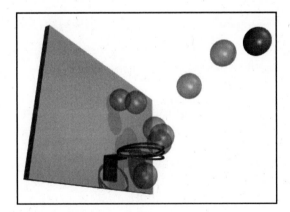

Studies of Animal Motion

The recognized reference on both animal and human motion is the collected work of Eadweard Muybridge, a photographer who took high-speed photographs of animals and people while they were performing various tasks. His book, *Complete Human and Animal Motion*, is a required reference for anyone who wants to animate living creatures.

Studying the photographs of Muybridge does not automatically make you ready to bring your animals to life. It is difficult to hold an audience's attention if you just duplicate the typical walk of an animal. Instead, you must give the creature a personality. Refer back to the paragraphs on anticipation and exaggeration and think about how you can employ those techniques to impart personality and life to your models. A few examples are adding an extra bounce to the walk of a puppy, adding frantic scrambling to the legs of a running mouse, or causing a duck to rear back in preparation of takeoff.

Studies of Human Motion

Everything stated about animal motion applies to human motion, except that you must be more careful with exaggerated effects. You are much more aware of how your own body moves. Because of this, you are less forgiving of exaggeration or movement that goes too far beyond what is really possible. The best way to get a feel for what is possible is to observe how the people around you move. Consider this an official license for people-watching.

You need to concentrate on two properties of human motion that often are overlooked: balance and curved motion.

Balance

With the exception of falling, the body is always balanced. If you extend your right arm, your left arm, shoulder, and torso, all pivot and move back. This action balances the extended mass of your right arm. Likewise, few people stand perfectly ramrod straight. Instead, they shift their weight to one leg, causing the hips and torso to twist as they shift to balance. The other leg carries little weight and acts as an outrigger to compensate for small changes in balance.

N O T E

Walking and running are special cases of falling. When you walk, you are constantly cycling through the process of falling forward, restoring balance, and falling forward again. Running works the same way except that you are spending most of your time falling forward.

Figure 4.11 demonstrates the difference between an unnatural straight pose and a realistic-looking balanced pose. Remember that every motion of one part the body is offset by a balancing motion in another part of the body.

FIGURE 4.11
A stiff, unnatural pose versus a natural pose.

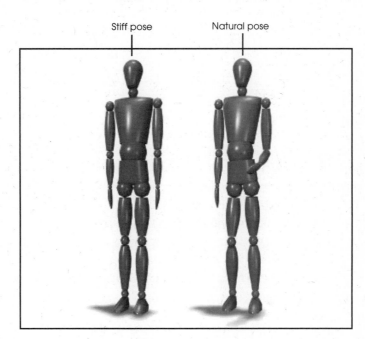

Stiff pose   Natural pose

Curved Motion

No straight lines exist in nature. This statement also applies to natural motion. The default animation controllers in 3DS MAX are set up to deliver curved motion, but remember that you use these to fine-tune a motion that you design manually. Two examples where curved motion often is missed are arm swings and head turns.

Watch a person as he swings his arm up for a handshake. Does the arm simply swing straight up? Usually the arm not only swings up, but it also swings out from the side and back in again. This subtle motion makes all the difference between an unnatural, robotic move and a move that appears lifelike.

See figures 4.12 and 4.13 for examples of two head turns. Many people may make the mistake of animating the head turn as it appears in figure 4.12. The features of the face follow a straight line as the head turns from side to side. The result is an unnatural, robotic head turn in which the features seem to slide across the face.

Figure 4.13 demonstrates a more realistic head motion. Notice that the head dips down and back up as it turns. The features of the face now follow a curved path from one side to the other. The greater the amount of dip, the more emotion conveyed by the turn.

FIGURE 4.12
An unnatural head turn.

Unnatural straight motion

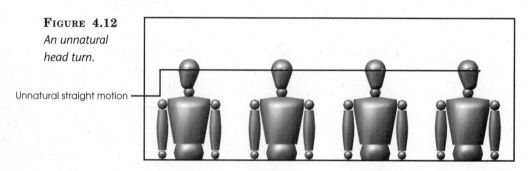

FIGURE 4.13
A natural head turn.

Natural curved motion

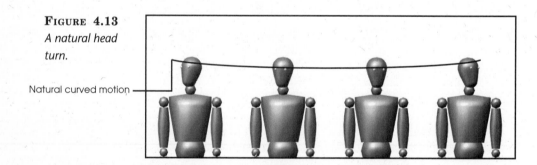

In Practice: Employing Good Animation Techniques

- **Use story boards** A story board aids planning your animation and leads to better results and less wasted time. Added benefits of story boards include helping explain proposals to clients, and saving a record of what type of animation a client approved.

- **Make motion believable** Use traditional animation techniques such as anticipation, squash and stretch, follow-through, and overlapping action to make even the wildest animation more believable.

- **Make motion visible** Use the concepts of staging ang exaggeration to ensure your audience doesn't miss the action you worked so hard to create.

- **Duplicate natural patterns of motion** Animals and people maintain balance in their motion and move in arcs rather than straight lines. If you ignore these traits your animation will appear mechanical and lifeless.

Image by Westwood Studios
Provided courtesy of Kinetix™

Chapter 5

PLANNING YOUR PROJECTS

An important time in any project is the time just before you start

production. If you have thought through the project, planned for

the important issues, and decided what is not so important, you

are likely to succeed. If, instead, you just jump in and start

building a scene, you are likely to experience extra errors and

wasted time and you will probably need to redo a greater portion

of your work. This chapter looks at the issues you need to consider

when beginning a project and shows you how to set up your scene

to get started.

This chapter covers issues that will help you plan your projects and avoid wasted effort. These issues include the following:

- Deciding the appropriate levels of accuracy, detail, and complexity in your scene.

- Understanding how 3D Studio MAX stores numeric values and how to avoid numeric round off.

- Defining units of measurement for efficient modeling and sharing of files.

- Setting up and navigating three-dimensional views.

- Managing the many file types used by 3D Studio MAX.

You have an idea for an animation. You have worked out the story and drawn the story boards. Now you have an empty scene waiting to be filled with animated objects. Your next step is to model those objects.

Modeling Decisions

Start any modeling effort by thinking about the objects you need to create. Do they need to be dimensionally accurate or can they just look good? Are they highly detailed or rough and schematic? How important is quick rendering time, and how much modeling can you replace with texture maps? When you can answer these questions, you have an idea about the levels of accuracy, detail, and complexity you need in your scene.

Accuracy

How accurate does the model need to be? Unlike CAD systems in which accuracy is slavishly adhered to, 3D Studio MAX can be more flexible. A good rule of thumb is, "If it looks right, it is right." This is not to imply that you can "fudge" dimensions in your models or ignore accuracy altogether. What it does mean is that you must be aware that 3D Studio MAX is, above all else, a visualization tool. The level of accuracy needed to properly display objects in a scene is far less than the level of accuracy needed to properly manufacture those same objects.

Most of the time, you can achieve appropriate accuracy by trusting your sensibilities. What makes a model appear accurate often has little to do with exact dimensions. The human visual system is not very good at distinguishing exact distances, lengths, and spacing; what your visual system excels at is comparing proportions and relationships. If you are comfortable with the proportions and relationships between the objects in your scene, your audience will be comfortable, too.

Sometimes, you must give extra attention to dimensional accuracy. Good examples are scientific animation, forensic presentations, and certain types of architectural or engineering presentations. You must realize, however, that even for projects that demand extreme accuracy, thresholds exist beyond which any extra precision is wasted. The two main thresholds you need to concern yourself with are:

- Image output thresholds
- 3DS MAX numeric thresholds

Image Output Threshold

One way to evaluate your threshold for precision is to examine your intended output media. Determine the visible width and height of your scene, and divide those values by the width and height of your output resolution. The result is the model dimension covered by one pixel. You waste effort by modeling to a precision that is less than one half of a single pixel's dimension.

NOTE

In an animation, the visible width and height of your scene varies depending on camera position and field-of-view (FOV). Calculate your precision requirements from the most critical scene in the animation.

The following example measures the image output precision threshold of a scene. Imagine that you plan to create a rendering of a low-rise office building to display on-screen at a resolution of 800×600 pixels. You want to know how precise to make the model.

MEASURING PRECISION THRESHOLD IN A SCENE

This example makes use of two types of helper objects— Grids and Tape Measures. The example also measures the size of the view Safe Frame. Details on how to create and use the helper objects are presented in the following chapter. A discussion of the Safe Frame is presented in Chapter 20, "Cameras and Setting the Shot."

The first step is to create a simple stand-in model and set up the primary camera view for the scene. Figure 5.1 shows a scene—PRECISE.MAX—that you can load from the accompanying CD-ROM to follow along with this example. The scene contains a stand-in for an office building 180' wide, 130' deep, and 34' tall.

FIGURE 5.1

Stand-in scene for calculating precision requirements.

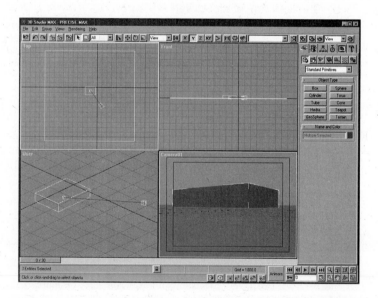

Study the camera view in the lower right viewport. Notice the concentric rectangles that border the view. These rectangles are the view Safe Frame. The outer rectangle at the edge of the viewport indicates the exact size of the final rendered image. To properly determine your precision threshold, you need to know the width and height of the Safe Frame in camera view, measured at the building. You take these measurements by creating a grid object aligned to the camera, and then creating tape measures on the grid.

1. Click Grid from the Helpers General category of the Create panel.

2. Drag the cursor in any viewport to create a grid.

   In figure 5.2, a 50' square grid was created in the Camera01 viewport.

3. Choose Views, Grids, Activate Grid Object to make the grid object you just created your active construction plane.

4. Choose Views, Grids, Align To View to align the grid with the Camera01 viewport.

   Figure 5.2 shows the results of the previous four steps. After using the Align To View command, the grid moves and rotates so it is aligned with the camera and centered on the camera's location.

FIGURE 5.2

Creating and aligning the grid object.

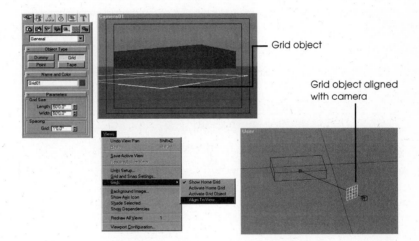

You now need to move the grid along the camera's line of sight until the grid is centered on the subject of the view (the building). You do this by moving the grid along its local Z axis.

5. Click Move and set the Transform Managers to Local coordinates and Z-axis constraint.

6. Move the grid so it is centered on the building as shown in figure 5.3. You can move the grid in any convenient viewport.

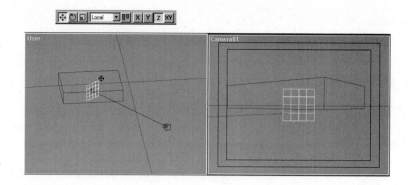

Finally, you are ready to create two Tape helpers to measure the height and width of the Safe Frame in the camera view.

7. Click in the Camera01 view to make it active.

8. Click Tape from the Helpers General category of the Create panel.

9. Create one tape that measures the width of the Safe Frame and a second tape that measures the height, as seen in figure 5.4.

10. From the Modify panel, select each tape one at a time. Note their lengths in the Length field.

11. Divide the measured width and height by the configured render width and render height. The results should be as follows:

    Width: 284'/800=0.36

    Height: 213'/600=0.36

FIGURE 5.4
*Creating Tape objects
on the aligned grid.*

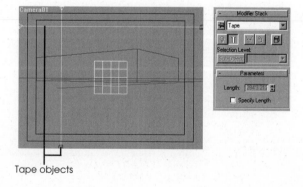

Tape objects

The result of 0.36', or just over 4", is that each pixel in the image covers a little more than 4" in the scene. If you assume that an object is centered on a pixel, then that object can move about 2" to either side and will still be within the same pixel. This model and camera view have an image output precision threshold of plus or minus 2".

Using the information from the previous example, you can determine that for the given camera angle and output resolution, modeling any detail less than 2" wide is a waste of effort. Also, you want to carefully consider whether any details less than 4" wide are really needed in the shot.

NOTE

In the preceding exercise, you calculated the same value of 0.36' for both the height and the width of the image. These values are equal only when the aspect ratio for your rendering device is set to 1.0.

When you specify rendering output resolutions, the aspect ratio reported in the Render Scene dialog is not always 1.0. The configuration for a video resolution of 512×486 yields an aspect ratio of 1.25. When this occurs, the result is two different values for the distance covered by one pixel—one result for when you measure horizontally and one for when you measure vertically. You must decide which value governs the most critical details in your scene.

You can employ a similar technique for projects in which precision is not that critical. Make some rough estimates about the size of primary views, and divide those sizes by the output resolution. These calculations provide an estimate of the precision threshold suitable for many projects.

TIP

The previous example uses a technique of aligning a grid object with a camera view to create objects on the perspective picture plane. You can use this same technique whenever you need to trace objects or create objects aligned with a perspective view.

3DS MAX Numeric Thresholds

3D Studio MAX uses single precision floating point numbers (floats) to store numeric values. This choice improves 3D Studio MAX performance at a slight cost of some precision when working with very large or very small models. Floats can represent incredibly large and incredibly small numbers, but they are limited to seven significant digits, resulting in 3D Studio MAX's ability to accurately track numbers over a range of seven digits, but after that range is exceeded, round-off errors occur.

How likely are you to be affected by numeric round-off? It depends upon the subjects you model, your modeling style, and the number of calculations needed to represent your object in the scene. The following are a few examples about where round-off occurs.

If your system unit is set to the default of 1.0", some approximate ranges of accuracy include:

- Accurate to 1" over a range of 60.8 miles

- Accurate to $\frac{1}{8}$" over a range of 7.8 miles

- Accurate to 1 centimeter over a range of 6.12 kilometers

- Accurate to 1 millimeter over a range of 765 meters

Notice that you can easily work with metric (SI) units even though the system unit is set to 1.0". Details about setting your working units are presented in the section "Setting a Unit of Measure" later in this chapter.

Because of the way floats are calculated, it is difficult to exactly determine where round-off occurs for any given model. The following list includes general guidelines to help avoid round-off:

- **Model at an appropriate level of detail for the scale of the scene.**   If your scene covers an entire city the size of Manhattan, for example, it makes no sense to model your door knobs.

- **Keep your model near the world origin.**   When you import models from CAD systems with much higher precision, it is not uncommon for objects to be located millions of units away from the world origin. Move these objects back to the world origin, either in the CAD system before you export or in 3D Studio MAX immediately after you import.

- **Change the System Unit Scale in the Preference Settings dialog only when absolutely necessary.**   You should rarely need to change the scale. More details are presented in the section "Setting the System Unit Scale" later in this chapter.

   For example, if you plan to model extremely small objects, using a molecular scale, you might consider changing the System Unit to millimeters. If you plan to model extremely large objects, such as at an astronomical scale, you might consider setting the system unit to miles or kilometers.

Modeling Detail

The issue of appropriate detail is closely related to precision. In the previous example scene, one pixel equals a distance of about 4". Detail smaller than 4" loses definition in the final rendering.

You also want to consider what is appropriate visual detail for your scenes. Many situations exist in which a detail is large enough to appear in a scene, yet you leave it out. Why? Because some details are not appropriate for the message that you are trying to convey. For instance, take the example of the office building described previously. You created the model of the building and located it on the site. Now you intend to add some people and cars in the foreground. You calculate the precision threshold for the cars and realize that details, such as windshield wipers and hood ornaments, would be visible. Do not model them. The details on the cars detract from the main subject of your rendering, the building. In this case, concerns about composition and focus overrule exact attention to detail.

You can also consider employing an artist's technique in your models. Often, an artist represents a detail with a suggestion of a shape or a shadow where something belongs. The viewer subconsciously fills in the details. You might be surprised at how little detail you actually need to model.

Another situation in which you should leave out detail is when you create animation for a courtroom presentation. Detail and extreme realism often cloud the issue at hand. Renderings that are too realistic can prejudice the jury and are often rejected as evidence. You must work closely with your client to determine the appropriate level of detail for such a project. In most cases, you should use the minimum amount of detail necessary to get the point across.

Model Complexity

Model complexity refers to the number of faces used to build models. A good rule of thumb is to use as few faces as possible in order to achieve the required level of realism because rendering speed is directly tied to the number of faces in the scene. The more faces in a scene, the longer that scene will take to render.

You can summarize the many different techniques for reducing model complexity into the following strategies:

■ Control the creation of faces through the various object parameters such as segments and sides for primitives, path and shape steps for loft objects, and tessellation controls for some modifiers. These settings directly control the number of faces used to display an object, and many of these parameters can be animated to add and reduce complexity as needed over the course of an animation.

■ Use the Optimize modifier to reduce the complexity of a model. The Optimize modifier uses multiple parameters to analyze an object and reduce the number of vertices and faces used. The Optimize parameters can also be animated to change the amount of optimization over time.

■ Use maps instead of actual geometry. You can represent many details in a model by applying a map, or picture, of the detail, rather than actually modeling the detail with faces. Figure 5.5 shows an example of this technique by using a model of a calculator. The extremely simple geometry produces a complex rendering through the careful use of maps. The rule here is to "Never model in geometry what can be represented with a map."

FIGURE 5.5
The wireframe model and mapped and rendered versions of a calculator.

Setting Up Units

There are two places where you control how 3D Studio MAX defines and measures units in your scene: the Units Setup dialog and the System Unit Scale in the Preference Settings dialog.

Your primary method for defining your working units is through the Units Setup dialog, which enables you to specify how units are measured and displayed.

The System Unit Scale sets the internal value for what a generic unit represents. This value should rarely, if ever, change.

Setting a Unit of Measure

Use the Units Setup dialog from the Views menu to define how you want to measure and display distance in your scene. The Units Setup dialog has four options, as shown in figure 5.6.

FIGURE 5.6
The Units Setup dialog.

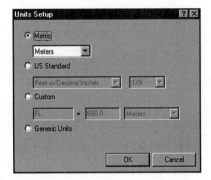

The first two options are Metric (SI) and US Standard (feet and inches) methods of measurement. These choices are pretty straightforward, and they offer sub-options within their specific methods. For example, two of the US Standard options are Decimal Feet (a civil engineering standard) and Feet with Fractional Inches (an architectural standard). The Metric method can measure in Millimeters, Centimeters, Meters, or Kilometers.

Use the third option, Custom, to define any custom unit of measurement that you want to use. The only restriction is that you must be able to describe the unit of measure using units that 3DS MAX already understands. Specify the suffix for the unit you want to define, followed by the amount of known units the custom unit equals.

The *3D Studio MAX User's Guide* uses an example of defining an ancient unit of measure know as a cubit, but custom units are handy for other modern measuring methods as well. For example, suppose that you wanted to model very small objects. A US Standard method expresses small measures in mils, which equals 0.001 inches. If you wanted to work in mils, you might define the following custom unit:

  Mil = 0.001 Inches

The last option is to use Generic Units. 3D Studio MAX doesn't assign any particular meaning to generic units and the size of your objects is governed by the current setting for the System Unit Scale.

Working in generic units is not a very good idea. Every time you create an object, you have in mind some particular unit of measure. People do not naturally think in terms of generic units. Look at the following three statements:

"My desk is 30 by 60 units."

"I'm 6 units tall."

"That bolt requires a 14-unit wrench."

These statements are vague and imply very odd spatial relationships—until you assign the correct unit of measure:

"My desk is 30 by 60 inches."

"I'm 6-feet tall."

"That bolt requires a 14-millimeter wrench."

The same confusion occurs when you model in generic units. This confusion is made worse when you arbitrarily decide that one generic unit represents something other than 1.0 inch (the system unit default). Working in generic units almost guarantees that you will have difficulty sharing files with other 3DS MAX users, because no one will know for sure what a unit is supposed to represent. Always define the unit of measure you want to use.

Setting the System Unit Scale

The setting for the System Unit Scale is buried on the General panel of the Preference Settings dialog for good reason. You should not change the setting as a matter of habit. 3D Studio MAX internally stores distances in generic units that have no particular meaning. The System Unit Scale is applied as the base scale when 3D Studio MAX displays measurements in various parameter fields. Changing the meaning of the System Unit Scale changes the meaning of all measurements in your scene.

The System Unit Scale is stored in the 3dsmax.ini file and not in individual MAX scene files. All measurements in a scene file are stored in generic units, and those units are multiplied by the current System Unit Scale when you open or merge a scene file. For example, create a cube with 10-inch sides by using the default System Unit Scale of 1.0". When you save the scene, the box is stored as having sides 10 units long. If you then change the System Unit Scale to 1 Foot, and open the scene containing the box, it now reports that the box is 10 feet to a side. The box never changed. It is still 10 units to a side; it's just that the meaning of the unit changed.

It is difficult to merge and share files between workstations using different System Unit Scales. You should try to leave the System Unit Scale at its default of 1.0" and only change the System Unit Scale after carefully considering its effect on the overall project and how the file might be used in the future.

The only reason you change the System Unit Scale is to avoid round-off problems when modeling extremely large or extremely small scenes. (See the discussion of numeric thresholds and single precision floating point numbers earlier in this chapter.) Round-off affects not only the precision of your scene, but also the capability to transform objects and zoom magnification levels.

For example, say you are modeling the entire Earth. Using a System Unit Scale of 1.0", the Earth's 24,900 mile circumference is more than 1.5 billion inches. Setting the unit of measure to miles helps you work with such numbers, but 3D Studio MAX is still working in inches. Single precision round-off occurs at about 40 feet, and you will encounter many problems working with such large numbers—the most obvious problem being that the maximum view is limited to a width of just less than four million units; you won't be able to view the extents of your scene.

If you change the System Unit Scale to 1.0 Mile, the numbers become much more manageable. The Earth's circumference is 24,900 system units; you have plenty of room to zoom the view, and your precision is still good to 40 feet.

Manipulating Views

3D Studio MAX provides a fast and efficient way to manipulate views of your model. The viewing tools range from specifying the screen layout to controlling view type and orientation to specifying how to optimize redraw performance while you work.

Viewport Arrangement

You can specify two viewport layouts and switch between them at will. Choose Views, Viewport Configuration from the menu bar, or right-click the viewport label and choose Configure from the pop-up menu.

Figure 5.7 shows the Layout panel of the Viewport Configuration dialog with the 14 standard viewport arrangements at the top of the dialog. At the right side of the dialog are two option buttons enabling you to choose whether you are working with Layout A or Layout B. Select the layout you want to specify and then click on one of the 14 standard viewport arrangements.

The layout option (A or B) that is active when you click OK is the layout displayed in the 3D Studio MAX application window. You can switch between Layout A and Layout B at any time by pressing | (the vertical bar key).

FIGURE 5.7

Layout panel of the Viewport Configuration dialog.

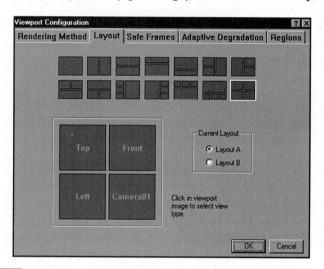

View Orientations

More important than setting the viewport layout is setting the various view orientations. 3D Studio MAX supports 13 view orientations. These view orientations can be organized into four functional groups:

- Standard orthographic views of Top, Bottom, Front, Back, Left, and Right
- Custom user-defined views of User (axonometric) and Perspective
- Object-based views of Camera, Spotlight, Grid, and Shape
- Track for displaying the animation tool, Track View, in a viewport

You can assign view types while specifying the viewport layout from the Viewport Configuration dialog. Clicking in a viewport of the sample layout at the left side of the dialog displays a pop-up list of available view types, as seen in figure 5.8. This same list is also available by right-clicking on a viewport label and choosing Views from the pop-up menu. Note that the

Camera and Spotlight view types do not appear in the list until you have created cameras and spotlights in your scene.

FIGURE 5.8

The view type pop-up list.

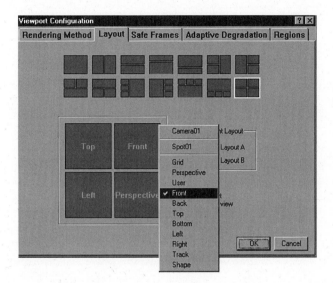

The fastest and most convenient way to change view type is to use the following single-letter shortcut keys to assign a view to the active viewport:

- **T**   Displays the Top view

- **B**   Displays the Bottom view

- **F**   Displays the Front view

- **K**   Displays the Back view

- **L**   Displays the Left view

- **R**   Displays the Right view

- **U**   Converts the current view to an axonometric User view. The angle of the view does not change. Converting a Front view to a User view preserves the same view alignment, but changes the active Construction Plane to the Ground Plane. See the discussion of construction planes in Chapter 7, "Basics of Creation."

  Pressing U is a convenient way to toggle between perspective and axonometric views without changing the viewing angle.

- **P**   Converts the current view to a perspective view. Like the User view, pressing P preserves the view angle and switches the Construction Plane to the Ground Plane. Unlike the User view, perspective projection always changes the appearance of the view.

- **C** Displays a Camera perspective view. If you have multiple cameras, a dialog appears in which you can select a camera by its name.

- **$** Displays a perspective view from a spotlight. If you have multiple spotlights, a dialog appears in which you can select a spotlight by its name.

- **G** Aligns the view with an active grid object. You can create grid objects and then specify one as the active Construction Plane. Working with a Grid view is similar to working in a Top view when the Ground Plane is the active construction plane. Pressing G when a grid object is not active aligns the view with the Ground Plane.

- **D** Disables the viewport. A disabled viewport prevents the real-time redraw of any scene geometry when the view is not the active view. An active disabled view behaves like any other view while you work in it. When you make another view active, the disabled view freezes its display until you make the view active again or choose Redraw All Views from the Views menu. This increases active view display performance at the expense of real-time update in the disabled views.

- **E** Converts a viewport to Track View display. Normally, Track View displays in a floating window above the 3D Studio MAX application window. This is just another display option. Why use E as the shortcut? Because just about every other letter in the term Track View had been used as a shortcut for something else.

- There is no shortcut key for Shape views. Choose Shape from the pop-up menu to align the view with a selected Shape object. Using a Shape view with Local or View coordinates is a convenient way to edit shapes that are not aligned with a construction plane or grid object.

NOTE

Most shortcut keys can be changed in 3D Studio MAX by using the Keyboard panel of the Preference Settings dialog. The view shortcuts just described are 3D Studio MAX shipping defaults.

Navigating Views

There are many ways to navigate through 3D space in 3D Studio MAX. The basics of using the view navigation buttons is presented in Chapter 4 of the *3D Studio MAX User's Guide*. The information in the sections that follow provides some extra insight into using views and shows you how to accelerate view navigation by using keyboard alternates.

Zooming Views

Most of the view navigation buttons are used to zoom the view. These buttons are available for all view types except Camera and Spotlight views.

The basic method of use involves clicking a Zoom button and then dragging in a view to define the zoom magnification. You can modify the effect of a zoom command by pressing the following modifier keys:

■ Ctrl while dragging accelerates the change in zoom magnification

■ Ctrl while dragging a Zoom All or clicking a Zoom Extents All excludes Perspective views from the command

■ Ctrl and right-click Zoom or Zoom All zooms in 2X

■ Alt and right-click Zoom or Zoom All zooms out 2X

You can perform the following keyboard shortcuts as stand-alone commands or interactively while you are in the middle of another command. For example, while you are dragging an object, you can press any of the following keyboard shortcuts to change your view without interrupting the move:

■ **Alt+Ctrl+Z**   Zoom extents in the active view

■ **Shift+Ctrl+Z**   Zoom extents in all views

■ **Shift+(Num+)**   Zoom in 2X in the active view

■ **Shift+(Num–)**   Zoom out 2X in the active view

■ **Shift+[**   Zoom in about half as much (1.414×) as Shift+(Num+); this is officially called Interactive Zoom In

■ **Shift+]**   Zoom out about half as much (0.707×) as Shift+(Num-); this shortcut is officially called Interactive Zoom Out

The following two zoom shortcuts are stand-alone commands only. They cancel any other active command.

- **Z**   Zoom active view

- **Ctrl+W**   Zoom region mode

You can assign a shortcut key to all of the Zoom commands. The shortcuts listed previously are the 3D Studio MAX shipping defaults. You can change the shortcut assignments or assign shortcuts to the other Zoom commands by using the Keyboard panel of the Preference Settings dialog.

Dragging up and down to zoom a view and using keyboard shortcuts are fast ways to set view magnification. Sometimes you might need to precisely adjust zoom magnification levels, and in those cases you can use your keyboard arrow keys to zoom the view.

The method for zooming with arrow keys begins differently than the normal zoom procedure. Using the normal method, you click the Zoom or Zoom All button and then drag in a viewport to adjust zoom magnification. If you want to use the arrow keys, you must click in a viewport, not drag.

The arrow keys have the following effect:

- Pressing the up or down arrow changes the zoom magnification by a small amount.

- Pressing Ctrl while pressing an arrow key changes the zoom magnification by a large amount. The amount of zoom magnification is about 100 times the magnification without the Ctrl key.

- Pressing and holding an arrow key zooms continuously.

To zoom a view by using arrow keys, do the following:

1. Click Zoom or Zoom All.

2. Click in the viewport where you want to perform the zoom.

3. Press the Up arrow to zoom in.

4. Press the Down arrow to zoom out.

5. Click to complete the zoom, or right-click to cancel.

Panning Views

The Pan command is also available for all views except Camera and Spotlight views. Actually, Camera and Spotlight views have a command called Pan, but it is a completely different operation.

You can use the following shortcuts with the Pan command:

- **Ctrl** while dragging accelerates the pan distance.

- **Ctrl+P (Pan mode)**   This command cannot be used interactively; it cancels the current command before activating Pan mode.

- **I (Interactive Pan)**   Pressing I pans the view so it is centered on your cursor. It is interactive and does not interrupt the current command. Interactive Pan is similar to a technique called edge scrolling but you have full control over when the scroll occurs.

Just as with the Zoom commands, you can Pan a view using your keyboard arrow keys. This technique gives you very precise control over Pan distance.

The arrow keys have the following effect:

- Pressing an arrow key pans the view a small amount.

- Pressing Ctrl while pressing an arrow key pans the view by a large amount. The distance panned will be about 100 times the distance panned without the Ctrl key.

- Pressing and holding an arrow key pans continuously.

To Pan a view using arrow keys, do the following:

1. Click Pan.

2. Click in the viewport where you want to perform the pan.

3. Press the Up or Down arrow to pan vertically.

4. Press the Left or Right arrow to pan horizontally.

5. Click to complete the pan, or right-click to cancel.

Rotating Views

The Arc Rotate button is available for all views except the Camera and Spotlight views. Use the Arc Rotate button to interactively rotate a view about any of the three coordinate axes. Arc Rotate has the added effect of converting an orthographic view to a User axonometric view.

The Release 1.1 version of 3D Studio MAX contains a bug that prevents Arc Rotate from behaving correctly in non-perspective views. When using Arc Rotate, view rotations are supposed to be performed about the center of each viewport, instead the center of view rotation is offset an amount from the World Origin that is roughly equal to the inverse distance from the World

Origin to the view center. The farther away your view is from the World origin, the less usable Arc Rotate becomes. Always use Arc Rotate Selected when you want to rotate a non-perspective view, because all view rotations with Arc Rotate Selected are centered on the selected object, the behavior is more predictable. Standard Arc Rotate works fine in a Perspective view.

Arc Rotate works in the following manner:

- Dragging the Left or Right tab rotates the view about a world Z axis passing through the view center.

- Dragging the Top or Bottom tab rotates the view about a horizontal screen axis passing through the view center.

- Dragging outside the Arc Ball rotates the view about a screen depth axis passing through the view center.

Turn on Angle Snap to restrict view rotations to the angle snap value set in the Grid and Snap Settings dialog.

As with zooming and panning, you can also rotate views using the arrow keys. This technique gives you very precise control over view angles.

The arrow keys have the following effect:

- Press the left or right arrow to rotate the view in 1.0-degree increments about a world Z axis passing through the center of the view.

- Press Shift with the left or right arrow key to rotate the view, in 1.0-degree increments, about a screen depth axis passing through the center of the view.

- Press the up or down arrow key to rotate the view, in 1.0-degree increments, about a horizontal screen axis passing through the center of the view.

- Press Ctrl with any of the above methods to rotate the view in 10.0-degree increments.

To Arc Rotate a view using arrow keys, do the following:

1. Click Arc Rotate.

2. Click in the viewport where you want to perform the pan.

3. Press an arrow key to rotate the view.

4. Click to complete the rotation, or right-click to cancel.

Working with Files

The final issue when setting up a project concerns strategies for finding, managing, and storing the many files that go into making a successful project. Issues such as saving files, merging files, backing up files, archiving files, and managing file structures are covered in the following sections.

Combining Multiple Scene Files

The first file management technique involves the construction of the scene and all of its supporting models. If your subject is simple, you can model the whole scene in a single MAX scene file. It is more likely, however, that your scene consists of many objects and that modeling these objects separately is an easier approach. Assuming that you have decided to model each object independently, you must decide how you want all of the objects to come together for the final rendering.

Scene File Strategies

Just like layering strategies with CAD systems, probably no one will ever agree on the best strategy for building a 3D model. It appears, however, that modeling strategies fall into two basic techniques.

Using one technique, you model each object separately and independently from the others. After all of the objects are modeled, you bring them together into a single file and arrange them as necessary. Such a technique works extremely well in the following two situations:

- **The scene is relatively simple and composed of common, well-known objects.**   You know what a coffee mug or a light bulb looks like, for example, so it is easy to start a new file and create them from scratch.

- **You already have an appropriate model on file.**   The model was used in an earlier project, was included on the accompanying CD-ROM, or was purchased from a third-party vendor. If you need a detailed mesh model of a coffee maker, for example, you could use a model from the Kinetix Residential 3D Props CD-ROM, rather than build one yourself (see fig. 5.9). In this case, make a copy of the file, edit it as needed, and merge it into your main scene.

NOTE

With version 1.1 of 3D Studio MAX, there are not many 3DS MAX models commercially available. This is not a problem because 3D Studio MAX can import mesh files in other formats.

FIGURE 5.9

A mesh model of a coffee maker from Kinetix Residential 3D Props.

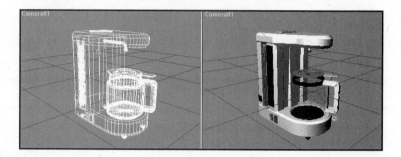

The other modeling technique requires you to set up the main scene first. You represent the objects in the scene by using simplified geometry or stand-in objects. The stand-in objects are copied out of the scene to serve as guides for the creation of detailed models. The detailed models eventually replace the stand-ins in the main scene. This approach offers the advantage of determining the basic shape, volume, and position of each object before you spend much time on modeling. A common mistake is to model an object in great detail only to have it end up far away in the background or, worse yet, completely obscured by a foreground object. This second approach is a necessity for almost any type of large, complicated scene.

As you may have guessed, most projects require a blending of these two techniques. Starting with a simplified stand-in scene, and then modeling detail only where needed, usually results in a better, more efficient model.

Merging and Replacing Objects in Your Scene

After you have built various models in separate files, you need to merge the files together into a scene. If you modeled a stand-in scene, you also need to replace the stand-in objects with the detailed objects. You perform both of these actions using the Merge command from the File menu.

Choose Merge from the File pull-down menu to combine objects from one .MAX scene file with the current scene. After you select the file to Merge, a second Merge dialog appears; select which objects you want to merge (see fig. 5.10). You can choose to merge all objects from the selected file or any number of objects you select from the list.

It is possible to have multiple objects with the same name in a 3D Studio MAX scene, so there is no problem if the objects you merge use the same names as objects already in the scene.

FIGURE 5.10

Selecting objects
to merge.

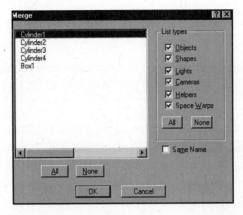

If you are using the stand-in method to build up the scene, you might want to automatically delete the stand-in objects when the same-named detail model is merged. To replace objects in the current scene with merged objects using the same name, check the Same Name check box near the lower right corner of the Merge dialog. When Same Name is checked, only objects in the merge file that have names matching objects in the current scene appear in the selection list. Selecting objects from the list replaces the same-named objects in the current scene.

One of the drawbacks to this method is that the Same Name option requires that the merged objects have the exact same name as objects already in the scene. If there is not a perfect name match, the unmatched objects are ignored.

You might frequently create a single stand-in object that will be replaced by a detail model made up of multiple objects. The Same Name option only merges the single object that has the same name as the stand-in object; all other objects with different names are ignored. The best way to get around this restriction is to avoid using the Same Name option and manually delete the stand-in objects after merging the detail models. Leaving the stand-in object in the scene provides a benefit in that the stand-in can be used as a size and position check against the merged object.

Coordination with Other Modeling Programs

Although 3D Studio MAX is one of the most powerful modeling tools around, you must sometimes resort to another program to get a job done. A common secondary modeler for 3D Studio MAX users is AutoCAD and the Mechanical Desktop from Autodesk.

Open models written with other formats using the Import command from the File menu. The files types supported in the 1.1 version of 3D Studio MAX include the following:

- **3DS** The standard 3D scene and animation file from 3D Studio R4 for DOS.

- **SHP** The 2D Shaper file from 3D Studio R4 for DOS. This file contains 2D splines that are converted to shape objects in the 3D Studio MAX scene.

- **PRJ** The standard project file from 3D Studio R4 for DOS. This file combines both the 3D and 2D information from 3D Studio. Only splines from the 2D Shaper and meshes and animation from the 3D Editor and Keyframer are imported into 3D Studio MAX. All other PRJ information, including the 3D Lofter, is ignored.

- **DWG** AutoCAD R13 and earlier 2D and 3D drawing files.

- **DXF** Autodesk Drawing Exchange Format. This file type is supported by AutoCAD and many other CAD and 3D modeling programs. It supports both 2D and 3D data.

- **AI** Adobe Illustrator 88 file format. Many spline-based 2D illustration programs support this file type. The splines in an AI file are converted to 3D Studio MAX shapes.

File Conversions

After choosing a modeling strategy—either creating all objects in one file or multiple files of individual objects—you must convert the file from its native format into the 3D Studio MAX scene format.

Because most CAD and modeling programs write DXF files, you can use 3D Studio MAX's built-in DXF reader to handle the conversion. The steps for loading a DXF file are as follows:

1. Within your CAD program, write a DXF file of your model.

2. Exit the CAD program and start 3DS MAX.

3. Choose Import from the File menu.

4. Choose *.DXF from the Files of Type list and select the DXF file that you just created.

At this point, 3D Studio MAX displays the Import DXF File dialog, which has options you can choose from to control how the DXF file is converted (see fig. 5.11).

FIGURE 5.11
Import DXF File dialog.

Maintaining File Coordination

A primary concern when using external modelers with 3D Studio MAX is how to maintain coordination between the modeling program and the 3D Studio MAX scene file. If all the design work in the external modeler is complete, this is a non-issue. Simply treat the converted files as your master models and begin building the scene. If, however, the models are part of an ongoing design process, you must take steps to ensure that your 3D Studio MAX model stays in synchronization with the design model in the other program.

The solution lies in always making design changes in the master file of the external modeler. Using the external modeler, you first identify discrete components of the overall project and write them out as independent DXF files. These DXF files are then converted to 3D Studio MAX files and are maintained as separate models. When design changes occur, you first change the master design file in the external modeler. After the change is complete, you write out only those components that were affected as DXF files and convert them to replace the corresponding 3D Studio MAX models. The key lies with the component models. If you converted the entire design model every time a change occurred, you would spend all of your time converting models and no time rendering and animating. Maintaining the component models enables you to convert only those components that have changed and thus preserve the work that you have completed on the rest of the model.

Managing Maps and Materials

Another organizational issue concerns where to store all of the bitmaps and libraries of materials that you apply to the surfaces of your model. The definitions of the materials are stored both in the 3D Studio MAX scene file and in a library file that uses the MAT extension. The material definitions contain the settings of all of the attributes that control color, shininess, transparency, and so on, as well as references to image files assigned as maps. When 3D Studio MAX renders a model, it reads the reference to the image file and searches specific directories on your hard disk to find the requested image. If the image is not found, a warning dialog appears, as shown in figure 5.12. You must either cancel the rendering or proceed without properly rendering that material.

FIGURE 5.12
Missing Map Files
warning dialog.

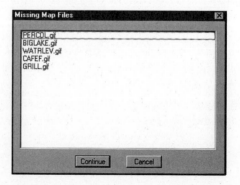

You can load image files from any directory or drive your computer is connected to. 3DS MAX stores the full path to every image file that you use. You can also specify any number of alternate directories for 3D Studio MAX to search should it fail to find the image in the stored path. Specify these alternate search directories by adding paths to the Bitmaps panel of the Configure Paths dialog. Choose Configure Paths from the File menu to display the dialog shown in figure 5.13.

FIGURE 5.13

Bitmap panel of the
Configure Paths dialog.

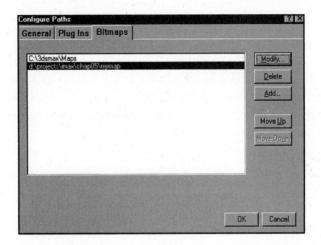

Depending upon your opinion, all of this flexibility is either a blessing or a curse. In one sense, you might never suffer the frustration of 3D Studio MAX failing to find a needed image file. On the other hand, it is now possible to create an incredible mess of directories from which your scenes pull image files from all over your hard disk and network. The following paragraphs describe techniques for how to make sense of these options.

Global Libraries

One technique is to create global libraries accessed by any project or scene. These libraries might consist of a global materials library directory where the master MAT files are stored, and a series of master image directories from which all of the image files are stored.

The default location for MAT libraries is the 3dsmax\maps directory that is automatically created when you install 3D Studio MAX. Separate MAT files can be stored in this or any other directory, with each file addressing a certain type of material. For example, some library files you might consider creating include the following:

- Metals.mat for metal materials

- Foliage.mat for grasses, leaves, and vines

- Blocks.mat for bricks, blocks, and tiles

The preferred strategy for organizing global image directories is to organize images by subject. This results in directories named WOOD, MARBLE, SKIES, BACKGRND, and so on. Such an organization makes it easy for you find images of a specific subject. Because 3D Studio MAX stores the path to any image and can alternately search many directories, you can organize your images into precise topics. A good example of this strategy can be seen in the arrangement of the map directories provided on the accompanying CD-ROM (see fig. 5.14).

FIGURE 5.14

Map directories on the accompanying CD-ROM.

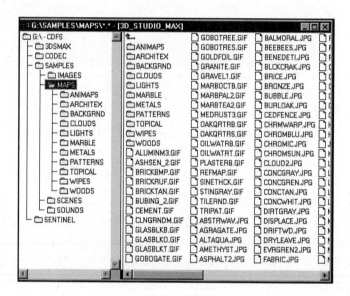

Project Libraries

Global libraries are great when you first put a project together, but what about later? It is terribly frustrating to restore an old project from backups, load it into 3D Studio MAX, and find out at render time that needed map files for critical materials are missing or have been altered. This is particularly troublesome when custom maps are created for a specific project.

The solution is to create separate libraries for each project. Each project should have its own directory for related scenes and image files. Right from the start, you can create a MAT file unique to that project and save it in the project directory. As materials are created and applied to the model, you can store their definitions in the project MAT file.

When you create an image file as a custom map for the project, store it in the project directory, not in one of the global directories. Later, if you feel that a custom map might be useful for other projects, copy the image file into the appropriate global directory. Also, after the final material definitions are set, copy all image files used by those materials from the global directory into the project directory. This might sound like a terrible waste of disk space, but this technique ensures that the global directory images your materials rely on won't be deleted or altered. And unless you place no value on your time, the cost of disk space is always cheaper than the cost to rebuild lost map files.

Managing Output

After you have built your scene, set up the cameras and lights, and applied materials, you are ready to render an image or an animation. The question now becomes an issue of what file format to use and where to place the files. One location for your output files is the project directory. Another, possibly better, solution is to create an output subdirectory below the project directory, on a separate removable drive, or on a large network drive.

Two concerns drive the decision to create a separate output subdirectory. First, rendering still images and animation creates several large files. Handling all of these files is easier if they are separate from everything else. The second reason is closely related in that you want to avoid placing rendered images in the same directory as your map images and scene files. Unless your file-naming strategies are very well planned, you might find it difficult to tell the difference between renderings and maps by looking at the file name alone.

Files for Different Types of Output

3D Studio MAX is very flexible when it comes to choosing an output format for renderings and animation. The choice of what file format to use has very little to do with 3DS MAX and is solely based on what you plan to do with the file once out of 3DS MAX. The following formats are currently supported by 3D Studio MAX:

- **TARGA** A 16.7-million-color (24-bit) format that supports a separate 8-bit alpha transparency channel. This format is supported by most high-end image processing programs and is a preferred format for output to video tape. The TARGA format is a good choice for general purpose 24-bit color files and is a standard for output to video.

- **TIFF** Another 16.7-million color format based on an international standard. Most image processing programs support the TIFF standard, making it an alternative to TARGA. Because the TIFF standard has many different variations, some compatibility problems between programs that offer TIFF support exist. TIFF is, however, the primary image format in the print and desktop publishing industry, and is common on the Macintosh platform. If you plan to send the images to a print service bureau, page layout program, or a Macintosh user, consider the TIFF format. 3D Studio MAX can create 24-bit color or 8-bit grayscale TIFF files.

- **BMP** This format is the image file standard for Windows. BMP format supports many color depths, from monochrome (1-bit) to true color (24-bit). 3D Studio MAX however, only writes 24-bit BMPs.

- **JPEG** The JPEG format provides true color with a variable quality compression scheme that degrades image quality as the compression level increases. Fortunately, JPEG allows for extreme levels of compression before most people can detect the loss of image quality. The JPEG format is supported by most high-end image processing programs. JPEG files are also found with increasing frequency on the Internet.

- **GIF** A 256-color (8-bit) format developed for CompuServe. Traditionally, this has been a very popular format for online services and the Internet. Previously, GIF files were an open royalty-free format; now programs that create GIF files require a license fee. For this reason, GIF files will probably fade from popular use and support for writing GIF files has been dropped from 3D Studio MAX.

- **PNG** In response to the licensing fee required to write GIF files, a new format was developed to take GIF's place. PNG files support multiple color depths (such as BMP), grayscale (such as TIFF), alpha channel (such as TGA), and lossless compression (such as GIF). This is a new file format, but it has the potential to become very popular. You should plan to keep informed of new developments.

- **RLA** This format was originally developed by SGI and was extended by the Yost Group for 3D Studio MAX. RLA files are used primarily to store multiple 8-bit effects channels (called the G-buffer). These channels can then be used for special post-processing effects in Video Post.

- **EPS**   A print format that is really a programming language. EPS stands for Encapsulated PostScript and is a common format in the print and illustration industry. 3D Studio MAX cannot read EPS files and can write only EPS bitmaps.

- **AVI**   This is an animation format widely supported for multimedia and Windows applications. AVI supports grayscale, 8-bit color, and inter-leaved sound. It also supports a variable compression scheme similar to JPEG. This is a popular format for multimedia presentations and animation delivered via the Internet.

- **FLIC**   This format was developed by Autodesk for the Animator and Animator Pro programs and includes the extensions of FLI, FLC, and CEL. It is a 256-color animation format that uses lossless compression. While FLIC files may be considered obsolete by many people, they are still very popular with multimedia and game developers.

File Conversions

What if the file format you need is not one of the options previously listed? 3D Studio MAX implements its image file support through external plug-ins that can be programmed using C++. It is quite possible that by the time you read this book, more file formats will be supported for 3D Studio MAX.

You can also use one of the many available file conversion programs on the market. Many high-end image processing programs can read and write files of many different formats, although it is a bit of an overkill to use a program such as Photostyler for format conversion. Other, inexpensive and simple conversion programs are available as shareware from CompuServe and many online services.

Preventing Disaster

No matter how fast you can build models or how many productivity techniques you know, they are all worthless if you lose your work. A program as powerful as 3DS MAX gives you unlimited opportunities to mess up. The following sections describe some strategies for protecting yourself from disaster.

Saving Files

As with any program, you should save your files often. 3DS MAX is unique in
the number and flexibility of its various file-saving strategies. There are
several commands for saving your work, including an option for saving
incrementally numbered files. Figure 5.15 shows a standard Save dialog that
identifies the File name field, the file format list, and the file increment button.

FIGURE 5.15
*A 3D Studio MAX
standard Save dialog.*

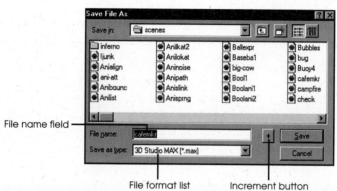

File name field

File format list   Increment button

You can enter any valid file name in the File name field. 3D Studio MAX uses
the current file name in the field as a default for convenience. If you click on
the file increment button, 3D Studio MAX appends a two-digit number to the
name in the File name field. This is a fast way to create incrementally
numbered files to use as a history of your progress.

You can use the following File menu choices to save all or part of your scene
to a file:

- **Save**   Quickly saves your scene without any extra prompts or dialogs.
  The first time you try to save a new file, however, the Save As dialog
  appears.

- **Save As**   Saves your scene to a new name and makes the new scene your
  current scene. This dialog contains the increment button for saving
  sequentially numbered files. When you click on the increment button, a
  two-digit number is appended to the name in the File name field.

- **Save Selected**   Saves your current selection of objects to a scene file.
  This dialog also contains the increment button. You can use Save
  Selected with the increment button to quickly split a large scene into a
  series of smaller, sequentially numbered files.

- **Export**   Saves your scene using a different file format. Export formats supported by 3D Studio MAX include 3DS (DOS), DXF, DWG, and VRML.

- **Archive**   Saves a scene file and compresses it, optionally including all of the map files used by materials assigned in the scene.

Backup Files

You can use two automated methods for creating backup files in 3D Studio MAX. One method creates backup files whenever you save a scene file to an existing file name. The other method saves backup files at regularly timed intervals.

When you save a scene to the same name as an existing file, 3D Studio MAX can create a backup file as well. Check the Backup File option in the File panel of the Preference Settings dialog to enable the writing of backup files. The *backup file* is a copy of the original file that uses the name MaxBack.bak. If you check the Increment on Save option in the File Preferences dialog, 3D Studio MAX creates sequentially numbered backup files rather than continually overwriting the same MaxBack.bak file. The MaxBack.bak file is always placed in the 3dsmax\scenes directory regardless of what directory from which your scene file was loaded.

If you check the Auto Backup Enable option in the Preference Settings dialog, 3D Studio MAX saves backup files at regularly timed intervals. The files are named Autobak1.mx through a maximum of Autobak9.mx and are placed in the 3dsmax\scenes directory. Once the maximum number of automatic backup files is reached, 3DS MAX starts over again at autobak1.mx. You can limit the number of Autobak files to create and specify the time interval in minutes between saves. The time interval field goes all the way down to 0.01 minutes, so if you're really worried about losing any work you can have 3D Studio MAX save backup files every 0.6 seconds!

Obviously, backup files certainly are not appropriate for long-term storage, and they were never intended for that purpose. The purpose for the backup files is to provide you with an escape route if you accidentally save a file to an existing name. If you realize the mistake soon enough, you can Alt+tab to the Window NT Explorer or File Manager and rename the backup file back to an appropriate 3D Studio MAX file.

Undoing a Mistake

The single most important development in the history of computing is the Undo command—or so it would seem. Most software users have come to rely heavily on the use of the Undo command, even to the extent of using Undo instead of regularly saving their work. If you have fallen into this trap, be warned. Relying on the Undo command can be an extremely painful mistake.

3DS MAX provides multiple Undo methods, as seen in the following list:

- Undo or redo screen changes
- Undo or redo scene changes
- Hold or fetch temporary files

Using Undo/Redo

3D Studio MAX supports five undo/redo buffers: one buffer for the scene and one buffer for each of the four viewports. You can use these undo/redo buffers to back your way out of most problems.

Use Undo/Redo from the Edit menu, or the Undo/Redo buttons on the toolbar, to reverse the changes you make to your scene. Almost anything you do in the scene can be undone. If you want to be sure about what effect Undo will have on your scene, use Edit, Undo rather than the Undo button. The Undo menu item usually includes the name of the action to be undone.

You can set how many commands to store in the scene undo buffer by changing the Undo Levels value in the General panel of the Preference Settings dialog.

WARNING

The most obvious actions that *cannot* be undone are the application or deletion of a modifier and the collapsing of the Modifier Stack. Think twice before performing these actions because they are permanent.

Use Undo/Redo from the Views menu to reverse viewport changes such as pan and zoom. Each viewport carries an independent undo buffer. The viewport undo buffers are fixed at 20 levels of undo each.

Note that changes to Camera and Spotlight viewports are really scene changes because you are changing camera and spotlight objects in the scene. Use the Edit, Undo command to reverse changes to Camera and Spotlight viewports.

Using Hold and Fetch

Another method used to reverse the effects of multiple commands is Hold and Fetch from the Edit menu. Choosing Edit, Hold saves the state of the current scene in a temporary file. You can then perform any number of commands and still return to the held state by choosing Edit, Fetch.

Hold and Fetch are much more convenient for reversing a sequence of commands than clicking the Undo button multiple times. Get in the habit of choosing Hold whenever you are about to try a complex technique. (Of course, a good, old-fashioned Save isn't such a bad idea either.) Then, if the technique doesn't work out, you can use Fetch to quickly return to your starting point.

Also, if your system should crash, preventing you from exiting 3D Studio as you normally would, you can still retrieve the contents of the temporary Hold file. The temporary Hold file is named maxhold.mx and is located in the 3dsmax\scenes directory. You can directly load this file into 3D Studio MAX or rename it as a normal scene file.

Archiving and Backing Up Your Files

You have heard this before, but it is worth repeating: Back up your data files! Nothing is more frustrating than turning on your computer and finding that the hard drive quietly passed to digital heaven sometime during the night. This frustration quickly turns to panic when you realize that your last backup is dated months before you started the project that is due next week. If you want to kill your chances as a professional animator, try explaining to a client that their presentation is not ready because you lost all of the files because of a disk drive failure.

Invest in a good, high-capacity backup device and use it regularly. Some devices are more versatile than others and can be used for more than backing up your data. For now, the most important feature of a good backup device is that it is removable. It does no good to have your backup on a second internal hard drive when your office catches fire and the whole system melts. Remove your backup media and store it away from your office.

3DS Archive Command

3D Studio MAX includes a convenient menu pick to combine a scene file with all of the referenced image maps into one compressed archive. 3DS MAX uses the PKZIP program for creating archives. Specify the location of your registered PKZIP program using the File panel of the Preference Settings dialog.

A drawback to the built-in Archive command is that it only saves a single 3D Studio MAX scene with all of its related image maps. Unfortunately, many projects use multiple scenes, external program files, and video post queues; these are left behind by the Archive command. Also, any special plug-ins used by the scene are not included in the archive. Every plug-in used to create a scene must be in place to effectively reload the scene. If you archive a file and then delete a needed plug-in, that part of the scene is lost. The best use of the Archive command is as a fast, convenient way to pack up your current work while you are still in 3DS MAX. Do not rely on it as a complete archive of your whole project.

WARNING

The current version of PKZIP (version 2.04g) does not support long file names. For compatibility with PKZIP use standard 8.3 file naming for your 3DS MAX scene and map files.

Manual Archiving

If you want to archive all of the various files associated with a project, you must still do it manually. Use your favorite archiving program to compress the files in your project directory into a single file. If you have created separate map or output subdirectories under the project directory, be sure to tell the archive program to recurse subdirectories and store the path names. This enables you to restore the project files back into the same directory structure later on. If you are archiving a completed project for long term storage, it is not a bad idea to archive 3D Studio MAX along with all its plug-ins with the project.

TIP

A handy trick is to use 3DS MAX's built-in Archive command as a map collector. It quickly pulls copies of all the referenced image maps into your project directory. Unzip the 3D-Studio-MAX-created archive to restore the maps. You then can archive the whole directory into one big file.

In Practice: Planning Your Projects

- **Modeling Decisions**   Determine your requirements for accuracy and detail to avoid unnecessary modeling work or creating overly complex scenes.

- **System Unit Scale**   Avoid changing the system unit scale unless absolutely necessary. Understand how the system unit scale affects numeric round off and how to avoid round-off errors.

- **Unit of Measure**   Set up logical units of measurement that fit your scene. Setting the right unit of measurement makes numeric entry easier and helps you avoid the trap of modeling unnecessary detail.

- **Viewport Layout**   Set up a comfortable viewport arrangement and change view orientation as needed.

- **Saving Files**   Save your files often and take advantage of the many 3DS MAX methods for backing up and protecting your data.

- **Organize Files**   Plan well organized global and project file directories. Well organized file directories save time and prevent lost files.

Image by Mondo Media for "Zork Nemisis" ©Activision
Provided courtesy of Kinetix™

Chapter 6

SELECTION, TRANSFORMS, AND PRECISION

Many of the things you do in 3D Studio MAX involve selecting and transforming objects. Remember, objects include much more than traditional geometry. Some examples of using selection and transforms include:

■ *Select and transform geometry*

■ *Select and transform geometry sub-objects, such as vertices, splines, and faces*

■ *Select and transform non-geometric objects such as a lights, cameras, and helpers*

- Select and transform modifier sub-objects, such as gizmos and centers
- Select and transform loft deformation vertices
- Select and transform animation keys

As you can see from the preceding list, selection and transformation are important tools. This chapter presents the basic techniques of selection and transformation. Because knowing how to transform objects is of little use unless you know how to put them precisely where you want them, this chapter also covers the set up and use of precision tools.

Using Selections

Because selections are so important, you find selection tools throughout the 3D Studio MAX interface. The basic 3DS MAX selection techniques should be familiar to anyone who has used a Windows-based CAD or modeling program. However, it might take a while for you to become proficient at identifying and using the many 3DS MAX specific selection methods.

To help you become familiar with the fundamentals of selections, this section explains 3DS MAX selection basics and then covers sub-object selection, selecting objects by property, and building named selection sets.

Selection Basics

Before you can perform any action you must select the objects that will be affected by that action. 3D Studio MAX uses a strategy called noun-verb selection. This means that you select your objects first and then choose an action to apply to the selection. This wouldn't be such a good idea if you were forced to use a single selection tool before you could use any other tool. 3D Studio MAX has a selection-only tool, but also includes selection as a function of all of its transform tools.

Using Selection Tools

Figure 6.1 shows the basic selection tool along with the transform buttons in the 3D Studio MAX toolbar. You can select objects whenever the selection button or any transform button is active. This selection capability is made painfully obvious by tool tips that display labels such as "Select and Move,"

"Select and Rotate," and "Select and Uniform Scale." Thankfully, this rather heavy-handed naming method is abandoned in other parts of 3DS MAX, where tools for transforming keys in Track View or transforming control vertices in loft deformations simply say "Move" or "Scale" even though they also double as selection tools.

NOTE

You can also select objects using the "Select and Link" button and the "Bind to Space Warp" button near the left end of the toolbar. The use of these buttons is so specialized that you rarely use them as general selection tools.

FIGURE 6.1
Selection and transform tools.

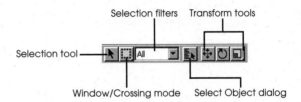

Whenever the selection tool or one of the transforms is active, you can tell what effect clicking or dragging will have by looking at the screen cursor. The appearance of the screen cursor, its meaning, and its effect, are as follows:

- **System cursor (arrow)**　The cursor is over empty space or over an object that is not valid for the current selection mode. Clicking deselects any currently selected objects; dragging performs a region selection.

- **Select cursor**　The cursor is over an unselected object that is valid for the current selection mode. Clicking selects the object and deselects any other selected objects; dragging selects and transforms the object while deselecting any other selected objects.

- **Transform cursor**　The cursor is over a selected object. Clicking keeps the object selected while deselecting any other selected objects; dragging transforms the object and all other selected objects.

TIP

If a selected object is in front of another object, you can deselect the front object and select the back object by clicking in an area where the objects overlap. Clicking in an area where objects overlap begins by selecting the front object. Every successive click deselects the current object and selects the objects deeper in the scene. This works for any number of overlapping objects.

Figure 6.2 shows all three cursors displayed with the Move transform. The left viewport shows the system cursor because the cursor is over empty space. The middle viewport displays the select cursor because the cursor is over a valid, unselected object. The right viewport displays the Move transform cursor because the cursor is over a selected object.

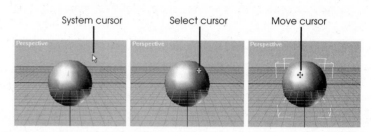

FIGURE 6.2
Selection and transform cursors for the Move transform.

You also have all the convenient global selection techniques available in the Edit menu. Select All selects all objects in the scene; Select None releases the current selection; Select Invert inverts the current selection so that all unselected objects are now selected and all selected objects are now unselected.

Using Region Selection

As mentioned previously, you can select objects by clicking them or by dragging a region that selects all of the objects contained by the region. Use the region select controls on the toolbar, prompt line, and Edit menu to set the shape and behavior of region selections.

The shape of a region selection is set by the region flyout on the toolbar (see fig. 6.3). The three types of region selection are

- **Quad**   Dragging defines a rectangular region in which one corner is located where you press down the mouse button and the opposite corner is located where you release the button.

- **Circle**   Dragging defines a circular region in which the center is located where you press down the mouse button and the radius is set where you release the button.

- **Fence**   Dragging defines the first segment of the fence boundary. Click to define more segments. Double-click or click on the start point to close the fence and complete the selection.

FIGURE 6.3

Choosing region shape.

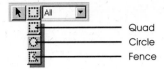

———— Quad
———— Circle
———— Fence

Region behavior is set by the region toggle in the prompt line or by choosing Region from the Edit menu (see fig. 6.4). The two types of region behavior are Window, which selects only objects that are completely within the region, and Crossing, which selects any object that touches the region boundary or is completely within the region.

FIGURE 6.4

Choosing region behavior.

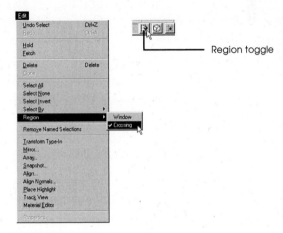

———— Region toggle

Adding and Removing Objects from a Selection

You can also use standard Windows modifier keys to add and remove objects from a current selection. Press the Ctrl and Alt keys while selecting objects to do the following:

Ctrl   To toggle the selection state of objects, press the Ctrl key while clicking. Clicking unselected objects adds them to the selection; clicking selected objects removes them from the selection.

Ctrl   To add regions of objects to the selection, press the Ctrl key while dragging a region. Selected objects within the region remain selected.

Alt   To remove objects from the selection set, press the Alt key while clicking objects or dragging regions.

Filtering a Selection

What do you do when you are working in a very complex scene and you want to select objects of only a certain type? For example, imagine you are lighting the interior of a convention center made of hundreds of objects. You want to select only lights so you can adjust their parameters and position them properly, but you keep accidentally selecting walls and furniture instead.

You could hide everything except the lights, but then you wouldn't know where to place the lights.

Or you could freeze everything except the lights, but then your shaded viewports would not show how the lighting changes affect the frozen objects.

Your best choice is to filter the selection using the selection filters on the toolbar (see fig. 6.5).

FIGURE 6.5

Choosing a selection filter.

If you choose an object type from the selection filters list, you can select only objects matching that type. The default filter is All, giving you the ability to select anything. The remaining filters match the first six creation categories from the Create panel: Geometry, Shapes, Lights, Cameras, Helpers, and Space Warps.

Locking a Selection

When you are working with a very complex selection or want to use the same selection for a sequence of commands, it is a good idea to lock the selection. Locking a selection prevents you from accidentally releasing the selection.

You can toggle a selection between being locked and unlocked by doing either of the following actions:

- Clicking on the selection Lock button in the status line at the bottom of the 3DS MAX window

- Pressing the spacebar

Sub-Object Selection

Many situations exist in which you can select just a few components of an object, or in other words, define a sub-object selection. All sub-object selection begins by first selecting an object and then clicking a Sub-object button to enter Sub-object selection mode. This is an important point; you first select an object and then turn on Sub-object mode to go deeper into that object. As long as sub-object mode is active, you can select only components within the original selected object.

The Sub-object button highlights in yellow to indicate that you are in Sub-object selection mode. If you find yourself trying to select objects and nothing happens, look at the command panel to see whether you are in a Sub-object selection mode. If so, click the Sub-object button to turn off Sub-object mode and return to normal selection methods.

NOTE

Sub-object selection mode is almost always accessed from the Modify panel either as part of a modifier or as the base parameters of an object. The only exception (as of Release 1.1) is Trajectories, which displays a Sub-object button in the Motion panel.

Remember, 3D Studio MAX is an object-oriented program, so sub-objects include far more than the components of geometry. Some examples of when you would encounter Sub-object selection modes include the following (see fig. 6.6):

■ **Geometry**   Click the Sub-object button in the base parameters of an Editable Mesh object or in an Edit modifier (Edit Mesh, Edit Spline, Edit Patch) to select vertices, edges, or faces of the geometry.

■ **Compound Objects**   Click the Sub-object button in the base parameters of a compound object such as a Loft or Boolean to select their internal shapes or operands. For some odd reason, you cannot sub-object select the internal objects of a Morph. Keep this restriction in mind when creating Morph objects.

■ **Modifiers**   Click the Sub-object button in a modifier to select its gizmo or center.

■ **Trajectories**   Click the Sub-object button while working with Trajectories in the Motion panel to select keys on an object's trajectory.

FIGURE 6.6

Examples of sub-object selection modes.

Selecting Objects by Property

Selecting single objects, or dragging a region to select multiple objects, becomes quite limiting when you have more than a handful of objects in your scene. You quickly realize that what you really need is the ability to select objects by property. For example, select all the objects using a certain material, or all the objects with names starting with the letter B. 3DS MAX has many tools for selecting both objects and sub-objects by their properties.

Selecting Objects by Type

Usually, the only time you want to select objects by type is when you want to select all objects of a particular type—for example, you want to select lights or cameras or shapes. You can select all objects of a given type in one of two ways: by using the selection filters or by using the Select Objects dialog.

To select all objects of a given type using selection filters, perform the following steps:

1. Choose an object type from the selection filters list in the toolbar.

2. Choose Select All from the Edit menu.

To select all objects of a given type using the Select Objects dialog, perform the following steps:

1. Press H to display the Select Objects dialog.

2. Click None in the List Display and then check the object type you want to select.

3. Click All below the selection list to select all objects of the displayed type (see fig. 6.7).

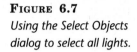

FIGURE 6.7
*Using the Select Objects
dialog to select all lights.*

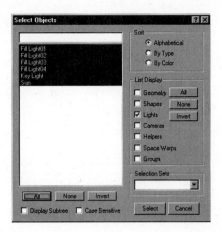

Selecting Objects by Name

Naming strategies play an important role in organizing any project. Whether you are organizing manila folders in a file drawer, word processing files on your hard disk, or objects in 3DS MAX, naming imposes a certain organizational strategy. If you are careful about how you name your objects, you can later quickly select groups of related objects using their names.

You select objects by name using the Select Objects dialog. You can display the Select Objects dialog by using any of the following actions:

- Press H.
- Click the Select by Name button on the toolbar.
- Choose Select By, Name from the Edit menu.

When the Select Objects dialog is visible, you can select an object by either clicking its name in the selection list or by entering a selection pattern in the edit field above the selection list as shown in figure 6.8. Selection patterns can use the following wild cards to expand the search:

- ?   Accepts any single character at that point in the search string. For example, B?x selects Box and Bix, but not Ball or even Box01.
- *   Accepts any number of characters at that point in the search string. For example, B*x* selects Box, Blox, Boxes, and Box01.

FIGURE 6.8

Selecting objects by name.

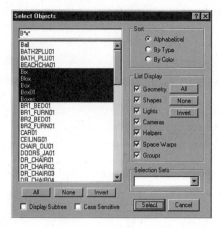

A second technique for selecting objects by name is to use the hierarchy list of the Track View window. The Track View hierarchy window displays the names of all objects in your scene under the Objects branch. Clicking the yellow cube icon to the left of an object's name also selects the object in the scene, as seen in figure 6.9.

FIGURE 6.9

Selecting objects in the Track View hierarchy list.

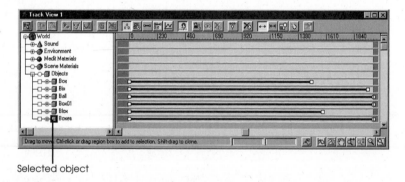

Selected object

Selecting Objects by Wireframe Color

One way to organize objects in your scene is to assign colors to each object. (This is an organizational strategy similar to layer colors in AutoCAD.) By assigning colors, you can then quickly select all the objects in your scene that share the same color.

A small color swatch is usually displayed beside the object name field in the command panel. Clicking this color swatch displays the Object Color dialog from which you can assign an object wireframe color (see fig. 6.10). Details about the full use of the Object Color dialog are found in Chapter 2 of the *3D Studio MAX User's Guide.*

FIGURE 6.10

Displaying the Object Color dialog.

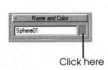

Click here

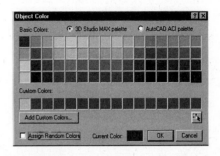

You need to know two important points about object colors. First, you need to plan a strategy to organize your scene by object color and stick to it. 3DS MAX supports two color palettes—you have 256 colors in the AutoCAD palette, and 64 fixed colors and 16 custom colors in the 3DS MAX palette. That's 336 organizational groups at your disposal. Second, you never want to turn on the Use Random Colors check box when working on a production project. The Use Random Colors option is an eye wash tool for people who make presentations. This option keeps the screen interesting by randomly switching colors while you create objects. Use Random Colors is incompatible with any kind of color organization strategy.

You can use two methods to select objects by color. One method is object driven—you pick an object and all objects assigned the same color are selected. The other method is color driven—you pick a color and all objects using that color are selected.

To select all objects assigned the same color as another object:

1. Choose Select By, Color from the Edit menu.

2. Click an object that contains the color you want.

3. All objects assigned the same color as the object you click are selected.

To select all objects using a specific color:

1. Click the color swatch beside any object name field in the command panel.

2. Click the color you want in the Object Color dialog.

3. Click the Select by Color button in the lower right corner of the dialog (see fig. 6.11).

4. The Select Objects dialog appears with all of the objects using the selected color highlighted in the selection list (see fig. 6.11).

5. Click Select to select the objects.

TIP

Click the Sort By Color radio button in the Select Objects dialog to quickly collect all of the highlighted objects at the same place in the list.

FIGURE 6.11

Selecting objects by color.

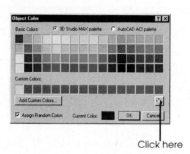

Click here

Selecting Objects and Faces by Material

You can select assigned material in either of the following ways:

■ Select complete objects using the Select By Material button in the Material Editor.

■ Select faces using the Select By ID button in the Edit Mesh modifier.

You can tell at a glance whether the material is assigned to objects in the scene by looking at the Material Editor. Material that is assigned to an object in the scene is called a *hot material*. Hot materials are indicated by white triangles in the corners of their sample slot. If the material is not hot, it is not assigned to any object and the Select By Material button is inactive.

Selecting objects by material is straightforward. You select a hot material in the Material Editor and then click the Select By Material button. The Select Entities dialog appears with all objects assigned the current material highlighted in the selection list (see fig. 6.12).

More often than not, what you really want to do is select all objects that use the same material as another object. You still use Select By Material in the

Material Editor to select the objects, but the trick is to start with the right material in the first place.

In the following example, imagine you have an object named Sample01 and you want to select all the objects in the scene that use the same material as Sample01.

FIGURE 6.12

Selecting objects by material.

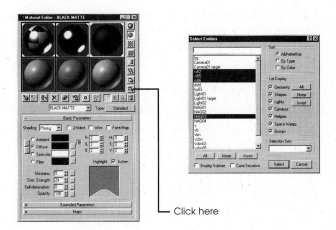

Click here

To select all objects using the same material as Sample01, complete the following steps:

1. Select the object Sample01.

2. Click Get Material in the Material Editor.

   This displays the Material/Map Browser dialog.

3. Choose Selected in the Browse From area of the Material/Map Browser dialog and then double-click the material in the material list.

   This places the material assigned to Sample01 (the selected object) in the current slot of the Material Editor.

4. Click Select By Material.

   The Select Objects dialog appears with all the objects that use the current material highlighted in the selection list.

5. Click Select to select the objects.

You use the other method of selecting by material when you have used a Multi/Sub-object material to assign multiple materials to the faces of an object and want to know which faces use a specific material. In this situation, you need to use the Select By ID button in the Edit Mesh modifier. Details about creating and using Multi/Sub-object materials are presented in Chapter 21, "Materials and Textures."

In the following example, imagine that you have an object named Racket, which uses a Multi/Sub-object material named RacketMat. You want to select all the faces of Racket that use the sub-material Black Grip.

To select faces by material, complete the following steps:

1. Make the Multi/Sub-object material RacketMat the current material in the Material Editor.

2. Examine the Basic Parameters of material RacketMat and determine the material number of the sub-material Black_Grip. For this example, assume that Black_Grip is Material 3.

The material number of a sub-material and the material ID of a face always match. Now that you know the material number for the sub-material Black_Grip, you can select all of the faces that use Black_Grip by selecting faces with Material ID 3. The following steps complete the process of selecting faces with Material ID 3 (see fig. 6.13).

3. Apply an Edit Mesh modifier to the object Racket.

4. Choose Face as the modifier sub-object selection level.

5. Drag the Modify panel up to the Edit Surface rollout.

6. Click Select By ID in the Material area of the Edit Surface rollout.

7. Enter 3 in the Select By Material ID dialog.

When you click OK, all the faces in the object Racket that use material ID 3 are selected.

FIGURE 6.13

Selecting faces by material ID number.

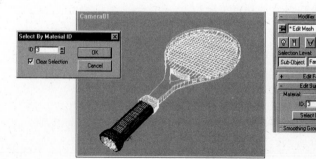

Selecting Faces by Smoothing Group

Later chapters describe how 3DS MAX uses smoothing groups to render smooth surfaces from faceted face meshes. You might find modeling situations in which you need to select all the faces of an object that use the same smoothing group.

Methods for selecting faces by smoothing group are similar to selecting faces by material. Details for this selection method are presented in Chapter 12.

Building Named Selection Sets

With all the selection capabilities in 3DS MAX, you may want to save and reuse some of the selection sets that you build. As mentioned previously, the two techniques for quickly selecting related groups of objects are to organize them by name and by color and then use the Select By Name and Select By Color commands. These are great techniques for high-level organization and selection, but what should you do if you need a more flexible method?

You can also name selection sets so that you can recall and reuse these sets at any time. The process of naming a selection set is quite easy.

To name a selection set:

1. Define a selection set of objects.

2. Click the named selection set field in the toolbar.

3. Enter a name for the selection. Press Enter.

Make sure that you press enter after typing the name of the selection. If you fail to press Enter, the selection name is not recorded and is discarded the next time you click anywhere in the 3DS MAX window.

Reusing a named selection is also easy. Whenever you want to reuse a named selection, you choose its name from the Selection Sets list. You can use either the list in the toolbar or the list in the Select Objects dialog, as seen in figure 6.14.

FIGURE 6.14
*Choosing a named
selection set.*

Renaming and Removing Named Selection Sets

If you make a typo while naming a selection or later decide to change its name, you must create a new named selection with the new name and then remove the old name. The process isn't as awkward as it sounds.

To rename a named selection, complete the following steps:

1. Choose the old name from the named selection list.

   The objects belonging to the named selection are highlighted.

2. Double-click the old name to highlight it, and enter a new name in its place. Be sure to press Enter when you are done.

   The selected objects now belong to two selection sets—the old name and the new name.

3. Again choose the old name from the named selection list.

4. Choose Remove Named Selections from the Edit menu.

Choosing Remove Named Selection from the Edit menu immediately removes the named selection visible at the top of the named selection list. Always double check that the named selection you want to remove is at the top of the list before you choose Remove Named Selection.

Named selections simply identify a group of objects. If you delete one of the objects in a named selection set, the selection set still exists and contains the remaining objects in the selection. In fact, you can even delete all the objects in a named selection set and the named selection will still exist—it just contains nothing. When you find you have an empty named selection set, choose it in the named selection list and then choose Remove Named Selection from the Edit menu.

Naming Sub-Object Selections

You can also name selection sets of sub-objects, such as a selection of faces or vertices. A named sub-object selection is saved with the Edit modifier that was used to create the selection. You cannot share named sub-object selections among Edit modifiers. In order to reuse the named sub-object selection, you must return to the same Edit modifier in the Modifier Stack.

Using Groups

Somewhere between named selection sets and permanently attaching multiple objects to form a single object lie groups. *Groups* are sort of hybrids of a combined object, semi-permanent selection set, and special linked hierarchy. A group is an object itself that contains other objects as *members* of the group. Groups can be animated, modified, and linked to other objects. Anything that you do to the group also affects the member objects inside the group. What makes groups unique is that you can open a group and individually animate and modify the objects inside.

Use groups whenever you want a collection of objects to behave as a single object, yet preserve the ability to edit objects in the group individually.

Everything you need to build, edit, and disassemble groups begins with the choices in the Group menu on the toolbar.

Building Groups

Two commands are used to build groups: Group and Attach. Use the Group command to define any selection as a new group. Use Attach to add any selection to an existing Group.

To create a new group from a selection of objects, complete the following steps:

1. Select one or more objects.

2. Choose Group from the Group menu.

3. Enter a name in the Group dialog (see fig. 6.15).

All of the selected objects become members of the new group. Because groups are objects, and an important organizational tool, you should exercise the same care in naming groups that you use when naming other objects.

FIGURE 6.15

*Creating a new group
object.*

All objects are valid choices for membership within a group. You can mix geometry, lights, space warps, and even other groups within the same group. When you place a group inside another group, you have what is called a *nested group*. Usually you don't want to nest groups more than one or two layers deep. Nesting any further makes it tedious to get to an object in the deepest group.

When you create a group, a special dummy object called the *group node* is created. This dummy object is normally invisible, but when you open the group, the dummy object appears as a pink colored box that surrounds the objects in the group. When viewing objects in Track View or any other display of hierarchy, the group node is represented as the parent of the member objects.

To add objects to an existing group, do the following:

1. Select one or more objects.

2. Choose Attach from the Group menu.

3. Click on any object that is part of an existing group.

The selected objects are added to the same group as the object you click.

Now it can be quite a trick to know which object to click unless you memorize which objects are members of which groups. The cursor changes to the cross-shaped selection cursor only when the cursor is over an object that is a member of a group—but that isn't a whole lot of help. The smart choice is to select a group by name. Groups appear in the Select Objects dialog with square brackets around the group name. The smart and easy replacement for step 3 in the previous example becomes:

■ Click Select By Name in the toolbar and then choose a group name from the Attach to Group dialog (see fig. 6.16).

NOTE

Here's one situation where the object-oriented design of 3DS MAX really shows. Because 3DS MAX knows that you are in a mode where you can only click a group object, the Select Objects dialog is replaced by the Attach to Group dialog and displays only group names.

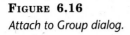

FIGURE 6.16

Attach to Group dialog.

Transforming and Modifying Groups

You can transform and modify groups in two ways. One way is to transform and modify the full group just as you would with any other object. A second way is to open the group and transform and modify individual objects inside the group.

You can transform or modify the full group by selecting any object in the group or by selecting the group name in the Select Objects dialog. Whichever method you use, all the member objects highlight as selected. Transforms and modifiers behave differently when applied to a group as compared to when applied to a single object:

- **Transforms applied to a group are carried by the group node.** Objects inside the group follow as children of the group node. When you detach an object from a group, it is also detached from the transforms applied to the group. This is especially noticeable when the group transforms are animated. Detaching an object from an animated group drops the object at its current place in the scene and the object no longer inherits any transform animation from the group.

- **Modifiers applied to a group are applied to the selection of all member objects.** Each object receives an instance of the modifier. An object retains its instanced modifier even after you detach it from the group.

You can transform or modify individual objects inside a group by first opening the group and then selecting one or more of the member objects.

After the group is open, you can work with the member objects the same as you would with any other object in the scene. Any animated effect that you apply to an object inside a group is preserved even after the group is closed.

To open a group:

1. Select any member object of the group you want to open.

2. Choose Open from the Group menu.

   When you do, a pink box appears around the group members. This box is the group node (see fig. 6.17).

3. Transform and modify individual members of the group.

FIGURE 6.17
The group node of an open group.

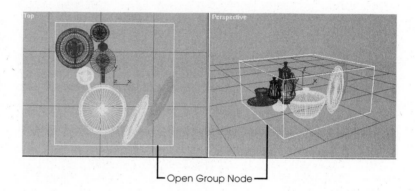

└─ Open Group Node ─┘

For example, imagine that you have modeled an insect inside a glass jar. You then select the insect, jar, and lid and place them inside a group named Bug_Zoo. You can open the group and animate the insect flying around inside the jar. After you close the group, you can animate the entire group moving around the scene while the insect continues to fly around (staying inside the jar).

When a group is open, you have access to the members of the group, but you can also transform with the full group. Transforming the pink group node transforms all of the members of the group in the same way as when the group is closed. You cannot, however, apply modifiers to the group while the group is open. Either close the group or manually select all members of the group to apply a modifier.

TIP

A quick way to select all the members of an open group is to double-click the group node.

If the open group contains any nested groups you can open the nested groups by using the same procedure. When you are finished working with the members of an open group, you close the group with the Close command.

To close an open group:

1. Select any member of the open group.

2. Choose Close from the Group menu.

The selected group and any open nested groups inside the selected group are closed.

Taking Groups Apart

After you create a group, you may decide that you want to remove some objects from the group or even completely dissolve the group. Take groups apart using three commands from the Group menu: Detach, Ungroup, and Explode.

Use Detach to remove one or more selected objects from an open group.

To detach an object from a group:

1. Open the group containing the objects you want to detach.

2. Select one or more objects to detach.

3. Choose Detach from the group menu.

4. Close the group.

Use Ungroup and Explode to quickly dissolve an entire group. You first select a group and then choose Ungroup or Explode from the Group menu.

The Ungroup command dissolves the selected group, thereby returning the group members to individual object status. Nested groups become separate groups. Any transform animation applied to the group node is lost.

The Explode command dissolves the selected group and all groups nested inside it. All members of the group become individual objects—no nested groups remain. All transform animation applied to group nodes is lost.

Grouping Strategies

Now you know what groups are, as well as how to create, modify, and dissolve them. The only question left is when to use groups. Like everything else in life, groups have benefits and trade-offs. Use the following guidelines to help decide when to use groups.

Use a group to combine objects when:

- You want to transform, modify, and animate the combined objects as a single object. Groups are more convenient than linking all of the objects to a dummy object because you can easily select all the members (children) of a group by selecting any one member.

- You want to animate the individual objects but also have the objects inherit the group animation.

- You want the combined objects to behave as a single object but still want access to the Modifier Stack and Base Parameters of each member of the group. If you combine objects using the Attach command of the Edit Mesh modifier, each attached object becomes a plain mesh and loses its Modifier Stack and Base Parameters.

Do not use a group to combine objects when:

- You will be animating individual objects more than you will be animating the group. Frequently opening and closing groups can become tedious and defeat the benefits of using groups.

- You are organizing related objects for selection purposes. Use named selection sets to organize collections of related objects. Named selection sets are much more flexible for most organizational purposes. For example, one object can belong to multiple named selection sets. If an object is a member of a group, it can be a member of only one group, and any named selection sets it belongs to must include all the members of its group.

- You need to weld vertices or smooth between the combined objects. The Attach command of the Edit Mesh modifier is the only way to combine objects so that you can weld and smooth between them.

Using Grids and Helpers

The first steps for building precision models involve setting up your reference grids and snap system. While you work in your scene, you can choose from three fixed grids, any number of custom grids, and two distinct snap systems. You also have a number of helper objects that you can create to locate points in space and measure distances.

The use of grids is an important modeling tool that, when used properly, can greatly increase your productivity. The following items are important points to remember about grids:

- The active grid defines where new objects are created in space. The active grid is also referred to as the *construction plane* because everything you construct is placed and aligned will the active grid.

- Grids define the default snap spacing.

- Grids and helpers define coordinate systems for transforming objects.

- Grids and helpers provide a visual reference for defining space and measuring distance.

Setting up the Home Grid

3DS MAX displays three permanent grids, called the *home grids,* for construction and visual reference. These three grids align with the world coordinate system and intersect at the world coordinate origin. The three home grids and their relationship to the world coordinate system are identified as follows:

- The Top/Bottom grid is aligned with the world X,Y axes. Because this grid is horizontal and often defines the floor of your scene, it is referred to as the *Ground Plane.*

- The Left/Right grid is aligned with the world Y,Z axes.

- The Front/Back grid is aligned with the world X,Z axes.

Display of Home Grids in Viewports

Only one of the three home grids is visible in any given viewport; which grid you see is determined by the viewport type. The visible grid also defines the construction plane for that view. The following are the three visible home grids:

- **Ground plane**   The construction plane for the Top, Bottom, User, Perspective, Camera, and Spotlight views

- **Left/Right grid**   The construction plane for Left and Right views

- **Front/Back grid**   The construction plane for Front and Back views

You can control the display of the Home Grid in the active viewport by any of the following methods:

- Choose Show Grid from the viewport pop-up menu.

- Choose Grids, Show Home Grid from the Views menu.

- Press Shift+G.

Setting Home Grid Spacing

You set the grid spacing for the home grids by using the Home Grid panel of the Grid and Snap Settings dialog (see fig. 6.18). You display the dialog by choosing Grid and Snap Settings from the Views menu.

FIGURE 6.18

Home Grid settings.

The Grid Spacing option sets the initial distance between grid lines and sets the grid snap value. When you set the grid spacing, keep in mind that you cannot snap to increments smaller than the grid spacing. The actual grid spacing varies for each viewport as you zoom in and out of a view. Look at the status line just to the left of the Animate button to see the current grid spacing for the active viewport.

The Major Lines every Nth option determines which grid lines are emphasized for visual reference. For example, if you set Major Lines every Nth to 10, every tenth line on the grid is emphasized as shown in figure 6.19. You need to choose this setting carefully because it also serves as a multiplier for the adaptive grid display used by 3DS MAX.

FIGURE 6.19

Identifying grid spacing and major lines.

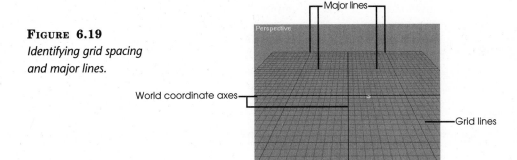

The adaptive grid display adjusts grid spacing on the fly so that viewports always display a usable grid regardless of their zoom magnification. When you zoom in or out of a view, the grid holds its grid spacing constant until the major lines are a certain number of screen pixels apart and then the grid is resized. The point at which the grid is resized varies with your screen resolution; at a screen resolution of 1024×768, the grid is resized when the major lines are about 50 pixels apart. The following rules control how the grid spacing changes:

- Grid spacing is multiplied by the Major Lines value every time the grid is resized during a Zoom Out.

- Grid spacing is divided by the Major Lines value every time the grid is resized during a Zoom In.

For example, say your grid spacing is set at 1.0 mm and your Major Lines value is set at 10 (emphasizing lines at every cm). As you zoom out, the first time the grid is resized, grid spacing is multiplied by 10 to be 1.0 cm with major lines at every decimeter.

Adaptive grid display ensures that you always have a visible, useful home grid in your viewports, but you are responsible for looking at the status line to check the current grid spacing value.

Adaptive grid display works exceptionally well for metric units of measure, but it is rather problematical for U.S. standard units. Imagine you are working with a grid spacing of 1.0 inch and a Major Lines value of 12 (1.0 foot). When you zoom out, grid spacing is resized times 12 (1.0 foot) and Major Lines are at every 12 feet—not a very common measuring scale. If you think carefully about your project, you can probably come up with Grid Spacing and Major Lines values that will even work well with U.S. standard units.

For example, a good choice for using U.S. Standard units for architectural modeling might be a Grid Spacing of 1.0 inch and a Major Lines value of 4. As you zoom out, your grid spacing changes from 1 inch, to 4 inches, to 16 inches all of which are standard building units. As you zoom in, the spacing changes from 1 inch, to $1/4$ inch, to $1/16$ inch, which again are standard divisions.

The next option in the Home Grid panel of the Grid and Snap Settings dialog is the Inhibit Grid Subdivision Below Grid Spacing check box. When you select Inhibit Grid, the adaptive grid display is prevented from dividing the grid below the Grid Spacing value. This means that if you set the grid spacing at 1.0 inch, the grid lines will never get any closer to each other than one inch. Adaptive grid display still works normally when you zoom out, regardless of the Inhibit Grid setting.

The remaining options control whether you can watch the grid update while you drag the grid spacing spinner.

Finally, there is a feature that controls adaptive grid display for perspective views. An adaptive grid can be nearly impossible to calculate for certain perspective viewing angles. When 3DS MAX detects such a viewing angle (such as rolling a camera 90 degrees), it switches to a non-adaptive grid that is 1000 units square and is centered on the eyepoint. When a non-adaptive grid is used, you notice that grid spacing does not resize as you zoom and that sometimes you can see the corners of the grid. If for some reason you decide that you always want to use a non-adaptive grid in a perspective view, you can press Ctrl+Shift+A to toggle the non-adaptive grid display. This option is only available for perspective views.

Setting Background and Grid Colors

You can set the viewport background color and grid intensity using the Viewports panel of the Preference Settings dialog (see fig. 6.20). To change the Viewport Background settings, choose Preferences from the File menu, click the Viewports tab and then change the settings in the Viewport Background area.

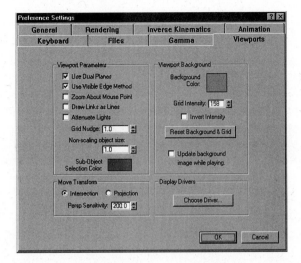

The default settings produce a medium gray background with a darker gray grid. These settings provide average contrast for most available wireframe colors. Depending upon your working style and project requirements, you may want to change the following background settings:

- **Background Color**   Click the color swatch to display the standard color selector. Choose any color you want as a viewport background. Another technique to consider is to set the viewport background color to the predominate background color of your scene. That way, the shaded viewports will display a more accurate approximation of the final rendered scene.

WARNING

Do not set your background color to pure white. Selected wireframe objects always display in white and will disappear against a white background.

- **Grid Intensity**   Grid lines are always drawn in shades of gray. The value in the Grid Intensity field sets the gray shade for standard grid lines. The values range from 0 (black) to 255 (white). Major Lines are drawn using a darker shade of gray—halfway between the Grid Intensity value and black. The world coordinate axes are drawn in black.

- **Invert Intensity** When this option is selected, the Grid Intensity value is subtracted from 255 to specify the shade of gray. High values now produce dark grid lines and low values produce light lines. Major Lines are drawn using a lighter shade of gray—halfway between the Grid Intensity value and white. The world coordinate axes are now drawn in white.

Figure 6.21 shows some examples of alternative background settings.

FIGURE 6.21
Alternative background and grid color schemes.

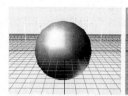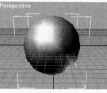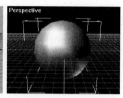

Using Grid Objects

Using the Home Grid is fine for most operations, but what if you want to construct something on top of a table or on the sloping side of a roof? That is when you need to use grid objects. Grids are helper objects that can take the place of the Home Grid for construction and transformation commands.

Uses for grids include the following:

- **As an alternative construction plane** You can align a grid object with the surface of another object and then create new objects sitting on the grid.

- **As an alternative transform coordinate system** You can place a grid object anywhere in space, such as on a slope and then use the grid's Local coordinate system for transforming other objects.

- **As a spatial reference** You can use grid objects to define planes and volumes in space. Because grid objects do not render they are very convenient for defining reference planes in your scene.

Create a grid object by clicking the Helpers category button in the Create panel and then clicking Grid in the object type rollout (see fig. 6.22). Dragging in any viewport defines the length and width of the grid object.

The remaining base parameter defines grid spacing. You may be surprised that nothing seems to happen when you change the grid spacing value. Grid objects display only their local X and Y axes until you make them active. You see the grid spacing only after you make the grid active.

FIGURE 6.22
Creating a grid object.

Grid objects can be used in place of the Home Grid, but they follow a few different rules:

- When a grid object is active, everything you create is placed on the active grid regardless of which view is active. Remember, the Home Grid switches between Top/Bottom, Left/Right, and Front/Back based on the active view to always present you with a usable grid. When a grid object is active, there may be some views that are nearly perpendicular to the grid, as shown in figure 6.23. These views are poor choices for use with the grid object; do not try to create objects in such views.

- Grid objects do not use adaptive grid display. The grid spacing and grid size are fixed. The grid size only controls the visible boundaries of the grid. This grid itself is infinite, and you can create objects outside the edges of the grid.

- Grid objects do not use the grid intensity setting in the Preference Settings dialog. Grid lines are always medium gray with black X,Y axis lines. Keep this in mind if you plan to use a grid object with a custom color background.

FIGURE 6.23
Good and poor views for an active grid object.

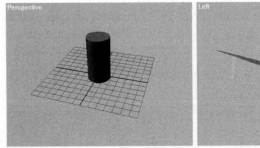 

Working with Grids

After you create a grid object, you must complete two steps to use the grid:

1. Position the grid using Move, Rotate, or Align.

2. Make the grid active.

You can use any transform command to position the grid object in your scene. You can even animate the grid, although it may be difficult to come up with many useful purposes for animated grids.

WARNING

Whatever you do, never scale a grid object.

As mentioned in Chapter 1, "Core Concepts of 3D Studio MAX," transforms, such as scale, are applied at the end of the dataflow and they are not reflected in an object's base parameters. This means that if you scale a grid object, the grid spacing value in the base parameters and the spacing you see on the screen no longer match. Even worse, the grid's scale transform is passed on to anything you try to create on the grid. Scaling grid objects can produce some very weird and unexpected results. You probably won't have much use for scaled grids.

An extremely useful method for positioning grid objects is to use the Align commands. After you position the grid object, you must make it active:

1. Select the grid.

2. Choose Views, Grids, Activate Grid Object.

You can immediately tell whether a grid object is active because grid lines appear on the grid object and disappear from the Home Grid (see fig. 6.24).

When the grid is active, everything you create is placed on the grid and aligned with the grid's local coordinate system.

Using Helper Objects

Other types of helper objects are as useful as are grid objects. You use these helpers to measure and define points in space and to establish alternate coordinate systems for transforms.

The three remaining helper objects are Tape Measures, Points, and Dummies.

FIGURE 6.24

Comparing the Home Grid and an active grid object.

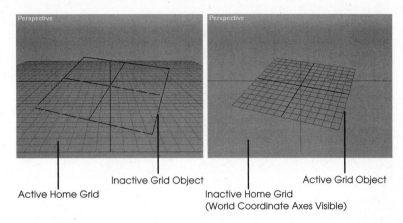

Inactive Grid Object   Active Grid Object

Active Home Grid   Inactive Home Grid
                                    (World Coordinate Axes Visible)

Using Tape Measures

A tape measure is a handy graphical device used to measure distances. To create a tape, click Tape in the Create panel and drag in any viewport. The triangular head of the tape is placed where you begin dragging, and the tape target is placed where you release the drag. After you create the tape, you can move either the head or the target to place the tape between points that you want to measure. The length of the tape is displayed in the length field of the tape's base parameters, as shown in figure 6.25.

WARNING

Never scale a tape object. Just as with grid objects, scaling a tape causes it to display false length values.

FIGURE 6.25

Reading a tape measure's length.

Tape object

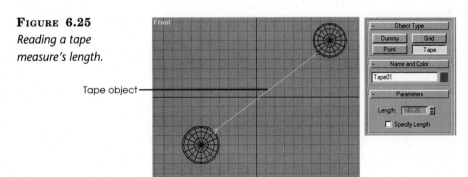

Keep in mind that the displayed length of the tape is a three-dimensional distance that can lead to inaccurate results if you concentrate on placing the tape in only a single viewport. Figure 6.26 shows an example of the wrong way to measure the width of an object. If you concentrate on only the Front viewport, you may think that you are properly measuring the object's width without realizing that the tape also runs back along the length of the object, as is evident in the Perspective viewport. In this case, you are not measuring the width of the object, but rather the diagonal distance across the top. You should always check the placement of the tape in at least two viewports to ensure you are measuring the correct distance.

FIGURE 6.26

Incorrectly measuring the width of an object.

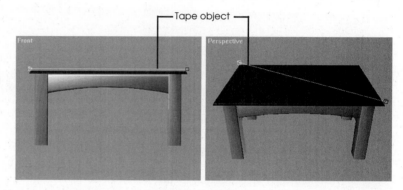

You can also use the tape to mark off a preset distance by checking the Specify Length check box in the tape's Parameters rollout. When you select Specify Length, the Length field jumps to a default value of 100 units. Set the length you want, and the tape grows or shrinks to that distance. It may look weird that the tape target does not move with the end of the tape, but just think of the target as an aiming handle—you move the target to aim the tape in the direction you want to measure.

Using a tape to mark off a preset distance is particularly useful when you want to position objects a known distance from a given base point. Place the head of the tape at the base point, check Specify Length, and aim the tape in the direction you want to measure. After setting the tape length, you can use 3DS MAX snap capabilities to position objects at the end of the tape.

Another good use for tape objects is to set up an alternate transform coordinate system. The local Z axis of the tape head is aligned with the length of the tape. You can create a tape object between any two points and then slide an object along the length of the tape by picking the tape head as the transform coordinate system and constraining movement to the Z axis. Details about choosing transform coordinate systems are presented later in this chapter.

Using Points

You use point helpers to define a point and coordinate axis orientation in space. You create a point by clicking Point in the Create panel and then clicking in any viewport. The point object appears as a yellow X with its local axis tripod displayed (see fig. 6.27). Use the point's base parameters to control the display and length of the axis tripod. The axes are aligned with the active grid axes for the viewport in which the point is created.

FIGURE 6.27

Creating a point object.

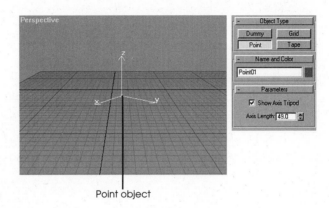

Point object

One very useful application for point objects is as object snap handles. The 3DS MAX snap system is designed to snap to vertices, edges, and intersections. The snap system does not work with an object's geometric properties such as the center of a sphere or the middle of a box face. If you find you need to frequently snap to an object's geometric properties, you can place a point object at that location and then place the object and the point in a group. The point defines a vertex that 3DS MAX can snap to, and the group keeps the point and object locked together.

The following example shows how to set up a point object as a permanent reference to the center of a sphere. The following example uses the Align command to place a point at the center of sphere. (The Align command is discussed later in this chapter.)

1. Select a point object.

2. Click Align on the toolbar.

3. Click a sphere.

4. In the Align Selection dialog, choose the following options (see fig. 6.28):

- Choose Pivot Point under Current Object (the point).

- Choose Center under Target Object (the sphere).

- Check the X, Y, and Z position boxes.

- Check the X, Y, and Z axis orientation boxes.

- Click OK.

The point is now centered inside the sphere and aligned with the sphere's local axes. To make sure that the point and sphere stay together, you can place them in a group. Simply select the sphere and the point and choose Group from the Group menu.

FIGURE 6.28

Placing a point at the center of a sphere.

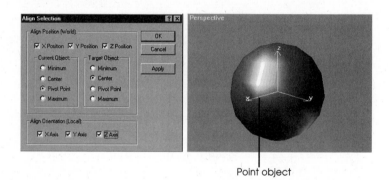

Point object

Using Dummy Objects

You can use dummy objects for many of the same uses as point objects. Traditionally, dummy objects are used as invisible link objects when building linked hierarchies. See Chapter 18, "Building Hierarchies," for more information about linking.

You create a dummy object by clicking Dummy in the Create panel and then dragging out the radius of a dummy cube in any viewport.

The main differences between point objects and dummy objects are as follows:

- Point objects display as an X with a single vertex that you can snap to.

- Dummy objects display as a cube with their pivot point at the center of the cube. The dummy has no snap vertex at its pivot.

- Point objects can be set to show orientation by displaying their local axis tripod.

- Dummy objects do not show orientation as well, but the simple cube is easier to see than the point's X and creates less visual clutter than the point's axis tripod.

Whether you use a point or a dummy object is mostly a matter of personal preference.

Choosing Snap Options

3DS MAX has a fairly complex snap system. You may find the snap system intimidating and confusing at first, but in time you will find it to be quite useful. Snap values control angle and percentage snaps. Position snaps are based on the following methods:

- Grid Snap uses the grid spacing value of the active grid.

- Spatial Snap uses the strength and priority settings in the Grid and Snap Settings dialog.

Which snap method is active at any given time is a function of the command mode you are in and your choice of snap modes from the prompt line. Figure 6.29 identifies the various snap controls in 3DS MAX.

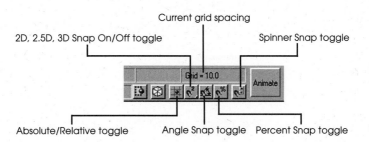

FIGURE 6.29
*Snap controls in
3DS MAX.*

Setting up Grid and Spatial Snaps

If you have read the previous topics about using grids and creating grid objects, you already know how to set grid snap. The Grid Spacing value also sets the grid snap. You set grid spacing for the Home Grid using the Grid and Snap Settings dialog; you set grid spacing for grid objects using their parameters rollout.

Set Spatial Snap options by using the Snap panel of the Grid and Snap Settings dialog (see fig 6.30).

FIGURE 6.30

Snap panel in the Grid and Snap Settings dialog.

Snap Strength sets the radius of a snap field around the cursor; geometry must be within the snap strength radius before the cursor will snap to that location. High values make the cursor very sensitive, jumping from snap point to snap point. Low values make the cursor less sensitive, so that you must move the cursor very close to a snap point before it "snaps."

Snap Priority sets which type of geometry you can snap to and the order in which snaps are evaluated. You can snap object vertices and edges as well as grid intersections and grid lines. Vertices and Grid Intersections snap the cursor to an exact point and hold the cursor there until you move it outside the snap strength distance. Edges and Grid Lines snap the cursor to a line but allow it to slide along the line.

If two snap objects are within each other's snap distances, the cursor snaps to the one with the highest priority setting; if the snap objects have the same priority, the cursor snaps to the one closest to the true location of the cursor.

The 2D, 2.5D, and 3D radio buttons control the snap mode and are similar to the snap mode flyout on the prompt line. The main difference is that the radio buttons in the dialog set the snap mode but do not turn it on. Use the buttons on the prompt line both to set the snap mode and to turn snap on and off.

Every time you click the snap mode buttons on the prompt line, you toggle the snap on/off state. Switching between modes can be frustrating if all you want to do is change the snap mode but leave snap on. For example, say you have snap turned on and are in 2D mode. If you press on the snap mode button and choose 3D mode, you also turn snap off. You must click the button a second time to turn snap mode back on again.

You can also press S to toggle snap mode on and off.

TIP

It is easy to forget that the snap mode on/off state gets switched when you change the mode from the prompt line. Get in the habit of double-checking the prompt line when using snaps to make sure that the on/off state is appropriately set.

The Relative/Absolute check box alters the snap mode for move transforms only and is also duplicated by the Relative/Absolute button on the prompt line. These buttons are discussed in the next section because they relate to using snap for creation and for moving objects.

Using Snap for Creation

When you use snap to create objects, you are using a mixture of spatial snap and grid snap. Spatial snap controls the location of points on the construction plane and grid snap controls height values along the Z axis of the construction plane.

When you create any object—except the Line object—creation snap works in the following ways:

- Relative/Absolute mode is ignored.

- Spatial snap is always in 2D mode, regardless of the snap mode setting. This means you can only snap to vertices and edges that lie directly on the construction plane.

- Height values such as Cylinder, Box, and Cone height snap to the grid spacing of the active grid.

When you create a Line object you can choose between 2D, 2.5D, and 3D snap modes:

- Relative/Absolute mode is ignored.

- 2D Snap mode constrains snaps to vertices and edges that lie directly on the construction plane.

- 2.5D Snap mode snaps to any vertex or edge in 3D space but projects the snap point to the construction plane. This forces the line to remain 2D but simulates the effect of tracing the 3D scene on a transparent plate held in front of the view.

- 3D Snap mode snaps to any vertex or edge in 3D space, creating a true 3D line. During construction, the pivot point is shown on the construction plane. After construction is completed the pivot point is located at the center of the line.

Certainly, a 2.5D or 3D snap for creating objects other than lines would be very helpful. Put it on your wish list, and with luck, that capability might appear in a future release of 3DS MAX.

Using Snap for Moving Objects

When you move objects, you can also use grid and spatial snap modes. Moving objects is the only time that the Absolute/Relative snap mode is used.

Relative Mode ignores the 2D/2.5D/3D value of the snap mode button and checks only that snap mode is on. When the button face is gray, and shows a dot inside the grid lines, Relative mode is active. When you move objects in relative mode, the distance moved is constrained to multiples of the grid spacing. This does not mean that the object is forced to the grid. If an object starts off the grid, it stays off the grid. In other words, the object maintains its relative offset from the grid.

Absolute Mode uses the full setting of the snap mode button. When the button face is highlighted and shows a dot on the grid intersection, Absolute mode is active. You can use Absolute mode only under the following conditions:

- You must be using either the Screen or View transform coordinate system.

- The active viewport must be an Orthogonal view or User view.

When Absolute mode is active, Snap behaves as follows:

- 2D Snap mode constrains snaps to vertices and edges that lie directly on the construction plane.

■ 2.5D Snap mode snaps to any vertex or edge in 3D space but projects the snap point to the construction plane.

■ 3D Snap mode snaps to any vertex or edge in 3D space.

In all three snap modes, the snap point is constrained by the active transform axis constraints. For example, say your transform constraints are set to the X,Y plane. If you 3D snap to a point, only the X,Y coordinates are used (the active constraint axes)—the Z coordinate is ignored. In this case, the 3D snap ends up working like a 2.5D snap.

Using Angle Snap

The Angle Snap setting is useful for object and view rotation. Enter a value in the Angle field of the Grid and Snap Settings dialog to specify a constraint angle for interactive rotations. The default setting is 5.0 degrees, but you might consider 15.0 degrees a more useful value. An Angle Snap of 15 degrees enables you to easily specify the major angles common to architecture and manufacturing: 15, 30, 45, 60, and 90 degrees.

Click the Angle Snap button on the Prompt line or press A to toggle Angle Snap on and off.

Angle Snap applies only to interactive rotations where you drag in a viewport. Angle Snap has no effect on angle fields such as bend angle.

Using Percent Snap

Enter a value in the Percent field of the Grid and Snap Settings dialog to specify a percentage increment for interactive scale operations.

Click the Percent Snap button on the Prompt line to toggle Percent Snap on and off.

Using Spinner Snap

Spinner Snap is set in the General panel of the Preference Settings dialog. This snap controls how much a numeric field changes when you click the up or down spinner arrows. You can quickly display the General panel of the Preference Settings dialog by right-clicking the Spinner Snap button.

Spinner Snap affects only the result of clicking the up and down spinner arrows. It does not constrain the values you type into a field, nor does it affect dragging a spinner arrow.

Click the Spinner Snap button on the Prompt line to toggle Spinner Snap on and off.

Using Transforms and Coordinate Systems

The term *transform* refers to the basic operations of Move, Rotate, and Scale. You can extend the functionality of these simple commands by choosing different transform coordinate systems, transform centers, and transform axis constraints. These extensions are called *transform managers*. The transform buttons and transform managers are located near the middle of the toolbar (see fig. 6.31).

FIGURE 6.31
Transform Managers
on the toolbar.

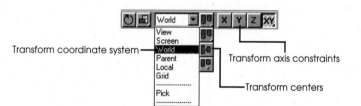

As mentioned in Chapter 1, "Core Concepts of 3D Studio MAX," transforms are always applied toward the end of the dataflow, after all of the modifiers in the modifier stack. Also, some objects give up their transforms when used for some purposes. Shape objects, for example, give up their transforms when used as a path or cross-section shape in a Loft object. Also, Mesh objects give up their transforms when used as targets in a Morph object.

Another way of looking at this is to realize that modifiers change the geometry within an object whereas transforms change only the location of the object in space. That's right. Technically speaking, a scale transform does not change geometry within the object. Scale changes the location of the object by varying its size, even if it varies size non-uniformly along each of the three local axes.

Apply transforms directly to an object when you want to size, rotate, or move an object into position without changing the object itself. To change the geometry of an object in a predictable and semi-permanent fashion, apply transforms at the sub-object level or use an XForm modifier.

The following sections describe how to apply transforms to objects and how to use the various transform managers.

Using the Transform Managers

Set the transform managers to constrain the behavior of the transform commands. These managers control three properties of transforms:

- **Transform coordinate system**   Controls which way is up

- **Transform center**   Sets the center of rotation and scale transforms

- **Constrain transform axes**   Locks the transform to a single axis or any pair of axes

3DS MAX remembers the transform manager settings you choose for each of the Move, Rotate, and Scale transforms. For example, when you click Move, the settings used the last time you moved are restored to the transform managers. Likewise, when you click Rotate, the last rotation settings are restored. This can be a productivity boost after you get used to it, but at first it is neither obvious nor intuitive. You should develop the habit of looking at the transform managers every time you use a transform.

Choosing a Transform Coordinate System

You cannot move or rotate an object in any arbitrary direction. All transforms in 3DS MAX are applied along the X,Y,Z coordinate axes. This would be incredibly restrictive if it were not for the fact that you can choose any arbitrary X Y Z coordinate system.

If you have a CAD background, you may be accustomed to specifying an arbitrary rotation axis or arbitrary mirror axis as part of a transform command. 3DS MAX includes this same functionality, but you set up the axis first by choosing your coordinate system. Then you proceed with the transform.

Keep in mind, the active grid (either the Home Grid or a grid object) only affects where objects are created and where snap points are projected.

Transform coordinate systems affect how you place an object in your scene after the object is created. The transform coordinate system can use the active grid, but it doesn't have to.

You can choose from the seven transform coordinate systems on the drop-down list in the 3DS MAX toolbar (see fig. 6.32). (For some odd reason the tool tip for this list calls it the Reference Coordinate System even though it works only for transforms.) The View, Screen, and World systems are permanently fixed and unchanging. The Local, Parent, Grid, and Pick systems vary according to the objects you select and your active grid choice. All of these systems are described in detail in the 3DS MAX User's Guide and Help system.

FIGURE 6.32

The Reference
(Transform) Coordinate
System list.

Of all of these coordinate systems, Pick is probably the most fascinating. By using Pick, you can use the local coordinate system of any object in your scene as the transform coordinate system for any other object. At first this might seem to be just an amusing oddity, but consider what you can do using the Pick coordinate system with Helper objects.

Place a point object and align it with any surface. Then, by using the Pick coordinate system, you can move or rotate any object along that surface or perpendicular to that surface. For example, you might pick a point object aligned with the side of a building as your coordinate system. You could then move windows, signs, and other fixture around the facade.

You can use a tape object to define a plumb line between any two points. By using the Pick coordinate system, you can move or rotate objects about that plumb line. For example, you might pick a tape object placed between two electrodes as your coordinate system. You could then move electrons along the tape by constraining movement to the tape's Z axis.

To use a Pick transform coordinate system, complete the following steps:

1. Position or align the object you want to serve as the coordinate system.

2. Choose Pick from the Reference Coordinate System list.

3. Click the object you want to use as the coordinate system.

4. Proceed to transform other objects.

Choosing a Transform Center

Use the three-button flyout to the right of the coordinate system list to define the transform center (see fig. 6.33). The center comes into play only for rotation and scale transforms. When you move an object, it really doesn't matter what center you use; the object just moves.

Figure 6.33

Transform center flyout.

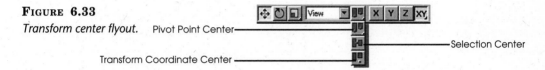

Pivot Point Center

Transform Coordinate Center

Selection Center

The three transform center choices are as follows:

■ **Pivot Point Center**   Uses each selected object's local pivot point as the center of rotation and scale. Each object rotates or scales an equal amount about its own pivot point.

■ **Selection Center**   Uses the geometric center of a bounding box surrounding all selected objects as the center of rotation and scale. The selected objects rotate and scale as a single unit, much the same as if you place the objects in a group.

■ **Coordinate System Center**   Uses the center of the transform coordinate system as the center of rotation and scale. This choice is quite useful when using the Parent or Pick coordinate systems. In those situations the center of rotation and scale is either the pivot point of the selected object's parents or the pivot point of the Pick object.

Pivot Point Center is the only valid choice if you want to animate a pure rotation or scale transform. The other two choices combine a move with the rotation and scale. That's why the transform center flyout is gray and cannot be changed when the Animate button is on.

The following three methods enable you to create the effect of an animated rotation or scale about an offset center:

■ **Linking**   You can link the object you want to animate to a Helper object and then rotate or scale the Helper using Pivot Point center. The end effect is an offset rotation or scale of the original object. This is probably your best solution for animated offset rotations and scales.

- **Preference Settings**   You can change an option in the Animation panel of the Preference Settings dialog that enables offset center animation. Choose Preferences from the file menu and uncheck the Local Center During Animate check box in the Animation panel of the dialog (see fig. 6.34). The end result is that the object scales or rotates about its own center and moves in a straight line to a location matching the offset scale or rotation—usually not what you want.

- **Pivot Point**   You can use features in the Hierarchy panel to change the position of the object's pivot point to an offset location and then rotate or scale the object using Pivot Point center. Changing the pivot point affects all transforms applied to the object and affects the way modifiers are applied after the pivot is changed.

FIGURE 6.34
Local Center During Animate option.

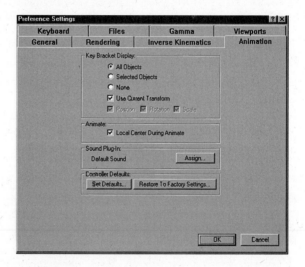

Constraining Transforms

Axis constraints are the final set of transform managers. You can choose from the three single axis constraints or from a flyout of three dual axis (planar) constraints (see fig. 6.35). The active transform axis constraint locks the transform effect to that axis or plane. For example, if the X axis constraint is active, you can move along only the X axis.

FIGURE 6.35
Transform axis constraints.

The keyboard shortcuts for choosing axis constraints are as follows:

- **`(grave)**   Cycles through choosing the four constraint buttons—X, Y, Z, and current dual axis.

- **~ (tilde)**   Cycles through the dual axis options without choosing the button.

- **F5**   Chooses X axis constraint.

- **F6**   Chooses Y axis constraint.

- **F7**   Chooses Z axis constraint.

- **F8**   Chooses dual axis constraint. If dual axis is already chosen, F8 cycles through the dual axis options.

Using the Keyboard to Transform with Precision

If you need real precision for Move, Rotate, and Scale operations, you can use the keyboard to perform the transform. You can choose either of the following keyboard techniques:

- Press arrow keys to transform the object rather than dragging.

- Use the Transform Type-In dialog to enter precise information values.

Using Arrow Keys to Transform

You can Move, Rotate, and Scale objects by using the arrow keys in much the same way you zoom and rotate views.

To transform objects using the arrow keys, complete the following:

1. Click a transform tool.

2. Select objects using the transform tool.

3. Position the cursor over the selection so the transform icon is visible.

4. Press an arrow key to transform the selection.

If, after making your selection, you decide you want to change one of the transform managers or viewports, you must right-click in an empty area of the viewport you want before proceeding with step three. The right-click is necessary to return system focus to the viewport after clicking on the toolbar or any other part of the user interface.

The type of transform you use determines which arrow keys you can use:

- **Move**   Uses both horizontal and vertical arrow keys. If a transform axis constraint limits horizontal or vertical movement, the arrow keys still move the cursor but the selection does not move along the constrained axis.

- **Rotate**   Uses only the vertical arrow keys. Up equals counterclockwise rotation and down equals clockwise rotation.

- **Scale**   Uses only the vertical arrow keys. Up equals increasing scale and down equals decreasing scale.

The arrow keys are actually moving the cursor on the screen—the same as if you were dragging the cursor—and 3DS MAX is translating that movement into transform values. This approach has the following effect on transforming with arrow keys:

- When you press the arrow keys, the cursor must move a few pixels before the movement is "read." After the object starts transforming, each key press is read as one pixel of cursor movement.

- When snaps are on, the cursor must move to a snap point before the object transforms. At first it might appear that nothing is happening, but as soon as the cursor reaches a snap point, the object transforms.

Using the Transform Type-In Dialog

You can use the Transform Type-In dialog to enter very precise values for Move, Rotate, and Scale transforms. This dialog floats above the 3DS MAX window and you can use it any time you are transforming an object. To use the Transform Type-In dialog, choose Transform Type-In from the Edit menu (see fig. 6.36).

The Transform Type-In dialog has two parts. The fields on the left side of the screen always show the absolute values for Move or Rotate in the World coordinate system and absolute Scale values in the Local coordinate system for the selected objects. The right side always shows 0.0 and is where you enter the transform offset using the current transform coordinate system. You can move, rotate, or scale selected objects by entering values on either side of the dialog.

FIGURE 6.36

The Transform Type-In dialog for Move, Rotate, and Scale.

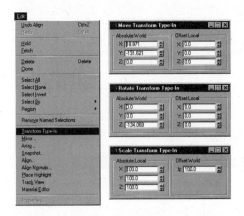

For example, open the Transform Type-In dialog, select an object, and click Rotate on the toolbar. Suppose the Absolute: World fields show a current rotation of 45.0 degrees absolute to the X axis. If you want the absolute rotation to be exactly 45.0 degrees about the X axis enter that value in the X: field under Absolute: World. As soon as you press Enter or click in another field, the rotation changes. Now click Move and the Transform Type-In dialog changes to show the object's position. If you want to move the object exactly 30.125 units along the Z axis from its current position, enter that value in the Z: field under Offset.

The Transform Type-In dialog has a secondary benefit of revealing the current transform values of a selected object. Because the dialog always displays absolute world values, you can examine the exact position, rotation, and scale values of an object at any time.

Mirror, Array, and Snapshot Transforms

There are only three transforms: Move, Rotate, and Scale. 3DS MAX combines these transforms and uses special dialogs to provide the special transform techniques of Mirror and Array. The Mirror and Array buttons are to the right of the transform managers, as shown in figure 6.37.

FIGURE 6.37

Mirror and Array buttons on the toolbar.

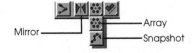

Mirroring Objects

Mirroring an object is a scale transform with a value of –100 percent. You can easily create mirrored objects by using the options in the Mirror dialog (see fig. 6.38). You interactively set options for mirror axis, mirror offset, and clone method.

FIGURE 6.38

Mirror dialog.

The Mirror dialog reports the current transform coordinate system as part of the dialog title. Make sure you set the transform coordinate system you want before you click Mirror. If you click Mirror and then realize that you want to change coordinate systems, you must cancel the Mirror dialog, change the coordinate system and then click Mirror again.

You have three decisions to make when mirroring an object:

- **Mirror Axis** Choose one of the six options for either single-axis or dual-axis mirroring from the Mirror Axis area of the dialog. The mirror axis passes through the current transform center point, and the axis orientation is set by the current coordinate system.

- **Mirror Offset** If you don't want the mirrored object to stay in its default location, you can specify an offset distance in the Mirror Axis area of the dialog. The offset moves the object an additional distance along the mirror axis from the default location. You can type the distance into the field or drag the spinner to watch the mirrored object move away from its original location.

- **Clone Method** Usually you mirror an object because you want a mirrored clone of the original object. This is useful when you model objects with symmetry. You model one half of the symmetrical object and then mirror it to get the other half. Choose Copy, Instance, or Reference from the Clone Selection area to create a new mirrored object from the original. Choosing No Clone mirrors the original object.

Tip

Even if you do not want to clone the mirrored object, you may find it handy to choose Copy while you experiment with various mirror axes and offsets. With Copy selected you always see the original object and the mirror result; this gives you a base reference to judge the effect of your choices. When you decide on the mirror axis and offset you want, choose No Clone before clicking OK.

Most people think of mirroring as a modeling tool, a way of flipping geometry end for end. Because mirroring is a transform, it is more a positional tool than a modeling tool. Mirroring an object can sometimes lead to unexpected results when you use that object with other features. Some examples of when mirroring causes problems include the following:

- **Loft Objects** When you get a shape for use in a loft object, the shape's transforms are discarded. This includes mirroring.

- **Morph Objects** When you select an object as a morph target, the object's transforms are discarded. This includes mirroring.

- **Inverse Kinematics** The negative scale value that produces mirroring can cause joint calculation problems when a mirrored object is used in an Inverse Kinematic chain.

The solution to these problems can involve a variety of techniques, but the root of the solution is to get the mirror (scale) effect out of the object's transformation matrix. You do this by manually applying negative scale values at the sub-object level. Unfortunately, Mirror only works at the object level, even when sub-object mode is active. You mirror something at the sub-object level by using the Scale Transform Type-In dialog.

To mirror an object using an XForm modifier, complete the following steps:

1. Select an object.

2. Choose Transform Type-In from the Edit menu.

3. Choose XForm from the Modify panel.

4. Choose Gizmo from the Sub-Object list.

5. Click Non-Uniform Scale.

6. Enter –100 in an axis field to mirror the object about that axis.

Mirroring the gizmo at the modifier sub-object level gives you the same overall effect as using the Mirror command but without the Mirror side effects. Mirroring the gizmo has the added advantage of being in the Modifier Stack, so you can go back and change or delete the mirror effect at any time.

To mirror sub-objects using an Edit modifier, complete the following steps:

1. Select an object.

2. Apply an appropriate Edit modifier for that object.

3. Click Sub-Object and define a selection.

4. Choose Transform Type-In from the Edit menu.

5. Click Non-Uniform Scale.

6. Enter –100 in an axis field to mirror the object about that axis.

By using this technique, you can mirror parts of an object. You can also use the Edit modifier to build the sub-object selection and pass it up to an XForm modifier. See Chapter 12, "Sub-Object Modeling," for full details about sub-object editing.

WARNING

Using Transform Type-In to apply negative scale values is a handy technique, but it does have a few glitches.

First, when you enter a negative scale value into any scale axis field, all fields report negative values. The end result is correct, but the fields indicate the wrong values.

A side effect of negative scaling is that the object normals will typically point in the wrong direction, making your rendered object appear inside-out. Check your object in a rendered viewport after applying negative scale. You can correct the inside-out affect by adding a Normal modifier and selecting the Unify and Flip check boxes.

Arraying Objects

Arrays are made by cloning objects with multiple repeated transforms. You can create arrays by using one of these two ways. The first method is to press Shift while dragging a transform to create any array based on a single Move, Rotate, or Scale operation. To use the second method, click the Array button on the toolbar to use the Array dialog.

Pressing Shift while dragging causes the Clone Options dialog to appear (see fig. 6.39). Choose the Clone Method of Copy, Instance, or Reference and set the number of clone objects you want to create in an array. This technique is handy for simple, quick, linear, radial, and scale arrays.

FIGURE 6.39

You can quickly build up complex geometry by using the Array dialog as shown in figure 6.40.

FIGURE 6.40

Array dialog.

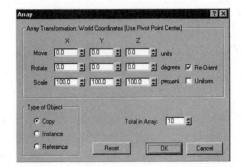

The Array dialog reports the current transform coordinate system and transform center. Make sure you set the coordinate system and center you want before clicking Array. If you click Array and then realize that you want to change coordinate systems or centers, you must cancel the Array dialog, change the coordinate system, and click Array again.

You have three decisions to make when creating an array:

- **Array Transformation** You can build arrays out of a single transform or by combining multiple transforms. Set the transform values for each axis in the Array transformation area of the dialog. The values you set are applied to each object in the array using the previous object as the starting point. Unlike Mirror, the Array dialog is not interactive. You must set up the array and click OK to see the result. If you don't like the result, you can click Undo and try again. Fortunately, Array remembers your last settings and uses them as the default when you repeat the command. This makes the trial and error approach much easier.

- **Total in Array** This single field sets the number of objects that are created.

- **Type of Object**   Choose an option in the Type of Object area to specify whether the array creates copies, instances, or references.

By varying the settings in the Array Transformation area, you can create many popular array types:

- **Linear**   Enter distances in the Move fields to create a linear array (copies aligned in a single row). The easiest way to create a linear array is to enter a distance in a single Move axis field. If you enter distances in more than one Move field, you get a linear array running at a diagonal to the coordinate system axes.

TIP

If you need a linear array running diagonally, it is often easier to align a point object with one of its axes pointing in the direction you want the array to take and then Pick the point object as your transform coordinate system. You can then define a linear array along a single axis.

- **Grid**   A grid array is a combination of two linear arrays. Create a linear array along one axis. Select all the objects in the linear array and create another linear array along either of the two remaining axes.

- **Volume**   A volume array is the result of three linear arrays. Create a grid array, select all the objects in the array, and create a new linear array on the third axis. Figure 6.41 shows examples of linear, grid, and volume arrays.

FIGURE 6.41
Linear, Grid, and Volume arrays.

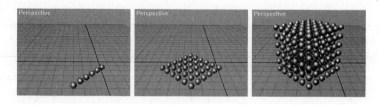

- **Radial**   Enter angles in the Rotate fields, usually with an offset center, to create radial arrays. If you use a pivot point center for a radial array, the object clones usually end up on top of each other. You usually want to use the coordinate system center or selection center. Use the Reorient check box to determine whether objects are positioned by the radial array or are rotated and positioned, as shown in figure 6.42.

Although you can define radial arrays using rotation about more than one axis, the results are difficult to predict. If you want to create a radial array about a diagonal rotation axis, it is easier to set up a point object to use as the coordinate system and perform a single axis rotation about the point. See the previous tip about diagonal linear arrays.

■ **Helix**   By combining move and rotate fields a helix array is formed. Define a radial array about a single axis and specify a Move value on the same axis. The result is a radial array that moves along its rotation axis, similar to spiral stairs or a DNA strand.

FIGURE 6.42
Affect of using Reorient with radial arrays

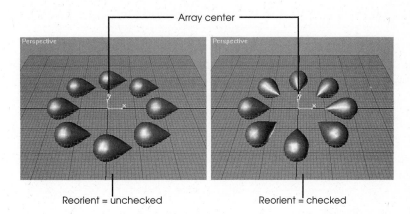

You may be tempted to try creating a flat spiral array by assigning a move distance on an axis other than the rotation axis. This does not work. You get a simple radial array that is offset by the move distance. Creating a flat spiral array requires you to employ multiple techniques. One possible method is described in creating snapshot arrays.

■ **Scale**   Enter values in the Scale fields to create scale arrays. Using a pivot point center or selection center on a single selected object usually creates a nested array. Using the coordinate system center often produces a result similar to a combined scale and linear array (see fig. 6.43).

FIGURE 6.43
Comparing pivot point center and transform coordinate center for scale arrays.

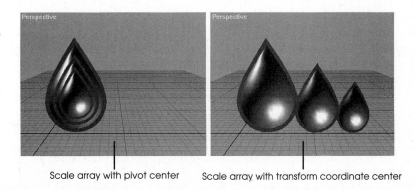

The following example demonstrates the advantage of using point objects as Pick coordinate systems for creating arrays along an arbitrary axis.

CREATING AN ARRAY ALONG AN ARBITRARY AXIS

Imagine that you have a fence post that you want to array along a line 30 degrees off the World X axis with a spacing of 4'0". By using trigonometry you could calculate that you need a linear array using the World coordinate system and the following distances in the Move fields: X=3'5.569" and Y=2'0". But who wants to do that much math?

The following technique uses a rotated point object to set up an array along a single axis:

1. Click Helpers in the Create panel.

2. Click Point under the General sub-category and create a point object in a top viewport. Name the point Fence-Line.

   This creates the point object aligned with the World coordinate system. The point object can be located anywhere in the top viewport.

3. Rotate the point object 30 degrees about the Z axis.

   The point's X axis is now pointing in the direction you want the fence post array to follow.

4. Choose Pick from the Reference Coordinate System list and click the point object.

The point now defines your current transform coordinate system. The next sequence of steps creates a linear array of fence posts using the point object as the transform coordinate system.

5. Select the fence post.

6. Click Array.

7. Enter 4'0" in the Move X: field, set the number of fence posts you want, and click OK.

An important advantage of the previous technique is that after you set up the point helper, you can go back and reuse it as a coordinate system any time. You just arrayed a row of fence posts, but you're also going to need fence rails, pickets, gates, and other objects where you can make use of the point's coordinate system. In this case you might also consider creating a grid object rather than a point so you can create objects on the grid as well as use the grid object as a transform coordinate system.

Snapshot Arrays

One last type of array uses the Snapshot button in the Array flyout (see fig. 6.44). A *snapshot* is a type of temporal array that creates clones based on an object's changes over time. Snapshot is the only array technique that can also capture and freeze modifier changes.

FIGURE 6.44

Snapshot dialog.

For Snapshot to be of any use, you must first animate an object's transforms or modifiers. You then use options in the Snapshot dialog to specify how many clones you want to create over time. Snapshot then creates clones at regular time intervals.

The options in the Snapshot dialog fall into two groups: Snapshot and Clone Method. With the Snapshot option, you choose the time parameters for creating the snapshots. Select Single to create a single clone at the time set by the Time Slider; choose Range to specify a time range and the number of clones to create over that range. With the Clone Method option, you choose the type of clone that you want to create. You can choose the three standard options of Copy, Instance, or Reference, or you can choose the special option Mesh.

The Mesh option collapses the modifier stack to freeze the modified form of the object at each time interval. This process wipes out all modifiers and base parameters, converting the object to a simple mesh. See Chapter 8, "Object-Level Modeling," for information about collapsing the Modifier stack.

Creating a flat helix array, as mentioned previously, is possible with snapshot. You first create a flat helix shape and animate an object following the helix as a motion path. Once the object is animated you can use snapshot to place copies of the object around the helix.

Alignment Tools

Use the buttons in the Align flyout (see fig. 6.45) to move and rotate objects to align with other objects. None of the Align buttons work with sub-object selections. The three buttons in this flyout each have a very specific purpose:

- **Align**   Aligns objects by comparing their local coordinate systems and the extents of their bounding boxes in the current transform coordinate system.

- **Normal Align**   Aligns objects surface to surface by matching face normals.

- **Place Highlight**   Aligns objects by matching the negative Z axis of one object with a face normal of another. This command was originally intended for use with light sources, but it can be used with any object.

FIGURE 6.45

Buttons in the Align flyout.

Align ——

Place highlight ——

—— Normal align

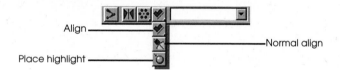

All three Align buttons employ the same sequence of operation:

1. Select objects to be aligned. These objects are called the *source objects*. They will move and rotate as a result of the align process.

2. Click an Align button.

3. Select a single object with which the source objects will be aligned. This object is called the *target object,* and it provides the reference used to move and rotate the source objects. The target object does not move or rotate as a result of the align process.

4. Set alignment parameters.

Alignment is just a transform technique for positioning objects according to specified relationships. Align forms no special connection to objects, and as soon as you complete the command you can use another transform to move the objects out of alignment. If you want aligned objects to stay aligned, you must group or link them.

Aligning Objects

Use the Align command to align objects based on their geometric extents (bounding box) or by their pivot points. This command is most useful for the following alignment tasks:

- Aligning objects by geometric extents. This works best with regular, straight-edged geometry such as boxes and cylinders.

- Aligning objects by pivot point. This is useful when setting up hierarchies and IK joints.

- Aligning helper objects to other objects.

Align uses two techniques:

- Align positions (move) based on the objects' bounding box in the current reference coordinate system.

- Align orientation (rotate) based on the objects' local coordinate system.

Select the source objects, click Align, and then click a target object to display the Align Selection dialog (see fig. 6.46).

FIGURE 6.46

Align Selection dialog.

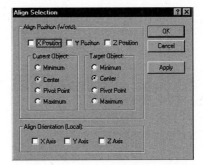

Aligning Object Position

Align the source object's position to the target using the options in the Align Position area. The Align Position title also indicates the current reference coordinate system because the align options depend upon the definition of the object's bounding box in the reference coordinate system.

The bounding box is the smallest three-dimensional box that completely encloses the object and has all of its edges aligned with the Reference coordinate system. Figure 6.46 shows the same object with its bounding box defined using three different reference coordinate systems.

When aligning objects using the Local coordinate system, the Local coordinate systems of the source objects are used, and the Local coordinate system of the target is ignored.

FIGURE 6.47
Bounding boxes for three different reference coordinate systems.

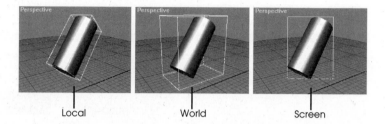

Local   World   Screen

To align the source object position to the target object position, you choose from three options: the active alignment axes, the source object alignment point, and the target object alignment point.

The alignment axis check boxes are similar to the transform axis constraints for the Move transform. These check boxes set which axes the source objects can move along to match up their alignment points.

The alignment points for the source objects and target object use the same four options. These options are calculated using the bounding boxes in the following way (see fig. 6.48):

- **Minimum**   Uses the edge of the bounding box in the negative direction of the active alignment axis.

- **Center**   Uses the geometric center of the bounding box.

- **Pivot Point**   Uses the object's pivot point. This is the only option that is independent of the current reference coordinate system.

- **Maximum**   Uses the edge of the bounding box in the positive direction of the active alignment axis.

As you choose different alignment axes and alignment points, the source objects move to show the current alignment result. Each source object uses its own alignment point based on its own bounding box. If you want to align the selection of source objects as a single object, you must first put them in a group.

FIGURE 6.48
The four alignment points using the World coordinate system.

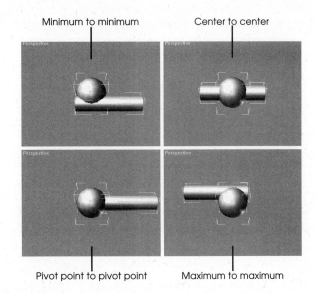

Minimum to minimum   Center to center

Pivot point to pivot point   Maximum to maximum

You can continue trying different options until you click OK to accept the alignment or click Cancel to discard it.

Aligning Object Orientation

The three check boxes in the Align Orientation area rotate the source objects to match the local axis orientation of the target object. Align Orientation is independent of the current reference coordinate system and always uses the local axes of both the source objects and the target object.

Aligning by Face Normals

Use the Normal Align button to align objects surface to surface. This is especially useful when you are working with very irregular geometry or need to place objects so that they are tangent to each other. After the objects are aligned, you can rotate or move the source objects about the aligned normal axis.

To align objects by face normals, complete the following steps:

1. Select source objects.

2. Click Normal Align.

3. Drag across the surface of the source objects to select the source normal.

As you drag over the source objects, a blue line appears at the cursor, showing the direction of the selected source normal. Release the drag to select the displayed normal.

4. Drag across the surface of a target object to select the target normal.

As soon as you release the drag, the selected objects move and rotate so that the source normal is aligned with the target normal and points in the opposite direction.

5. Set parameters in the Normal Align dialog.

Figure 6.49 shows the procedure for selecting source and target normals, and the Normal Align dialog.

FIGURE 6.49

Aligning objects by face normals.

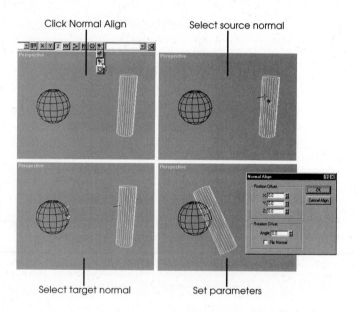

Use the options in the dialog to move and rotate the source objects with respect to the aligned face normals:

- **Position Offset** Moves the source objects. Entering a distance in the Z field moves the source objects in and out along the aligned normals. Entering distances in the X or Y field moves the source objects along the local X or Y axis of the face that contains the source normal. It can be difficult to predict the orientation of the X and Y axes, so your best technique is to drag the spinners and watch how the source objects move.

- **Rotation Offset**   Spins the source objects by using the aligned normals as the rotation axis. This also has the side effect of rotating the orientation of the X and Y position offset and can be used to align the position offset axes to another direction.

- **Flip Normal**   Flips the source objects so that the normals are aligned and point in the same direction.

TIP

An extremely useful technique is to align a grid object to another object using Normal Align. Doing this creates a construction plane aligned with the surface of an object. You can the use the grid as a reference coordinate system to transform objects aligned with the surface or as the active grid to create new objects aligned with the surface. Grid objects are the only helper objects that work with Normal Align.

Aligning with Place Highlight

You use Place Highlight to align source objects' negative Z axes with the reflected line of sight off a face of the target object. The result produced by Place Highlight is dependent upon the view in which you select the target face.

The original purpose for Place Highlight was to help place lights to create specular highlights at specific locations on an object's surface. Any object can be used as the source object for Place Highlight, which makes the command useful for other techniques as well.

You can use Place Highlight to do the following:

- Locate lights to create specular highlights at specific points on an object's surface. If you are a technical illustrator, you recognize this technique as creating "farkles."

- Locate objects so that their reflection appears at a specific point on a reflective object's surface.

To use Place Highlight, complete the following:

1. Select the source objects to be placed. You can select multiple source objects, but because they all end up in the same place, it is usually best to work with one source object at a time.

2. Click Place Highlight.

3. Drag across the surface of the target object.

4. As you drag across the target object, a blue line appears at the cursor, showing the normal of the selected face. The source objects move and rotate to align with the reflected line of sight off the selected face.

In Practice: Selection, Transforms, and Precision

- **Selecting Objects**   The transform tools can also be used for selection. Press Ctrl to add to a selection and press Alt to remove from a selection.

- **Named Selection Sets**   Use named selection sets as a way to manage and organize the objects in your scene.

- **Select by Property**   Use selection filters and options in the Select Objects dialog to efficiently select objects based on common properties such as color, object type, and name.

- **Grouping Objects**   Use groups to combine objects so that they can be manipulated as a single object. Groups are more permanent than named selection sets but more flexible than attaching objects with an edit modifier.

- **Using Helpers**   Use helper objects to build connections between objects (through linking) and to define alternative coordinate systems and snap points.

- **Work Precisely**   Set grid and snap options to work to regular spacings. Use numeric fields and Transform Type-In to set precise values.

- **Transforms**   Use transform managers to work with alternative coordinate systems, alternative center points, and to constrain transforms to selected axes.

Part II

BUILDING 3D SCENES

Image created by Peter Noldt
Arch Image
Houston , TX

Chapter 7

BASICS OF OBJECT CREATION

This chapter discusses the basics of object creation along with the characteristics and uses of the basic geometric primitives. Although we are talking about the simplest of objects, the same rules apply for the most complex of objects. In addition, the simple primitives often serve as the building blocks for creating even the most complex or organic of models. In particular, this chapter will discuss the following points:

- *Basics of creating 3D primitive objects*

- *Using the Home Planes and Grid Helpers in creation*

- *Achieving accuracy*

- Understanding creation options coming to many object types
- Exploring the basic primitives
- The concept of geometric classes in 3D Studio MAX

The Basics of Creating Objects

Although objects in 3D Studio MAX may seem quite complex, creating them is a fast and easy process. Every object you create is *parametric* in nature, meaning that its form is defined by a series of parameters. The act of creating objects usually involves three basic steps:

- Choose the plane upon which you want the object to rest (most often this just means activating a particular viewport).
- Pick the point on the plane for the beginning point of the object (this is just a click in the viewport at the desired spot).
- Drag your mouse to define the remaining parameters for the object.

Creating Interactively

Creating geometry is intended to be an interactive experience in 3D Studio MAX. As such, the conventional method for creating an object is to click in a viewport and drag the cursor to define the remaining parameters. 3DS MAX draws the resulting geometry simultaneously in all viewports as you define distances and create.

The plane upon which objects are created is determined either by the viewport or an active construction Grid helper object. The location of an object is a characteristic of the object's definition. Most objects rest on the creation plane and define a height from it. Cylinder primitives, for example, locate their bottom circle caps on the creation plane and the height parameter extrudes perpendicular from that plane. Because Sphere, GeoSphere, Torus, and Hedra primitives are defined by their centroid, these primitives are exceptions to this rule and locate their centroid on the construction plane. While other objects sit on the construction plane, these three will bisect it.

The plane about which a primitive begins is also the location for its pivot point. The *pivot point* is the center of the object's local axes, and it determines the point about which the object rotates. This initial creation also defines the object's permanent bounding box orientation.

NOTE

The preceding descriptions are standard for 3DS MAX primitives. Objects created by third-party developers (and perhaps yourself) can follow these conventions or can have different creation methods and locate their pivots elsewhere.

Using the Ctrl Key in Creation

The Ctrl key performs a special, and somewhat hidden, service when creating various primitives. With the exception of Box, every primitive enables you to adjust its initial rotation by pressing the Ctrl key any time between the first and final defining points. This enables you to quickly orient your objects while you are creating them. In the case of the Box, the Ctrl key constrains the initial creation to a square rather than affecting its rotation.

Creating with the Keyboard

Keyboard entry is provided for all primitives as a stark alternative to the interactive method. With it, you must enter all the parameters that would normally be derived from your interactive input. Creating a box, for example, is usually a matter of picking a start point, dragging to define its opposite corner, and dragging once more to define its height. Figure 7.1 shows how keyboard entry requires six entries for what would otherwise take only three steps, and no visual clue is given until you commit to create. In practice, you will probably reserve keyboard entry for times when exact placement is crucial and you have the relevant data at hand. Although keyboard input is available for all primitives (except Hedras), this book will always assume that you are creating objects interactively.

While keyboard entry may appear more accurate, the same accuracy can be obtained by creating the object interactively and adjusting its parameters from the Modify panel and its location from the Transform Type-In dialog. The same accuracy can also be obtained using Snap with appropriate grid settings. In most cases, interactive creation with subsequent modification will be faster, because usually only one or two parameters are critical.

FIGURE 7.1

Keyboard entry for creating Box objects.

T I P ───

Keyboard creation can be faster than interactive creation when the world origin is an acceptable location for the object and you know the dimensions. This fact may be familiar to you already if you've used one of the various programs that mandate that objects be created at the origin.

Creation Panel Influence

After you have defined an object, whether interactively or with the keyboard, the parameters in the Create panel are "live" and will continue to influence the object you just created. If you want to adjust a parameter, change it at this time in the Creation panel. This relationship between the Create panel and the recently created object is broken as soon as you click in a viewport or switch to another operation. If you wish to edit the object's creation parameters after this initial point, simply go to the Modifier panel with the object selected.

When adjusting spinner arrows, remember that pressing the Ctrl key accelerates your mouse, whereas the Alt key decelerates it. When editing number fields, replacing the field with an "r" plus a value and pressing Enter adds that value to the original. The "r" in this case stands for "relative" because you are adding a value relative to the original. The process for relative entry is shown in figure 7.2, where the Height parameter of 96.0 is increased by R24, for a final value of 120.0.

FIGURE 7.2

The steps for changing edit fields by relative amounts.

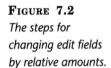

Creating with Home Grids

The world coordinate system is fixed in 3DS MAX, with the X,Y,Z axes always intersecting at absolute 0,0,0. Through this permanent point run three infinite construction grids known as *home grids*. These three orthogonal home grid planes are each parallel to one of the three world axes as shown in figure 7.3. Views other than the six orthogonal views always use the X,Y home grid. Because of this grid's prominence and because in modeling it nearly always represents the plane of the earth, this grid is often called the *ground plane*. Perspective, User, Camera, and Spotlight views always display the ground plane when the home grid is active.

TIP

A general rule to remember is that "If you can see an active grid (the grid lines are visible), then that grid is the active construction plane for that viewport."

When creating objects with the home grids, the view in which you begin defining the object determines the construction plane. When you create an object in an Orthogonal viewport, you are determining the placement of two of the pick point's three coordinates. The third is determined by the remaining home grid. For example, when you create objects in a Right or Left view, you are defining the Z and Y positions with the X component being placed on the home XY home grid at 0. Figure 7.3 shows the planes and their XYZ designations.

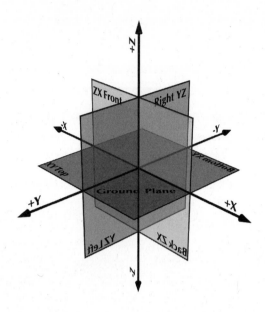

FIGURE 7.3
*The default
home grids.*

NOTE

When you create in a non-orthogonal viewport, you are always defining the X,Y position, and the Z component is zero (as long as the home grid is active). Thus, when you create in Perspective, User, Camera, or Spotlight views, the objects are always placed on the ground plane.

Creating with Grid Helpers

Grid helper objects are available when you need to construct on planes other than the home grid or wish to use the same plane in all viewports. You may find the default home grids sufficient when using 3DS MAX to create independent, isolated models. You will, however, find grid objects very useful when your models grow in complexity and you need to coordinate with other assemblies, possibly from other programs. Grids prove invaluable for defining construction planes that are aligned to views, faces, and objects.

TIP

When working with scenes located far from the world origin, it's good practice to create grid objects where your modeling will take place and use them instead of the home grids. This will prevent the undesirable situation of creating lights and cameras long distances from their intended location.

Grid helpers are manipulated like any other object, so you can move, rotate, and align them quite easily. The Normal Align function is particularly valuable when building in relation to models. To use a grid object, you must first activate it by selecting a grid object and either right-clicking (as shown in figure 7.4) or by choosing Grids/Activate Grid Object from the Views menu. Once activated, the home grids disappear, and the grid lines of the grid object are displayed. For discussion purposes in this chapter, the *currently active grid* refers to either an activated grid object or the visible home plane grid in the current viewport.

FIGURE 7.4
Activating a grid object by right-clicking on the grid object.

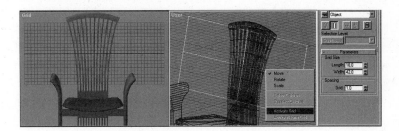

WARNING

It is not advisable to Scale grid objects. When you scale a grid object, its Grid spacing remains unscaled. The relationship between the visual grid and the snap grid is now disconnected. If you want a larger grid, you should *always* change its creation parameters. If you have accidentally scaled a grid, you can reset the scale to 100 percent with Transform Type-In.

A viewport can be assigned to be Grid viewport and will display the XY-plane (plan) view of the currently active grid object (as shown in the left of figure 7.4). When the home grids are active, Grid viewports display the XY-plane home grid (ground plane). Grid views dynamically update as you position and rotate the active grid object. You now have a permanent elevation view perpendicular to the plane. Grid views are particularly useful when creating splines at angles to the world axes. In this sense, Grid views can be thought of as picture planes upon which to draw in the traditional perspective sense.

TIP

Grids are the only objects capable of being aligned to a view. If you need to align other objects to a view, create a grid object and align it to the view first. The grid can now be used to align other objects with either Align or Normal Align.

Grid objects are not limited to aiding only in creation. Referencing the active Grid object as the current coordinate system for transforms, alignment, arrays, and mirroring is often very useful and is especially common for objects that were created on or aligned to the grid.

NOTE

Importing models from other programs sometimes places the models extremely far from the world origin because they were modeled there in the other program. This location can have the undesirable effect of causing round-off errors in 3DS MAX. One solution is to move the entire scene closer to the origin. This solution, though, is equally undesirable if you plan to continue coordination with the external database. In this case, you need to increase the System Unit Scale under General Preferences (see Chapter 5, "Planning Your Projects," for more detail).

Accuracy in Creation

3D Studio MAX provides grids and the snap system as its primary tools for creation accuracy. Readouts at the bottom, as shown in figure 7.5, indicate the current state of your cursor's X,Y,Z location or the current offset in position, rotation, or scale. During creation, the readout shows the cursor's coordinate location. In transforms, the readout reports the relative translation distance, rotation angle, or scale percentage. For accuracy, pay careful attention to the coordinate display as you drag, or set the active grid's settings to an appropriate increment. Access the Grid and Snap Settings dialog (see fig. 7.5) by right-clicking over the various snap icons, choosing it from the Views menu, or choosing it from an assigned key alternate.

TIP

An appropriate grid size aids immensely when creating objects. Assigning the Grid and Snap Settings dialog to a familiar keyboard alternate makes adjusting these helpful settings fast (such as Ctrl+A from 3DS DOS).

Although the snap system gives options for snapping to vertices, edges, grid intersections, and grid lines in 2D, 2.5D, and 3D space, the availability of these options varies depending on the situation. When creating 3D primitives, the snap system is always in 2D mode with the active grid supplying the missing coordinate component. The other snap settings of 2.5D and 3D are applicable only to Line spline object creation. Vertex and edge snapping is respected, but only to vertices and edges that lie on the active grid. Geometry is always being compared to the grid's location. Given these limitations, your tool for creation accuracy really rests in the grids.

FIGURE 7.5

The Grid and Snap Settings dialogs.

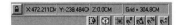

NOTE

Absolute snap is a projection into screen space and is only available when the Screen or View coordinate system is active. When working in World, Parent, Local, Grid, or Pick coordinate systems, the Absolute snap setting will revert to Relative Snap.

Grid viewports are invaluable aids to using grid objects. These viewports stay perfectly in line with your active grid, even as you rotate and position the grid objects. They make it possible to have a constantly updated and centered plan view of your construction plane.

NOTE

AutoCAD users accustomed to user coordinate systems (UCSs) will find grid objects very similar in use with the exception that grids are objects and can be manipulated as such. Changing the active coordinate system to a grid is very similar to creating and modifying with a named UCS in AutoCAD.

Creation always occurs on the active grid. Many modelers find that orienting the grid is more accurate and faster than constructing off the default home grids and then repositioning the objects.

To create objects parallel to a User, Perspective, Camera, or Spotlight view, you must use an active grid object because only the X,Y ground plane is respected when the home planes are active. With an active grid object selected, choose Views, Grids, Align to Views, and the grid will be aligned to that view. The grid is now ready for construction.

Creating Parametric Primitives

Knowing the basics of how construction occurs and how accuracy is achieved enables you to explore how primitives are defined and their parameters are manipulated. The 3D Studio MAX geometric primitives (see fig 7.6) supply the building blocks from which many other forms can be made. Many modelers use primitives as the starting point for mesh and vertex sculpting. Primitives commonly serve as sculpting or modeling tools when used to create Boolean compound objects. The standard geometric primitives available within 3DS MAX include the following:

- Box (as a cube or rectangle)

- Sphere (based on quadrilateral polygons)

- GeoSphere (based on triangular polygons)

- Cylinder (in solid or hollow form)

- Tube (the hollow form of the cylinder)

- Cone (a pointed variation of the cylinder)

- Torus (a donut)

- Hedra (of five geometric families and diverse possibilities)

- Teapot (classic computer graphics icon)

- QuadPatch & TriPatch (flat Bézier patches)

All primitives have parameters to control their defining dimensions—resulting complexity, smoothing, and mapping coordinate generation. Initially, you can be very free with all these parameters, because you can always modify them to be whatever is required by adjusting their values from the Modify panel or Track View at a later date.

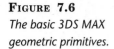

FIGURE 7.6

The basic 3DS MAX geometric primitives.

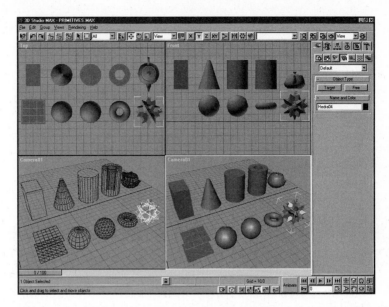

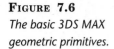

NOTE

Unlike most 3D programs, you never have to commit when initially defining creation parameters in 3DS MAX. You can adjust creation parameter values to whatever is required at a later time by using the Modify panel. These values cannot be adjusted after you perform an operation that collapses the object's stack. Before executing such an option (such as EditMesh/Attach), examine the creation parameters and consider how much detail will be required of the object in the scene.

Creating geometric primitives is a straightforward procedure. You simply pick a base point, and then drag to define the remaining dimensions. When home grids are active, the viewport in which you choose to create determines the placement of the object. Each primitive comes with defining dimensions and segmentation, and some include slice and chop options for defining only a portion of the original primitive.

Most objects have an established limit of 200 segments for any one dimension. This is actually a very high limit that you will rarely need to approach. A box with 200 segment sides, for example, contains 480,000 faces, whereas a teapot with its maximum of 74 sides has 272,144 faces. What's fantastic about parametric geometry is that although it has an impact on scene and rendering memory, the amount of disk space required for the MAX file is the same, regardless of segmentation levels for as long as the object remains parametric.

To manage scene size and interactive speed, a useful approach is to keep parametric objects at minimal segmentation settings and increase them only when necessary. One method using this approach is to model and position on one frame with very low settings, and then render on another frame with very high settings. The impact on your file size is minimal because you are only adding animation keys for the segmentation parameters.

Parametric Creation Parameters

Parametric objects, by definition, have a set of controlling parameters that dictate their result. These parameters will vary depending on the object, but most can be grouped into the following categories (the first four—dimensions, segments, smoothing, and mapping coordinates—being available for all objects).

Dimensions

Dimensions define the size of the parametric object, as measured from its creation point. Common dimensions include height, length, and width, whereas circular objects usually contain radius parameters. Alternative possibilities from other developers might include perimeter, volume, and mass.

When you scale an object with a transform, its creation parameters will not reflect the resulting overall dimensions. If the object retains its parametric definition, you should adjust the creation parameters instead. Scaling parametric objects should be reserved for when the scale needs to occur along different axes or about different points.

Segments

Segments define how dense the object's mesh is in various dimensions. Curved dimensions require higher segmentation for higher resolution, but linear dimensions only require increased segmentation if you plan to deform the object about that dimension.

Smoothing

Smoothing parameters control whether or not smoothing groups are automatically added to the object. Some objects, such as the Torus, provide convenient options for smoothing that would be tedious to perform in a nonparametric manner. Custom smoothing to specific faces selections can be assigned with the EditMesh or Smooth modifiers.

Mapping Coordinates

Mapping Coordinates controls whether or not parametric mapping coordinates are added to the object. The default primitives create mapping with a fixed tiling of 1.0 in each direction. Objects from other developers may include the capability to control the tiling and extents of their parametric mapping. Custom mapping can be assigned with the UVW Map modifier.

"Portions" Parameters

"Portions" control how much of the object is created. Common examples include Cylinder & Tube slicing, Sphere chopping, and Teapot parts. Objects from other developers may include the number of teeth a gear has or the components of a window or an automobile.

"Variations"

"Variations" manipulates the dimensional and segmentation values in various ways. These are usually "extras" for various objects and are included to create interesting variations that would otherwise be very difficult to do. The Rotation and Twist options for the Torus are examples of this group. Other possibilities from other developers might include wind, gravity, age, and so on.

"Family"

"Family" changes the entire result of the other parameters. Common examples include the Type for GeoSphere and Family for Hedra objects. Other possibilities from other developers might include genus, species, race, manufacturer, line, product, and so on.

Dimensional Center Points

Each primitive has a point from which its dimensions are measured. This dimensional center is also the initial location for the object's pivot point. While the pivot point can be relocated at any time, the dimensional center can never be changed because it is integral to the object's definition. Figure 7.7 shows the dimensional center locations for the basic primitives.

FIGURE 7.7

The dimensional centers and initial pivot points of primitives.

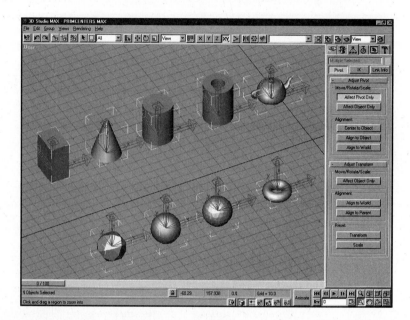

Bounding Box Orientation

Parametric objects will always begin with the same Local coordinate system orientation. The initial X axis of a Teapot, for example, always centers on its handle and spout, regardless of how or where you create it.

This orientation determines the bounding box orientation of the object for as long as the object retains its parametric definition. Unlike other programs, an object's bounding box does *not* indicate the orientation of its internal axes—this is controlled entirely by its pivot point orientation, the currently active coordinate system, or both.

TIP

At times you may find it preferable to work in Box mode—when adjusting complex geometry that would otherwise incur significant screen refresh delays, for example. In situations comparable to this, having consistent bounding box orientations can be important. To reorient an object's bounding box, you can attach it to a meshable object with the preferred bounding box orientation (using EditMesh/Attach). After attaching, you are free to detach the newly reoriented element or delete the target element. This process should be performed only when necessary because it collapses the stack of the attached object and causes the attached object to inherit the pivot point of the object it is attached to. An alternative method is to use the Reset Transform utility in R1.1 to apply an XForm modifier to the object to accomplish the same effect without removing the object's data history.

Slice and Chop Parameters

Primitives having definable slice lines typically have Slice or Chop parameter options. The Slice On option enables the Slice From and Slice To parameters to define the beginning and end locations of a "pie" slice centered on the object's creation center as shown in figure 7.8. The slice parameters are expressed in angles with the resulting cut always being along the sides. An important feature of slice is that the same number of segments is maintained when animating the slice, giving an "unfolding" appearance.

FIGURE 7.8

Using Slice and Chop parameters for Sphere, Cylinder, Torus, Cone, and Tube primitives.

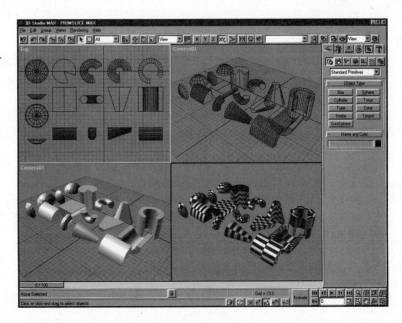

The Sphere primitive differs by having a Hemisphere parameter, with a range of 0–1 (which defines the percentage of the sphere). The Squash option maintains the same number of segments for the resulting sphere section. The Chop option sections the sphere at the same location as Squash but leaves the remainder of the originally defined sphere segments. Figure 7.9 shows spheres with the same Hemisphere values in both Squash and Chop. The Base to Pivot option changes the effect of Hemisphere considerably. With Base to Pivot checked, the base of the sectioned sphere will always rest on the creation plane. When animated, the sphere appears to emerge from the plane, much as if it were breaking the surface of a liquid. With Base to Pivot unchecked, the top of the sectioned sphere remains stationary, and the sphere seems to grow away from it, as shown in figure 7.9.

Parametric Mapping Coordinates

3D Studio MAX primitives generate default mapping coordinates as an aid in getting textures on them quickly. This option is not automatic because mapping coordinates do have an impact on file size because extra data is added. Default coordinates are fixed in projection method and are usually one tile unit in each direction. Although they cannot be adjusted (because they are parametrically defined), the material assigned to them can have the offset and tiling for its mapping adjusted as needed. For more control or to change the type of mapping, a UVW Map modifier can be added to the object for custom coordinates. Figure 7.10 shows the default mapping for the basic primitives.

FIGURE 7.9

The effect of Base to Pivot on sphere sections.

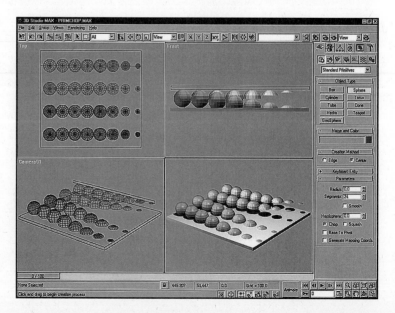

FIGURE 7.10

The default parametric mapping coordinates for the basic primitives.

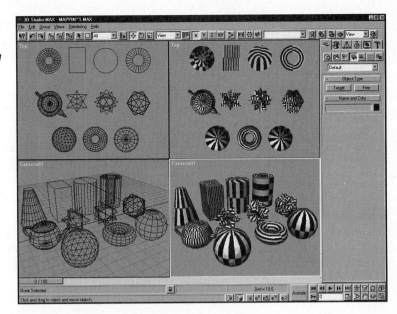

Parametric Smoothing Options

For surfaces to be rendered in computer graphics, they must be converted to triangular faces. This is true of all programs, even those that work entirely in seemingly freeform surfaces. When rendered, these surfaces are converted to faces (although this fact may not be presented to the user). Three-dimensional arc and curve surfaces are not directly supported, but rather are approximated with segments, which in turn are made up of faces. The smoother the curve, the more segments and faces are required.

To minimize this modeling overhead and maintain speed, 3DS MAX includes the concept of *smoothing*. Smoothing affects an object by rendering it as if the geometry were actually spherical. Edges that exist between the smoothed faces are essentially ignored by the Renderer as the mesh is smoothed. The rendered effect of smoothing differs between the interactive renderer and the production renderer due to rendered shading level. The production renderer primarily uses Phong or Metal shading models, which create very smooth highlights by averaging the color space of every pixel. This is in contrast to the Gouraud shading model used in 3D Studio MAX's smooth, shaded viewports in which shading is interpolated between vertices. Therefore, the resulting quality of highlights is dependent upon the mesh density because more definition requires more vertices to shade between. Figure 7.11 compares the same smoothed geometry as seen in a shaded viewport and the production renderer. Figure 7.12 then shows the same geometry without the smoothing option.

FIGURE 7.11
*The effect of
smoothing on
different mesh
densities.*

FIGURE 7.12
*The same geometry
without smoothing.*

The effect of smoothing is most dramatic on spherical meshes, which is the form that the smoothing function approximates. Although spheres created with dramatically different face counts have center sections that render amazingly alike, the extra detail becomes important at the sphere's profile. Figure 7.12 shows how the apparent "roundness" of any curved form's perimeter is always determined by the number of faces that go into making it. As a modeler, you must balance the number of faces in a scene against the amount of detail you need. Remember that smoothing does not affect an object's true geometry—only the way its surface is rendered.

NOTE

Smoothing should not be confused with the MeshSmooth modifier (introduced in Release 1.1), which actually affects the topology of the surface and not just its rendering characteristics.

Smoothing creates this illusion of roundness by assigning *smoothing groups* to the appropriate faces. All adjacent welded faces that share a common smoothing group are smoothed across their bordering edges. You must keep in mind that smoothing can work only between welded faces. So while an object may have several smoothing groups assigned to its various parts, the effect of smoothing cannot extend between areas that are not connected— even if the faces are assigned the same smoothing group.

TIP

Smoothing groups created by procedural methods are usually organized quite well and provide a convenient method for selection when using the EditMesh modifier.

For most primitives, when the Smooth option is off, no smoothing groups are assigned. Boxes, cylinders, and cones are exceptions and still assign a smoothing group to their flat caps. Later modeling operations can commonly deform these edges. A common smoothing group over these planes ensures that they continue to render smooth (and presumably flat). This is something to remember when you begin to deform these sides from their original plane and may no longer want them to be smooth.

NOTE

When you begin to modify objects, especially at the Sub-Object level, the original smoothing group assignments are very likely to be incorrect. In this case, you will need to assign a Smooth modifier or assign smoothing via the EditMesh modifier.

Manipulation Components

When you manipulate an object or a selection, several components aid, guide, or control the outcome of the process. The components described in the following sections do not actually exist per se, but are used temporarily in the course of performing operations.

Bounding Box

The Bounding Box is a rectangular box whose size is defined by the extent of the object or the current, temporary selection set. When Adaptive Degradation is active, 3DS MAX uses a bounding box as a stand-in when dragging selections during commands. A selection's bounding box extents and center are used as the basis for the Align command. The orientation of an object's bounding box is determined by the object's relation to the world coordinate system at creation. The bounding box can be reoriented only indirectly, not directly, through reorientation of the object.

Selection Center

The Selection Center is the bounding box's geometric center, and a common transform point from the transform manager.

Transformation Matrix

This matrix is a table of numbers maintained by 3D Studio MAX to keep track of changes to the location, orientation, and size of objects. The location of an object is determined by the intersection of three planes in the center of the bounding box. Its use is completely transparent to the user, but can influence the effect of certain materials and Keyframer transformations.

Local Coordinate System

The Local Coordinate system (or object space) is unique to the object and is maintained in a table of numbers called a *transformation matrix* 3DS MAX that keeps track of changes to the object's location, orientation, and size. The location of an object is determined by the intersection of three planes in the center of the bounding box as defined at the object's creation. While the transformation matrix use is completely transparent to the user, the local coordinates influence materials using 3D map types and various transformations.

Coordinate System

The Coordinate Systems defines the orientation of the X,Y,Z planes and are the basis upon which (non-animated) transforms are conducted. You have a choice of determining which coordinate system to use from the toolbar's Reference Coordinate System drop-down list. The active coordinate system controls every action you make when you use the toolbar (move, rotate, scale, mirror, array, and align).

Pivot Point

The Pivot Point defines the origin and orientation of an object's local axes and thus its local coordinate system. The pivot point defines the orientation of the object's local coordinate system and the point about which the object is transformed. As such, the pivot point is very important for animation. The pivot point is often the default location for modifier gizmo centers. Unless overridden with the Local Center During Animate preference, the pivot point is always used as the location for an object's animated transform. You can relocate and reorient an object's pivot from the Hierarchy panel. Although this gives you control over the object's local coordinate system, it does not reorient the bounding box.

Basic Primitives

3D Studio MAX provides several geometric primitives with parametric definitions. While often useful in and of themselves, these usually act as the building blocks for more complicated models. Because the 3DS MAX Software Developer's Kit (SDK) provides all of these as source code, they are sure to act as programmatic building blocks as well, assisting developers (and perhaps yourself) in creating entire new object classes.

The most modest primitives (boxes, cylinders, and tubes) can actually be thought of as raw bar, rod, and tube stock—ready for the blacksmith's anvil, metal worker's break, or glass blower's fire. Nearly everything that is formed from raw stock in the real world can be made from these basic primitives with deformation modifiers in 3DS MAX. Examine objects in the world around you. Nearly all the iron work, spindles, and glass work you see can be formed from primitives.

Boxes

Boxes are the simplest of objects (see fig. 7.13), yet they are often the most useful. You commonly use box objects to quickly define floors/ground planes as well as walls and backdrops. Boxes can be used as quick tools for alignment purposes and are often-used operands for slicing objects in Boolean operations. Boxes can also be thought of as raw stock, ready for bending or twisting.

Boxes are the only object besides Hedras that do not have a smoothing option. Instead, each of the six sides is assigned a smoothing group. This means that when you begin to distort boxes, their sides remain smooth.

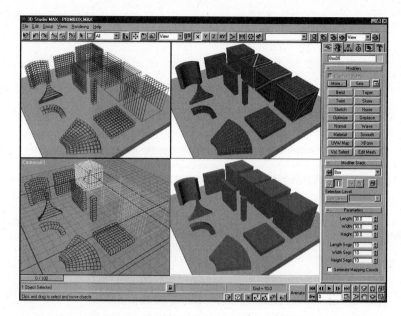

Cylinders and Tubes

You can create both Cylinders and Tubes (hollow cylinders) as parametric objects. These objects are a common starting point for many model parts because they are akin to bar and tube stock. With non-uniform scale and limited deformations, these simple forms can be bent, milled, lathed, and pinched into many common objects. Many of the manufactured pieces that surround you in the world can be traced back to these simple shapes.

The segmentation required for cylinders and tubes (as with all circular objects) will vary according to how closely you intend to view their ends and how pronounced these objects are in the scene. Figure 7.14 shows how the perceived roundness of circular objects varies with their segmentation. If the ends cannot be seen, you can create a minimum of sides; if the profile is obvious (as is common with the tube interiors), then you will need to increase the number of segments.

NOTE

If you find that a 200-sided cylinder is not smooth enough for your needs (which is possible for high-resolution images or very large objects forming shallow arcs through the scene), you'll need to loft or extrude circles that contain more segments and steps.

FIGURE 7.14
*Cylinder and Tube
objects with varying
creation parameters.*

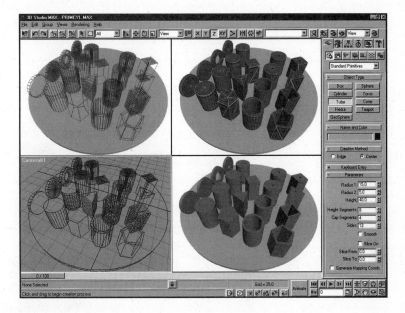

The number of height segments required for cylinders and tubes will vary depending upon what you need to do with these objects. The more you deform these primitives, the more segments they require to be convincing and smooth. Height segments only affect the rendering quality of the cylinder if it is later deformed. Of course, the planning for this is not critical because you can change the segmentation at a later time. Planning does become critical, though, when you are about to perform an operation that collapses the object's stack.

Cones

Cone objects are actually very similar to cylinders, because a cone is essentially a cylinder with different sized ends. Cones are often used for creating common shapes—much like cylinders—yet their two radii provide the capability to impose a controllable taper on the resulting object at any time. Another common use is for basic pyramidal shapes as included in figure 7.15. In practice, cone is chosen over a cylinder when you want to have parametric control over the top and bottom radii.

Cone objects will always have two ends—you can never eliminate the faces from the sharp tip of a cone. While at first this might seem like a waste of faces for sharp cones with zero radius tips, this feature is actually very helpful. The extra set of faces at the tip of the cone ensures that sides of the cone will only smooth with adjacent sides. If the sides share a single vertex at the tip, all side faces share a common smoothing group. This has the effect of smoothing over the tip of the cone as if it were a sphere (see fig. 7.16).

FIGURE 7.15
Cone objects with varying creation parameters.

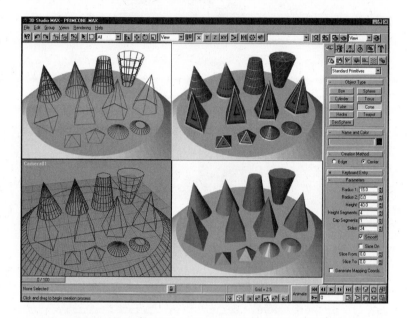

FIGURE 7.16
The smoothing effect of cones meeting at one vertex.

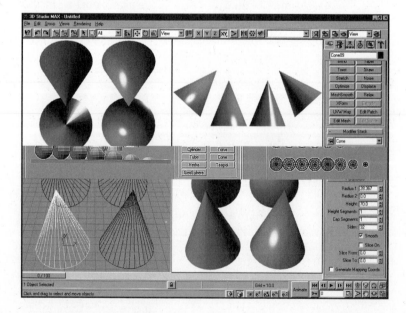

The cone object amplifies a characteristic of 3D Studio MAX smoothing. Because the Renderer's smoothing algorithm tries to approximate a sphere, "smoothed" sides will appear somewhat faceted if they taper to a sharp point—something that is quite typical for a cone. To increase the rendered smoothness of a cone, you need to increase its segmentation to reduce the average angle between faces. Figure 7.17 shows the resulting smoothing of cones with varying height segments.

FIGURE 7.17
The effect of height segmentation on rendered Cone smoothness.

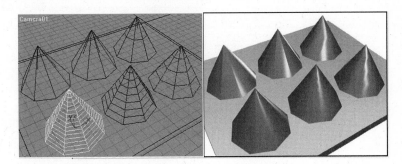

Spheres and GeoSpheres

Sphere and GeoSphere parametric objects represent different ways of defining spherical volumes and together give you four different sphere and dome geometries (see fig. 7.18). The basic Sphere object creates quadrilateral sections similar to the latitude and longitude lines of a globe. GeoSphere creates triangular sections in the method of geodesic domes (made popular by Buckminster Fuller).

The Tetra, Octa, and Icosa options all create triangular facets but organize their geometry in different methods. The Icosahedron sphere is the classic geodesic dome design, forming pentagons of triangles at critical points. In contrast, the Octahedron and Tetrahedrons form squares and equilateral triangles at similar junctures.

In use, the GeoSpheres are the most efficient, providing the smoothest profile for the least number of faces. The Sphere object is the easiest to slice and is usually the choice when you need to interact with other rectilinear objects. When carving out sphere chunks as Boolean operands, you will probably be more satisfied with the results of Spheres than GeoSpheres. When standing alone, especially as domes, you'll most likely want to use GeoSphere objects.

FIGURE 7.18
*Sphere and
GeoSphere objects
with varying
creation parameters.*

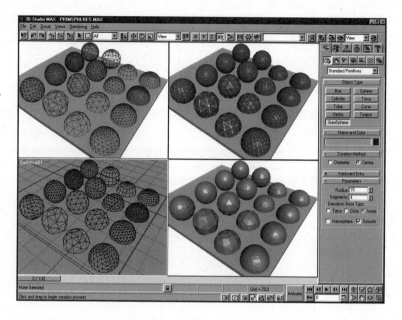

Torus

Torus objects are often called donuts, tires, or rings. Although it appears simple, this object has some interesting parameters. As figure 7.19 shows, the Twist parameter twists the radial lines (sides), which spiral around the Torus, while the Rotation parameter rotates the cross sections (segments). The effect of the Twist parameter is quite evident in a still image, whereas the Rotation parameter is best seen in animation.

NOTE

Because Twist has a definite beginning point, a definite pinch at the twist's start will exist unless the twist makes a complete revolution to allow the start and end to match. Unless you have activated the Slice option to insert a break at this point, you should use Twist values with increments of 360 to avoid the pinch.

FIGURE 7.19

Torus objects with varying creation parameters.

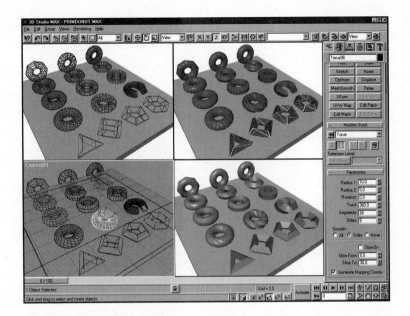

FIGURE 7.19

Torus objects with varying creation parameters.

Complex Objects (Hedras and Teapots)

The Hedra and Teapot objects provide a hint at what is possible with 3DS MAX objects. Hedra provides limitless permutations, whereas Teapot is an example of a complex parametric object that contains parts (see fig. 7.22 later in this chapter). You can expect to see many more parametric objects that fall into these two classes from developers. Trees, plants, vegetation, landscapes, and clouds are actually similar to Hedra, whereas parametric doors, windows, chairs, and even suits of armor would be similar to Teapot.

The Hedra object provides five families of Polyhedrons with numerous controlling parameters. The possibilities with these parameters can seem endless, and because they can be animated, provide for some very interesting geometry (especially for the third-party particle systems that can accept referenced objects as particles). Figure 7.20 shows just a fraction of what is possible with this object; figure 7.21 diagrams the defining parameters.

FIGURE 7.20
Hedra objects with varying creation parameters.

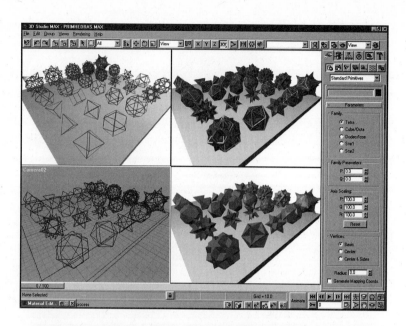

FIGURE 7.21
The varying Hedra families and basic parameter variation.

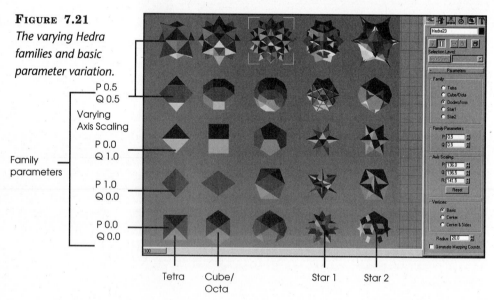

P 0.5
Q 0.5

Varying
Axis Scaling

P 0.0
Q 1.0

P 1.0
Q 0.0

P 0.0
Q 0.0

Family
parameters

Tetra   Cube/   Star 1   Star 2
          Octa

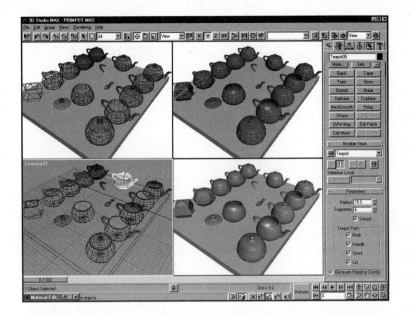

The Teapot object is a computer graphics classic. Known in the industry as the "Utah Teapot," it was one of the first subjects ever rendered. It is now an icon for 3D graphics in general (hence its usage as the rendering icon). Although it may seem humorous, the humble teapot is actually quite valuable for testing materials and modifiers thanks to its geometric variations and appropriate mapping coordinates as shown in figure 7.23.

Understanding Geometric Classes

The parametric objects supplied with 3D Studio MAX are actually of two basic geometric classes, because they can all convert to triangular meshes and Bézier patches. As 3DS MAX evolves, and more geometric classes are added, the way the modifiers interact with geometry will become more important. The 3DS MAX architecture can accommodate any geometric definition. Included in the base product are parametric, mesh, patch, and spline objects.

NOTE ─────────────────────────────────

Although 3D Studio MAX does not directly include NURBS creation objects or editing tools, it does include a NURBS object class for users of the 3DS MAX SDK to build applications upon. 4D Vision, a 3DS MAX Developer, has announced a NURBS plug-in for 3DS MAX—titled "Sculptor"—that promises to be a very capable NURBS modeler.

Everything Becomes Faces

Models in 3DS MAX are based upon geometric classes. In general, objects begin at a high level and convert themselves to simpler levels as required. A parametric object may convert to a patch which then converts to a mesh of triangular faces for example. Unextended 3DS MAX includes the following geometric classes and their associated tools:

Geometric Class	Possible Editing Tools
Parametric Objects	Base parameter manipulation only (can convert to patch or mesh)
Spline Objects	EditSpline, Extrude, Bevel, Lathe, and so on (can convert to mesh or patch through other modifiers).
Bézier Patch Surfaces	EditPatch, Extrude, Bevel, Lathe, and so on (can convert to mesh)
Mesh Objects	EditableMesh, EditMesh, MeshSmooth, Optimize, and so on (base mesh class or subdivide into patch)

A geometric class defines how the derived object is displayed and how it can be edited. 3D Studio MAX currently ships with only four classes; however, developers are adding custom classes quite rapidly. Because of these rapid additions, understanding how geometry evolves as you model is important.

Working with Patch Versus Mesh Primitives

By default, the 3DS MAX primitives convert to meshes when edited by modifiers. The same primitives can be worked with as patches if you apply an EditPatch modifier directly after creation parameters. Therefore, EditPatch is the first modifier in the stack. Remember that you can go back later and insert the EditPatch modifier after other modifiers have been applied. As figure 7.24 shows, Box, Cylinder, Tube, Cone, Torus, and Teapot objects convert to square patches, and Spheres convert to triangular patches, whereas Hedras and GeoSpheres convert every face to triangular patches.

Unfortunately, the slice parameters for primitives are ignored when adding an EditPatch modifier directly after creation parameters in the stack. If you want to edit objects with slice options, you will have to place a modifier that converts it to a mesh first (such as XForm) and then apply EditPatch to work with the interpolated patches.

FIGURE 7.24
The patch geometry of the geometric primitives.

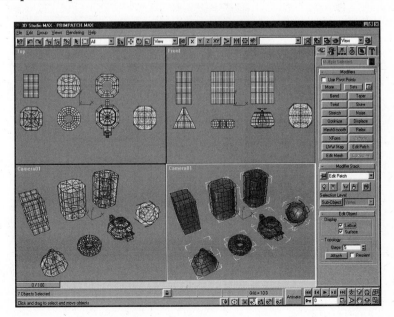

When adding an EditPatch modifier to convert primitives to patches, turning off the Sub-Object selection state immediately after application is best if you intend to apply modifiers to the entire object. Edit modifiers always begin in a Sub-Object selection state. If you immediately proceed to add an additional modifier, you will not be able to see its effect because the stack is not showing the object, but rather an *empty* selection set. You must take it out of Sub-Object selection (or select something) before you can see the effect of other modifiers in the stack.

Patch objects react differently to modifiers than mesh objects do. Figure 7.25 shows how the resulting curves of deformed patches are much more subtle than if the same object was deformed as a mesh. This is because a mesh's vertices are explicit, whereas a patch is the result of an equation.

FIGURE 7.25

The difference in deforming Patch and Mesh geometry.

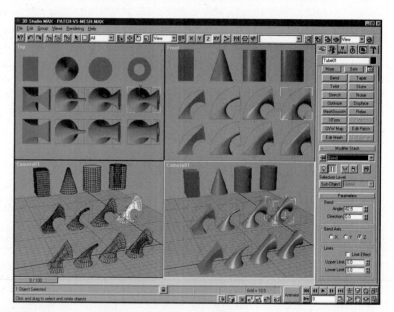

Usually when modelers work with objects as patches, the modelers want to preserve the patch geometry for as long as possible. Knowing when an operation will force the geometry to convert from patches to faces then becomes very important. Most modifiers work with either geometry, but some do not. The following modifiers will always convert the geometry to faces: EditMesh, Material, Normal, Smooth, VolSelect, MeshSmooth, and Relax.

A New Geometric Class

Understanding geometric classes is somewhat easier if you can imagine an entirely new one. For the sake of discussion, we'll call it the FOO class. The first thing to decide is how the FOO class is defined, or what it is composed of. 3DS MAX's mesh objects are composed of faces built on vertices with edges, whereas its Bézier patch objects are made of patches with control vertices and tangent handles. The FOO class can be composed of anything we wish. It may have knots, widgets, handles, curves, meridians, curves, sweeps, contours, grids, lattices, or whatever. For discussion, we'll say that FOO objects have "grids" that are composed of "contours."

To be seen in the viewport and eventually rendered, the FOO object must know how to convert the FOO class geometry to a mesh (or more properly a TriFaceMesh). In fact, every object class in 3D Studio MAX must be able to convert to a triangular mesh. This requirement provides a common denominator for all modifiers to revert to so every modifier can operate on any object. The next question is whether it's appropriate, or even possible, for FOO geometry to convert to Bézier patches or perhaps third-party additions. For now, we'll say that the FOO object cannot convert to anything but faces.

The FOO class is added to the creation menu, and you are able to create FOO objects. But once created, how are the objects edited? With a FOO object selected, go to the Modifier panel. Only tools that model the FOO object appear. Because every geometric class can convert to a mesh, several modifiers such as Bend, Taper, Twist, and EditMesh are available. EditSpline, Extrude, and Lathe only work on splines and are grayed out. The EditPatch modifier is grayed out as well because FOO objects cannot convert to Bézier patches. When you apply the Bend modifier, it looks at the geometry at the end of the pipeline and, not knowing what a FOO is, requests patches. FOO returns that it cannot convert to patches, so Bend requests a mesh. The FOO object converts to a triangular mesh object, and the Bend tool proceeds as normal. After the bend, the EditPatch modifier is ungrayed and available for use. This is because 3D Studio MAX's mesh class knows how to convert to Bézier patches.

If you wish to edit the FOO object in a FOO-like manner, your current option is to go to the bottom of the Edit History stack and adjust the FOO creation parameters. What you really need are modifiers that know how to manipulate FOO geometry. To edit the FOO object, you need to have FOO editing tools. A FOO modifier class is created that preserves and modifies the native FOO grids and contours. Because the basic axial deformations are so useful, the Bend, Taper, Twist, Skew, and Stretch commands are modified to also accept and manipulate the FOO class. Now when you bend the FOO object, it stays in FOO geometry and the EditFOO modifier is still available after the Bend. Apply an EditMesh at this point, and the geometry is a mesh.

A real possibility would be a new NURBS object that can convert to Bézier patches and meshes. As long as you work with the newly supplied NURBS modeling tools, your model will stay as NURBS. As soon as you apply a basic modifier (that knows nothing of NURBS), the model would convert to patches and, if necessary, faces. The same would apply to solids and polygonal modeling.

Whether for a new or existing object, the system for its geometric class representation is the same. When you apply a modifier to an object, the modifier finds out what geometric class the object can represent itself as and works at the highest level possible. If the modifier understands the current geometric class, no conversion takes place—the modifier simply affects the model as it wishes. If the current geometry is a class the modifier does not understand, the modifier will convert it to a simpler class that it can manipulate and then continue.

After additions by developers, a possible geometric hierarchy might look like this:

Geometric Class	Possible Editing Tools
Parametric Objects	Base parameter manipulation (can convert to any)
Solid Objects	EditSolid, Fillet, and so on (can convert to NURB)
NURB Surfaces	EditNURB, Trim, and so on (can convert to Patch)
Bézier Patch Surfaces	EditPatch, Blend, and so on (can convert to Polygon)
Polygonal Faces	EditPoly and so on (can convert to Quad)
Quadrilateral Faces	EditQuad, GameOut, and so on (can convert to Triangles)
Triangular Faces	EditMesh, Optimize, and so on (bottom class)

Geometry in 3DS MAX evolves as called upon. Objects stay at the highest order possible until required to convert to a lower, simpler class. Higher order geometry converts itself to simpler geometry when a modifier is applied that cannot operate on that geometric class. The common denominator for all objects is the triangular mesh. Because all 3D Studio MAX objects must be able to convert to these calls, all modifiers can work on any given object—although they may have to convert it to a mesh to do so. Most of the 3DS MAX modifiers can process either meshes or patches, preserving whichever is handed to them and passing along the modified result in the given geometric class.

In Practice: Basics of Object Creation

- **Object creation** Creation is designed to be an interactive process in 3DS MAX, with the fastest mode of operation tending to be to create the object and then adjust base parameters for accuracy.

- **Grid helpers** Grid helpers are extremely useful when establishing planes of construction at odd angles or in relationship to existing geometry. Any number of grids can be maintained so many relationships can be established and returned to. Special capabilities of Grids include the ability to define snapping, transforms, and have views perpendicular to them.

- **Snap system** The Snap system is your primary tool for creation accuracy, with the Align system being your best tool for positioning objects in relation to one another.

- **Base parameters** You can adjust base parameters of objects at any time in the Modifier Stack, enabling you to make their display as simple or as complex as your rendering requires. Primitive objects require the same amount of disk space, regardless of how many segments you specify for them.

- **Primitives** The basic primitives should be viewed as the building blocks for more complex models. They are the raw materials from which nearly any form can be eventually modeled.

- **Conversion** Every object class within 3D Studio MAX that has a renderable surface must have the capability to convert to a triangular mesh. Higher order geometry, such as Bézier patches, can be modeled as patches or converted to a mesh. Other geometric classes will be added by developers over time. Therefore it becomes important to understand which modifiers cause a conversion to various geometric classes.

"The Daedalus Encounter"
Image by Mechadeus, for "The Daedalus Encounter"
Provided courtesy of Kinetix™
©Mechadeus®

Chapter 8

OBJECT-LEVEL MODELING

In 3D Studio MAX, objects are meant to be modified and animated. Even the most complex or intricate model begs to be animated once inside 3DS MAX. This chapter covers the basic concepts of modification and editing the edit history with the Modifier Stack. This discussion contains the basics for understanding how all modifiers operate within the Modifier Stack concept. The modifiers themselves are explained in terms of daily use rather than their specific dialog descriptions. This chapter serves as the basis for more advanced discussions later in this book. Specifically, this chapter covers the following topics:

- Applying modifiers to objects

- Issues involving single and multiple object modifications

- Understanding the Modifier Stack

- Manipulating modifier gizmos and centers

- Controlling modifier influence with extents

- Understanding the difference between transforms and modifications

- Using axial deformation modifiers

Basics of Applying Modifiers

Modifying single objects is straightforward. Select the object and click on the modifier you wish to apply. The modifier is assigned at the current level in the object's Modifier Stack and is ready for receiving values. Modifiers usually begin with their default settings, which often have no values, or with the effect's first iteration. Other modifiers, such as Bevel and Extrude, remember the values previously used and assign these as the beginning defaults. Once applied, adjust the parameters of modifiers from their dialogs in the Command Panel (screen interaction is rarely required). Additional modifiers for an object accumulate sequentially in the Modifier Stack. Figure 8.1 shows steps in an accruement of modifiers on a tube primitive.

FIGURE 8.1

Three modifiers applied to a Tube primitive.

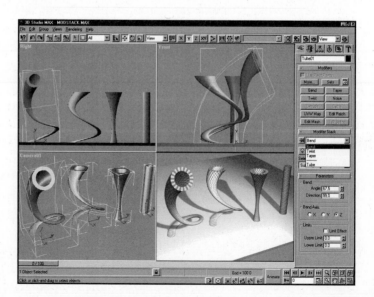

Modifying multiple objects changes significantly when the Use Pivot Points box is checked. When active, this option makes the modifier perform as if it were affecting the selected objects individually. As the right of figure 8.2 shows, each object is given a gizmo that reflects its geometry with the gizmo's center located at the pivot point. Although these appear as individual modifiers, they are instances—adjusting one's parameters will affect them all. You can immediately tell when you are affecting instanced modifiers because the gizmos for every object of the original selection are displayed.

Applying a modifier to a set of objects and then later having to adjust one of them differently from the rest is common. Making instanced modifiers unique is the purpose of the Modifier Stack's Make Unique button. Figure 8.3 shows a chair modeled from similar modifiers and finished with a common bend. During an animation the front legs needed to "walk," so the Bend modifiers for the front were made unique and adjusted for the walk.

FIGURE 8.3
Making common modifiers unique to allow for individual animation.

TIP

Modifying a selection is an accurate and fast method to locate a common gizmo center for a given modifier. The chair slats in figure 8.4 were assigned a Bend modifier as a selection and then, while a selection, were made unique. Each slat then had the exact same center location for their concentric bends.

FIGURE 8.4

*A selection bent
without Use Pivot
Points to ensure
common gizmo centers
and then made unique
to make concentric
bends.*

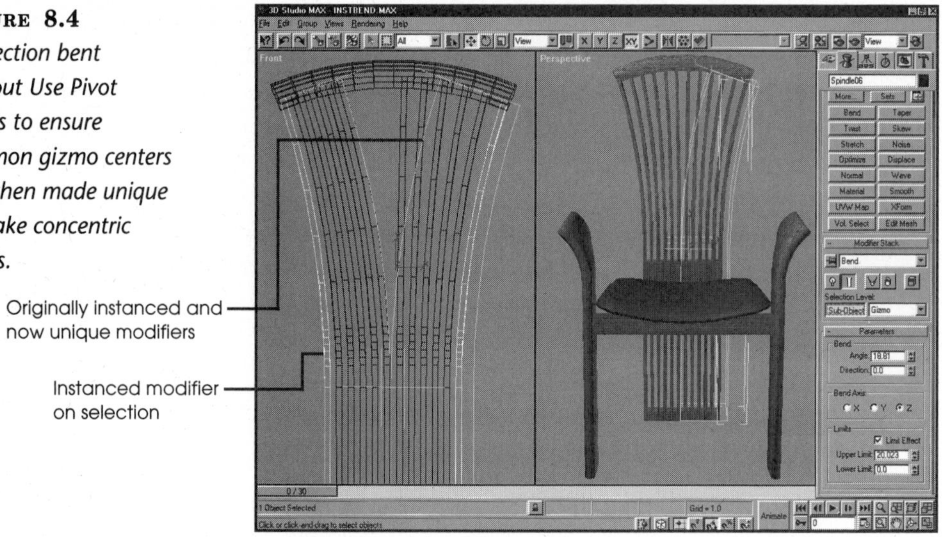

Originally instanced and
now unique modifiers

Instanced modifier
on selection

When you make a selection with the Modify Panel open, 3DS MAX examines the selection to determine if any common modifiers exist. If found, the common modifiers are presented in the stack. If none are found, the drop-down list is blank. You do not have to select all the objects of the shared modification to adjust an instanced modifier. If, for example, ten objects were tapered, the Taper modifier would be shown if you selected 1–10 of the objects. But if an object other than the ten were included in the selection, commonality would not occur and the stack list would be blank.

Using the Modifier Stack

Of all the areas in 3DS MAX's interface, the rollout entitled *Modifier Stack* containing a small section of seven buttons and two drop-down lists (see fig. 8.5) is by far the most powerful. If you become proficient in using the Modifier Stack and the toolbar, you are well on your way to mastering 3DS MAX. The Modifier Stack provides access to an object's modeling history. Every modeling operation you perform on the object is stored there for you to go back to for adjustment or removal. Operations in the stack are stored with your scene for as long as you wish, enabling you to change your mind at any time.

FIGURE 8.5
*The Modifier Stack
rollout.*

The Modifier Stack itself is housed in a drop-down list (see fig. 8.6). When you select an object, the last modifier added to the object is displayed at the top of the stack and next to the drop-down arrow. The first modifier added to the object—the earliest information 3DS MAX has on the object—is shown at the bottom of the stack. In the case of geometric primitives, their parameters are always at the bottom of the stack. Models imported from other programs (such as 3DS files) usually have Mesh, Editable Mesh, Patch or Bézier Spline as their first (bottom) stack entry. Because this is the beginning state of an object, you can never place a modifier below it in the stack.

FIGURE 8.6
*The Modifier Stack
drop-down lists.*

 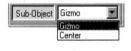

TIP

TIP

As with all drop-downs in 3DS MAX, the arrow button is actually redundant to the field itself. For speed, most modelers simply click on the name field to display the list and choose the entry they want, rather than trying to click on the small button.

The buttons surrounding the stack drop-down have distinct rolls to play in managing the stack. Each entry in the stack can be worked on and displayed individually:

- **Pin Stack (state)**   Freezes modifier's current state, enabling you to transform other objects in the scene while the pinned modifier for the original selection is still active. Pin Stack thus provides an exception to the way 3DS MAX normally works because the Modify panel is not reflecting what is currently selected. This exception can be useful for coordinating a modifier's result with the position and orientation of another object. Many modelers use Pin Stack as a method to maneuver "template" objects as guidelines for modifier operations.

The Pin Stack state will not enable you to transform another object if your current modifier is in Sub-Object mode.

 ■ **Active/Inactive (toggle)**   Toggles whether the result of the current modifier is passed along the modifier pipeline. The modifier still displays its gizmo but no longer has an effect on the geometry. This attribute can be very useful when you assign an intensive modifier (such as Displace or MeshSmooth) and want to manipulate the object in a simpler form later in the stack.

 ■ **Show End Result (toggle)**   Toggles whether the remaining modifiers in the stack display their results, enabling you to return to a state in your model's history and adjust its effect without being distracted by what happens later. Modelers often turn off Show End Result when adjusting a modifier and toggle it back on to check its relevance. Turning off Show End Result can save time when the remainder of the stack is memory intensive and interactivity is impeded.

 ■ **Make Unique (action)**   Makes an instanced modifier unique to that object. Make Unique is used to eliminate the dependency of other objects sharing the same modifier—it breaks the connection to the rest of the objects. This button can be confusing because no check is made to see if a modifier is actually instanced and the button is always available for use. Make Unique should not be clicked unless you are sure that you want to break the shared relationship to other objects with the same modifier because the action cannot be undone.

 ■ **Remove Modifier (action)**   Deletes the selected modifier from the stack. The result is as if the modifier had never been applied. This button should be used with caution because the deletion cannot be undone.

 ■ **Edit Stack (dialog)**   Brings up the Edit Modifier Stack dialog shown in figure 8.7 and enables you to make unique, remove, or collapse selections of modifiers and rename individual ones. Operations in the Edit Stack dialog need to be done with *great* care because nothing can be undone except renaming.

As a rule, only edit field changes can be undone when adjusting modifiers. Make Unique, Remove Modifier, and collapsing the stack options can never be undone. In general, if you can't animate it, you can't undo it.

FIGURE 8.7
The Edit Modifier
Stack dialog.

Renaming modifiers is done by simply selecting the modifier and entering a new name at the bottom of the dialog. That name is now present in the stack and in Track View. Making a modifier unique resets the modifier's name as it breaks the connection to other dependent modifiers. If the modifier is already independent, the Make Unique option is still active and can be used as a method for quick renaming. Removing and making modifiers unique work the same with selections as their buttons do with individual modifiers.

The first (bottom) entry in the stack cannot be affected within the Edit Stack dialog and cannot be renamed. This entry is its geometric class and renaming the base object type would cause considerable confusion. Geometric classes include the parametric objects, Editable Mesh, Patch, Bézier Spline, Loft, Boolean, and Morph. The first entry cannot be collapsed or removed because nothing is below it to which to collapse. The first entry will often be modified, however, as the result of a stack collapse.

Collapsing the Stack

Although an object's Modifier Stack is quite valuable, it does come with a cost—RAM. Every step in the stack takes a bit of RAM, with Edit modifiers costing by far the most because they contain actual copies of the object as modified to that point. The more modifiers in the stack, the more RAM that is required to evaluate them.

To have your object consume less RAM, you can collapse its stack. Collapsing the stack causes an evaluation of the geometry pipeline and reduces the object to its highest geometric class. The effect of each modifier is maintained, but its effect is now explicit and frozen in time. What you see in the viewport is the result you are going to have from the collapse.

This does not mean, however, that collapsing saves disk space. Primitives, for example, require the same disk space regardless of their segmentation and resulting face count because the primitives are only storing parameters in the file. When fully collapsed, objects become explicit meshes (or patches) and the entire mesh must be saved to disk.

Collapsing the stack causes an evaluation of the geometry pipeline and reduces the object to its highest geometric class. The effect of each modifier is maintained, but its effect is now explicit and frozen in time. What you see in the viewport is the result you are going to have from the collapse.

Warning

What you see in the viewport is *exactly* what the resulting collapse will deliver. If the stack is at an intermediate level and is not showing the end result, the rest of the stack will not be evaluated. If modifers in the stack have their effects turned off, they will not be taken into account. If animation is occuring within the modifiers, the state shown at the current frame will be the one result.

Clicking Collapse All in the Edit Modifier Stack dialog eliminates all modifiers and reduces the object to what you see in the interactive viewport. After you have selected one or more modifiers (above the bottom one) in the stack, the Collapse To button is available. Clicking Collapse To collapses the stack from the point of your selection to the bottom of the stack. Collapsing the stack can be confusing when you have a selection of modifers because you may believe the stack will collapse only within your selection. Figure 8.8 shows that when collapsing a selection, the last (top) modifier in the selection determines from which point the stack is collapsed, while the bottom of the collapse is always the bottom of the stack. To collapse a primitive to base geometry, apply an appropriate Edit modifier (EditMesh, EditPatch, or EditSpline) and immediately collapse the stack. This collapses the stack to a Patch, Editable Mesh, or Bézier Spline class object.

Tip

Adding an Edit modifier takes RAM for storing edits and time because you are immediately placed in Sub-Object mode. Unless you are collapsing to Patches, adding nearly any other modifier (such as a Bend or XForm) will be faster for collapsing to an Editable Mesh or Bézier Spline class.

The result of the collapse depends upon what modifiers have been applied to the object. If you began with an EditPatch modifier the result of the collapse is a Patch, if you have not added a modifier that caused the object to convert to a mesh. Otherwise, the object most likely collapses to an Editable Mesh. Typical modifiers that cause a conversion to a mesh are EditMesh, Optimize, Displace, Relax, and MeshSmooth.

FIGURE 8.8

The result of collapsing a "selection" of modifiers.

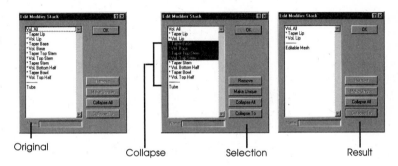

Original   Collapse   Selection   Result

NOTE

The Editable Mesh class is visible only if you have enabled it (as stated in the 3D Studio MAX readme.wri file) by adding the following lines to your 3dsmax.ini file:

    [EditableMesh]
    Enabled=1

Enabling this option has no adverse effect and doing so enables you to perform explicit mesh editing significantly faster and with substantially less RAM than using the EditMesh modifier. This book assumes that you have enabled this option in your 3dsmax.ini file.

When you collapse portions of the stack you are indicating that you are finished with that portion of the model. Again, undo is not an option. Therefore, collapsing should not be done for experimentation unless you have cloned the object or saved the file as a precautionary backup. Using Save Selected on objects before collapsing their stacks is a prudent measure so you have a copy of the object in a modifiable form. Collapsing the stack always eliminates a primitive's base parameters, for example, and returning to them is often quite useful. The Merge command provides an easy method for this replacement if you have the originals for reference.

Navigating the Modifier Stack

After you have added a modifier to an object's stack, you need to consider where in the stack, or more properly, that object's history the next modifier should go. Mapping, for example, is often easier and more appropriate to apply early in an object's history, before the geometry is deformed. An understanding of how modifiers are saved, their order is evaluated, and their sub-object elements are used is essential to making proper use of this powerful capability.

How Modifiers Are Saved

Everything in your 3DS MAX scene is actually the result of a series of operations. What you see on the screen or, in some cases, a rendering is the result of those operations at that point in time. When you save your scene to a file, you are actually saving the beginning state of your objects and then a "script" of every modification you have applied to them. The resulting geometry is never saved in a MAX file directly. Instead, the original object and all the steps to create that geometry are saved, allowing you to change your mind at any time in the future while modeling.

The calculation of the stack is performed only when necessary. The result is termed a *validity mesh,* and the period of time that result is valid is termed the *validity interval.* When you first load a scene, each object's Modifier Stack is evaluated and the result is displayed. This state is cached and will not be reevaluated unless the object is modified—by adding a new modifier, adjusting a parameter in the stack, or moving to a point in time when a parameter changes. Performing transforms on an object does not require a reevaluation of the stack; just one reason why moving, rotating, and scaling objects are so fast in 3DS MAX.

Modifier Order

The order in which you apply modifiers has paramount impact on your results. You need to plan the order in which you apply them. Figure 8.9 shows the dramatic differences between two identical modifiers placed in a different stack order.

While the Modifier Stack enables you to go back to any point in time and place a new modifier at any location, it does not enable you to reorder them. One common misconception is that you can reorder stack entries through the Edit Modifier Stack dialog or Track View—you cannot. If a modifier is applied in the wrong order, you must delete the incorrectly placed one, situate yourself at the appropriate place in the stack, and apply the modifier again. If the original settings need to be maintained, you have to record and then copy them to the new modifier manually. Luckily it is a fairly rare circumstance. You can usually tell immediately when a modifier is placed at the wrong point in the edit history because the interactive viewport telegraphs your error.

FIGURE 8.9
The effects of reversing modifier orders in the stack.

Bend, Taper

Taper, Bend

Twist, Bend

Bend, Twist

Manipulating Gizmos

In general, you should move a gizmo only to establish a new visual reference but not to control its effect. Instead, move the center. Moving the gizmo's center is nearly always the same as moving the gizmo except that the gizmo's extents remain intact with the modified object. Moving the gizmo creates a visual departure that can be confusing during the life of the model. Figure 8.10 shows the same model with equal Bend modifier values. The right Bend modifier's center was moved to the object's top while the gizmo was moved up on the left. The center is in the same location after both operations but, as can be seen when the gizmo is moved, its boundary no longer matches what is being deformed. When the center is moved, the gizmo boundary respects the deformed object.

FIGURE 8.10

The difference between moving the center and moving the gizmo on the gizmo's boundary.

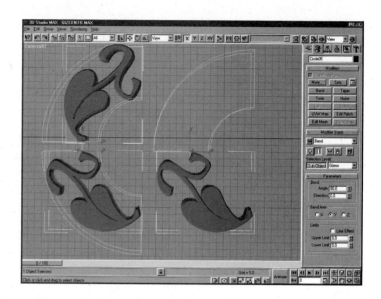

NOTE

The Align function does not work with gizmos or their centers because it does not see the Sub-Object level. When you use Align in Sub-Object mode, the entire object is aligned.

The location of an object's pivot point determines the initial location of the axial modifier's center and orientation of the gizmo's own Local coordinate system. Many modifiers provide the parameters necessary to rotate their effect. If available, such as with Bend and Skew, they should be used because they keep the gizmo's boundary in better relation to the modified object. Figure 8.11 shows the effect of using a Bend's Direction parameter and rotating the gizmo.

When using modifiers that do not have a directional component, such as Taper, Stretch and Twist, your only choice is to rotate the gizmo. Many times a model's orientation is not conducive to the direction you wish to apply the modifier. Figure 8.12 shows such a model. The cannon is orientated to the world, but the barrel is tilted. The middle cannon shows the effect of applying the modifier according to the default axis, while the near cannon has its Taper gizmo rotated to match the barrel's incline.

Gizmo rotated 90°

FIGURE 8.11

The difference between using a Direction parameter and rotating a gizmo on the gizmo's boundary.

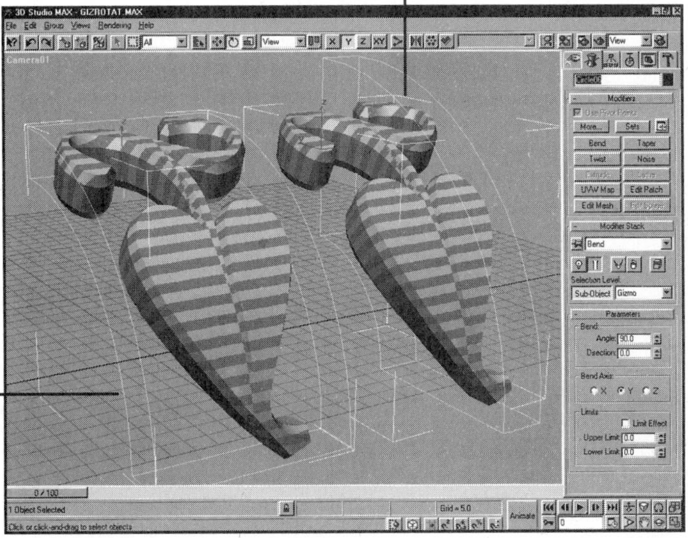

Modifier with a direction of 90 degrees

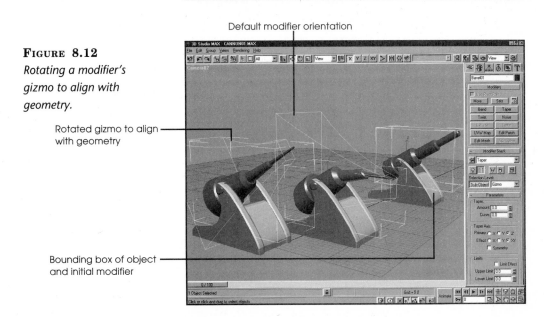

Default modifier orientation

FIGURE 8.12

Rotating a modifier's gizmo to align with geometry.

Rotated gizmo to align with geometry

Bounding box of object and initial modifier

Scaling Gizmos

Scaling a gizmo magnifies the modifier's effect. Performing a uniform scale is identical to increasing the modifier's strength. The top two objects in figure 8.13 show the same end result—the first from scaling the gizmo and the second from increasing the modifier's strength.

FIGURE 8.13
Scaling a modifier's gizmo.

Scaled gizmo ⎯

Modifier with increased angle ⎯

Gizmos with non-uniform scale ⎯

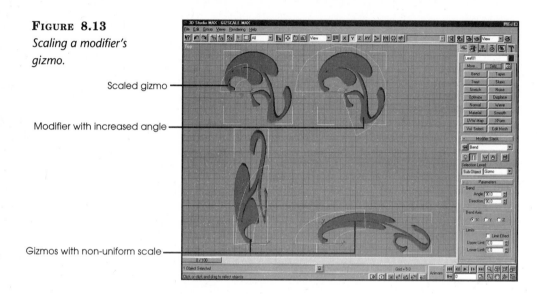

Performing a non-uniform scale to the gizmo, however, produces different results. The bottom two objects in figure 8.13 show the results of non-uniform scales on the gizmos. This effect cannot be duplicated by either adjusting the strength or placing the center.

TIP

When using modifier limits, the maximum or minimum effect of a modifier may not be strong or subtle enough. To amplify the modifier's effect, perform a uniform scale on the gizmo about its center.

After scaling gizmos, determining exactly how much they have been scaled and along what axes can be difficult. This process can be frustrating when comparing similar modifiers. Transform Type-In does not display the current location of gizmos as it does for objects. Your only option is to use **Track**

View's Key Info. Key Info is available only for keys, however, and no keys exist unless animation occurs. Thus, the gizmo's transform must be animated for its values to be examined. Because the transformation is not too common an occurrence, the following is a quick way to add a key in Track View and adjust a gizmo's absolute scale:

1. With the object selected, enter Track View and find the selected object. If your scene is large, click Filter and choose Show Only Select Objects.

2. Right-click on the object's name and choose Expand Tracks.

3. Enter Add Keys mode by clicking on the Add Keys icon and click anywhere along the gizmo's scale track to create a key.

4. Right-click on the new key to bring up Key Info with the gizmo's scale values as shown in figure 8.14.

    Adding this key did not create an animation. It created only a single key, so interpolation will not occur between other keys over time.

5. You can adjust the scale values and see the results interactively in the viewports. Optionally, you can delete the adjusted key and the values will remain.

FIGURE 8.14
Adjusting a gizmo's scale through Track View.

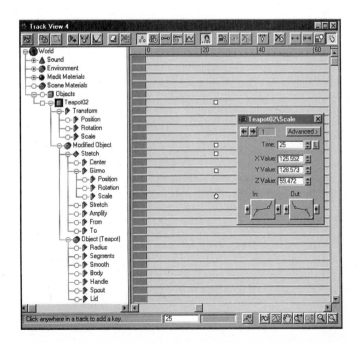

Using Modifier Limits

Many modifiers include the capability to limit the location of their effect with parameters termed *limits*. They are controlled by Upper and Lower (sometimes referred to as From and To) parameter limits and the location of the gizmo's center. Limits differ from sub-object modification because they influence the entire object but place their deformation only within a given range.

A bent straw is a good example of when to use limits. Figure 8.15 shows several attempts to bend a straight straw (a tube primitive). Starting from the left, the first bend affects the entire straw, which was not the intent. The second bends just the top half of the tube (using a Volume Select modifier), but doesn't allow for a straight section after the bend. The third tries to bend a middle section of the straw (again with Volume Select) and meets with bad results. The fourth bend is applied to the entire straw (just like the first straw), but the effect is localized with limits to produce the classic bent straw.

FIGURE 8.15

Attempts at bending a straw.

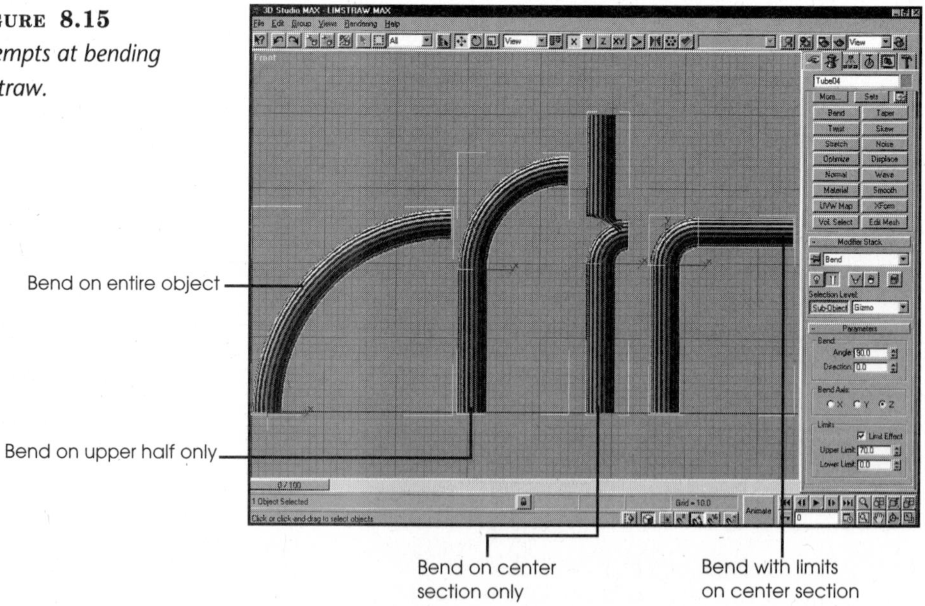

Bend on entire object

Bend on upper half only

Bend on center section only

Bend with limits on center section

BENDING A STRAW USING LIMITS

Modifier Limits are based on the gizmo's center. The Upper and Lower Limit parameters indicate the distance from the center the modifier is affecting. The location of the center then determines where along the axis the limited effect takes place. Because they are based on the center, the Upper and Lower limits "travel" with the center as it is moved. Duplicating the bend of the straw demonstrates this concept well.

FIGURE 8.16

The five steps in bending the straw.

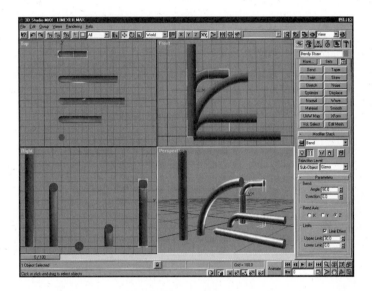

1. Begin by creating a cylinder on the ground plane with a radius of about 5 units and a height of about 100. This is your straw.

2. Add a Bend modifier to the straw and give it an angle of 90 degrees.

   Because the cylinder's pivot point is at its base, the (orange) gizmo arches from the base to form a 90-degree arc. The cylinder tries to match the gizmo's arc but is limited by the number of height segments it has been assigned.

3. Click on the stack, choose Cylinder, and increase the height segments to at least 50.

4. Return to the previous Bend modifier (do not apply another one) and activate the Limit Effect check box.

The straw is bent "flat" because the Upper distance is zero and the entire bend modification is occurring immediately at the gizmo's center (which is located by default at the pivot point).

5. Drag the Upper Limit value spinner upward until the desired "elbow" size is created (30 for example).

    This Upper Limit defines the size of the bend from the gizmo center. The Upper and Lower Limit values are actually the distance from the gizmo's center as measured in an undeformed state. If you were to make the Bend angle 0, the gizmo line indicating the Upper Limit would be 30 units above the center. To locate the bend along the straw, you need to move the center.

6. Click on Sub-Object and choose Center from the drop-down list.

7. Click on the Move transform, choose World as your coordinate system and constrain to the Z axis.

8. Move the Center along the length of the straw until it places the bend at the desired point (note that locking your selection by pressing the spacebar is very convenient when moving centers).

    The straw should now resemble the left of figure 8.17. Now that the Center has been moved from the base, within the cylinder, you can see the effect of using the Lower Limit.

9. Drag the Lower Limit spinner downward until its value is the negative equivalent of the Upper Limit (–30, for example).

    The bend becomes more shallow and the cylinder seems to "rise" from the ground plane (see the center of fig. 8.17) because the bend angle of 90 degrees is being stretched along a longer portion of the straw. The angle is still 90 degrees; it's just that the center of the bend has changed.

10. Increase the Bend angle to 180 degrees.

    The elbow becomes a u-joint, as shown figure 8.17. The bend is still constrained by the upper and lower limits, but the increased bend angle returns the upper portion to the 90-degree bend it had previously.

11. You can now add more limited bends to turn the straw into a pipeworks. While you probably want to continue to bend along the Z axis, you can always change direction and bend angle to create very intricate bends as shown in figure 8.18.

FIGURE 8.17

*Adjusting the Bend's
Lower Limit value.*

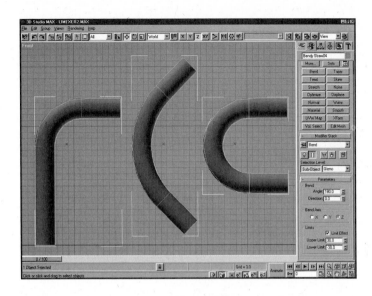

FIGURE 8.18

*Many limited bends on
a single cylinder.*

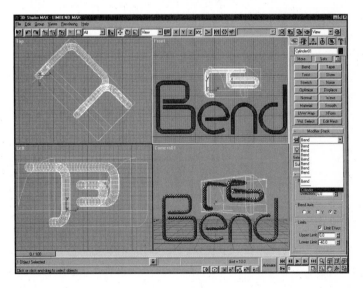

Modifiers with limits typically affect the entire object. The influence of one limited modifier can adversely impact that of another because they may overlap. The order in which modifiers are applied have an effect as well. In general, limited modifiers should be "stacked" along the object's length in order to avoid conflicts. When applying multiple, limited modifiers, applying the farthest modifier first and working backwards is always best. If your object's pivot point is in the center, you conceivably have two "stacks" to work with—Upper Limit modifiers above the pivot and Lower Limit modifiers below the pivot.

While simple in concept, modifiers limits provide a capability that is not possible in most other programs. Although useful, they are also extremely efficient. In terms of modeling, you only need to adjust one modifier for the effect—not a modifier and a previous Sub-Object selection modifier. In terms of memory, they require no more than a single modifier (which is quite small) and far less RAM than an Edit modifier. Finally, in terms of file size, modifiers are just a list of a few parameters and require little storage. On the other hand, each Edit modifier significantly increases the size of the file.

The Differences between Transforms and Modifiers

As described in Chapter 1, "Core Concepts of 3D Studio MAX," the geometry pipeline evaluates objects by first processing their creation parameters, applying any modifiers in stack order, accumulating transforms (as assigned from the toolbar), and finally applying any space warps bindings (world space modifiers). This process means that transforms are always processed after all modifiers have been applied. It doesn't matter when you apply a transform in regards to the object's edit history—the transform is always applied last. The result is not a problem with translation, rotation, and uniform scale but can be a problem with non-uniform scale.

Non-Uniform Scale

When you scale an object about only one or two of its axes, the operation is termed a non-uniform scale (or nu-scale for short) because all three axes are not consistently scaled. The object is said to "stretch" or "shrink" in one or two directions while the third direction stays constant.

You should be careful when you apply a non-uniform scale. Figure 8.19 shows the vast difference between performing a nu-scale as a modifier and as a transform. In both cases the Z-axis scale occurs before the bend. The surprising distortion is because transforms are always applied at the end of the pipeline, after all modifiers. The order you apply transforms in regard to modifiers doesn't matter—transforms are always applied after the entire stack of modifiers.

Mistaking this transform operation as a modification is easy. After all, the object did appear to permanently distort. In reality, it did not. Transforms are known in computer graphics as affine operations. An affine operation can be applied to an object over and over again, but the effects can always be reversed by applying more countering operations.

FIGURE 8.19
Non-uniform scale XForm versus non-uniform scale transform.

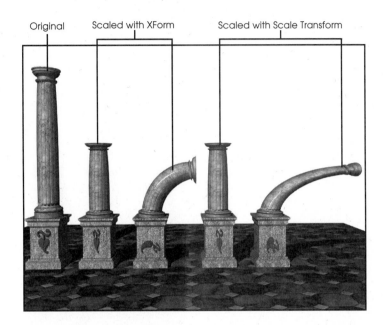

The commands located on the toolbar (Move, Rotate, Uniform Scale, Non-uniform Scale, Squash, and even Mirror) all affect what is known as the object's transformation matrix (or TM for short). The results of these commands are stored in the object's TM as position, rotation, and scale keys, if animated. After the connection is made that these operations are all manipulating the same nine numbers of the TM, any operation can be reversed at a later date.

While transforms are affine, modifiers are almost always non-affine operations. Modifiers usually distort the object and can even alter topology. Performing a second operation can rarely reverse the previous one. 3DS MAX blurs the distinction between affine and non-affine operations by enabling you to adjust the parameters of a given operation after it is applied and even remove it from the stack. Most modeling programs are not so lenient. Once applied, a modifier usually has a significant effect on the object's future. 3DS MAX gives you the luxury of changing your mind for any operation.

Using XForm Instead of Transforms

The XForm modifier is used to apply the effect of a transform (move, rotation, or scale) as a modifier— meaning that non-uniform scaling is treated as a modifier and not a transform at the object level. Chapter 9, "Modeling with Shapes," shows this modifier also used as the primary method for animating sub-object geometry.

The concept of the XForm modifier is simple. It produces a gizmo that encompasses the selection set and immediately places you into Sub-Object mode. All adjustments to the XForm modifier are done by simply transforming the gizmo.

XForm is an interesting modifier because it doesn't appear to have a user interface. The Sub-Object drop-down contains the gizmo and the gizmo's center. You find no other parameters because XForm relies entirely on the transform tools in the toolbar for control. After all, XForm is just taking transforms and making them part of the data history.

As with all modifiers, XForm has an effect on the objects to which it is applied when it is current in the Modifier panel. If Sub-Object mode is active, your transforms are being recorded on the gizmo, and they behave like a modifier. If Sub-Object mode is inactive, you are performing transforms as normal. When you first apply an XForm, it immediately enters Sub-Object mode because it assumes you want your adjustments to be recorded in the stack.

The effect, then, is occurring as a modifier in object space, and subsequent transforms do not affect it—an important idea. Essentially, if you want a transform to have a permanent effect on your model, you should use it in conjunction with XForm.

Using Axial Deformations

The basic geometric modifiers of Bend, Taper, Twist, Skew, and Stretch make up what are known in computer graphics as axial deformations. Each of these modifiers affects objects along their current axis. Because this modifies the shape of the axis for subsequent modifiers, the order in which you apply axial deformations has a profound effect on the resulting geometry.

All axial deformations have a gizmo and center that influence their results. A gizmo can be thought of as the modification itself embodied as an object. As an object, it has a full transform matrix and can be moved, rotated, and scaled. Its orientation determines which axis (many times secondary axis) is being affected on the object. The axial modifiers all have radio buttons for X, Y, and Z. These buttons are quick aids in reorienting the gizmo because you could rotate the gizmo to achieve the same modification.

TIP

While you can rotate a gizmo to duplicate a modifier's X, Y, Z axes check boxes, the axis options scale orients the gizmo to the object's extents along the chosen axis and quickly readjusts the center. Doing so is most often faster and returns a gizmo with a more conforming shape than rotating the gizmo itself.

The center is the gizmo's pivot point, and it is used to locate the centroid of the modifier's effect. Moving the center is much like moving an object's pivot point. Unlike a pivot point, a center defines only a single point and does not have a set of axes that can be rotated or scaled. You may also think of the center as a child of the gizmo because moving the gizmo moves the center as well. The process for using axial deformers and getting the desired result is often as follows:

1. Assign the modifier.

2. Increase the top value in the dialog to see the orientation and location of the modifier (the amount is not important at this time unless the result is already what is desired).

3. If the direction of the effect is inappropriate, cycle through the Axis radio buttons to locate the correct direction. Again, don't be too concerned with the finished result because you are determining the overall axial direction of the modifier.

4. If the effect is in the correct plane but the wrong direction, you need to adjust the Direction parameter (if one exists) or try reversing the sign of the first parameter (positive to negative for example).

5. If the desired direction cannot be attained with steps 3 and 4, the gizmo needs to be rotated to define the correct axis. Click Sub-Object, choose Gizmo, and rotate the gizmo 90% as needed about the modified axis. Remember that the current transform center affects this rotation: Use Pivot Point rotates about the gizmo's center (usually the most appropriate choice); Use Selection Center rotates about the center of the object being modified (if only modifying one object); and Use Transform Coordinate System Center rotates as its name states.

6. If the location of the effect is not correct, Click Sub-Object, choose Center, and move the gizmo's center to the desired location (most often constraining movement to one axis).

The location of the center has a tremendous effect on the result of the modifier. This effect can lead you to believe you must rotate the gizmo when all that is required is to move the center.

Using Bend

The Bend modifier "rotates" the vertices of the selection about a default point and along one axis. The effect is very similar to bending malleable material over a rigid cylinder. The diameter of that "cylinder" varies as the Bend angle increases and the gizmo center is repositioned. A 360% Bend will rotate the object over until it forms a circle. The size of the circle is dependent upon where the gizmo center is located, as shown in figure 8.20.

Figure 8.21 shows that while moving the gizmo's center keeps the gizmo's shape adhered to the deformed object, moving the entire gizmo actually locates the bend's center of rotation. This figure shows how moving the center has an impact on the effect of the bend along the three axes.

FIGURE 8.20

Successive use of the Bend modifier.

Y-axis Bend

X-axis Bend

Z-axis Bend

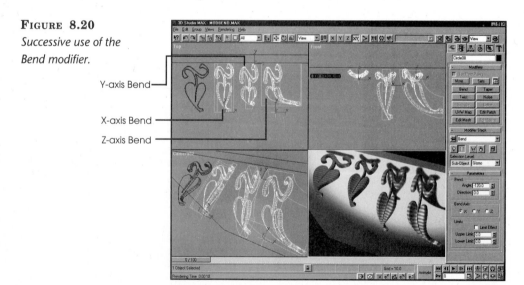

FIGURE 8.21

The radius of the Bend in relation to the Bend's center and gizmo.

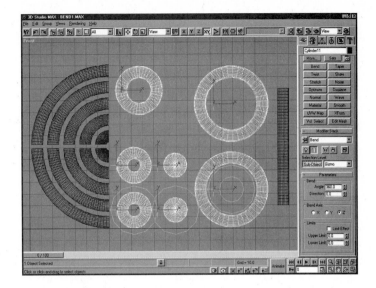

The single most important parameter for Bend (and actually for all axial deformations) is the axis about which the effect occurs. If the bend you want occurs in the plane of the modifier's axes, you can orient the bend by choosing the Bend axis and adjusting the Directional angle. Figure 8.22 shows how the three axes and 90% adjustments to them locate the bend's effect.

FIGURE 8.22

Directing the Bend with the Axis and Direction parameters.

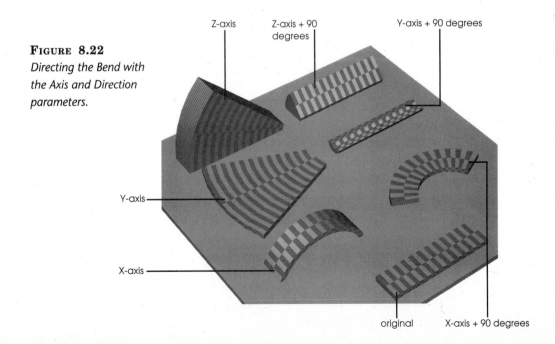

When working on single objects or multiple objects with the Use Pivot Points option, Bend locates its gizmo's center on the object's pivot point. When acting upon generic selections of objects or sub-objects the center is located at the centroid of the selection's bounding box. Figure 8.23 shows the effect of locating the Bend's center at different distances and along different axes.

The usefulness of Bend has increased significantly with 3DS MAX. Now with the capability to animate and limit its effect, Bend can define objects that could only have been lofted previously. Figure 8.24 shows some of the possibilities of modeling with Bend limits.

FIGURE 8.23

The effect of the Bend's center location on the three axes.

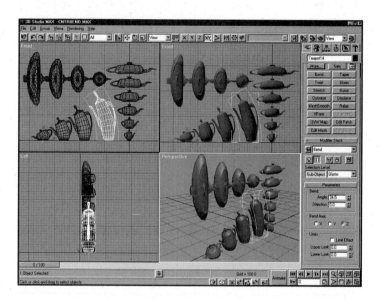

Using Taper

The Taper modifier parallels Bend as being an extremely flexible, all purpose tool. Taper bases its effect on the gizmo center, with opposite scaling occurring above and below the center. The center acts as a stable location where no scale occurs. Taper's Curve option enables you to bulge out or sweep in what would otherwise be a straight taper. Figure 8.25 shows the Taper modifier being used successively. Figure 8.26 illustrates the effect of Taper's center on the three axes.

Taper is unique among the basic modifiers because it gives you the option to taper along any combination of axes. The effect of these combinations is shown in figure 8.27. This figure also shows the effect of the Symmetry option, which centers and mirrors the effect of the taper about the axes. Note that because a Teapot's pivot point is at its base, changing the Symmetry option for the primary Z axis has no effect.

The Taper command becomes particularly useful when used with limits. Figure 8.28 shows just a sample of what can be created with limited tapers. Note that the history stack only contains Tapers and no EditMesh or VolSelect modifiers. Therefore, the model is very efficient. Because all modifiers have been applied at the object level, you are free to modify any of the Tube parameters without having an adverse impact on the model, enabling you to adjust the segmentation at any time. You can then easily include models of varying complexity in the scene.

FIGURE 8.24

The use of multiple, limited Bends to create complex forms from cylinder primitives.

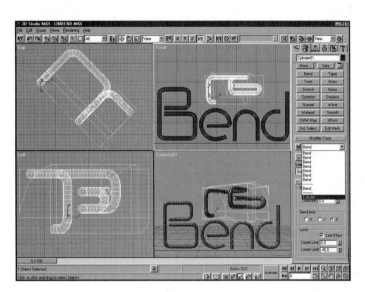

Using Skew

The Skew modifier is actually less of an axial modifier and more of a scale effect. Skew scales the selection in opposite directions based on the location of the gizmo's center. The center acts as a stable location where no skew occurs (see fig. 8.29).

Skew affects a selection's geometry by "stretching" or "sliding" the locations of the mesh's vertices along one axis. The direction of the skew is controlled by the Direction parameter and the axis chosen. If the gizmo center is in the middle of the selection, the object is skewed in both directions with the center becoming the fault line (see fig. 8.30).

FIGURE 8.25
*Successive use of the
Taper modifier.*

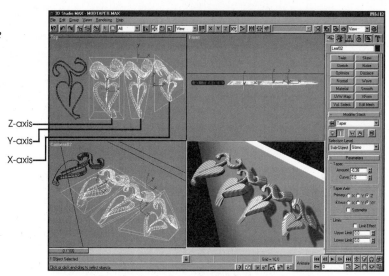

Z-axis
Y-axis
X-axis

FIGURE 8.26
*The effect of Taper's
center location on the
three axes.*

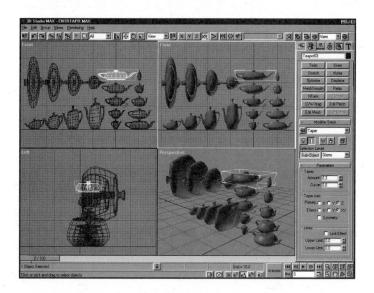

To restrict Skew so that it flares only one side, you must position the gizmo center at the extremity of the side you wish to remain stable. Placing the center enables you to give more "weight" to one side or the other. Figure 8.31 shows the use of Skew with limits. Because Skew performs a scaling, or flattening, of the selection, you may not find it as universally useful as the other axial deformations.

FIGURE 8.27

Using the various axial combinations with the same Taper strength.

Primary axis

Symmetry

Off

On

Off

On

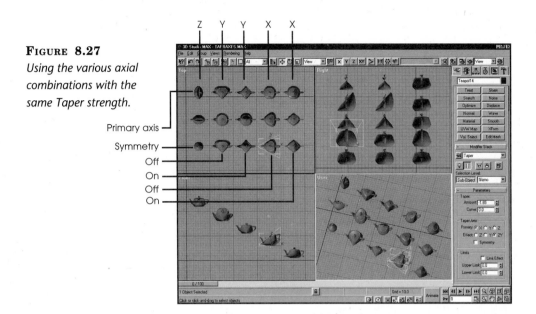

FIGURE 8.28

Using several Tapers with limits on a Tube primitive to create a goblet.

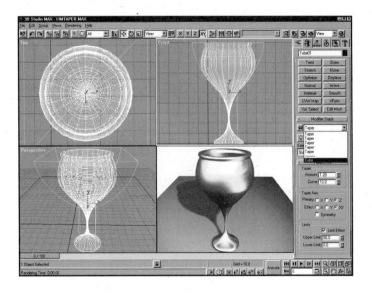

FIGURE 8.29

*Successive use of the
Skew modifier.*

Z-axis   Y-axis   X-axis

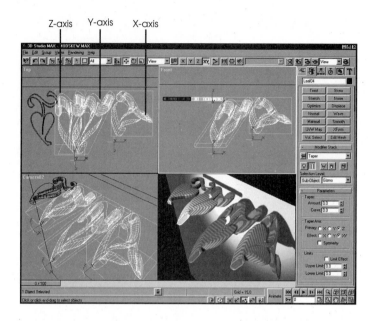

FIGURE 8.30

*The effect of Skew's
center location on the
three axes.*

Gizmo center

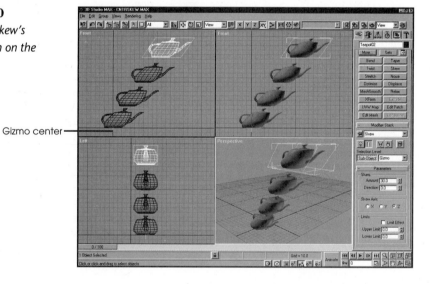

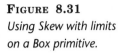

FIGURE 8.31

Using Skew with limits on a Box primitive.

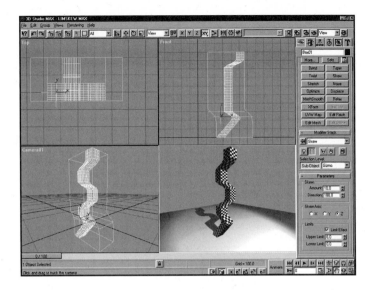

Using Twist

The Twist modifier essentially takes an axis and creates a spiral or cork screw. The effect is similar to what happens to a rope that hangs straight from your hand, when you quickly rotate your wrist. Figure 8.32 shows the use of several twists on the same object.

Much of Twist's impact is dependent on the location of its gizmo's center. When centered on the object, Twist creates geometric spirals—much like a barber pole or candy cane. If the center is moved away, the geometry is twisted to form a spiral. The cylinders in figure 8.33 show the effect of a centered gizmo center and one that is offset. The location of the center along the affected axis controls the Twist's rotation. Figure 8.33 shows that in lowering the center, the twist rotates the object (the two rows of teapots have the same gizmo center location).

Using Twist with limits has a lot of potential. Decorative iron work, twisted wire, and, as figure 8.34 shows, even jewelry can use limited twists. When animating characters, the twist can be limited to just the head and neck to produce cartoonish results.

Y-axis   Z-axis   X-axis

FIGURE 8.32
*Successive use of the
Twist modifier.*

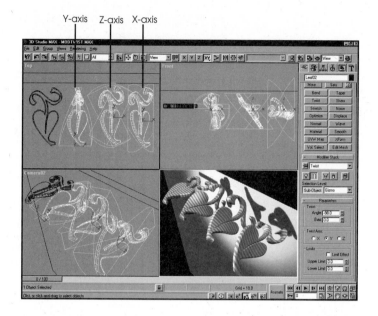

FIGURE 8.33
*The effect of locating
the Twist's center.*

Common center——

Offset center——

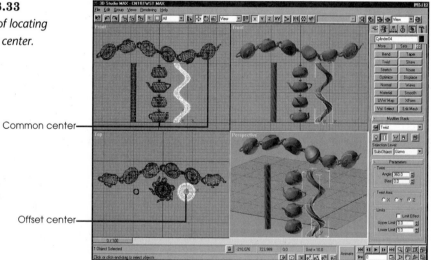

FIGURE 8.34

FIGURE 8.34
Using limited twists on box primitives to create twists common in jewelry.

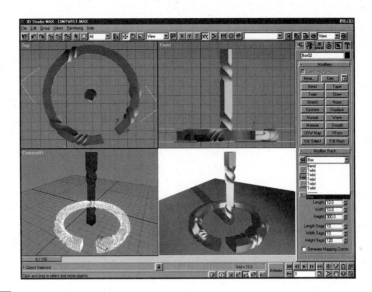

Using Stretch

The Stretch modifier was added in Release 1.1 to complete the axial deformations. In many ways, it's a cross between the Squash transform and the Taper modifier. Squash is a non-uniform scale that scales one axis up as it scales the other two out. Stretch does much of the same except it creates curve in the stretched axis, similar to Taper's Curve option. Figure 8.35 shows the effect Stretch has in a limited manner.

The location of Stretch's gizmo center influences to which side the effect will occur. Usually, you want the gizmo's center centered on the object, but figure 8.36 shows how offsetting this center can create some interesting effects for giving weight and character to the deformation.

Although Stretch is used primarily as an animation tool, it does have potential for modeling when used with limits. Figure 8.37 shows how a simple Tube was made into an intricate vase with several limited stretches. Stretch should be used in this manner with the understanding that one axis is going to scale beyond the limits of the current geometry.

Z-axis   Y-axis   X-axis

FIGURE 8.35
*Successive use of the
Stretch modifier.*

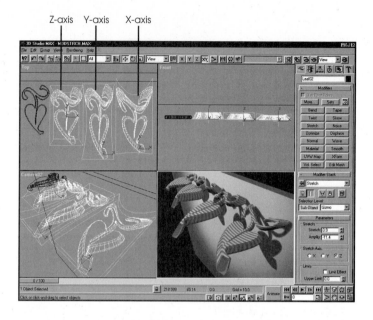

FIGURE 8.36
*The effect of Stretch's
center location on the
three axes.*

Common center——

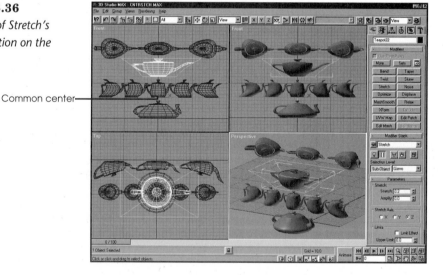

FIGURE 8.37
*Using limited stretches
to create a vase from a
tube primitive.*

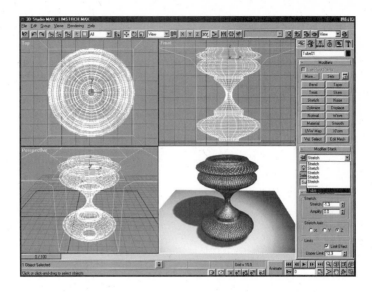

In Practice: Basics of Object Level Modeling

- **Editing objects** An object's Modifier Stack contains the modifiers you apply to the object, enabling you to adjust any of your modeling decisions at a later date. Each modifier entry is essentially an object, with its own effect and animation capabilities.

- **Collapsing the stack** Collapsing the stack flattens every modifier you have applied into one, static model. The resulting geometry of the collapse depends on the modifiers collapsed. A partial collapse will always collapse every modifier from the selected one down to the bottom of the stack.

- **Sub-object gizmos** Many modifiers contain sub-object gizmos that enable you to adjust and animate the modifier's effect as if it were an object with standard transforms.

- **Modifier limits** Modifier limits enable you to control the extents that a modifier's effect has on an object. This gives you the control that would otherwise require sub-object selections and numerous edits.

- **Modifier order** The order modifiers are applied is paramount to the resulting effect. An object's creation parameters are evaluated first, and the Modifier Stack is evaluated from bottom to top, then the cumulative transform is applied, and finally Space Warp bindings are added.

- **Non-uniform scale transform** A nonuniform scale transform appears to be a modification—although it's not—and can have surprising results because the scale transform is applied after the Modifier Stack. In practice, it is best to use an XForm modifier in conjunction with this to make the scale part of the Modifier Stack.

Created by Kim Lee
Design Systems
Provided courtesy of Kinetix ™

Chapter 9

MODELING WITH SHAPES

Shape tools in 3D Studio MAX include objects such as Lines, Circles, and Rectangles. These sound more like they belong in a drawing or CAD program than a three-dimensional modeling and animation product. How do shapes fit into the scheme of 3D modeling?

You create shape objects in 3DS MAX to use as source geometry for creating other objects. You can create shapes that form the foundation of other objects in much the same way that a painter stretches a canvas over a frame, or a sculptor builds a wire armature to hold the clay. Because 3DS MAX is also an animation tool, you can create shapes that control motion.

This chapter looks at the general issues behind creating shapes and introduces some shape-based 3D modeling techniques. These issues include:

- Understanding what shapes are and the terms used to describe them

- Exploring how decisions you make when creating shapes can affect the complexity and performance of your scene

- How to create and edit shape objects

- Applying modifiers to shape objects

- Special techniques for employing shape objects as precision tools

Of course, the place to start is with the creation of shape objects

Creating Shape Objects

Create shape objects by clicking the Shapes category in the Create panel and then clicking a shape button in the Object Type rollout (see fig. 9.1). Drag in a viewport and set shape parameters in the Create panel to complete the shape. The following sections explain how to create shapes and what the shape parameters mean.

FIGURE 9.1
Shape button in
the Create panel.

Before creating and editing shapes, it helps to have a basic understanding of shape terminology. The following list defines shape terminology used in 3DS MAX and figure 9.2 illustrates these terms.

- **Vertices** The points at either end of spline segments. You can set vertex properties to define whether the vertex is a corner, smooth, or Bézier type. Vertices are shape sub-objects.

- **Tangent Handles** Shape vertices set to the Bézier vertex type display tangent handles. Drag tangent handles to control the curvature of the spline segment as it enters and leaves the vertex. Tangent handles are properties of a vertex.

- **Segments** The part of the spline between two vertices. The curvature of spline segments is controlled by changing the properties of the vertices at either end of the segment or by changing the properties of the segment itself. Set the segment properties to define whether the segment is a line or a curve. Line segments ignore vertex properties. Segments are shape sub-objects.

- **Steps** The number of segment divisions used to represent a curve. When you use shapes to create geometry, the curves in the shape must be converted into triangular faces. The step setting controls how many face edges, or facets, are generated by the shape. High step values create smooth curves that generate many faces. Steps are a shape parameter.

- **Splines** A collection of connected segments. Splines are a type of smooth adjustable curve, but 3DS MAX includes options for inserting corners and defining linear segments. Splines are shape sub-objects.

- **Shapes** A collection of splines defines a shape object. Restrictions on the number and type of splines in a shape vary with the shape's intended use. Shapes are named objects.

- **Paths** A term used to describe a shape. A path invariably describes a shape containing a single spline that you use as a track for something. Examples include Loft paths, Path Controller paths, and Path Deform paths. Remember that whenever 3DS MAX refers to a path, what is really being described is a single spline shape.

Creating Lines

Click the Line button in the Create panel to create the most basic type of shape. Creating lines involves more than picking points on the screen. You should remember a number of features:

- All the segments created in a single Line command are part of the same spline and same shape. If you want to create separated line segments, you must right-click to complete the first Line command and click in a viewport to begin another line.

- You can create lines flat on the construction plane by clicking in a viewport or in full three-dimensional space. If you use 3D Snap or Keyboard Entry you can also vary the Z value of spline vertices.

- Lines can be either straight or curved depending on your Creation Method choices and whether you click or drag as you create vertices.

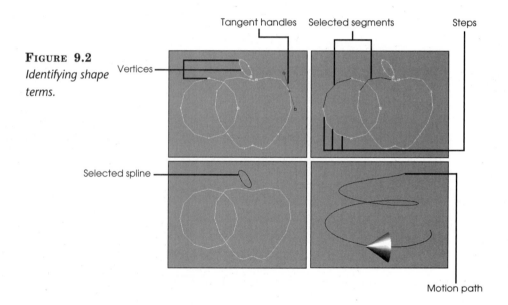

FIGURE 9.2
Identifying shape terms.

Line Creation Methods

The choices you make in the Creation Method rollout are critical to controlling the initial properties of Lines. Choose options to control the type of vertex you get when you click or drag while creating lines. Figure 9.3 shows the two Creation Method types and their supported vertex types.

- **Initial Type**   These options should really be called Click Type because they set the type of vertex created when you click. The default is Corner. Corner vertices produce segments that are linear as they enter and leave the vertex.

Smooth vertices produce a curve through the vertex in which the amount of curvature on either side of the vertex is equal. The tangent of a smooth vertex is always parallel to a line drawn between the two vertices to either side of the smooth vertex.

■ **Drag Type**   These options set the type of vertex created when you drag. The choices include Corner and Smooth, just like Initial Type, and Bézier. In all cases the vertex is placed at the location where you first press the mouse down. Dragging the mouse activates the chosen drag type for the vertex. The direction and distance that you drag before releasing the mouse only matters if your drag type is set to Bézier.

Drag direction sets the tangent direction of the curve as it passes through the vertex. *Drag distance* sets the magnitude of the curve at the vertex.

FIGURE 9.3
Line Creation Method and vertex types.

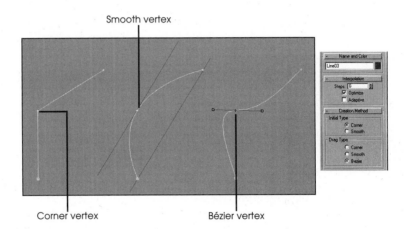

Smooth vertex

Corner vertex

Bézier vertex

Interactive Creation

The most common method for creating Lines is interactively clicking in a viewport. The following rules govern interactive line creation:

■ Line creation can only occur in a single viewport. You cannot switch viewports after starting to create a line. You must right-click to complete the command before you can switch to another viewport.

■ Vertex type is set by options in the Creation Method rollout. Be careful when using the Bézier drag type. You rarely, if ever, want to drag the first vertex of a line. You might also find it easier to create all vertices and then use Edit Spline to convert them to adjustable Bézier vertices.

- Lines lie flat on the current construction plane unless 3D Snap is active. If 3D Snap is active, Line vertices snap to the edges and vertices of other objects in 3D space.

- Regardless of how the line is created, its Local coordinate system is placed on, and aligned with, the current construction place.

Keyboard Creation

Another method of creating lines is to use features of the Keyboard Entry rollout (see fig. 9.4). Type X, Y, and Z coordinates and then click Add Point for each vertex of the line. When you are finished, click Close to connect the last vertex to the first, closing the line, or click Finish to leave the line open.

FIGURE 9.4
Keyboard Entry
rollout for Line
creation.

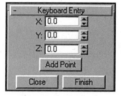

The following rules govern creating lines with Keyboard Entry:

- All vertices use the Initial Type (click) option in the Creation Method rollout.

- The Local coordinate system is placed on, and aligned with, the current construction plane.

- All line segments are invisible until you click Close or Finish.

The last rule makes precision line drawing with Keyboard Entry difficult to use. With luck, a future release will display each line segment as it is created.

Creating Parametric Shapes

The remaining shapes are parametric objects. The vertex locations and types are set by parameters in the Create panel. The shapes can be further distinguished according to their creation technique. With two exceptions, you create shapes by defining either a radius or a rectangle. The exceptions are arcs and text.

Create most shapes by first dragging out a radius. The shapes that use this technique are donut, circle, helix, NGon, and star. The creation technique for these shapes is as follows:

1. Choose a Creation Method. Choose Edge to define by diameter or Center to define by radius.

2. Drag in a viewport to define shape location and Radius 1.

3. If necessary, click in the viewport to set remaining parameters.

   Donut and star: Click to set Radius 2.

   Helix: Click to set Height. Click again to set Radius 2.

4. Set any remaining parameters in the Parameters rollout.

You create rectangles and ellipses by dragging the diagonal of a rectangle. The creation technique for these shapes is as follows:

1. Choose a Creation Method. Choose Edge to define by corner to corner or Center to define by center to corner.

2. Drag in a viewport to define shape location and the diagonal of a rectangle that defines Length and Width.

3. Set any remaining parameters in the Parameters rollout.

Creating Circles and NGons

Create circles and NGons by dragging a single radius. Circles always use four vertices to define the circle.

Use the sides parameters for NGons to vary the number of vertices and sides. Use an NGon with the Circular option checked whenever you need a circle with more than four vertices, as shown in figure 9.5.

Creating Donuts and Stars

Create donuts and stars by dragging out a first radius and then clicking to define a second radius. Stars have two extra parameters that are to set the number of points in the star and the amount of distortion.

The distortion parameter for a star rotates the vertices on Radius 2 around the local Z axis for the star. Positive values rotate the vertices counterclockwise, and negative values rotate the points clockwise (see fig. 9.6).

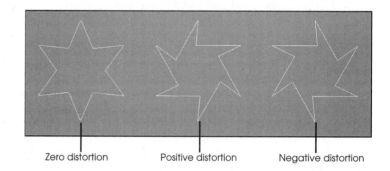

FIGURE 9.5
Comparing flat and circular NGons.

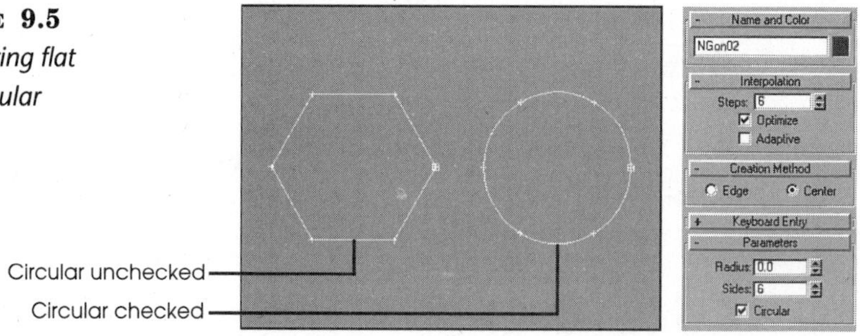

Circular unchecked
Circular checked

FIGURE 9.6
Changing star distortion.

Zero distortion   Positive distortion   Negative distortion

Creating Rectangles and Ellipses

Create rectangles and ellipses by dragging a diagonal. The diagonal defines the Length and Width parameters used by the rectangle or ellipse.

If you press Ctrl while dragging, you are constrained to creating a square rectangle or a circular ellipse. Why would you want a circular ellipse when you could just create a circle? The answer is that you can animate the length and width of an ellipse. If you want to animate a shape from a circle to an ellipse, start with an ellipse created with the Ctrl key option.

Creating Arcs

The way you create arcs depends greatly on your Creation Method choice. You can define an arc using one of two methods:

- **Center-End-End**   This is the most familiar method and is useful when you want to hit an exact center and starting point. You can't precisely predict the location of the second end point because it is a function of the arc radius.

To create a Center-End-End arc, drag to define the arc center (mouse down) and radius and start point (mouse up). Click to define the second endpoint.

■ **End-End-Middle**   Use this method when you want the arc to exactly hit two endpoints. The method for creating an End-End-Middle arc is as follows:

To create an End-End-Middle arc, drag to define the first endpoint (mouse down) and the second endpoint (mouse up). Click to define the radius of the arc.

Whichever technique you use, the arc parameters are stored as a radius, a From angle, and a To angle. Only the center point of the arc is fixed. Changing any of the three parameters causes the endpoints of the arc to move.

Creating Helixes

You create a helix by dragging out a first radius, clicking to set the height of the helix, and clicking again to set a second radius. You can then set three other parameters for Turns, Bias, and turn direction. A helix is very useful as a loft path for creating objects such as corkscrews, curved stair railings, and heating elements.

The method for creating a Helix is as follows:

1. Drag to define the center, radius, and starting point.

    The start point is always located in the positive X direction from the helix center on the current construction plane.

2. Click to set the Z axis distance off the construction plane for the helix endpoint.

3. Click again to set the radius for the helix endpoint.

After you have created the basic helix, you can set the following parameters:

■ **Turns**   Sets how many 360 degree revolutions to make from the start point to the endpoint.

■ **Bias**   Sets where the turns occur in relation to the helix height.

    The default value of 0.0 spreads the turns evenly from start to end.

Positive values move the turns closer to the endpoint; negative values move the turns closer to the start point.

- **CW/CCW Options** Set the direction of the turns as they leave the start point. CW = clockwise; CCW = counterclockwise.

Figure 9.7 shows a simple helix with its parameters on the left. The helixes on the right show what you can achieve by changing the Helix parameters.

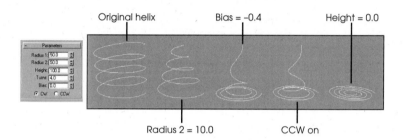

FIGURE 9.7
Various helix forms.

Creating Text

Text is the easiest shape to create. Click in any viewport and text is placed on the current construction plane. You can also drag to see the text as you move the cursor around the viewport; the text is dropped wherever you release the mouse. You then set parameters to change the font, style, size, and displayed text string as follows:

- **Font** 3DS MAX can use any True Type font installed in your Windows NT system and any Adobe Type 1 PostScript font that you have placed in the 3dsmax\fonts directory. Click in the font list to choose any available font.

- **Style** Clicking the two buttons below the font list toggles the use of italic style and underlined text. If you want bold text, you must choose a bold font.

- **Size** Sets the height of the text. Setting text height is a little tricky at first because 3DS MAX uses the full font height from the font file to calculate height. Most commercial font files define height as being the distance from the top of the ascender to the bottom of the descender plus a default leading (or shoulder), as shown in figure 9.8.

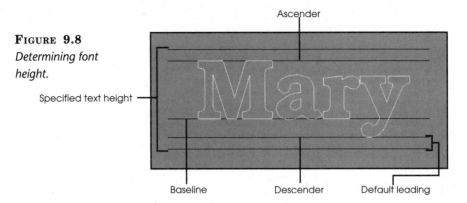

FIGURE 9.8
Determining font height.

Because of the way font height is defined, no text string ever fully fills the specified size. You must experiment with the Size value until the text string is the height you want. After you find a good height, all text created using the same font and the same size have uniform letter heights.

Type the text you want to place in the 3DS MAX scene. Although the text field is many lines tall, you can type only a single line of text. If you type text longer than the width of the text field, the text scrolls to the left.

You can also paste text from the Windows clipboard with the following restrictions:

- The font, size, and style of the text from the clipboard is ignored. 3DS MAX uses the current font, style, and size in the Parameters rollout.

- Only the first full line of text is read from the clipboard; 3DS MAX ignores all text following the first line break.

WARNING

You can create text with a null string (no text in the text field). What you get is an invisible pivot point that can be selected only if it falls inside a region selection or if you select it by name. Always make sure you have something in the text field before you click in a viewport.

Text in 3DS MAX has an interesting split personality. The text is parametric, so you can go back and edit the text as text. Because the text is also a spline, you can edit text as geometry. This dual nature of text objects gives you the best of both worlds. The following example shows how to edit and transform text objects to create a justified paragraph.

No one would ever mistake 3DS MAX for a word processor, but some animation jobs might require that you create a few lines of text with a certain justification. For example, you need to create a logo or a sign with a few lines of text. This example uses Array and Align to lay out three lines of left-justified text for a shop named Cameron's Camera Shop:

1. Create the first line of text.

2. Click Text in the Shapes category of the Create panel.

3. Choose a font, leave Height at 100, and type **Cameron's** in the text field.

4. Drag in the Front viewport to place the text.

You need three lines of text, but manually placing text and getting even line spacing is rather difficult. Use the Array tool to quickly create more lines.

5. Select the text object and choose Local as the reference coordinate system.

6. Click Array in the toolbar.

7. Click Reset in the Array dialog.

8. Set the Move Y field to **–90.0** and set Total In Array to **3**.

9. Click OK.

The preceding steps create three lines of text spaced 90.0 units apart, as shown in figure 9.9. The text size is usually a good starting value for the Array spacing. You can adjust up or down from there. For most fonts you may want to reduce the spacing, especially if your text has very few descenders, as is the case with Cameron's Camera Shop.

Arraying the first line of text is the fastest way to lay out multiple lines of text. Next, edit the two new lines using the Modify panel.

1. Select the middle line of text.

2. In the Modify panel, change the text field from Cameron's to Camera.

3. Select the bottom line of text and change it to Shop.

FIGURE 9.9
Creating multiple lines of text.

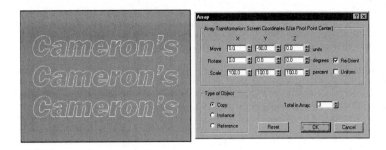

If you want center justification, you are finished. 3DS MAX places the pivot point for text in the center of the text string giving you default center-justified text. Use the Align command for left or right justification.

4. Select the bottom two lines of text and choose Local as the reference coordinate system.

5. Click Align in the toolbar and then click the top line of text.

6. Check the X Position check box.

7. Choose Minimum for both the Current object and Target object.

8. Click OK.

The text is now left justified with the position of the first line of text, as shown in figure 9.10. The combination of parametric text, Array, and Align makes it easy to lay out multiple lines of justified text for 3D signs and logos.

FIGURE 9.10
Justifying lines of text.

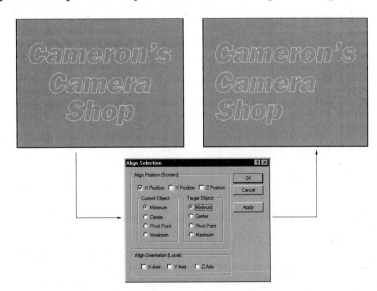

Creating Multiple Splines in the Same Shape

By definition, donuts and text contain multiple splines in the same shape. Such shapes are called *compound shapes*. A donut shape contains two circular splines; a text shape contains at least one spline for each letter, and many letters require multiple splines.

Create compound shapes by unchecking the check box next to the Start New Shape button (see fig. 9.11).

- When the box is checked, the Start New Shape button is always on, and everything you create becomes a separate shape object.

- When the box is clear, the Start New Shape button pops out, and every thing you create becomes a spline in one big compound shape.

- You can manually start a new shape by clicking the Start New Shape button.

FIGURE 9.11

The Start New Shape check box and button.

You can always go back to any shape and add to it, using one of the following two techniques:

- Select a shape object and then clear the Start New Shape check box. Any shapes you create after that are added as splines to the selected shape.

- Apply an Edit Spline modifier to a shape and use Attach to add other shapes to the selected shape. Edit Spline is discussed in the section "Using Edit Spline" later in this chapter.

The Start New Shape button is fast and convenient, but Edit Spline provides greater control over how the splines are located. Also, using the Start New Shape button prevents you from going back and accessing any shape parameters after you finish creating the shape. By using Edit Spline, you can preserve parameters for at least one of the splines in the compound shape.

Understanding Shape Interpolation

All the basic shape objects contain a parameter rollout labeled Interpolation (see fig. 9.12). This rollout contains three parameters that control the number of steps in each spline segment. Understanding and properly using the interpolation parameters is critical to the efficient use of shapes.

FIGURE 9.12

Shape

Interpolation

parameters.

As mentioned earlier in this chapter, steps are divisions along a spline segment. Steps control two properties of a shape: smoothness of the shape curves and the number of faces generated by the shape. With the smoothness of the shape curves, high step settings produce a smoother curve; with the number of faces generated by the shape, higher step settings generate more faces.

The Interpolation parameters control the number of steps in a shape:

■ **Steps** Enter a value in this field to manually specify the number of steps used for all spline segments in the shape. Use the Steps parameter to gain exact control over the number of faces generated when the shape is used to create 3D geometry. The Adaptive check box must be clear to use the Steps field.

■ **Optimize** When checked, steps are reduced to 0 for all linear spline segments in the shape. Because steps are used to represent curves, they are not needed to accurately represent linear segments and can be removed. Optimize should remain as the default setting.

However, you may want to turn off Optimize if you plan to deform the spline along the linear segments. The segments may be linear now, but if you plan to bend or twist them, you need the extra segments removed by optimizing. You may also want to turn off Optimize if you plan to generate Morph targets from the shape. All Morph targets must have the same number of vertices. Optimization removes shape segments that would generate mesh vertices for a morph target, making it difficult to generate morph targets from shape containing flat sides and other shapes containing curved sides.

The Adaptive check box must be clear to use the Optimize check box.

■ **Adaptive** Automatically calculates steps for each spline segment in the shape. The steps are set so that a change in angle from one step to the next is no more than 2 degrees. Linear segments receive no steps.

Use Adaptive when you want to see smooth, accurate splines used as motion paths or loft components. Adaptive is not a good choice for splines used to generate 3D geometry with modifiers such as Extrude or EditMesh. The smoothness of an adaptive spline generates an inefficient number of faces.

Checking Adaptive disables the Steps and Optimize parameters.

Figure 9.13 shows three text shapes using the letter D that have been converted to a mesh by applying an EditMesh modifier. All three shapes are identical except for their interpolation settings. The face edges are displayed to emphasize the difference.

FIGURE 9.13
Changing interpolation settings.

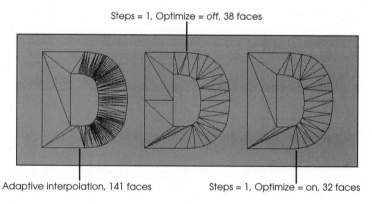

Steps = 1, Optimize = off, 38 faces

Adaptive interpolation, 141 faces

Steps = 1, Optimize = on, 32 faces

The letter on the left side of figure 9.13 uses Adaptive interpolation. You can barely tell that the letter is smoother than the others. Applying EditMesh creates a mesh object using 141 faces.

The letter in the middle of figure 9.13 also uses a Steps setting of 1 and Optimize is unchecked. Applying EditMesh creates a mesh object using 38 faces. The middle letter has 73 percent fewer faces than the letter on the left.

The letter on the right of figure 9.13 uses a Steps setting of 1 with Optimize checked. Applying EditMesh creates a mesh object using 32 faces. The letter on the right has 16 percent fewer faces than the middle letter and 77 percent fewer faces than the letter on the left.

More faces consumes more disk space, more memory, and, most importantly, more rendering time. You always want to use the fewest faces necessary to produce a given image quality. In the preceding example, the Adaptive setting may be appropriate if you plan to fly a camera in and around the letter. For most situations, however, using the Steps setting and Optimize is your best choice.

Using Edit Spline

Use the Edit Spline modifier to edit and transform the sub-objects of shapes (Yes, it's really an Edit Shape modifier). The following information about Edit Spline focuses on basic shape modeling techniques.

To apply an Edit Spline modifier to a shape, select a shape object. Next, click Edit Spline in the Modify panel.

The next four sections describe techniques common to all levels of spline Sub-Object editing.

Working with Shape Sub-Objects

Shape terminology and definitions of shape sub-objects were presented at the beginning of this chapter. By using the Edit Spline modifier you can select and edit the following shape sub-objects:

- **Vertices**   The lowest level of shape sub-objects. Vertices carry Bézier curve information. Working with vertices is the only way to exercise full control over shape curves.

- **Segments**   The middle level of shape sub-objects. There are few segment editing tools, and many segment editing techniques are simply a convenient way of working with vertices.

- **Splines**   The top level of shape sub-objects. Many shapes contain a single spline, so editing at the spline Sub-Object level may seem to be the same as editing the object, which is not the case. All sub-object editing occurs in object space and has no effect on the object's Local coordinate system or object transformations.

Select these shape sub-objects by clicking the Sub-Object button and choosing the Sub-object level you want to edit. Then select a sub-object by using the standard selection tools.

Using Undo with Edit Spline

You can undo any action performed with Edit Spline as long as you do not access any other modifier. Choosing another modifier in the Modifier Stack, or applying another modifier, clears the Undo buffer. After the Undo buffer is cleared, the only way to reverse the effects of an Edit Spline modifier is to delete the modifier from the Modifier Stack.

Detaching Sub-Objects

You can detach segments and splines from a shape to create new shape objects. When you detach selected sub-objects, the location and orientation of the original shape's pivot point is copied for the new shape. Figure 9.14 compares pivot point locations between an original shape and a new shape created by detaching some of its segments.

Both the Edit Segment and Edit Spline rollouts contain a Detach button with two options: Copy and Reorient.

When the Copy option is checked, the selected segment or spline is left undisturbed and copied to a new shape object. This technique is useful when you want to duplicate parts of a shape as a starting point for another shape.

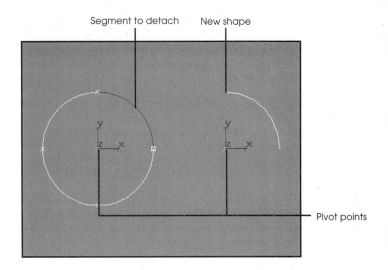

FIGURE 9.14
Comparing pivot points between original shape and detached shape.

When unchecked, the selected segment or spline is removed from the shape to create a new shape. Even after detaching a segment or spline, the Edit Spline modifier keeps a record of the detached sub-objects. If you use Undo, the new shape is deleted, and the original shape is restored. You can also restore the shape to its original form by deleting the Edit Spline modifier from the Modifier Stack. The new shape created by detaching the sub-objects is not affected by deleting the Edit Spline modifier.

When the Reorient option is checked, the detached objects are moved and rotated to align with the current construction plane (active grid). The pivot point of the new object is located at the origin of the construction plane, and the pivot point axes are aligned with the construction plane axes (see fig. 9.15). The pivot point of the new object is copied from the creation pivot point of the original shape.

When unchecked, the new shape with detached sub-objects is left in its original location. Telling the difference between the new shape with the detached sub-objects and the original shape when reorient is unchecked can be difficult. The tip-off to telling the difference is that the new shape changes color and cannot be selected as long as the Edit Spline modifier remains selected in the Modifier Stack, and Sub-object mode is active.

A point to keep in mind is that the new shape object created by a detach operation has no base parameters. The new object is a simple Bézier spline, not a parametric shape. So, you do not have access to any interpolation parameters for the new shape. Make sure that the interpolation parameters for the original shape are set the way you want before you detach any sub-objects.

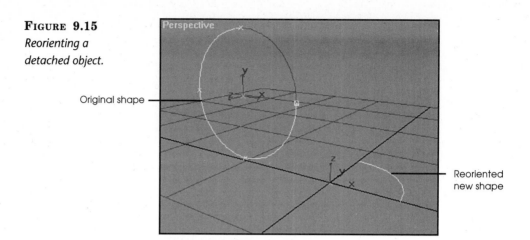

FIGURE 9.15
Reorienting a detached object.

Original shape

Reoriented new shape

Deleting Sub-Objects

It is possible to delete any shape sub-objects by selecting the sub-objects and then clicking the delete button, or pressing Del, on the keyboard. The Edit Vertex, Edit Segment, and Edit Spline rollouts all contain a delete button.

Similar to detaching sub-objects, the Edit Spline modifier keeps a record of all sub-objects that you delete. You can restore the shape to its original form by deleting the Edit Spline modifier from the Modifier Stack.

Transforming Sub-Objects

Use the transform tools of Move, Rotate, and Scale with shape sub-objects the same as you use them with full objects. The special transforms of Mirror, Array, and Align, however, work only on full objects.

Choosing a sub-object transform center and transform coordinate system follows the same rules as for transforming objects with the exceptions of using Pivot Point center or the Local coordinate system. The behavior of sub-objects using these transform managers is as follows:

- **Pivot Point Center** Ignored for all sub-object coordinate system choices, except when transforming vertices with the Local coordinate system. In all other situations, Pivot Point center is the same as Selection center.

- **Local Coordinate System** Uses the World coordinate system and the World origin as the transform center, except when transforming vertices. In this reason, you should avoid using the Local coordinate system when you are transforming sub-object segments and splines.

Minimizing Edit Spline System Overhead

As mentioned previously, Edit Spline keeps a record of all sub-objects that you detach or delete. Edit Spline also records every change you make to every sub-object. This recording technique is what enables Edit Spline modifiers to exist anywhere in the Modifier Stack and is why you can delete an Edit Spline from the stack and have the object revert to its previous form. The price you pay for this flexibility is increased memory and file space usage.

General techniques for the use of Edit Spline include the following:

- **Use Edit Spline only if other methods do not work.** If you are contemplating changes at the spline Sub-Object level, you can often achieve the same result by applying an XForm or other modifier to the entire shape. This usually uses less memory than using Edit Spline.

- **Use Undo every time you change your mind while editing with Edit Spline.** Because Edit Spline records each change you make, the common habit of making many minor changes to zero in on the final result consumes a lot of memory.

- **Separate Edit Spline modifiers used for modeling from those used to pass sub-object selections up the stack.** Edit Spline modifiers used to pass selections up the stack use little memory and are useful for animating shapes.

- **Place Edit Spline modifiers used for modeling near the bottom of the Modifier Stack and collapse them when modeling is complete.** You cannot animate the modeling changes you make with Edit Spline. After you finish modeling the static form of the shape, collapse the Edit Spline modifiers to save memory.

The following example shows how much memory is consumed by moving a single vertex a few times and how you can conserve memory by using Undo:

1. Apply Edit Spline to a shape and save three copies of the file.

2. Leave one file alone so the Edit Spline contains no edits.

3. Open the second file, select a vertex, move the vertex multiple times, and drag the vertex handles a couple of times. Save the file.

4. Open the third file and perform the same edits, but use Undo between each change. The last move should place the vertex in approximately the same location as the last move in the previous file. Save the file.

5. Examine the file sizes and note the differences. In one case, the third file (using Undo) was only 1.5 KB larger than the unedited file, whereas the second file (no Undo) was 9.7 KB larger. That's an increase of 546 percent!

Edit Spline is a powerful tool, but you must use it carefully. Plan the steps you will use with Edit Spline. Use Undo regularly. Collapse the modifier when you finish modeling. Using these techniques can save a considerable amount of memory and improve the overall performance of 3DS MAX.

Editing at the Object Level

If you turn off Sub-object mode of an Edit Spline modifier, you can use two features at the object level. These features are found in the Edit Object rollout as shown in figure 9.16.

FIGURE 9.16
*Buttons in the
Edit Object
rollout of Edit
Spline.*

Using Attach

You use Attach to add other shapes to the selected shape with the Edit Spline modifier. Keep the following important points in mind when you use Attach:

■ The attached shape gives up its identity as a separate object. This means that the attached shape is collapsed into a simple Bézier Spline.

■ You can no longer access the attached shape's base parameters or any of the modifiers that were on the attached shape's Modifier Stack.

■ If the Reorient check box is unchecked, the attached shape stays where it is but becomes part of the selected shape.

■ If Reorient is checked, the attached shape moves and rotates so that its former pivot point and Local coordinate system match the position and orientation of the selected shape's pivot point.

Using Create Line

Click the Create Line button to begin drawing lines on the current construction plane. Any new lines you create are considered to be part of the selected spline. Because the new lines are part of the selected spline, this method is a convenient shortcut to create a line and then attach it to the shape.

The main difference between the regular Line tool and Create Line in Edit Shape is that you have no control over the creation vertex type when using Create Line. You always create a Bézier vertex when you drag and a Corner vertex when you click.

Editing at the Vertex Level

The first Sub-Object level in the Edit Spline sub-object list is Vertex. Choosing the Vertex Sub-Object level displays the Edit Vertex rollout of Edit Spline (see fig. 9.17).

FIGURE 9.17

Buttons in the Edit Vertex rollout of Edit Spline.

Working with Vertex Properties

You can control the curvature of your shapes by setting vertex properties. Select some vertices and right-click the selection to see the Vertex properties menu. You have four choices—Corner, Smooth, Bézier, and Bézier Corner—to set the curve type for a vertex; you may recognize the first three choices as the Creation Method options from the Line tool. The four choices are described in the following list and are illustrated in figure 9.18.

- **Corner**   Produces segments that are linear as they enter and leave the vertex.

- **Smooth**   Produces a curve through the vertex where the amount of curvature on either side of the vertex is equal. The tangent of a smooth vertex is always parallel to a line drawn between the two vertices to either side of the smooth vertex.

- **Bézier**   Produces a curve through the vertex with an adjustable tangent. Changes you make to the direction of the tangent and the amount (magnitude) of the curve are applied equally to both sides of the vertex.

- **Bézier Corner**   Produces an adjustable curve through the vertex that can have a sharp corner. Both the tangent direction and magnitude of the curve can be set independently for each side of the vertex.

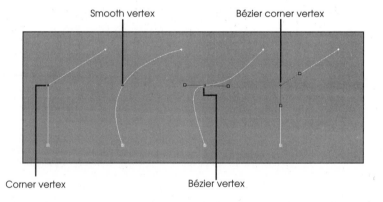

FIGURE 9.18
Shape vertex properties.

Smooth vertex   Bézier corner vertex

Corner vertex   Bézier vertex

You can easily convert from one vertex type to another. When you convert from a Bézier Corner vertex to a Bézier vertex, one handle is moved to align with the other handle. What you usually want is both handles to move so that they are averaged between the vertices on either side. That's the definition of a Smooth vertex. When you want to convert from Bézier Corner to Bézier, consider first converting to Smooth and then to Bézier. The result is usually a useful vertex.

Making a Vertex the First Vertex

Each spline within a shape contains a first vertex. The first vertex is used for many purposes and can be critically important in some situations. The first vertex is used as the following:

- The starting point for splines that are used as paths. Features that use shape splines as paths include Loft paths, Path controllers, Motion Trajectories, and Path Deform space warps. The initial condition or starting point for these features is set by the first vertex.

- The vertex ordering point for geometry. This is especially important for geometry generated from multiple shapes or shapes with multiple splines. The first vertex of each spline is used as the starting point for constructing the mesh. You can often improve the spacing and regularity of the generated mesh by aligning the first points.

To specify the first vertex of a spline, select a single vertex on a spline. If the spline is closed, you can select any vertex on the spline; if the spline is open, you must select one of the end points. Click Make First.

You can identify the first vertex by the small box drawn around it, as shown in figure 9.19.

FIGURE 9.19
Identifying the first vertex of a spline.

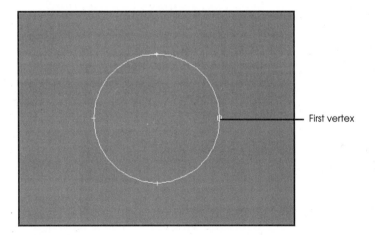

First vertex

Connecting Vertices

Use the Connect button to drag from one vertex to another to connect them with a segment. Both of the vertices must be located at the end of an open spline. The new segment always appears linear. You must change the vertex properties to make the segment appear curved.

Adding Vertices

You can choose from three different methods for adding vertices to a spline:

- **Insert**   Use Insert to build details or extensions off an existing spline. Click Insert and then click anywhere on a spline segment to insert a vertex into that segment. When you click, the new vertex remains attached to the cursor, and you can move it into position. At this point you have three options.

  The first option is to click to drop a corner vertex at its current location and insert another vertex following the new vertex. To perform the second option, drag to drop a Bézier vertex at the current location and insert another vertex following the new vertex. The remaining option is to right-click (or press Esc) to cancel the current vertex insert and exit the insert operation.

  Unlike other modes in 3DS MAX, you cannot exit Insert by clicking another button. You must right-click or press Esc to exit Insert.

- **Refine**   Use Refine to add extra vertices to a spline without changing its form. Click Refine and click anywhere on a spline segment to insert a Bézier vertex at that location. The direction and magnitude of the Bézier handles are automatically adjusted to preserve the original shape of the curve.

- **Break**   Use break to split apart spline segments by replacing a single vertex with two unconnected vertices in the same location. You first select vertices and then click Break. Each selected vertex is replaced by two unconnected vertices of the same type.

Welding Vertices

Although the Edit Vertex rollout contains only one Weld button, you can choose between two methods for welding vertices.

- Click Move and drag one end vertex to within about five pixels of another end vertex. When you release the drag, a dialog pops up asking if you want to weld the coincident vertices. This technique only works when dragging end vertices to other end vertices. The resulting vertex is always a Bézier Corner vertex except when both vertices were originally smooth vertices; then, the result is another smooth vertex.

- Select a group of vertices, set the Weld Threshold distance, and click Weld. Selected vertices within the weld threshold that meet the other weld restrictions weld at a single averaged point.

However, the following restrictions to welding vertices apply:

- End vertices can weld only to other end vertices.

- Vertices in the middle of a spline can weld only to other vertices on the same spline.

- Welded vertices in the middle of a spline cannot "skip over" a vertex. For example, you could never weld every other vertex of a spline.

Transforming Vertices

You can transform vertices, and the tangent handles of both types of Bézier vertices, by using the standard selection and transform tools on the toolbar. These types of transforms are static and cannot be animated.

As mentioned previously in this chapter, Pivot Point centers do not work when transforming vertices about any coordinate system other than Local. With other transform coordinate centers, Pivot Point centers behave the same as Selection center. When you choose the Local coordinate system, you are locked to using only Pivot Point centers (you can choose another center type, but the type always behaves as a Pivot Point center). Transforming vertices by using the Local transform coordinate center is very convenient when you are working with Bézier vertex tangent handles.

NOTE

Spline vertices cannot exist by themselves. They must always be part of a spline with at least one other vertex. Because of this restriction, you cannot use the Shift-Clone technique to copy vertices.

Transforming Bézier Vertex Handles

When you select vertices of the Bézier and Bézier Corner type, you also see their Bézier tangent handles. You can assume complete control over the direction and curvature of a segment by manipulating the tangent handles:

- **Tangent direction**   Each segment is tangent to its handle at the vertex location. If both handles are parallel, forming a straight line, the curve passes smoothly through the vertex. If neither handles form a straight line, the curve contains a kink, or sharp point, at the vertex location. Figure 9.20 shows tangent handles for both a smooth curve and a kinked curve.

  Bézier vertices are always smooth, with the tangent handles locked to form a straight line. Vertices in which the tangent handles form a kink are always Bézier Corner vertices.

- **Magnitude**   The length of a tangent handle sets the magnitude (degree of curvature) for its corresponding segment. The longer the handle, the greater the curvature of the segment. Figure 9.20 shows segments demonstrating both long and short tangent handles.

  Although technically incorrect, you may find it helpful to think of the length of the tangent handle as the radius of an arc. A long tangent handle creates an arc with a large radius as the segment leaves the vertex. An extreme amount of curvature is necessary to bend the segment back around to the direction of the next vertex.

FIGURE 9.20

Comparing tangent handle direction and length.

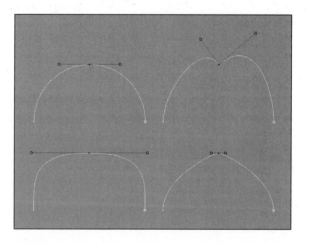

The most common way to transform vertex handles is to use the Move tool. To transform a tangent handle, drag on the green box at the end of the handle rather than on the vertex itself. Even if you have multiple vertices selected, you can drag only one tangent handle at a time. Dragging a tangent handle works in the following way:

- If the vertex is a Bézier type, dragging one handle affects both handles.

- If the vertex is a Bézier Corner type, you can drag each handle individually.

- Dragging parallel to the direction of the handle changes the handle's magnitude.

- Dragging perpendicular to the handle rotates the handle around the vertex, changing tangent direction.

- Pressing Shift while dragging converts a Bézier vertex to a Bézier Corner vertex so you can drag a single handle.

You can also drag the handles of a selection of vertices or lock Bézier Corner handles together by using the Lock Handles options (see fig. 9.21). The Lock Handles options rely on the concept of vertex order. Each spline stores its vertices in order, starting with the designated first vertex and progressing to the last vertex. The tangent handle is then identified as the incoming handle for the one pointing back to the previous vertex and the outgoing handle for the one pointing forward to the next vertex. You can't tell the difference by looking at them, but it makes a difference when using the Lock Handles Alike option.

FIGURE 9.21
The Lock Handles options in the Edit Vertex rollout.

The lock options of Alike and All behave differently depending on whether you are working with a selection of one or multiple vertices.

- Lock Handles All for a single vertex causes both handles of a Bézier Corner vertex to be affected by dragging either handle.

- Lock Handles All for multiple vertices causes all handles of all selected vertices to be affected by dragging a single handle.

- Lock Handles Alike for a single vertex has no effect because a single vertex has two handles, one incoming and the other outgoing, both different.

- Lock Handles Alike for multiple vertices causes the matching handle of all selected vertices to be affected by dragging an incoming or outgoing handle. This difference is noticeable only if the selected vertices are Bézier Corner vertices. For Bézier vertices, dragging either handle affects both.

- Press Shift while dragging with Lock Handles Alike to convert all selected vertices to Bézier Corner vertices.

A drawback of dragging tangent handles is that it is difficult to control the drag when you want only to change one property, such as direction. A handy solution is to rotate or scale a selection of vertices using the Local transform coordinate system.

- Rotating a vertex using the Local coordinate system rotates the tangent handles without affecting the magnitude of the curve.

- Scaling a vertex using the Local coordinate system changes the magnitude of the curve without changing the tangent direction.

Animating Vertex Transformations

None of the features of the Edit Spline modifier can be directly animated. You can animate the effect of transforming vertices, however, by passing selected vertices up the Modifier Stack to an XForm or Linked XForm modifier.

To animate vertex transformations:

1. Select vertices with Edit Spline.

2. Leave Sub-Object Vertex active and click the More button in the Modify panel.

3. Choose XForm from the Modifiers dialog.

   A yellow rectangle appears around the selected vertices. This is the XForm gizmo.

4. With Sub-Object Gizmo activated for the XForm modifier, turn on the Animate button and move, rotate, or scale the XForm gizmo.

   When you animate the XForm gizmo, it carries the selected vertices with it.

You can use this same technique to animate the effect of transforming vertex tangent handles:

1. Select a single vertex by using Edit Spline.

   If you want to animate tangent handles for more than one vertex, repeat this process for each vertex.

2. Leave Sub-Object Vertex active and click the More button in the Modify panel.

3. Choose XForm from the Modifiers dialog.

   The yellow XForm gizmo is placed around the single vertex, making it almost impossible to see.

4. With Sub-Object Gizmo active for the XForm modifier, click the Lock Selection Set button in the middle of the Status Line at the bottom of the 3DS MAX window.

   This selection enables you to drag anywhere on the screen to transform the Gizmo, rather than having to drag on the incredibly small Gizmo itself.

5. Turn on the Animate button, and rotate the Gizmo to animate the direction of the tangent handles. Scale the Gizmo to animate the magnitude of the tangent handles.

Editing at the Segment Level

The next sub-object editing level in the Edit Spline modifier is Segment. Choosing the Segment Sub-Object level displays the Edit Segment rollout of Edit Spline (see fig. 9.22). The Edit Segment rollout has far fewer options than the Edit Vertex rollout.

Detach and Delete have already been described for all Sub-Object levels at the beginning of the Edit Spline discussion. The remaining options are described in the following sections.

Breaking Segments

The Break button has an effect similar to Break in the Edit Vertex rollout, although you apply it somewhat differently. Instead of splitting two segments apart at a selected vertex, you are now able to split a segment into two pieces anywhere along the segment. After clicking Break, click anywhere on a segment to insert two unconnected vertices at the point you click.

Refining Segments

The Refine button is moonlighting from the Edit Vertex rollout and works exactly the same. Click Refine and then click a segment to insert a single vertex.

Working with Segment Properties

You can also control the curvature of segments by setting segment properties. Select some segments and right-click the selection to see the Segment properties menu. You have the following two choices for segment properties:

- **Curve**   Choosing Curve doesn't necessarily cause the segment to curve. Rather, this property causes the segment to follow the properties set for the vertices at either end of the segment. If the vertices are corner vertices, the segment appears linear; if the vertices are Smooth or Bézier, the segment appears curved.

- **Line**   Choosing Line causes the segment to ignore the vertex properties and create a straight line. You can tell when a segment is using the Line property because tangent handles for Bézier vertices at either end show an X rather than a box. The X indicates that the tangent handle is ignored by the segment, as shown in figure 9.23.

FIGURE 9.23
*Linear segments
ignore tangent
handles.*

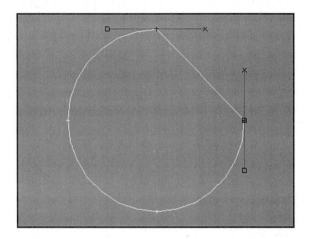

Using the Line segment property is a convenient way to flatten a segment without affecting the curvature of the segments to either side of it. You can get the same result by converting the vertices to Bézier corner vertices and then adjusting the tangent handles to make the segment linear, but this process requires a lot of work.

Transforming Segments

You can transform segments by using the standard selection and transform tools on the toolbar, including the Shift-Clone technique to make copies of segments. These types of transforms are static and cannot be animated.

If you want to animate the effect of transforming segments, you can use the XForm technique described previously for vertices.

As mentioned earlier in this chapter, Pivot Point centers do not work when transforming segments about any coordinate system. Also, choosing the Local coordinate system locks you into the World coordinate system with a World Origin center.

Editing at the Spline Level

The final Sub-Object level of Edit Spline is Spline. Choosing the Spline Sub-Object level displays the Edit Spline rollout of Edit Spline (see fig. 9.24).

Detach and Delete have already been described for all Sub-Object levels at the beginning of the Edit Spline discussion.

FIGURE 9.24

*Buttons in the
Edit Spline rollout
of Edit Spline.*

Closing Splines

This simple command draws a segment from the last vertex of an open spline back to the first. Select a spline and click Close.

Outlining Splines

Outlining a spline is a fast and convenient way to produce multiple, concentric copies of a closed spline or to produce a double-line version of an open spline. These copies are handy when you need to create outline text, hollow logos, or similar shapes. The Outline feature can be tricky at first, but after you get used to it, you see that it has a lot of flexibility.

Clicking the Outline button puts you into outline mode. As long as the button is active, you can continue to select and outline any spline in the selected shape. To exit Outline mode, click another button or right-click in the active viewport.

The Center check box determines how the outline is generated from the outline distance.

■ When unchecked, the original spline remains, and the outline is placed the Outline Width distance away from the original.

- When checked, the original spline is deleted, and two outlines are placed one-half the Outline Width's distance to either side of the original.

After you select a spline to outline, proceed with one of the following techniques:

- Drag the selected spline to define the outline location. As you drag, the outline appears. When you release the drag, the outline drops into place. When you drag a spline, you can define only a positive outline width— the outline can go in one direction only, and that direction is determined by the vertex order of the spline. Outlines for clockwise splines always drag out, away from the spline center; outlines for counterclockwise splines always drag in, toward the spline center. If the direction the outline takes is not the one you want, cancel the operation by right-clicking and use one of the other techniques.

- Drag the spinner next to the Outline Width field. You can drag the spinner to define both positive or negative outline widths. When you release the spinner, the outline drops into place, and the spinner value resets to 0.0. Do not click the spinner. Each click creates a new outlined spline.

- Type a value in the Outline Width field. When you press Enter, the outline is created, and the spinner is reset to 0.0.

The type-in method is convenient for setting precision outlines and for generating repetitive multiple outlines. For example, imagine you need to outline a letter multiple times with each outline being exactly 5 units away from the previous outline. This is easy using the type-in method:

1. Select the spline that forms the letter.

2. Click Outline.

3. Set Center to unchecked.

4. In the Outline Width field type **5**, press **Enter**, type **10**, press **Enter**, type **15**, and press **Enter**.

Each time you press Enter, an outline is created, and the Outline width field is reset. These steps create multiple outlines with a spacing of 5 units between each copy (see fig. 9.25).

FIGURE 9.25
*Creating
concentric
outlines.*

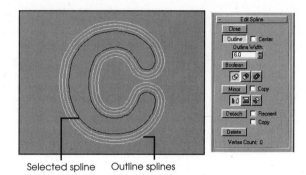

Selected spline   Outline splines

Boolean Operations

The Boolean command combines two source splines and always deletes both sources in the process of creating the Boolean spline.

Before you can perform a Boolean operation on splines, the source splines must meet the following requirements:

- Splines must be part of the same shape. You often need to attach one shape to another before you can Boolean the splines.

- Splines must be closed.

- Splines cannot intersect themselves.

- Splines must overlap. A spline completely enclosed within another is not considered an overlapping spline.

Beyond these restrictions, the Boolean command is a very easy and stable tool. Figure 9.26 shows examples of invalid and valid splines for Boolean operations.

To perform a Boolean operation between two splines, complete the following steps:

1. Select a single spline.

2. Click Boolean.

3. Click the Boolean operation type Union, Subtraction, or Intersection.

4. Click a second spline.

If your chosen operation was Subtraction, the second spline is always subtracted from the first.

FIGURE 9.26
Valid and invalid splines for Boolean operations.

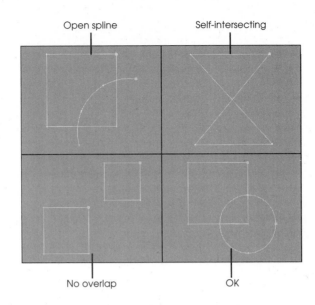

Open spline   Self-intersecting

No overlap   OK

Mirroring Splines

Mirroring splines produces results similar to those produced by using the Mirror object command on the toolbar. In both cases, you are flipping an object over one or two axes, with an option to copy at the same time.

Two important differences between mirroring splines and mirroring objects are as follows:

- Splines always mirror about their local centers regardless of the transform center option.

- Splines always mirror about the shape's local axes regardless of the transform coordinate system chosen.

To mirror a spline, complete the following steps:

1. Select a spline.

2. Set the Copy check box for whether or not you want to make a copy.

3. Click a Mirror axis button for the direction of the Mirror.

4. Click Mirror.

Each time you click Mirror, the selected splines flip about their local centers.

Transforming Splines

You can transform splines by using the standard selection and transform tools on the toolbar, including the Shift-Clone technique to make copies of splines. These types of transforms are static and cannot be animated.

If you want to animate spline transformations, you can use the XForm technique described previously for vertices.

As mentioned previously in this chapter, Pivot Point centers do not work when transforming splines about any coordinate system. Also, choosing the Local coordinate system locks you into the World coordinate system with a World Origin center.

Using Shape Modifiers

As with most objects in 3DS MAX, you can apply modifiers to shapes. Of course, the whole previous discussion about Edit Spline concerned a special-purpose modifier designed to work exclusively with shape objects, and the sections about animating Sub-Object transforms made use of the XForm modifier.

The modifiers that ship with 3DS MAX do one of two things when applied to a shape object: they modify the shape geometry leaving the shape still a shape, or they convert the shape to a mesh and modify the mesh geometry.

Applying Geometric Modifiers to Splines

Applying geometric modifiers to a shape is similar to applying a modifier to any other object. Figure 9.27 shows examples of applying modifiers to shapes. Applying and animating modifiers to shape objects opens up many modeling possibilities. Imagine the possibilities of animating a shape used to create a surface of revolution or animating a Loft path.

One important point to remember about applying modifiers to shapes is that most shapes are flat (or at least they start out flat); the shape has no dimension along its local Z axis. By coincidence, most modifiers default to acting on an object's local Z axis.

If you apply a modifier to a shape object and the modifier seems to have no effect, check the modifier's active axis. If the shape is a flat shape, set the active axis to X or Y.

FIGURE 9.27
Bending a helix and skewing text.

Converting Shapes to Flat Meshes

A common technique for modeling signs, surface patterns, or very thin objects is to convert a flat shape into a mesh. You may wonder why you wouldn't use a texture map in the case of signs and labels. Texture maps are great for most labels and signs, but if you need to view the label closely or need very sharp edges, creating flat geometry may be a more efficient choice.

Many modifiers convert a shape to a mesh object, the most obvious one being the EditMesh modifier. Other modifiers that you may consider using to convert shapes to meshes include any of the surface modifiers, such as Normal, Smooth, or Material. The surface modifiers are simple and don't carry the potential for memory overhead that the Edit Mesh does.

Extruding Splines

Use the Extrude modifier whenever you have a shape you want to extrude along a straight line. The next chapter describes how to create Loft objects that can extrude any number of shapes along almost any kind of spline. But for a single shape along a straight line, Extrude is your best choice.

You can extrude virtually any shape, including shapes with open splines that form sheets or ribbon-like surfaces. Some shapes, however, work better than others. For example, shapes with overlapping splines or splines that intersect can produce odd results when capping is turned on. Figure 9.28 shows examples of extruded shapes.

FIGURE 9.28

Examples of extruded shapes.

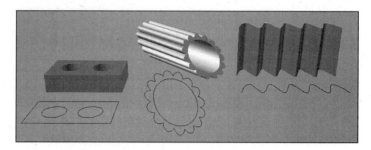

Your two primary concerns when extruding shapes are the Extrusion amount and the number of segments:

- **Amount**   Set the length of the extrusion as measured along the shape's local Z axis. Most shapes lie flat on their local XY plane, creating flat-topped extrusions. If you extrude shapes containing splines rotated off their local XY plane, you can create skewed or diagonal cut extrusions. Figure 9.29 shows the result of extruding a shape when you use Edit Spline to rotate one of the splines off the XY plane.

- **Segment**   Set the number of divisions along the length of the extrusion. Increase segments if you plan to bend or otherwise deform the extrusion with another modifier.

You can choose from the following options when extruding a shape:

- **Capping**   You can choose to cap either or both ends of the extrusion and choose between Morph or Grid capping methods. Morph capping uses fewer faces but does not deform as well as Grid capping. Morph capping is necessary if you plan to use variations of the extruded object as Morph targets.

- **Generation of Mapping Coordinates**   Checking this option applies mapping coordinates to the extruded sides for use with mapped materials. You need to manually apply mapping coordinates to the caps of the object.

- **Output**   Chooses whether the result of the extrusion should be a mesh object or a patch object. The proper choice is highly dependent on what you plan to do with the object. The default choice of Mesh should be appropriate for most purposes.

FIGURE 9.29
Extruding non-flat shapes.

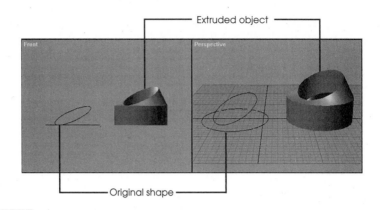

Lathing Splines

Apply Lathe to a shape object to generate a surface of revolution. Surfaces of revolution are also something that you can create as a Loft, but as with Extrude, if you are revolving a single shape around an arc, Lathe is a better choice.

Also (as with Extrude), you can Lathe virtually any shape. Figure 9.30 shows examples of lathed shapes.

FIGURE 9.30
Examples of lathed shapes.

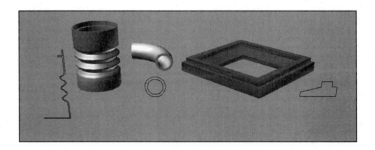

Your most important decisions when lathing shapes are setting the Lathe axis options and setting surface of revolution options.

Setting the Lathe Axis

The default location for the Lathe axis runs through the shape's creation center and is aligned with the shape's local Y axis. The creation center is the default location of the pivot point when the shape was created.

WARNING

Because of a bug in 3DS MAX, the Lathe axis appears to run through the pivot point of the shape but the actual Lathe center is located at the original creation center of the shape. The placement of the Lathe axis is correct only if you haven't manually moved the pivot point before applying the Lathe. Do not move the pivot point of a shape object if you plan to apply a Lathe modifier later. Otherwise, the Lathe axis will appear in the wrong place.

If you need to change the position of a spline with respect to a shape's pivot point, you are better off using Edit Spline to move the spline rather than using Adjust Pivot to move the pivot.

If you want to use something other than the default axis location, you have four choices:

- **Min** Click to locate the axis at the negative X axis boundary of the shape.

- **Center** Click to locate the axis at the geometric center of the shape. Depending on what type of editing you performed on the shape, the geometric center may or may not be the same as the default creation center.

- **Max** Click Max to locate the axis at the maximum X axis boundary of the shape.

- **Sub-Object** Click and manually move or rotate the axis to any place you want. You can also non-uniform scale the Lathe Axis to produce elliptical surfaces of revolution (see fig. 9.31). Usually you want to scale along the Lathe's active axis.

After you use any of these four methods to change the location of the Lathe axis, there is no guaranteed way to reset the axis to its default location. You must delete the Lathe modifier and reapply it if you want to return to the default axis location.

You can set the orientation of the Lathe axis by using the three orientation buttons. Click the X, Y, or Z button to align the Lathe axis with the Local axis of the selected shape. You need to consider the following issues when selecting the Lathe axis:

- The default orientation of the Lathe axis is aligned with the shape's local Y axis.

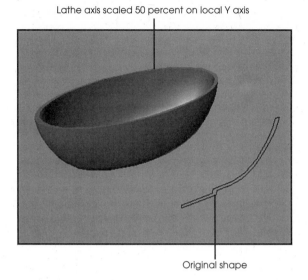

Lathe axis scaled 50 percent on local Y axis

FIGURE 9.31
*Result of scaling
a Lathe axis.*

Original shape

- If you choose to align the Lathe axis with the shape's local X axis, you cannot use the Min, Center, or Max buttons. You must manually move the Lathe axis if you align with the local X axis.

- Most shapes that you lathe are flat, making the Y axis and X axis your primary choices. Lathing about the Z axis is useful only if the shape does not lie flat on its local XY plane.

Controlling the Surface of Revolution

Three surface of revolution options control the degree of revolution and the complexity of the mesh generated:

- **Degrees** Sets the number of degrees of revolution. If you use values less than 360 degrees, you will probably want to check capping for both the start and the end of the lathe.

- **Segments** Sets the number of intermediate copies of the shape you want to create around the lathe. High segment values produce a smoother round lathe, whereas lower values produce rougher surfaces or even geometric frames.

  If you want a round shape, you usually need 16 segments or higher for 360 degrees of revolution. Lower values (between 4 and 8) are useful for creating regular geometric frames, as shown in figure 9.32.

- **Weld Core**   Core vertices are vertices of the shape that lie on the Lathe axis. Each core vertex of the shape is duplicated for each segment of the lathe, causing many vertices to "stack up" at the center of the lathed object and leading to rendering errors. Check Weld Core whenever a shape vertex lies on the Lathe Axis.

You may want to uncheck Weld Core when you are creating Morph targets and you need to preserve a predictable vertex count.

FIGURE 9.32
Using different segment settings.

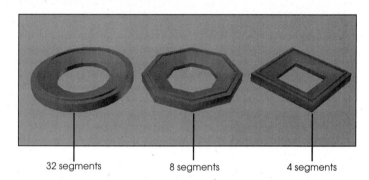

32 segments   8 segments   4 segments

Capping options and the choice between Mesh and Patch output is the same as for Extrude.

Lathe also includes the Generate UV Coordinates check box to apply mapping coordinates to the sides to the Lathed object. If you do not use a full 360 degrees, you need to manually apply mapping coordinates to the caps of the object.

Beveling Splines

A new modifier introduced for 3DS MAX R1.1 is the Bevel modifier. Use this modifier to both extrude and bevel a shape. The primary use for this modifier is the creation of classic beveled text and logo treatments, as shown in figure 9.33.

Just as with Extrude and Lathe, you can create beveled objects as lofts. For most classic bevel situations, the Bevel modifier is your best choice.

Your main considerations when beveling a shape include:

- Setting Bevel values.
- Choosing edge treatment.
- Cleaning up edge intersections.

FIGURE 9.33
Beveled text and logos.

Setting Bevel Values

Create the beveled object by setting the following bevel values:

- **Levels**   All beveled objects require a minimum of two levels, a start, and an end. The Start Outline field is the only parameter for the start level. Think of the start level as being Level 0. Level 1 is the default end level for a two-level object. You can optionally enable two more levels for a total of four levels. The highest numbered level used is always considered the end level.

The classic bevel treatment uses all four levels. Figure 9.34 shows a classic bevel and identifies one possible level arrangement.

FIGURE 9.34
Four levels for a classic bevel.

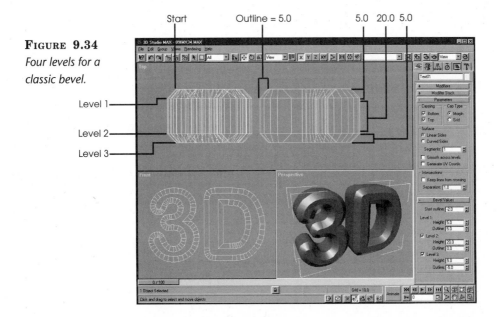

■ **Outline** Specifies how much larger or smaller a level is, compared to the previous level's shape. The value represents the distance in current units from the edge of the previous shape to the edge of an outlined copy of the shape. The start outline represents the difference between the start shape and the original shape.

The key to setting outline values is to remember that the value always represents the change from the previous shape. For example, a classic beveled object with a 5.0-unit bevel uses the following outline values:

Start Outline: 0.0 (no change from original shape)

Level 1 Outline: 5.0 (bevel out 5.0 units)

Level 2 Outline: 0.0 (hold the same size as Level 1)

Level 3 Outline: –5.0 (bevel back to the original shape)

Looking at the preceding list, you see the basic rules for creating classic four-level bevels:

The Start Outline sets the base size of the bevel.

Levels 1 and 3 are the same value but have opposite signs.

If you want a 45-degree bevel, the Height for Level 1 and Level 3 is positive and equal to the Outline value.

Level 2 is always zero.

Recognizing that the Start Outline sets the base size of an object, you can set up the bevel conditions for levels 1, 2, and 3 and then experiment with the overall size of the object by changing the Start Outline.

■ **Height** Sets the distance from the previous level to the current level as measured along the shape's local Z axis. For classic bevels, the Height values are always positive and usually equal. You can create interesting bevel variations by combining positive and negative highest values. Figure 9.35 shows an object with the following bevel values:

Start Outline: 3.0

Level 1 Outline: 0.0, Height: 20.0 (rises straight up, no bevel.)

Level 2 Outline: –5, Height: 0.0 (creates a flat top 5.0 units wide)

Level 3 Outline: 0.0, Height: –5.0 (sinks into the shape 5.0 units.)

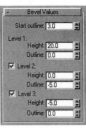

FIGURE 9.35
Effect of combining positive and negative height values.

Choosing Edge Treatment

The options in the Surface area of the Parameters rollout set how the edge surfaces are treated. The options primarily control whether the sides are flat, chamfered sides or smooth, rounded sides:

- **Linear or Curved Sides** Choose the option for the type of side interpolation you want. Curved Sides uses a spline curve to interpolate from one level to the next. You must set Segments greater than 1 to see the effect of choosing Curved Sides.

- **Segments** Increase the segments if you are using Curved Sides or plan to deform the object with another modifier.

- **Smooth Across Levels** Applies smoothing groups to smooth the side faces of the object. Bevel never tries to smooth from the sides into the face of the object. Check this option if you are using Curved Sides or multiple segments.

The options for UV (Mapping) coordinates and capping are typical for all objects, with a small exception for the meaning of Top and Bottom capping. Most capped objects are labeled Start and End. The objects don't care about the spatial relationship of the caps. Bevel checks the local Z axis heights of the start level and the end level. Checking Top caps the level with the greatest local Z axis value, whereas checking Bottom caps the level with the least local Z axis value.

Cleaning Up Intersections

A common problem with beveling text shapes occurs on serifs and where the shape comes to a point sharper than 90 degrees. When a bevel is applied, these areas tend to "shoot off" to great distances and intersect other parts of the object, as shown in figure 9.36.

FIGURE 9.36
*Problem
intersections on
beveled objects.*

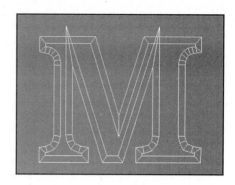

Employ one of two techniques to correct problem intersections. Use the Bevel modifier Intersection parameters or manually edit the shape.

The options in the Intersections area of the Parameters rollout automatically prevent levels from intersecting.

Check the Keep lines from crossing check box to turn on intersection checking.

Enter a value in the Separation field to set the minimum distance to be maintained between edges. You can set this value as small as 0.01 units, creating a bevel that appears to come to a point. Figure 9.37 shows the result of checking Keep lines from crossing for the previous beveled object with crossing intersections.

FIGURE 9.37
*Using the Keep
lines from
crossing option.*

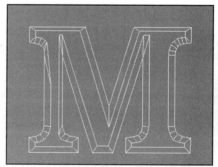

NOTE

The Keep lines from crossing option can take considerable time to calculate all the intersection constraints, especially with complex serif letters. After you have the bevel set the way you want, you may want to consider collapsing the Modifier Stack to convert the bevel to a mesh and prevent the need to recalculate.

You can also manually fix many intersection problems by using Edit Spline. Most intersection problems are caused by shape edges coming to a sharp point. If you flatten the point, even by a small amount, you can fix many bevel intersection problems.

Use the following technique to manually fix crossing intersections:

1. Apply a Bevel modifier to a shape and identify the crossing intersections.

2. Apply an Edit Spline modifier below the Bevel modifier.

3. Use Refine to add a vertex to both sides of the problem corner.

4. Delete the corner vertex.

5. You can optionally set the segment between the two new vertices to linear.

6. Choose the Bevel modifier from the Modifier Stack and check the results.

Figure 9.38 shows the object in figure 9.37 after applying this technique.

FIGURE 9.38
Manually correcting intersections.

Delete this vertex ——

Add vertices using Refine ——

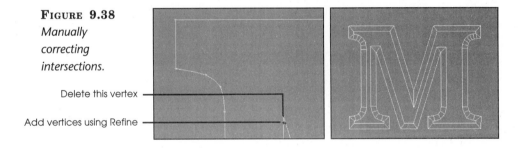

Bevel also includes the Generate UV Coordinates check box to apply mapping coordinates to the sides of the beveled object. You need to manually apply mapping coordinates to the caps of the object.

In Practice: Modeling with Shapes

- **Shapes are used as components for other objects.** Shapes do not render as visible surfaces. A shape is always modified or used as a Sub-Object to define a visible 3D surface. Shapes can also be used to define animation paths.

- **Text shapes can be edited as text or geometry.** You can change the parameters of a text shape to edit spelling and change fonts. You can also apply modifiers to text shapes to deform them like geometry.

- **Attached shapes are non-parametric.**   If you attach shapes, or use the Start New Shapes button, to build shapes containing multiple splines the attached shapes give up their parametric properties.

- **Shape interpolation settings affect object complexity.** Your choices for shape interpolation have a great impact on the face density of objects generated from the shape. Carefully consider your choices for shape steps setting and other interpolation parameters.

- **Collapse Edit Spline modifiers.**   Edit Spline modifiers can generate enormous memory overhead. Once you are certain that you want your Edit Spline Sub-Object changes to be permanent, collapse the Edit Spline modifier. Collapsing the modifier saves memory and improves system performance.

- **Animate shape sub-objects using the XForm modifier.**   Shape sub-objects cannot be directly animated. Use an Edit Spline modifier to define a Sub-Object selection and then apply an XForm modifier to the selection. You can then animate the XForm gizmo.

Created by Andrew Murrall
Murrall & Lang
West Midlands, England

Chapter 10

BUILDING LOFT OBJECTS

Loft objects are some of the most complex and interesting types of objects you can build in 3D Studio MAX. You create loft objects by combining any of the cross-section shapes with a single path shape. Because everything about creating loft objects is dependent on the source shape that you use, it would be helpful to read Chapter 9, "Modeling with Shapes,"—if you haven't already done so.

This chapter presents the following discussions about creating loft objects:

- Strategies for creating source shapes

- Two ways to create the initial loft object

- How to build the loft by adding additional shapes

- Controlling loft parameters for detail and appearance

- Using special loft deformation tools

- Editing the loft

- Animating the loft

- Using Fit Deformation

Before you proceed with creating loft objects, you should be familiar with the basic concepts behind creating lofts.

Concepts of Creating Loft Objects

During the life of 3D Studio MAX, the description of building a ship's hull as an analogy for lofting has been used repeatedly. Yes, the loft path can be thought of as a keel and the loft shapes as the ribs of the hull arranged along the keel. Unfortunately, this description implies a limited approach to lofting that doesn't do justice to the modeling options available with Loft objects.

Another way of looking at the lofting process is to examine the way industrial designers or sculptors build up study models. These professionals use a form of spatial sketching to build three-dimensional models by arranging lines in space. The lines usually take the form of cross sections of the object and are held in place by a central core. As the design progresses, a surface is formed by filling the spaces between the cross sections with a sculpting material (like clay) or by stretching a skin over the cross sections (like plaster soaked cloth).

Creating Loft objects works much the same way. You create a central core (the path) to support any number of cross sections (the shapes). As you edit the path and the shapes, you can use the loft surface parameters to display the surface in both wireframe and shaded form.

Loft Terminology

Loft objects employ special terminology along with the basic terms used to describe Shape objects. The following definitions review shape terminology as applied to Loft objects and introduce new, loft-specific terms. Detailed definitions for shape terms are presented in Chapter 9.

- **Vertices**   Defines cross-sectional shapes and paths. Vertices can have the properties of corner, smooth, and two types of Bézier. Vertices also have special meaning for paths as they define path levels.

- **Segments**   The part of the spline between two vertices. You control the curvature of spline segments by changing the properties of the vertices at either end of the segment or by changing the properties of the segment itself.

- **Steps**   The number of segment divisions used to represent a curve. The number of steps you use defines the smoothness and mesh density of the loft surface. Lofts use their own step settings for the path and cross section shapes, ignoring the interpolation settings of the shapes themselves.

- **Splines**   A collection of connected segments. Splines are a type of smooth adjustable curve, but 3DS MAX includes options for inserting corners and defining linear segments.

- **Shapes**   A collection of splines defines a shape object. A path shape can contain only a single spline. Cross section shapes can contain any number of splines as long as all cross section shapes on the path contain the same number of splines. In a loft, shapes become sub-objects.

- **Paths**   Describes the one shape that defines the central core of the loft.

- **Level**   Intermediate positions along the loft path. At the very least, each vertex on the path defines a level. Shape locations and deformation curve control points can also define additional levels.

- **Control Point**   Vertices on the deformation curves. Control points appear and behave like shape vertices with a few added restrictions on their use.

- **Deformation Curve** Defines the basic form of a loft by placing shapes on the path. Allows you to further modify the loft using deformation curves to adjust scale, angle, and size of the shapes.

- **First Vertex** All shapes have a first vertex. 3DS MAX builds the loft surface by matching the first vertices of each shape on the path and stretching the skin from the first vertex to the last vertex. You can gain control of this process by choosing how the first vertices line up.

Creating Source Shapes for Cross Sections and Paths

You can use virtually any shape as a source for a cross section shape or a path. By observing a few restrictions and suggested techniques, you can greatly improve your success at creating source shapes for lofts.

Path shapes have only one restriction—path shapes can contain only a single spline. 3DS MAX refuses to accept any shape containing more than one spline as a path (such as a donut). If you are trying to create a loft and 3DS MAX won't accept the shape you want to use as the path, check to make sure that the path you want is not part of a shape with multiple splines.

Two restrictions apply to cross section shapes. All the shapes on the path must contain the same number of splines, which is not as restrictive as you might think. You can easily make what appears to be a single shape split into multiple shapes by building the "single shape" out of a series of unconnected splines. Figure 10.1 shows a fork that uses this technique. The shapes that make up the handle of the fork are made of two splines. One spline each for the left and right side enables the loft to split when it reaches the tines of the fork.

All shapes on the path must have the same nesting order. If the first shape on the path contains two splines inside another spline, then all shapes on the path must contain two splines inside another. You can get around this restriction by opening the outer spline. Open splines, even if their endpoints are touching, do not nest. The odd object in figure 10.2 shows the use of this technique. The outer rectangle of the loft shape has been opened by breaking a corner vertex using the Edit Spline modifier.

FIGURE 10.1
Splitting a single shape into multiple shapes.

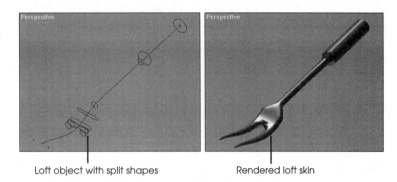

Loft object with split shapes   Rendered loft skin

FIGURE 10.2
Changing nesting order.

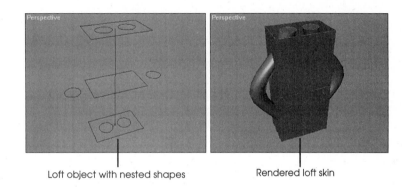

Loft object with nested shapes   Rendered loft skin

Both methods mentioned for avoiding restrictions on the spline number and the nesting order involve using shapes containing open splines. The main drawback to using open splines is that they cannot be capped using the loft capping parameters. If you need to cap loft objects with open splines, consider using the following techniques:

■ Create other objects to serve as caps and then group, link, or attach the objects to the loft.

■ Apply an Edit Mesh modifier to the loft and manually build faces to create a cap. Use of the Edit Mesh modifier is discussed in Chapter 12, "Sub-Object Modeling."

■ Use loft scale deformation to abruptly scale the loft shape down to zero percent at the ends of the loft. Loft scale deformation is discussed in the section "Using Scale Deformation" later in this chapter.

The following sections introduce other techniques to make your loft modeling more successful.

Transforming Shapes

A great source of confusion when creating loft objects concerns the effects of transforms applied to the source shapes. Transforms applied to shapes at the object level are ignored when the shape is added to a loft object.

With the exception of moving or rotating the first shape used to create a loft, shape transforms are not part of the loft. Chapter 1, "Core Concepts of 3D Studio MAX," discusses the object dataflow and how information about the object progresses from the base parameters through the modifiers, on to transforms, and finally to space warps. When you use a shape in a loft, the dataflow for that shape splits off after shape modifiers and before the shape transforms. Transforms such as Move, Rotate, and Scale do not travel with the shape into the loft.

Use the following two rules when applying transformations to shape objects that will be used as loft shapes:

- Use Move and Rotate to place shapes in convenient locations in your scene. Keep in mind that moving or rotating a shape has no effect on how the shape behaves in a loft.

- Never scale a shape! This is good advice for just about any object but is especially important for shapes used in lofts. The scale factor is not carried into the loft. The shape appears in the loft using its original non-scaled size.

If you need to Move, Rotate, or Scale a shape as part of the loft design, you have several options.

- **Change base parameters**   Many scale functions can be handled by changes to a shape's parameters. Change the radius of a circle or the height of a helix rather than using scale.

- **Apply an XForm modifier**   Any time you want to Move, Rotate, or Scale an object as part of a modeling operation use an XForm modifier. Because an XForm is a modifier, it carries the effect of a move, rotate, or scale operation into the loft.

- **Use Loft Sub-Object mode**   You can Move, Rotate, or Scale a shape as a sub-object operation within the loft. Click the Sub-Object button and transform shapes on the loft path. These transforms are carried within the loft.

- **Apply an Edit Spline modifier**   Using Edit Spline Sub-Object mode you can Move, Rotate, or Scale sub-objects such as vertices and splines.

Which technique you employ depends on your modeling style and what you are trying to do with the loft. In any case, do not transform shapes at the object level and expect the transform to show up in the loft.

Creating Shapes In-Place

You can create source shapes for Loft objects in any viewport and any orientation. Lofts are assembled using the Local coordinate systems of the source shapes, so 3DS MAX really doesn't care in which viewport the shapes are created. However, you might find it helpful to follow a few techniques for laying out loft shapes in a predictable manner.

The generation of the loft surface begins at the first vertex of the path and progresses to the end vertex. Shapes are placed on the path so that their local Z axis is tangent to the path and pointing in the direction of the path end. What you might consider to be the face or front of the shape is pointing to the end of the path.

Using this information, you can form a couple of helpful rules:

■ Draw the path shape from the base of the loft object to its top; in the case of horizontal objects, draw the path from the back of the object to the front.

■ Draw shapes in the viewport that most closely matches the top or front view of the loft object.

Drawing the path and the cross section shapes all in the same view can make it difficult to predict how the shapes and the path will align. Use different views for creating the shapes and the path. The following examples help to illustrate this concept.

Imagine that you want to loft a simple column. The column's base and capital use squares and the rest of the column uses a circle. Most columns (unless you are modeling ruins) stand vertically on the ground plane. A good approach to laying out the shapes for the column is to do the following:

1. Create the path for the column in the Front view. Start at the bottom of the viewport, near the ground plane, and finish near the top.

2. Create the cross section shapes in the Top view. Creating the cross section shapes in the Top view orients the face of the shapes in the same direction as the top of the column.

Next, loft some text next to the column. In this case, the path runs horizontally. Lay out the lofted text in the following manner:

1. Create the path in the Top view running from back to front. Start near the top of the viewport (the back) and finish toward the bottom of the viewport (the front).

2. Create the text in the Front view. Again, this orients the face of the text shape toward the front of the loft.

With some practice, you can quickly get the feel for how shapes and paths work together and confidently predict the orientation of Loft objects.

Changing the Cross Section Shape Pivot Point

When you add cross section shapes to a Loft object, the shape is placed with the path running through the shape's pivot point location. You can preset where the path intersects a cross section shape by moving the shape's pivot point.

For example, imagine you are lofting a series of stars along a path, and you want the path to pass through the top point of each star. You use the Affect Pivot Only button in the Hierarchy panel to move the pivot of each star before adding it to the loft. When you use Get Shape to add the stars to the loft, the path passes through the shape's pivot location. Figure 10.3 shows a loft shape with its original pivot location and what happens if you change the pivot location and get the shape a second time.

The pivot location is examined only at the time the shape is added to the loft. Changing a shape's pivot point after the shape is added to a loft has no effect.

FIGURE 10.3

Changing the pivot location for loft shapes.

The pivot point orientation of a shape is also ignored by the loft. Rotating a shape's pivot point has no effect when the shape is added to a loft. If you want to rotate a shape with respect to its local coordinate system and have that rotation show up in the loft, you must rotate the shape at the sub-object level.

Loft Creation Methods

Once you have created your source shapes, you are ready to create the Loft object. Access the Loft Creation Methods by clicking the Geometry button in the Create panel and choosing Loft Object from the category list. If you have not selected a shape, the Loft button is inactive. Once you select a shape, you can click the Loft button to display the Creation Methods rollout as shown in figure 10.4.

FIGURE 10.4

Accessing the Loft Creation methods.

The first two shapes you use to create the loft must be the path shape and a cross section shape. After those, you can continue to add more cross section shapes or even replace the path shape. The basic steps involved in creating a loft object are:

1. Create your source shapes.

2. Select a shape to start the loft.

3. This first shape is very important because it sets the position and orientation of the loft object.

4. Access the loft object Creation Methods.

5. Get a path or a cross section shape.

Your choices in this rollout set the shape clone method and determine whether you are starting with a path or a cross section shape.

Starting with the Shape First

If you want to start with the selected shape as the first cross section on the path, you must click the Get Path button to select a path shape. Click Get Path when you want to build the loft using the position and orientation of a selected cross section shape. When you click Get Path, you are put into a pick mode in which you can select only a single shape. The cursor changes to display the Get Path cursor whenever it is positioned over a valid path shape. Clicking a shape when the Get Path cursor is displayed accepts that shape as the Loft path.

The shape picked as the path is moved to the pivot point and rotated to align with the selected shape's original local coordinate system. Use this technique when you have created, or aligned, a shape exactly where you want to locate the base of the loft. Then, use Get Path to bring the path to the shape.

For example, you might want to loft a docking hatch projecting from the side of a space ship. Create the outline shape of the docking hatch and use Normal Align to align the shape with the surface of the ship. Use Get Path to begin building the loft at the shape's location. Figure 10.5 shows the steps used for this example.

Starting with the Path First

If you want to start with the selected shape as the path, you must click the Get Shape button to select a cross section shape. Click Get Shape when you want to build the loft using the position and orientation of a selected path shape.

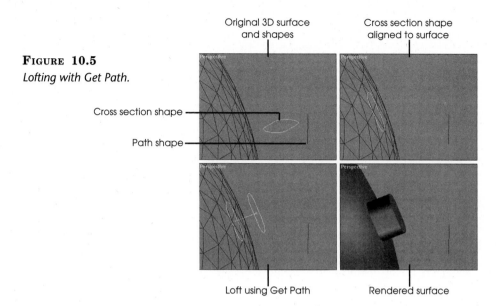

Original 3D surface
and shapes

Cross section shape
aligned to surface

FIGURE 10.5

Lofting with Get Path.

Cross section shape

Path shape

Loft using Get Path

Rendered surface

When you click Get Shape, you are put into a pick mode in which you can select only a single shape. The cursor changes to display the Get Shape cursor whenever it is positioned over a valid cross section shape. When you first create a Loft object, every shape is a valid cross section shape; only when you add more shapes to the path do you begin to see invalid cross section shapes (see the section "Adding Shapes to the Path" later in this chapter). Clicking a shape when the Get Shape cursor is displayed accepts that shape as a cross section on the path.

NOTE

Occasionally, you begin creating a loft and find that the Get Shape button is inactive. This happens only when your initial selected shape is invalid as a path shape. For example, if you select a donut shape and click Loft, your only choice is Get Path because the donut contains two splines and is, therefore, invalid as a path. Either click Get Path and pick a path shape or cancel the Loft creation process to start with a different shape.

The shape picked as the cross section is moved and rotated to align with the selected path. Use this technique when you have created, or aligned, a path shape exactly where you want to locate the loft. Then, use Get Shape to bring cross sections to the path. For example, you might want to loft a spring for a coil-over shock absorber. Create a helix as the spring path and position it around the shock absorber cylinder. Use Get Shape to bring a cross section to the path. Figure 10.6 shows the steps used for this example.

NOTE

When using both Get Path and Get Shape, you can flip the default shape alignment by pressing Ctrl while picking a shape. If your first attempt at getting a path or cross section shape comes in with an undesired orientation, press Ctrl and get the shape again.

FIGURE 10.6
Lofting with Get Shape.

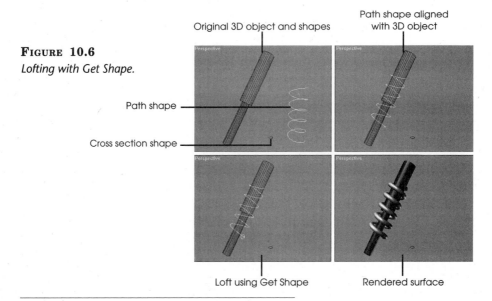

Original 3D object and shapes

Path shape aligned with 3D object

Path shape

Cross section shape

Loft using Get Shape

Rendered surface

Choosing the Clone Method

When you bring shapes into the loft, you can decide whether the shape is absorbed into the loft, or whether it is cloned as a copy or an instance. The choice you make affects how you edit the loft later on. Don't worry too much about making a wrong choice; 3DS MAX contains plenty of options you can use if you change your mind later.

Instancing the First Shape

You must select a shape object before you can click Loft. Your choices after clicking Loft determine whether that selected shape becomes the path or the first cross section shape. Regardless of what you do, an instance of the selected shape is placed inside the loft.

The loft and your original shape occupy the same space in your scene. If you move the loft to a different place in the scene, the original shape is left behind.

After creating a loft, you should consider moving the original shape to a new location to make it easier to find. Moving the original shape also prevents you from accidentally selecting both the loft and the shape when you want to modify only the loft.

Choosing Move, Instance, or Copy

When you use the Get Path or Get Shape buttons to add shapes to the loft, you can choose whether the added shapes are moved, copied, or instanced into the loft.

- **Move**   The original shape is moved into the loft and ceases to exist as an independent object. Once a shape is moved into a loft, the only way to edit the shape is through the Loft Sub-Object mode. While Move might seem to be an attractive choice for keeping your scene uncluttered, it can lead to difficulties when you want to edit the shape later. Use Move only if you are reasonably sure you will not need to make any more changes to the shape.

- **Copy**   The copy of the original shape that is placed in the loft. The copy and the original do not share any connections. You should avoid using this choice for the same reason you avoid using Move. The only difference is that Copy leaves the original shape in the scene to use with other objects.

- **Instance**   An instance of the original shape is placed in the loft. Any change you make later to the original shape is also reflected in the instance inside the loft. Instance is the default, and preferred, way of adding shapes to a loft. If you need to edit the loft shapes, you can edit the instances instead and watch the changes appear on the loft. A loft and its instances can eventually clutter your scene. You can avoid this clutter by hiding the shapes or deleting them once you finish modeling the loft.

Moving from the Create Panel to the Modify Panel

After you have created the basic loft (a path with a single shape) you can proceed to add more shapes and change the surface and skin parameters, although it is usually more convenient to move to the Modify panel to complete the loft. You should use whatever technique you find most comfortable, but using the Modify panel has the following advantages:

- You don't have to worry about dropping out of creation mode if you click a transform or some other button on the toolbar.

- The Modify panel displays the Loft Parameters anytime the loft is selected.

- You can use Sub-Object mode only in the Modify panel.

- You can use Loft deformations only in the Modify panel.

The Modify panel gives you a more stable environment, with more features, to finish your loft. Figure 10.7 compares Loft Parameters in both the Create and Modify panels.

Building Lofts with Multiple Shapes

You can create many Loft objects using a single shape on a path, but many more interesting and complex objects can be created by placing multiple shapes on a path, as shown in figure 10.8.

The following sections present the commands and techniques you need to know to successfully build lofts with multiple shapes. The main issues involve adding shapes at specified locations on the path, using shapes of differing form, and a technique for making one shape appear to split into two shapes.

FIGURE 10.7
Comparing Loft parameters in the Create and Modify panels.

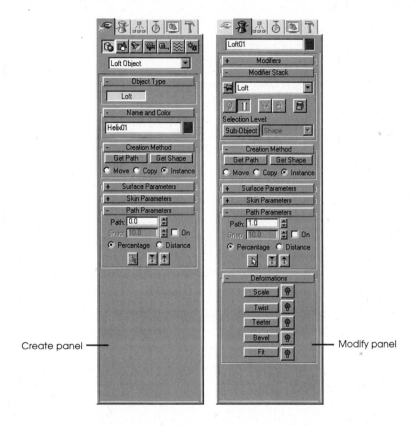

Create panel —   — Modify panel

FIGURE 10.8
Objects created by placing multiple shapes on the path.

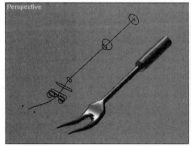
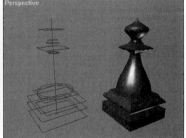

Adding Shapes to the Path

You can add shapes to a loft while you are still in creation mode, or at a later time by selecting the loft and accessing its parameters in the Modify panel. The basic procedure for adding shapes to the loft path is as follows:

1. Set the current path level in the Path Parameters rollout to specify where on the path the shape will be added.

2. Click Get Shape in the Creation Methods rollout.

3. Set the clone method for Move, Copy, or Instance.

4. Pick a shape.

Setting the Path Level

Set where on the path a shape is added using the options in the Path Parameters rollout (see fig. 10.9). The current path level is represented by a small X on the path.

You set the current path level by entering a value in the Path field. This value can be specified as a percentage of the path length or as an absolute distance along the path. Set which method is used by choosing the Percentage or Distance radio buttons in the Path Parameters rollout.

- Choose Percentage to enter a value between 0 and 100 percent of the path length.

- Choose Distance to enter a value in current units to specify the distance measured from the first vertex of the path.

Regardless of which method you use to add a shape to the path, the shape is always stored using the percentage method. If you change the length of the path, the shapes move to maintain their percentage on the path, even if they were placed by absolute distance.

You may encounter situations in which you want to know the length of a spline. Using the Path Parameters rollout for Lofts is currently the only way to read a spline's length in 3DS MAX.

FIGURE 10.9

*Options in the Path
Parameters rollout.*

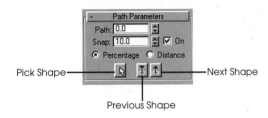

Pick Shape ——

—— Next Shape

Previous Shape

To measure the length of a spline:

1. Make a copy of the shape you want to measure.

2. Select the shape and click Loft in the Create panel.

3. Click Get Shape and click any shape in the scene.

    You can even select the same shape again.

4. Choose the Distance option in Path Parameters and drag the Path
    spinner to its maximum value.

    The value in the Path field is the length of the Path.

In both Distance mode and Percentage mode you can check the Snap check
box to specify a Distance or Percentage snap value. Unfortunately, there is
no way to snap to vertices on the path.

Using Get Shape

After you set the path level, click Get Shape to pick a shape to place at that
level. When you click Get Shape, you are put into a pick mode in which you
can pick one shape at a time. The cursor changes to display the Get Shape
cursor whenever it is positioned over a valid cross section shape. Valid
shapes are defined as shapes that contain the same number of splines and
same nesting order as the first shape used to create the loft.

If you use Get Shape at a level where a shape already exists on the path, the
new shape replaces the current shape.

If you change your mind and decide to use shapes with a different number
of splines or a different nesting order, you must first delete all the current
shapes from the path.

Navigating Path Levels

After you have placed some shapes on the path, you can use the remaining three buttons on the Path Parameters rollout to navigate to path levels containing shapes.

- **Next Shape**   Moves forward along the path to the level of the next shape.

- **Previous Shape**   Moves backward along the path to the level of the previous shape.

- **Pick Shape**   Click any shape on the path to jump to the level of that shape.

The main reason to use these navigation controls is to quickly jump to a shape's level to replace that shape with a Get Shape operation.

Changing from One Form to Another

Usually, creating a Loft object involves placing multiple shapes of varying forms on the path. For example, you might loft a screwdriver using a combination of circles, squares, and custom shapes. You can place shapes of almost any form on the path and 3DS MAX will figure out how to generate a surface between them.

The following two techniques will help you exercise control over how the surface is generated.

Matching the First Vertex

3DS MAX builds the loft surface by matching the first vertex of each shape on the path. If the first vertices are not aligned, there is a twist in the surface as the edges shift from vertex to vertex. Figure 10.10 shows two Loft objects to compare the difference between misaligned and aligned first vertices.

Two ways of aligning the first vertices of your Loft shapes are as follows:

- Apply an Edit Spline to each shape. Use the Make First button in the Edit Vertex rollout to assign a new first vertex that aligns with the other shapes. See Chapter 9 for information about using Edit Spline.

- Enter the Loft's Shape Sub-Object mode in the Modify panel. Select shapes on the path and rotate them until their vertices align. Transforming shapes at the Sub-Object level is discussed later in this chapter.

FIGURE 10.10

Results of lofting with misaligned versus aligned first vertices.

Misaligned first vertices ———

Aligned first vertices ———

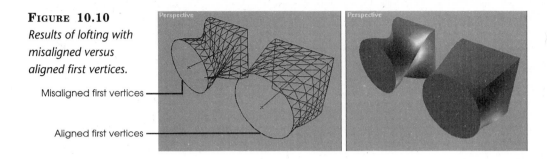

Sometimes you need to combine both of these techniques to achieve the result you want.

Matching Vertices

You do not need to have the same number of vertices in each cross section shape used in the loft object. 3DS MAX can interpolate between shapes with varying numbers of vertices. This feature is extremely helpful while you are building the loft object, but usually you want to match vertex counts and vertex positions between shapes to gain the maximum amount of control over the loft surface.

When shapes on the path are irregular or have widely varying vertex counts, the loft skin can twist and stretch in unpredictable ways. Such twisting of the loft skin can lead to rendering anomalies and difficulty when modifying the loft with other modifiers. Figure 10.10 shows how the loft surface twists when using irregular shapes with varying vertex counts.

You cannot expect to limit your loft modeling to regular shapes, or shapes that all share the same vertex count, but you can analyze the loft skin after creating the loft to decide where you might want to edit your shapes to improve the surface. Your main technique for improving the loft skin involves inserting vertices into the loft shapes to control how the skin is generated.

Figure 10.11 shows a loft object that uses two very irregular shapes. The object on the left uses 3DS MAX defaults to interpolate from the four vertices in the circle to the 12 vertices in the cross. The interpolation creates a slightly irregular surface on the left object. The object on the right uses Edit Spline to add vertices to the circle that match the vertices in the cross. The right object has a more regular surface.

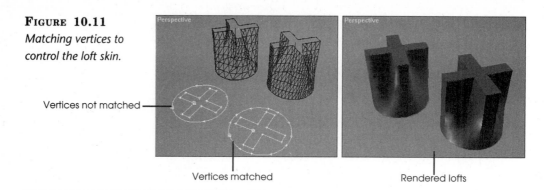

FIGURE 10.11
Matching vertices to control the loft skin.

Vertices not matched

Vertices matched

Rendered lofts

Combining Open and Closed Shapes

You can also loft objects using shapes that transition from open to closed. This technique is useful for modeling objects with slits or ruptures in their surfaces. Keep the following points in mind when combining open and closed shapes in the same loft:

- All shapes in the loft must contain the same number of splines. A closed shape is a single spline. If your open shape has only one opening then it is also a single spline.

- If you want to use shapes with multiple openings, you must divide the closed shape into an equal number of splines. See the following section for details about this technique.

- The first vertex at one of the ends of the open shape is matched to the first vertex of the closed shapes, increasing the importance of matching first vertex locations when combining open and closed shapes in the same loft.

Figure 10.12 shows an example of combining open and closed shapes in the same loft.

Splitting from One Spline to Two

Another useful loft technique is to split the loft from what appears to be a single shape into multiple shapes. You cannot break the rule that requires every shape in the loft to contain the same number of splines; instead, resort to a little sleight of hand. Splitting a loft relies on using Edit Spline to divide what appears to be a single spline into multiple splines. You do this using Break in the Edit Vertex or Edit Segment rollout of the Edit Spline modifier.

FIGURE 10.12

Combining open and closed shapes in the same loft.

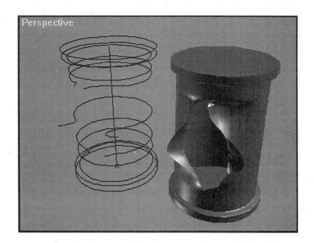

Remember that the Break command splits a spline without changing its location or curvature. Break behaves differently depending upon whether you use it from the Edit Vertex or Edit Segment rollout of the Edit Spline modifier.

- In the Edit Vertex rollout, Break inserts a second vertex at the selected vertex and breaks the spline between those two vertices. Use this method when the spline already contains a convenient break point.

- In the Edit Segment rollout, Break inserts two vertices at the point you click and breaks the spline between those two vertices. Use this method when you want to break the spline in the middle of a segment.

Details on using the Break command of Edit Spline are presented in Chapter 9.

To split a loft from one spline into multiple splines:

1. Create all the shapes needed for the Loft object.

2. Count the number of splines in the shape containing the greatest number of splines.

3. Apply Edit Spline to the remaining shapes and use Break in the Edit Vertex rollout to divide the shapes into the same number of splines.

4. Select a path and get the shapes to the loft.

The key to how well this technique works lies in your choice of break points and first vertices for all the splines. Because you are working with multiple splines in each shape, you need to match the first vertices of all the splines in one shape with the matching splines in the next shape on the path. Two basic issues drive your decisions about where to break a spline and where to locate the first vertices.

■ Place first vertices in a shape as close as possible to matching first vertices in the next shape.

■ Divide splines to eliminate any ambiguity about how the loft skin transitions from one shape to another. This step often requires dividing splines into more pieces than seems necessary.

■ Match up the first vertices of all the splines within the shape to avoid twisting.

This technique is tricky and not for the faint of heart, but it can pay off with incredible loft models.

You will also need to apply an Edit Mesh modifier to the loft so you can weld the seams created by all of the split shapes and unify normals. See Chapter 13, "Mesh Modeling," for details of using Edit Mesh.

Controlling the Loft Surface

In the previous exercise, you checked an option to display the loft skin in wireframe viewports. The Skin Parameters rollout contains many options that affect not only the display of the loft skin, but also the mesh density and interpolation methods used. A second rollout named Surface Parameters contains the options to control how the loft surface renders. Figure 10.13 shows both of these rollouts.

FIGURE 10.13

Skin Parameters and Surface Parameters rollouts for loft objects.

Setting Skin Detail

Some of the most important decisions you make regarding Loft objects concern the density of the surface mesh (or skin). As mentioned in previous chapters, you choose between a number of tradeoffs when making the decision about how complex to make a Loft object.

- Dense meshes show more detail than sparse meshes.

- Dense meshes deform more uniformly than sparse meshes.

- Dense meshes can render a smoother profile than sparse meshes.

- Sparse meshes consume less memory and display faster than dense meshes.

- Sparse meshes are often easier and faster to work with than dense meshes.

- Sparse meshes render faster than dense meshes.

You achieve the best all-around solution by creating the most sparse mesh possible to satisfy the deformation and rendering requirements of your project. You can also use the Optimize modifier to display a low-resolution model for modeling, while storing a high resolution model for final rendering. See Chapter 15, "Using Advanced Modifiers," for information about the Optimize modifier.

Notice that many of the settings discussed next are similar to options you can set in the Shape Interpolation rollout when creating shapes. Remember that shape interpolation settings are not used when getting shapes into a loft. Instead, the Loft object overrides shape interpolation settings with its own settings. For this reason, you can use the Adaptive interpolation setting while creating loft shapes, to work with the smoothest shapes possible, and control mesh density using the loft options.

All of the following parameters are found in the Skin Parameters rollout for Loft objects.

Setting Path Steps and Path Level Interpolation

Path Steps set the number of interpolated steps between each level of the Loft path. Path levels and Path steps combine to define the number of divisions along the length of the path in much the same way Height segments define the number of divisions along the height of a cylinder. The higher the number of steps and levels on the path, the more dense the final mesh.

You control how path levels affect the skin using the Adaptive Path Steps option. When Adaptive Path Steps is checked, a level is created along the path at the following locations:

- At every vertex on the path shape.
- At the location of every shape on the path.
- At every control point on a loft deformation curve.

When Adaptive Path Steps is unchecked, path levels are only created at path vertices, making for a more efficient surface. You might lose detail, however, if some of your shapes are not located at a vertex or at an intermediate step setting.

The idea behind the Adaptive Path Steps option is to automatically create path levels wherever you might need them. 3DS MAX assumes that if you have placed a shape at a certain point along the path, or inserted a vertex or control point, that shape or point must be an important feature, and you want it represented exactly on the loft surface. This is generally the case, but

Adaptive Path Steps can sometimes create more path levels than necessary. An example is when vertices on the path do not match up with important shape locations in the loft. In such cases, levels are created at both the vertex locations and the shape locations with the vertex levels possibly being unnecessary. Figure 10.14 shows the same loft comparing the difference between Adaptive Path Steps checked and unchecked. Both lofts use the default Path Steps setting of 5.

FIGURE 10.14

Comparing Adaptive Path Steps checked versus unchecked.

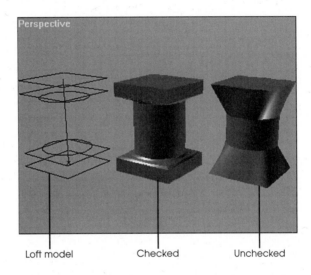

Loft model   Checked   Unchecked

After you decide how you want to handle path levels, set the Path Steps field to specify how many intermediate divisions you want between each level. The higher you set this value, the smoother the path curves are represented in the loft skin, but you also increase memory requirements and rendering time. Some useful guidelines for setting path steps are:

■ Set path steps lower if the path has few curves.

■ Set path steps lower if Adaptive Path Steps is checked. (Usually the added path levels make up for the lower step setting.)

■ Set path steps higher if you plan to deform the loft either through deformation curves or with modifiers.

■ Set path steps higher if Adaptive Path Steps is unchecked.

One feature missing from the path steps equation is an Optimize option. If you remember from Chapter 9, checking Optimize removes intermediate steps from straight segments. If you need to make your loft surfaces as efficient as possible, you can use one of the following techniques to simulate optimization on the path:

- **Edit Spline**   Apply an Edit Spline to the path and use Refine in the Edit Vertex rollout to add extra vertices along curved segments. After adding the vertices you can reduce the path steps to near zero. The extra vertices you added to the path provide surface detail at the curves while the reduced path steps optimize the straight portion of the path. Some benefits of this technique are that you can see exactly where on the path you are adding the extra vertices, and it works regardless of whether Adaptive Path Steps is checked or unchecked. The biggest drawback is that it is difficult to remove an added vertex if you change your mind later.

- **Loft Deformation Curve**   Use a deformation curve to add extra levels when Adaptive Path Steps is checked. Details about using deformation curves are presented later in this chapter. The trick is to employ an otherwise unused deformation curve to insert extra levels. Leave the control points at the default values to prevent the curve from deforming the loft and reduce the Path Steps setting. For example, you could insert control points in the Teeter deformation curve but leave all the control point values at zero degrees of teeter. Teeter is a good choice for this technique because almost no one uses teeter deformation. The main advantages of this technique are that the control points are easily moved or deleted if you change your mind about where you want a level, and the control points can be animated. A relatively minor drawback is that you specify control point locations by percentage along the path rather than picking exact locations on the path.

Setting Shape Steps and Optimization

The Shape Steps field and Optimize Shapes check box set the number of interpolated steps between each vertex of a cross section shape. These parameters apply to all shapes on the path and override the steps and optimize settings in each shape's base parameters. See the discussions of "Steps and Optimize" in Chapter 9 for more information.

Checking Optimize Shapes when you have both curved and linear shapes on the path can produce interesting results as 3DS MAX attempts to construct a surface between shapes with widely varying numbers of steps. Using Optimize Shapes in such situations reduces surface complexity but might make the mesh more difficult to deform.

Capping

The capping parameters determine whether 3DS MAX covers the ends of your lofted object and how those ends are constructed. Because 3DS MAX is a surface modeler, everything you create is hollow. The illusion of solidity is created by capping the ends of objects. If you want your object to appear open and hollow, uncheck the capping parameters to leave one or both of the ends uncapped.

You can choose between Morph or Grid capping methods. Morph capping uses fewer faces but does not deform as well as Grid capping. If you plan to use variations of the loft object as Morph targets, Morph capping is necessary.

If you do not cap your Loft objects, the side walls appear thin and unrealistic. You might have to apply a Normal modifier for the object to render properly. Applying the Normal modifier is covered in Chapter 15.

NOTE

If you loft an object on a closed path, 3DS MAX ignores the Cap Start and Cap End check boxes. Examples of closed paths are circles or rectangles. A closed path has no ends, so the settings of the Cap check boxes have no meaning.

Setting Surface Characteristics

Surface characteristics affect the shape of a loft surface without changing the number of faces created. Parameters that affect surface characteristics are found in the Skin Parameters rollout.

Contouring the Surface

The Contour check box controls whether the shapes on your path turn to follow curves. In many ways, Contour is like the difference between the Skew and Bend modifiers. If Contour is checked, shapes turn as they follow curves in the path. Contour forces the shapes to stay perpendicular to the path, resulting in smooth bends where the path curves. If Contour is unchecked, the shapes remain parallel to the shape at path level 0, regardless of how the path curves, producing an object that is skewed from side to side rather than bent. Figure 10.15 shows the difference between a Loft object with Contour checked and with Contour unchecked. Usually, if you design a path with a curve, you want your object to bend. In such cases, check Contour.

FIGURE 10.15
A loft object with Contour checked versus unchecked.

Checked ———   ——— Unchecked

Banking the Surface

The Banking check box controls whether cross section shapes spin about the path (bank) as the path turns and climbs along its Z axis. The Banking parameter is used only when Contour is also checked. If Contour is unchecked, Banking is ignored.

When Banking is checked, 3DS MAX twists cross section shapes around the loft path based on the sharpness of the path bend and the rate of the path climb. When Banking is unchecked, cross section shapes hold a constant orientation to the path as defined by the shape at path level 0. Figure 10.16 shows the difference between a Loft object with Banking checked and an object with Banking unchecked.

If you want complete control over the bank angle, leave Banking unchecked and apply manual banking using Twist deformation. Loft deformations are described later in this chapter.

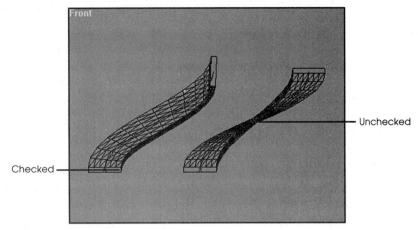

FIGURE 10.16

A Loft object with Banking checked versus unchecked.

Choosing a Linear or Curved Surface

The Linear Interpolation check box controls how the skin is interpolated between shapes on the path. When Linear Interpolation is checked, the skin is stretched tight between the cross section shapes. When Linear Interpolation is unchecked, the skin appears looser and follows a spline curve through the cross section shapes.

Consider checking Linear Interpolation when you create machined objects. Uncheck Linear Interpolation when you create organic or sculpted objects. Figure 10.17 shows the difference between a Loft object with Linear Interpolation checked and an object with Linear Interpolation unchecked.

If you want complete control over skin curvature, leave Linear Interpolation unchecked and apply manual skin curvature using Scale deformation. Loft deformations are described later in this chapter.

Setting Surface Rendering Properties

The final set of surface properties affects neither the number of faces nor the shape of the skin. The parameters in the Surface Parameters rollout control how the surface appears when it is rendered.

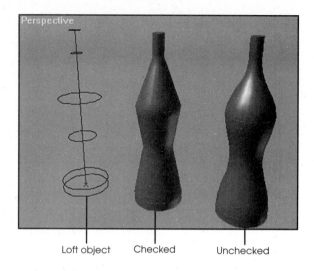

Loft object   Checked   Unchecked

Smoothing the Surface

Two smoothing check boxes determine whether your object appears as a smooth or faceted surface. This is similar to checking or unchecking the Smooth check box in a cylinder's base parameters. The difference is that you have control over whether the length, the width, or both are smoothed.

Checking Smooth Length instructs 3D Studio MAX to smooth the object along the length of the path. This produces smooth bends as the object follows a curved path, but it renders the cross-sectional shape as faceted. Smooth Length is checked for the top left object in figure 10.18.

Checking Smooth Width smoothes the perimeter of the shape. This setting produces smoothly curved cross sections but renders curves in the path as faceted. Smooth Width is checked for the middle object in figure 10.18.

Checking both parameters renders a fully smoothed object. Figure 10.18 shows three 90-degree bends rendered as fully smoothed, smooth length only, and smooth width only. Both smoothing options are checked for the bottom right object in figure 10.18.

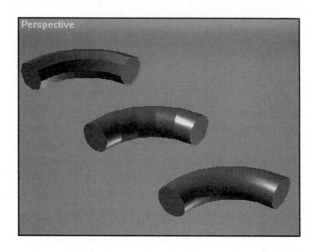

Figure 10.18
The effects of smoothing.

Mapping the Surface

Many Loft objects you create might be rendered with mapped materials. Chances are that all but the simplest objects defy the capabilities of the standard mapping types found in the UVW Mapping modifier. Use a Loft object's own mapping parameters to apply mapping coordinates that follow the path and surface deformations of a loft object. Figure 10.19 shows an example of a child's straw mapped with lofted mapping coordinates. This effect would be nearly impossible to duplicate using other mapping techniques.

Figure 10.19
Example of using lofted mapping coordinates.

To use lofted mapping coordinates, you must first check the Apply Mapping check box in the Surface Parameters rollout. When Apply Mapping is checked, the following parameters are enabled:

- **Length Repeat**   Sets the number of times the map repeats along the length of the path.

- **Perimeter Repeat**   Sets the number of times the map repeats around shapes on the path.

- **Normalize**   When checked, mapping is scaled evenly along the length of the path and around the perimeter of the cross section shapes. When unchecked, mapping is scaled unevenly based upon the spacing of levels and vertices. Most of the time, you want Normalize Length checked.

TIP

You may consider setting both repeat fields to 1.0 and checking Normalize. You can then use the UV Tiling fields in the map Coordinates rollout of the Materials Editor to control the number of map repetitions. Using this technique, you can animate the map tiling, whereas the loft repeat fields cannot be animated.

Editing Loft Shapes

After you have placed cross section shapes on the path, you might need to edit those shapes. Edit shapes on the loft path by entering Shape Sub-Object mode in the Modify panel, as shown in figure 10.20.

FIGURE 10.20
Accessing Sub-Object Shape mode of a loft object.

To edit loft shapes, select a Loft object. Choose Loft from the base of the Modifier Stack in the Modify panel. Click the Sub-Object button and choose Shape as the Sub-Object level.

Select shapes on the loft using standard selection techniques and use features in the Shape Commands rollout.

The following sections describe the various ways to edit loft shapes. These editing techniques include using the alignment commands in the Shape Commands rollout, transforming the shapes, and accessing the shape's Modifier Stack to apply modifiers and Edit Spline to the shape.

Comparing Shapes

If you place multiple shapes on the path, you often need to compare the position, orientation, or vertex alignment of one shape to another. If your path is perfectly straight, you can easily compare them by setting up a user view that looks down the path. But what if you have a curved path? Click Compare in the Shape Commands rollout to display two or more shapes in a window based on their spatial relationship to the path.

When you click Compare, it displays an empty Compare window. Shapes are displayed in the Compare window by clicking the Pick Shape button in the window's toolbar and clicking the shapes you want to display. The Compare window displays each shape on its own local XY plane, ignoring the effects of path curvature, Contour, and Banking. The path is represented as a cross that is common for all displayed shapes. Figure 10.21 shows an example of a Loft object with a curved path and how the shapes appear in the Compare window.

FIGURE 10.21

A loft object and shapes in the Compare window.

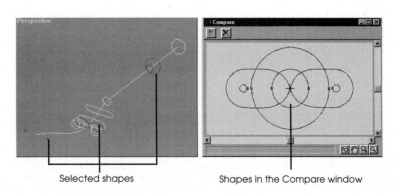

Selected shapes   Shapes in the Compare window

You primarily use the Compare window to examine and compare the first vertex location of shapes on the path. The first vertex of each shape appears as a small box.

Positioning Shapes

There are many ways to change the position of a shape on the path. You face your first shape position decision when you specify the Path Level before getting a shape. After that you can change shape positions using techniques in Shape Sub-Object mode.

Remember that a shape is placed on the Loft path with its local X and Y axes perpendicular to the path and its local Z axis tangent to the path. Changing the position of a shape is performed in the shape's Local coordinate system.

Changing Path Level

Change the path level of a shape by selecting the shape and changing the Path Level in the Shape Commands rollout. You can also change the path level of a shape by moving it along its local Z axis. See the discussion about transforming shapes in the following topics.

Using the Alignment Buttons

Use alignment buttons of Align Left, Align Right, and Center to change the position of the shape with respect to the path. Select shapes and click one of the alignment buttons. The alignment buttons move a shape in its local XY plane in the following manner:

- **Align Left**   Moves the shape so that its negative X-axis boundary is on the path, and the shape is centered along its Y-axis extents.

- **Align Right**   Moves the shape so that its positive X-axis boundary is on the path, and the shape is centered along its Y-axis extents.

- **Center**   Moves the shape so that both its X-and Y-axis extents are centered on the path.

Figure 10.22 shows a shape in the Compare window with its original orientation after Get Shape and the results of using each of the alignment functions.

FIGURE 10.22

Using the loft shape alignment buttons.

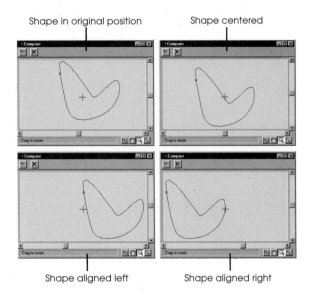

One alignment button absent from the Shape Commands rollout is a button that would restore a shape to its original Get Shape alignment with the path. When you get a shape to the path, it is originally aligned with its pivot point on the path. Return a shape to this alignment by using one of two techniques:

- After using one of the alignment buttons, click Undo to return the shape to its previous position, assuming that the previous position was the default Get Shape alignment.

- Put the shape to the scene and use Get Shape to replace it at the current level. The drawback with this technique is that you lose any other transforms you have applied to the shape at the Shape Sub-object level.

Deleting Shapes

The only way to remove shapes from the path is to delete them in Shape Sub-Object mode. After entering Shape Sub-Object mode, select the shapes you want to delete and then click the Delete button in the Shape Commands rollout or press Del on the keyboard.

Using Transforms

Transforming shapes on the path is similar to transforming any other object. The main difference is that the transform coordinate system is locked to the shape's local coordinate system and the transform center is the point where the path intersects the shape's local XY plane. Transforming loft shapes in Shape Sub-Object mode follows these special conditions:

- Moving shapes along the X or Y axis moves them perpendicular to the path.

- Moving shapes along the Z axis moves the shapes along the path and changes the shapes' path level. Each shape is constrained to stay between the shape that precedes it on the path and the shape that follows it.

- Rotating shapes along the X or Y axis is similar to using teeter deformation.

- Rotating shapes about the Z axis spins the shapes about the path and is similar to using twist deformation.

- Scaling shapes is similar to using scale deformation.

- You can remove all Scale and Rotate transforms applied to a loft shape by clicking Reset in the Shape Commands rollout. Reset does not affect the results of moving or aligning a shape.

- Transforms applied to shapes on the path are internal to the Loft object and are not reflected in any instances of the shapes elsewhere in the scene.

This last point is important to remember. Scale and Rotate transforms applied to shapes in the scene are discarded when you use Get Shape to bring them into a loft. If you want to scale or rotate loft shapes, consider using Get Shape first and then scaling or rotating the shapes on the path using Shape Sub-Object mode.

Modifying Shapes

You can also apply modifiers to shapes in a loft such as Bend, Twist, or Edit Spline. You must be careful not to apply any modifiers that convert the shape to another object type such as a mesh or a patch. Examples of such modifiers include Extrude and Normal. Modifiers that convert a shape to another object type make the loft object invalid and cause the loft to disappear from the screen. You can still select the loft object by name using the Select Objects dialog, and deleting the offending shape modifier to restore the loft to a valid object.

Apply a modifier to a loft cross section shape using one of the following two techniques:

To apply a modifier directly to a loft shape:

1. Select the shape using Shape Sub-Object mode.

2. Choose the Shape object below the Loft object in the Modifier Stack. The Shape object appears in the Modifier Stack only after you have selected a shape in Shape Sub-Object mode.

3. Apply a modifier to the shape.

Working directly on shapes in a loft can be confusing because of differences between the shape's and loft's local coordinate systems. Most people find it easier to apply modifiers to an instance of a loft shape somewhere else in the scene, which is the main reason for using the Instance option with Get Shape.

To apply a modifier to an instance of a loft shape, complete the following steps:

1. Select an instance of the shape in the loft rather than selecting the loft itself.

2. Apply a modifier to the instance.

If you did not use the Instance option with Get Shape, you can put an instance of the loft shape back to the scene using the Put button in the Shape Commands rollout.

Animating Shapes

You can create many animated effects by animating the shapes on the loft path. Three techniques for animating loft shapes include:

- Animating the base parameters of a parametric loft shape.

- Animating modifiers applied to loft shapes.

- Using XForm modifiers with Edit Spline to animate individual vertices of loft shapes.

Notice that all of these methods involve working with a shape's modifier stack. Animating instances of a loft shape is the easiest way to set up this kind of animation.

Editing Loft Paths

You can edit a loft path in much the same way you edit loft cross section shapes. Edit the loft path by entering Sub-Object Path mode in the Modify panel (see fig. 10.23).

FIGURE 10.23

Accessing Sub-Object Path mode of a Loft object.

To edit loft paths, complete the following:

1. Select a loft object.

2. Choose Loft from the base of the Modifier Stack in the Modify panel.

3. Click the Sub-Object button and choose Path as the Sub-Object level.

The path is automatically selected when you enter Path Sub-Object mode because each loft object has only one path. You don't have many options once you enter Path Sub-Object mode. There is only one button in the Path Commands rollout for putting the path to the scene and all but one transform is inactive in the toolbar. The only transform available is rotation about the local Z axis of the path shape at path level 0.

Applying modifiers to path shapes follows the same procedure described for modifying cross section shapes. As with modifying cross section shapes, the best method is to modify an instance of the path shape somewhere else in the scene and observe the effect on the loft.

The following topics describe a few techniques involving the creation and modification of loft path shapes.

Closed Paths

A closed path is any path in which the first and last vertices are welded together. You can create a path that appears closed but does not have its first and last vertices welded. As far as 3DS MAX is concerned, such a path is open.

Closed paths exhibit two important traits, as follows:

- They are not capped because they have no beginning and no end.

- When smoothed along their length, they show no seam where the first and last vertex meet.

Backtracking Paths

An extremely powerful but seldom mentioned option is the capability of a path to backtrack over itself. The best way to demonstrate this is to examine an object that uses this technique. Figure 10.24 shows a model of a mechanic's socket created using a backtracking path.

FIGURE 10.24

Example of an object using a backtracking path.

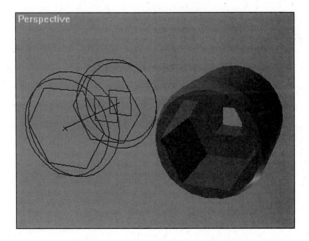

At first glance, this loft seems to use a straight path. Only when you examine the skin of the loft, or manipulate the vertices on the path, do you suspect the truth. What had seemed to be a simple, straight path is actually a three vertex closed path that doubles back on itself. Figure 10.25 is a diagram of the object with the backtracking path pulled apart to show the shape locations. Table 10.1 describes what is happening with this object.

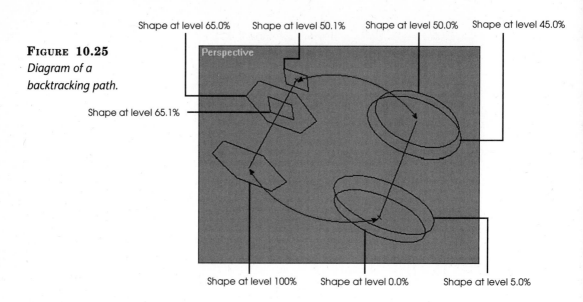

FIGURE 10.25
Diagram of a backtracking path.

Shape at level 65.0%   Shape at level 50.1%   Shape at level 50.0%   Shape at level 45.0%

Shape at level 65.1%

Shape at level 100%   Shape at level 0.0%   Shape at level 5.0%

TABLE 10.1

Analysis of the Socket Path

Lvl	Inside Description	Lvl	Outside Description
0.0%	Circle solid. Forms front face of socket.	50.1%	Square hole. Path changes direction back toward level 0.0%. Shape transitions from circle solid to a square hole.
5.0%	Circle solid. Forms outer surface of socket.	65.0%	Square hole. Continues drive hole of Socket.
45.0%	Circle solid. Continues outer surface of socket.	65.1%	Hexagonal hole. Transitions to socket hole of Socket.
50.0%	Circle solid. Forms back face of socket.	100.0%	Hexagonal hole. Path closes with level 0.0%. Shape transitions from hexagonal hole to circle solid.

A convenient way to visualize this type of path is to think of an athletic tube sock. Stretch the sock out, and the path runs down its center—the fabric represents the surface created by shapes on the path. If you roll the open end of the sock back on itself, the path doubles back as well; what was once the inside of the sock becomes the outside. Closing the path is like snipping off the toe of the sock and stitching the two ends together.

By examining the Socket path, you can see that at the location where the path doubles back on itself, the shapes on the path become holes drilled back into the object. Many people use Booleans to create such forms. Using this loft technique, you can create more efficient and predictable objects.

An interesting side effect of backtracking paths is their effect on smoothing. If you render the Socket, you find that 3DS MAX tries to smooth around the flat end where the path doubles back on itself. When lofting backtracking paths, uncheck the Smooth Length option and manually smooth the object by applying a Smooth modifier.

Animating Loft Paths

You can create many animated effects by animating the loft path shape. Three techniques for animating a loft path shape include the following:

- Animating the base parameters of a parametric loft path shape.

- Animating modifiers applied to a loft path shape.

- Using XForm modifiers with Edit Spline to animate individual vertices of a loft path shape.

Notice that all these methods involve working with the shape's modifier stack. Animating instances of a loft path shape is the easiest way to set up this kind of animation.

Using Loft Deformation Curves

You can accomplish only so much by manipulating the path or by placing different shapes along the path. A vital tool for creating lofts is the use of Deformations. This section looks at the first four deformations of Scale, Twist, Teeter, and Bevel. The last deformation option, Fit, is discussed in its own section later in this chapter.

Before moving on to specific deformation commands, you should be familiar with the general aspects shared by all the deformation grids. Figure 10.26 shows a typical deformation window. In general, the vertical lines represent the levels on the path (solid lines for levels containing shapes, and dotted lines for path vertices and other levels). The horizontal lines represent values on the deformation grid. The curve is a deformation control curve. A deformation window can display up to two curves, a red curve for X axis deformation and a green curve for Y axis deformation.

FIGURE 10.26

Example of a loft deformation window.

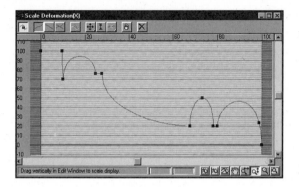

The following list points out a few general rules to keep in mind when working with deformation grids:

- Snap works with the vertical grid values. If your snap spacing is set at 10 units and Snap is on, you are constrained to increments of 10 percent in the Scale grids and increments of 10 degrees in the Twist and Teeter grids. Snap has no effect on horizontal path position in the graph.

- Always check the setting of the Make Symmetrical button. Scale and Teeter both use the Make Symmetrical button in the deformation window toolbar. Always decide whether you want your adjustments to be independent or symmetrical about the X and Y axes, and examine the Make Symmetrical button before you begin making adjustments.

- Remember that the deformation curve is not the path. It is easy to fall into the assumption that the deformation curve is the same as the path. The shape and control point spacing of the deformation curve are completely independent of the path. Though the shape of the deformation curve controls the shape of the lofted object, it does not necessarily look like the final lofted object.

- The number of Path Steps and the setting of the Adaptive Path Steps check box control how closely the deformation grid is followed. The value of the deformation curve is applied at each path step and path level. If Adaptive Path Steps is checked, new levels are inserted for every control point added to the deformation curve.

You can create fantastic animated effects by animating the value and path percent of the deformation curve control points. An example is animating a bulge moving through an object by animating scale deformation. To animate a deformation control point:

1. Select a control point on a deformation grid.

2. Turn on the Animate button.

3. Drag the time slider to a new frame.

4. Move the control point or enter new path percent and deformation amount values in the fields at the bottom of the deformation window.

Using Scale Deformation

Use the Scale deformation window to alter the X and Y scale factor of the shape. The scale base point is always on the path. A powerful modeling option is to use scale deformation on shapes that are not centered on the path. Figure 10.27 shows an appliance handle lofted by scaling a shape with its edge aligned to the path.

FIGURE 10.27
Scale deformation for an appliance handle.

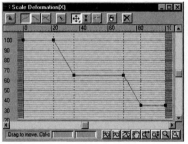

Using Twist Deformation

The Twist deformation grid controls rotation of the shape about the path. You can create similar effects by placing multiple shapes on the path and rotating the shapes at the Shape Sub-Object level, but most people find the Twist deformation grid easier to use.

Using Teeter Deformation

Teeter enables you to rotate the shape about the X and Y axes perpendicular to the path. You often can use teeter with a shape offset from the path to generate objects that are difficult to create by any other means. Figure 10.28 shows an arch lofted with an X axis Teeter.

FIGURE 10.28

Teeter deformation for an arch.

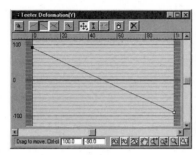 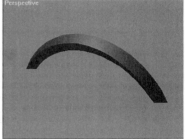

Using Bevel Deformation

The Bevel deformation window performs a function similar to the manufacturing process of chamfering. You use the deformation curve to specify the exact units to cut back or push out a shape from its original size. Bevels work best with large blocky shapes. Thin shapes or shapes with sharp points are difficult to bevel. For such shapes you should consider using the Bevel modifier or other modeling methods.

Sometimes your attempted bevel causes a shape to self-intersect and produce rendering errors or even causes some faces on the object to disappear. Remember that you can use the Bevel deformation curve to add size to a shape, as well as cut it back. Often, changing the direction of a bevel enables the operation to succeed.

Figure 10.29 shows two different Bevel deformation grids. Both create an object with 10 units of inward bevel. The first grid begins by cutting the shape inward 10 units and enabling it to expand back out to its original size. The second grid starts with the shape at its original size and then expands out an additional 10 units. The resulting mesh objects are very similar, yet one bevel might succeed where the other one fails.

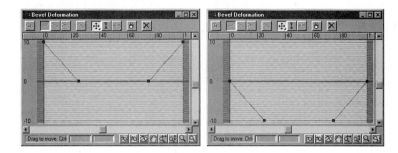

Creating with Fit Deformation

The final deformation is Fit deformation. You use this deformation type to create three-dimensional objects by specifying the profile of the top, side, and front view of the object. This command has a few restrictions, but it is still an extremely fast and powerful technique for generating complex geometry.

Fit deformation relies on your specifying three shapes that serve as the profiles of the three-dimensional object. 3DS MAX refers to these three shapes as Fit X, Fit Y, and the Loft Shape. *Fit X* and *Fit Y* represent the top and side views of the object and actually serve as scaling limits for the Loft shape. The *Loft shape* can be thought of as the front or cross-sectional view of the object, and it is the shape actually passed along the path.

When you create these shapes, arrange the shapes the way a draftsman would draw them by hand. That is, draw the top view first, project the side view out to the right or left, then project the front view down. This technique makes it easy to check that the top view and side are the same length. Figure 10.30 shows an example layout of shapes ready for import into the Fit Deformation window.

Fit X shape ——

Fit Y shape ——

Cross section shape

TIP

Fit deformation aligns the local X axis of the fit shape with the length of the path. The most predictable results are produced when you draw your fit shapes in the Top view with the X axis aligned with the length of the shape.

Setting up the Fit deformation in the 3D Lofter requires creating a Loft object and picking fit shapes in the Fit Deformation window. The steps involved are as follows:

1.   Create the fit shapes, a front or cross section shape, and a shape for the path.

2.   Select the path shape and click Loft in the Create panel.

3.   Click Get Shape and pick the cross section shape.

4.   Go to the Modify panel, expand the Deformations rollout, and click the Fit button.

5.   Check the status of the Make Symmetrical button. Most often, you have separate fit shapes for the top and side of the object; therefore, Make Symmetrical should be off.

6.   In the Fit Deformation window, click Display X Axis, click Get Shape, and pick the top view shape to import into the Fit Deformation window as the Fit X shape.

7.   Click Display Y Axis, click Get Shape, and pick the side view shape to import into the Fit Deformation window as the Fit Y shape.

8.   Click Generate Path to have 3DS MAX process the fit shapes and generate a lofting path for the object.

Figure 10.31 shows the Fit Deformation setup and the Loft object created from the shapes in Figure 10.30.

FIGURE 10.31

A fit deformed Loft object.

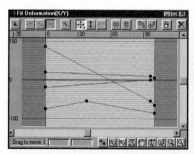

You can improve your chances for a successful Fit deformation by adhering to the following rules of thumb:

■ The top view shape (Fit X) and the side view shape (Fit Y) should be the same length. This is not an explicit requirement, but if the two shapes are of unequal length, 3DS MAX scales the first Fit Shape that is imported to match the length of the second Fit Shape.

■ A level is placed on the path for every vertex in both the top view (Fit X) and side view (Fit Y) shapes. You can greatly reduce the complexity of your final object by making the vertices in the two shapes line up.

■ You can place multiple front view or cross-sectional shapes on the path. If the cross section of your object changes along the path, import another shape at that level. Many users overlook this capability. See the example on lofting a rowboat later in this chapter for an example of this technique.

■ You can edit the path after clicking Generate Path. In fact, you can ignore the Generate Path button altogether and use the fit shapes on any path that you manually create.

Four basic restrictions for the Fit X and Fit Y shapes are outlined in the *3D Studio MAX User's Guide*:

■ The fit shapes must be a single spline. No outlines or nested shapes are allowed.

■ The fit shape must be closed.

■ No curved segment can extend beyond the first or last shape vertex in the X axis.

■ The fit shapes cannot contain undercuts. An easy way to check for undercuts is to imagine a line aligned with the shape's local Y axis passing through the shapes. If you can place the line in a position so that it cuts through the shape in more than two places, you have an undercut. Figure 10.32 shows undercuts revealed by this technique.

Only the first restriction, shape must contain a single spline, prevents the use of the shape as a fit shape. Shapes with extremely curved segments or undercuts can be selected as fit shapes and 3DS MAX flattens the curves and ignores the undercuts.

The following example shows you how to use Fit deformation to loft the hull of a rowboat. An important variation is the use of multiple shapes on the path to enable you to carve out the seating area.

FIGURE 10.32

Invalid undercuts in fit shapes.

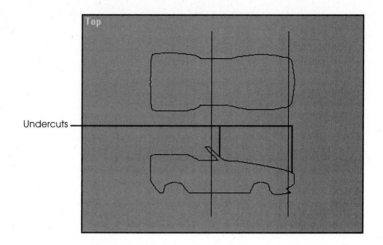

Undercuts ⎯

LOFTING A ROWBOAT WITH FIT DEFORMATION

The first step is to create the source shapes that define the path, cross sections, and fit shapes. All the shapes are drawn in the Top view.

1. Draw top view and side view shapes of a rowboat hull; make both shapes 240 units long.

2. Draw two cross section shapes for the rowboat.

    One shape is solid and the other is hollowed out. Remember the first vertex location is important when using multiple shapes on a path. The first vertex for the cross section shapes is at the keel. Also, if you remember from the previous section on "Matching Vertices," you do not have to match the number of vertices between the two shapes, but matched vertices provide more control over the loft surface. In the case of this rowboat, adding extra vertices across the top of the simple solid shape to match the vertices of the hollowed shape creates a cleaner surface.

3. Draw a straight horizontal line to be the path.

    You can turn on Snap to make drawing the path easier.

The shapes, and their first vertex locations, are shown in figure 10.33.

Next, create the loft object and pick the fit shapes.

4. Select the path shape and click Loft in the Create panel.

5. Click Get Shape and pick the solid cross section shape.

   You now have the basic loft object. You might want to choose Smooth with Highlights shading in a Perspective view so you can see the loft skin as you proceed with the rest of the exercise.

6. Go to the Modify panel and click Fit in the Deformations rollout.

7. In the Fit Deformation window do the following: turn off Make Symmetrical, click Display X Axis, click Get Shape, and click the top view (Fit X) shape for the rowboat.

8. Click Display Y Axis, click Get Shape, and click the side view (Fit Y) shape for the rowboat.

9. Click Generate Path and close the Fit Deformation window.

Step 9 isn't necessary if you drew the path 240 units long (to match the fit shapes), but it is a convenient way to ensure that the path is the same length as the fit shapes.

The next step involves placing more cross section shapes on the path. Place the solid shape at the bow and the stern to form the bulkheads. Then position the hollow shapes next to the solid shapes to form the seating area of the rowboat.

10. In the Path Parameters rollout, set the Path Level to 15.0%.

11. Click Get Shape and click the solid cross section shape.

12. Set the path level to 15.01% and get the hollow cross section shape.

   Placing the hollow shape so close to the solid shape makes the loft skin seem to drop straight down into the hollow.

13. For the stern bulkhead, place a hollow cross section at path level 90.0%, and a solid cross section at 90.01%.

14. In the Surface Parameters rollout, uncheck Smooth Length.

   The quick transition from solid to hollow causes surface rendering errors when Smooth Length is checked. You can apply a Smooth modifier later to fine-tune the surface smoothing.

FIGURE 10.33
*Source shapes for
the rowboat.*

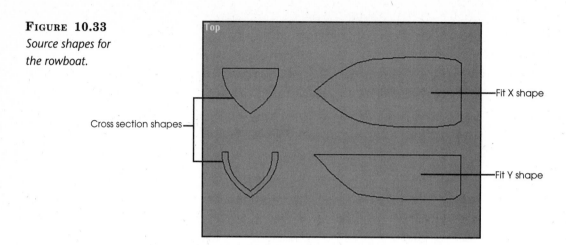

Cross section shapes—

—Fit X shape

—Fit Y shape

Your Loft object should look similar to the object in figure 10.34. If your shapes do not seem to be aligned properly on the path, enter Shape Sub-Object mode, select all shapes, and click Center in the Shape Commands rollout.

FIGURE 10.34
*Completed rowboat
scene.*

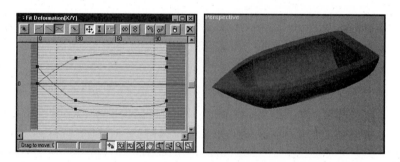

In Practice: Lofting Objects

- **Creating Source Shapes** You can use almost any shape as a path, cross section, or fit shape with only a few critical shape restrictions. Path shapes must contain a single spline. All cross section shapes on the path must contain the same number of splines and same nesting order. Fit shapes must contain a single spline.

- **Creating a Loft** Create a loft by starting with the path shape or the first cross section shape. The method you choose sets the original position and orientation of the loft object. You can also choose to add the original shape to a loft or add a copy or instance of a shape. Usually adding instances is the best choice for ease of editing.

■ **Editing Loft Shapes**   Enter Shape or Path Sub-Object mode in the Modify panel to edit shapes in the Loft object. If you added shapes as instances, you can apply modifiers to the instanced shape outside the loft and see the changes reflected in the shapes inside the loft.

■ **Using Deformations**   Use the Deformations rollout in the Modify panel to apply changes in scale, rotation, and beveling to the shapes on the path. You can also use Fit Deformation to create complex objects based on top, side, and cross section profiles.

■ **Animating Lofts**   You can animate the sub-object shapes that make up a loft and animate the control points on the deformation curves. The easiest way to animate loft shapes is to animate the modifiers applied to instances of the shape.

Andrew M Phelps -copyright 1996

Sector 76
Created by Andrew Phelps
Bowling Green State University
Bowling Green, OH
aphelp@bgnet.bgsu.edu
http://www.bgsu.edu/~aphelp/

Chapter 11

Boolean Modeling

Modeling with Boolean operations is a common and often favorite technique of many modelers because Boolean operations come close to simulating traditional sculpting and modeling techniques. 3D Studio MAX makes Boolean modeling even more useful by implementing its Boolean compound object. Unlike a modeling modifier, a Boolean compound object is composed of the two objects, called operands, *that perform the Boolean operation. These operands remain as objects for as long as you wish, giving you the ability to access their parameters and modifier stacks.*

The Boolean compound object is different from many programs' concept of Boolean operations because it does not permanently change the defining operands' geometry. You can reposition, redefine, or swap the geometry of the defining operands at any later time. Because the operands remain objects, you interact with them as you would any other. You can even animate them, creating amazing effects. 3DS MAX's shaded viewports allow you to see the result of the Boolean as you change the operands. This is an interactive benefit and makes it feel as if you are really using one object to carve another. While extremely useful and fun, Booleans may become complex when you nest them within one another. This chapter provides insight that makes the general use of Boolean operations easier, as outlined in the following:

- Basics of Boolean operations and how to make them as interactive as possible

- Working with nested Boolean objects

- How different types of Boolean operations are used to sculpt and model

- Considerations for achieving successful Boolean operations

Boolean Operation Basics

As with many computer graphics terms, the term Boolean is derived from the name of the person who introduced the concept (in this case, George Boole). In mathematics, the term *Boolean* has come to mean a comparison between sets; with 3D Studio MAX, this comparison is between geometric objects. Although a Boolean operation may seem like a modifier, it is found in the Create panel rather than in the Modify panel because you *are* defining a new object from two existing ones (similar to a Loft or a Morph). A Boolean operation in 3D Studio MAX is done by creating a Boolean compound object from two existing objects, termed *operands*, and follows these steps:

1. Select the initial object for the Boolean operation.

2. Choose Compound Objects from the Geometry selection list in the Create panel and then click Boolean.

    The selected object is now Operand A for the compound Boolean object. You are now ready to select Operand B.

3. Choose the type of Operation you wish to perform.

4. Click Pick Operand B and then select the second object.

    The objects are compared to determine whether they are valid (from a Boolean standpoint) and if valid, the Boolean operation is performed.

    You can now change the Operation type and see the different Boolean results.

The operation types are similar to many traditional techniques. Union joins the object like clay modeling; subtraction carves one object from the other like sculpture; intersection leaves what would have been carved or punched out from a subtraction. Union and intersection always return the same result, regardless of the order in which the operands are chosen. Subtraction does depend on the order. Two options are provided (A–B and B–A) so that you can switch the result quickly in case you accidentally start with the wrong choice. The results of these basic operations are shown in figure 11.1.

Figure 11.1
The four types of Boolean operations.

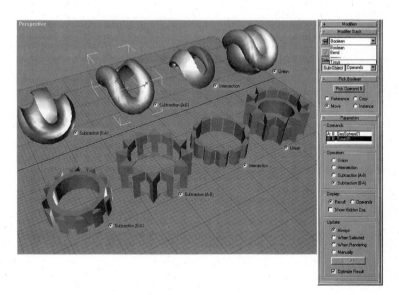

Warning

You can click the Pick Operand B button and pick another Operand B as many times as you want. If you pick a new Operand B, the original operand is deleted from the scene. If you pick the wrong object as Operand B, click Undo before picking another Operand B.

Booleans as Compound Objects

What is extremely flexible about Boolean operations in 3DS MAX is that the objects comprising the Boolean operands still exist as objects. Each operand maintains its original Edit History stack and can be modified from the Command panel. The operands can even be transformed at the Sub-object level. Figure 11.2 shows the result in Track View after a Boolean object is created.

FIGURE 11.2

A Boolean compound object's Track View listing.

Original object —

Selected object for Boolean operation —

Original object types displayed when modified —

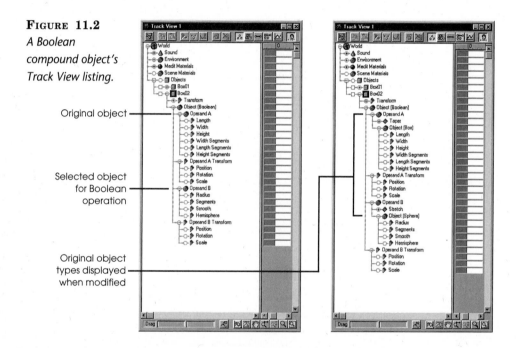

The 3DS MAX instance and reference architecture shows its power with Booleans. When first creating a Boolean compound object, you have the option to move, copy, instance, or reference the object selected as Operand B. The default option is Move, and appears to cause an explicit action because only the Boolean result remains. Both objects selected for the Boolean are now sub-object operands. The remaining options perform the Boolean result with either a copy, instance, or reference of the selected object. In all three cases, the object chosen for Operand B remains unchanged, and the Boolean result is performed with the new operand object. In these cases, it could appear that nothing has happened until you move or hide one of the two objects.

NOTE

An object chosen for Operand B will have any transform animation applied to it removed, whereas Operand A's (the initial object's) transform animation remains. If Operand A has transform animation, the current frame's location, position, and scale are used for the now static operand.

Although you can make a copy, instance, or reference of the Operand B, no such option exists for Operand A (the object selected when you click Boolean). A flexible method of working around this is to clone all the objects you intend to Boolean to the side as instances. Then use the default Move option for Operand B selections, providing the capability to modify any of the objects in the Boolean and preserving a duplication of their relationship to one another.

TIP

To make an instance from an object that is already an operand, enter Track View. Copy the operand's object definition (indicated by a blue circle) to the clipboard and paste it into another object's definition as an instance. You can use this technique in reverse as well, completely redefining the geometry of the defining operands—changing all the square holes to circles, for example.

After a Boolean object has been created, you can change the choice of Operand B from within the Boolean object's Modify panel with the same choices that were present at creation. Use this option with caution because it eliminates the originally chosen Operand B from the scene. Eliminating the original can be a problem if you originally used the Move option and a representation of that geometry no longer exists as a separate object. Choosing another operand is the same as replacing the operand's object definition in Track View except that you have the option to make a reference, which is not present in Track View.

After you create a Boolean object, you can return to each operand's modifier stack in the Modifier panel (see fig. 11.3). The first time you enter a Boolean object's Modify panel neither of the operands is selected, so the Modifier Stack shows only itself in the stack. To modify a particular operand's stack, you need to choose it from the Operand's listing. The operand you select now displays its stack. You can adjust any modifier in the stack and add new ones that affect the operand object before the Boolean. There are no additional restrictions on what parameters can be animated. To transform an operand, you must activate the Sub-object mode for the Boolean object. In this way, you can think of the operands as being similar to gizmos, with the exception that, unlike gizmos, operands have their own modifier stacks.

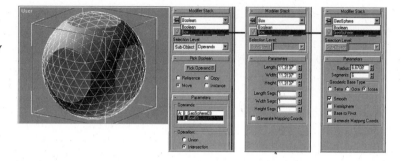

FIGURE 11.3
Using the Boolean's Modify panel to manipulate the operands.

Update Options

The Boolean Update options control how the Boolean calculations are actually performed. For complex objects the Boolean calculations can be time consuming. These calculations also slow the editing of other objects, if these objects are instances or references to Boolean operands. If you are experiencing a pause in your modeling, change the Update method from automatic to one of the other options. The Manual option is the most conservative method, and it provides you with the most control over when the operations are evaluated. This mode is highly encouraged for complex models. The When Rendering method does not evaluate the operation until a production rendering is performed and then returns the updated result to the scene. The When Selected method is somewhat unreliable in when it actually updates the result and should not be your first choice.

To speed modeling operations, keep the operands simple. When you complete your Boolean operations and modifications, return to the operand's earlier definitions and increase their density. If these are instances, increase all their complexity and then manually update the result all at once.

TIP

You can terminate a lengthy Boolean calculation by using the Escape key while the wait cursor is being displayed. When you terminate the calculation, the Update mode is automatically changed to Manual so you can now control the exact time an update should be calculated (because most likely the geometry you are adjusting is complex).

Interactive Booleans

When you enter a Boolean's Sub-object mode, you can transform the operands independently of one another. Whichever operand has its name selected is the one eligible for movement, rotation, or scale. When the operand is manipulated at the Sub-object level, you are literally performing an interactive Boolean because as you move either operand the other remains stationary, and the display updates the Boolean result as you move the operand. For small models or fast machines, this is often in real time.

NOTE

For complex Boolean operations, you should put the Boolean into Manual Update mode so that you can position the operands without being delayed by time-consuming calculations. After the operand is in place, click Update to see the new result.

Understanding the Boolean Display options is the key to making interactive changes. The default option, Result, shows the result of the Boolean operation. If you change to the Operands option, both A and B operands are displayed as if no Boolean occurred. Although easy to see, the fully displayed operand obscures the Boolean result, which makes you work blind to some extent. In practice, the best combination is usually to choose Result with the Show Hidden Ops option enabled. This displays the missing operands as wireframes (but *only* in shaded viewports) and provides you with the information of exactly where the operand is and its current influence to the Boolean operation.

NOTE

Remember that you can always assign an operand to another object's controller or a unique Path, Look At, or Expression controller for effects such as animated drill bits or laser burns.

Nested Boolean Objects

You are not limited to one Boolean operation per object. You can perform as many as you like, with each operation creating its own set of operands—one nested inside the other. The only "limit" is the practical number you wish to navigate.

After creating a Boolean object, you can perform additional Boolean operations to the same geometry by selecting the object as Operand A for a new Boolean compound object. Each time you perform a Boolean operation on an object, you are actually making the original an operand of a new Boolean object. You are thus creating a "Boolean tree" composed of single branches — a very linear progression of steps. Every Boolean operation you conduct can be accessed at a later time, although the method for doing so takes a bit of practice because it all occurs in the Modify panel. Figure 11.4 shows the results of making three successive Boolean operations. A Box subtracts a Sphere, then subtracts a Cylinder, and finally subtracts a Cone.

FIGURE 11.4

Navigating a Boolean tree containing three operations.

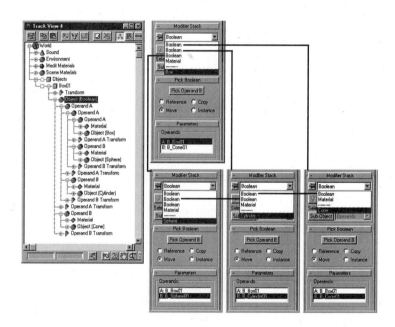

TIP

To advance deeper into a Boolean tree, continue to choose the Operand A and then go to the next Boolean in the stack. You can use Operand B's stack to go forward, but you can use only Operand A's stack to go backward in the edit history.

You need to be careful when performing several Boolean operations, one after the other — a common situation when you are chamfering or filleting all the corners of an object and have the pieces all arranged. After you complete an operation and so complete the Boolean compound object, you must leave the Boolean dialog or your subsequent pick will replace the operation you just performed and delete that object from the scene. Although it takes extra button clicks, you should exit the Compound Object's list by selecting another Geometry type (such as Patch Grids) and then return to Compound Objects to define the next Boolean object.

When navigating a Boolean tree in Track View, keep in mind that only items that have animatable parameters appear. When a Boolean object is made from a raw mesh or patch, only the operand's transform is shown because it has no creation parameters to adjust. When the same object is given a modifier, a new entry is given for the modified object. What may be confusing is that it has the same Operand label as the Transform (with a blue modifier circle instead of a green controller triangle). When traversing a deep tree as pictured previously in figure 11.4, keep your eye on the blue Operand circles. Only the deepest Operand A contains an object definition; all other object definitions are within previous Operand Bs.

TIP

When using primitives as operands, Track View lists their parameters under the generic Operand title. Giving the primitive a modifier, such as Material, moves the creation parameters to a modified object sphere beneath the operand, with a label denoting its object type.

Boolean Characteristics

When creating a Boolean object, the smoothing groups and material IDs of the separate objects are preserved. Mapping, unfortunately, is totally removed and needs to be applied after the final Boolean result. If your object's mapping was assigned with UVW modifiers, you are able to restore it. If you make a copy—not an instance—of your original object or modifier, assign a new UVW Map after the Boolean, and use the modifier's Acquire function to restore it. Note that this operation does not work for procedural mapping assignments.

Mapping coordinates are removed because the vertices of the Boolean result are always welded. Also, if you were intending to separate the original operands after the operation, you need to use EditMesh to detach them. Having unique material or smoothing groups per operand assists greatly in making the face-level selection for the detachment.

Material IDs are probably your most valuable tool in controlling the final surface results of a Boolean object, especially for nested Booleans. Giving each operand a Material modifier with a separate ID means you have a guaranteed method of selecting the faces after the Boolean operations are complete. Although useful for sub-object material assignment, keeping operands as face selections is also valuable in selecting faces for smoothing group assignments and UVW Mapping modifiers to restore lost mapping.

Sometimes a Boolean result appears to have kinked or warped imperfections. These imperfections are often caused by similar smoothing groups acting with each other in ways they shouldn't, or vertices not being welded so smoothing cannot occur. If you see these imperfections, apply an EditMesh modifier, select all the vertices, and perform a Weld Selected. If the imperfections persist, you need to analyze your smoothing group assignments (before or after the Boolean operation).

In most cases, it is far easier to select critical regions before they become part of a Boolean operation. If you know a portion of the model will require unique smoothing (for example, the chamfer in figure 11.5), assign those faces a unique smoothing group or material ID so that after the Boolean operation they have the proper smoothing.

FIGURE 11.5

Assigning surface characteristics before Boolean operations occur.

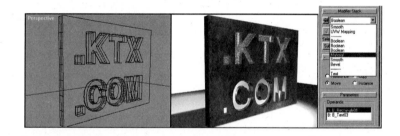

This discussion may make it seem as if you must put in a considerable amount of forethought and planning before you can even perform a Boolean operation, when in fact, the Modifier Stack enables the process to be much less structured. It is common practice to create the Boolean objects quickly and then return to earlier in the operand's history to make smoothing and material assignments as necessary. Note that this is *much* easier to do if you have instanced the objects before they became operands.

Considerations for Better Booleans

The Boolean code in 3DS MAX is extremely general, enabling it to work between arbitrary surfaces. This generality means, however, that not every object forms a valid Boolean and that some "valid" results may have artifacts (such as long splinter faces) or undesirable results. The following checklist should assist you in troubleshooting and building models that are Boolean-friendly:

- The normals for the entire surface must be unified without any rogue faces pointing the wrong direction. Face normals are used in determining the direction of the surface and the resulting Boolean.

- The mesh must be properly built, meaning that faces that share an edge must share two vertices, and that an edge can be shared only by two faces. (The inner vertex core faces from a lathe is a typical nightmare situation for the latter rule.)

- Ensure that all vertices are welded. Welding all the vertices manually with EditMesh may be necessary, even between consecutive Boolean operations.

- Coplanar faces, especially those within the same operand, are troublesome to deal with and should be avoided. One of the worst cases is back-to-back coplanar faces (easily created by making a primitive with a zero height).

- Booleans work reliably only between single elements. If either operand is composed of multiple elements (such as the Teapot or Hedra), only one element can be successfully acted upon at a time.

- If the operation is not successful, turn off the Optimize Result option at the bottom of the rollout so the final pass that checks for coplanar faces is not calculated. This can sometimes make an invalid result valid.

- If the operation is still not successful or is producing splintered faces, try a slight adjustment between the two operands.

- Change the operand's level of detail, especially at the area local to the actual Boolean operation.

Do not let this checklist scare you into avoiding Boolean operations. Most of these options work on the first try, especially if your geometry adheres to the first three rules—which it probably will if it was built within 3DS MAX.

When animating Boolean operations, you may encounter a sudden "flash" or surface "twitch" on a frame or two—most likely the result of the Boolean operation failing or creating odd faces on that one frame. Considering the drama and impact of an animated Boolean, it is worth the time to advance the animation frame by frame to examine the Boolean result. If a condition arises that causes a rendering error, simply adjust the geometry slightly on that frame to get a better result and continue. If numerous adjustments are needed, you may be better off assigning a Linear controller to the operand's position track and adjusting nearly every frame.

Carving with Boolean Subtraction

Boolean subtractions tend to be the most commonly used of the operation types and is, therefore, the default. These subtractions can be thought of as "taking a bite from," "sculpting," "carving," "removing from," "drilling," "punching," or whatever analogy makes the most sense to you.

Successful sculpting with Boolean subtractions begins with an understanding of what shape you want the eventual subtraction to be. This form leads you to think of what geometry is required to accomplish that pattern. Many times the object being subtracted bares little resemblance to the finished result; the object simply provides the shape of the carving knife that slices the surface. The second operand can be thought of as a "chisel" or "router bit" that creates a particular "groove" in the first object. A Boolean subtraction is also a good—if not the primary—method for creating chamfers and fillets on existing objects.

NOTE

You may find it useful to maintain a selection of "carving tools" as Bézier shapes that you can extrude, loft, or lathe for Boolean subtractions. More complex Boolean cutting forms can be saved as meshes and merged when needed.

Scooping New Objects with Boolean Intersection

A Boolean intersection creates the object that would have otherwise been "carved out" with a Boolean subtraction. The result is sometimes difficult to visualize, but can create geometry that would have otherwise been very difficult to model (see fig. 11.6). In this situation, the second operand is acting like a six-directional cut.

FIGURE 11.6
Complicated geometry formed from a Boolean intersection.

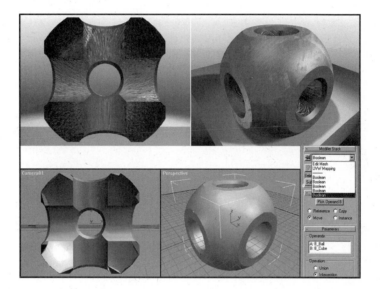

One of the primary uses for a Boolean intersection is to retrieve what would be taken "out" in a Boolean subtraction. Often you'll find it necessary to use the piece that "fell on the floor" in an animation. You may want to show the piece that is punched out from a metal die, for example. To do this, copy the original objects and perform two Boolean operations, thereby creating the "cut" object and what was "cut out."

Modeling with Boolean Union

A *Boolean union* operation combines the two operands and removes any overlapping geometry. Before performing a union, you should consider carefully whether the union is even necessary. If the underlying intersection can be seen, then using the union is the correct choice. If the intersection of the two is hidden, you may be better off allowing the objects to simply intersect. A common use of union is when you need smoothing groups to continue across the joint. In this case, the Boolean union is probably just the first step in a more complex modeling sequence.

A Boolean union is most commonly used with objects that appear to be "solid." The surface is closed, and there is no need for an interior structure, so the object is only one face thick. Many times a Boolean union is performed in order to achieve the effect of a subtraction. One operand trims the other, enabling it to be used for another purpose without harming the one that trimmed it. This operation can be useful when the "trimming" object has a particular form that needs to be adhered to on the other object.

You also can use a Boolean union to create two elements that could be separated for other uses with Detach function in EditMesh. When you use a Boolean union operation to edit objects, no mesh is formed where the geometry once overlapped. As the resulting elements are pushed apart, there is a hole in the mesh where the two objects were joined. To use this technique effectively, it is best to assign each operand a unique Material ID# so you can select the faces easily (by Material ID#) from within EditMesh when performing the detachment.

In Practice: Boolean Modeling

- **Operands**   Boolean operations comprise two objects and keep them as editable operands. Each operand can be transformed, edited, and animated like any other object.

- **Nested Boolean operations**   Boolean operations can be nested by creating a Boolean compound object that uses another compound object as an operand. The Modify panel interface of the Boolean object only gives access to one pair of operands at a time. You can traverse the Boolean history by selecting an operand and making one of its previous Boolean operations current from the Modifier Stack.

- **Calculating Boolean operations**   You can choose when the Boolean operation is calculated. This can be important when the operands contain complex geometry, the calculation is intensive, and interaction is impaired. When performance become sluggish, it's best to change the Update mode to Manually or When Rendering.

- **Material ID#s**   Assigning defining Material ID#s to each object before they become Boolean operands is a useful technique for being able to select the separate pieces after they are welded in the Boolean operation.

■ **Boolean operations** These operations depend on correctly constructed geometry to achieve desirable results. Of primary concern are unified normals, adjacent faces sharing two vertices, and edges not being shared by more than two faces.

Image by Mondo Media for "Zork Nemesis" ©Activision
Provided courtesy of Kinetix™

Chapter 12

Sub-Object Modeling

Although many objects can be modeled from primitives or defined by a loft, many more can be created by manipulating the basic geometry of vertices, faces, edges, and patches. This is where computer modeling becomes more like sculpting. Modelers adept at these techniques are often called vertex sculptors. In 3D Studio MAX, this is the area known as sub-object modeling.

When you affect anything less then the entire object, you are sub-object modeling in 3D Studio MAX. There are essentially two forms of sub-object modeling: manipulating the sub-object entities themselves and restricting modifiers to sub-object selections. In the first form, you are actively pulling, scaling, and rotating sets of vertices, and possibly changing the topology by adding or deleting sections. In the second form, you define a selection of vertices with one modifier and pass that selection along up the stack for subsequent modifiers to affect.

The chapter will specifically address the following concepts of sub-object modeling:

- Using selection modifiers
- Selection levels within edit modifiers
- Defining sub-object selections for other modifiers
- Basics concepts of sub-object modeling
- Common terms and concepts for mesh editing

NOTE

Because every object class contains vertices as its most basic component, this chapter often refers to generic sub-object selections as *vertices*.

Editing at the Sub-Object Level

Sub-object modeling takes place whenever you are manipulating discrete entities or regions within an object. To model at the vertex, face, edge, spline, segment, or patch level, you must add a modifier that gives you access to the desired sub-object level. The sub-entities an object has and the modifier used to edit those sub-entities vary depending on the geometry of the object (see fig. 12.1):

- Bézier Spline shapes contain vertices (with tangent handles), segments, and *splines* and are edited with the EditSpline modifier
- Loft objects contain shapes and paths (made of Bézier splines), which are edited within the Loft object definition
- Mesh objects contain vertices, faces, edges, and elements and are edited with the EditMesh modifier

- Bézier Patch objects contain vertices (with tangent handles) and lattices with edges and patches, and are edited with the EditPatch modifier

- Boolean compound objects contain operands made of other objects, which in turn are edited within the Boolean object definition

FIGURE 12.1
Sub-object components of the primary object classes.

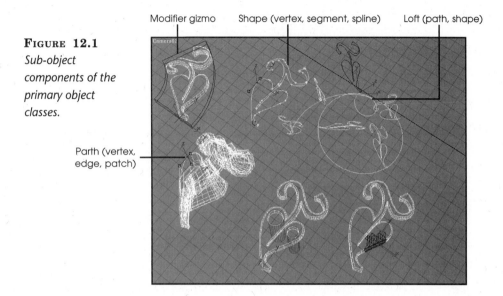

When working in most modeling programs, editing discreet sections of a model is nearly always a permanent decision. This was the method with 3DS DOS—every time you edited vertices and faces, you were making explicit changes to the model that could not easily be reversed. This method is very similar to sculpting from a block of stone. Decisions must be planned carefully, and the chisel needs to strike with confidence lest the sculpture be gouged or lose a nose. But in 3D Studio MAX, you do not have this permanence unless you want it. Modeling with the EditableMesh object is explicit, whereas modeling done within EditMesh and with selection modifiers is reversible.

Using Selection Modifiers

You might find it easier to think of there being only *two* types of modifiers in 3D Studio MAX—those that define selections and those that act upon selections handed to them. This book refers to these as *selection modifiers* and *modeling modifiers* respectively. Understanding this basic difference will enable you to plan the sequence of your Edit Modifier Stack quite well.

Currently, only a few 3DS MAX modifiers define selections, and these are known as *selection modifiers*. These are the Edit modifiers (EditMesh, EditSpline, and EditPatch) and Volume Select. These modifiers give you the capability to select specific portions of your model to pass along for manipulation by the remaining modifiers. The exception to this is the new EditableMesh object, which enables you to define a sub-object selection without adding a modifier. For discussion purposes, EditableMesh can be considered a selection modifier, even though it's an object class.

Because of their usefulness, other selection modifiers are sure to be added by developers. When introduced, these selection modifiers will most likely follow the same rules laid down for Volume Select and EditMesh.

The Stack's Active Selection

The Edit Modifier Stack passes along what is termed the *active selection*. This is the geometry that subsequent modifiers "see" and apply their effect to. The contents of the active selection can change throughout the stack by adding other select modifiers, with the other modifiers applying their effect to whatever selection is passed to them. This fact may not be apparent to you when modeling at the object level because the active selection is the entire object, and the fact that a selection is being passed along is not obvious. The power of this concept is that you can define what is being modified at any point in the stack by adding or adjusting a selection modifier.

N O T E

Sub-object selections are active only when the Edit modifier's Sub-object button is depressed and yellow (yellow always alerts you to the fact that you are in Sub-object mode). In contrast, VolSelect modifiers are always active because their Sub-object mode is for gizmo manipulation and not selection levels.

The stack's active selection can change from modifier to modifier. The goblet shown in figure 12.2 illustrates this concept because the stack began as a Tube primitive and was the result of five tapers following five different volume selections. Each selection replaced the previous one and defined a new active selection for the stack. An EditMesh was added at the end to finalize the smoothing and perform the bulged grip. The stack enables you to return to any previous selection and change what the active selection at that point in the stack is. Subsequent modifiers operating on that selection affect the new selection immediately. You can see the impact subsequent edits have on selection adjustments—a fairly unique and amazingly useful technique.

FIGURE 12.2
Multiple active selections within the same stack.

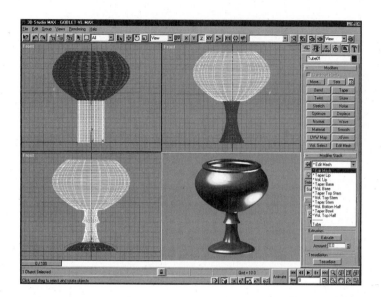

The "Edit" Modifiers

Although innocent in appearance, the simple buttons preceded by the word "Edit" arguably contain the most power in Modifier panel. The three Edit modifiers (EditMesh, EditSpline, and EditPatch) each serve two roles in 3D Studio MAX: they enable sub-object editing of their respective geometry, and they define sub-object selections for future modifiers in the stack to act upon. The buttons are as follows:

OTE

The EditMesh modifier actually does triple duty by containing face-level surface property tools.

For 3D Studio veterans, the single EditMesh modifier is the equivalent of what used to be the entire 3D Editor module, whereas the EditSpline modifier is equivalent to the entire 2D Shaper module. All the commands that used to comprise mesh editing and spline editing within 3DS DOS are now within these two modifiers.

The Edit modifiers automatically disable the stack's Show End Result button when you are working with them. This is because modifications at the Sub-object level need to occur in the space defined by that modifier at that point in the history. You can examine the end result by clicking and holding on the Show End Result button, but you cannot model with this result showing. After you release, the button will return to the off state as you return to editing in Sub-object mode.

Defining Selections with Volume Select

When created, the Volume Select modifier establishes its gizmo at the extents of the active selection. This is a one-time-only adjustment; unlike other modifiers, Volume Select does not adjust the extents of its gizmo as the active selection below it changes. Of course, you wouldn't want this readjustment to occur because it makes the resulting selection nearly worthless. Unfortunately, the Volume Select gizmo does not have an adjustable center. Its pivot point is always its centroid. Because of this, you will find it useful to use another object (most likely a dummy helper) as the pick coordinate system when you're adjusting volumes. The most common thing to adjust with volume is the gizmo's scale. Because the modifier does not have size parameters, the only way to adjust its defined volume is with the scale transform. Use a pick coordinate center to scale about is often critical to making accurate, and quick, adjustments of the volume.

NOTE

When a Volume Select or an Edit modifier defines the entire object as the active selection, subsequent modifiers locate their centers at the object's pivot point rather than the selection center.

TIP

When working with a sub-object selection, you can locate a subsequent modifier's center at the object's pivot point by first assigning a Volume Select modifier, leaving it at the object select level, and then assigning the modifier. You can now either use the Volume Select modifier, or delete it and use the original Edit modifier. The newly added modifier will conform its gizmo to the new selection while leaving its center at the object's pivot point.

You need to realize that Volume Select modifiers are not deformed by modifiers that are previous in the stack. Although this is a trait shared by all modifier gizmos, it has incredible impact with Volume Select. Say, for example, you make a Volume Selection at the top of a cylinder and proceed to make tapers on the top. If you then go to the base of the stack and bend the entire cylinder, the Volume Select gizmo remains stationary and the vertices of the cylinder bend through the selection volume. The selection set for the subsequent tapers then changes as the bend increases. In this case, you should have added another Volume Select modifier at the end of the stack to return the selection to the entire object. The bend should have been applied after that to ensure that the selection volume remained consistent as the entire object was bent. This trait is not unique to the Volume Select modifier, but actually occurs with all modifier gizmos. It's just that the impact is far more noticeable with a selection modifier.

Edit Modifier Mechanics

The Edit modifiers are actually quite amazing in that they record every action you ever do within them. This is not just an undo list, but an actual progression of every decision you make. Although you can undo only what is in the current 3DS MAX session, all of your edits are preserved by the Edit modifier in the MAX scene file. This enables you to return to earlier portions of the stack and adjust previous modifiers or the creation parameters and have all your previously applied sub-object modeling propagated through the new history. This capability is amazingly powerful, but it comes with a price—increased file sizes and RAM.

Every Edit modifier you add to the stack adds this overhead in RAM, so all edits are interactive and changeable. Thus, applying a dozen Edit modifiers to the same object increases the RAM requirements of that object by more than twelvefold, although it may have the same number of faces throughout its history and even far less at the end. Because of this overhead, you will want to use Edit modifiers with extreme discretion and perhaps for limited periods of time.

NOTE

The overhead incurred in using EditMesh was the reason that the EditableMesh object was introduced in Release1.1 and why new EditableSpline and EditablePatch objects are likely to follow.

Each Edit modifier records your actions a bit differently. EditMesh records a delta for every vertex you affect, so the size of the modified object can double in size "only" if you transform all vertices. EditSpline and EditPatch are quite different in that they record every single edit operation you perform and keep it in the order you applied it. Thanks to this record-keeping, the important curve and tangency relationships of spline geometry are properly adjusted when you affect items earlier in the stack. Such extensive record-keeping also has implications for memory overhead. When using EditSpline, you should collapse the stack often to reduce your RAM consumption and file size.

Within each Edit modifier is a "DeleteObject" that records all the destruction you've done to the object. This is why you can go to an earlier stage in the stack and find your entire model, or remove the modifier and the "deleted" portions reappear. To make the deletions within an Edit modifier permanent, you must collapse it. This characteristic of keeping a record of deleted geometry also enables you to detach and explode portions into new objects and then restore the original object by removing the Edit modifier.

NOTE

It's good practice to collapse the Edit portion of the stack when you are finished with it to save RAM and file size. Many modelers perform a Save Selected on the object to preserve a copy before making the collapse—just in case they need to return to the earlier states of the model.

Selection Levels Within Edit Modifiers

Edit modifiers each contain separate and distinct sub-object selection levels for their entities. Each selection level acts as a separate selection set and does not influence other selection levels (with the exception of hidden faces and vertices). As it happens, each of the Edit modifiers maintains three selection levels:

- EditMesh: Vertices, Faces, and E

- EditSpline: Vertices, Segments, and Splines

- EditPatch: Vertices, Edges, and Patches

Because an Edit modifier determines the active selection at a given time, it is of paramount influence on subsequent modifiers. The selection level (Vertex, Face, or Edge for EditMesh, for example) defines both the content and type of geometry the next modifier in the stack "sees." This can be important because some modifiers work only with certain types of geometry. A Normal modifier, for example, will act upon only an active selection of faces and will ignore selections of vertices or edges.

Edit Modifiers as Selection Sets

An Edit modifier can be thought of as a selection set container. When its Sub-object level is active, the currently defined selection is passed as the current selection for future modifiers to act upon. This can be tricky because your current sub-object selection state can be influencing future modifiers. Changing the EditMesh level from Vertex to Face will most likely change the selection and future results dramatically.

NOTE

When an Edit modifier is placed in Sub-object mode and nothing is selected for the current selection level, future modifiers in the stack will not show any result because the active selection is empty.

Edit modifiers are used to edit the discrete sections themselves or define a selection that is passed along to other modifiers in the edit pipeline. The active selection is active until another selection modifier, such as an Edit or Volume Select modifier, is added in the pipeline. As long as you want to model with the same selection, you can continue to add modifiers to it. If, however, you want to change the selection, you will need to add another select modifier to alter the selection.

In practice, it's safest (and sanest) to use Edit modifiers to either edit the model *or* define a selection—but not both. Editing and defining the selection can lead to confusion when you change the selections for the purpose of editing and later modifiers are acting on the selection. If you want to pass a selection you defined in an Edit modifier up the stack and you are editing in that modifier as well, you should immediately assign another Select modifier. If the selection is definable by a volume, assign a Volume Select modifier, and assign an Edit modifier only if the selection is irregular or discontiguous.

NOTE

Remember that every Edit modifier you add to the stack adds substantial overhead to your model's RAM and disk space requirements.

Named Sub-Object Selection Sets

When you define a sub-object selection, you have the opportunity to store it as a named selection set (see fig. 12.3). These sets act just like object-level selection sets, except they are seen only by the modifier in which they were defined. Each Edit modifier (and the EditableMesh object) enables you to maintain as many selections per selection level as you like. To avoid confusion, named sub-object selections cannot be seen between selection levels. This means, for example, that named selections of vertices will not appear when you are at the Face level. When you remove an Edit modifier or collapse an EditableMesh object, you are also removing any named sub-object sets you may have made.

FIGURE 12.3

Using named sub-object selections to record decisions.

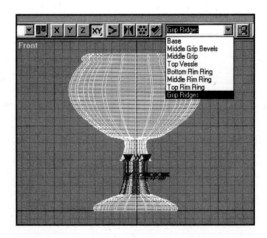

NOTE

Remember to press Return when you enter named selections in the toolbar because this is the only time they are recorded.

Other methods for storing sub-object selections include Material ID numbers greater than 1 (for objects *not* assigned a Multi/Sub-Object material) and Smoothing Group assignments (for objects that are entirely smooth anyway). Although not intended as selection sets, smoothing groups and Material IDs do provide the capability to store face level selections that are seen by all subsequent modifiers in the stack, and they continue to exist after the stack is collapsed.

Defining Sub-Object Selections for Other Modifiers

As previously described, modifiers act upon the stack's active selection. There is actually a bit of an art to defining the correct selection at the appropriate point in edit time. When modifying sub-object portions of an object, you will be most efficient if you define the selections for the modifier using the following priorities:

1. Use Modifier Limits when you want to influence the entire object but affect only a portion of it (a bent straw, for example).

2. If you need to change a sub-object selection to be the entire object, add a Volume Select modifier (at the object level) before the modeling modifier.

3. Use Volume Select when you are modifying selections definable by one or more rectangular, cylindrical, or spherical volumes. This enables previously defined topology to change, but does not work if the previous geometry changes dimensions.

4. Use EditMesh selections when you are modifying selections that are irregular or noncontiguous. This enables previously defined dimensions to change, but does not work if the previous topology changes.

Adjusting Modifiers with Sub-Object Selections

Modifiers treat sub-object selections in the same way they treat multiple objects—by locating their gizmo centers at the centroid of the selection.

Gizmo centers are located only at the pivot points when they modify a single, entire object. Modifiers conform their gizmos to the extents of the active selection. As the selection beneath them changes, so do the extents of the gizmo. The gizmo's center, however, does not move when the selection changes. The center remains where it began, with the initial selection or where you placed it afterward.

Relocating a gizmo's center after applying a modifier to a sub-object selection is extremely common. A typical procedure is described in the following list and shown in figure 12.4.

1. Apply the modifier to the sub-object selection.

2. Increase the amount value(s) to view the effect.

3. Activate the modifier's Sub-object mode and choose Center.

4. Choose Move and constrain the transform axis as appropriate.

5. Move the gizmo center to a defining position. For Bend and Taper, for example, this is often the edge of the selection.

6. Return to adjusting and finalizing the modifier's values.

FIGURE 12.4
Adjusting a gizmo's center for a sub-object selection.

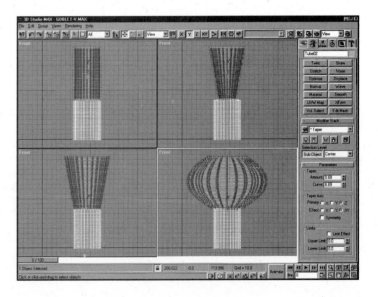

TIP

To position gizmo centers more easily, press the spacebar to lock the selection on the Center and proceed to move it without first having to select it with your cursor. Note that if you switch the selection level to the gizmo, you will be locked on the gizmo, and if you leave Sub-object mode, your locked selection will be the entire object.

Using EditableMesh Selections with Other Modifiers

When you are working within EditableMesh, you are most likely making permanent modeling decisions. If this is your preferred manner of working, the Modifier Stack can seem a bit foreign to you. To deform just a portion of an object, such as adding a Bend or Taper, you select the vertices you want to modify within EditableMesh and, without ever leaving Sub-object mode, apply the modifier. The modifier affects whatever is the active selection in the pipeline, and because you never left Sub-object mode, the vertices you just selected are now modified. You then adjust the modifier to see the result of the selection. Unlike other programs, such as 3DSDOS, you can revisit your selection, modify it, and return to the modifier. When performing explicit modeling, the following is a common procedure:

1. Make the sub-object selection for vertices or faces (edges are actually selections of vertices).

2. Add a modifier to the stack to influence the selection and apply an amount to view the effect.

3. If needed, position the modifier's gizmo center in relation to the sub-object selection.

4. Adjust the modifier's values until you are satisfied.

5. Return to the EditableMesh and adjust the selection if needed.

6. After the selection and modifier are correct, collapse the modifier in the stack.

7. Return to EditableMesh to make another selection (your previous sub-object selections are still remembered) or apply another modifier.

As the preceding method implies, when modeling with EditableMesh, it is common to apply modifiers and collapse the stack often. The stack is somewhat like a water level that rises and falls with the number of edits you perform. When you have many decisions, the level is high. When you are comfortable with various stages, you usually collapse them, and the level falls. When you begin to animate the parts of finished objects, there are often many modifiers, and all of them need to be maintained. Therefore, edit histories commonly fluctuate in size.

Another useful method with EditableMesh is to define selections, add a Volume Select whose extents will automatically encompass the selection. The selection can then be cleared at the EditableMesh and other modifiers can then be placed between the EditableMesh and the Volume Select. This has to be done with some forethought because you cannot reorder the stack, and the selections must be made in the correct order to be usable. However, you can copy the transform, and thus the defined selection volume, of Volume Select modifiers between the modifiers' track entries in Track View.

Locating Gizmo Centers on Sub-Object Selections

For a modifier applied at the Sub-object level, the default location of its gizmo center is the centroid of the selection. Such placement, however, can make the coordination of several modifiers difficult because the gizmo centers will shift as the selection changes. Overriding the default—placing the gizmo centers at the pivot point instead of the centroid—makes coordination easier. The following steps can be used to place a modifier's gizmo center at the pivot point instead of the centroid of a sub-object (see fig. 12.5):

1. Make the desired sub-object selection within the Edit modifier or by the Volume Select modifier.

2. Deactivate the Edit modifier's Sub-object mode (its Sub-object button is no longer yellow) or switch the Volume Select modifier to the Object level.

3. Apply the desired modifier.

   The modifier's gizmo fits the entire object, and the gizmo center is located at the pivot point.

4. Return to the Edit modifier, re-enter Sub-object mode, and choose the appropriate selection level for your selection. If using a Volume Select, switch from Object to Vertex or Face level.

5. Return to the modifier you just applied in the stack.

The modifier's gizmo fits the active selection, but the gizmo center is still located at the pivot point.

6. Proceed to adjust the modifier's parameters.

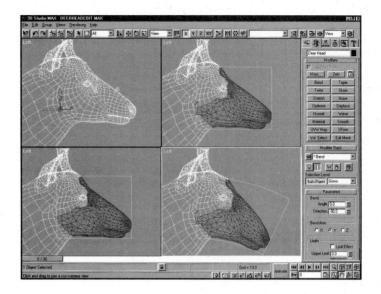

The preceding method is the most reliable one for locating the gizmo center at the pivot point of a sub-object. You can use this method with all the selection modifiers, keeping in mind that turning off their sub-object selection may enable yet another sub-object selection to return to an active state. In such a case, you will want to add a Volume Select modifier at the object level, between your Edit modifier and modifier.

NOTE

When sub-object selections are defined by the EditableMesh object, the next modifier locates its center at the object's pivot point. This occurs as long as you add the modifier as the first in the stack. Modifiers added after the first will treat the selection as described previously, locating their gizmo centers on the active selection.

The gizmo center is such a critical manipulation point that it is often useful to locate the pivot point for the sole purpose of locating gizmo center. Unlike sub-object selections or gizmos, pivot points respect the Align system, but can snap only to the vertices belonging to other objects.

To locate the pivot point at a vertex on the same object, snap a Point helper to the vertex and then align the pivot to the helper. This gets around the anomaly of pivots being able to snap to the vertices of other objects but not to those of their own.

Basics of Sub-Object Modeling

Previously, the discussion has been on how the sub-object selections defined by EditMesh, EditableMesh, and the other Edit modifiers are passed to other modifiers. But passing selections is just a by-product of what the modifiers were intended to do—sub-object modeling. EditMesh and EditableMesh were designed for direct mesh editing, where you manipulate the raw mesh by its vertices, faces, and edges. New mesh parts are constructed and others are refined or deleted. Finally, the surface characteristics of what is seen, how light is reflected, and what material is present are all assigned through mesh editing. All of this editing is performed at the Sub-object level.

Many subtleties of realistic and efficient modeling are at the vertex and face level. After an object is created, you may need to stretch vertices, turn or align faces, and build additional faces. Smoothing groups are perfected and face normals are best analyzed at the Sub-object level as well. Many modelers spend the majority of their time working at Sub-object level, using mesh editing tools and perfecting their surface properties. The rest of this chapter analyzes the functions that manipulate these finite entities and give specific character to models. The next chapter builds on these basic principles as it explores the details and techniques of using each of the sub-object modeling tools.

Concepts Common to Edit Modifiers

The Edit modifiers have many things in common because each manipulate sub-object geometry and work in a manner that is usually thought to be explicit (when performed in other modeling programs). Because of this, numerous procedures are the same between the Edit modifiers. These include attaching objects in order to work with them, the way pivot point centers work with different selection types, the use of angle thresholds, and principles of animating sub-object selections. Several efficiency techniques are also commonly used by modelers to make working with the Edit modifiers convenient. These include the use of grid objects, point helpers, and numerous keyboard shortcuts. When reading these common methods, you will find EditMesh and EditableMesh to have many more capabilities than EditSpline and EditPatch.

Object Level Attaching

The Edit modifiers contain one function that does not involve sub-object selections: Attach (see fig. 12.6). The Attach function joins two objects, with the result that one becomes the active object and one becomes the attached object, an element of the active object. This action of joining objects together is required for actions that "stitch" sub-object geometry together, with the most common need being for vertex welding between separate objects.

NOTE

The only method to attach more than one object to another in one step is with the EditableMesh's Attach Multiple function.

FIGURE 12.6

The Attach options for the Edit modifiers.

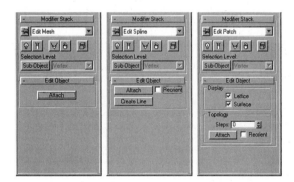

NOTE

Attaching should be done with care because the process collapses the stack of the attached object. If the attached object is a parametric or patch object, the object is collapsed to a mesh. Any animation or Modifier Stack information is lost during the collapse. When performing an attach, you should examine which object's edit history and animation you wish to keep because only that of the active object is kept.

If you want to keep the attached object's history and animation, you should either group or link the objects together instead of using Attach. The primary reason for attaching objects is to build faces between them. Faces can only be built upon, and vertices can only be welded to vertices of the same object. If you want to build faces between objects but do not want to attach them, you will need to create a duplicate set of vertices to build faces upon.

When attaching objects, several decisions are made as to material and mapping assignments. If neither of the objects have been assigned a material, nothing happens; but if materials are assigned to one or both of the objects, the effects are as follows:

- If only one object has a material, its material is inherited by the other object as well.

- If the object being attached to does not have a material, it inherits the material of the object being attached.

- If both objects have materials, the materials are combined into a multi-material.

A strange situation occurs when the objects being attached have material IDs that do not reference a multimaterial. Boxes, for example, are created with six different material IDs (one for each side) for convenience. When attaching it to other objects, the different IDs suddenly become relevant, and the various sides of the box have different materials. To avoid this situation, assign the entire Box object a single material ID (with either a Material or EditMesh modifier) before attaching it.

Averaged Pivot Point Centers for Contiguous Selections

Several functions refer to contiguous selections. A selection is said to be contiguous so long as the selection contains adjacent faces or edges that share vertices. Adjacent faces belonging to separate elements do not qualify as being contiguous. A noncontiguous selection is formed when you select separate areas of a mesh that do not touch one another or are parts of different elements. In all cases of selection adjacency, the axis tripod is your key to seeing which point and axis is currently active. The move, rotate, and scale transforms obviously obey the orientation and position of these individual icons. Functions specific to EditMesh, with Extrude being the most obvious, rely on these icons for the direction of their result.

NOTE

EditMesh and EditableMesh calculate pivot centers in very different manners, with EditMesh having much more flexibility. The EditPatch and EditSpline modifiers are similar to EditableMesh in this regard.

When using EditMesh, individual selections of faces are given their own pivot center at each face's center. The center's orientation depends upon the current coordinate system. If the coordinate system is anything other than Local, the orientation of the icon matches that of the coordinate system. As figure 12.7 shows, if Pivot Point Center is active, an axis is displayed per selection, and an averaged axis is made otherwise. If the coordinate system is Local, an axis is displayed per selection—regardless of the current transform center choice. The icon's X-orientation is always in the World XY plane, the Z-orientation matches the face normal, and the Y is perpendicular to the X and Z axes.

FIGURE 12.7

The transform icons for discontiguous selections.

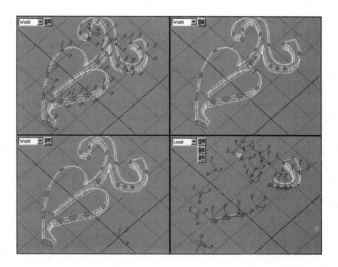

For contiguous selections, the location of each pivot center is averaged to establish a common center point (see fig. 12.8). If the coordinate system is Local, the directions of the individual normals are averaged into a common normal vector.

FIGURE 12.8
*Averaged center
points for
contiguous
selections.*

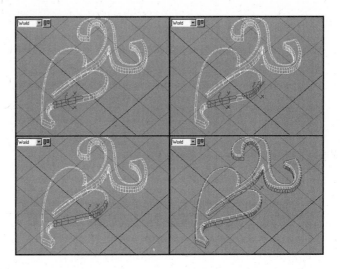

Vertex selections differ from face selections in that they are always considered discontiguous. When working in any coordinate system other than Local, the center is always the averaged location of the selected vertices, as shown in figure 12.9. When working in the Local coordinate system, each vertex presents an axis that represents the averaged normals of all the faces that share it.

FIGURE 12.9
*The transform icons
for vertex selections.*

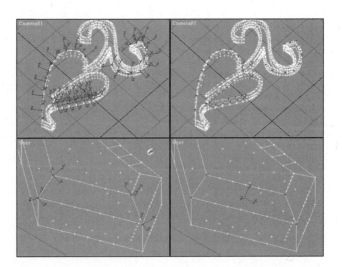

The previous discussion of transform center options pertained to EditMesh. It's important to note that EditableMesh, EditSpline, and EditPatch depart significantly from those very flexible options just described for EditMesh. In the case of EditableMesh, the choice to make this change from EditMesh was to increase interactive speed while sub-object modeling. If you need the transform flexibility just described, use EditMesh. If you want speed, use EditableMesh. There currently is no equivalent option for EditSpline and EditPatch. The rules for the way the remaining Edit modifiers transform centers are located is much simpler:

- When the transform center choice (in the toolbar) is set to Pivot Point Center, only one axis tripod is generated, and it is located at the center of the vertex/face/edge selection set. The Pivot Point Center option is now identical to the Selection Center option.

- When the coordinate system is Local, the axis tripod is still located at the center of the selection set; however, its orientation depends on the selection level. The orientation of the axis is an average on the selection's normal vectors.

    This difference in calculating transform center points may be the single largest reason for using EditMesh over EditableMesh. If you want to manipulate separate selections at the same time (simultaneous extrusion or rotations, for example), you need to use EditMesh. If you are modeling single areas of the mesh at one time, you're better off using EditableMesh.

Using Points and Grids Instead of Pivots

The object's pivot point provides a naturally relevant point about which to scale and rotate the object when working at the Object level. But when working at the Sub-object level, not only is the object's pivot not available as a center option, but this point is usually not as relevant to the various sub-object selections you make.

T I P

You can transform about the object's pivot by selecting the object as the Pick coordinate system and using the Coordinate System Center.

In Sub-object mode, the transform manager's Pivot Point Center option ignores the object's pivot point and uses the selection center instead. Therefore, you have two options—the selection center and the coordinate system center. The transform manager's Pick option thus becomes extremely important because it provides the capability to use any object as the center point. To control the manipulation point, simply choose an object you don't mind positioning as the Pick coordinate system and place it where you want to rotate and scale (see fig. 12.10).

FIGURE 12.10
Rotating vertices about a Point Helper object.

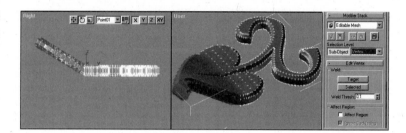

> **TIP**
>
> Point Helper objects are invaluable tools for sub-object modeling because they can be aligned and snapped to vertices and then used as the coordinate center. Modelers commonly link Point helpers to their objects so the manipulation points are always there.

Using a Point helper as the coordinate center is very similar to the 3DS DOS practice of locating the Global Axis in the 3D Editor. Point helpers provide the added benefits of multiple points, linking, alignment, and animation. For accurate placement, a Point helper can be placed with 2.5D vertex snap or the Align function. For a true 3D vertex snap, you currently need to snap the Point to the desired vertex in two perpendicular viewports.

It may take a little time to align a Point helper to the correct spot, and you must decide whether this accuracy is indeed needed. Some modelers prefer to modify the selection quickly and worry about its placement later. At the Sub-object level, this approach does not usually work because entities within the object are being rotated and scaled, and it is not easy to go back if your manipulation point has moved. The careful placement of a Point helper axis thus becomes a major aid when manipulating vertices and faces.

> **TIP**
>
> You can save a few steps when adjusting helper objects by pinning the stack (with the Thumb Tack button), leaving Sub-object mode, and then transforming the helper.

Grids are the other valuable tool for sub-object modeling because, like a Point helper, their pivot point can be used as the transform coordinate center. In addition, Grid objects provide a customizable snap grid for creating vertices. A subtle, but valuable, feature of grids is Grid Nudging— a capability assigned (by default) to the number pad's + and – keys. When a grid is active, pressing these keys will "nudge" the grid along its Z axis by a given distance. The default distance for the move is one system unit, although you can set it to be whatever you like with the Grid Nudge value located in the Preferences Viewports tab.

Angle Thresholds

Several functions within EditMesh and EditableMesh base their operation on the angles formed between adjacent faces. The AutoEdge, AutoSmooth, and Explode functions use what is called an *angle threshold* value, which refers to the angle formed between the faces. Every pair of faces that shares an edge is analyzed to determine the angle between the faces. Internally, this is done by comparing the included angle formed from the face normals. Although correct, this can be a bit difficult to visualize. Instead, you can determine the angle by visually projecting one face's side and noting the included angle formed to the other face. Figure 12.11 shows both methods.

FIGURE 12.11
Angle thresholds by face normal and included angle.

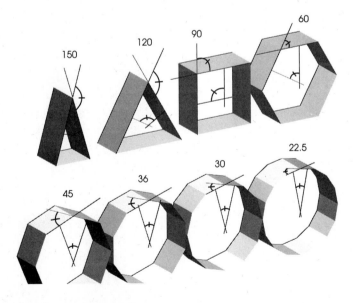

Any pair of faces whose included angle is less than the angle threshold value is acted upon by the function using it. The more acute the angle, the higher the angle threshold needs to be for it to qualify; lower thresholds work on shallower angles. Faces that do not fall within the range are simply ignored by the function.

Animating Sub-Object Transforms

For all their capabilities, none of the Edit modifiers produce an animation track in Track View. When you work with these modifiers, you are either making explicit modeling decisions or are defining sub-object selections that are passed up the stack for the next modifier to affect and possibly animate. Animation does not occur within the Edit modifiers—this is one of the few times when the Animated button has no effect.

NOTE

The Linked XForm and XForm modifiers provide you with the ability to perform transform animation on the sub-object selections passed to them.

The procedure for animating vertices, edges, elements, patches, and splines is to make a selection and apply a subsequent modifier to manipulate the selection. The desire is often to animate what you are performing in the Edit modifier itself. Because this is almost always a transform, the XForm modifier is commonly applied to animate the selection with a standard transform. If a selection made within the Edit modifier does not qualify as a geometric selection, it cannot be passed up the stack and cannot be animated. Common examples of this are vertex and lattice control handles and vertex region curves. These cannot be directly animated and must be approximated with other method.

Modifiers other than XForm, such as Bend or MeshSmooth, will act as they do upon the entire object except they now constrain their effect to what was just selected (as shown in earlier in this chapter). Animating the modifier's parameters will animate the discreet, active selection. If the selection changes, so does the modifier's animated result. Although you cannot animate an Edit modifier's selection, you can use a Volume Select modifier and animate what selection is defined by its size and placement.

Useful Keyboard Shortcuts

When modeling at the Sub-object level within any of the Edit modifiers, you will find it most efficient to use familiar keyboard shortcuts for several of the most common functions:

- Select All, Select None, Select Invert, and Selection Lock

  Because selection manipulation is key to sub-object modeling, you need to quickly convert the current selection to be efficient.

- Backface Cull, Edges Only, Hide Unselected, Unhide All, and Unhide By Name

  Having these Display panel commands as keyboard alternates enables you to work within the Edit modifier without having to leave it, forfeit your place in the stack, and loose time.

- Move, Rotate, Scale, Cycle Through Scale Modes, Center Point Cycle, Constraint Direction Cycle, and Constraint Plane Cycle

  With Edit modifiers you are nearly always working with transforms and need to switch the coordinate system type, center point, and axis constraint often. By having these as keyboard shortcuts, you will save many visits to the toolbar.

- Select, Cycle Selection Method, Snap, Angle Snap, Absolute/Relative Snap, and Window Crossing

  These selection method options enable you to change selection methods while not having to move your mouse. You can keep concentrating on the selection itself and not lose your place as you click on option buttons.

- Cycle Sub-object Level and Sub-object Selection Toggle

  It is very common to cycle between the various selection levels (such as faces, vertices, and edges) and making these selection level options shortcuts speeds navigation.

Common Terms and Concepts for Meshes

The complexity of models possible in 3D Studio MAX is staggering, and it's easy to be taken aback by their apparent complexity. But as you look closely at even the most complex models, you'll notice that they're made of simple, discrete pieces that are knitted together. In fact, 3D Studio MAX uses only a few very basic geometric types to define the many worlds created within it (see fig. 12.12). EditMesh, EditableMesh, and Volume Select all use the same geometric terminology when making selections.

Mesh editing relies on the capabilities contained within the EditMesh modifier. The same capabilities, with a few exceptions, are also present in the EditableMesh object definition. The choice of which to use and when is discussed next.

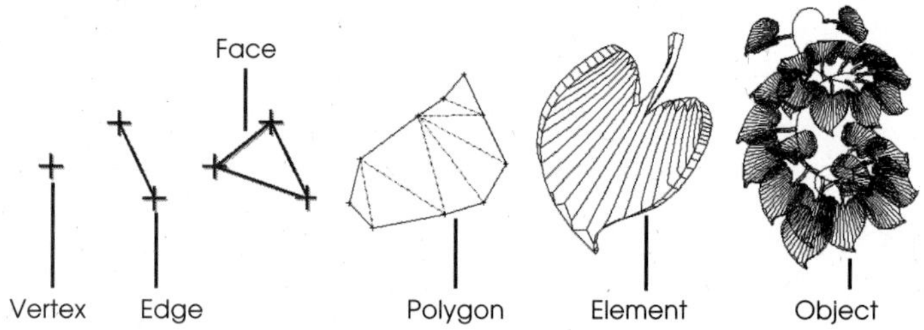

FIGURE 12.12

The geometric components of 3D Studio MAX meshes.

Vertex   Edge   Polygon   Element   Object

A *mesh* generically refers to a mesh object or a collection of its faces. The term mesh is used when referring generically to geometry and is not a specific entity type. Meshes are composed of triangular faces that in turn define any combination of flat, curved, or bent surfaces. (A mesh is equivalent to an AutoCAD PFace or polyface mesh.)

Vertices define points in three-dimensional space and are the most basic of entities. A vertex defines no geometry except the location of a point in space. It has no surface or properties of its own, and so cannot be seen in a rendering. The sole purpose of vertices is to build faces upon. A vertex that is not connected to other vertices by faces to form a mesh is known as an *isolated vertex*. 3DS MAX stores mapping coordinates with vertex locations so that when vertices move, the associated mapping moves with them.

Faces are triangular surfaces formed by connecting three vertices. Because each face has only three points, each defines a geometric plane, and each is flat by definition. Each face defines a *normal*, a direction that is perpendicular to the face's surface and that points away from the face's visible side. Faces are what "skin" a model, give it form, and enable it to have materials and reflect light. As you assemble faces, they define surfaces and identifiable forms. (A face is equivalent to an AutoCAD 3DFace that has only three sides. A conventional four-sided 3DFace is the equivalent of two 3D Studio faces.)

Edges are the lines that connect two vertices and form a face's border. Each face, therefore, has three edges. Adjacent faces that share two vertices are also said to *share an edge*. Edges are not created directly, but rather are the result of creating faces. Edges are used to manipulate faces or serve as the basis for creating new faces. A face always possesses three edges, and these edges can be either visible or invisible. Edge visibility influences redraw speed, clarity, and the boundaries of polygon selections. Visible edges are used primarily for clarity and influence only the mesh's rendering when given a wireframe material.

Polygons are coplanar sets of welded faces that make up the facets, sides, and ends of meshes. 3DS MAX uses the term *polygon* to define coplanar sets for faces within a mesh for the purpose of face selection. A polygon's definition stops at visible edges or at a planar threshold. In 3DS MAX, polygons are a tool only for selecting faces—they are not entities with special manipulation capabilities. When you select and transform polygons, you are really just selecting and transforming the selection of faces.

Elements are 3D Studio MAX's term for a discrete mesh. When adjacent faces build off of the same vertices, they are said to be *welded* together. Vertices used by more than one face are said to be *shared* or *welded* vertices. An element extends as far as the mesh has welded faces. Often, elements within the same object appear to be continuous, when in fact they use a duplicate set of vertices along the common edges. Such vertices are known as *coincidental vertices* and are required when you want a distinct break in the mesh but still want it to appear continuous. An element can be quite large or as small as a single, isolated face. Any number of elements may occupy the same object. Although separate meshes, elements cannot be animated themselves without a modifier.

Mesh objects contain one or more elements and can be thought of as an organization of elements. Unlike an element, an object does not need to be a continuous mesh. An object is commonly composed of widely separated elements, and it may contain isolated vertices (which are, in turn, individual elements). Objects are named and colored, and only objects have transforms, pivot points, data history stacks, and animation tracks.

Therefore, a geometrical hierarchy for mesh objects exists within 3D Studio MAX. This hierarchy is shown the following order (from lowest to highest):

1. Vertex (can be isolated)

2. Face (built upon three vertices)

3. Edge (result of a face, and connects two vertices)

4. Polygon (contains coplanar, welded faces)

5. Element (which contains continuously welded faces)

6. Object (contains elements of continuous faces and possibly isolated vertices)

The EditableMesh Object

The EditableMesh object was introduced in Release 1.0 as a not fully implemented and hidden feature that needed to be enabled with an entry in the 3ds.max.ini file. 3D Studio MAX Release 1.1 brings the finished version of this much needed object class as a standard feature (see fig. 12.13).

FIGURE 12.13
The EditableMesh object command panel.

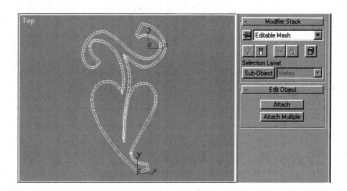

Because of its capability to edit and define a selection, the EditableMesh falls under the category of selection modifiers. Technically, however, EditableMesh is not a modifier—it's actually the object class for all mesh objects. The interface for EditableMesh will appear as the stack's first entry.

Any object that has a raw mesh as its creation parameters (the master object) is an EditableMesh object in Release 1.1. This means that when you import a 3DS file, every object imports as an EditableMesh object, and you can immediately begin editing in Sub-object mode without applying a modifier (similar to the way editing was performed in 3DSDOS).

You can convert objects you create in 3DS MAX into EditableMesh objects by collapsing their stacks. If a modifier in the collapsed stack converts to mesh, the result is an EditableMesh object. Objects without an edit history cannot be collapsed. If the object is a brand-new primitive, loft, or Boolean, you'll need to add a modifier (any modifier other than EditPatch, that is) to be able to collapse the stack to an EditableMesh. If the object is a patch object, you'll need to add a surface modifier (Normal, Smooth, Material, UVW, or EditMesh) to the stack to change the outcome to a mesh. Otherwise the object will collapse to a Patch object.

NOTE

Working with EditableMesh is similar to working in programs without an edit history concept (3DS DOS, for example).

Using EditableMesh Versus EditMesh

So what is an EditableMesh, and why is it here? Many times the modeling you are doing is explicit. You are working on the model at its root level by pulling vertices, building faces, and dividing edges. When this is all that you are doing, and you do not need to pass selections up the stack to other modifiers or preserve operations as distinct, retrievable operations, you can use the base functionality of the EditableMesh object.

EditableMesh is actually somewhat of a step backward in computer modeling because you cannot reverse your decisions. When you are using an EditableMesh, you are performing explicit deformations to the entities within the object. Unlike EditMesh, the history of your actions in EditableMesh is not recorded because the actions are explicit (although undo is still available). EditMesh records your actions so it can propagate changes from lower in the stack. Because EditableMesh is the master object, there cannot be anything lower in the stack. You should think of everything you do with EditableMesh as being permanent because your Undo buffer is of finite size and does not last between sessions. Each method obviously has its advantages and disadvantages. The following table outlines the most important aspects of each:

EditMesh Modifier	EditableMesh Object
Full Mesh editing functionality	Full Mesh editing functionality
Capability to use local coordinate centers for selections	Can use selection center of coordinate system center only

continues

EditMesh Modifier	EditableMesh Object
Can only attach objects one at a time	Can attach multiple objects at the same time
Full undo to the current limit	Full undo to the current limit
Each operation performed is remembered by the modifier and saved in the file	Only the resulting mesh at the end of the session is saved in the file
File size grows with editing and extra Edit modifiers	File size affected by resulting mesh size only
Detached and deleted geometry is defined within the modifier and saved with the file	Detached and deleted geometry is discarded after the undo limit is reached
Deleting the modifier removes all changes, even the deletion of geometry	Object definitions cannot be deleted without deleting the object itself
Modifier's effect can be turned off	Object definitions cannot be turned off
Can define active selection anywhere in the stack	Can define active selection only at the beginning of the stack
A copy of the object is made in RAM for each EditMesh, along with the processing of all the steps	Only the result, which is the master object, is kept in RAM
Detaching faces and vertices can be very slow on large meshes	Detaching is fast, even for large meshes
Initiating the modifier takes time with large meshes	Entering Sub-object mode is fast
Operations may seem sluggish with large meshes	Operations feel fast
Intended for animated modeling	Intended for static modeling
No keyboard shortcuts	Has keyboard equivalents if activated in the 3dsmax.ini file

NOTE

Because the keyboard shortcuts for Editable Mesh are fixed and may conflict with your choices for 3DS MAX itself, enabling them has been made an option which must be enabled with the following addition to your 3dsmax.ini file:

    [EditableMesh]
    KeyAccelsEnabled=1

The keyboard shortcuts themselves are detailed in the 3D Studio MAX R1.1 readme.wri file.

Mesh Graphical Components

Besides their geometric classifications, objects tend to have graphical characteristics that are referred to often. This book and the 3D Studio MAX documentation refer to the same terminology when describing parts of an object as shown in figure 12.14 and in the following list:

FIGURE 12.14
Graphical components of objects.

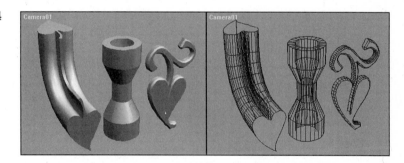

- **Segments**   The cross-sectional divisions along a dimension of an object. Each segment provides an opportunity to deform the mesh at that section. You should base an object's need for segments on your need to bend, push, or break the mesh. Sides are the same as segments but refer to the meshed subdivisions of a curve, arc, or circle.

- **Caps**   Refer to the ends perpendicular to the an object's extrusion. The extrusion may be a height parameter, an extrusion distance, or a loft path.

- **Sides**   Usually associated with the steps that form an arc—one side for each step. Sides can also refer to two coplanar faces that share an edge; many people call these facets.

- **Steps**   The spline subdivisions of curve, arc, and circle segments.

Mesh Surface Definitions

Within EditMesh and EditableMesh is the capability to influence what the surface of your model looks like. This is done with smoothing group assignments, face normal orientation, and material ID assignments. All of these are located within the Face level's EditSurface rollout shown in figure 12.15.

FIGURE 12.15

The EditSurface rollouts of EditableMesh and EditMesh.

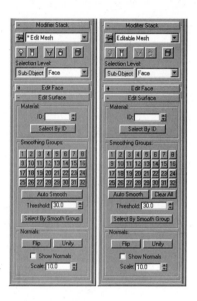

Smoothing is greatly affected by the consistency of the mesh because the effect of smoothing can occur only over welded faces. Edges that meet without sharing both vertices will form a seam, whereas redundant faces can cause very odd effects.

In Practice: Sub-Object Modeling

- **Defining selections**   The Modifier Stack allows different selections to be defined at any point in the edit history, with each modifier affecting the active selection at its point in the stack. The selection can be the entire object, or one of a variety of sub-object selection types (vertices, faces, edges, and so on). The stack allows the contents of the selection to be changed at later times.

- **Edit modifiers**   The Edit modifiers combine powerful modeling with sub-object selection capabilities, with and overhead in RAM being required for their flexibility.

■ **EditableMesh versus EditMesh** The EditableMesh object is designed for fast, explicit, modeling with a minimum of RAM usage, whereas EditMesh modeling decisions can be changed at any time and introduced at any point in the stack, with the cost being RAM. The EditMesh modifier provides more flexible methods for locating the sub-object selection centers and is a reason why it becomes a choice over EditableMesh when this flexibility is required.

■ **Defining selections with Volume Select** Whenever possible, use the Volume Select modifier to define a selection instead of EditMesh to minimize RAM requirements. A selection defined by EditMesh can often be assumed by a subsequent Volume Select modifier, allowing the costly EditMesh modifier to be removed.

■ **Choosing selection methods** Volume Select is ideal when you want to adjust the topology and density of your underlying model but do not need to change its size (changing the segmentation of the original cylinder for example). EditMesh becomes the preferred selection method when the underlying topology is fixed, but its dimensions will change (change the radius of the original cylinder for example).

■ **Helper objects** Helper objects are convenient for sub-object modeling. Combining the Pick coordinate system with a Point Helper object enables you to define the transform center for sub-object transforms. Grid Helpers can be nudged while in Sub-object mode allowing for fast, layered vertex creation.

"Underwater Castle"
Created by Samati Boonchitsitsak for "Bug II"©
    Sega of America
Realtime Associates, Inc., El Segundo, CA

Chapter 13

MESH MODELING

The majority of current 3D Studio MAX modeling tends to be with meshes. Although this is partly because most 3D Studio veterans became accustomed to meshes, a larger reason is because 3DS MAX's major strength still lies in its mesh editing roots. Mesh editing involves modeling at the sub-object level with explicit vertex, face, and edge selections. Whereas the definitions of these selection levels were defined and discussed at the end of Chapter 12, this chapter focuses on how to manipulate these discreet pieces with the EditableMesh object and the EditMesh modifier.

Major topics for this chapter include:

- Mesh editing at the sub-object level, also referred to as "traditional" mesh editing or vertex "sculpting."

- Modeling at the vertex level, including selecting, hiding, creating, transforming, using effect region, and affecting topology.

- Modeling at the face level, including selecting, hiding, creating, transforming, extruding, and topology changes.

- Controlling surface characteristics at the face level, including smoothing, normals, and materials.

- Modeling at the Edge level, including transforming, visibility, dividing, and turning.

Modeling with Vertices

We begin with vertex manipulation because it is the most basic and often the most appropriate control you have on a mesh. The vast majority of 3DS MAX (and computer graphic) operations manipulate vertices, with the faces simply being pulled along. Faces that share vertices are always manipulated by them. Every time you create or clone a mesh, you also create vertices, because the faces are defined by their vertices.

Transforming vertices is very similar to moving, rotating, and scaling faces or edges. The reason for this similarity is that mesh editing always affects vertex locations. Mesh editing in 3DS MAX manipulates vertices—not faces, elements, or edges. Faces and edges that make up the mesh follow along to the new positions dictated by the vertices. When you scale an element, you are scaling the location of its vertices. When you rotate faces, you are rotating the vertex locations, and the faces change orientation based upon the new locations. Thinking of this when you perform any mesh editing operation, or any modification for that matter, should make the results more predictable and obvious.

Vertex Level Basics

As soon as you enter the Vertex selection level, all vertices are displayed as ticks (see fig. 13.1). Unlike faces, vertices are displayed even if they are on parts of the mesh whose face normals point away from you. At this point, every selection you make consists of vertices, with transforms affecting them only. As always, adjusting vertices pulls the faces that are built on them.

FIGURE 13.1

*The Vertex Level
common to both
EditableMesh and
EditMesh.*

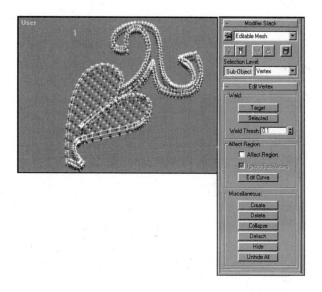

Isolated and solitary vertices usually exist for only one reason—to build faces on. Isolated vertices rarely have any other purpose. Vertices never define a mesh by themselves and cannot be independently rendered. When faces are deleted, 3DS MAX prompts whether you want to delete the orphaned vertices at the same time. Unless you plan to build new faces on these vertices in the future, your answer should always be yes.

Selecting Vertices

Selecting vertices is quite simple, because the window and crossing options don't apply. Clicking on a vertex selects it. Also, a region selection (either rectangular, circular, or fence) that encloses a vertex selects it. As always, pressing the Ctrl key enables you to add to a selection, whereas pressing the Alt key subtracts the selection. Most often you will be using a region selection and removing stray vertices with another region or selective clicks.

Hiding Vertices

Hiding vertices is a method of removing them from accidental editing. Hidden vertices hide their display ticks, but do not hide the mesh they define. When hidden, vertices are no longer selectable and are no longer affected by your actions. In this state, vertices are very similar to frozen objects. Hiding vertices is an extremely valuable tool when you want to preserve a certain area of the mesh but modify other parts—especially those that are close to the hidden vertices. Hidden vertices can also be used to segregate areas of the mesh from face level operations. Hidden vertices cannot have faces built upon them and are not considered in face selections when using the By-Vertex face selection option.

Warning

When you hide a selection of vertices, these vertices are still considered the active selection and can be accidentally deleted or, if you press the spacebar lock, transformed. To be safe, it is best to perform a Select None, or click in the viewport to empty the selection after hiding vertices to ensure that they are not affected by mistake.

Due to their size, vertices can be difficult to see. Before selecting vertices for an edit, it is good practice to perform a Select None to ensure that your selection will be only what you intend. Because selections are passed up the stack, it is easy to forget about an earlier selection that is now active—especially when the selection was established by a much earlier modifier.

Transforming Vertices

The toolbar's Move, Rotate, and Scale transforms are your principal method for manipulating vertices, and the subtleties described earlier in the "Common Terms and Concepts for Meshes" section of Chapter 12 are of particular importance. The capability to edit meshes at the vertex level is actually quite powerful. As you manipulate vertex positions, you pull, stretch, and scale the faces that are built on them. Much of the secret to manipulating vertices effectively is in selecting the correct vertices to be edited and leaving the others alone.

Although you can edit vertices individually, most vertex editing is done with selections. Passing single vertices up the stack as the active selection rarely has much—if any—effect. If you are rotating or scaling a single vertex, you must use the coordinate system center to have any effect as well. Otherwise, you are rotating and scaling about the vertex itself and nothing occurs.

SCALING A CYLINDER INTO A DUMBBELL

It is very common to take 3D primitives and convert them to entirely different objects through vertex editing. This exercise takes a basic cylinder and creates a dumbbell with just a few vertex edits and then perfects the surface with smoothing group assignments.

1. Create a cylinder with 24 sides and 9 Height segments on the home plane. The radius of this cylinder will be the radius of the dumbbell.

2. Add an EditMesh modifier and select the middle two cross-sections of vertices (most easily done with a rectangular selection window).

3. Click Non-Uniform Scale, choose the World coordinate system, the Selection Center, and the X,Y axis.

4. Scale the vertices down to form a center handle grip, as shown in the first viewport of figure 13.2.

5. Select the middle four cross-sections. Switch your axis constraint to Z.

6. Scale the selection upward until the cross-sections are close to the next rows of vertices, as shown in the second viewport of figure 13.2.

7. Select the top and bottom rows of vertices and scale these as close to their next rows as you did the others in step 6, as shown in the third viewport of figure 13.2.

   You now have two skinny segments next to one broad segment at each end.

8. Press your Ctrl key to add to your current selection and select the other vertices bordering the opposite skinny segments.

9. Switch your constraint to X,Y and scale these inward until they form a bevel, as shown in the fourth viewport of figure 13.3.

10. Switch the axis constraint to Z and scale the middle two rows of vertices out until they form a reasonable slant to the barbell's edges, as shown in the first viewport of figure 13.3).

11. Switch to Shaded mode.

    The top right view of figure 13.2 shows how the dumbbell looks odd. This is because the cylinder began with one smoothing group along its sides, and scaling the vertices angled the faces in a way that doesn't make sense for smoothing.

12. Exit Sub-object mode, add a Smooth modifier at the end of the stack, and check the AutoSmooth box. Accepting the default value of 30 degrees.

The bevels and sides are now crisp (see the lower views of fig. 13.3), because adjacent rows no longer share the same smoothing group.

FIGURE 13.2
*Creating a dumbbell
from a cylinder
primitive.*

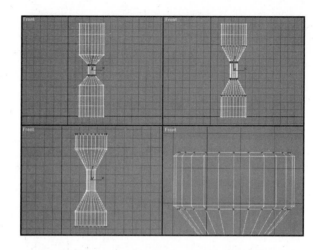

FIGURE 13.3
Finishing the dumbbell.

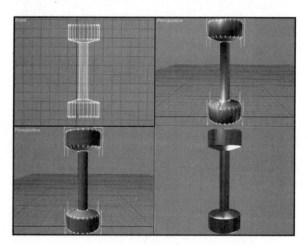

ROTATING VERTICES

As the following exercise's basic Sphere object shows, you do not need a complicated model to investigate the powerful effects that vertex manipulation can have.

1. Create a 16-sided sphere on the home plane and add an EditMesh modifier to it.

2. From a side viewport, select every other row (latitude), skipping the top vertex (as shown in the top of figure 13.4).

3. Name this selection "Lat."

4. Begin another selection in the Top viewport by selecting every other row (longitude/meridian) of the sphere. You can do this most easily by using the Fence selection method (see the bottom of fig. 13.4).

   Note that for a very interesting effect you can select the faces in a similar manner and assign individual smoothing groups to achieve the smoothing effects shown in figure 13.4.

5. Name this selection "Long."

FIGURE 13.4
Making the preliminary vertex selections.

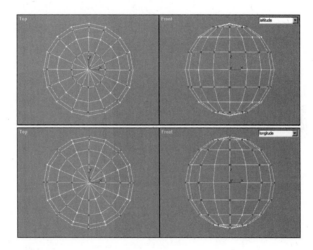

6. Click Rotate and choose the World coordinate system, the selection center, and the Z axis.

7. Select "Lat" from the Named Selection Set drop-down and rotate the selection from any viewport.

   The sides of the sphere twist in a chevron pattern, as shown in the top viewports of figure 13.4B.

8. Select "Long" from the Named Selection Set drop-down and rotate the selection from any viewport.

9. The chevroned sides of the sphere rotate together, decreasing the sphere from 16 to 8 sides, as shown in the lower viewports of figure 13.5. Note that although the pole vertices are selected, they are coincidental with the selection center, spinning in place without effect on the mesh. You can now switch between selection sets to perfect the appearance of your chevrons.

FIGURE 13.5
Rotating the vertices of a sphere primitive.

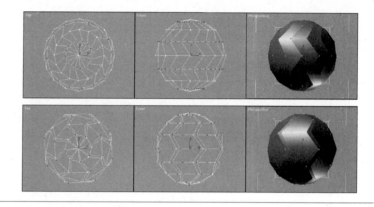

Modeling with Affect Region

The Affect Region function enables you to influence an entire region of vertices with a much smaller selection or, more often, only a single vertex. When you check the Affect Region check box, every transform you perform affects a region of vertices instead of only the ones you selected. Checking this box fundamentally changes the way vertex editing works, because a single vertex now acts like a magnet by pulling others when it changes position by a Move, Rotate, or Scale transform.

Affect Region works in conjunction with its controlling region curve. The *region curve* is a visualization of the result of moving a single vertex from a flat grid. Clicking Edit Curve brings up the Edit Affect Region Curve dialog (see fig. 13.5). As you can see, the Falloff setting defines the radius of a selection "sphere." Every vertex within this sphere is affected according to the values of the region curve.

2'-0"   2'-0"

FIGURE 13.6

The Edit Affect Region Curve dialog's meaning.

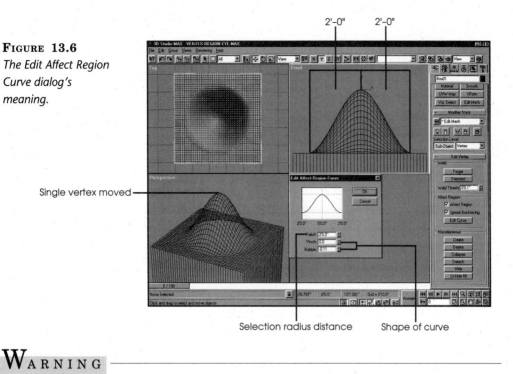

Single vertex moved

Selection radius distance   Shape of curve

WARNING

The Affect Region Function mode does not respect the status of hidden vertices. Every vertex within the falloff radius is affected.

The influence of the region curve is best shown by a single vertex's influence on a box grid. Figures 13.7 and 13.8 show the effect of moving a single vertex by the same amount on a cube 100 units in size. The top rows in both figures show how the shape of the region curve is duplicated by the displaced vertices. With this result in mind, you should be able to predict the impact of the region curves you define. To pull smooth curves with Affect Region, you want to manipulate single vertices, or isolated faces, and pay close attention to the controlling region curve.

The result of editing vertices with Affect Region is similar to working with patches because moving a single vertex is much like pulling a patch vertex. The major difference, of course, is that a subsequent vertex move does not restore the previous mesh, whereas reversing the vertex move of a patch does. Figure 13.9 compares the results between pulling the central vertex of mesh and patch cylinders.

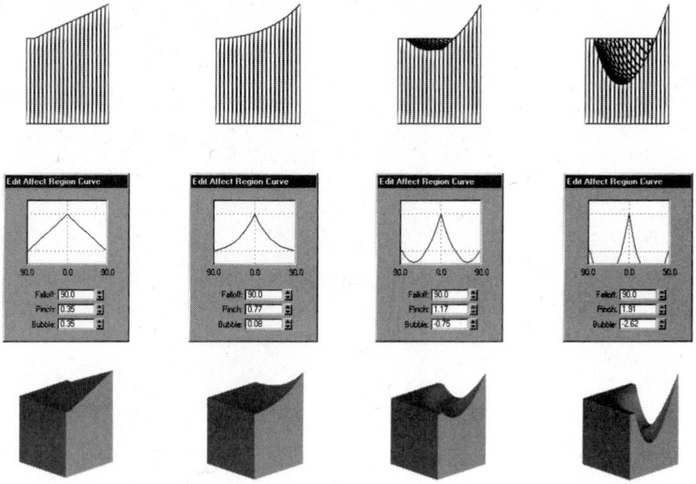

FIGURE 13.7
The effect of using concave region curves.

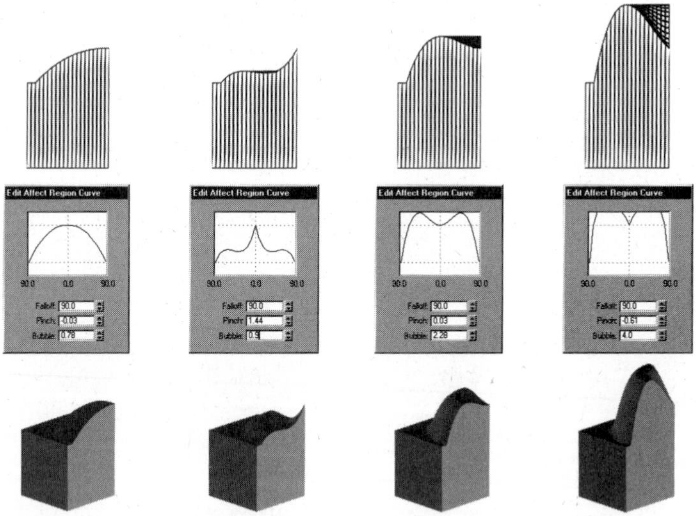

FIGURE 13.8
The effect of using convex region curves.

The Ignore Backface option controls which vertices within the falloff radius are affected. When the Ignore Backface option is off, every vertex within the falloff radius is affected. When Ignore Backface is on (the default), the faces that share the selected vertices are analyzed to see which way their normals are pointed. An averaged normal of the faces is determined and compared against every other face within the falloff radius. If the averaged normal can "see" the other faces (the compared angle is less than 90 degrees), the vertices that share those faces are affected. Vertices shared between backface and visible faces are considered seen and are affected.

Mesh   Patch   Mesh   Patch

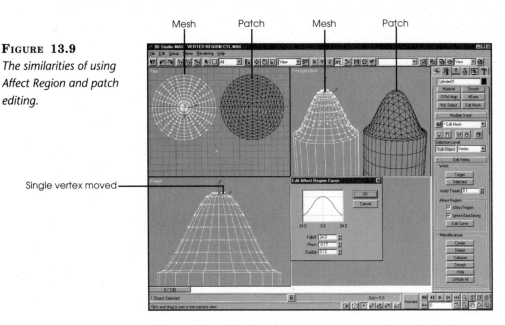

FIGURE 13.9

The similarities of using Affect Region and patch editing.

Single vertex moved

TIP

To be absolutely sure of Affect Region's impact, clone one or two faces off the original mesh, and use these three or four vertices as your vertex pulling "magnet." This process gives you a clear understanding of which faces can be seen when using Ignore Backface.

WARNING

Isolated vertices are poor choices to use with Ignore Backface, because they do not have any faces from which to derive a normal; they use a default normal direction instead. An isolated face is a better choice to use with Ignore Backface.

If the normals are pointed away, their faces cannot be "seen" by the vertex, and the Affect Region does not select their vertices. Faces whose normals are "on edge," at exactly 90 degrees, are affected. Figure 13.10 shows the effect of moving the middle vertex of a cube's top front edge within a falloff radius that exceeds the cube's height. The first cube shows the result with Ignore Backface turned off—every vertex is displaced, even those on the bottom. The middle cube shows the result with the Ignore Backface option turned on—the bottom vertices are not moved because they cannot be seen, whereas the edge vertices are at 90 degrees and are selected. The last cube has the

Ignore Backface option off, but moves a vertex from the second row—the side vertices are no longer affected because they are now presenting a backface to the vertex.

FIGURE 13.10

The effects of using Ignore Backface.

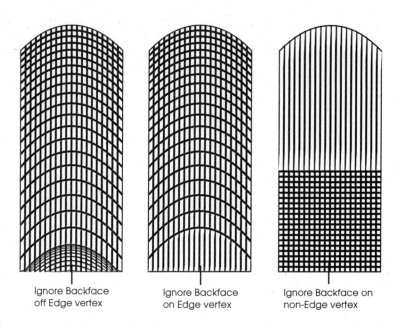

Ignore Backface
off Edge vertex

Ignore Backface
on Edge vertex

Ignore Backface on
non-Edge vertex

Because the face normal that Affect Region uses is an average, surprising results occur when the faces shared by selected vertices have diverse face normals (such as picking vertices from opposite sides of a box). In this case, the averaged normal may not include vertices that would be included if the vertices were selected individually. If the resulting affected vertices are very different from what is needed, it may be better to clone faces from the selection and use this new, isolated selection for the operation. This will produce an averaged normal which does not include the extra faces that originally made the averaged normal unsuccessful.

Many situations call for using several gradual moves or rotations rather than one large one. The first cube in figure 13.11 shows the effect of rotating a vertex 90 degrees in one move where the resulting distortion is linear. The remaining cubes show the successive small rotations whose sum is 90 degrees and results in a curved distortion. The middle cube is not ignoring backfacing so it pulls every vertex in its range. The last cube has its Ignore Backfacing checked and is missing vertices at critical times.

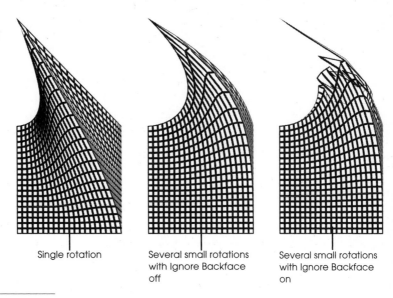

Single rotation   Several small rotations   Several small rotations
                       with Ignore Backface   with Ignore Backface
                       off   on

Creating Vertices

Every time you create or clone a mesh, you also create vertices because the faces are defined by them. Although this method often provides the vertices you need for other modeling, you may need to create others independently, and at exact locations, for creating stitching faces.

Vertices cannot be created in isolation. They must be added to an existing object from within the EditMesh modifier. Within EditMesh you can create vertices individually with the Vertex/Create function, or you can clone vertex selections as part of the object or as a new object. Cloning vertices of an existing mesh is the only method for creating isolated vertices as objects.

The Vertex/Create function places you in a mode in which every click on the screen creates a new vertex at that location on the active grid. Creating vertices in this manner is especially useful when used with an active Grid object and the nudge keys. This nudging enables you to move the active grid, without leaving your current sub-object command, and create layers of vertices at controllable heights.

Using Existing Meshes for Vertices

Your greatest source for creating vertices is existing meshes. You can either "strip" the faces off a mesh by deleting them and leaving the vertex "cloud," or select their vertices and clone them when performing a transform. Cloned vertices are just that—they leave their faces behind and create an object without surface. If you need to clone the mesh, you should clone face selections instead. When cloning, you have the choice of whether to make the selection a new object or isolated vertices within the current object.

Commonly, you need to duplicate an existing mesh's vertices in place so that these vertices can become the building blocks for another mesh that relates to the first. If you are going to add vertices to an object and want the vertices to correlate to existing vertices, clone them in place, or to the side, for use as a source. This method is usually easier and more accurate than carefully placing an active Grid for each level of new vertices.

NOTE

To clone a selection of vertices in place (or any other selection), activate a transform, press the Shift key, and click once on the selection. This clones the selection without a displacement.

Using Vertex Create

Vertex Create is the only method for creating vertices from scratch, other than cloning. The vertices you create are always part of the original object, and usually serve as the building points for future vertices. When creating vertices, each point you pick defines two coordinates, with the third being supplied by the viewport's active grid. This can be overridden when using vertex and edge snapping.

Vertex Create works well with vertex and edge snapping. Setting your vertex snap priority to 1 and the others to Off (see fig. 13.12) ensures that you will only be snapping to vertices. When using 3D Snap, Vertex Create enables you to create the framework on which to build bridging faces. When using 2.5D Snap, you create a projected template of vertices onto the viewport's active grid. Although rarely needed, flattened projections of other meshes can be created from these projected templates.

FIGURE 13.12

*The Snap settings for
3D Vertex snapping.*

FIGURE 13.12

*The Snap settings for
3D Vertex snapping.*

Vertex Topology

With vertices you work with the defining points of your mesh, and it is only natural to affect the topology with them as well. Besides the ever-available Delete, several functions are unique to vertices, with the most often used being Weld.

Welding Vertices

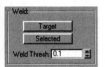

Welding fuses two or more vertices together to form a single vertex, which drags with it any faces built upon the original vertices. Welding is used for knitting together separate faces to form an element, or consolidating faces of an element into a simpler mesh. The Weld function is by far the most commonly used button in the Vertex level, and with it you can weld either precisely or generally.

NOTE

Although you can assign a single EditMesh to multiple objects, you can weld only vertices of the same object, because welding changes the object definition. If you want to weld between objects, you must attach one to the other first.

Although mapping coordinates can extend over unwelded faces, smoothing groups cannot. Without the capability to properly smooth, a mesh never looks quite right. Edges that meet without having shared, and thus welded, vertices cannot be smoothed over and always form an edge.

Weld's Target method places you in a mode in which you select vertices and drag them over a target vertex as shown in figure 13.13. Your cursor determines the vertex to which you are welding and changes to crosshairs when over a vertex on the same object. What determines a targeted vertex is the proximity of your cursor in screen pixels. This pixel sensitivity is fixed and is approximately a five-pixel radius. Your active viewport thus has a great influence over what you are welding. Working in an orthogonal viewport enables you to weld vertices that are a great distance apart (in screen depth) which can be either ideal or unwanted. Working in a User or Perspective view usually gives you a clearer understanding of vertex relationships when welding. An often convenient method is to select vertices in orthogonal views and perform the Target weld in a User or Perspective view.

FIGURE 13.13

Welding a selection with Weld Target.

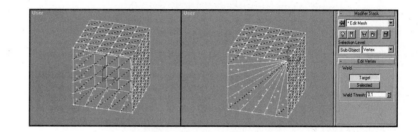

NOTE

Weld Target is commonly combined with Edge Turn and Divide to sculpt defining lines in your mesh.

The Weld Selected method examines your current vertex selection and uses the Weld Threshold value as a range "string" to swing about each of the selected vertices. If any vertices fall within each other's threshold range, they are welded together. If all the vertices are out of each other's threshold range, none are welded and the alert shown in figure 13.14 appears. The locations of all vertices that fall within the threshold are averaged to form the new location for the resulting, welded vertex. The resulting vertex remains selected for quick manipulation. Because an averaging of locations occurs, welded vertices move unless they are already coincidental. If you want to weld only coincidental vertices and do not want any chance of the vertices shifting, set your Weld Threshold to zero. With very large thresholds, Weld Selected can be similar in function to performing a Vertex Collapse on the same selection.

FIGURE 13.14
Weld Selected's Weld Threshold alert.

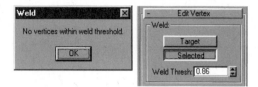

TIP

If you want to weld a selection of vertices about an averaged point, Uniform Scale the selection until the vertices are close and then perform a Weld Selected. This is often faster than adjusting the Weld Threshold and then resetting it.

In practice, Weld Selected is most often used when you are welding portions of a model that are aligned with coincidental vertices, or have vertices that are very close to being so. Perhaps these separate elements used to be together, are the result of a Boolean object, or are from another program that did not afford the capability to weld meshes. In these cases, performing a Select All and welding with a low threshold works well. For accurate welding, Weld Target should be your choice, because with it you can be confident of obtaining positive results.

Collapsing Vertices

Collapse

The Collapse function is destructive but very useful. When you click Collapse, the current selection of vertices is welded into one, common vertex. The location of the new vertex is the average location of the selected vertices. This location is quite predictable when the collapsed vertices are coplanar, as shown in figure 13.15. When not coplanar, the averaged position of the new welded vertex will usually cause a "dent" in the surface. Unlike Edge or Face Collapse, Vertex Collapse does not work on a single vertex because there is nothing with which to average. In actuality, Edge and Face Collapse are supersets of Vertex Collapse, affecting two and three vertices respectively.

FIGURE 13.15
Collapsing a coplanar set of vertices.

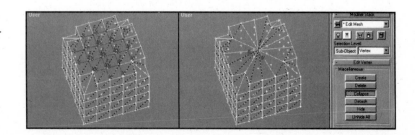

Collapse welds every vertex you have selected, regardless of how far the vertices may be spaced or that they may belong to separate elements. This feature is illustrated in figure 13.16, where the central vertex of each side was selected for the collapse. The only time Collapse ever treats selections separately is if you applied an EditMesh to a selection of objects, in which case each object is welded separately.

FIGURE 13.16

Collapsing separate sets of vertices into one.

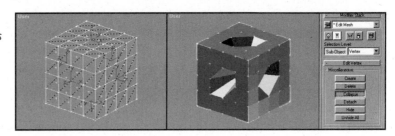

Collapse can also be used as a quick method to weld elements about a common point, as shown in figure 13.17. This capability emphasizes the fact that Collapse can be used to locate important construction points because of the way it averages differences. A midpoint can be established from collapsing two vertices, for example. Creating isolated vertices for the purpose of collapsing to find such points is not unheard of. Similarly, the EditMesh modifier can be removed after other objects have been aligned to collapsed vertices.

FIGURE 13.17

Collapsing vertices from separate elements to form one.

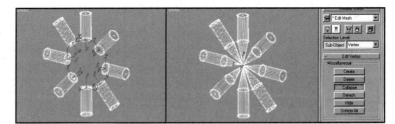

Detaching Vertices

| Detach |

Detaching vertices breaks the vertices and every face they define from the mesh into a new object. Detaching vertices is similar to detaching faces except that when detaching vertices, you are more certain of the mesh's extent. You can easily miss a face and not select one whose normal was facing away from you. With vertices you can be sure you're defining the entire mesh.

If you want to detach vertices and not faces, you need to clone the selection instead of detaching it. Cloning is done by performing a Transform (most often Move) and pressing your Shift key. This creates a vertex cloud without faces. When cloning, you have the option to make the selection a new object. If the selection of cloned vertices is made into a new object, you are not able to build faces onto it from the original object. If you do not create a new object, the new vertices remain selected for you to manipulate. Unlike detaching, cloning does not automatically prevent the vertices from moving. If you want to ensure the cloned vertices do not move, enable your snap, press Shift, and click once over the selection.

Deleting Vertices

Delete

Vertex deletion is a fast way to clear unwanted sections of a mesh, because nothing is left behind, and you aren't slowed down by prompts. When you delete a vertex, you also delete any and all faces that share it. Deleting the central vertex of a cylinder's cap, for example, deletes the entire cap. You may find this surprising, but remember that the criteria for making a crossing selection of faces is to enclose any of their vertices. As always, the Delete key is the keyboard alternate for the Delete function.

Modeling with Faces

This section moves from vertices to faces, the second major component of mesh editing. Manipulating face locations is much like working with vertices in sets of three, but faces define much more information than vertices. Vertices define the location of a face's boundary; faces define a directional normal and a surface that can have material, mapping, and smoothing assignments. When editing vertices, you are modeling the object's form and are concerned only with position. When editing faces, you are also concerned with how the surface reflects light.

TIP

Minimizing the Modifiers rollout provides valuable Command Panel real estate that is useful when working at the Face level. If you make Sub-object cycle and Sub-object mode keyboard alternates, you can collapse the Modifier Stack rollout as well.

Face Level Basics

The face level (see fig. 3.18) provides several modes for selecting and manipulating faces. Navigation of the face level—one of 3DS MAX's longest rollouts—can quickly become an art. But the rollout is long for a reason— faces have many properties, and you cannot edit a face without at least thinking about the ramifications to the rendered surface. When you manipulate faces, you are actually working with vertices in locked sets of three, so much of what you have learned with vertex modeling is directly applicable to face modeling.

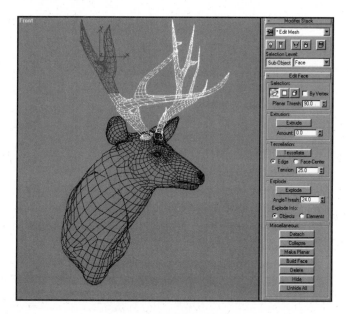

FIGURE 13.18

The Edit Face rollout of both EditMesh and EditableMesh.

Selecting Faces

You can select faces in a variety of ways: singularly, by region, by mesh extents, by coplanar relationships, or even by material and smoothing assignments. Selecting the quickest, most accurate method from among these alternatives is part of the art of good modeling. As always, selection methods are for controlling the results of the selected item; the current selection mode never affects the result of subsequent functions.

Face selection is categorized into three geometric definitions: face, polygon, and element.

Face selection selects a single, triangular face, and is the fastest selection method offered, being much faster than Polygon or Element when working with very large meshes. Face selection displays all edges of selected faces, even if normally invisible.

 Polygon selection selects welded faces that are not separated by visible edges and fall within the Planar Threshold value. Often, it is convenient to select by polygon and then switch to Face Select mode to display every edge of the selection.

 Element Selection selects all faces that can trace a path of shared (welded) vertices. Element selection ignores edge visibility and Planar Threshold, concerning itself only with mesh extents. Element selection is always in Crossing mode.

 By Vertex changes the manner in which your selection is evaluated. When By Vertex is not checked (the default), clicking anywhere within a face, polygon, or element selects that sub-object. When By Vertex is checked, you must click (or enclose) a vertex of the desired sub-object in order to select it. Activating the By Vertex option is primarily for window selections, because there is no longer an initial selection with your first pick. When By Vertex is active, selection is done according to vertices, so the hidden state of vertices is respected. This situation is the only one in which the hidden state of one selection level influences another.

Every time you click and drag, you begin a region selection. The shape of the selection is controlled by the toolbar's flyout. It can be either rectangular, circular, or fence. Changing the region shape is common and makes for a very convenient keyboard alternate. Region selection works hand in hand with the window and crossing selection methods. A window selection must enclose the entire geometry of the selection—all three vertices of a face or all the vertices of a polygon. A crossing selection needs to enclose only a single vertex to select every face, polygon, or element that shares that vertex. Crossing mode is most useful for fast selections, whereas window is best for careful ones.

WARNING

The window selection mode is not consistent. Elements always ignore window and always use crossing, whereas irregularly shaped polygons often do not need to be fully enclosed to be selected. In addition, the By-Vertex option ignores window mode and makes all selections by crossing mode.

Region selections project back into the viewport and select faces that you might not be able to see; there's no filtering of back faces. Therefore, it is good practice to always check your selection in various viewports to confirm what has been selected. The axis tripod is a reliable signal of an accidental selection. If the axis is not correctly centered or more than one axis appears, you have probably selected more than you want.

TIP

When using the By Vertex option, the hidden state of vertices is respected and their faces are excluded from selection.

The By Vertex option becomes very important with region selections performed within a mesh. Without it, your first mouse click to define the region selects the face, polygon, or element—a result you rarely want. With By Vertex on, nothing is selected with your first click, so your region selection performs an accurate region selection of the vertices you then enclose.

NOTE

The By Vertex option ignores the state of the Window/Crossing button and *always* places you in crossing mode.

When working with large meshes, the interactive response may seem slow when moving selections, faces, or elements, because all four viewports are being updated for the mesh. For maximum speed, disable all your viewports so only the active one updates. You can then right-click in another viewport to see the result.

NOTE

You commonly work interchangeably between the Face and Vertex selection levels. When doing so, remember that when you select faces, you do not select their vertices.

Hiding Faces

Hiding faces does more than remove them from view. When hidden, faces are no longer selectable and are no longer affected by your actions. Hiding faces is an extremely valuable tool when you want to protect certain areas of the mesh from selection or modification, especially when you are selecting or modifying nearby faces. Hidden faces can also be used to segregate areas of the mesh from vertex and edge level operations.

NOTE

Although hidden faces are protected within the Edit modifier, they can be affected by modifiers added later in the stack. Volume Select does not ignore them, and object level actions always affect them.

After hiding faces, you can Select All the remaining faces and perform an operation without affecting the hidden ones. Hidden faces are unaffected by the deletion of any or all other faces. Hidden faces are affected only when the vertices upon which they are built are modified. If you transform faces that are welded to hidden faces, the welded vertices of the hidden faces are transformed as well. Vertices unique to the hidden faces cannot be influenced while at the face level. Figure 13.19 shows how a selection of faces was hidden and the remaining faces moved, with the result being that the hidden faces are stretched.

FIGURE 13.19
The effect on hidden faces of transforming visible ones having shared vertices.

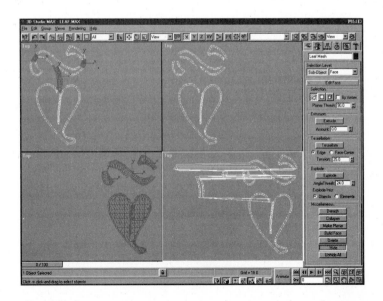

You'll find it convenient to hide faces when assigning sub-object material IDs and smoothing groups. After you assign your carefully made selections, hide them and proceed to select the next ones without fear of affecting the ones you just assigned. Hiding the faces makes subsequent selections faster, because there are fewer and fewer faces to sort through.

Note

Hidden faces do not affect the selection status of elements. If the faces were elements before they were hidden, they remain elements after they are hidden.

Transforming Faces

The toolbar's Move, Rotate, and Scale transforms are your principal methods for manipulating faces. Transforming faces is very similar to moving, rotating, and scaling the equivalent vertex selections with one enormous difference—faces enable you to transform about individual centers if you are using EditMesh. This capability is one of the fundamental differences between using EditMesh and EditableMesh.

With EditMesh, when you are in Pivot Point Center mode, each selection of faces determines its own coordinate system based on the averaged normals of the selection. This enables you to move, rotate, and scale discontiguous face selections all at once, as if you were manipulating them one at a time.

Tip

It is often convenient to use the Local Coordinate System when using Pivot Point Center on face selections. This option ensures that the axis orientations of the selections are consistent with one another, with Z always pointing in along the normal.

Creating Faces

Faces can be created in numerous ways within the Face level. They can be extruded, tessellated, cloned, and even built one at a time. Of these options, Extrude is the most powerful, Build the most common, and Tessellate the most face count intensive.

Extruding Faces

The Extrude function creates faces by moving the selected faces outward and building sides or "walls" connecting the selection and its perimeter. Clicking Extrude places you in an extrusion mode and takes you out of your current toolbar transform.

TIP

The best way to exit Extrude mode is to click the desired toolbar button. Exiting the mode by clicking Extrude automatically changes your toolbar state to Move, even if you were previously in Pick, Rotate, or Scale.

Extrude is one of the rare 3DS MAX functions that actually enables you to define its result within the viewport. In Extrude, your cursor turns into an Extrude icon when it is placed over a selection. You then can define the extrusion by dragging your cursor; the Amount field reports the height of the extrusion.

TIP

The fastest way to use Extrude is to use the Extrusion spinner with a selection, which extrudes the faces but does not affect your toolbar status. You can move between extrusion and transforms without delay.

An extrusion cannot be adjusted. After you make an extrusion it is set. Trying to "adjust" the extrusion results in an additional extrusion on the same selection. Therefore, you should analyze your extrusion carefully before releasing the spinner arrow or dragging cursor. Adjusting an existing extrusion is a great time saver when you want to quickly give successive segments an extrusion. Figure 13.20 shows how to give objects sequential extrusions to add segments.

FIGURE 13.20
Using multiple Extrudes to add height segments.

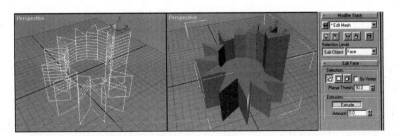

Extrude moves the selection of faces according to its averaged normal. If the selection is flat/coplanar (probably the result of a polygon selection), the extrusion is perpendicular to the plane. If the selection is not coplanar, the normals of the selected faces are averaged and the extrusion follows this vector. Selecting the adjacent sides of a box, for example, extrudes the sides at 45 degrees. For controlled results, Extrude is best used with coplanar selections.

The Extrude function ignores the state of the toolbar's selection center and always treats it as if you were using Pivot Point Center. Each discontiguous selection of faces has its own normal. You can make discontiguous selections and extrude them all at once, and they extrude as if you extruded them one by one. Figure 13.21 shows the creation of a complex form through a series of extrusions and intermediate non-uniform scale transforms on discontiguous selections.

FIGURE 13.21
Using Extrude and non-uniform scale on an octagon primitive.

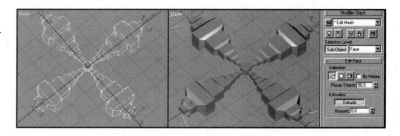

The normals of Extruded faces face outward if the extrusion is positive and face inward if negative. Mapping coordinates are "stretched" along the length of the new sides. Remember that it's usually best to apply mapping after an EditMesh modifier because of all the topological changes you may make.

When you apply an EditMesh modifier to a closed shape (text, for example), the shape is immediately capped with a mesh. The Extrude function can then be used to quickly give depth in a manner very similar to the Extrude modifier. Unlike the Extrude modifier, with the Extrude function a cap is not created on the other side. The Extrude function is thus very useful when the shape is already a mesh (either through a collapse or import from another program) and you want the result the Extrude modifier provides for closed shapes.

NOTE

Flat shapes sometimes contain peculiar edges and faces that cause incorrect extrusions if you perform a Select All. If this error occurs, selecting the faces by Polygon usually results in a correct extrusion.

Tessellating Faces

Tessellation is primarily used to increase mesh density; it is used on selected areas to create additional vertices and faces for manipulation or to increase overall detail for future modifiers. For example, a mesh may not have enough segments to bend properly, or a Displace modifier may require a denser mesh to achieve more detail for its displacing bitmap.

Tessellated faces assume the smoothing group(s) of their parent. If you're using Edge tessellation with Tension, you need to examine the resulting geometry to see whether an AutoSmooth operation is in order. The newly created edges of tessellated faces are always displayed, regardless of the parent's visibility. Using AutoEdge with a value of 1 after tessellating cleans up the mesh's appearance by making coplanar edges invisible. Faces created by tessellation conveniently assume the material assignment and mapping coordinates of the original faces. The only time that there is a noticeable change is when the mesh is assigned a face map material.

Tessellation's Face-Center option splits each selected face into three faces. The new edges actually bisect the angles of the original face, and the new vertex is the original face's centroid. Faces created with this option are always coplanar with the originally selected faces. This method creates an interesting pattern that can be useful in its own right, as shown in figure 13.22. Repeated applications of Face-Center continue to add density to the same selected region—the affected area does not grow in the way that Edge tessellation does.

FIGURE 13.22
Patterning geometry with Face-Center tessellation.

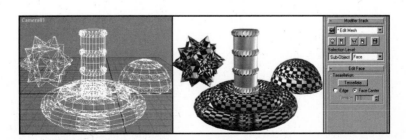

Tessellation's Edge method splits each selected face into four by dividing each edge in half and connecting the new vertices with a central face. If the edge is shared with another face, the addition of the new vertex causes that face to be divided into two faces. This explains how edge tessellation propagates its effect to adjacent faces. Such propagation may seem to create more faces than necessary, but you really need the adjacent faces to be created in order to deny a seam. Smoothing cannot occur between adjacent vertices that do not share two vertices. Figure 13.23 shows tessellating the top of a vessel so a rounded lip can be modeled there.

FIGURE 13.23

Edge tessellating specific regions for modeling.

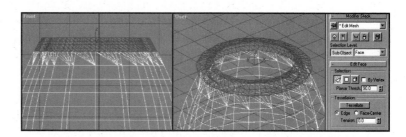

The Edge method also works with the Tension value (grayed out when Face-Center is active), which controls the location of the newly created vertices. The vertices of the original faces are unaffected while new vertices project outward, or "inflate," with positive tension, and project inward, or "deflate," with negative tension. Tension is a value from –100 to 100, with 0 having no effect. If you want your tessellated faces to remain coplanar (as with Face-Center), use a Tension of zero.

Without Tension, tessellation increases only the mesh density; it does not affect the profile. If your object has curves, you might want the new vertices to conform to the projected curve. The reference (default) value for Tension is +25. This value projects the new vertices to follow a circle or sphere. Edge tessellating an entire sphere with a Tension of 25, has the same effect as doubling its segmentation (see fig. 13.24). The correct choice for the Tension value depends on your geometry's curvature. Performing multiple tessellations, especially with extreme Tension values, is a great method for "crumpling" and roughening a surface.

The new vertices projected by the Tension value do so to produce a curve across all the affected faces. If you are tessellating a totally flat surface, Tension has no effect. Figure 13.25 shows the propagation of successive edge tessellations, in which the surface does not deform until it reaches the corner and has faces between which to average a curve.

FIGURE 13.24

Tessellating spheres with a Tension value of 25.

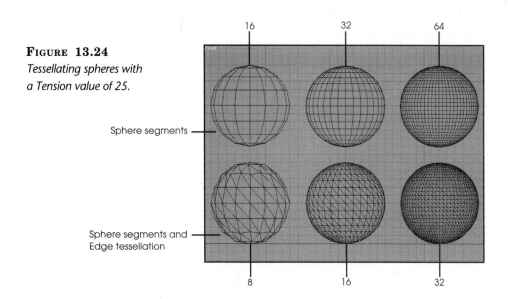

Sphere segments

Sphere segments and Edge tessellation

FIGURE 13.25

The propagation of successive Edge tessellations.

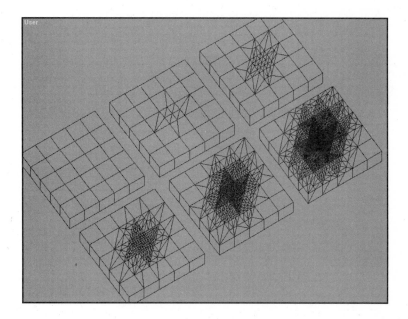

NOTE

The MeshSmooth modifier (introduced with Release 1.1) provides a superior method for adding mesh density with more accurate curvature than tessellation with tension does.

A useful technique to use with tessellating meshes is to select the vertices of the faces before tessellating them. After tessellation, this selection of original vertices can be convenient for controlling the surface, because you can now move or scale the original vertices, or invert the selection and manipulate the new vertices. Performing a uniform scale on the inverted vertex selection is often very similar in effect to using the Tension control. Figure 13.26 shows an example of a GeoSphere in which you select all the vertices, tessellate all the faces, and scale the original selection of vertices inward.

FIGURE 13.26
Creating a spiked ball by scaling vertices after a tessellation.

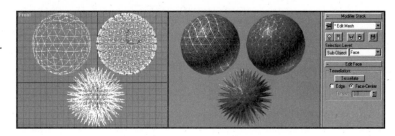

Building Faces

The Build Face enables you to create triangular faces, one by one, upon existing vertices. Clicking on Build Face places you in a mode for stitching faces, which is the only method in 3DS MAX for creating faces by hand. This mode switches the vertex display to ticks, so your target vertices are easily seen.

Building faces is a "connect-the-dots" procedure using three vertices that determine the new face. All three vertices must belong to the same object and must be unhidden to be used because only the visible vertices of the selected object display as ticks. Building faces does not create or alter the vertices, so the new faces are automatically welded to faces already sharing the vertices. Your cursor turns into a cross-hair whenever it is over a valid vertex.

TIP

Selecting the last vertex of a long, tapering, "splinter" face can be somewhat difficult because the rubber-band triangle tapers to such a sharp point. In building such faces, you will find it easier to select the longest sides first, thereby reducing the acuteness of the rubber-band triangle. You likely will need to zoom close and pan interactively as you build the face to make sure you hit the correct vertices.

The normal direction of the newly built face is dictated by the order in which you select the three vertices. Picking the vertices in a counterclockwise manner makes the face visible to you, whereas a clockwise selection order points the face away from you.

NOTE

Sometimes it is more convenient to build faces with Backface off in order to see both sides of the mesh and not worry about face normal orientation and the order in which you pick vertices. After you finish, switch Backface mode back on and either flip incorrect normals or unify the mesh.

Newly built faces are given the default assignments of Material ID#, and, if any mapping is assigned to the mesh, box-mapping coordinates. But newly built faces are devoid of smoothing groups. Although the Material ID#1 assignment is often correct, the mapping and lack of smoothing are rarely what you want. Usually, you will want to complete your face building and then assign the correct smoothing and mapping coordinates.

For any three vertices, there are two faces—one facing in each direction with opposite face normals. If you try to create a face that already exists, the alert shown in figure 13.27 appears, and you cannot proceed with the creation. This prohibition exists because meshes with duplicate faces cause problems, including rendering anomalies and failed Boolean operations.

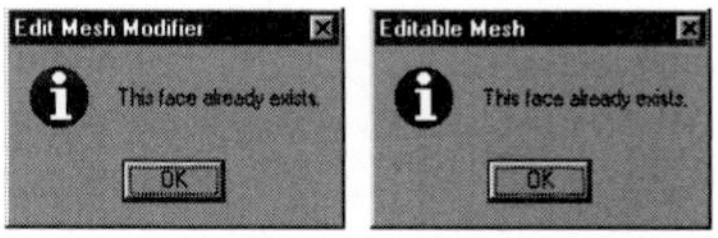

FIGURE 13.27

Alert messages warning of attempts to create a preexisting face.

Face Topology

Several functions enable you to change the surface topology of your mesh through explosion, detachment, collapsing, making planar, and deletion. These functions tend to be destructive and are primarily used when you want to substantially change the surface of your model.

Exploding Faces

Consider Face Explode a tool for breaking apart or dissecting meshes. Explode separates meshes by creating duplicate vertices and "unwelding" the faces. Whether the exploded mesh breaks into faces or elements depends on the accompanying Angle Threshold value.

Faces whose angular relationship to one another falls below the Angle Threshold form elements to be exploded into. An angle of 0 degrees explodes all faces, whereas a 180 degree angle breaks objects by elements. When applied to a cube, for example, an angle threshold of 90 degrees leaves the cube intact, whereas 89 degrees separates it into six elements (one for each side), and 0 degrees separates it into individual faces. When you are comfortable with analyzing the angle threshold, use Explode to separate portions of your model for use as pieces elsewhere.

The option to explode into objects or elements is simply that. If you want the exploded pieces to have their own edit history and animation tracks, choose objects. If you want to keep exploded pieces part of the same object, explode the pieces into elements.

TIP

Exploding an object with an angle threshold of 180 degrees splits every element into a new object—a timesaver when you want to give numerous objects sequential names. Simply attach all of the objects to one (use EditableMesh's Attach Multiple option), select all the faces, and explode with 180 degrees into objects. Each object is now named sequentially.

Remember that when using EditMesh, the history of your actions is maintained with the modifier. If you explode an object into other objects, you can later delete the EditMesh modifier. The original object reappears intact, whereas the objects created from the explosion remain. This is one method for splitting portions off a model without harming the original.

Detaching Faces

The Detach function is used to create new objects from pieces of the selected one. The entire selection becomes one object, even if it results in numerous elements. The new object inherits the bounding box orientation of the original object.

TIP

To detach faces to an element without making an object, explode the face selection with an Angle Threshold of 180 degrees. This procedure also enables you to create multiple objects in one step.

Collapsing Faces

Detach

The Collapse function simplifies a mesh by using a unique method of deleting faces. The selected faces are deleted and replaced by a centered vertex. Every adjacent face that shared a vertex with a deleted face is stretched (and welded) to the new vertex location. If an adjacent face shares two vertices with a deleted face (an edge), it is deleted. Collapsing a single face can delete a maximum of four faces at one time—the collapsed face and three with shared edges. Collapsing a selection of faces results in very quick model face reduction while preserving a meshed surface, which is especially useful for eliminating coplanar faces. Collapsing faces that are adjacent to corners pulls the faces from the adjacent sides. You can chip away at corners easily, as shown in figure 13.28.

FIGURE 13.28

"Chiseling" a mesh by collapsing selected faces.

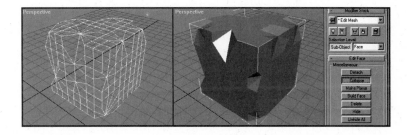

What may be surprising is that Collapse treats your selection as one, even if it is discontiguous, similar to the way Vertex Collapse works. With discontiguous selections, the collapsed vertex is still located by averaging the locations of every selected face. This is not usually desirable unless you are carefully planning the collapse by analyzing where the resulting vertex will be. For most modeling, you want to restrict your collapse to a contiguous selection.

Collapse is often used as a sculpting tool, acting like a chisel in the way it "chips" away at a mesh's profile and face count. Collapse is best used on meshes that contain a considerable number of faces with which to work. The function can prove useful on fractally generated landscapes and organic meshes that you need to refine and individualize. When used on a mesh with a regular surface, Collapse provides pinched points where new vertices are located. See this chapter's earlier discussion of Vertex Collapse for a more controlled method and further examples.

Making Faces Planar

The Make Planar function examines the normals of the selected face and determines an average based on their face's overall size (e.g., faces at a right angle to one another will only form a 45 degree angle if they are the same size). The faces are then rotated to align on the same plane. Figure 13.29 shows how even discontiguous face selections are angled to form a common plane. This function is most commonly used to flatten out irregularities in what should be a flat plane. With skill, the Make Planar function can be used to create planar relationships among numerous elements to make critical relationships quickly (see fig. 13.30).

FIGURE 13.29
Using Make Planar to align faces along a common plane.

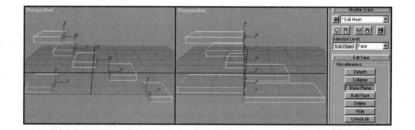

FIGURE 13.30
Using Make Planar to stretch elements to a common plane.

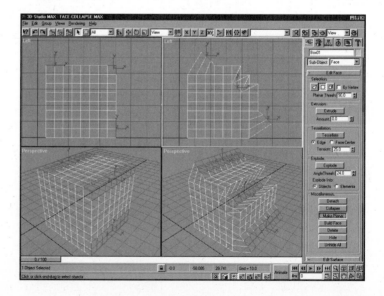

TIP

Use Make Planar on an entire mesh to flatten the mesh. This can create an interesting morph target for an animation.

Deleting Faces

`Delete`

The Delete function does exactly what it's name says—it performs the exact same function as the keyboard's Delete key. The effect of Delete is obvious except in conjunction with hidden faces.

Immediately after a selection is hidden, its perimeter remains highlighted in red, because the hidden faces are still in a selected state and will be deleted if you press or click Delete. Faces that are hidden but not yet deleted can act as a delete "preview" of sorts. You can hide faces and add to the selection by keeping your Ctrl key depressed. You can continue to select and hide faces, all the while building a "hidden" selection. After you are comfortable with the result in the viewport, press Delete, and what was hidden is removed.

Surface Control with Faces

What faces really define are surfaces that reflect light. The color of the light depends on the material assigned to it and the color of the light illuminating it. If no material is assigned, the object color is used to reflect light. The way the color is shaded across a surface is further controlled by smoothing. If it is not smooth, each face reflects light as an independent plane. If it is smoothed with adjacent faces of the same mesh, the shared edges are smoothed over, and the geometry renders much rounder than it really is.

Smoothing Faces

The correct use of smoothing groups can make a simple model intricate and a complex model perfect, whereas the incorrect use of smoothing groups causes odd streaks or eliminates detail. By carefully assigning smoothing groups to select faces within a mesh, you can create economical and visually correct models. The basic concept of smoothing was described in Chapter 7, "Basics of Object Creation," with respect to objects, but you also need to understand how to assign smoothing at the face level if the mesh is at all irregular.

Remember that smoothing is a rendering illusion that always attempts to approximate the shading of the same form—a sphere. No "degrees" of smoothness exist. Faces are either smoothed, or they are not.

Understanding Face Smoothing

Smoothing can occur only between welded faces, and therefore cannot occur between elements or objects. Faces will continue to smooth with one another as long as they can trace a line of welded faces that contain the same smoothing group.

Each face assigned one or more smoothing groups checks each shared vertex to see whether the adjacent, welded face has a matching smoothing group. If a match is found, smoothing occurs across the two faces. Multiple matches of smoothing groups have no effect on the amount of smoothing because there are no "degrees" of smoothness. A surface is either smooth or it is not. Assigning a face more than one smoothing group only causes the faces to match that many more groups on other faces. If no match is found, an edge is produced between the faces if they are not coplanar.

The Smoothing function always tries to approximate the effect of a spherical form. Figure 13.31 shows how smoothing faces that meet at angles more acute than 60 degrees—especially 90 degrees—can result in unrealistic effects because the program attempts to smooth the corners in a spherical fashion. The objects with acute angles in this figure reveal awkward smoothing on their vertical surfaces because the shading is pulled diagonally across the mesh's sides. As a mesh gains more sides and those sides become progressively smaller, the diagonal highlight sharpens in angle and approaches a vertical, revealing more natural-looking smoothing. As a rule, smoothing angles sharper than 120 degrees (which equals an Angle Threshold of 60) produces undesirable results.

Using AutoSmooth

The AutoSmooth function provides the easiest method for assigning smoothing groups to a selection of faces. AutoSmooth compares its accompanying Threshold value to the angle between selected, welded faces. If the angle between selected welded faces is less than the Angle Threshold, AutoSmooth assigns a common smoothing group to those faces.

FIGURE 13.31

The effect of smoothing the sides of various angled meshes (tops and bottoms have no smoothing assigned).

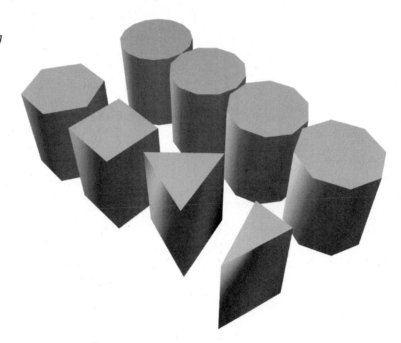

The AutoSmooth function is an enormous timesaver and works for most meshes. Coplanar faces are assigned unique smoothing per face if the Threshold is 0 degrees. A Box, for example, is given one smoothing group to all its faces with a Threshold of 90 degrees, alternating groups for each side with thresholds >0 degrees and <90 degrees, and alternating groups for every face with a 0 degree threshold. AutoSmooth is quite efficient with its assignments and usually assigns the bare minimum. The smoothed box receives three, not six, smoothing groups because the three can be alternated so they do not touch. This efficiency often makes the faces assigned by AutoSmooth convenient selection groups for other operations.

NOTE

If smoothing appears incorrect, check the mesh's construction. Coincidental vertices or adjacent faces may cause seams, and redundant faces may cause rendering irregularities such as "flashing."

AutoSmooth works best when the mesh's faces form angles that are consistent with their smoothing needs. A mesh that has many 45-degree chamfers, some of which need to be smoothed and some of which need to stay sharp, is an example of a poor candidate for AutoSmooth.

TIP

For AutoSmooth to work appropriately on meshes with varying angle transitions, move the vertices of the shallow angle areas (with snap) to create sharper angles that are more easily separated by the overall Angle Threshold. AutoSmooth will now assign groups that correspond to the geometric lines of your model. Once assigned, you can return the temporarily moved vertices to their original position. The alternative is to detach the face regions into elements so that smoothing cannot occur between them.

Although AutoSmooth works on selections, it is most effective when applied to entire elements. AutoSmooth begins with the lowest of the 32 smoothing groups and works upward. Performing several AutoSmooths on differing selections in the same element increases the likelihood that the more popular, lower number groups are shared between faces of separate operations. This results in smoothing where it might not be desirable, and most likely would not have occurred if the entire element had been selected for the AutoSmooth operation. The best time to perform AutoSmooth on a selection is when you have removed smoothing from the entire element and want to AutoSmooth discrete parts that do not meet. This way the common smoothing groups do not touch, and unwanted smoothing does not occur.

Identifying Smoothing Groups

The array of 32 Smoothing Group buttons is your first clue to identifying which smoothing groups are assigned to which faces. When you select a face, any smoothing groups assigned to it are shown as depressed buttons. In a selection of faces, the buttons are depressed if the group is shared by all of them, and the button is grayed-out (but not depressed) if the group is assigned to just some of the faces in the selection.

NOTE

Odd streaks and overly darkened edges are often signs of incorrect smoothing assignments. If an object does not seem to be rendering correctly, check to see that its smoothing group assignments are appropriate.

The Select By Smooth Group function presents a dialog (see fig. 13.32) that shows every smoothing group currently assigned to the object. Depressing a numbered button and clicking OK selects every face assigned to that group.

The Clear Selection option performs a Select None and then selects by the smoothing groups you have chosen. Leaving this option off adds the selection by smoothing to the current selection of faces.

FIGURE 13.32

The Select By Smooth Groups dialog.

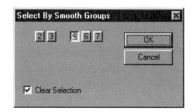

TIP

You can select every face that has no smoothing assignments by selecting every smoothing group and then performing an Invert Selection.

Manual Smoothing Assignments

A selection of faces can be assigned or cleared of smoothing group assignments with the 32 Smoothing Group buttons. This manual assignment gives you complete control over the result rather than the automatic method afforded by AutoSmooth. To clear a smoothing group, click on its button to undepress it. If the button is grayed out and, therefore, not common among the selection, you need to click the button twice—once to assign the group to the entire selection and again to remove it.

When assigning smoothing groups, you need to consider several questions about your model's form. What pieces should render round? Which sections should have crisp edges? Which planes should be faceted? After making these decisions, assigning smoothing groups manually becomes a study in face selection.

When smoothing intricate shapes, such as ornate iron work or beveled fonts, it's common to make multiple selections involving regions, deselection, invert, and face hiding. A common strategy is to identify flat surfaces first. The flat surfaces should be selected, assigned a unique smoothing group, and then hidden to make way for further selections. Making subsequent selections becomes increasingly fast because there are fewer unassigned faces with each pass.

Another common method is to Select All, perform an AutoSmooth, and then correct only the incorrect faces. The smooth shaded viewports report the state of smoothing and give you a clear account of how well the smoothing is assigned. If you spot errant smoothing, select the face and check its group numbers. Select adjacent faces, compare, and decide how to proceed. Often the best route is to clear all the smoothing from these difficult areas and start assigning to a clean slate.

When choosing smoothing group numbers, you have complete freedom— don't be overwhelmed by the choice of 32 groups. That number is provided so you can organize your selections without confusion, and it ensures even the most complex models have enough groups. There is no significance to choosing low, high, or consecutive numbers. Lower numbers are filled by AutoSmooth first, so you may want to use the higher numbers to avoid a conflict. You will probably find that most meshes need only between two and six smoothing groups. More groups usually means that the mesh is very intricate or that separate groups are being maintained to double as selection sets.

T I P

Some modelers assign the same smoothing group number for a given geometric condition so the groups become convenient selection methods. Consistently assigning group 32 to caps, for example, would provide a fast method for selecting caps later on. The same goes for bevels, sides, round areas, fillets, and so on.

Controlling Face Normals

Each face possesses a normal that emanates perpendicular from its center. The normal points away from the side of the face that can be seen. The inability to see the other side of the face is termed a *backface cull*, a method that is commonly used to speed graphics and is the default mode for 3DS MAX's interactive and production renderers. Face normals are also an important indication of the geometry because consistent normals define a surface's direction and in so doing, whether it's an interior volume or exterior surface. Because of these reasons, face normals are used by several functions to make both rendering and modeling decisions. A mesh that has consistent normals throughout its surfaces is said to be *unified*.

NOTE

When an object appears to be "backward" or "inside out," the cause is usually reversed normals. This incorrect facing is common when working with surfaces of revolution. What you may see as "in," the normals make "out." Figure 13.33 shows several objects with reversed normals.

FIGURE 13.33

The visual impact of reversed normals.

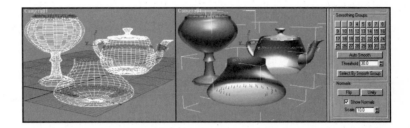

Normals determine far too much within 3DS MAX for you to ignore them. With EditMesh, normals define a face's Pivot Point Center, the direction of extrusion, and the angle thresholds used by Explode, AutoSmooth, and AutoEdge. Other modifiers, such as Optimize, Displace, MeshSmooth, and Relax, calculate their effects by normals as well. Having unified normals is critical when creating Boolean compound objects. Some materials, including face maps and many procedural textures, base their results on face normals.

NOTE

The option to ignore face normals and render both sides (with 2-Sided materials or the Renderer's Force 2-Sided option) is a poor choice considering how many modeling operations depend on correct normals. It often takes less time to correct the normals caused from poor modeling than to use the 2-Sided option and render the extra faces, not use backface cull, and fight the irregular modeling that results.

Unifying Normals

The Unify function resets a selection of face normals according to the 3DS MAX default—reorienting the normals to face out from the selection's center. This function is a fast method for unifying an entire mess (working well with Select All) and should usually be your first step with an incorrect mesh. For Unify to work correctly, a mesh's faces and vertices must already observe the golden rule of mesh building: every face that shares an edge with an adjacent face must also share two vertices.

NOTE

A misleading situation occurs when adjacent faces have coincidental vertices and appear to be welded only. If an apparently correctly built mesh is having problems with normal unification, make sure its vertices are actually welded and that no duplicate faces exist.

Unify works best when you have an entire element selected and that element has a minimum of opened ends. Unifying selections within an element is not nearly as reliable as unifying an entire element because the selection may not extend far enough to give Unify a clear picture of the mesh. Coplanar selections will unify, but the direction in which they unify has a 50/50 chance of being wrong because coplanar faces afford no sense of direction.

Showing Normals

The Show Normals option displays the normals of every face you select as a blue-to-white vector. This designation makes a misdirected normal easy to spot. Therefore, using Show Normals to identify misdirected faces can be more efficient than examining the faces. The accompanying Scale parameter in Show Normals scales the size of the normal vector and has no impact on the mesh. With some geometries, it can be useful to increase the Scale dramatically to see the intersection of normals (for example, the normals of an interior dome will intersect at the dome's center). Normal vectors are for display only and cannot be manipulated directly (you must use the Flip function on selected faces instead).

Flipping Normals

Normal Unify will not work with every mesh. Coplanar, interior, revolved, or imported meshes must have their normals adjusted manually. This task can be quick, as when the normals are simply facing the wrong direction, or quite tedious, as when the mesh is built incorrectly (most likely in another program) and the normals are haphazard. A common situation is when you want to see inside an object you created. Unifying the normal always faces the normals outward from the selection's center, and you have to manually flip the entire mesh to face them inward.

When the mesh is unified but pointed in the wrong direction, select by element or Select All and click Flip. The normals now face in the opposite direction. This procedure works well for quickly flipping coplanar meshes, surfaces of revolution (such as a lathe), and objects meant to be viewed from the inside.

If the mesh has random normals throughout and does not unify consistently, it is probably built incorrectly (faces sharing edges do not also share two vertices). This situation is almost always the result of importing models made elsewhere. Many modeling programs that create DXF files (such as AutoCAD) have no method for storing face normals and do not promote mesh modeling basics. When presented with an incorrect model you must decide, based on your plans for the model, whether to take the time to flip the normals. If your plans are just to assign mapping, materials, and render, you can probably avoid flipping the normals and get by using 2-Sided materials. Note that this choice has negative implications for rendering time and memory requirements. On the other hand, if you plan to do any modeling, especially Boolean compound objects, you should take the time to unify the normals by either correcting the unconventional modeling and using Unify or by flipping the normals yourself.

Although *flipping normals* may sound like a game, it can be a tedious endeavor. Applying and combining several face selection techniques and display options is the usual method for attacking this chore. Making Backface Cull a keyboard shortcut is very convenient, because you often need to compare the flipped and unflipped representations in this process.

Begin flipping normals by hiding areas of your mesh that have correct normals. If the majority of the remaining mesh is facing the wrong direction, Select All and click Flip. You are now at least working with less than half the faces. Proceed to select the faces that are incorrectly facing you and flip the selection. As the mesh's normals become more unified, you might find it easier to flip faces that are facing you rather than away from you. You can either switch to an opposite view or Select All and flip the entire mesh.

TIP

It's often much easier to flip the entire mesh's normals to the wrong direction and work "backward" by flipping faces you can see. After all the rogue faces are flipped and you can no longer see your mesh, Select All and flip it back again for a unified mesh.

Unifying Normals Versus Two-Sided Materials

You always have the 2-Sided option to render both sides of a face and thus skip the time required to correct face normals. This can be done by the property of a material, or the Renderer can be forced to treat the entire scene as two-sided. This modeling "shortcut" does cost rendering time because each face is calculated in both directions. The memory requirements of the 2-Sided option have an increasing impact if your rendering is casting shadows or calculating reflections.

NOTE

Making objects 2-Sided gives them the appearance of infinitely thin shells—something that does not exist and looks odd when rendered. Because nearly everything constructed has thickness, you should consider modeling both the inside and outside of your models unless it is made up of a thin material, such as a dollar bill.

In order to convey believably the natural properties of certain materials—notably glass—a 2-Sided material is necessary. Meshes visible on both sides and not close enough in the scene to be perceived as infinitely thin, such as leaves, flags, paper, cloth, and bags, are also good candidates for two-sided materials. The backs of objects that reflect into mirrors are often given 2-Sided materials to make up for their one-sidedness. For specific, troublesome objects that refuse to render correctly, you can assign 2-Sided materials as an alternative to rendering the entire scene in Force 2-Sided mode.

It's easy to conclude that a 2-Sided material takes only twice the resources to render as a one-sided material and is thus not too much of an expense. Reality shows, however, that closer to four times more faces are calculated by the renderer, by each shadow casting light, and by each reflecting surface within the scene. These extra faces are result of rendering both sides of what is facing you (2×) and then both sides of what is not facing you (perhaps an additional 2×, but possibly more).

Assigning Material IDs

Each face begins, by default, with material ID #1 assigned to it. Faces do not keep a record of the actual material name but rather the ID#. If the material is *anything* except Multi/Sub-object, the material ID has no impact. When you assign the object a Multi/Sub-object material, the material ID dictates which submaterial in the material definition is assigned.

When deciding how to assign a sub-object material to selected faces, you should first consider whether the selected faces should remain part of the larger object. If your modeling is complete and you do not require the selected faces to be smoothed with other faces having different materials, you may be better off detaching the selected faces as independent objects and assigning the new objects a Standard Material. Usually when part of an object requires a different material than the rest of the object, a visible break appears in the surface, at least a seam, between the two materials. You avoid this difficulty by detaching the faces selected for sub-object material assignment.

A typical situation where you need to smooth and must use Material IDs with a Multi/Sub-object material is with separate paints or finishes on a continuous surface. A bumpy wall with differing paint colors, a chrome handle with a knurled grip, and a vase with changing glazes are all examples of where you need smoothing to continue but are examples that require different materials.

Selecting by ID

The consideration of Material IDs concludes for now by noting that the assignment of IDs still enables face selection and selection set storage. Selecting by Material ID creates a selection of the faces with the chosen ID, enabling you—when you are using multi-materials—to see what part of your mesh is assigned what material. If you are not using a Multi/Sub-object material, you can safely store selection sets of faces with different ID#s. Storing the selection sets has no impact on the material but creates very convenient face level selection sets.

Modeling with Edges

The third of the three major elements of mesh editing is edges. *Edges* are a byproduct of creating faces and cannot exist without them. Although edges are not a piece of geometry unto themselves, 3DS MAX enables you to use them to manipulate the faces which they are a part of and form the basis by which additional faces can be created.

Edge Level Basics

The Edge rollout shown in figure 13.34 is by far the simplest of the selection levels. Edges obey the same rules of window and crossing region selections as face selection does. You will find, however, that unless you display all the edges, it is difficult to select only what you intend. This is especially true when making region selections within a mesh's interior. Whereas face selection has a By Vertex option, edge selection does not. When defining a region, your first mouse-click to define the region performs a selection and can easily hit an unwanted invisible edge.

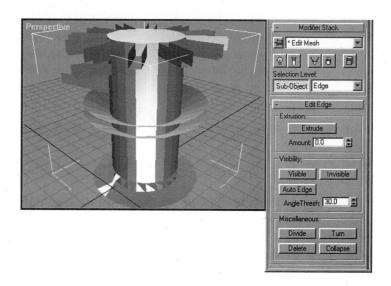

FIGURE 13.34
The Edit Edge rollout common to EditMesh and EditableMesh.

WARNING

Be careful when using Select All option with edges. Unlike hidden faces and vertices, invisible edges are acted upon as if they were selected, and Select All does select invisible edges. Any modification you apply after Select All with Edges affects invisible and visible edge selections with likely undesirable consequences.

Transforming Edges

When you transform an edge, you are actually transforming the two vertices that define it. Edges are a way to lock two vertices in relationship to one another as you manipulate the edge. You can think of an edge as a rigid barbell that moves the weights at either end without deforming itself. The way an edge locks two vertices in relationship is similar to how a face locks a selection of three vertices.

With EditMesh, each edge possesses a local axis so you can use the pivot point center. As with faces, each contiguous selection determines a selection center. This capability is not available with EditableMesh.

Controlling Edge Visibility

Edges are not hidden but rather are made "invisible." Invisible edges behave differently from hidden faces and vertices. On the other hand, hiding faces and vertices "protects" them from further modification; making edges invisible does not. You can select, transform, extrude, divide, turn, collapse, and delete edges without ever seeing them. Although modifying invisible edges can be convenient, it can also be dangerous because you may be affecting far more than you want.

Edge visibility affects few things in your model. In modeling, visible edges define the boundary for polygon selection. In rendering, only visible edges are rendered when the faces they belong to are given a wireframe material (see fig. 13.35). Also, hidden edges influence the orientation of face mapped materials. For the most part, however, the only differences between visible and invisible edges are organizational and visual clarity. Invisible edges often make your model cleaner and more understandable because only prominent lines are displayed. In addition, invisible edges increase redraw speed because fewer lines need to be drawn.

You can display invisible edges with the Edges Only option, found under Display Optimization in the Display panel (see fig 13.36). If you plan to work with edges, you will want to enter the Display panel and turn off Edges Only before you perform much editing. The Edges Only option has no influence on rendering.

FIGURE 13.35

The effect of hidden edges on wireframe materials.

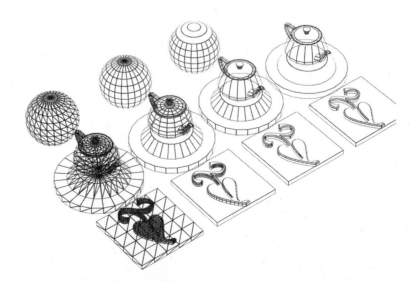

FIGURE 13.36
Edges Only control.

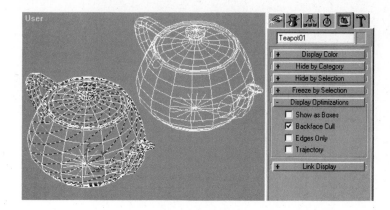

T**IP**

If you don't want to leave the Edit panel to turn off the Edges Only option, perform a Select All on the edges and perform an AutoEdge with an angle of zero to display every edge. You can later use AutoEdge to make edges invisible.

Manual Visibility Assignment

You can control the display of edges precisely with the Visible and Invisible option. Decide which edges should be visible, select them, and click Invisible or Visible to change their status. Whereas selecting visible edges to make them invisible is straightforward, selecting invisible ones to make them visible may not. Remember that, unlike hidden faces and vertices, you can select invisible edges even though they are not displayed. To be sure of what you are selecting, turn off the Edges Only option. To make this easy, you are highly encouraged to make Edges Only a keyboard alternate so you do not have to leave the Modify panel to change it.

Using AutoEdge

Although manual visibility assignment gives you control, it can be tedious. AutoEdge examines your edge selection and compares the normals of faces sharing those edges to the accompanying Angle Threshold value. As with AutoSmooth and Explode, the higher the Angle Threshold value, the more edges qualify to be made invisible. The higher you make the threshold, the more acute the angle that falls within its range.

By working on a selection, you can control what part of your model is
evaluated with the current Angle Threshold value. This evaluation can be
important when different parts of your model have different angularity and
a general AutoEdge would display too much or too little in a given area.

Creating Faces with Edges

Although edges are not a geometric entity in their own right, 3DS MAX
enables you to create faces based on face edges, with Extrusion and Dividing.

Extruding Edges

Extruding an edge is similar to extruding a face except only one side is
created. Each extruded edge moves the vertices of the edge and creates two
new faces. The extrusion direction is determined by the plane formed by the
selected edges. Adjacent edges that lie on a plane reliably extrude at 90
degrees to that plane.

Extruding individual edges is unpredictable because two vertices cannot
define a plane. The function attempts to determine an extrusion direction
based on faces adjacent to the edge, but this rarely produces the desired
angles. A similar difficulty occurs if you extrude discontiguous selections of
edges. Your best method for extruding edges is to work with contiguous
edges. Every contiguous group of edges determines its own extrusion
direction.

As with Face Extrude, you can extrude interactively with your mouse or the amount spinner. Every drag and release of the mouse or spinner creates another extrusion, enabling you to quickly create stripes of extruded faces.

TIP

The fastest way to use Extrude is to use the Extrusion spinner with a selection. This choice extrudes the faces but does not affect your toolbar status. You can move between extrusion and transforms without any delay.

Dividing Edges

The Edge Divide function affects a single edge by inserting a new vertex at its midpoint and splitting the original face into two. If the edge is shared between two faces, both are split, resulting in four faces. The newly created edges are always made visible so you can see the results. Edge Divide is similar to EditSpline's Edge/Refine function and may be thought of as "insert vertex at midpoint." Regardless of what it is called, its capability to create a vertex and faces at midpoint locations can be valuable. The geometry shown in figure 13.37 was created from a Box with Edge Divide and subsequent vertex scale transforms.

FIGURE 13.37

Creating geometry with Edge Divide.

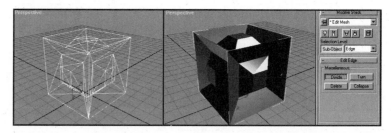

Dividing edges is a convenient way to introduce a vertex and add a face at mesh areas that need to be welded. Many models created in other programs are improperly tessellated and may have dissimilar vertex counts at transition points (AutoCAD's 3DS export of ACIS solids is an example of this). For these surfaces to smooth properly, vertices need to be created to balance the vertex counts at joints. Once a similar number is achieved at the transition, the vertices from either side need to be welded to allow smoothing to continue and deny the seam.

Faces that are newly created by Divide inherit the parent's mapping coordinates but do not acquire any smoothing groups. If your model uses smoothing, you need to assign smoothing groups after you finish dividing edges.

NOTE

When dividing edges on smoothed models, you can select the newly created faces by using Select by Smooth to select every smoothing group and performing a Select Invert.

Edge Topology

Although seemingly a minor function, Edge Turning is one of the most basic mesh editing tools. This tool often is often used before and after Edge Divide, Vertex Collapse and Weld, and Face Extrude to produce the correct surface topology for the mesh.

Turning Edges

Edge Turn affects a single, shared edge by redirecting the edge to the other vertices of the two faces. Edge Turn has no effect on isolated faces or perimeter, unshared edges. Because mapping coordinates are actually stored with the vertices, turning edges does not affect mapping. You can reverse an edge turn quickly by turning the same edge again.

NOTE

The direction of an edge changes the way face-mapped materials render and can be a critical tool in adjusting their appearance.

Turning an edge is a subtle modeling tool that is often used to alter a mesh's profile. Turning is a readjustment that does not make the mesh any more complex because it simply reorients what already exists. If a mesh's area needs to be roughed or smoothed a little, turning an edge can help. If a Boolean operation is not working, turning an edge on coplanar faces may readjust the geometry enough for it to work without otherwise changing the object's position or complexity. But the most common uses of edge turning are to establish patterns within a mesh (see fig. 13.38) and to orient edges for subsequent modeling operations.

Collapsing Edges

Edge Collapse acts on the current edge selection. Collapsing an edge is similar to collapsing a vertex or face but is much less predictable than the other two. Collapsing an edge eliminates one of the vertices on the edge and "pulls" all edges that previously shared that vertex to the remaining one. The two faces that shared the original edge are removed and covered by the adjacent faces' stretch. Unfortunately there's no way to determine to which vertex an edge is going to collapse.

FIGURE 13.38
Creating geometric patterns by turning and dividing faces.

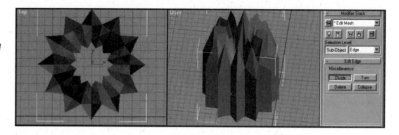

When collapsing a selection of edges, each contiguous selection collapses to a single vertex. This vertex tends to be at an extremity of the selection, but its location cannot be predicted reliably. What constitutes a contiguous selection may be difficult to see as well because every face that shares the selected edge is considered for the collapse.

Deleting Edges

Edge Delete works on the current selection of edges. When you delete an edge, you are actually deleting the faces that share the edge while leaving the vertices intact. This deletion explains why you never receive a "Delete Isolated Vertices" message when deleting edges, in contrast to deleting faces. You can select, and thus delete, invisible edges. As always, be careful after performing a Select All because invisible edges may still be active. You can be most confident of your deletion if you perform a Select None before building your edge selection.

In Practice: Mesh Modeling

- **Affecting vertices** Most mesh modeling is affecting vertices. Face, polygon, element, and edge selections are often just alternative methods for affecting the vertices that comprise them. When you adjust vertices, you adjust all faces that are built upon them.

- **Face level functions and normals** Many face level functions base their effect on face normals or the averaged normal of the selection. Making faces coplanar, extrusion, and the vertex level's Affect Region are just some functions that make proper, and unified, normal orientation critical for mesh editing. Other modifiers, such as Boolean compound objects and MeshSmooth, depend on proper normals for their results as well.

- **Vertex editing**   The vertex level's Affect Region option radically changes the way vertex editing works. When active, vertex selections act as "magnets" that push and pull regions of other vertices as defined by the shape of an adjustable region curve.

- **EditMesh**   The individual transform centers provided by EditMesh provide a significant modeling advantage over EditableMesh. This is especially true when transforming discontiguous selections in place or extruding faces and edges.

- **Preventing accidental editing**   Hiding faces and vertices is a method to segregate from other selections and "protect" them accidental editing. This should not be confused with edge level visibility that does not impact the selectability of the edges.

- **Smoothing groups**   Smoothing groups are key to perfecting a surface's quality. AutoSmooth works well for models with distinct transitions, while manual smoothing group assignments are needed when the model is very irregular or subtle in its transitions. Smoothing can occur only between welded faces.

- **Mesh functions**   Although the edges are a byproduct of face definitions, there are functions that are often used by serious mesh artists. In practice, Edge Turn and Edge Divide are among the most often used mesh functions besides transforms.

- **Material IDs**   Material IDs must be assigned at the face level for objects to contain more than one material definition (through the use of a Multi/Sub-object material). Material IDs can also be used as a means of storing face selections when only single material is being used on the object.

- **Storing selections**   Named sub-object selections are a convenient method to store selections for a series of actions within a modifier. Named selections can not, however, be used between modifiers.

- **Mesh construction**   Proper mesh construction is critical for numerous operations and other modifiers within 3DS MAX. The primary rule is that every face must share two vertices with any face that it shares an edge with. Some operations in 3DS MAX (such as Boolean Compound objects and MeshSmooth) require that an edge can be shared by a maximum of two faces.

Created by Greg Phillips
Phillips Design Group
Indianapolis, IN
http://www.pdg.com

Chapter 14

PATCH MODELING

Modeling with Bézier patches is a complete alternative to traditional mesh editing. Computer modeling programs tend to be mesh, patch, nurb, or solids-based in their approach. 3D Studio MAX is somewhat different in that it enables any object class to exist and introduces the basics of patch editing with its Patch class and EditPatch modifier. Although patch editing can be extremely artistic and organic, it is also, admittedly, limited. The patch functionality currently included in 3DS MAX is best thought of as a solid foundation on which other developments are built. Because this is the groundwork, however, much of this new world of patch modeling can be learned now and applied to later breaking creations as they appear.

Although 3DS MAX is basic in its patch modeling capabilities, you can create some impressive work with its current patch tools. This chapter will explain patch modeling and will cover the following areas:

- Characteristics of patch models and types of patches in 3DS MAX

- Understanding how Bézier curves are defined and how they relate to Bézier patch editing

- Using the patches formed from a variety of creation methods, such as primitives, Extrude, Lathe, and meshes

- Techniques in using the EditPatch modifier for sub-object patch modeling and the Vertex, Edge, and Patch levels

- Procedures for keeping your model as patches without converting to meshes until you need to

Patch Type Basics

There are currently two types of patches with 3DS MAX, QuadPatches and TriPatches, both of which are based on Bézier curves. The QuadPatch and TriPatch primitives (found under Patch Grids in the Create Panel's Geometry drop down list) create single patches of these types to which you can add additional patches with the EditPatch modifier. Modifiers such as Lathe and Extrude can export their objects as patches and meshes can be converted to patch objects as well. The important thing to realize is that the various creation methods can produce either Tri or Quad patches and that these two basic patch types produce different results when edited. Figure 14.1 shows two patches and their resulting forms after a few basic edits. The vertices and tangent handles of both patches were positioned in the same manner. As can be seen, the TriPatch object mesh tends to bend evenly, much like a piece of paper. The QuadPatch object tends to bend more like rubber than paper because QuadPatches affect a "quad" of adjacent control vertices—vertices at a diagonal affect each other's surface. In contrast, TriPatches only influence vertices with which they share an edge, and the surfaces from diagonal vertices aren't affected.

FIGURE 14.1

Differences between TriPatch and Quad Patch deformations.

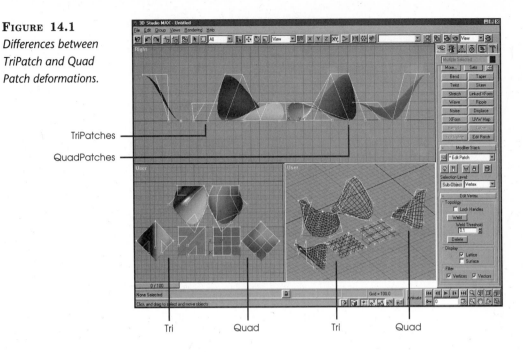

TriPatches

QuadPatches

Tri   Quad   Tri   Quad

Patch Display Options

Patch objects are defined by a *lattice* that produces a *surface*. The lattice is a grid of the control vertices, vector handles, and intermediate vertices (see fig. 14.2). You have the option of displaying either the lattice or the surface or both. In practice, you will probably want to hide the lattice when working at the Vertex level and show the lattice at the Edge or Patch level.

Edges and Patches are only "seen" on the lattice itself. When working at the Edge or Patch level, all your selections are indicated on the lattice and no selection indication is made on the surface. If the lattice isn't present, your selections are still made, but they aren't visible (a sometimes dangerous situation). The controls for the lattice and surface display are provided at all levels because you turn them on and off constantly as you work.

The patch surface is a result of the lattice and can't be edited directly. This is a great asset, not a limitation, because it enables you to define the density of the patch surface at any time. As a result, you can work with a very simple representation and increase it when editing becomes more subtle or your rendering output requires it.

FIGURE 14.2

Display elements of patches.

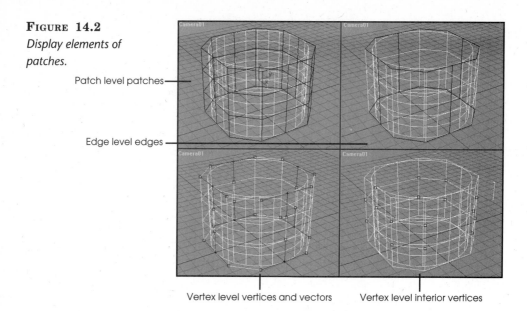

Patch level patches

Edge level edges

Vertex level vertices and vectors   Vertex level interior vertices

Understanding Bézier Curves

Bézier patches behave in much the same way that Bézier splines do. The classic Bézier spline uses four points to determine its curve. The curve passes through the first and last points and interpolates between the middle two. Figure 14.3 shows how, with patches, the vertices are the spline's end control points and the patch vectors are the spline's intermediate control points.

The concept of two intermediate control points is essential to understanding exactly what the patch lattice is. Patch vertices are the endpoints through which the Bézier spline passes. These vertices are the easiest to relate to because they're part of the object's surface. The vectors on the lattice are thus the defining splines' other two control vertices.

Patch edges comprise the perimeter of a patch, whether Quad or Tri, and have three connected line segments. Although they may look boxy and somewhat odd, they actually connect the four defining points of the Bézier curve. Each edge begins and ends at a vertex, with the segments being defined by the vector handle locations. Patches are thus composed of either three or four edges, depending on whether they are a QuadPatch or TriPatch. These edges define the Bézier splines that in turn define the patch.

Vectors are the lines that connect patch handles to vertices. The handles are actually the intermediate control points for the Bézier spline that defines the patch edge, meaning that there are two vector handles between each patch vertex, with a vertex having as many vectors as it has edges intersecting it. Vectors are often referred to in other programs as nodes, knots, or control points. This chapter refers to vectors as the visual line and handles as the control point at the end of the vector.

FIGURE 14.3
Bézier curve path shape.

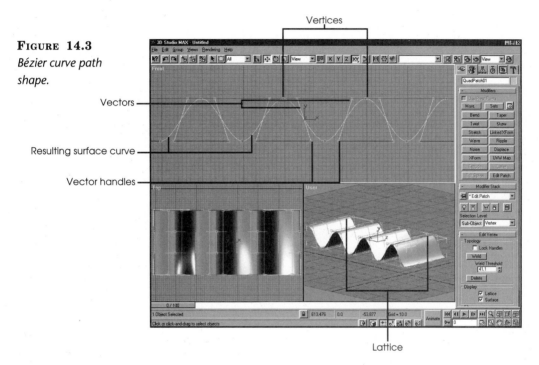

Vertices

Vectors

Resulting surface curve

Vector handles

Lattice

NOTE

Manipulating the vertices with the lattice turned off can be confusing. The vectors appear to be properties of the vertex with the lattice turned off, when, in fact, they are the interpolation points for the defining spline edge.

Interior Vertices

Other lines of the patch lattice crisscross the patch. These interior "edges" end at vector handles and pass through what are termed *interior vertices*. These vertices are actually secondary control handles that influence the curvature across the patch. (Calling these "vertices" is extremely misleading, and you are best off thinking of them as interior handles or interior control points.) These interior control vertices behave much like vector handles, controlling the Bézier curvature in a more subtle way. Note that although patch edges form true Bézier splines (passing through the patch vertices), the interior lattice "splines" don't because their end points are vector handles that don't have to be on the surface.

Interior vertices can be important because they enable you to distort a single patch in a manner that would otherwise require additional vertices and thus more patches. Figure 14.4 shows how adjusting the interior vertices deforms a single patch in a manner that would normally require the vertices of four patches.

FIGURE 14.4
Adjusting interior vertices versus vertices from additional patches.

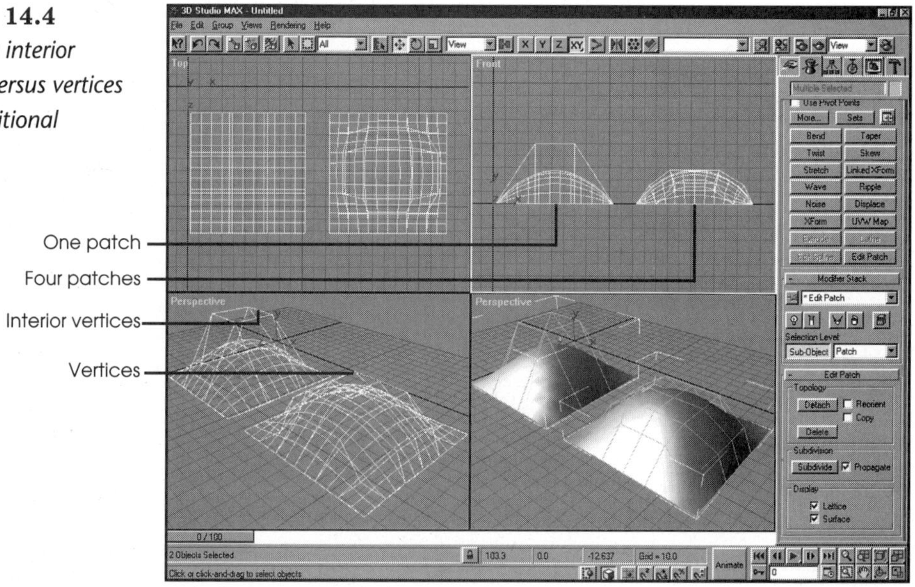

One patch
Four patches
Interior vertices
Vertices

Interior Vertices/Handles

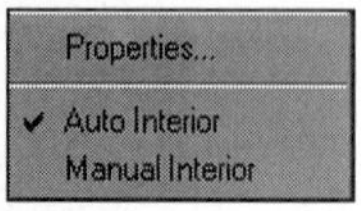

Although interior vertices may be useful, they are a bit difficult to get at. When first editing a patch, the patch is in Auto Interior mode, and the interior vertices are invisible because the interior control points are being moved when you adjust vector handles, edges, and patches. The interior vertices don't appear until you change the patch(es) to *Manual Interior* mode by right-clicking on them while in the Patch sub-object selection level.

When you place a patch in Manual Interior mode nothing visually happens until you return to the Vertex selection level. Then, all the interior vertices appear in yellow (four vertices for a QuadPatch and three for a TriPatch) for every patch currently in Manual Interior mode (see fig. 14.4). Unlike with vector handles, you don't have to select anything first to manipulate them—they're always available for manipulation.

What may not be obvious is the effect Manual Interior has on Edge and Patch editing. When you're in the default Auto Interior mode, the interior vertices are moved when you manipulate edges and patches. Manual Interior, on the other hand, effectively freezes the interior vertices to where they are. They can now be edited *only*, by hand, at the Vertex level. Figure 14.5 shows the moving of an edge in Auto Interior versus Manual Interior.

FIGURE 14.5

Moving an edge with the patch in Auto Interior and Manual Interior modes.

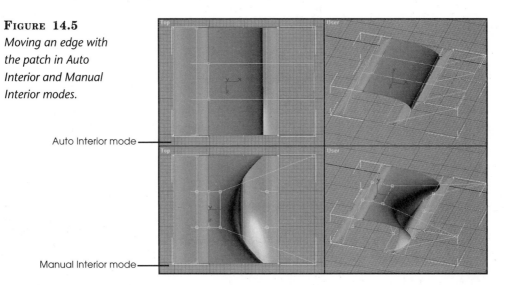

Auto Interior mode

Manual Interior mode

Editing vertices is also different when the patch is in Manual Interior mode because the interior vertices are no longer pulled along. Figure 14.6 shows the same vertex edits in both modes. Moving vertices without their neighboring interior vertices results in sharp-edged surfaces. Of course, editing just the interior vertices results in equally useful surface qualities, as shown in figure 14.7.

Transforming a patch or edge transforms the vertices and vector handles of the edge or patch, but leaves the interior vertices behind. Although this can be useful, it also can be very confusing if you aren't prepared for it. When you're prepared for the result, Manual mode can be quite useful.

FIGURE 14.6
Moving single vertices with the patch in Auto Interior and Manual Interior modes.

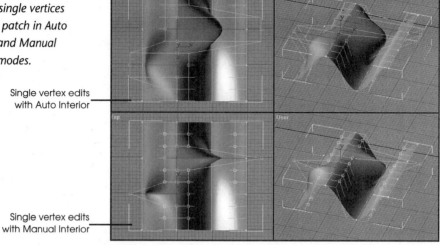

Single vertex edits with Auto Interior

Single vertex edits with Manual Interior

FIGURE 14.7
The effect of moving just interior vertices.

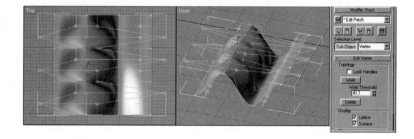

WARNING

Changing a patch from Manual Interior to Auto Interior cancels any editing you've done to the interior vertices. (Luckily this is reversible by clicking on Manual Interior again.) If you begin manipulating interior vertices you must keep the patch in manual mode to maintain your edits.

Subdividing and Propagation

Subdividing a patch divides every selected patch into four. The new patches, whether Quad or Tri, have edges at the midpoints of the original patch's edges. As figure 14.8 shows, this doesn't necessarily mean that the entire object quadruples. Only the patches that border divided edges themselves divide, and many divide just once.

FIGURE 14.8
Repeated subdividing with Propagation on.

Original —

One subdivision —

Two subdivisions —

Three subdivisions —

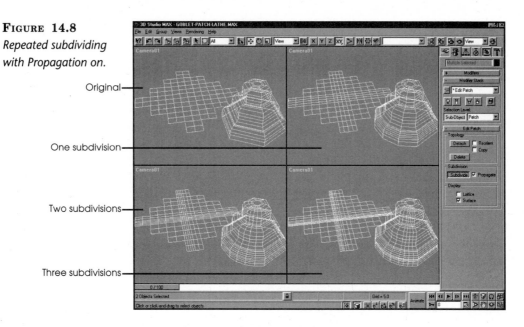

The Propagate option divides patches as necessary to maintain consistent vertices along edges. Unless you want a visual break in the model, you should *always* propagate your patch subdivisions. Without propagation, smoothing can't continue over the edge. The reason is simple—the new vertices have nothing with which to weld. The visual effect is a ridge at the seam because smoothing cannot continue across the edge. This makes the area similar to a "flap" that is ready to be peeled away, without affecting neighboring patches, as shown in the lower right of figure 14.9.

Creating Patches

Patches can be created in many ways. You can create them as raw rectangular patches, change Extrude or Lathe output to be patches, or convert 3D primitives to patches. Finally, 3DS MAX enables you to convert any arbitrary mesh to a patch and any patch to a mesh. This is accomplished through the use of two different types of Bézier patches—rectangular (bicubics) and triangular (quartics). These basic forms enable patches and meshes to change into one another.

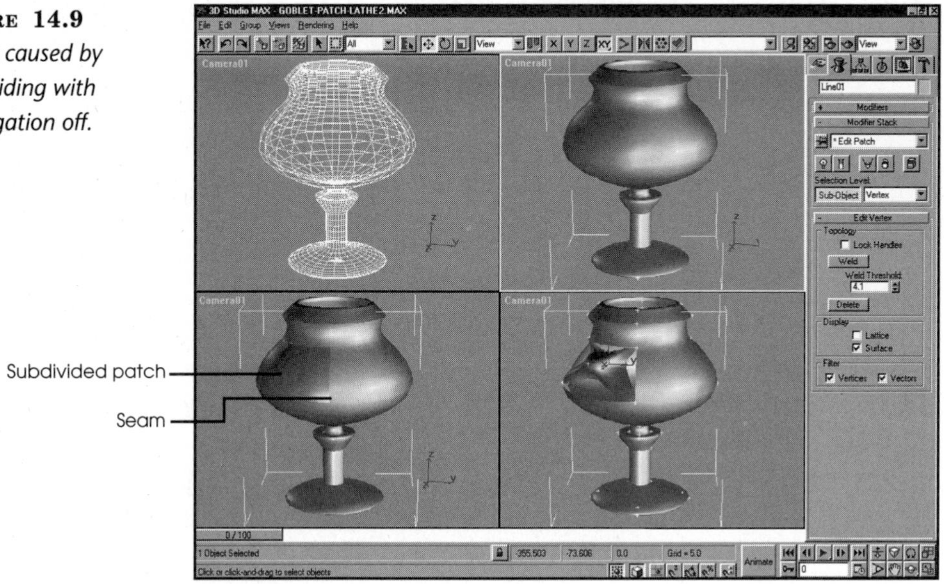

FIGURE 14.9
*Seams caused by
subdividing with
Propagation off.*

Subdivided patch ——

Seam ——

Using Patches from Primitives

You may often be forced into working with one type of patch over the other. When meshes are converted to patches (by adding an EditPatch modifier) they are always converted to TriPatches, even if their topology produces quadrilateral polygons. QuadPatches, which are often more preferable, are formed as the result of a creation parameter. Most of the standard primitives, as well as splines given an Extrude or Lathe modifier, produce QuadPatches. Figure 14.10 shows the resulting patch geometry after immediately giving primitives an EditPatch modifier.

TIP

Creating primitives with negative heights creates patches with reversed normals. This can be a very convenient method for creating patch objects for containers, vessels, and rooms from Boxes, Cylinders, Tubes, and Cones.

As figure 14.10 shows, every primitive except spheres and GeoSpheres converts to QuadPatches. Spheres convert to TriPatches due to a problem of QuadPatches "pinching" at the poles (a condition you can reproduce by lathing a half circle as a patch). The patch density of primitives is fixed. You can increase the density by using EditPatch's Subdivide function with the

Propagate option. This shouldn't be an inconvenience because an EditPatch has to be initially added to convert primitives to patches.

FIGURE 14.10
The patch equivalents for the standard primitives.

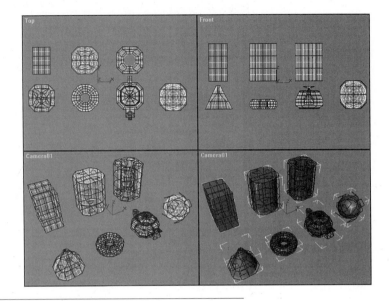

Using Patches from Extrude and Lathe

Extrude and Lathe both have the option to output patches rather than meshes. In doing so, they become two of the most convenient methods with which to begin patch modeling. Figure 14.11 shows the patch models, beginning as splines, converted to QuadPatches by Extrude and Lathe.

Splines are natural starting points for patch models because they both base themselves on the same geometric form—the Bézier spline. Splines can be converted into patches by using the Extrude or Lathe modifier. Unfortunately, the Lofter doesn't produce patches as an option.

TIP

Ironically, you can create patch objects from lofts if you have 3D Studio Release 4. The 3DS models created by the 3DSR4 3D Surfer module are translated into 3DS MAX patches on import, as shown in Figure 14.12.

FIGURE 14.11
*Using Extrude and
Lathe for generating
QuadPatches.*

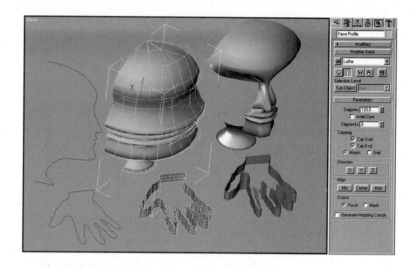

FIGURE 14.12
*A 3D Studio R4 3D
Surfer loft by 3DS
import.*

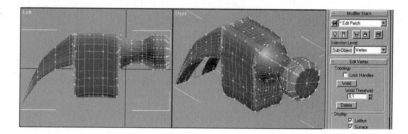

The Lathe modifier is extremely useful for creating basic forms for patch modeling. Lathe can be thought of as a potter's wheel, spinning a spline into soft, malleable patch clay. The tricky thing about using Lathe is directing its normals. Unlike meshes, you can't redirect the normals of a patch. If a patch's normals are facing the wrong way, you either have to change the manner in which the normal was created, reorient the existing patch, or use two-sided material. The last option is one to be avoided because turning Backface Cull off makes anything but the most basic of patch editing difficult.

Capping Patches

Patch objects formed with Extrude and Lathe are not as easily capped as their mesh equivalents. If the end cap is three-sided, it's capped with a TriPatch, and if it's four-sided, it's capped with a QuadPatch. If the cap has more sides, which is most likely, a more elaborate analysis should be done with the following rules:

- Nested shapes can't be capped (an extruded donut, for example).

- A clear line of sight must exist from each vertex to the shape's center.

In practice, it's the second rule that usually prevents capping and can be a bit frustrating. Figure 14.13 shows this situation, where the interior vertices just cross one another and invalidate the cap. To prevent this, place the star with the vertices in the left position and then edit with EditPatch to arrive at the position that previously canceled the capping.

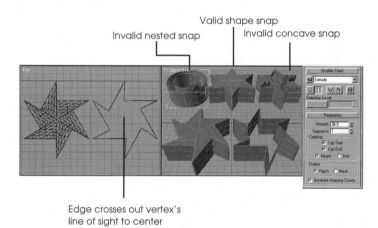

FIGURE 14.13
Line of sight checking for capping.

Valid shape snap
Invalid nested snap
Invalid concave snap

Edge crosses out vertex's
line of sight to center

For more elaborate shapes, such as the hand shown in figure 14.14, you need to cap the shape yourself. In this case, patches were added to the exposed edges (with EditPatch's Add Quad function) and then their vertices were welded to the vertices across from them. This is actually preferable for organic shapes because you now have control over where the patch lines occur and what type of patch is generated (automatic capping usually produces TriPatches). Most importantly, the patches you add and stitch across the face of the object have continuous smoothing—something that doesn't occur along automatically capped edges. The next section discusses capped edges in detail.

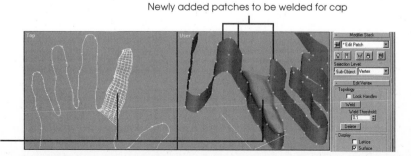

Newly added patches to be welded for cap

FIGURE 14.14
Manually capping a complex shape by adding patches to edges and welding.

Manually added and
welded cap patches

Smoothing Continuity

A spline's vertex type dramatically impacts the resulting smoothing of the patch extrusion or lathe. Although Smooth or Bézier vertex types result in smooth patches, Corner or Bézier Corner vertex types result in crisp edges over which smoothing cannot continue. This situation is similar to that described for primitives, although, unlike primitives, you can return to EditSpline to change these vertices to either Smooth or Bézier (see fig. 14.15). If you collapsed the stack for a patch object created with Extrude or Lathe and now have a patch object, the smoothing continuity of the object is fixed and can't be changed. You should, therefore, carefully analyze your models before collapsing them to see if the spline vertices need reclassification.

FIGURE 14.15

Vertex type's influence on smoothing continuity.

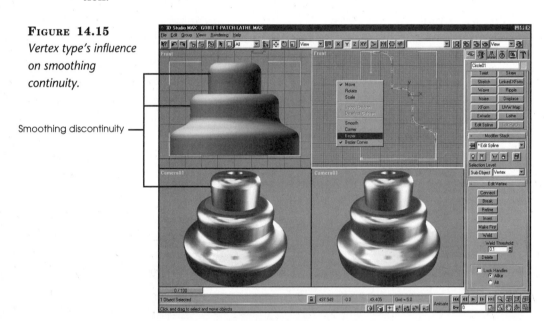

Caps created by Extrude and Lathe modifiers, or defined as part of a parametric object, always exhibit a smoothing discontinuity along their capped edges. This is exactly the same situation previously described for splines with corner vertex types. The only difference is that there is no way to change this for caps; the edge always renders as a ridge.

If you need a smoothing to continue across the capped edge of an Extrude or Lathe, first remove the cap by either deleting the patches or removing the cap option in the modifier. Then add patches to the edges, stretch the exposed vertices to the opposite edges, and weld.

The patches generated by the standard primitives have a property that can't be duplicated with other patch modeling and, unfortunately, can't currently be changed. Primitives that begin with caps (crisp, hard edges such as the top of a cylinder or sides of a box, for example) maintain those hard edges for the life of the patch. Unlike Extrude or Lathe cap edges, patches added to primitives along originally capped edges always render as an edge. Figure 14.16 shows the situation where the top vertex of a cylinder was deleted and the newly exposed edges given QuadPatches. Because the cylinder's top was originally "hard," an edge exists, even though the patch vertices are later welded and remain tangent. This is a unique situation because this smoothing discontinuity can't be introduced for other patches, nor can it be eliminated for these. Knowing this, you can either plan to avoid it or use it to your advantage when you want to introduce a break in smoothing but don't want to convert the patch model to a mesh to do so (by having to add a Smooth or EditMesh modifier).

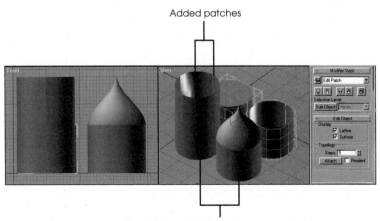

Added patches

Hard edges with discontinuous smoothing

FIGURE 14.16
Smoothing break between "hard" edges unique to caps.

Using EditPatch

EditPatch is your primary tool for patch editing. It's similar in concept to EditMesh and EditSpline, although admittedly less robust. As with the

EditSpline, EditPatch saves every edit you perform in sequence, meaning that the longer you work with the modifier, the larger the file (and the larger your RAM requirements) becomes. As you arrive at stages where you're comfortable with your model, you're definitely encouraged to collapse the stack. Models with large edit histories might even have their file sizes increase by a factor of 100 or more. As long as you do not include a modifier that converts the model to a mesh, the result of the stack collapse will be a Patch object, upon which you can apply the EditPatch modifier and return to patch modeling.

EditPatch is your only tool for establishing sub-object patch selections. Unlike mesh modeling, the Volume Select modifier doesn't work for patches; it unfortunately converts them to a mesh instead, and the sub-object animations must have their selections established with EditPatch. Because of its overhead, you are best off defining these selections in EditPatch modifiers that don't perform any editing—only selection. Adding specific EditPatch selection modifiers should be your standard method, whether animating transforms with XForm, modeling with modifiers, or animating that modeling.

Adding EditPatch as the very first entry in a primitive's edit history converts the primitive to a patch object. The primitive remains a patch until you add a modifier that requires it to convert to a mesh (such as Normal or Volume Select). Adding *any* modifier, other than EditPatch, as the lowest stack modifier converts a primitive to a mesh and removes any patch editing you may do with subsequent EditPatch modifiers. To add a UVW Map (for example) before the first EditPatch, you must add an EditPatch first.

You will find that navigating EditPatch is very similar to the other Edit modifiers. The next four sections describe adjusting the EditPatch object and using the tools found within the three selection levels of EditPatch.

Working with Patches at the Object Level

The Object level of EditPatch (see fig. 14.17) enables you to add other patch objects and contains your control for the mesh density of the entire patch object. It's not uncommon to return to the Object level while modeling at other levels to adjust the Steps setting for faster or more accurate vertex modeling.

FIGURE 14.17
*The Object level of
EditPatch.*

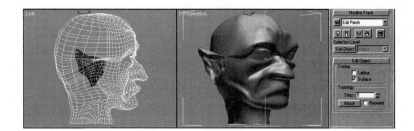

NOTE

Unlike EditSpline or EditMesh, cloning is not supported at any level within EditPatch—you can forget about using your Shift key when patch editing. Your only method for creating something similar to a clone is to detach patches with the Copy option.

Patch Topology

The Steps parameter influences how many subdivisions are made within all the patches of the object. As with everything in 3DS MAX, geometry must be converted to faces for rendering. The Steps parameter dictates how many subdivisions, and thus how many faces, are made within every patch of the object. This is very much like the steps settings for spline primitives, where adjusting the steps makes the spline rounder. Unlike splines, however, patches always give you control over their steps, even after they have been collapsed. Just add an EditPatch modifier and you can always adjust the patch steps at that point in time (see fig. 14.18). This is one of the most powerful aspects of patch modeling because the model's complexity (and the resulting RAM requirements) can be adjusted as needed. Because this is an animatable value, the density of your patch model can adjust as its prominence in the scene changes.

Although the amount of disk space your patch model requires is independent of its Steps setting, the RAM required for displaying and rendering is not. The number of faces generated is (steps + 1)^2 for every patch. A high Steps setting can thus bring your system to its knees if you are not careful. The maximum value for Steps is 100, creating more than two million faces for the model. Do not use the Ctrl accelerator key when adjusting the Steps spinner!

One step; 840 faces

*Changing the patch
density by adjusting
Steps.*

Zero steps; 210 faces

Three steps; 3,360 faces

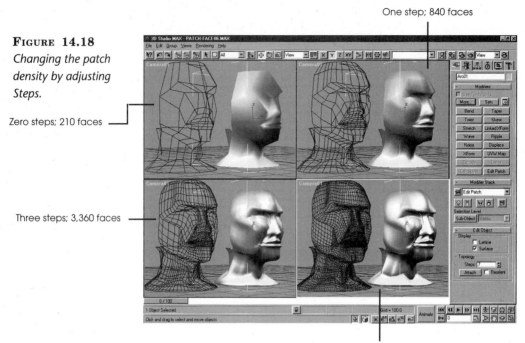

Seven steps; 13,440 faces

Attaching Patches

Attach enables you to bring another patch object into the same patch object definition. This is usually done for the purpose of welding patches together because welding can occur only within the same patch object. Objects attached that are not patch objects are translated into patch objects during the attachment. Figure 14.19 shows how a cylinder primitive is converted to a patch as part of the attach. You should be careful of attaching large mesh objects when your steps setting is high because doing so dramatically inflates the size of the model.

Unlike EditMesh, but similar in action to EditSpline, the Attach function provides a Reorient option. If checked, the selected object is reoriented so its transform matches that of the EditPatch object as shown in figure 14.19. The Reorient option centers the selected object according to its creation center onto the creation center of the active object. The rotation and scale values of the active object are simply copied to the attached object. For rotation, this has the effect of aligning the attached object, and is usually desirable. The same cannot be said for scale transforms, which affect your model's geometry. To prevent this scaling, you should use the XForm modifier rather than a transform to perform the scale of the base object.

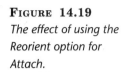

Cylinder primitive   Primitive converted to patch

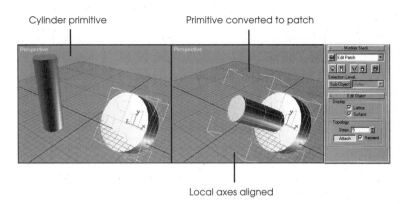

FIGURE 14.19
The effect of using the Reorient option for Attach.

Local axes aligned

NOTE

Because the Reorient option can be a bit surprising, it's advisable to use the Align function to center your objects before attaching to ensure that the reoriented result is desirable.

Patch Modeling at the Patch Level

The Patch level (see fig. 14.20) provides the basics of patch control. Here you make broad transforms, change the status of interior vertices, and surgically detach, delete, and subdivide. Ironically, some patch level operations (such as deletion and subdividing) affect far less then either the vertex or edge levels do. In practice, the Patch level is used primarily for detaching and subdividing patches and defining the status of interior vertices.

FIGURE 14.20
The Patch level of the EditPatch modifier.

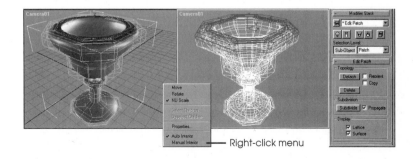

Right-click menu

Transforming Patches

When you move, rotate, or scale a patch, you're actually transforming all its vertices as a locked selection. In general, working at the Patch level is limited to initial, broad adjustments. The finer detail is provided at the Edge level, or especially the Vertex level. Deleting at the Patch level is the most controllable method for deleting patches because only what you selected is deleted—patches that share edges are not deleted.

WARNING ─────────────────────────────────

Patches treat the Local coordinate system as being the world and always rotate and scale about the world origin. Using the Local coordinate system is thus discouraged for the Patch level.

The one thing to be very careful about when transforming patches is the status of interior vertices. When using the default Auto Interior method, the interior vertices always move with the patch. If Manual Interior is active, however, interior vertices are frozen in place and can't be moved. Figure 14.21 shows the effect of scaling patches that have their interior vertices in Manual Interior mode.

WARNING ─────────────────────────────────

Changing a patch's mode from Manual to Auto removes the state of your interior vertices, regardless of when or how their positions were established. Interior vertices will return to their default positions whenever an EditPatch is added and the patches are placed in Auto mode (collapsing the stack does *not* protect interior vertex locations from this reset).

Detaching Patches

Unlike EditMesh, detaching a patch always results in the creation of a new object. Detach is the only way to "clone" a patch off of a model because standard cloning isn't supported by the EditPatch modifier. Unlike EditMesh, the option to keep the new patch as an element isn't available. If you need the new patch to be part of the same object, you need to use Attach at the Patch Object level.

Like Attach, Detach provides a Reorient option that attempts to move the detached patch object to an aligned position on the active grid. Due to the nature of patches, however, the result of using Reorient usually isn't desirable, and you're better off not using this option and using the standard Align function instead.

Interior vertices

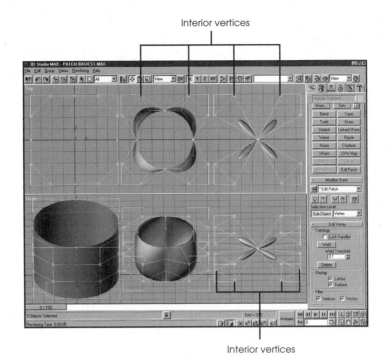

FIGURE 14.21
Scaling patches in Manual Interior mode, leaving their interior vertices unaffected.

Interior vertices

Patch Modeling at the Edge Level

Working with a patch edge is similar to manipulating two vertices at the same time. Edges can be a bit difficult to identify because you nearly always have to be viewing the lattice to ensure that you have the correct edge. Notice that figure 14.22 doesn't have a Delete function because you aren't able to delete at the Edge level. In practice, you will probably be using the Edge level for adding new patches more than anything else.

WARNING

Using the Delete key with a selected Edge deletes the *entire* patch object because there isn't a Delete function and the Delete key is being used at the object level instead.

Patch edges of original lathe selection

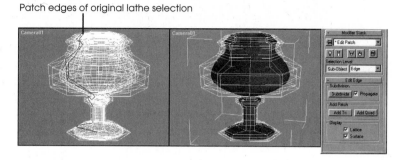

FIGURE 14.22
The Edge Level controls of EditPatch.

Transforming Patch Edges

You may be surprised by what can be accomplished by transforming edges, especially when you rotate them. Figure 14.23 shows the formation of a wave from a flat strip by simply rotating the edges as individual selections. In this case, not a single vertex was relocated—they still remain on the original flat plane. The interior vertices, however, were displaced by the very nature of Bézier patches.

Like patches, edges can't affect interior vertices that are currently in Manual Interior mode. These vertices are "left behind" as you transform the edge. Returning the patch to Auto Interior mode reverts interior vertices to their default locations and edge transforms will now affect them.

Roated edges

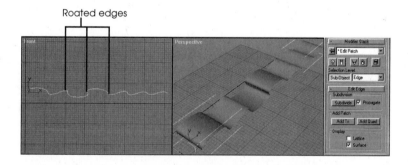

FIGURE 14.23
Rotating edges to form a ribbon of waves.

Patch edges treat the Local coordinate system as the world, and always rotate and scale about the world origin. Using the Local coordinate system is thus discouraged for the edge level.

Adding Patches

Your primary reason for being at the Edge level is to add patches. Adding edges is the only way to extend a patch object's boundary other than welding. Added edges weld themselves to the selected edge. The remaining vertices of the new patch (two for a Quad or one for a Tri) are then free to be manipulated. In most cases, you weld these to other patches.

Adding edges isn't quite as basic as it might seem at first. After selecting an edge, you click either Add Tri or Add Quad to add the appropriate patch type. What may not be obvious is that *every* selected edge receives a patch. This can be a problem when the same duplicate patches are created when there appears to be only one. Figure 14.24 shows a typical situation where extra patches are accidentally added because too many edges were selected. As the lower right viewport shows, the duplicate edges can be peeled from one another to expose the duplicates.

The correct method to add patches in interior corners is to select single edges with an eye as to how far they will extend (see the lower-left viewport of figure 14.25). After new ones are added, return to the Vertex level, perform a Select All, and weld the entire patch so that the newly added patches share the adjacent edges. You don't have to be this careful when adding patches to exterior edges because it's usually obvious where the new patches will be placed. Figure 14.26 shows adding TriPatches to a QuadPatch and then moving the vertices to create the beginnings of a flower.

Patches are added tangent to the patch belonging to the selected edge. When you're adding patches to more organic models, as shown in figure 14.26, the resulting patches might easily project at odd angles. When you're closing holes or knitting between parts, the edge you select to receive the new patch dictates this direction. Happily, it doesn't matter which edge you select because when you weld to the next patch, the new patch assumes its continuity. Your choice of edges to add to should be based on whatever produces the most convenient result. If the patch results at a sharp twisted angle, undo and select another side to which to add. Your aim is usually to create a patch that has vertices that are easily selectable for any subsequent transform or weld operation you may need to perform.

FIGURE 14.24
Duplicate patch creation from selecting adjacent edges.

Duplicate edges

Correctly selected edges

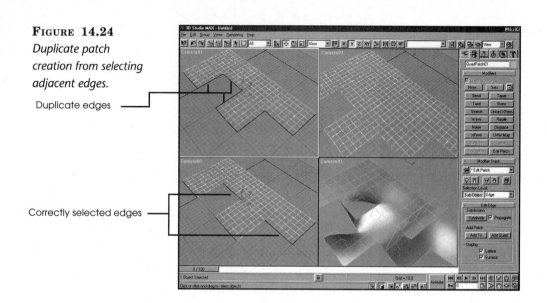

Four TriPatches added

FIGURE 14.25
Adding TriPatches to begin a flower.

Original patch

Eight TriPatches added

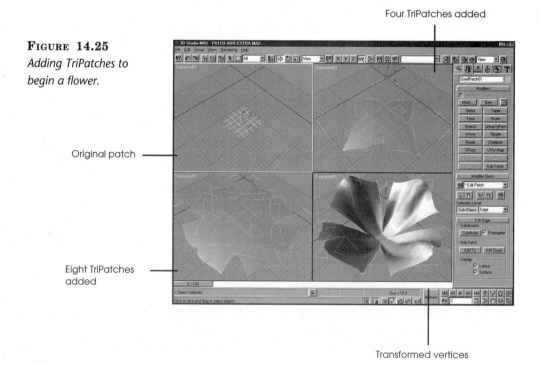

Transformed vertices

New QuadPatches

FIGURE 14.26
*Tangent patches
added to selected
edges.*

Selected edges —

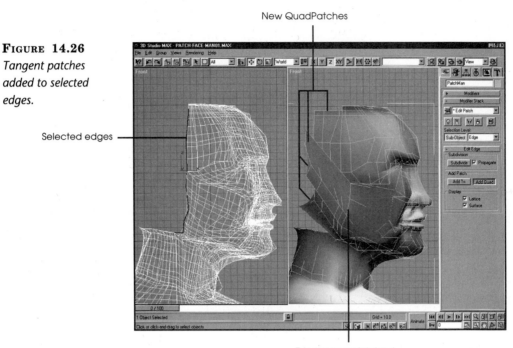

Tangency maintained

As the beginning of the chapter indicated, the type of patch you add impacts
how it deforms and behaves. Although perfectly legal, you should be very
cautious about mixing the two patch types because editing methods differ
across your model. When closing an organic object based on QuadPatches,
for example, it may appear simpler to use TriPatches at certain junctures.
This can result in areas that have challenging edge smoothing conditions
because the different patches on either side of the edge bend in fundamentally different ways. Figure 14.27 shows a situation where a TriPatch was
added in the midst of QuadPatches. The result is an edge that still needs
some vertex vector handle adjustment to smooth out the resulting ridge.

Patch Modeling with Vertices

The Vertex level (see fig. 14.28) is where the vast majority of patch modeling
occurs because it is at this level only that the critical tangent vectors are
accessible. Unlike mesh vertices, a patch vertex and its vectors have a
tremendous impact on the surrounding surface. In fact, adjusting single
patch vertices is similar to transforming single mesh vertices with the Affect
Region option.

FIGURE 14.27
A TriPatch added in the midst of QuadPatches.

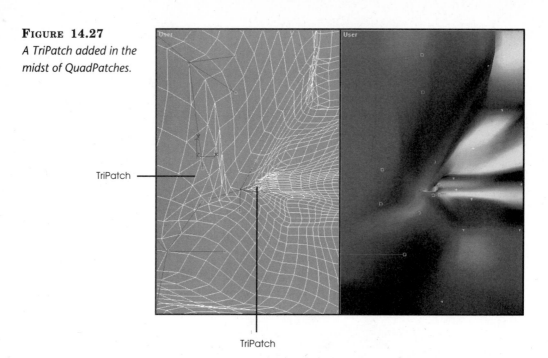

TriPatch

TriPatch

FIGURE 14.28
The Vertex Level rollout of EditPatch.

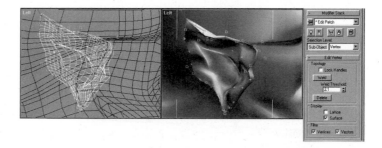

TIP

You are likely to find that when editing vertices you have no need to ever show the patch lattice because all vertices are part of the patch surface, and their influence is quite apparent. When working with vertices, it's usually best to turn off the lattice.

The density of the patch, controlled at the object level by the Steps setting, has no impact on your vertex edits. Low step levels can betray the effect of your editing because not enough faces are produced to show the resulting curvature. When making final edits to your model, you want to increase the Steps so the shading subtleties, dictated by tangencies, are apparent as you edit. Remember, you can always lower this setting without harm. Higher settings don't impact file sizes, only RAM.

Vertex filters are quite useful, although their check box options can be a bit confusing. When both options are checked (the default) then both the vertices and vector handles can be selected. Clicking on Vertex filters out the vertices so that only vector handles can be selected, and clicking on Vectors filters vectors out so that only vertices can be selected. The somewhat odd toggling of these options is to prevent the filtering of both because in that case, nothing can be selected. Even so, if you filter Vertices before selecting any, you won't be able to affect vectors because they're displayed only when their vertices are selected. To work with just vector handles, you need to perform a Select All and then check Filter Vertices. Filters are primarily used when vector handles are coincidental or close to their vertices, and you need to ensure the selection of one over the other.

Transforming Vertices and Vector Handles

Nearly all of your edits with patches involve transforming vertices and their tangent vectors. Each vertex should really be thought of as a cluster of points, never just one because each vertex has a vector handle for every edge that shares it. When you move, rotate, or scale a patch vertex you're also transforming its handles. Rotations and scale, operations that do nothing for single mesh vertices, can have a significant impact on patch vertices. Vector handles can be adjusted only when their vertex has been selected, and it's common to select several vertices and adjust their handles independently.

When adjusting vertex tangent handles, it's important to remember that you can't animate them. Sub-object patch animation always takes place with either the XForm or Linked XForm modifier, and both of these only see vertices. When you're designing your patch model for animation, this needs to be taken into account. If you need to animate a vector handle, you can subdivide the patch and animate the resulting vertices instead. You will find that the new vertices react in a manner similar to that of the handles. You can animate *all* of a vertex's vector handles by applying an XForm scale or rotation to a single vertex. The vectors then scale and rotate about the vertex in a uniform manner without disturbing the vertex itself.

TIP

The newly introduced FFD (Free Form Deformation) modifiers can animate patch surfaces in a manner that is very similar to adjusting the tangent handles. The FFD modifiers preserve the model as a patch and are extremely valuable tools for manipulating patch models.

Vector handles are interesting and extremely valuable controls because they usually impact the curvature of two patches (those that share the edge to which they initially "point"). Vector handles are all that matter. The vector is just a "lifeline" of sorts that visually shows you what vertex the handle belongs to. All that matters is the location of the handle. Vector handles concern themselves only with position. When you rotate or scale a vector handle, the handle simply rotates about or scales to the vertex to which it belongs.

TIP

To move a single vector handle perfectly along its vector, scale the handle and it moves co-linear to the parent vertex.

Right-clicking on a vertex, or selection of vertices, enables you to edit their vector type. This procedure is similar to spline vertices, except there are only two options—*Coplanar* and *Corner*. The Corner option enables you to adjust each vector independently, so editing one doesn't impact the others. This does *not* influence path smoothness or continuity. The Coplanar option adjusts the Vertex handles to be coplanar with one another and then locks the vectors so that they maintain their coplanar relationship. What may be surprising is that this doesn't ensure or enforce tangency of the affected patches; it aligns only the vector handles on a common plane.

After the Coplanar option is applied, all handles adjust when one is manipulated, to maintain the coplanar relationship. The only way to move one handle and not affect the other is to scale it. Vertices having only two vectors (those on outside corners) are always treated as Corner because three points are required to define a plane. Although changing a vertex from Corner to Coplanar often changes the curvature a bit, changing from Coplanar to Corner has no initial effect on the patch surface.

TIP

When modeling organic forms, you will probably want to be using corner vectors, and perhaps change them to Coplanar after you're nearly finished. You will find that this gives you more freedom for each vertice's manipulation as you concentrate on the form.

Transforming patch vertices is different from transforming patches or edges, when using the Local coordinate system. When Local is active, your vertices rotate and scale about a local axis that has the same axes alignment as the object itself. This is regardless of the current pivot point center option.

This means that when using the Local coordinate system with vertices, the Use Selection Center option has *no* effect. Although a bit confusing, this capability enables you to independently rotate and scale vertices—with the effect being that the vector handles spin around and move to and from the static vertices. If you need to rotate them about a collective center, you will need to choose another Coordinate system type (such as Parent).

The Lock Handles option locks handles so that adjusting one influences the other. Only when a handle moves along its vector (scaled) are the others not affected. Lock Handles is a global setting for the patch object that is identical in operation to the way handles adjust when their vertices have Coplanar settings. In practice, you probably will not want this setting on. Its primary use is for adjusting Corner vertices that require their handles to maintain the same relationship.

Weld

Welding vertices is your method for joining patches to one another or sealing the open edges of patches newly added to edges. Weld works in conjunction with its Threshold value. This value indicates the distance vertices must be from one another to be welded. Vertices found to be within each other's threshold have their positions averaged to arrive at a new location for the welded vertex. Unlike mesh vertices, a few more rules apply to welding patch vertices:

- Welding can't be done to two vertices on the same patch.
- Patches must belong to the same object.
- Welding can occur only between open edges.
- No weld can take place if the result would form an edge that would be used by more than two patches.
- If you attempt to weld a vertex that isn't on an exposed edge, it is ignored, enforcing the above restrictions.

The positional averaging that occurs between welded vertices can be exactly what you want, or form a horrible mess. Although EditPatch doesn't have a Weld Target option (as with EditMesh), it gives you control through a somewhat hidden method. You can keep a vertex anchored and force the other vertex to move to it by simply selecting the patch (at the patch level) to which the target vertex belongs. Selected patches can't move their vertices during a weld operation unless the other vertex being welded is also part of a selected patch.

TIP

Selecting patches for vertices you don't want to alter is critical when adding patches to areas of an already finished section of your model.

Welding patches may seem a bit "magical" because of the way the welded patches are adjusted to be tangential and smooth. When welded, the edges that the vector handles and vertices define have new points through which to interpolate. The Bézier curves then produce a naturally smooth surface. Figure 14.29 shows how several added patches, which start out smooth on their attached edges, are given continuity when their corner vertices are adjusted to be close to one another and welded. This is a wonderful property of Bézier curves, in that they maintain continuity between adjacent curves, and in this case patches.

Newly added patches   Vertices welded

FIGURE 14.29
Continuity created between welded edges.

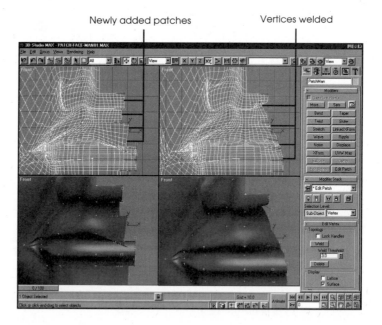

When working on symmetrical models, such as noses and faces, it's very convenient to model only half of the form. After you're to a point where it becomes necessary to see the other side, mirror the model about the central edge and make the new object an instance or reference. As a result, when you work on one side, the changes are duplicated on the other. Figure 14.30 shows this technique with a head, where all edits done to one side are dynamically updated on the other as you work. After you're finished, attach the second side to the first and weld the seam shut (as was done in the lower right view of figure 14.30).

FIGURE 14.30
Patch modeling with a mirrored instance.

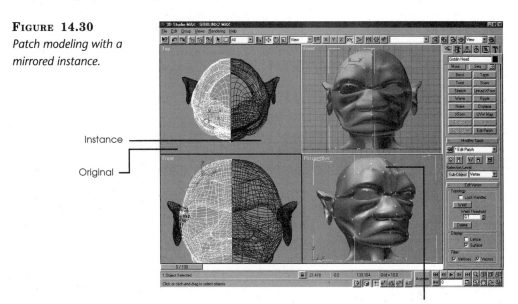

Instance

Original

No seam after attach and center vertices have been welded

TIP

If you have begun modeling on an entire model that is symmetrical and wish to use this technique, simply detach or delete one half of the model and mirror the remainder. Weld's averaging of vertex positions is often an aid in creating a straight mirror seam.

Delete

Deleting a vertex deletes all the patches that share it. In this way, it is very similar to deleting mesh vertices, where every face that shares a vertex is deleted. Deleting patches by their vertices is not nearly as surgical as deleting individual patches. Remember that you aren't allowed to delete at the Edge level.

Staying in Patch Mode

When working with patches, the last thing you usually want to do is introduce something in the Modifier Stack that causes the patch object to convert to a mesh. Certain modifiers do this every single time and should be used only at the very end of the stack, so your patch modeling can continue below it without harm. Modifiers that are designed to work with meshes or faces (nearly anything dealing with a surface) must convert the object to a mesh. In Release 1.1, the following always convert patches to meshes when applied:

EditMesh	Material
Smooth	Normal
VolumeSelect	MeshSmooth
Relax	Optimize

As a result, it's very prudent to create a button set that includes only modifiers that can work with patch objects. Figure 14.31 shows a "Patch Edit" button set that includes such commands, as well as the ones for spline editing because the two go very well together.

FIGURE 14.31
A Patch Edit button set to ensure Patch geometry does not go to mesh.

The only surface-related modifier that you can apply is a UVW Map modifier. Internally, this is because both the mesh and patch object classes belong to the "mappable" object class, which enables modifiers to store mapping without affecting topology. The same capability is unfortunately not afforded smoothing, materials, and normals, pointing to a very significant aspect of patch editing—the smoothness of your model is entirely dependent on the tangencies of your model and how it was constructed.

Using Modifiers on Patches

Modifiers can be added in your edit history in much the same way that you add modifiers to meshes. Remember to avoid Optimize, Relax, and MeshSmooth modifiers. Although modifiers operate in the same way for patches and meshes, their effect is usually different. Both meshes and patches are actually modified by their vertices. The difference between patches is that the vertices are the control points and not the surface. Thus, a modifier is manipulating patch vertices, which obviously has a more dramatic impact on the surface than mesh vertices. Figure 14.32 shows the moving of a Displace modifier diagonally across a patch surface. In all four frames, the modifier was level and its values constant. The reason for the dramatically different effect is that the control vertices of the patch were displaced and because they define the patch surface through interpolation, the surface is displaced considerably.

FIGURE 14.32

A Displace modifier's effect on patch vertices.

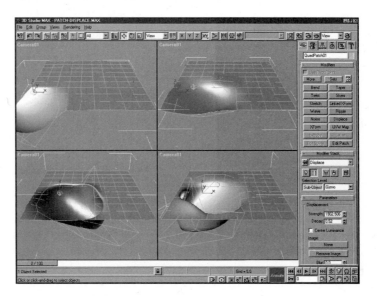

NOTE

If you have a patch model and need the result to behave like mesh instead of patch, place a simple modifier, such as Normal, at the end of the path editing stack to convert the model to a mesh. Figure 14.33 shows the same model four frames as figure 14.32 except that a Normal modifier has been placed between EditPatch and Displace to turn the patch into a mesh for the displacement.

FIGURE 14.33

The Displace modifier's effect on the same surface as a mesh.

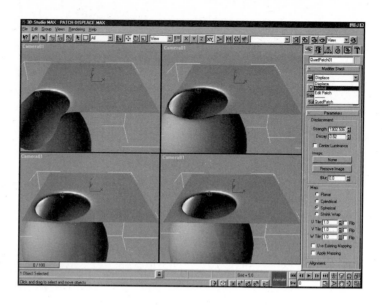

Switching from patch modeling to mesh is fairly painless because your model's surface complexity doesn't change. The surface defined by the EditPatch Steps setting is used to define the resulting mesh. Adding an additional EditPatch modifier after mesh editing increases your model's geometry significantly because every face is turned into a TriPatch. Ideally, you should perform all your mesh editing after your patch editing and return to patch editing by going lower in the Edit History stack.

NOTE

Be careful returning to EditPatch after mesh modeling because its Steps setting affects the vertex and face ordering used by subsequent mesh modifiers.

In Practice: Patch Modeling

■ **Patch models**   Patch models are ideally defined from the beginning as patches or derived from Lathe and Extrude modifiers. Deriving patches from meshes should be a secondary choice because the conversion is to Tri instead of Quad patches.

■ **Interior vertices in Manual mode**   Switching interior vertices to Manual mode should be viewed as a permanent setting because returning the patches to Auto Interior mode will reset manually positioned vertices to their default locations.

- **Adding modifiers to patch models** Remember that Optimize, MeshSmooth, Relax, Normal, Smooth, Material, and Volume Select will convert the model to a mesh.

- **Patch edge smoothness** Welding patches together at an edge automatically gives the two patches a smooth continuity across the edge. Smoothing can occur only between patches that share edges with one another.

- **Patch surface smoothness** Vertex positioning and tangent handle adjustment are the only methods to influence the smoothness of a patch surface. The concept of smoothing groups is available only to meshes.

- **FFD modifiers** The FFD (Free Form Deformation) modifiers work very well for deforming patch models and can overcome the limitation of not being able to animate tangent handles.

Pavlov Lantern Room from the Palaces of St. Petersburg Exhibit
Created by Harold Kalmus
Articus Media Labs, Inc.
Philadelphia, PA
Exhibition designers: Charles Muck Associates/Quenroe Associates

Chapter 15

Advanced Modifiers

Each modifier can bring an amazing amount of capabilities to your modeling. Some are very complex, whereas others are very straightforward. The key in using any modifier, but especially those in this chapter, is understanding the order in which to apply them in the stack. As with most modifiers, nearly all of them can (and should) be used in conjunction with others in the stack for maximum flexibility. Although each modifier is presented on its own, it rarely works in isolation. You often have to define selections, optimize the result, perfect smoothing, and assign mapping as you modify the object. This chapter points out situations when this synergy is important and when it is not.

This chapter organizes modifiers according to how they treat the geometry handed to them in the stack. This is an important trait to learn because several modifiers will convert splines and patches to meshes when you do not want the conversion to occur. The modifiers are classified here as those that work with any geometry, those that work only with meshes, those that work solely with transforms, and those that work on surfaces. This is done to reinforce what can and cannot be done with patch and spline models. In this regard, the chapter is separated into the following sections:

- Geometry modifiers
- Mesh modifiers
- Transform modifiers
- Surface modifiers

Geometry Modifiers

Some of the most versatile modifiers are those that work with a variety of geometry. The axial deformation modifiers (Bend, Taper, Twist, Stretch, Skew) described in Chapter 8, "Object-Level Modeling," were of this type. To this crowd we add Displace, Noise, Wave, Ripple, and FFD. Each of these modifiers is a bit more complex than the those described before but bring with them some incredible modeling opportunities.

Using Displace

Displace is a modifier that pushes or pulls the vertices of your model according to mapping coordinates. The mapping coordinates can be those applied previously in the Modifier Stack, or those applied by the Displace gizmo itself. The direction of the displacement is determined by the averaged face normal for each vertex and the mapping projection. The strength of the displacement is controlled by the modifier's strength spinner and, optionally, a referenced bitmap.

TIP

The Escape key cancels Displace during long calculations and returns you to your previous settings.

The Strength parameter controls the distance, in units, that the affected vertices move, according to their mapping projection. Mapping coordinates striking normal to the surface, at 90 degrees, displace the vertices a distance equal to the Strength amount. Figure 15.1 shows the effect of using Displace's Spherical and Planar projections with strengths of 5 on a box with a width of 10. The planar projection displaces its entire square by 5 while only the area 90 degrees to the sphere's center reaches 5 units in displacement.

FIGURE 15.1
The Strength setting's impact on displaced distance.

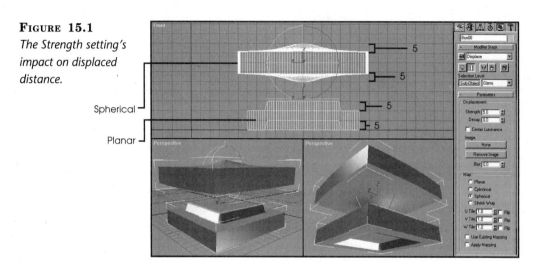

NOTE

The surface you are displacing must have enough vertices located at critical areas of detail in order for the modifier to have a visible effect (that is, displacing a 1-segment box will have no effect).

The Displace modifier's uniqueness comes with its Image button. Clicking the Image button (labeled "None") enables you to select any bitmap with which to modulate the modifier's strength. In all cases, bitmaps are read as intensity maps, where the luminance is used and color images are treated as grayscale. White pixels have full effect, black none, and grays a proportional effect. Figure 15.2 shows this in its top views. The white cross is projected the full strength of 15, the 50% gray surroundings half of that, and the black areas have no effect.

FIGURE 15.2

The impact of a bitmap image on strength.

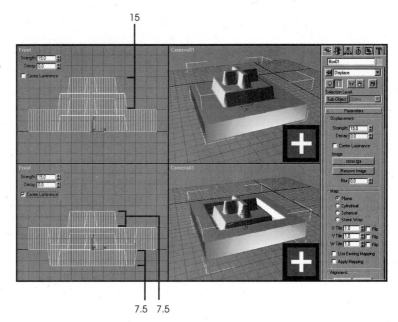

The Center Luminance option has an impact on the strength setting and is used when you want your bitmap to displace your surface inward as well as outward. When checked, white and black are treated as having equal but opposite strengths. White is now 50% percent of the Strength setting, black is –50%, mid-gray has no impact, and light or shades of gray have proportional effects. Figure 15.3 shows the impact of this option in its lower viewports, where the previous flat black areas are now carving a crevice, and the mid-gray area is even with the original surface. If you aren't using a bitmap image, checking Center Luminance cuts the overall Strength in half but doesn't force any to go negative.

NOTE

3D Studio MAX uses only the RAM necessary to process the color depth of your bitmaps. Whenever you reference an intensity map, an 8-bit grayscale version requires $1/3$ the RAM as the same image in 24-bit color. Grayscale images also are more intuitive because it's easier to compare depths of gray than imagining the grayscale equivalents of color.

The Blur option has a value of 0–10 and affects the bitmap image by passing it through a blur filter. The effect is similar to the blurring you get in the Materials Editor, and the contrasting edges of your image are softened. The top views of figure 15.3 show how a small blur amount can anti-alias coarse edges whereas the bottom views of the figure show how larger blur amounts can completely weather a displacement.

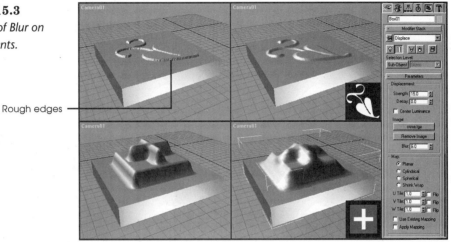

When using Displace's own mapping, the gizmo is your control for the placement, orientation, and scale of the displacement map. Displace always treats the mapping as a "decal" where the extents of the gizmo dictate the extents of the mapping and thus the displacement. (You can't "tile" past the extents of the gizmo when using the Displace gizmo for mapping.) Figure 15.4 shows the results of using the four displacement options (gizmo shapes) available in Displace.

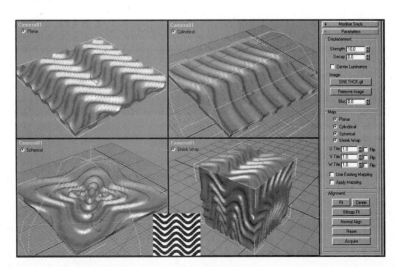

When you check the Use Existing Mapping option, the current projection of Displace is ignored, and the existing mapping coordinates—however they may have been applied—are used to control the displacement. Figure 15.5 shows displacing a spherical image with different tiling rates. The two mapping types Displace does not afford (Box and Cylindrical Cap) are also shown. The existing mapping option also enables you to displace according to very intricate coordinates, whether they were lofted or the result of numerous deformations, as shown in figure 15.6.

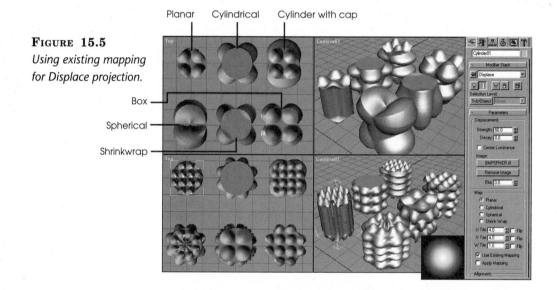

FIGURE 15.5
Using existing mapping for Displace projection.

FIGURE 15.6
Using existing mapping after other deform- ations or from a loft.

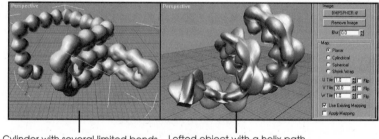

Cylinder with several limited bends   Lofted object with a helix path

NOTE

When using existing mapping, Displace respects your object's mapping coordinates as the object animates or changes shape, enabling you to create extremely intricate animations or make modeling decisions while seeing the impact on a later displacement.

Displace is often used without existing mapping to influence a model or, more likely, specific portions of a model. In this mode, the Displace gizmo becomes much like a "thumb" probing into the model or a "magnet" pulling the surface from the model. Figure 15.7 shows how a spherical gizmo (which is actually unequally scaled to be an ellipsoid) is ideal for this analogy, regardless of whether it has positive or negative strength.

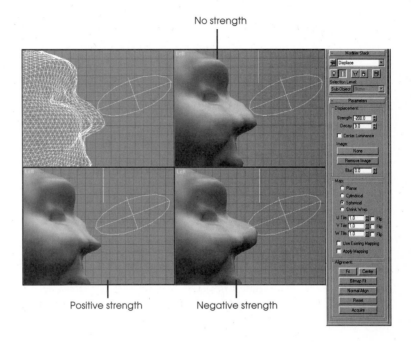

FIGURE 15.7
Using Displace as a modeling "thumb" or "magnet."

When used for localized effects (such as the wiggling of a nose), the Decay parameter becomes very important to keep Displace from affecting the entire object. Decay is used to limit the range the Displace gizmo's strength has. As the Decay is increased, the impact of the Strength is decreased. The values for Decay are not easily described, especially because they impact Strength at the same time. The best approach is to increase the Decay and then the Strength in tandem until the desired result is achieved.

TIP

It's often easiest to set a very high Strength setting so that the impact of the Decay range can be seen and then adjust Strength downward for the desired result.

The tiling options for Displace have an impact on both existing and applied mapping. Values greater than one cause the pattern to repeat within the gizmo's extents. If existing mapping is used, the previous tiling value is respected, but only for the first repeat of the pattern. Previous tiling thus has the effect of scaling the region of the Displace gizmo. Previous map tiling can be confusing and isn't recommended.

When working with existing mapping, the current Displace Map Type influences its interpretation. When set to Planar, only the first tile repeat of the mapping is respected—with Cylindrical as the first row—and with Spherical or Shrink Wrap, both rows and columns are read. You can thus control the extents of previous mapping by choosing the Displace gizmo shape.

The Apply Mapping option is included if you want to quickly apply the mapping within Displace as actual coordinates for materials (or future modifiers) to use. The W Tile field is supplied for this purpose alone because it has no effect on Displace itself. The Alignment options within Displace are identical in use to those of the UVW Mapping modifier.

TIP

You can animate a Displace gizmo by assigning it a path or Look At controller. This often gives more control than using the space warp version of the modifier in world space.

In practice, you probably need to use extremely fine meshes for Displace to give you the detail you need. This detail may come from the object's surface parameters, an EditMesh tessellation, or possibly a MeshSmooth modifier. After Displace accomplishes its deformation, it is often followed with an Optimize modifier (discussed later in the "Mesh Modifiers" section) to reduce the geometric overhead. A Smooth modifier also is a common companion after Displace or Optimize, ensuring the proper smoothing group assignments for the newly modeled geometry. A common sequence for using Displace in the modifier stack becomes: MeshSmooth, Displace, Optimize, Smooth.

Using Noise

The noise modifier is invaluable for roughening up your model in a random and fractal manner. Sometimes you want your model's surface to shake, shiver, and twist, but actually modeling that type of deformation might make you cringe. Noise is perfect for affecting your model without harming its careful modeling. It's also ideal for creating fractal landscapes and uneven surfaces, such as a crinkled paper bag or watercolor paper. The Noise modifier is similar to the Noise controller except that the effect is governed by the gizmo's transform in 3D space instead of by time.

The Strength parameters control the amount of noise displacement along a given axis. The strength values are actually the maximum distance (in units) that the displacement will occur (when Scale is at 100%). Every vertex is displaced according to the axis strength and the global Seed and Scale settings. Introducing a scale value along one axis moves all the vertices along that axis.

The lower left (Top) view of figure 15.8 shows how the noise isn't seen when viewed down the affected axis, which in this case is the Z axis. The effect is evident when viewed from the other two sides as Noise makes its standard displacement—a sine curve along the other two axes. When the same strength is given to each axis, a sine wave is sent along each axis, as shown in the upper views of figure 15.8. The initial phase of the curve is controlled by the Seed value, so changing this value is a quick way to give similar objects very dissimilar noise displacements. It isn't possible to constrain the displacement along one axis (to do so, see the Wave modifier).

FIGURE 15.8
The default sine wave displacement of the Noise modifier.

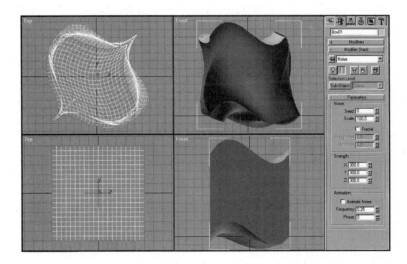

NOTE

Regardless of how radically you displace your geometry with Noise, the vertices at the extremities of the Noise gizmo remain stationary because they're the end points of the displacement spline curve.

The Scale parameter affects all the axes' Strengths and should be thought of as a three-axes strength adjustment. Scale starts at 100 (percent) with lower values decreasing the size of the displacement curve and higher values increasing it. As the curve grows it flattens, so you need to compensate with a larger Strength if you want the same displacement distance. The opposite is true for lower values.

When the Fractal option is checked, a fractal curve is applied to the originally smooth sine wave, and the results can be seen in figure 15.9. In practice, this is the most common application for Noise because creating and animating this effect by hand is extremely tedious. With Noise, it's a simple matter of interactively adjusting a few parameters. Fractal landscapes are usually generated along just one axis because using more than one shifts the vertices horizontally. The Iterations setting controls how many "peaks" occur within the sine curve, with 1.0 doing nothing (because the initial sine curve is the first iteration) and 10.0 giving nine additional variations. Be careful with large meshes because increasing the iterations increases the computation time. The accompanying Roughness parameter adjusts the sharpness of the fractal curve by acting as vertical adjustment to the vertex displacements. The higher the Roughness, the sharper the noise.

FIGURE 15.9

Applying fractal noise along one and then three axes.

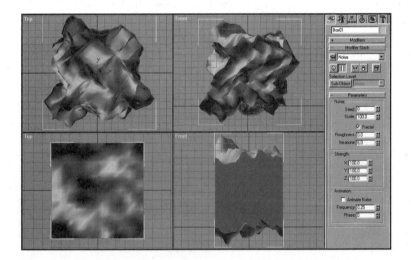

TIP

Fractal Noise can be an intensive modifier because it affects every vertex. If you want your model to only shake and shudder, modifying the Scale transform with a Noise controller is much more efficient.

Unlike the Noise controller, there is no graph that describes the noise function. Instead, the modifier's gizmo represents the noise curve quite well and in three dimensions. Manipulating the gizmo's center is very similar to adjusting the Seed or Phase values, and animating it produces smooth deformations. To affect the phase, move the center perpendicular to the strength axis you wish to modulate (for example, if it's Z, move it in the XY plane). Scaling the gizmo is similar to simultaneously adjusting the Scale and Strength settings. Rotating the gizmo changes the direction the vertices are pulled. For animations, you're much better off animating the gizmo and its center than the Seed, which causes a very abrupt change per interval. Animating the noise gizmo and center presents many interesting opportunities, as shown in figure 15.10.

FIGURE 15.10
An animated body of water using Noise on a box.

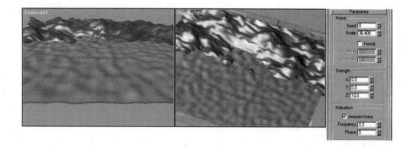

Noise animation is further controlled with the Animate Noise option. When checked, the Phase controls the animation cycle of the displacement curves. When Animate Noise is first checked, a key is placed at each end of the active time segment. You can now add more keys by conventional methods. If you turn off Animate Noise, the track is ignored by Track View; if you turn it on, your keys are returned to being active. Although the accompanying Frequency setting can't be animated, it does affect the "speed" of the given phase.

NOTE

When animating complex noise effects, you will want to modulate the noise animation with ease and/or multiplier curves. Because noise is fractally generated, looping is not available and you will need to have the noise animation at least equal the active time segment.

Using Wave

The Wave modifier deforms an object by sending a sine wave along a single axis, as shown in figure 15.11. By default, this is applied along the object's Y axis, but it can be oriented anywhere by rotating the Wave modifier's gizmo. When animated, the Wave modifier can create everything from graceful bends in the wind to a swimming manta ray.

FIGURE 15.11
The Wave modifier's default sine curve distortions.

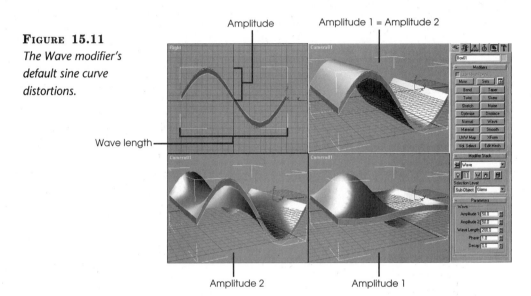

The Amplitude values express the distance the wave will crest from the original surface. When set to the same value, Amplitude 1 & 2 produce a uniform wave, as shown in the top of figure 15.11. Amplitude 1 controls the height at the gizmo center (by default the center), and Amplitude 2 defines the wave height at the two edges. Note that the width of the wave is *always* the entire width of your selection. The Wave modifier repeats along its primary axis only. The amplitudes give you the ability to modulate that one wave along its width—something that's essential for a manta ray.

The width curve being defined by Amplitude 1 and (by default along the object's X axis) is actually a single, infinite curve that doesn't repeat. The gizmo center defines the center of the curve, as shown in figure 15.12. The height defined by Amplitude 2 is relative only when the center is actually in the middle of the gizmo's width. As figure 15.12 also shows, moving the center to either side "slides" the curve and projects the edge heights considerably. The gizmo center is thus defining the location and center of the first wave with the amplitudes determining the height.

Amplitude 2   Shifted curve

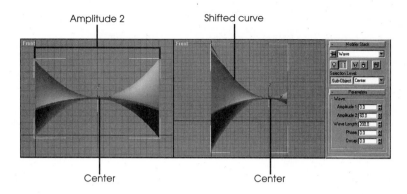

FIGURE 15.12
*Gizmo center
determining curve
location.*

Center   Center

The Wave Length parameter controls the distance between wave crests or, more properly, the frequency of the wave. This property is also mimicked by scaling the gizmo along its Y axis. The Phase parameter controls the position or cycle of the wave as it travels along the Y axis. This is the parameter to animate if you want a rolling wave. The Phase parameter also can be achieved by moving the gizmo center along the Y axis.

The Decay parameter enables you to fade out a wave (if it is less than 1.0), or amplify it (if it's greater than 1.0). Decay values tend to be quite small (most often below 0.1) and control only the decay across the length of the wave because the wave height is constant across the width and modulated only by the amplitude settings. The source of the decay is the gizmo center, so placing it appropriately is very important. The lower views of figure 15.13 show the results of using decay. Manipulating the gizmo gives you even more variations on what can be created, as shown in the upper views of figure 15.13, because rotating the gizmo orients or slants the waves.

FIGURE 15.13
*Manipulating a wave's
effect with gizmo
orientation and decay.*

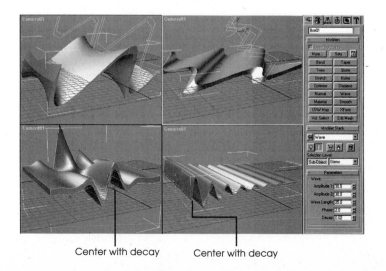

Center with decay   Center with decay

Using Ripple

The Ripple modifier is identical to the Ripple space warp except that it acts in local, rather than world, space. It's very similar to the Wave modifier in that it displaces the vertices according to a sine curve. The difference is that Ripple projects its sine curve radially from the gizmo center, as shown in figure 15.14, rather than linearly along one axis as Wave does.

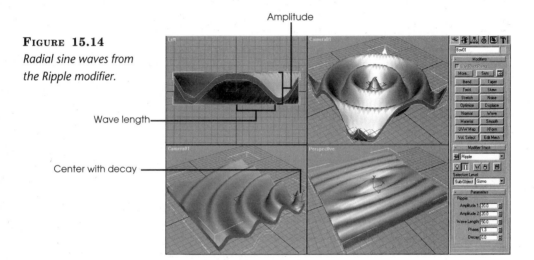

FIGURE 15.14
Radial sine waves from the Ripple modifier.

By default, Ripple modifies the object's Z axis, with Amplitude 1 affecting the X axis and Amplitude 2 affecting the Y axis. For nearly all liquid ripples, you want these values to be the same. Different values usually mean you're modeling an effect, as shown in the lower right of figure 15.14 (whose gizmo was unequally scaled to further dramatize the effect).

The Wave Length, Phase, and Decay settings are similar to those of the Wave modifier. The impact of the gizmo center's location is much more straight-forward because it defines the center of the ripple and can be thought of as the pebble thrown onto the liquid surface. As always, the gizmo's orientation dramatically impacts the deformation. Using multiple Ripple and Wave modifiers that crash into one another can often create convincing water or mottled surfaces.

Using Free Form Deformation

The Free Form Deformation (FFD) modifiers are a recent addition to 3DS MAX, being added as free downloads from www.ktx.com as soon as the legal arrangements from Viewpoint DataLabs (the owners of the FFD concept patent) were finalized. Included in this initial offering are three FFD modifiers or varying lattice densities (2×2×2, 3×3×3, and 4×4×4). FFD modifiers affect vertices, whether they be of meshes, patches, or even splines.

WARNING

For FFD modifiers to work correctly, they must be assigned to objects having three dimensions. Although not usually a problem, it can become one when you attempt to deform coplanar splines and other flat objects.

In principle, the FFD displacement is elegantly simple. A lattice of control points is placed about a surface, and when you move a control point the surface is deformed. The actual deformation relates to a Bézier curve (as shown in figure 15.15) when a 4×4×4 FFD lattice is used. With a 4×4×4, the end control points "stick" to the surface whereas the intermediate control points form a Bézier curve when they are moved. The 3×3×3 modifier works in much the same way except it has only one middle point with which to interpolate. The 2×2×2 modifier has only corner control points and generates a linear interpolation.

NOTE

With the advent of the FFDs, several other 3DS MAX modifiers lose their importance. The 2×2×2 modifier all but eliminates the need for using skew, and the 4×4×4 reduces the need for wave.

The strengths of the FFDs lie in their capability to localize their effect. When you scale the lattice, only the vertices within the lattice's volume will be deformed as long as the Deform/Only In Volume option is active (see the upper viewports of figure 15.16). The lattice volume defines its selections *before* any control points are moved, enabling you to move the control points however you wish without affecting the selection. The lower viewports of figure 15.16 show that when you scale the lattice to a small region and then switch the selection to All Vertices, the resulting displacement can be quite large due to interpolation.

FIGURE 15.15
The three FFD modifiers and the shape of their displacements.

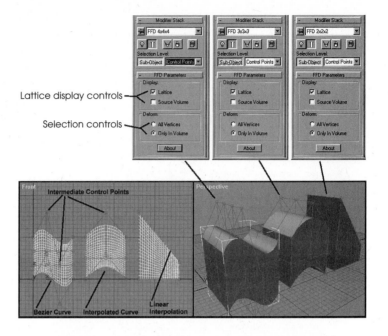

FIGURE 15.16
Using the Deform Only In Volume option versus All Vertices.

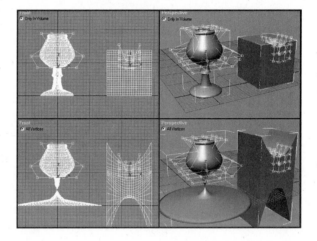

When working in Volume mode, it can be a bit confusing as to exact volume extents after making several control point adjustments. You can show what the true lattice volume is by changing the Display option from Lattice to Source Volume. When Source Volume display is active, control point adjustments appear as relative movements while moving the cursor and return to their starting position after the move. The movement has been added to the control point's cumulative position; it just isn't currently being shown. The resulting deformation is shown regardless of the lattice display option.

TIP

The lattice should be scaled and positioned *before* any control point adjustments are made. If the control points are at their default locations, nothing will deform as you position the lattice. If, however, control points have been moved, the model will continue to deform as you move the lattice.

If you do not want to be concerned with the lattice's extents, you can define a sub-object selection (with an Edit modifier or Volume Select) and assign an FFD modifier after it. The FFD modifiers respect the active selection like most other 3DS MAX modifiers do. Choosing Deform/All Vertices ignores the lattice extents and affects all vertices that are within the current, active selection. You will probably find this option best when working with sub-object selections. The FFD modifiers can also be layered in the stack, each working with a different selection. This enables you to place the FFD deformation exactly where you need it and as often as necessary. Figure 15.17 shows how three FFD modifiers are placed to animate the subtleties of ear movements and nose twitches.

FIGURE 15.17

Using FFDs on selection sets to achieve fine, local control.

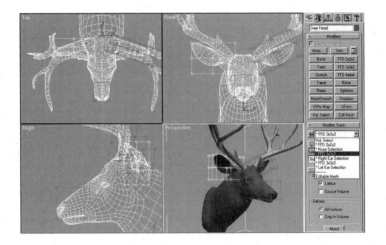

FFD modifiers can also be animated at the lattice or control point level. Animating the lattice moves the control points and their effect, enabling you to move the lattice through your object for special, animated effects. Until an FFD space warp is available, this will be the technique necessary for "through the keyhole" effects. But the real animation power of the FFD lies in animating the control points. Whenever the Animate button is active, every transform you perform on a control point generates a key (see fig. 15.18). Control point animation tracks are not added until you animate the points, similar to how tracks are added to the Lofter's deformation grids as you animate them. Animating control points, especially on local discreet selections, gives you fine-tuned control. FFD modifiers should be your choice whenever you want to animate the few things in 3DS MAX that cannot be readily animated (such as EditMesh's Affect Region vertex displacement or the tangent handles of EditPatch vertices).

FIGURE 15.18

Track View's display of animated tracks after FFD control points have been animated.

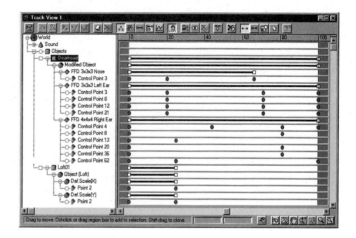

Mesh Modifiers

Several modifiers can read and produce only mesh information. These modifiers ask the object to convert to a mesh. Because every object in 3DS MAX has the capability to convert to a mesh as a requirement of being displayed and rendered, assigning these modifiers to a patch or spline model will convert them to a mesh from that point on in the Modifier Stack. Although there is no warning of this conversion, you can always return earlier in the edit history and edit the object as a spline or patch before it was converted to a mesh.

Using Optimize

Optimize is the primary 3DS MAX tool for reducing face count. It's also a method to speed the redraws when manipulating large models. In either case, Optimize analyzes the angle each face has to adjacent faces and compares it to a threshold value. Optimize is commonly used after another modifier generated or required a large number of faces (such as MeshSmooth or Displace) as shown in figure 15.19. You can easily compare the optimized result to the original by temporarily disabling the Optimize modifier's light bulb icon.

FIGURE 15.19
Using Optimize after Displace to simplify the model.

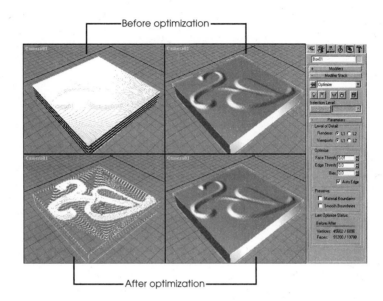

TIP

The Escape key cancels Optimize during long calculations and returns you to your previous settings, which is important because Optimize can take a long time on large meshes. An accidental action that causes a recalculation (such as Undo) can thus be aborted.

The Threshold parameters are the key to Optimize because they control which faces are eliminated. Faces are determined to be within the threshold by the same method described for EditMesh's AutoEdge, AutoSmooth, and Explode functions in Chapter 13, "Mesh Modeling."

The Face Threshold affects faces that share three edges with other faces. The Edge Threshold value controls the optimization of only faces with exposed, non-shared edges. The value for edges can't be higher than that for faces, with higher values simply being ignored. The default value of 1.0 for edges optimizes those that are colinear. As figure 15.20 shows, different values for edges and faces cause different results. If you want to preserve the profile of your model, the edge threshold should be very low; if you're trying to achieve maximum optimization, both thresholds should be the same.

FIGURE 15.20

The impact of the Edge threshold on the Optimized mesh.

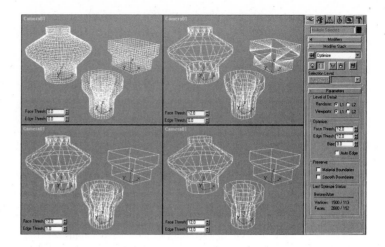

TIP

Threshold values just above zero (0.01 to 0.1) reduce all coplanar faces and don't disturb the profile of your model. This may need to be increased to 0.1 or 1.0 for round-off errors.

The Bias value controls the shape of the resulting faces, with 1.0 nearly eliminating optimization and 0.0 having no effect. Low values (less than 0.1) eliminate splinters whereas higher values leave enough vertices for other deformations. Figure 15.21 shows the impact of Bias on the resulting mesh. The default Bias value of 0.1 eliminates the long tapering faces that can cause rendering artifacts, but if you want maximum optimization, the Bias should be placed at zero.

FIGURE 15.21

The impact of Bias on the resulting tessellation.

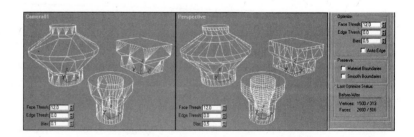

Optimize is unique among the 3DS MAX modifiers because it enables you to have separate values for interactive and production rendering. This means that a complex model can be optimized for viewport manipulation, yet always rendered at the highest level of detail. Figure 15.22 shows how the same model can be viewed with a low face count and rendered with the original count. When you switch the viewport between Level 1 and Level 2, the settings change (they both have the same initial defaults). This means that if you're using Level 1 in the viewports, you still have to temporarily switch the viewports to Level 2 to edit the values. The reason is simple—you need to see the results as you make changes to the values. Using this method can greatly speed up interaction with dense models. Remember, however, that as long as Optimize is in the Modifier Stack, the entire model is being calculated and saved to disk.

FIGURE 15.22
Using Level of Detail 1 for interactivity and Level 2 for production rendering.

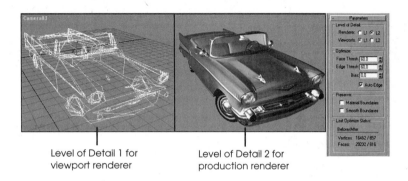

Level of Detail 1 for viewport renderer

Level of Detail 2 for production renderer

TIP

You can optimize your scene without incurring any rendering overhead by applying an Optimize modifier whose rendering level of detail is set to 0.0; no calculations are done when the value is zero.

The Preservation options for Material Boundaries and Smooth Boundaries should be strongly considered if your model has sub-object material or import-smoothing group assignments. When checked, Optimize treats each material ID or smoothing group as an independent region. Amazingly, edge conditions where the differing regions meet still have matching vertices. As mentioned, material and smoothing groups usually have important reasons for being assigned and often define characteristic areas of the model. You should, therefore, use these options if you want these areas to maintain their prominence in the model after Optimization. Figure 15.23 shows the impact of using and not using this option for smoothing groups.

The Auto Edge option is used to preserve the visible edge status of your model as close as possible to the way it was before it was optimized. It is not the equivalent, however, of the similarly named EditMesh function. The intent of this function is to prevent previously invisible edges from suddenly appearing. The Auto Edge option is entirely for visual clarity and has no impact on the resulting face count.

FIGURE 15.23

Preserving regions by smoothing group during optimization.

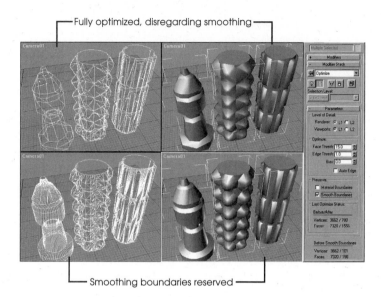

Fully optimized, disregarding smoothing

Smoothing boundaries reserved

Using MeshSmooth

MeshSmooth was added in Release 1.1 and provides the capability to round the corners of mesh models. MeshSmooth increases geometry by tessellating mesh edges in a way that is usually far more useful than the tessellation performed by EditMesh. Adding MeshSmooth to a low face count model is often similar to adding steps to a patch or spline model, as shown in figure 15.24.

When applied, MeshSmooth creates additional faces by essentially "offsetting" each edge to either side and "trimming" the result, as shown in figure 15.25. This results in each original vertex being the center of a new polygon, whose number of sides matches the number of edges originally sharing the vertex, creating beveled, and sometimes beautiful, edge patterns.

The Iterations buttons perform another MeshSmooth calculation. Every iteration is the same as adding another MeshSmooth modifier to the stack. You need to use caution, however, because the number of vertices quadruples (at the least) with every iteration. Your model can get very large, very fast.

FIGURE 15.24
Using MeshSmooth to add level of detail.

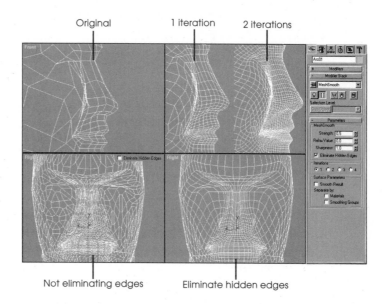

Original   1 iteration   2 iterations

Not eliminating edges   Eliminate hidden edges

FIGURE 15.25
Face tessellation patterns from MeshSmooth.

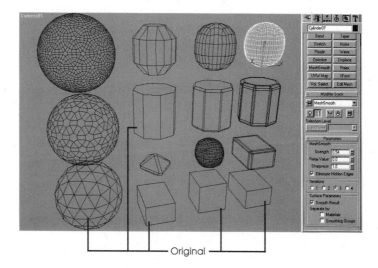

Original

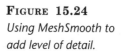

T I P

MeshSmooth respects the Escape key. If you accidentally went from one to four iterations (and your model just grew by over 50×), you can abort the process instead of waiting for the result.

The Strength parameter is actually the offset proportion from the original vertex. A value of zero negates the MeshSmooth effect by placing all the new vertices at their original locations. Increasing the Strength to 1.0 moves the vertices until they meet their opposite pairs at a mid-point location. Values between 0.0 and 1.0 proportion the distance accordingly. Figure 15.25 shows that if you're looking to create eased edges, a trait common in manufactured goods, a low Strength does just that. High strengths tend to make more crystalline forms as the edges collapse to midpoints. The default value of 0.5 creates a rounded shape with a couple of iterations. Figure 15.25 also shows that a value of 0.54 creates a nearly spherical shape from a cube.

The Eliminate Hidden Edges option, which is on by default, ignores hidden edges while tessellating. This is one operation where the visible status of your edges *does* make a difference. Figure 15.24 showed the same geometry with and without this option. Without it, the size of the model is growing much faster and the resulting form may not be as appropriate.

It's very important for your mesh to be constructed properly in order for MeshSmooth to work because the function traverses the edges to determine tessellation and direction. If the mesh isn't constructed correctly, MeshSmooth disables itself by turning off its light bulb and changing its name in the Command Panel to "MeshSmooth Error - See Help" as shown in figure 15.26. When this occurs, you need to examine and correct your model according to the following rules:

- Any given edge can be shared only by two faces.

- Faces that share an edge must have consistent normals.

FIGURE 15.26
Improperly built meshes that cause a MeshSmooth error.

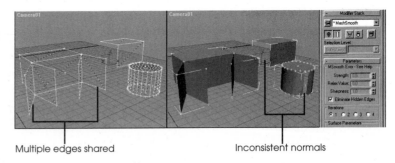

Multiple edges shared   Inconsistent normals

Using Relax

The Relax modifier affects the apparent "tension" of your mesh's surface by moving the vertices closer to or away from vertices of adjacent faces. Figure 15.27 shows how the vertices migrate from one another to soften the mesh.

The Relax parameter makes the resulting relaxed surface concave with values from 0 to 1.0 and convex with values from –1.0 to 0. The Iterations parameter performs an additional Relax iteration. As figure 15.28 shows, numerous iterations can be used to create "shrinking" effects.

FIGURE 15.27
Using Relax to soften an object's surface.

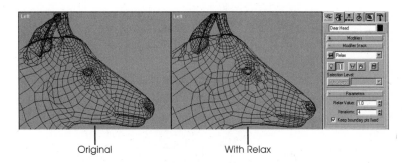

Original   With Relax

FIGURE 15.28
The result of using Relax with 16, 4, and 0 iterations.

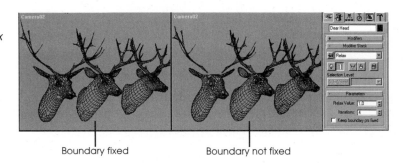

Boundary fixed   Boundary not fixed

As the vertices migrate, separate elements within the object pull away from one another. This is prevented with the Keep boundary points fixed option, as shown in figure 15.28, after many Relax iterations. Unlike MeshSmooth, iterations within Relax are not expensive because the geometry isn't increasing, and only the existing vertices are being moved. Very little, if any, overhead is needed in using high numbers of iterations.

Transform Modifiers

There are several modifiers designed to work as simple move, rotate, and scale transforms. The reason they are modifiers is that it is often desirable to have the transform evaluated within the Modifier Stack rather than after it.

Selecting with Volume Select

Volume Select is designed to make sub-object selections that are based on a defined region/volume, as shown in figure 15.29. It's a complete alternative compared to making explicit selections of vertices or faces with EditMesh, whose aspects need to be understood because using them is essential to efficient modeling.

FIGURE 15.29

Selection volumes defined by Volume Select.

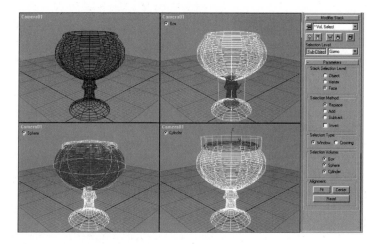

The first reason to use Volume Select is that it requires minimal RAM and disk space when compared to the expensive EditMesh modifier. A volume selection is dependent upon the area it encloses and is independent of topological changes. Put another way, Volume Select doesn't care how many vertices and faces there are in the object, only where they are located.

By contrast, EditMesh depends on the given topology and is independent of where the selection may be. It doesn't care where the selection is located, only how many vertices and faces there are in the object. Thus, if you want to be able to change the overall density of your model (the segmentation of a primitive or loft, for example), you need to use Volume Select to define a volumetric selection rather than an explicit selection. This allows volume selections to work after EditMesh, Optimize, and MeshSmooth modifiers and be independent of their changes. If you intend to change the defining dimensions of your model (the parametric dimensions of primitives for example), you need to use EditMesh to define an exact selection.

NOTE

Volume Select works only with mesh objects. Assigning it to a patch model or a closed spline converts the object to a mesh.

When first assigning Volume Select, the gizmo assumes the extents of the stack's active selection at that level. Often, this active selection is the object level and the gizmo assumes the object's extents, forcing you to transform the gizmo at the subject level if you want to define a sub-object selection. If the active selection is a selection of vertices, faces, or edges, the gizmo acts like most modifiers and conforms to the sub-object selection. Unlike other modifiers, Volume Select's gizmo doesn't change shape or position if the previous stack selection changes because doing so would corrupt your carefully placed volume. In this way, the establishment of a Volume Selection's gizmo extents is similar to how a standard modifier's gizmo center is first placed. The first assignment determines the placement and subsequent selection adjustments do not readjust it.

TIP

A quick method for accurately locating Volume Select gizmos is to define the sub-object selection extents with EditMesh, apply a Volume Select, and then remove the EditMesh modifier from the stack. Although this may seem expensive, it is often faster and more accurate than the alternative of transforming the Volume Select gizmo.

You can define the selection volume to be either a box, cylinder, or sphere. Your choice produces a different gizmo, similar to the different forms of the UVW Map modifier. Because it's a gizmo, you can position, orient, and scale it as you wish, enabling other forms such as rectangles, ellipses, and ellipsoids.

The Stack Selection Level defines what level of geometry is being selected (the object, faces, or vertices). By default, this is the Object level, which selects the entire object regardless of the gizmo's extents. Because the entire object is selected, the remainder of the Volume Select controls have no effect—everything is being selected. At the object level, you never need to be concerned with the gizmo's position, size, or shape because the entire object is always being selected. Using Volume Select on multiple objects only creates volume selects at the face or vertex level. If left at the object level, all objects are chosen, regardless of other modifier options.

The Selection Method determines how the previous stack selection is treated. By default, this is set to Replace, which discards any current stack selection and makes the gizmo's volume the current selection. The selection options become powerful with the next options because Add and Replace interact with the current stack selection. This means that you can use Volumes for Boolean selection methods, as shown in figure 15.30. In this example the first modifier replaced, the second subtracted, and the third added. An XForm was then added, moving and scaling the resulting selection. Volume Selects enabled the original box to be maximized in segmentation without disturbing the selection shape or the final modification.

FIGURE 15.30

Using three Volume Select modifiers to perform a complex "Boolean" selection.

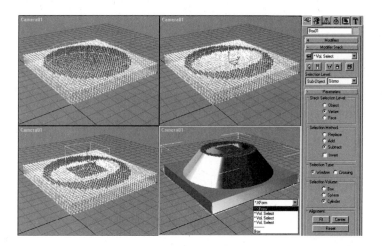

NOTE

The Invert option actually modifies the option chosen above it (notice that it's a square option box and not a round radio button). The volume selection is evaluated and then the resulting selection is inverted if this option's chosen. (In practice you may want to maneuver your gizmo with this option off and invert at the end because seeing an opposite selection can cause confusion.) The Selection Level is thus somewhat like an equation from top to bottom:

Previous Selection *plus/minus* Volume Selection *yes/no* Invert = Selection

Unlike the Object selection level, face and vertex levels work with the Selection Method and Volume Type. The face level also respects the Selection Type choices of Window and Crossing, behaving like they do for EditMesh (the vertex level treats window and crossing as being the same). If multiple sub-object selections exist in the stack, only the current Selection

Level is affected. Stack selections of different types (edges or faces when you're selecting vertices, for example) are unaffected by a volume selection, so you can interact with them in a future modifier if you wish.

TIP

The Selection Level choice changes the current selection state of the Modifier Stack. A selection level established as faces by a preceding EditMesh modifier is changed to vertex if the Volume Select was set to the vertex level.

You can select faces based on vertices, or vertices based on faces, by defining the Volume Select gizmo's extents with one and then switching the selection level to the other.

The Alignment options quickly orient the volume gizmo, similar to the UVW Mapping modifier. Fit extends the gizmo to the extents of the object according to the object's current orientation and scale. The Reset option reorients the gizmo so that its Z axis matches the object's and resets the scale to be uniform and match the object's extents.

Transforming with XForm and Linked XForm

Chapter 8 described the basics of the XForm modifier and its use whenever you want to unequally scale your model in a more permanent way. Although this is true, the XForm modifier's real use is animating sub-object selections and storing gizmo transforms as editable, animated actions.

When you assign the XForm modifier, you're immediately placed into its sub-object Gizmo mode. This should be expected because the purpose of XForm is to interact with the Move, Rotate, and Scale transforms. When working with the entire object, the result of transforming the XForm gizmo is identical to a standard transform; however, actually transforming the object's vertices and not the object definition is very different. This means that no matter how much you rotate the object, the local axis maintains the same orientation. When you move the XForm gizmo, you're moving the object's vertices and the object's pivot point remains stationary. When you scale the XForm gizmo, you're scaling the vertices, and the object's Scale tracks are unaffected. Because the local axis is unchanged, the bounding box orientation (visible when you're in Box display mode) doesn't change either.

———————————————————————————

The XForm modifier isn't the same as the Reset-XForm command in 3DS DOS, which resets the Local coordinate system according to the object's current orientation to the world axes. The XForm modifier can be used to produce the same result, and 3DS MAX does this automatically for you with the Reset Transform utility shown in figure 15.31 and supplied in Release 1.1.

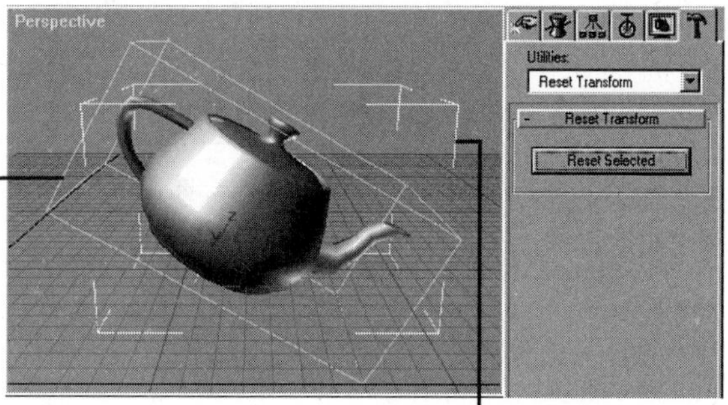

FIGURE 15.31
The Reset Transform utility.

XForm modifier applied

Resulting reset bounding box

The XForm gizmo's center acts as the gizmo's pivot point. When you're manipulating the gizmo, you don't have ready access to the object's pivot point (unless you set the coordinate system to pick, pick the object, and use the transform coordinate center). As with most modifiers, the center is placed at the pivot point when acting on the entire object and is placed at the selection center if assigned to a sub-object selection.

The XForm modifier is extremely efficient when paired with Volume Select modifiers. In this case the Volume Select defines the selection and the XForm acts on it, enabling you to model and animate discrete portions of your model—even a single vertex. If you're using a patch or spline model, the Volume Select method doesn't work. In these cases you need to use an EditPatch or EditSpline modifier to define the sub-object election. Remember that these modifiers are quite expensive and that you want an absolute minimum of edits performed within them. When used to define selections for XForm modifiers, they should ideally define only the selection and nothing else.

———————————————————————————

An XForm modifier should be used when you've performed a transform modification that you want to be able to revisit or animate. Sub-object transforms about which you are confident and want to have made permanent should be done within the Edit modifiers.

Animating an XForm modification is just like animating any other gizmo. Unlike an Edit modifier, the active selection in the stack below the XForm can be changed and alter what is being modified. In this way you can define a transform (a scale, for example), return to the previous Volume Select, change the selection, and watch the resulting scale update dynamically with the changing selection. Place a Smooth modifier at the end of the stack (in AutoSmooth mode), and you're able to see the smoothing change as well.

You can control the animation of sub-object selections with other objects by using the Linked XForm modifier. Linked XForm works just like the XForm modifier except that the "gizmo" you move, rotate, and scale is another object you select. This enables you to animate an object with an underlying bone structure. Chapter 16, "Building Systems," shows how Linked XForm is used for exactly this purpose with the Bones systems.

Surface Modifiers

A class of surface modifiers that are really subsets of the massive EditMesh modifier is provided so that you can make basic assignments without significant RAM overhead. All these modifiers (except UVW Map) operate only on faces and convert patch objects and closed splines to a mesh so they can adjust their (face) surface properties. These modifiers are simple in concept, acting upon the active selection of faces in the edit history pipeline. If the active selection contains only vertices or edges, the sub-object selection is ignored and the surface modifier acts upon the entire object instead.

In practice, these modifiers usually act on the entire object or face selections defined by a Volume Select modifier. EditMesh is sometimes used to define highly irregular selections and is useful when you want to have a clear separation between selection and effect. This flexibility has to be weighed against the cost of adding the EditMesh modifier, of course. Using EditMesh for this purpose will become obsolete when other selection modifiers become available.

Normal Modifier

The Normal modifier (see fig. 15.32) provides the face normal flipping capabilities of the EditMesh modifier, with the exception of not being able to physically display the normals as directional lines.

The Normal modifier is ideal for situations where you need to flip surface direction but don't want the overhead, or time delay, of using an EditMesh. Flying inside an object is a common situation where you want to be able to quickly flip the normals. Unfortunately, this act still has to occur manually because the Normal modifier can't be animated.

The Unify Normals option unifies the normals of the active selection in a manner similar to EditMesh. Use this option carefully for sub-object selections because the function assumes your model is closed and ready for unification.

The Flip Normals option simply reverses the normals of the active selection and is the more commonly used of the two options. Unlike Unify, Flip is totally reliable to use with sub-object selections.

Smooth Modifier

The Smooth modifier (see fig. 15.33) provides the smoothing group assignment ability of the EditMesh modifier. Unlike EditMesh, Smooth can be animated, which is its largest asset. With Smooth, you can dynamically adjust the smoothing of your model as it changes form. In practice, this is similar to the "Morph Smoothing" option in 3DS DOS, except that this is much more general, can work with selections, and can adjust the AutoSmooth threshold angle over time. In practice, a Smooth modifier is ideal to have at the end of the stack so it adjusts your surfaces as you work.

The Smooth modifier begins by clearing *all* smoothing groups currently assigned to the active selection. It is assumed that you want to assign or clear your smoothing and because face selection isn't part of this modifier, keeping smoothing groups would be more frustrating than clearing them. Once cleared, you have the option of either assigning a smoothing group number or using AutoSmooth.

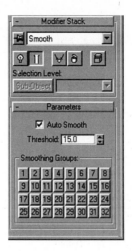

If the AutoSmooth option is checked, the active selection is smoothed according to the accompanying threshold value, as described in Chapter 12 in the section "Angle Threshold." The modifier evaluates the surface being passed to it and dynamically adjusts the smoothing group assignments as dictated by its threshold angle. This enables you to return earlier in the stack, make modeling changes, and see the resulting AutoSmooth applied dynamically—something that's not possible with EditMesh.

When AutoSmooth is on, the grid of 32 smoothing group buttons is locked and can't be chosen. With it off, you can assign the active selection of a particular group. The assignment of a smoothing group number is an explicit action and can't be animated. Although it's common to make multiple smoothing group assignments with EditMesh, it's very rare to assign more than one group to the same selection with a Smooth modifier. Assigning one group makes the selection smooth to itself, whereas assigning other groups only has an effect if you're trying to match the groups assigned to adjacent, welded faces as well.

Material Modifier

The Material modifier (see fig. 15.34) provides the material ID assignment capability of the EditMesh modifier. Unlike an explicit assignment done in EditMesh, the assigned Material ID can actually be animated. Because it's an integer, the material ID change occurs suddenly on a given frame (it doesn't occur gradually). If you're animating Material ID assignments, you will want to analyze their occurrence as a function curve in Track View and adjust the curve so that the materials transition exactly when you want them to do so.

FIGURE 15.34
The Material modifier's rollout.

UVW Map Modifier

The UVW Map modifier assigns mapping coordinates to the active face or patch selection in the stack. For all objects, vertex and edge selections are ignored and the entire object is considered the face or patch selection instead. This modifier enables you to combine numerous mapping coordinates of varying types at different locations in the object's edit history. You most often do this when the object portrays its geometry at orientations and configurations that are more convenient for mapping assignments. The UVW Modifier is detailed in Chapter 21, "Materials and Textures," because of its tight integration with material assignments.

TIP

For gradual material transitions, use an animated Blend material or a Mask or Mix map type instead of animating the Material ID#.

In Practice: Advanced Modifiers

- **Displace, Noise, Wave, Ripple, and FFD**   The geometry modifiers of Displace, Noise, Wave, Ripple, and FFD work equally well on splines, patches, and meshes.

- **Noise, Wave, Ripple, and FFD modifiers**   These modifiers all base their distortions upon Sine and Bézier curves, with several of their control parameters acting as intermediate tangent handles for the distortion curves.

- **Mesh modifiers**   The mesh modifiers of MeshSmooth, Optimize, and Relax will always convert the stack's geometry to a mesh for their operations.

- **Volume Select modifier**   Volume Select is the ideal modifier for defining a sub-object selection when the geometry below it in the stack will not change dimensions. EditMesh must be used when the earlier geometry will change size but not topology.

- **Surface modifiers**   The surface modifiers of Normal, Smooth, Material, and UVW Map are low-cost alternatives to the memory-expensive EditMesh, with Smooth and Material being capable of animation that cannot be done with EditMesh.

Image by Warner Interactive (Manchester)
Provided courtesy of Kinetix™

Chapter 16

BUILDING SYSTEMS: THE BIPED EXAMPLE

The Create panel in 3D Studio MAX has a Systems button.

A system is really a piece of software that creates objects that

are preprogrammed to do something; that is, they are a

combination of geometry and behavior. The Systems cat-

egory is intended to be a convenient place for third-party

developers to plug in their programs. The kinds of plug-ins

that you'll see manifesting as systems will range from the

most simple to the most complex. 3DS MAX Release 1.0

ships with two very simple plug-in systems: Ring Array

and Bones.

Ring Array is a sample system shipped as a programmer's example. This plug-in creates an array of objects with a variety of parameters. By animating the phase and cycle, you can make cubes do all kinds of circle dances. Attach objects to the cubes and then hide the cubes for animating complex geometry such as merry-go-round horses.

Bones is a system with a more obvious practical value. You can use bones to easily set up a hierarchical framework for animation. For example, you can create a humanoid figure from simple objects linked to the underlying bones, as shown in figure 16.1. In this illustration, the bones are on the left, the objects are in the center, and the bones and objects ready for animation are on the right. The bones create a hierarchical framework that you can use to suspend the renderable objects (bones are helper objects that do not render). As you click to create the bones, a hierarchy is generated automatically, with the first bone at the top of the tree. Each new bone is added as a child of the previous bone.

FIGURE 16.1

A set of bones used to animate a simple hierarchy.

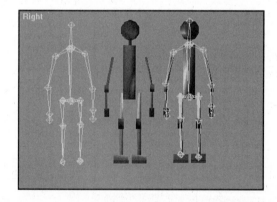

Bones have another use, which is to serve as a framework for the Physique modifier, one of the plug-ins that make up Character Studio from Kinetix. (A complete discussion of Physique is outside the scope of this book, although this chapter does contain an introduction to it.) Basically, the Physique modifier can be attached to the root bone of a hierarchy of bones placed inside a mesh model. Physique can then deform the mesh. This is a useful modeling technique rather than an animation technique. Meshes with Physique are intended to be animated with Biped, the other Character Studio plug-in, which is the subject of this chapter. Figure 16.2 shows a torso that uses bones for its framework modeled in Physique.

FIGURE 16.2

A set of bones used as a framework for the Physique plug-in modifier.

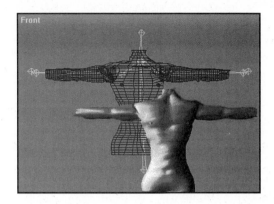

Biped is the first major 3DS MAX plug-in to be released as a system, and it is an excellent example of what a system can be. The remainder of this chapter shows how you might use Biped to manage a real animation project. Along the way, you'll see how Biped integrates seamlessly with 3DS MAX and how it adds a tremendous amount of new functionality to the program, making Biped truly a system in its own right.

The Biped Solution to Creating Lifelike Movement

Biped is a character animation plug-in that generates realistic movement for two-legged creatures. Before you look more closely at how it works, you should know that you're not forced to create lifelike movement with Biped. You can create surreal or fantastic movement or animate dancing gas pumps or jumping credit cards if you like. However, Biped is especially good at realistic motion because it has intelligence built into it that takes into account the dynamics of motion, the law of gravity, and so on. You can look at Biped as a software solution to the problem of animating the human body in 3D. There are other solutions to this problem, but these tend to be hardware solutions that are expensive or brute-force solutions that are time consuming.

For example, say that you want to animate a jumping figure sequence for a game you're working on, and you want the movement to be as realistic as possible. What are your options? If you have a large budget, you can buy or rent motion capture equipment. Motion capture tracks the movement of real people by means of optical/electronic sensors attached to the limbs of the people. The sensors then translate that movement into a useable format.

You may need to do some manual adjustment to the motion data before you can use it, but the end result is likely to be extremely realistic. You'll also need to hire someone who can do a good high jump. Make sure you have plenty of room in the studio.

If you have a low budget but do athletics in your spare time, you can act out the motions yourself and animate a model by using inverse kinematics. The main drawbacks here are time and quality. Animating even a few seconds of lifelike motion using manual keyframing is highly labor intensive. Getting a good sense of forceful forward motion and a lifelike contact with the ground is especially difficult. After all your effort, you're unlikely to approach the realism of motion capture.

If you have neither a large budget or a great deal of time, you can use Biped and rotoscope a video sequence of Olympic hurdling recorded from your own TV and brought into your PC with an inexpensive video capture board. With Biped you can approach the quality of motion capture at a fraction of the cost. Timewise, too, Biped speeds up the animation process and takes a lot of the drudgery out of manual keyframing. Biped's solution is based on three main ideas:

- A biped figure "skeleton" with inverse kinematics and biomechanical laws built into it

- Footstep-driven animation to control the biped figure

- A special file format for storing and loading movement from one biped figure to another

You'll see how these three elements work together as you read through the rest of this chapter, but because they are such important concepts in Biped, we'll take a little time to look at them individually.

The Biped Skeleton

After you install the Biped plug-in, creating a biped figure or skeleton is a simple matter of drawing a box in any viewport. The default figure that Biped creates has human characteristics, but you can easily change this structure to create other two-legged creatures, as shown in figure 16.3. The default biped is on the right, whereas the other biped figure has been modified to fit into a mesh model of a kangaroo. In this illustration, you can also see the Biped structure parameters as they appear in the 3DS MAX Create panel. You set these parameters to determine the number of fingers and toes, height of the biped, whether it has a tail, and so on.

FIGURE 16.3

Biped figures with different structures.

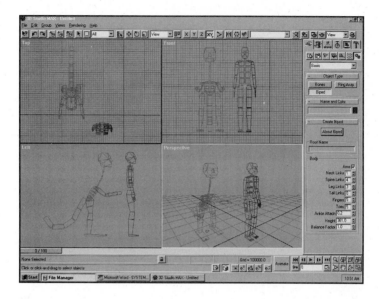

The biped figure has its own advanced system of inverse kinematics, so if you click and drag its hand or foot with the 3DS MAX Select and Move tool, for example, the entire arm or leg will move as well. Figure 16.4 shows a biped posed using the Select and Move tool. You don't have to turn on the 3DS MAX Inverse Kinematics tool to use IK with Biped. Biped's IK system is actually more precise than the one 3DS MAX uses. If you grab the biped's hand, move it, and return it to the same spot, you'll find that it returns to *exactly* the same position rather than to approximately the same position.

FIGURE 16.4

Biped posed using inverse kinematics.

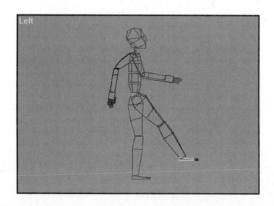

You may notice that the various parts of the biped are colored differently. This coloring is not arbitrary—like the random object color assignments that 3DS MAX uses. The colors have a definite meaning: the left side is colored blue, and the right side is colored green. This relates to the biped footsteps, which use the same color convention, as discussed in the next section.

The biped is a color-coded, jointed armature that you can put into any kind of posture. You can set different poses at different frames, and 3DS MAX will interpolate between them, just as it will for any animated hierarchical structure. However, the biped can do far more than this. The biped really comes to life when you generate footsteps for it.

Footstep-Driven Animation

Next to some of the bus stops in the city of Seattle, there are metal footsteps set into the sidewalk. These footsteps are arranged to show the sequence of steps for popular dances so that while you are waiting for the bus, you can follow the steps and practice your tango or waltz. Biped is based on this same principle. You place footsteps in front of the biped in the viewport. When you activate the footsteps, the biped follows the steps, adapting itself to the kind of movement you specify—walking, running, or jumping. You can place the footsteps manually, which is best if you are creating something such as a dance sequence that contains many twists and turns, or you can place the footsteps automatically by using the Create Multiple Footsteps dialog. By using this dialog, you can generate as many footsteps as you want at the same time and you can also control the acceleration or deceleration of the biped over the course of the footstep sequence. Automatically generated footsteps are laid out in a straight line, but you can bend these steps afterward. You can also move and rotate individual footsteps. Figure 16.5 shows a frame of the default walk sequence generated by Biped. Note that the footsteps are colored (you should be able to see the difference even in grayscale; right is green; left is blue) and numbered (right is odd; left is even).

The default walk sequence that Biped generates is quite realistic. If you look at the trajectory of the biped center of mass object (which is the small octahedron in the pelvis area), you'll see how the motion follows a gentle wavelike path that reflects the slight differences in the elevation of the center of mass at the points of heel touchdown and toe liftoff.

FIGURE 16.5
Default walk sequence generated by Biped.

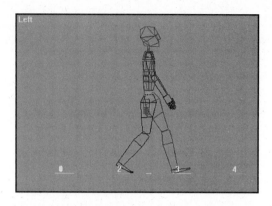

FIGURE 16.6
Trajectory of the biped's center of mass object.

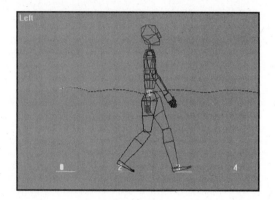

The center of mass object (also called the biped root object) is important in calculating the proper position and balance of the biped as it moves. After you create and activate footsteps for the biped, the center of mass object, together with the legs, behaves very differently from the way it behaved before. Activating footsteps generates keys for the center of mass and the legs, constraining these objects to follow Biped's internal rules for keyframe interpolation. Figure 16.7 shows the biped before footstep activation (left) and another biped after activation (right). Both bipeds have the center of mass object rotated in the X axis, Y axis, and Z axis. The first biped rotates completely, but the second biped maintains contact with the ground while rotating its trunk in a realistic manner.

Likewise, if you select and move the root object down, the biped without footsteps simply goes through the ground plane, whereas the biped with active footsteps bends its knees to remain in the correct relationship to the ground (see fig. 16.8).

FIGURE 16.7

Effect of rotating the root object before and after footstep activation.

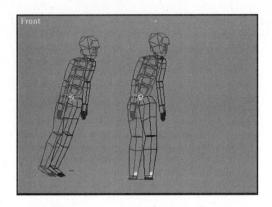

FIGURE 16.8

Effect of moving the root object before and after footstep activation.

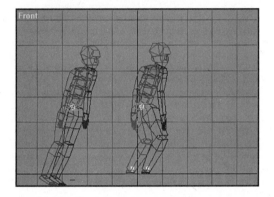

Bipeds, therefore, are entirely driven by their footsteps. This doesn't mean that you have no freedom to create expressive animation. You should take the motion that Biped generates as a kind of "motion sketch" that you can then adapt by adjusting footsteps and by adding keys for the upper body, such as the arms and head. Biped doesn't constrain these keys as it does for the leg and center of mass. You can also turn off the effect of the footsteps by creating "free-form" areas between footsteps. In these free-form areas, the biped is not attached to the ground and can be animated into any position.

Biped footsteps have their own special track in the 3DS MAX's Track View (see fig. 16.9). The footsteps are displayed in this track as colored blocks: pale blue for the left foot and pale green for the right. You can also see the number of each footstep (in boldface) and its start and end frames. In this example, which shows the same default walk sequence as in figure 16.5, the footsteps overlap slightly—that is, the start frame of each step falls before the end frame of the previous step. This overlap is called the *double-support period* and is characteristic of the walking gait. If you get up and walk around now in slow-motion, you'll be able to sense the double-support period. Double-support is absent in the running and jumping gaits, in which there is an airborne period in between the footsteps.

FIGURE 16.9

3DS MAX Track View showing the Biped footstep track.

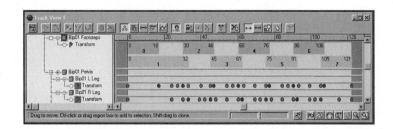

Below the Biped footsteps track are the tracks for the left and right leg (Biped treats all the parts of the leg from thigh to toes as one unit so there's only one track for each leg.) Biped generates all the keys in these tracks automatically when you activate footsteps. Some of the keys are marked with a red dot to signify that those keys are locked. Biped locks keys for the leg tracks so that it can perform its calculations properly. If you rotate the leg at a locked keyframe, the leg just snaps back into place. You can unlock these red keys inside Track View, but you do so at your own risk. You can move the footsteps in the Track View, lengthen and shorten them, and so on. When you do this, Biped recalculates the footstep relationships and generates new keys. Internally, Biped performs collision detection between the foot and the ground plane and uses this point of contact as the basis for computing the other positions of the foot. At any frame in an animation, each foot can be in one of four states (see fig. 16.10):

- **Touch** Frame at which the heel of the foot contacts the ground

- **Plant** Frames during which the foot is in contact with the ground; includes the frames where the weight of the body is supported by that foot

- **Lift** Frame immediately before the foot leaves the ground

- **Move** Frames during which the foot is airborne (has no contact with the ground)

FIGURE 16.10
The four Biped foot states.

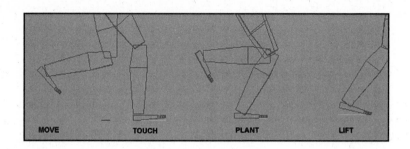

MOVE   TOUCH   PLANT   LIFT

A *footstep cycle* is the time in frames it takes to complete a single footstep. By default, this is 15 frames (half a second) for both walking and running and 20 frames for jumping. Biped measures the footstep cycle from the touch frame of one footstep to the touch frame of the following footstep. If you look again at the walk cycle as it appears in the Track View (see fig. 16.9), you can verify this. The locked keys occur in the touch and lift positions, which are the first and last frames of each footstep. Because these frames are numbered, you can easily see how many frames are in each cycle. So for example, the walk cycle—from right foot to left foot after the biped is in full stride—goes 45, 60, 75, 90, and so on. Having a sense of the cycle time is useful when you are matching a particular movement captured on video. The four states are labeled for the left and right feet in the command panel directly under the General rollout. These labels shift throughout the footstep cycle, but they cannot be edited in the command panel by typing the states.

Saving and Loading Biped Files

The Biped file format (BIP file) is a special format that stores all the key information for the biped. The file stores both the footstep-key information and the upper-body-key information. The only motion that does not get stored unchanged in the Biped file is motion created with inverse kinematics because IK uses the object space parameter. An IK relationship occurs when you attach the hand to a ball, for example. The biped file format doesn't know anything about the ball, but it stores the motion of the hand bouncing the ball by itself. To save the relationship of hand and ball, save as a MAX file.

After you store the Biped file, you can load and apply it to other bipeds. This means that you can use this file format to create whole libraries of movements in much the same way that you can create libraries of textures in 3DS

MAX. You can store different kinds of jumps, runs, and walks, dances, leaps and kicks, categorized in any way you want. For example, the Character Studio CD-ROM includes a set of six animations done from the classic animation reference book *The Human Figure in Motion* by Eadweard Muybridge. After you have a collection of movement clips stored in this way, you can load and splice them together, adding motions onto one another to create more complex sequences. The biped animations can be loaded onto any biped of any size and proportions, and the animations correct themselves in adjustment to the new character.

The Save and Load Biped file controls appear in the General rollout of the Motion panel (see fig. 16.11).

FIGURE 16.11
*Save and Load Biped
file buttons.*

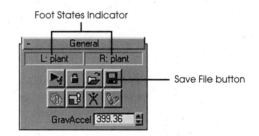

After you animate a biped to your satisfaction, select it and click the Save File button. Give the file a unique name and store it in your motion library. When you want to apply the movement to another biped, select the biped in the scene and click the Load File button. Biped loads the saved footsteps and other key information and automatically adapts the selected biped to the new data. You can think of the biped file as your "finished product" in most cases. The biped skeleton is essentially a repository for the stored motion data.

Muybridge Project

The remainder of this chapter shows you how to use Biped to complete a real animation project but is not a tutorial as such. Purchasing Character Studio is not necessary; we assume only that you're interested in finding out what the program can do and how you could use it. If you have purchased Character Studio, this section offers an approach that you won't find in the documentation that ships with the product. In either case, you should have no difficulty in applying the instructions in this section to your own work. The particular method of rotoscoping explained here is by no means the only, or even the preferred way, of working with Biped. However, it does enable us to demonstrate many of the fundamental Biped procedures in their proper order while focusing on what Biped does best—lifelike animation of the human figure.

Capturing the Source Material

Copying commercial video tapes for public viewing or redistribution is, of course, illegal, but the FBI probably won't bother us for capturing a few seconds of the great moments in athletics for self-education purposes. With a VCR you can tape from television broadcasts for your own use. If you have a video camera, the whole world of movement is open to you; all you have to do is to go out and shoot it. Add to that the cost of an inexpensive video capture card and you're ready to bring any kind of movement into 3D Studio MAX. Of course if you intend to use what you shoot for some commercial project, legal issues may still come up and you'll need to check out the laws where you live. 3DS MAX also supports high-quality video input from devices such as the Accom Work Station Disk, but for the purposes of providing video frames as a background for a biped sequence, a simple AVI file works almost as well. Video capture and compression is an art in itself and is one that frequently changes with the introduction of new compression/ decompression technologies. For the latest information on video capture, talk to someone you know who has experience in digital video or refer to a recent book or trade magazine article on the subject.

Common low-cost video capture cards include Intel's Smart Video Recorder Pro, ATI's VideoIT and UMAX Maxmedia. These types of cards typically record at 320×240 or smaller resolutions between 15 and 30 frames per second. These cards are available from a few hundred to $1000. For higher resolution capture, more expensive products such as Digital Processing Systems' Perception Recorder and Truevision's Targa 2000 are commonly used. These boards usually cost more than $1000 and also require a dedicated hard drive for capture and playback. Diaquest makes a plug-in for 3DS MAX called 3d/av just for this purpose.

T I P

For the latest information on products and processes try *Digital Video Magazine* or *PC Graphics and Video.*

Setting Up 3DS MAX and Biped for Rotoscoping

Rotoscoping is the process of bringing video frames into 3DS MAX to serve as a background for the alignment and synchronization of elements in the scene. From this point, you'll learn step by step how to set up the 3DS MAX and Biped environment for rotoscoping.

1. Use the Viewport Background dialog (choose Views, Background) to specify the AVI source file or device (Accom) for the video frames. Figure 16.12 shows the dialog settings for an AVI file.

FIGURE 16.12

The Viewport Background dialog and the first video frame.

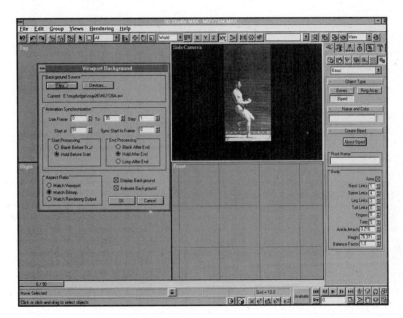

Note that the video input isn't scheduled to start until frame 51. Because of this delay, you have plenty of frames to adjust the biped so that its stride is in synch when the video starts. When you render, you can leave out these frames.

Remember to check the Animate Background as well as the Display Background boxes. After you specify the source, you can display the background video frames in any viewport by using the View Background toggle in the right-click viewport menu.

2. Create a biped in the same viewport as the background. Draw the box that defines the biped's height the same size as the figure you're tracing or a little bigger if the figure is on the small side. Adjust the biped's height

to make the figure 6' tall. If the background is dark, as in this case, you'll need to change the wireframe color of the biped to a bright color, such as yellow, so that you can see it properly.

3. Create a camera in the scene and use the Orbit, Truck, and Pan Camera controls to approximately match the perspective of the biped to the figure, as shown in figure 16.13.

FIGURE 16.13

Matching the biped's perspective to the video.

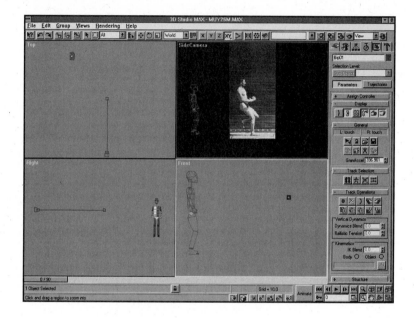

At this point, you've set up the 3DS MAX environment and are ready to start matching the movement in the video.

Analyzing the Movement and Creating the Footstep "Sketch"

Now it's time to leave the computer and do some paperwork. What you want to do is look at the video closely, analyzing it frame-by-frame so that you can draw a diagram on paper of the frame numbers of the footsteps in the video. If you play the video a dozen times or so, you'll get the feel of where the footsteps fall, even if it is not obvious or if the video is blurred in places. Sometimes you won't be able to make out the exact frame that a figure's foot lifts off or touches down, but usually you'll be close, which is good enough.

1. Make your notation by using the same format that the Track View uses: frame numbers along the X axis and numbered blocks of frames for the footsteps. You'll use this diagram as a cheat sheet to set up the biped's footsteps in Track View. Figure 16.14 shows the diagram for the hurdling video.

FIGURE 16.14

The hardcopy diagram of the footsteps in the video.

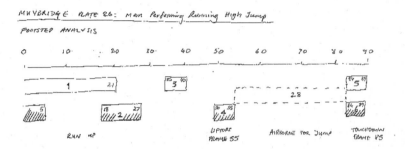

In this video, the figure starts with a run (only one step is shown in the video, but we can extrapolate the steps before that one), jumps off the right foot, pulls up both legs to make the leap, and then lands with both feet together.

2. Generate several default footsteps for the biped—starting at frame 0—to occupy the 50 empty frames at the beginning of the animation. You'll edit these later in the Track View to make sure they match exactly. At this point, the only thing that's important is to check that when the figure in the video has his right foot on the ground and his left foot traveling through the air, the biped foot states match with the move and plant of the figure respectively.

3. Place the landing footstep in the top view a good distance away from the other footsteps (see fig. 16.15). Move or rotate the new footsteps if you need to before you activate them. Play back the animation as you develop it by scrubbing the Time Slider to make sure the movement is reasonable.

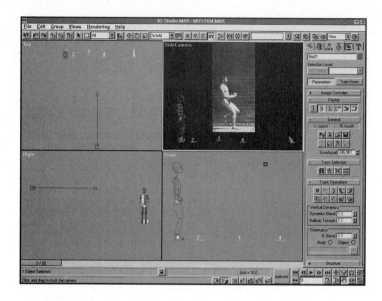

4. Armed with the footstep analysis you drew, go into the Track View and start moving and stretching the footsteps so that the start and end frames match those in the diagram. Figure 16.16 shows the edited Track View (compare this to the original drawing in figure 16.12). Play back the animation to check it.

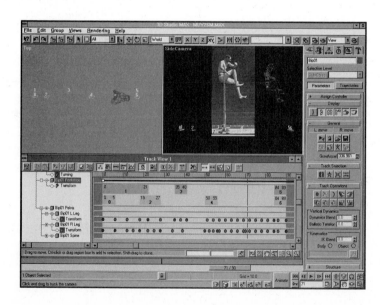

5. When you finish, go through the animation and check how closely the biped's footsteps match the figure in the video (checking every 10 frames will probably be sufficient). Use the Foot States Indicator in the General rollout to see what the foot is doing at a particular frame.

If your original analysis was reasonably accurate, you'll be surprised to see how closely the footsteps match. Getting this right is the biggest step toward capturing the motion in the video. Of course, you still have no upper body keys or any fine-tuning of the movement. However, you have created a good initial motion sketch, which you can now start to refine.

6. Adjust the Gravity Acceleration parameter as you scrub along the Time Slider. This adjustment establishes the correct height for the jump (see fig. 16.17). By default, the biped jumps fantastically high. By adjusting the gravity, you can precisely control the height of the jump relative to the distance covered.

FIGURE 16.17

Setting the keys for the vertical position of the biped.

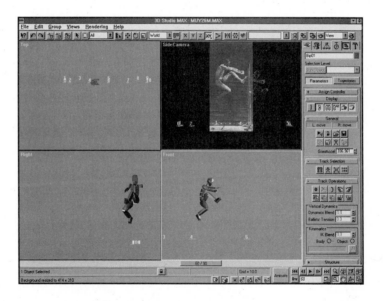

At this point, you've already completed a lot of the work. The rest involves traditional keyframe animation.

Completing the Animation by Setting Body Keys

What you do next is go through the animation keyframes and adjust the position of the upper body keys to match the figure in the video. This is the more creative part of the project because now you're free to use your animation skills to develop the movement—you can capture the motion exactly, exaggerate it, or use it as a basis for whatever effect you want to create. To some extent, the video has already served its primary purpose, which was to establish the correct footstep cycle.

Completing the animation from this point is fairly straightforward. You use traditional keyframing to adjust the leg positions and set new keys for the arms, spine, and head. You can spend as much time as you want on this, depending on the degree of refinement you want and need to achieve.

1. Select one of the legs, turn on Key Mode and Animate, and proceed to click through the keyframes. At each leg keyframe, rotate the biped's leg joints to match the video.

2. Rotate the other leg into position and then adjust the arms and head. Proceed in this way from one keyframe to the next.

3. As your animation nears completion, use Make Preview with the video in the background to see how well the movement matches. The Biped Playback button is useful in the early stages for checking the movement because it gives you instant, real-time feedback; Make Preview is more useful at this later stage because it includes the video background. Figure 16.18 shows the Biped playback and figure 16.19 shows a frame from the preview. The preview shows exactly what the movement looks like and how it relates to the video. You can step through it frame by frame and make notes of any problems that still need to be fixed in the animation—sudden jerkiness, bad positioning of the hand, and similar glitches.

4. Fine tune the animation according to your notes from the preview. The amount of time and effort you can spend at this stage is virtually unlimited; it's almost always possible to improve an animation to make it that bit more lifelike. Some of the corrections that were made to the highjump animation at this stage included:

   ■ Using the Apply Increment feature in the Biped Track Properties dialog to raise the arms over a series of frames

- Correcting jerkiness in the leg position during the jump, caused by too many keys too close together

- Adding more backward lean in the run up by rotating the spine object

FIGURE 16.18

The Biped playback button provides real-time motion without any other elements in the scene.

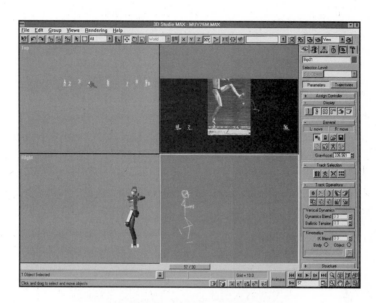

FIGURE 16.19

The Make Preview command shows the video in the background.

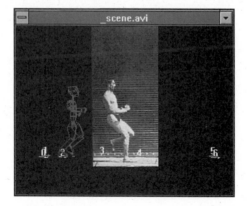

5. Save the completed movement as a Biped file.

Now that you have the stored movement, you can apply it to a mesh model using the other Character Studio plug-in: Physique.

Skinning the Biped

Normally you can store your completed Biped movement in a Biped file (BIP file format) that you can then apply to any other biped figure, which may already be skinned (meaning that it has a mesh attached to it). However, if you have established an IK relationship to some object in the scene, with a hand holding a ball, for example, you need to store the animation in a standard MAX file to preserve the relationship. You can still save a Biped file, and it will store the steps and all the body keys. The only aspect of the animation that the Biped file can't save is the IK Object Space keys, which are reset to body space. In this case we have no IK, so we can just save the animation out of the scene as a Biped file. We could equally well merge a mesh model into the scene and then use the mesh to skin the biped.

We won't cover the process of skinning a biped in detail, because the Physique modifier is outside the scope of this chapter. (See the Character Studio documentation for a more thorough discussion.) The following is a summary of the process:

1. Select the biped and go into Figure mode, which is a special mode that enables you to modify the structure of the biped without affecting the animation you've already done.

2. Use the 3DS MAX transform tools to fit the biped into the mesh model. This process includes positioning the pelvis object and scaling and rotating the arms and legs. The biped doesn't have to fit perfectly inside the mesh. In fact, it's good if the biped objects stick out of the mesh slightly, especially at the finger and toe tips and the head (see fig. 16.20).

NOTE

Ideally the mesh should be standing with its arms stretched out from the shoulders pointing to either side, palms down. If you have a mesh in a different pose—arms straight down at the side, for example—you should reposition them before you skin the mesh.

FIGURE 16.20

Fitting the biped into the mesh.

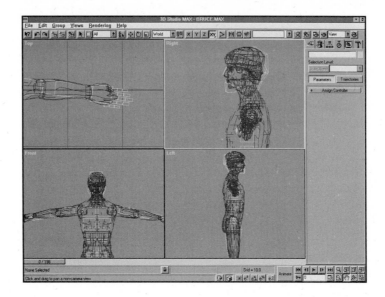

3. After you fit the biped to your satisfaction, apply a Physique modifier in the Modifier panel and attach it to the biped. The modifier generates a series of links throughout the mesh and establishes the relationship between the mesh and the underlying biped skeleton (See fig.16.21). Now when you rotate the biped limbs, the mesh moves along with it.

FIGURE 16.21

Physique modifier applied to the mesh.

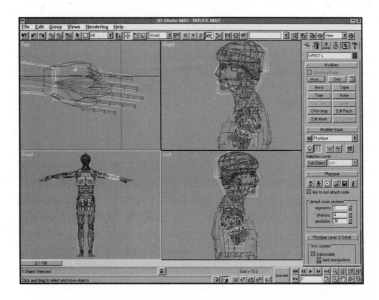

4. Test the mesh by rotating the biped arms and legs. Usually you'll have to do some manual clean-up at this point. Physique assigns the vertices of the mesh to the biped links based on their cylindrical distance from them. This doesn't work perfectly, so Physique provides vertex-level tools to enable you to finish the job. Figure 16.22 shows the correct assignment of the vertices of the head. Manual vertex assignment takes a little time, but after it's done, the mesh is fully animatable and will follow any movement of the underlying biped, including movement stored in biped files.

NOTE

Vertices can be assigned as rigid or deformable. Use these options to control the creasing of the skin where the arms and legs meet the body. Further refinements can be achieved by using Physique's cross section editor to add muscle bulges based on angles between the biped bones and tendon editor to create additional links of influence to stretch, pull, and pinch the skin.

FIGURE 16.22

Manually assigning vertices in Physique.

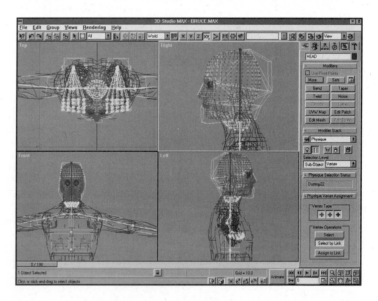

5. Hide the biped, leaving just the figure mesh and any other scene elements that you want to render.

6. Add lights, adjust the camera, and render. Figure 16.23 shows a frame from an animation of a mesh model composited over the video, created in Video Post. You can see the complete animation in the ch16all.avi file.

FIGURE 16.23

Composited frame from Video Post rendering.

For purposes of comparison, we've included the following AVI files on the CD-ROM as well:

Ch16bip.avi   Shaded biped with video background

Ch16bip2.avi   Shaded biped with video background
                     (different view)

Ch16step.avi   Shaded biped with footsteps and no background
                     (Preview quality)

Character Studio is a product that promises to make character animation much simpler. To a large extent, it lives up to that promise by delivering tools that take a lot of the drudgery out of the animation process. By leaving you free to focus your attention on the subtleties of adding realistic motion to your models, Character Studio advances the state of the art and provides an exciting new way to work. Biped and Physique are well worth getting to know if your work involves a lot of character animation or if you are interested in studying the human figure in motion.

In Practice: Working with the Biped System Plug-In

- **Biped creation** By default, Biped creates an upright humanoid creature with no tail. However, you can easily change the biped's structure by using the properties in the Modifier panel and by scaling and rotating the various pieces of the biped. You can have several bipeds with different characteristics in the same scene.

- **Automatic footstep generation** The single biggest time-saving feature in Biped is the capability to generate a whole series of walking, running, or jumping footsteps at once. Use the Generate Multiple Footsteps dialog whenever possible and then manipulate individual footsteps manually afterward. By using this dialog, you can have the biped climb stairs by setting the vertical interval between steps. You can also make the biped speed up or slow down between the first and last step.

■ **Gravity and ballistic tension** Take advantage of Biped's built-in capability to simulate human movement fairly accurately. You can control the height of the airborne biped during runs and jumps through the Gravitational Acceleration parameter. Dynamics Blend controls the amount of "spring" or "knee-bend" when the biped takes off and touches down.

■ **Advanced IK** You'll want to learn to use Biped's IK features because they enable you to do things that you can't do in 3DS MAX. For example, using Biped, a figure can hold an object for a number of frames and then drop it. The "letting go" of the object can be a blend of inverse and forward kinematics, which creates a very realistic effect.

■ **Motion mapping and splicing** These are two key concepts. Motion mapping means that when you apply a movement stored in a biped file to another biped, the movement adapts itself to the characteristics of the new biped. For example, if you apply movement generated for a human-oid figure to a duck, the movement will adapt the placement of the footsteps to the smaller leg and pelvis dimensions. Motion splicing means that you can create more complex sequences by copying, pasting, and inserting shorter sequences.

■ **Skinning a biped** The two components of Character Studio—Biped and Physique—are completely different but work well together. Biped is intended to generate full-figure animation, which you can then use with a mesh model. Physique is the means by which you attach the model to the underlying structure provided by the biped. Physique is a modeling tool; Biped is purely an animation tool.

Visual for TVR at the Birmingham Motorshow
Created by Andrew Murrall
Murrall & Lang
West Midlands, England

Chapter 17

Using Space Warps

Animators often want to create major distortions in their scenes that affect some or all of the objects, such as a shockwave hurtling through space or dust particles getting whipped around in a tornado. In 3D Studio MAX, you can create these types of effects with space warps. The best way to think of space warps is to think of them as invisible force fields that act on other objects.

Ever wanted to simulate dust flying around? How about smoke or rain? In the 3D world, such conditions are produced by particle systems. A *particle system* is a collection of particles that can produce a variety of animated effects when emitted. In 3DS MAX, particle systems are objects and the particles emitted are actually sub-objects. You can animate a particle system as a whole and you can adjust the particle system's properties to control each particle's behavior over time.

In this chapter, you learn how space warps work and how to use them. Specifically, this chapter explains the following:

■ The difference between space warps and modifiers

■ Using the universal space warp called Displace

■ Using object space warps such as Ripple, Wave, Bomb, and Path Deform

You create space warps by clicking the Space Warp category button on the Create panel. For example, to create a Ripple space warp, click in the Object Type rollout and drag in any viewport to set the Ripple radius. After releasing the mouse, move up or down and click to set the Ripple amplitude. Most space warps follow this drag-click creation technique.

Not all space warps affect all types of objects in 3D Studio MAX. Displace is a universal space warp that affects all types of objects. Ripple, Wave, Bomb, and Path Deform affect only objects, whereas Gravity, Wind, and Deflector work only with particles. (Spray and Snow particle systems are covered in Chapter 25, "Building and Animating Particles.") Before the specific space warps are explained, however, the following section provides you with background information on how space warps differ from modifiers and how space warps work in the stack.

The Difference Between Space Warps and Modifiers

Many of the space warps available are also available as modifiers. So why would you choose one over the other? The choice depends on the effect you want to achieve. Modifiers are carried by the object and apply deformation in the object's local space. Space warps exist as independent objects and apply deformations to other objects based on the object's world space location. For example, applying a Ripple modifier to a selection sphere has quite a different effect than binding the spheres to a Ripple space warp (see fig. 17.1).

FIGURE 17.1

Objects with the Ripple modifier applied versus the Ripple space warp binding.

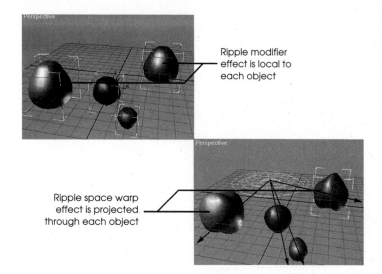

Ripple modifier effect is local to each object

Ripple space warp effect is projected through each object

When you apply a ripple as a modifier, the ripple is applied as a gizmo to the object. The effect of the ripple depends on the relative position of the gizmo with respect to the object. Moving the object does not affect how the ripple modifies the object; however, a ripple as a space warp has quite a different effect. As seen in figure 17.1, the ripple is projected from its center outward to all objects bound to it—in this case, the spheres. The ripple's position in space, as well as its orientation, directly affect the objects bound to it. If you transform the Ripple space warp, its effect on the bound objects changes. If you move one or several of the bound objects, the relation of their position and orientation in 3D space to the space warp affects the object's appearance.

This is the behavior of all space warps. The only difference between one space warp and another is the design of the space warp itself. Both Ripple and Displace affect objects based on 3D position, but have clearly different effects.

Space Warps and the Stack

Objects are bound to a space warp with the Bind to Space Warp button located in the toolbar (see fig. 17.2). Any number of objects can be bound to a single space warp. To bind objects to a space warp, click the Bind to Space Warp button, select the object you want to bind, and then drag from the objects to a space warp.

FIGURE 17.2
The Bind button.

Space warps are the last thing to be evaluated in the object history stack. It's easy to forget this, but 3DS MAX has a way of telling you that the space warp is evaluated last. Figure 17.3 shows how space warp bindings are displayed in the stack. All bindings are listed after all modifiers and are further separated by double dotted lines. Sub-object bindings are displayed with an asterisk before the binding name. This occurs only if the last modifier in the stack is sending sub-object selections out of the pipeline.

Space warp bindings are the last things in the object dataflow.

FIGURE 17.3
Space warp bindings as displayed in the modifier stack. The Sub-object binding is indicated by an asterisk.

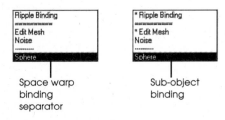

Universal Space Warps: Displace

Universal space warps are those that can affect anything bound to them. This could be any type of deformable object from particles to geometry. Although not as common as the other two types of space warps, universal space warps can be just as useful.

The only universal space warp to ship with 3DS MAX is Displace. Displace uses grayscale image information to physically displace both geometry and particles in 3D space. The intensity of the grayscale values dictate how far the object or particle is displaced. Much like a bump map, the lighter, or more toward white, the image is, the further the displacement. You can use Displace to create multiple types of effects—from cookie-cutter modeling to animated geometric distortion. Figure 17.4 demonstrates what a simple image of a white ring can do to simple geometry in 3DS MAX to create a rather intricate object. Figure 17.5 demonstrates another usage of the Displace space warp on two objects.

FIGURE 17.4

The Displace space warp bound to a torus. The displace map used is projected using planar mapping in this example.

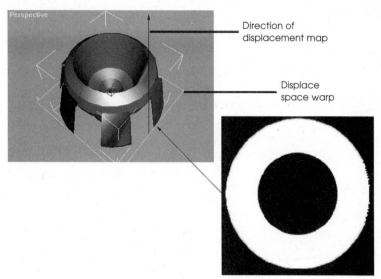

Direction of displacement map

Displace space warp

Displacement map

Using Displace on a particle system has a different effect. Rather than displacing geometry, the Displace space warp actually distorts the particle system's path. You can use multiple Displace space warps to alter a particle system's direction several times. Unlike Deflector, which can do the same thing, Displace can allow some particles to pass through or even deflect unevenly based on the grayscale of the image (see fig. 17.6). As you can see, Displace space warps act much like a force on a particle. Using the Displace space warp can actually cause a particle to accelerate based on the strength of the warp.

FIGURE 17.5

Use Displace space warp to displace a terrain object and a road. The effect of using one space warp on two objects creates a road that twists and turns as it adheres to the contour of the terrain.

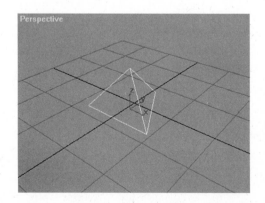

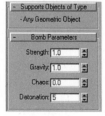

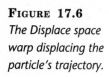

FIGURE 17.6
The Displace space warp displacing the particle's trajectory.

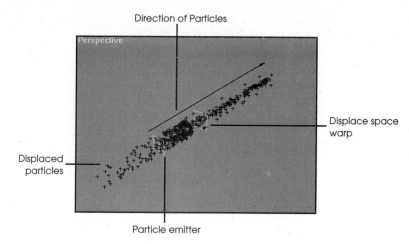

Direction of Particles

Displace space warp

Displaced particles

Particle emitter

Object Space Warps

Object space warps deform geometric objects but do not affect particles. For example, you could use the Ripple space warp to deform a sphere, but it would have no effect on the spray or snow particles. You may also find object space warps useful for animating many effects—from wave deformations to explosions. You can also use a single object with multiple space warps to produce a compound effect. For example, you could bind a sphere to both Bomb and Ripple space warps. The resultant animation would be an exploding sphere in which the the pieces exploded in a rippling pattern.

In this section you explore the three space warps dedicated to deforming geometry: Ripple, Wave, Bomb, and Path Deform.

Ripple

The Ripple space warp sends concentric waves from its center out to infinity. Use Ripple to model organic geometry or create effects such as ripples on a pond.

Any geometric object can be bound to a Ripple space warp. What's more, you can also bind lights, cameras, and helpers to a Ripple space warp. Lights, cameras, and helpers are deformed the way geometric objects are but are instead transformed to move with the ripple effect. You can simulate such things as a camera on a ship at sea by binding a Free camera to a Ripple space warp.

You can also deform part of an object by binding sub-object selections to a space warp by using an edit modifier or the Volume Select modifier. The key to this technique is placing the Edit or Volume Select modifier at the top of the Modifier Stack after any other selection modifiers.

Phase

The Phase parameter tracks the change in amplitude from the highest point in the ripple to the lowest point and back again. Changing the phase has the effect of moving the ripples along the local XY plane of the Ripple space warp. Both the Ripple and Wave space warps use a Phase parameter to position and animate their effect. To make a ripple or wave appear to move, animate the Phase parameter. A whole number change, from 0 to 1 for example, represents a complete cycle in the wave. With that in mind, remember to keep the changes in Phase small if you're looking for subtle movement. For more radical movements, change the parameter more radically. The values you use depend on the size of the objects you are working with. Large phase changes, for example, will have a great effect on small objects and will have a much more reduced effect on a larger object.

TIP

To make Ripple or Wave appear to animate in the opposite direction, animate the phase from zero to a negative value.

Using Ripple to Animate a Lava Lamp

In this exercise, you see how to use a regular sphere to create lava for a lava lamp. Through a combination of multiple space warps with varying orientations, you can easily create lava snaking upward in the lamp. Ready to return to the sixties?

MAKING LAVA WITH RIPPLE

1. Open imx17rp1.max.
2. Click on the Lava object or select it by using Select By Name.

3. Click the Bind button in the toolbar.

4. Use Hit By Name to bind the Sphere to Ripple01 and Ripple02.

Figure 17.7 shows the Bind By Name dialog that is used to select the valid space warps in your scene.

Flexibility

A common parameter between ripple and wave is Flexibility. As a matter of fact, Flexibility is used only with Ripple and Wave. Flexibility is a binding specific parameter; it doesn't apply to the space warp, but rather specifies how much effect the space warp has on each object. The Flexibility parameter is located in the Modify panel.

5. With the object selected, go to the Modify panel.

6. Alter the Flexibility value.

7. Notice that increasing the value magnifies the effect of the ripple on the sphere, whereas decreasing it has the opposite effect.

Figure 17.8 shows two values of the Flexibility parameter and how the value is displayed in the Modify panel.

Flexibility is entirely animatable. This means that a space warp's values can remain constant, and you can animate the amount of effect the space warp has on a single object by changing the Flexibility value. That way, other objects bound to the same space warp can be affected differently as well. If you want to change the effect globally, adjust the space warp's values.

8. Set the Flexibility to 0. Click Ripple Binding in the modifier stack, and select the first Ripple Binding.

9. Set the Flexibility to 0.

10. Go to frame 20, and turn on the Animate button.

12. Set the Flexibility to 1.

13. Repeat this process for the second Ripple Binding.

14. Make a preview of the animation.

With Flexibility, you can specify when and how much the space warp affects the object. In this example, the lava starts out as a squashed sphere, and changes into an undulating lava shape as it travels up the lamp.

FIGURE 17.8

The Modifier panel with the Ripple Binding chosen from the stack. The Flexibility parameter is the only editable and animatable value.

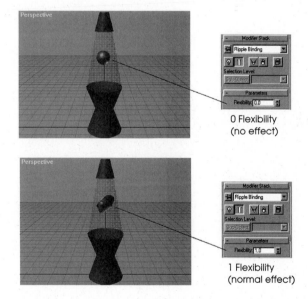

0 Flexibility
(no effect)

1 Flexibility
(normal effect)

NOTE

The *3D Studio MAX User's Guide* specifies that changing Flexibility is like adding or removing vertices, when actually this is not the case. Changing Flexibility is more like changing the multiplier value on a light. At 1, the values for amplitude, for instance, are 1 to 1. At 2, the effect is twice as great, and so on.

Wave

Wave is much like Ripple in the sense that it distorts geometry in a wavelike pattern. Rather than its distortion being concentric such as Ripple, Wave is linear. The waves travel in only one direction.

> **NOTE**
>
> Remember that all space warps are based on 3DS MAX units, so their scale and detail affects variously sized objects in different ways.

Both Ripple and Wave contain parameters called Amplitudes 1 and 2. The primary purpose of having these two amplitudes is to enable you to specify different amplitudes for the X and Y axes of a space warp (Amplitude 1 is X; Amplitude 2 is Y). For instance, if you wanted to make a crease through the center of a wave, set one of the amplitude values to 0. By default, when you're creating a Ripple or Wave space warp, both values are created with the same value. Manually edit one value or the other either immediately after creation or later in the Modifier panel.

> **NOTE**
>
> Both Wave and Ripple have a display section, which is purely for controlling the display of the space warps in the viewports. The display section has no effect on the space warp of the objects bound to it.

You can use Wave to create multiple types of scenes. In the following exercise, you learn how to distort geometry for both modeling and animation purposes. You have a scene that contains a yacht traveling on the high seas. Unfortunately, the scene has come upon some nasty weather, and the waves have become increasingly choppy. To simulate this weather, you need to use Wave for two things: modeling the waves on the seas and the boat riding the waves. Hope you're not easily disturbed by violent up and down movements!

MODELING AND ANIMATING WITH WAVE

When you load the scene, the first things you see are the boat, a box, and a line. Start by creating waves that bind the Wave space warp to the box.

1. Open imx17wav.max.

2. Go to the Create panel and click the Space Warps button.

3. Click on Wave, and click-drag a wave and its amplitude in the Top viewport. (Don't worry about the values for now. You'll change them later.)

4. Rotate the Wave 90 degrees in the Top viewport.

5. Click on the Bind button, choose the box, and then drag to the wave.

6. Select the wave, and go to the Modify panel.

7. Alter the wave's parameters so that Amplitude 1 reads 5, Amplitude 2 reads 7, and the Wavelength reads 120. Phase and Decay should be set to 0.

Notice that moving the wave up and down in the Top viewport has no effect on the box, but moving it side to side does. This movement is a result of the linear distortion that the wave provides. Both Wave and Ripple have no effect on the objects bound to them if you move them along the axis of amplitude.

Both Wave and Ripple work on all types of geometry, including 2D splines. In this part of the exercise, you bind the spline to the wave, and have it deform just like the box object. The yacht is using the spline as a path controller with the Follow option on.

8. Scroll the Frames slider back and forth to see the animation.

9. Click on the Bind button, and then choose the spline object.

10. Drag to the Wave space warp.

The spline deforms to the wave and, consequently, so does the ship's movement. See figure 17.9.

The spline must have a sufficient number of vertices to properly deform to the wave. If not, the result is a much less smooth deformation and animation.

Wave space warp bound to
2D spline (path)

FIGURE 17.9

The yacht traveling along both the ocean and spline path bound to the Wave space warp.

Wave space warp
bound to ocean

Suppose you wanted the yacht to gradually enter the rough seas. That's what the Decay parameter is most useful for. Here's how it works for wave.

11. Go to the Modify panel and select the Wave space warp.

12. Change the Decay parameter to .005.

The wave tapers off as it gets farther away from the space warp icon because for both Wave and Ripple, Decay causes the effect to gradually decrease as you get farther away from the center of the space warp. The size of the space warp has a direct effect on this Decay parameter. Figure 17.10 shows two of the possible Decay settings for this scene.

Decay is based on scale. As the objects to which that wave is bound get larger, larger Decay parameters are needed to see an effect.

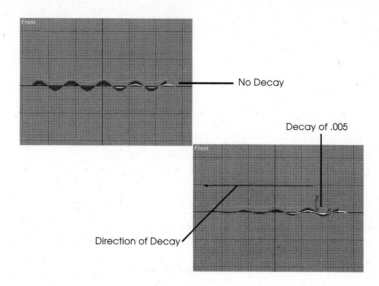

No Decay

Decay of .005

Direction of Decay

Bomb

Bomb produces an "egg shell" type explosion; it will explode an object into tiny faces. The result is that you're exploding what appears to be an object with no volume—a shell.

Bomb's real usefulness lies in its parameters. Through manipulation of the Bomb space warp's settings, you can use Bomb to create many types of effects. Several of the values associated with Bomb can be negative, such as strength. You can implode objects rather than explode them. You can also give the appearance of little, no, or reverse gravity through effective use of the Gravity parameter.

Most people think bombs are used to blow objects up; however, 3DS MAX has the capability to put things back together by using Bomb. In this exercise, a soda can starts out in hundreds of tiny little pieces.

USING BOMB TO PUT THINGS BACK TOGETHER

1. Open imx17bom.max.

2. Go to the Create panel and create a Bomb space warp underneath the can.

3. Bind the can to the Space Warp.

4. Move the Bomb to about 50 units above the can.

5. Move the Frames slider back and forth to see the animation.

As you can see, the bomb's force is causing the can to break apart starting at frame 5 and forces the can downward. The number one reason why it's doing that is because of the strength. If you set the strength to –1, you see a different result. With a negative strength, the bomb actually pulls the objects bound to it toward the bomb center, and then forces them outward, much like a jet engine.

6. Select the Bomb, and go to the Modify panel.

7. Change the Strength to –1.

Notice how the can implodes rather uniformly. There is an obvious pattern to the explosion. The Chaos variable works well to diminish the uniformity of the bomb's force. For this example, set the Chaos to 1. This will randomize the pattern enough to not make the implosion so canned (pun intended).

8. Set the Chaos Value to 1.

9. Scroll the Frames slider to see the result of the animation.

10. Now make some changes to the gravity to alter how the can will come together. Gravity will affect the motion of the exploded geometry after the detonation frame (discussed next). For now, set the gravity to 0.

11. The detonation frame specifies when the Bomb affects the geometry with the strength variable set. The default is frame 5, which means that the can will implode starting at frame 5. This is the opposite effect from what you want. What you want is for the object to explode at frame 0, and reform by frame 100. In order for this to happen, the detonation frame needs to happen before frame 0, so set the detonation parameter to –30.

The last step is to animate the Strength parameter. To have an object start exploded or imploded and reform to the original object, animate the strength going from whatever strength you specify at frame 0 to no strength by the frame you want.

12. Go to frame 100, and click the Animate button.

13. Set the strength value to 0.

14. Make a preview of the animation.

15. Notice how the can comes together by frame 100. You can further tweak this animation by going into Track View and editing the function curves for the Strength parameter. Figure 17.11 shows the result of using Bomb with the preceding steps.

FIGURE 17.11

Four frames from the completed can animation showing the various Bomb space warp parameters.

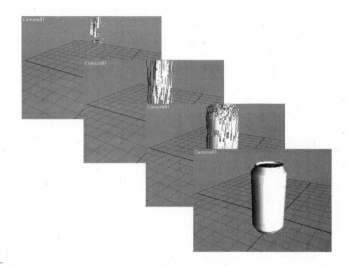

Path Deform

The latest addition to the 3DS MAX space warp set is Path Deform. You can use Path Deform to twist and turn objects based on some 2D spline. A great example of how this works is to create some text, and then bind it to a Path Deform space warp.

Path deform acts a bit differently from the other space warps. As a matter of fact, after you create the Path space warp, you really never work with it. The space warp serves only as the deforming shape. All changeable parameters are accessible through the binding options in the modifier stack.

Understanding how path deform works can be a bit tricky. First of all, the object deforms in its local space about its pivot point. It does not immediately "snap" to the path as you might expect. Furthermore, the path deformation takes place in local space by using the space warp as a reference.

The best way to understand path deform is to use it. A common example is deforming text along a path.

USING PATH DEFORM TO MODIFY TEXT

1. Open imx17pat.max.

2. Go to the Create panel and click the Space Warps button.

3. Click Path Deform.

4. Click Pick Path, and choose the helical spline object.

You have just created a Path Deform space warp. At this point, you can bind an object to the space warp, and the object will deform along it.

5. Click the Bind to Space Warp button in the 3DS MAX toolbar.

6. Click the 3DS MAX text, and drag to the spline object and release.

As you can see in figure 17.12, the object re-orients itself. What's happening at this point is that the object is using the space warp shape to deform, but the deformation is taking place in the object's local space.

FIGURE 17.12

The path assigned as a space warp, and the 3DS MAX text bound to it.

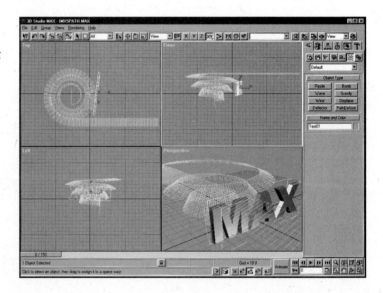

By default, the object deforms along its Z axis. The X axis runs along the length of the text, so you need to change the axis of deformation. All controls for the object using the space warp are located in the Modify panel.

7. Go to the Modify panel.

8. Change the Path Deform axis to X.

9. Check on the Move Object to Path option.

10. Set the rotation value to 180.

At this point, the object is on the path and deforming on the proper axis. To animate the object traveling along the path or any other option, you need to change the values by using the Animate button.

11. Click on the Animate button, or press the N key on your keyboard.

12. Move the frames slider to frame 150, and change the Percent value to 97.

13. Change the Rotation value to 225.

14. Make a preview and then play it back to see the results.

Figure 17.13 shows four frames from the final animation.

FIGURE 17.13
Four frames from an animation of text using a Path Deform space warp.

Other values include Stretch and Twist. You can use these values to alter the shape of the deforming object on the path. Use Stretch when you want to give the object the appearance of shrinking or growing along the path. The Twist value actually twists the object the number of degrees set in its value over the length of the path. If you had a straight line path and a twist value of 360, the object would twist along the path 360 degrees from one end to the other.

WARNING

The Move object to path option is animatable. Use caution when toggling this option on or off while the animate button is on.

Particle Space Warps

Particle space warps enable you to apply such things as real-life dynamics to particle systems. You can put the spray particle system in a wind storm or suck snow upward using the Gravity space warp. For more information on particle systems and space warps, refer to Chapter 25, "Building and Animating Particles."

In Practice: Using Space Warps

- **Space Warps work in world space**   Unlike modifiers, space warps affect objects in world space. Both the object's and space warp's position in space are important. The effects of a space warp changes as a bound object moves through a scene.

- **Space Warps are evaluated last in the stack**   When you bind a space warp to an object, remember that the binding is evaluated after all modifiers are applied. If you want to bind a space warp to a sub-object selection, make sure it's the last modifier in the stack.

- **Universal Space Warps**   Universal space warps affect both geometry and particle systems. 3D Studio MAX only ships with one universal space warp, Displace. You can use displace to model or animate distortions through the usage of map intensity values.

- **Object Space warps**   With object space warps, you can distort any deformable object. This includes both 3D and 2D objects. For example, you can use a object space warp on a 2D spline and have an object use that as it's animation path.

Image created by Frank DeLise
Autodesk, Inc.
Provided courtesy of Kinetix™

Chapter 18

BUILDING AND ANIMATING HIERARCHIES

Many of the objects that you will build and animate with 3D Studio MAX will be comprised of many parts. Take a look at real world objects surrounding you, very few of these objects are made from a single part. Also, for many real-world objects, their component parts are held together with movable joints or links. Examples of such objects include the sliding tray of a CD player, the hinged doors of a car, and the jointed limbs of your body.

You simulate these joints and links in 3DS MAX by building linked object hierarchies. After you have built a hierarchy, you can animate it by combining the techniques of Forward and Inverse Kinematics. This chapter covers the building and animation of object hierarchies including details about the following topics:

- Linking objects to build hierarchies

- Controlling link behavior by adjusting pivot points

- Using dummy objects

- Animating hierarchies with Forward Kinematics

- Using Inverse Kinematics

- Defining IK joints

- Animating with Inverse Kinematics

The next few sections describe what object hierarchies are and how to begin building them.

Using Object Hierarchies

Build an object hierarchy to set up a relationship in which a single parent object is linked to one or more child objects; the transforms of Move, Rotate, and Scale are passed between a parent and its children. Linking parent objects as children to other objects enables you to quickly build a complex hierarchical structure that is many levels deep. Such structures simulate the complex joint structure of real-world objects.

The process for creating linked hierarchies uses the following steps:

1. Select objects to link as children of another object.

2. Click Link in the toolbar and drag from the selected objects to a single parent object.

3. Repeat steps 1 and 2 until you have linked all of the objects you want in the hierarchy.

4. Adjust the location and orientation of pivot points for the linked object.

5. Specify link inheritance.

6. Define Joint Parameters if you plan to use Inverse Kinematics.

Building linked hierarchies is a very powerful technique that can save you much time and effort when used properly. Linking objects has two important functions:

- **Simulates the real world by linking objects together in some sort of jointed assembly**   A good example of this is a machine or a human figure. If you move the figure's upper arm, you want the lower arm, hand, and fingers all to move with it. Manually moving all the pieces throughout an animation is nearly impossible. Linking takes care of all that work and makes it easy.

- **Assists in the definition of complex motion**   Imagine that you want to animate a block tumbling down a slope. Manually moving and rotating the block is quite difficult. Use linking to link the block to an invisible dummy object. You can then rotate the block and drag it down the slope by moving the dummy object. Dummy objects are the key to many complex motion solutions.

The controls for creating and manipulating hierarchical links are found in the Hierarchy panel and in two buttons on the toolbar (see fig. 18.1). The toolbar buttons are used to create or break the links between objects. The controls in the Hierarchy panel are used to adjust links and define link parameters.

Parent, Child, and Root Objects

Any object that has another object linked to it is a *parent object*. A parent can have any number of other objects linked to it, and these other objects are called its *children*. The children of an object can also have children of their own. All objects connected through any number of links to a parent object are called *descendants* of the parent.

Parent objects can also be linked as a child to another parent object. Any translation that affects a parent also affects the descendants attached below that parent.

Child objects are one of any number of objects linked to a parent. Although a parent can have any number of children, a child can have one and only one parent. If you try to link a child object to a second parent, the link to the first parent is destroyed and replaced with the link to the new parent.

FIGURE 18.1
Linking controls.

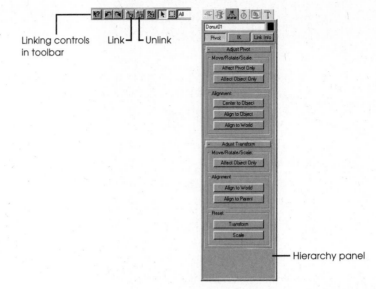

Linking controls
in toolbar

Link

Unlink

Hierarchy panel

If you trace the links from child to parent to the parent's parent, and so on, you will eventually reach the root of the hierarchy. All of the objects that are linked from a child back to the root are called the child's *ancestors*.

All hierarchies contain only one root object. The *root* of a hierarchy is the one object that claims all other objects in the hierarchy as its descendants and has no ancestors above it. An object that has no children and no parent can be considered a root object as well—it is the root of itself.

Hierarchies and the World

Technically speaking, the scene itself (called the *World*) is the root of all hierarchies. That means that you are always working with a hierarchy because every object in your scene is either linked as a child of another object or the object is a child of the world.

This "hidden hierarchy" becomes apparent in the following situations:

■ Manipulating pivot points for root objects works because the pivot point defines the link between the root object and the world.

- Choosing the Parent transform coordinate system for a root object returns the World coordinate system because the world is the parent of all root objects.

- When IK is active, you cannot transform root objects unless you release them from the world or define joint parameters between the root object and the world.

Viewing the Hierarchical Tree

As you create links between objects, the linked objects are arranged in a tree structure. This tree structure takes the form of a list, where the names of the child objects are indented below and to the right of their parent objects. You can view this list in Track View or by choosing the Display Subtree option in the Select Objects dialog (see fig. 18.2).

FIGURE 18.2
Displaying object hierarchies.

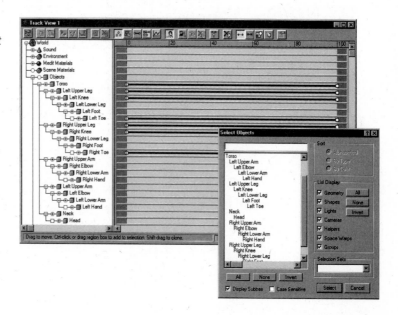

Use the Link and Unlink buttons on the toolbar to build and modify the structure of the hierarchy. These buttons are described in the next section.

Linking Objects

Use the Link and Unlink buttons on the toolbar to create and break links between objects. All other commands for manipulating links are found in the command panels.

Click the Link button in the toolbar to specify which objects are linked to other objects. You always drag from a selection of child objects to a single parent object as shown by the prompt at the bottom of the 3DS MAX window. Note, however, that it's easy to get this backward and drag from what you want to be the parent to a child.

When you specify links, it is very easy to get the wrong parent object when you release the drag, especially if your model is even the slightest bit complex. After selecting child objects with the Link button active, you can click the Select by Name button to display the Select Parent dialog. Figure 18.3 shows an example of using Select Parent dialog to select the object Right Lower Leg as a parent for another object, probably the object Right Foot. This dialog is really the Select Objects dialog with a new name to help remind you of what you are doing. Select any parent in the list box and click Link in the lower-right corner of the dialog to complete the link process.

FIGURE 18.3
Selecting a parent object.

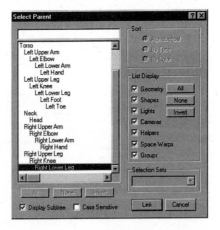

Click the Unlink button in the toolbar to sever the link between selected child objects and their parents. The Unlink command is one of the few commands in 3DS MAX that forces you to select objects before you activate the command. Click the Select Object or Select by Name buttons on the toolbar to select objects, then click Unlink.

Setting Link Inheritance

Set link inheritance options in the Hierarchy panel to define which transformations are passed from a parent to a child:

1. Select a single child object.

2. Click Link Info in the Hierarchy panel.

3. Expand the Inherit rollout and check or uncheck the inheritance options (see fig. 18.4).

In figure 18.4, the checked link inheritance options are active. The transform axes represented by the active options pass transform information from the

FIGURE 18.4

Link inheritance options in the Hierarchy panel.

parent to the selected child, causing the child to transform with the parent. Unchecked options release the child on those transform axes so the child is no longer affected by the parent.

This capability is particularly useful when you model mechanical linkages. Often an object is linked to its parent so that the object is fixed about one or two axes and is free about another. Examples of such linkages are connecting rods in an engine and buckets on a conveyor belt. Both of these objects are linked like a door hinge; they are fixed and immobile on two axes, yet are free to rotate about the single axis which is defined by the hinge pin (pivot point).

Displaying Links

When you link objects, especially complex hierarchies, you may find it difficult to visualize which objects are linked to which and how they are linked. As previously described, you can use Track View or the Select Object dialog to display the hierarchical tree structure, but there is a third technique for displaying the links in the scene.

Set options in the Link Display rollout of the Display panel to control link display for selected objects (see fig. 18.5). The two display links options work as described in the following list:

- **Display Links**   When checked, a three sided cone is drawn from the pivot point of selected objects to the pivot points of the selected objects' children. The link cone is wide at the parent and tapers to a point at the child (see fig. 18.5).

- **Link Replaces Object**   When checked, the selected objects disappear and are replaced by small tetrahedrons located at the objects' pivot points. Checking Link Replaces Object forces the Display Links option to become checked as well.

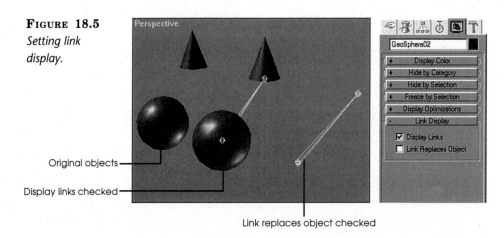

FIGURE 18.5
Setting link display.

Original objects

Display links checked

Link replaces object checked

Avoiding Nonuniform Scale with Hierarchies

Linking is designed as a way to pass transforms from one object to another. Transforming a parent object passes the transform information to any children of the object. This process works extremely well for Move, Rotate, and Uniform Scale transformations. Linking does not work well with objects that have been nonuniformly scaled.

A child object linked to a nonuniformly scaled parent will squash and skew as you rotate the child (see fig. 18.6), which is almost never the result that you want. As stated throughout this book, you should almost never apply nonuniform scale directly to an object. Always apply nonuniform scale to sub-object selections or use the XForm modifier.

You can remove the nonuniform scale link effect from a parent object in many ways. Two of the easiest methods to remove the effect are as follows:

- Select the child of the nonuniform scaled object and uncheck the affected scale axis in the Link Inheritance rollout. You will need to do this for every child of the nonuniform scaled parent object.

- Reset the transform of the nonuniform scaled object after you unlink any children. After the transform is reset, you can re-link the children to the object. Techniques for resetting an object's transform are presented later in this chapter, in the "Adjusting Transforms" section.

Working with Pivots

An object's *pivot point* defines where the link between a parent and a child occurs. Think of the three-sided cone that you see when Display Links is checked. Imagine that the cone is a rigid arm welded to the pivot point of the parent object and connects to the pivot point of the child with a joint. The joint enables the child to move, rotate, and scale independent of the parent, but when you transform the parent the cone moves and drags the child along with it.

WARNING

Changing the pivot point of an object after you specify any animated transforms can lead to unexpected side effects. Make any changes to your pivot points before you start animating your objects.

Although the pivot commands are in the Hierarchy panel, they can be used with all objects—not just those objects that are linked. Remember that objects that have no parent or children are still considered linked to the world. The pivot point defines the orientation of an object's Local coordinate system and is the point about which all object rotation, and scaling, is centered.

The following sections describe how to change the position of pivot points within their objects.

Adjusting Pivots

Use the commands in the Adjust Pivot rollout to transform and align pivot points and their objects. Click the Pivot button in the Hierarchy panel to display the Adjust Pivot rollout (see fig. 18.6).

FIGURE 18.6

The Adjust Pivot rollout.

The top two buttons in this rollout—Affect Pivot Only and Affect Object Only—are critically important. Click one of these buttons to choose whether you want to transform an object independent of its pivot or transform the pivot independent of its object. The following list describes the effects of clicking the Affect Pivot Only and Affect Object Only buttons:

- When Affect Pivot Only is active, transforms and alignment are applied only to the pivot leaving behind the object and any linked children. Use this button when you want to move an object's pivot to a new location.

- When Affect Object Only is active, transforms and alignment are applied only to the selected object leaving behind the pivot and any linked children. Use this button when an object's pivot is just where you want it, and you want to move the object to a new location.

- When either of the buttons is active, the pivot point is visible as a large three-axis icon (see fig. 18.7).

- When neither button is active, transforms and alignment are applied normally to both the object, the pivot point, and any linked children.

- Clicking a button to make it active automatically deselects the other button.

- Clicking a button that is already active, deselects the button so that neither button is active.

FIGURE 18.7
The Pivot Point icon.

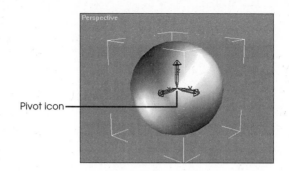

Pivot icon

Aligning Pivots

You use the remaining three buttons in the Adjust Pivot rollout to align the object or the pivot point. The button labels change depending on whether Affect Pivot Only or Affect Object Only is active. The effects of the three buttons are as follows:

- **Center to** If the button reads Center to Object, clicking the button moves the pivot to the geometric center of the object. The orientation of the pivot does not change. If the button reads Center to Pivot, clicking the button moves the object so that its geometric center is at the pivot. The orientation of the object does not change.

- **Align to** If the button reads Align to Object, clicking the button rotates the pivot to align with the original Local coordinate system the object had when it was created. The position of the pivot is not affected. If the button reads Align to Pivot, clicking the button rotates the object to align its original Local coordinate system with the pivot. The position of the object is not affected.

- **Align to World** The object or the pivot (depending on which Affect Only button is active) is rotated to align with the World coordinate system. The location of the object or pivot does not change.

Aligning Pivots with the Align Command

Another interesting way to align an object's pivot is to use the toolbar's Align command with one of the Affect Only buttons in the Adjust Pivot rollout. By using the Align command on the toolbar bar, you can align an object or its pivot with any object in the scene, including itself. See Chapter 6, "Selection, Transforms, and Precision" for details about using the Align command.

When Align to Pivot is active, the Current Object in the Align dialog should be set to Pivot Point to achieve the most predictable results. Furthermore, you can select the object to which the pivot belongs as the target object and then use the options of the Align dialog to align the pivot to the boundaries of the object.

When Align to Object is active, you can select the object's pivot as the target object. Then you can use the options of the Align dialog to align the boundaries of the object to the pivot.

Adjusting Transforms

You use the commands in the Adjust Transform rollout to transform and align a parent object (including its pivot) independent of any linked children. The buttons in the Adjust Transform rollout temporarily suspend link inheritance while you transform a parent object. Click the Pivot button in the Hierarchy panel to display the Adjust Transform rollout (see fig. 18.8).

FIGURE 18.8

The Adjust Transform rollout.

NOTE

The buttons in the Alignment and Reset areas of the Adjust Transform rollout work with any object and are convenient for adjusting the transforms of any object in your scene.

Click the Affect Object Only button in the Adjust Transform rollout to move, rotate, or uniform scale a parent object without affecting any of its children. (Do not use nonuniform scale with linked objects.) To align selected objects with the World or with the selected objects parents, click either of the alignment buttons in the rollout.

When the Affect Object Only button is active in the Adjust Transform rollout, you can use the Align command on the toolbar to align selected objects with any other object in the scene without affecting the selected objects' children.

Resetting Transforms

The two buttons in the Reset area of the Adjust Transform rollout reset the rotation and scale transforms of an object so that its current condition is considered its original condition. The reset buttons always pass on the change in transform to any linked children. If you want to reset the transform of an object without affecting its children, you must first unlink the children from the object and then re-link them after resetting the transform.

The two Reset buttons have the following effects:

■ **Transform** Reset Rotation would be a better name for this button because it rotates only the object's pivot to align with the World coordinate system. In other words it resets the object's rotation transform back to zero degrees of rotation for each axis. The main difference between Reset Transform and Align To World is that Reset Transform affects the object's children and Align to World does not.

■ **Scale** Absorbs the object's current scale setting and declares it to be the 100% scale condition.

Reset Scale can get confusing because it causes a disconnect in the way an object reports its condition. If you have a sphere with a 50-unit radius and a 150% uniform scale, the sphere in the scene has a radius of 75 units. If you reset the Scale of this sphere, you have the odd condition of the radius parameter reporting 50 units and scale reporting 100%, but the sphere in the scene still has a radius of 75 units. Reset Scale hides the original scale factor from the rest of 3DS MAX.

Reset Scale is one way to fix nonuniform scaled objects so they work properly with hierarchical linking. Be sure to unlink any children from the object before applying Reset Scale.

Resetting Transforms with the Reset Transform Utility

You can also use a new utility in 3DS MAX R1.1 to reset an object's transforms in another way. Choose Reset Transform from the category list of the Utility panel shown in figure 18.9. When you click the Reset Selected button, the object is returned to its initial orientation and scale, and any rotation and scale transforms are placed into an XForm modifier.

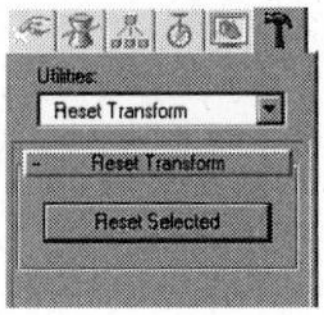

FIGURE 18.9
*The Reset
Transform utility.*

Using the Reset Transform utility has the added benefit of segregating rotation and scale transform values from the base object while leaving those values accessible in the XForm gizmo.

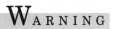WARNING

Because the Reset Transform utility uses a modifier, applying Reset Transform cannot be undone. Choose Hold from the Edit menu before using the Reset Transform utility. Then, if you don't like the result of Reset Transform, you can use Fetch to restore your scene.

Setting Object Transform Locks

You can use options in the Locks rollout of the Hierarchy panel to prevent an object from being transformed about any selected local axis. You access object locks by clicking the Link Info button of the Hierarchy panel and expanding the Locks rollout (see fig. 18.10). Although the Locks rollout is located under Link Info, locks have nothing to do with links between objects. Setting a lock affects only transforms applied directly to an object.

FIGURE 18.10
*Setting object
transform locks.*

The Locks rollout contains three sets of X, Y, and Z check boxes—one set each for the Move, Rotate, and Scale transforms. Checking an axis check box prevents transformation about the specified axis. For example, the locks set in figure 18.10 prevent the selected object from moving along its Z axis or rotating about it X and Y axes.

Using Dummy Objects

Dummy objects are invisible, non-rendering objects whose main reason for existence is to be linked to other objects. Dummy objects are used as placeholders or support structures for other objects that must perform complex motions. You create dummy objects from the Helper category of the Create panel (see fig. 18.11). Click the Dummy button and drag anywhere in your scene to create a cube-shaped dummy object.

FIGURE 18.11

The Dummy button in the Create panel.

Earlier in this chapter, an example for the use of a dummy object described a box tumbling down a hill. Another example is an atomic structure. Imagine modeling the motion of electrons as they travel around the nucleus of an atom. Manually specifying the various rotational and positional keys for the electrons would be a daunting task. The following exercise shows how to create an atomic model with linked dummy objects.

A LINKED ATOMIC STRUCTURE

This exercise uses dummy objects hidden inside a model of an atom with electrons linked to the dummies. You can follow along with this exercise by loading the exercise file in step 1. You can also read through the steps and then examine the completed model by loading the file atom.max.

1. Open the file atom-ex.max.

The model begins with a dummy object centered on the nucleus of the model and a single electron linked as a child of the dummy object (see fig. 18.12a).

Two more linked electrons are created in steps 2–4.

2. Select both the dummy object and the electron.

3. Press Shift while rotating the dummy object 120 degrees about its Local Z axis.

4. In the Clone Options dialog, set the Object option to Copy, set the number of copies to 2, and click OK (see fig. 18.12b).

   Two more sets of dummy objects with linked electrons are created as seen in figure 18.12c.

Animate the electrons using steps 5–7:

5. Turn on the Animate button.

6. Drag the Time Slider to the end time of the animation.

7. Rotate each dummy object about one of the dummy's local axes (see fig. 18.12d). Choosing different local axes produces different orbits.

You can examine this completed model yourself. Open the file atom.max from the CD-ROM and play atom.avi to see the animation.

FIGURE 18.12
Steps involved in creating an atomic model.

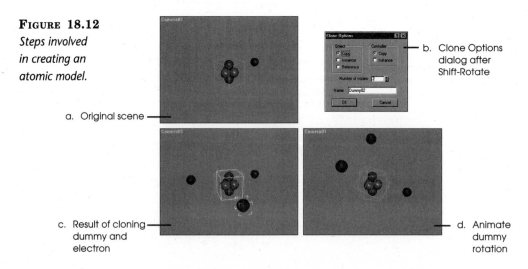

a. Original scene

b. Clone Options dialog after Shift-Rotate

c. Result of cloning dummy and electron

d. Animate dummy rotation

The preceding example demonstrated how simple it is to set up complex motion with a few dummy objects. You could argue that this same exercise could have been completed without using dummy objects by placing each electron's pivot point at the center of the nucleus, and you would be correct. The drawback to this approach occurs if you later decide to map a texture to the electrons and show them spinning about their own centers. The offset pivot point becomes a problem because now you no longer have a rotation point at the center of the electrons. The linked dummy objects are easier to understand, easier to manipulate, and leave more options open for other effects.

Using Inverse Kinematics

As pointed out in the previous sections, hierarchical linking is a one-way effect. Objects are linked from parent to child, and animation effects applied to a parent are passed along to its children. Effects applied to a child do not pass up the chain to parent objects.

This type of linking is useful, but it does not closely simulate jointed objects in the real world. As you know, when real objects are linked together, moving one linked object affects all of the linked objects based on their positions and the properties of their connecting joints. You simulate this behavior by using Inverse Kinematics (IK).

You use IK to manipulate an entire linked chain by moving or rotating a selected child object. When IK mode is active, moving or rotating an object in a hierarchy has the following effects:

- The selected object is called the IK *end effector*.

- Descendants linked to the end effector inherit the transforms applied to the end effector in the normal fashion for hierarchies.

- Ancestors of the end effector define a kinematic chain back to the root of the hierarchy or back to a special terminator object. Moving or rotating the end effector moves and rotates all of the ancestors in the kinematic chain based on their IK parameters.

To enable IK behavior, click the IK mode button on the toolbar. To set up IK parameters, click the IK button in the Hierarchy panel (see fig. 18.13).

FIGURE 18.13

The IK controls.

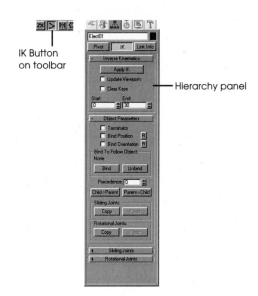

IK Button
on toolbar

Hierarchy panel

The following sections present preliminary IK concepts that will help ensure you of successful animations with IK. Your first step in successfully using IK is to understand how IK interacts with the objects in your hierarchy.

Coordinate Systems

When using IK, an object's joint parameters are driven by the local coordinate system of that object's parent. The relationship between the orientation of an object's Local coordinate system and the Local coordinate system of that object's parent is important. The most predictable IK hierarchies occur when you set up the initial hierarchies with the local coordinate systems aligned with their objects and all of the objects aligned with the World.

Figure 18.14 shows a figure properly laid out and ready for linking and IK set up compared to a figure that will have problems with IK. The figure on the left has all of its components laid out square to the World coordinate system, and the Local coordinate systems of each component are aligned with their objects. The figure on the right is not laid in any kind of alignment, and some local coordinate systems are obviously out of alignment with their objects. It will be difficult to set joint parameters for the figure on the right, and some joints might not work at all.

FIGURE 18.14
*Comparing an
object laid out
properly for IK to
one improperly
laid out.*

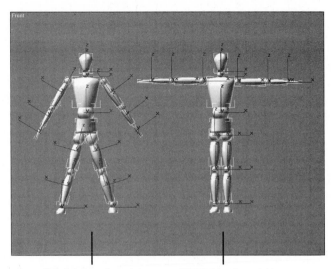

Poorly laid-out model   Well laid-out model

Because the relationship between an object's Local coordinate system and its parent's Local coordinate system is so important, you need to be aware of how various commands alter Local coordinate systems and plan for how those changes will affect your animation. The following actions change the Local coordinate system of an object:

- Rotating an object also rotates the object's Local coordinate system. IK joint axis alignment is based on the relationship of an object to its parent when both the object and its parent are aligned to the World.

- Modifying objects at the sub-object level affects the sub-objects but does not change the Local coordinate system.

- Attaching objects always sacrifices the Local coordinate system of the object being attached and uses the Local coordinate system of the selected object.

- The various forms of Reset Transform always align an object's Local coordinate system with the World coordinate system.

- Any of the Adjust Pivot commands in the Hierarchy panel change the position and orientation of an object's Local coordinate system.

Situations to Avoid with IK

IK works great for almost any task you throw at it, but a few situations are just beyond the capabilities of IK. Most of these unworkable situations occur when you use non-standard controllers with IK or apply the dreaded nonuniform scale transform to an object in the IK hierarchy.

Techniques to use when using IK include the following:

- Euler XYZ rotation controllers work best with IK. Quaternion rotation controllers, such as TCB and Smooth rotation, do work with IK, but they are not as accurate as Euler XYZ controllers and can sometimes freeze up when using joint limits.

- Do not disable Move or Rotate link inheritance for any object you plan to use with IK. IK calculations are based on Move and Rotate transforms passed through the hierarchy.

- Do not use the Follow option on any Path controllers assigned to objects in the IK hierarchy. IK cannot calculate rotation caused by using the Follow option.

- Parametric controllers such as LookAt, Noise, Audio, or Expression controllers do not normally work with IK. (In other words, 3DS MAX doesn't prevent you from using these controllers, but you probably won't get very useful results.)

Defining IK Joints

After you link your objects, you can begin specifying their IK joint behavior. The heart of IK is the definition of how the links between the objects (their joints) are constrained.

To define IK joint behavior, select an object in the hierarchy you want to animate and then adjust IK controls in the Hierarchy panel. You access the IK controls by clicking the IK button in the Hierarchy panel (see fig. 18.15).

FIGURE 18.15

IK controls in the Hierarchy panel.

The following sections discuss the IK controls for joint behavior. These controls are the Joint Parameters and Joint Precedence.

Setting Joint Parameters

When you first set up a hierarchy, all default joints are free to rotate in all directions but are prevented from sliding. If you want a controllable, realistic effect, you must specify constraints on how the joints operate. There are two types of joints available in IK—rotational joints and positional joints. Any joint can have freedom of motion for rotation, position, or both. You also have independent control over how much the joint rotates or moves about all three axes of the Local coordinate system.

Two rollouts in the Hierarchy panel contain the joint controls and current joint parameters for a single selected object (see fig. 18.16). If you select more than one object, the joint parameters rollouts do not display. The joint parameters rollouts are named as follows:

- **Rotational Joints** Always available for any type of rotating joint. Contains three sets of joint parameters—one set for each of the three rotational axes of X, Y, and Z.

- **Sliding Joints** One of two standard positional joint types. Sliding Joints is the default type used for most Position controllers. Contains three sets of joint parameters—one set for each of the three positional axes of X, Y, and Z.

- **Path Joints** Second standard positional joint type. Used whenever the selected object is assigned a Path position controller. Contains one set of joint parameters controlling the position of the object along the path.

All these joint types contain controls for three basic joint properties: joint active status, joint limits, and joint friction (called easing and damping). The following sections describe these joint properties.

FIGURE 18.16
The three standard joint parameters rollouts.

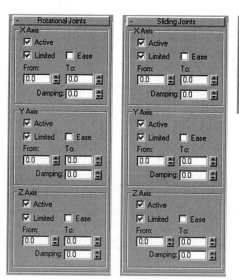

Activating Joints

If you want the selected object to rotate or move on a joint axis, you must check the Active check box for that joint axis. Most real world joints are active on only one axis but are occasionally active on two axes.

Some examples of real world joints that you can model with 3DS MAX IK include the following:

- A door hinge is active on only one rotational axis and zero sliding axes.

- A drawer slide is active on only one sliding axis and zero rotational axes.

- Your shoulder joint is active on all three rotational axes and zero sliding axes.

- A bead on a ring (path) is active on possibly one rotational axis and active for the path joint.

Remember that joint axes are defined by the Local coordinate system of the selected object's parent. Consider choosing Parent and the transform coordinate system. You can then use the displayed transform coordinate icon as a visual reference.

Limiting Joints

If a joint is active on a given axis, the joint is probably limited as well. For example, if a rotational joint is not limited, the object spins freely. Wheels and gears may use an unlimited rotational joint, but most other joints, such as hinges, shoulders, and knees, have definite limits.

To set joint limits, do the following:

1. Check the Limited check box for the active joint axis you want to limit.

2. Enter values in the From and To fields to set the maximum range of motion for the object on that axis (refer to fig. 18.16).

   The selected object moves while you drag the field spinners to indicate the location of the limit. You can also press the mouse button over the From or To label to cause the object to jump to that limit position. In both cases, the object returns to its initial position after you release the mouse.

Joint limits are measured in different ways. Rotational joint limits are measured as the angle from the active axis of the parent's Local coordinate system to the matching axis of the selected object's Local coordinate system. Sliding joint limits are measured as the distance from the parent's pivot point to the pivot point of the selected object. Path joint limits are measured as a percentage of the path from the first vertex of the path.

WARNING ———————————————————————————

If your selected object uses a quaternion rotation controller (TCB, Linear, or Smooth) and its initial position is outside the rotational limits, the object can freeze when you try to apply IK. To fix the problem, either expand the limits to contain the object's initial position or turn off IK mode and rotate the object until it is within the limits. Euler XYZ rotation controllers do not exhibit this problem.

Easing and Damping Joints

In a perfect world, joints would not have friction or resistance to motion. Our cars would last longer, and our wrists wouldn't hurt from writing large computer books. Unfortunately, joints do have friction. 3D Studio MAX simulates resistance in IK joints with two settings called *Ease* and *Damping*.

You can think of Ease as being similar to trying to move your arm or leg through its maximum range of motion. Most of the range is easy to move, but as you approach your limits, you experience greater resistance and the motion becomes more difficult. Checking the Ease check box for an axis increases resistance to motion on that axis as the joint approaches its limit. The more resistance there is at a joint, the more other joints in the IK hierarchy must contribute to the solution.

Likewise, you can think of damping as being similar to a rusted or very tight joint. The damped joint resists all motion and lets other joints in the IK hierarchy do most of the work. Damped joints begin to move as the other joints approach their limits. Setting a value in the Damping field applies resistance across the entire range of motion. A Damping value of 0.0 applies no resistance, whereas a maximum Damping value of 1.0 cancels all motion for that axis.

Copying and Pasting Joints

Quite frequently you will want to use the same type of joint, with the same settings, on multiple objects in your hierarchy. You can set parameters only for one joint at a time, but you can copy a joint's parameters and then paste them into another joint. Rotational joints and Sliding joints each have their own custom Copy and Paste buttons in the Object Parameters rollout (see fig. 18.17). These joints also have their own clipboard memory so you can store one rotational joint and one sliding joint at the same time.

NOTE

3DS MAX does not support Copy or Paste for Path joint parameters.

FIGURE 18.17
*Joint parameter
Copy and Paste
buttons.*

To copy and paste rotational or sliding joint parameters, complete the following steps:

1. Select an object.

2. Click copy in the Object Parameters rollout for either sliding joint or rotational joint parameters.

3. Select a different object.

4. Click paste for the joint type you want to paste.

Setting Joint Parameters for Root Objects

You might think that you don't need joint parameters for the root object of a hierarchy. By definition, the root object is not linked to a parent, so it doesn't have a joint—right? No. Remember that a root object is always considered to be a child of the World. The joint parameters for the root of a hierarchy define how the root object moves with respect to the world while IK mode is active.

When joint parameters are inactive for a root object, it cannot move or rotate. The root object acts like an anchor, remaining unaffected by any IK solution. Also, you cannot directly select and move or rotate the root object. It is locked solidly in place.

When joint parameters are active for a root object, it can only move or rotate according to the joint parameters of its active axes. The world now acts as the anchor for the hierarchy. If you try to select and Move or Rotate the root object, is only able to move or rotate as allowed by its joint parameters.

Sometimes, you want the joint parameters of a root object to be inactive, so it acts as an anchor for any IK solution, but you also want the ability to directly select and Move or Rotate the root object. 3DS MAX provides this capability through the Always Transform Children of the World option in the Inverse Kinematics panel of the Preference Settings dialog. When Always Transform Children of the World is unchecked, transforming root objects is constrained, and only follows the object's joint parameters. When Always Transform Children of the World is checked, you can freely transform root objects, but any IK solution for the root object is constrained to follow the object's joint parameters.

Joint Precedence

The setting of *joint precedence* controls how motion is distributed between the joints. Joints with a high precedence absorb a greater share of the overall motion than joints with a low precedence. The absolute value of the joint precedence makes no difference; all that matters is whether one joint's precedence value is higher than another.

You set Joint precedence in the Object Parameters rollout. The default precedence starts with all joints having equal precedence of zero. When joints have the same precedence values, joints closer to the end effector move more than joints further away.

You can manually set the precedence for each joint by selecting objects and entering a value in the Precedence field. This method gives you precise control over motion distribution along the kinematic chain, but the process can be very tedious to set up. Most of your needs can probably be handled by one of the following two presets:

■ **Child->Parent**   The preset choice that provides the typical solution for most situations. You select a child object and its ancestors and click Child->Parent to assign joint precedence that decreases from child to parent. This setting causes child objects closer to where the transform is applied to move more than parent objects further away.

■ **Parent->Child**   Select a child object and its ancestors and click Parent->Child to assign joint precedence that increases from child to parent. This setting causes child objects closer to where the transform is applied to move less than parent objects further away.

Defining the Kinematic Chain

As stated at the beginning of the IK sections, transforming an object with IK mode turned on affects all of the object's ancestors back to the root of the hierarchy. The chain of ancestors from the selected object back to the root is called the *Kinematic Chain*. Because each object in the hierarchy can have only one parent, there can be only one possible Kinematic Chain from any object to the root of the hierarchy.

Sometimes you won't want the Kinematic Chain to go all the way back to the root of the hierarchy. An example might be when you are animating the arms of a figure and you want the IK effect to stop at the shoulders. You can stop the Kinematic Chain before it reaches the root by specifying an object as an IK terminator. You specify an object as an IK terminator by selecting the object and checking the Terminator check box in the Object Parameters rollout (see fig. 18.18).

FIGURE 18.18
*Checking the IK
Terminator check
box.*

Animating with Inverse Kinematics

After you complete the setup steps linking a hierarchy, setting joint parameters, and specifying any terminator objects, you are ready to begin animating with IK. The two primary forms of IK animation are listed as follows:

■ **Interactive IK**   Involves manually selecting and transforming an end effector at keyframes you specify.

■ **Applied IK**   Involves binding an end effector to an animated follow object and having 3DS MAX calculate an IK solution for every frame.

Using Interactive IK

Use Interactive IK when you want more freedom and artistic control of the IK motion and are willing to let 3DS MAX interpolate between your keyframes. To activate Interactive IK mode, click the IK button on the toolbar. You then manually position your end effectors, while viewing the results of your changes in real-time. Turn on the Animate button, move to different frames, and move or rotate end effectors at will until you have set up your desired animation.

Using Applied IK

Use Applied IK when you want your hierarchy to mimic the motion of another object in the scene. With Applied IK, 3DS MAX calculates a complete IK solution for every frame of the animation, yielding greater accuracy than the Interactive method. Applied IK can be more flexible to use because you can quickly change the animation by choosing different follow objects or by changing the animation of a follow object.

To use Applied IK you first bind selected end effectors to animated follow objects and then click Apply IK in the Hierarchy panel.

Binding Object Position

Check the Bind Position check box when you want an end effector to point at or even touch a selected follow object. To bind end effector position to a follow object, complete the following steps:

1. Select an end effector from the hierarchy.

2. Check the Bind Position check box in the Object Parameters rollout.

3. Click the Bind button in the Bind to Follow Object area.

4. Drag from the end effector to an object in the scene.

   The cursor will change to the Bind cursor (it looks like a push pin) when the cursor is over a valid follow object.

TIP

Trying to drag from the end effector to a specific follow object can be difficult if there are many other objects near the follow object. You can also specify the follow object using the Select Pin dialog. When this is the case, replace step 4 with:

Click the Select by Name button in the toolbar and select the name of the follow object from the Select Pin dialog.

3D Studio MAX attempts to match the pivot point of the end effector with the position of the pivot point of the follow object. The kinematic chain is still constrained by the settings of the joint parameters, so it may not be possible for the end effector to actually reach the follow object. In this case, 3DS MAX places the end effector as close as possible to the follow object.

Clicking the R button to the right of the Bind Position check box causes the end effector to mimic the motion of the follow object without actually trying to point at or reach the follow object itself. This option is useful for animating gestures and secondary motions.

If you check the Bind Position check box but do not bind the end effector to a follow object, the end effector is considered bound to the World. In this case the bound object tries to stay put and does not move until other transforms in the Kinematic Chain force it to move to complete an IK solution.

Binding Object Orientation

Check the Bind Orientation check box when you want an end effector to match the orientation of a selected follow object. To bind end effector orientation to a follow object, complete the following steps:

1. Select an end effector from the hierarchy.

2. Check the Bind Orientation check box in the Object Parameters rollout.

3. Click the Bind button in the Bind to Follow Object area.

4. Drag from the end effector to an object in the scene.

    The cursor will change to the Bind cursor (it looks like a push pin) when the cursor is over a valid follow object.

3D Studio MAX attempts to rotate the pivot point of the end effector to match the orientation of the pivot point of the follow object. The Kinematic Chain is still constrained by the settings of the joint parameters, so it may not be possible for the end effector to actually match the orientation of the follow object. In this case 3DS MAX rotates the end effector to match the orientation of the follow object as closely as possible.

Clicking the R button to the right of the Bind Orientation check box causes the end effector to mimic rotational changes of the follow object without actually trying to match the orientation of the follow object itself. This option is useful for animating gestures and secondary motions.

If you check the Bind Orientation check box but do not bind the end effector to a follow object, the end effector is considered bound to the World. In this case the bound object tries to hold its original orientation and does not rotate until other transforms in the Kinematic Chain force it to rotate to complete an IK solution.

Applying the IK Solution

Your final action after binding end effectors to animated follow objects is to Apply the IK solution. The controls for applying IK are found in the Inverse Kinematics rollout of the Hierarchy panel.

To apply an IK solution, complete the following:

1. Select any object in your IK hierarchy.

2. Set the start time and end time for the IK solution in the Start and End fields.

3. Click Apply IK.

While 3DS MAX calculates the IK solution, a progress bar is displayed at the bottom of the 3DS MAX application window. Click the Cancel button to the right of the progress bar to halt the IK calculations at any time.

There are two other options in the Inverse Kinematics rollout that affect the applied IK solution. These options are listed as follows:

- **Update Viewports** When checked, 3DS MAX displays the IK solution for each frame in the viewports. You can watch the progress of the IK solution but at the expense of slowing down the IK calculations.

- **Clear Keys** When checked, all position and rotation keys are deleted from objects in the IK hierarchy before beginning the IK calculations. If you are making only small changes to an existing IK solution, leaving Clear Keys unchecked can speed up the IK calculations. If you are making large changes, you should check Clear Keys to ensure the most accurate IK solution.

In Practice: Building and Animating Hierarchies

- **Building Hierarchies** Use hierarchical linking to simulate assemblies of objects connected with mobile joints. Consider using Group or Attach to simulate assemblies that are glued or welded together.

- **Complex Motion** If a complicated motion can be broken down into multiple simple motions, use a hierarchy of linked dummy objects. Each dummy object carries one of the simple motions and inherits the other motions from its ancestors.

- **Children of the World** Remember that if an object is not linked to another object it is considered to be linked to the World.

- **Never Scale Linked Objects** Nonuniform scale produces undesirable side effects in the children of the scaled object. Any scale disrupts IK calculations. Always use XForm modifiers to apply scale transforms to linked objects.

- **Pivot Points** Adjust an object's pivot point to change the location and orientation of an object's Local coordinate system and to define the location of the joint between an object and its parent.

- **Interactive IK** Use Interactive IK mode to manually position and animate IK hierarchies. 3DS MAX uses simple interpolation to animate between your IK keyframes.

- **Applied IK** Use animated follow objects with Applied IK to have 3DS MAX calculate an accurate IK solution for every frame of your animation.

Philadelphia International Airport improvements project
Created by Harold Kalmus
Articus Media Labs, Inc.
Philadelphia, PA
Architect: DPK&A, Philadelphia PA

Chapter 19

LIGHTING AND ATMOSPHERE

Good lighting—and moody atmosphere—is an area that separates superb work from average. You can have a scene with magnificently designed models, amazing animation, and photorealistic textures, but a washed out or inadequately lit scene can turn art into a waste of pixels. Filmmakers know it, video producers know it, and theater lighting directors know it, but many 3D animators don't know it. Avoid good lighting and a sense of atmosphere, and your work is sterile, without life.

This chapter discusses the following topics relating to lighting and atmospheric environments:

- *Default lighting in 3D Studio MAX*
- *Basic lighting styles*

- 3DS MAX lighting methods
- Types of lights, and example uses
- Creative use of attenuation
- Controlling shadow settings
- Projector lights
- Volumetric lights, fog, and combust
- Architectural lighting types and concepts

Lighting is something we naturally take for granted. Everywhere we go, we have a lit path already established. The sun illuminates our world quite simply—but effectively. Whether in our own lives or in the movies or TV shows we watch, we don't have to worry about lighting; it's done for us. But with 3D, it's a different story. In 3D environments, things are rarely set up for us. Like modeling, texturing, and animation, lighting takes thoughtful work to establish a meaningful, well-lit scene.

Setting Up Standard Lighting

This section discusses some basic lighting styles that are often the foundation of designing a thoughtful light design that accentuates and gives depth to your scene. You will also learn about 3D Studio MAX's default lighting, which provides good overall lighting; basic illustration styles, such as three-point lighting; and the concept of reflected light.

3DS MAX Default Lighting

When no lights are present, 3DS MAX provides a default lighting setup so that the scene can be viewed effectively. This lighting can be thought of as the "house lights" that provide enough illumination for you to work, but are not intended for the final rendered result. The default lighting provided is simply two omni lights placed at diagonal corners of your scene. Assuming your scene is centered at the origin, the lights are placed up in front at –X, –Y, +Z and the other is down in back at +X, +Y, –Z.

When you first add a light to your scene, 3DS MAX removes the default lighting so that you can see the illumination of what you introduced. Your scene will become darker when you do this because two lights have been removed and replaced by one new light. You can now introduce additional lights as required. The default lighting is left off as long as light objects exist in the scene, regardless of whether they're on or off. When all lights are deleted from the scene, the default setup is returned automatically. You can, however, override the scene's illumination with the default lighting setup with a keyboard alternate (assigned to Ctl+L by default). This override is on a viewport basis and is saved with the scene. In practice, this is useful when there is no illumination from a certain angle and you need to model the darkened side.

NOTE

The interactive renderer can show a maximum of 12 lights. In a scene using more than 12 lights, the earliest 12 are used for the interactive illumination. This limitation has no impact on the production renderer's lighting.

Although the interactive renderer is useful, it is not a replacement for making test renderings with the production renderer. Because the interactive renderer uses Gouraud-based shading, the highlights you see are dependent on each surface's mesh density. A box having only 12 faces, for example, may have intense highlights, but none are shown in the viewports because the shading is being averaged across just two faces. Other subtleties, such as attenuation, atmosphere, and true material effects, can only be seen effectively in a full rendering.

Basic Illumination Styles: Triangle and Zone Lighting

Lighting is always a stylistic issue, but two different illumination styles are often used to build upon: triangle lighting and zone lighting.

Triangle lighting (also called *three-point lighting*) uses three lights to provide illumination. The primary light, called the *key*, is generally the brightest light and illuminates most of the scene (see fig. 19.1). The key is usually the light that casts a shadow in the scene.

A second *backlight* is used to separate an object from its background and reveal more depth. This light is generally behind and above the object and of lesser or equal intensity than the key (see fig. 19.2).

A third light, the *fill,* is generally left of the camera and fills dark areas missed by the key (see fig. 19.3). The fill light is used to control contrast between the brightest areas of the scene and the darkest. A bright fill creates even lighting whereas a dim fill increases the contrast and makes the scene more uneasy. Your selection of lighting intensities helps to create an overall mood. Just as happy cartoons are bright and well illuminated, spooky castles are dimly lit and full of contrast. Figure 19.4 shows the arrangement of the lights used in figure 19.3.

FIGURE 19.3
Key, backlight, and fill lights.

FIGURE 19.4
Arrangement of key, backlight, and fill lights.

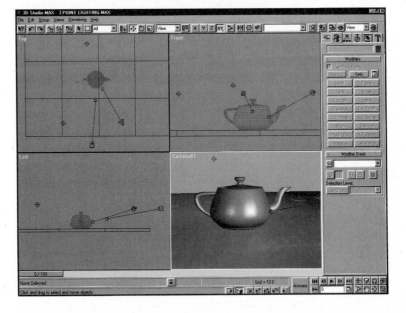

Sometimes a large scene cannot use basic triangle lighting effectively so a slightly different approach to lighting is needed. *Zone lighting* occurs when an area is broken down into zones, and each zone is illuminated individually. Selection of zones can be chosen by areas of importance or similarity. After a zone is selected, basic triangle or three-point lighting can be applied. Sometimes, however, zone lighting doesn't create the proper mood so a free-form lighting scheme is used. When used carefully, *accent lights*—used to illuminate key objects or areas—are often used for drawing attention to something important.

Each visual art has several styles of lighting, and all can be used in 3D space. In fact, 3D lighting isn't limited to available power or the brightness of a bulb. The lighting isn't limited by where it can be placed, what it illuminates, or where its shadow is cast. 3D lights can animate their brightness and color and move with complete freedom.

NOTE

For good theory, lighting tips, and techniques, look to books and magazines from the traditional visual arts, such as photography, film, theater, and video. Real-world light design can easily be used in 3D space.

Reflected Light

3DS MAX bases its illumination on the angle the light source is to the surface and *not* its distance to it. When a light source is square to a plane and far away, the angles of the light's rays that fall on the plane's surface are nearly parallel, and the resulting illumination is very even. If the same light is placed close, the angles of the light's rays that strike the surface vary considerably and produce a pronounced hotspot. It usually is desirable to shade objects gradually across their faces and not to create such hotspots. To do this, you must place the light sources at an angle to the object (to create gradations) and at a significant distance (to minimize hotspots). The resulting basic setup is composed of two omni lights placed at a diagonal to the model—the formula for the 3DS MAX default lighting setup.

The amount that a light illuminates a surface depends completely on the light's angle to the surface, not on the light's proximity. This is the light's *angle of incidence* to the surface. If the surface is at a right angle to the light, it is illuminated at full effect. As the surface tilts away from the light source, this angle is lowered, and the illumination received diminishes. This means that as a light is placed further away, it illuminates the scene more and more evenly—each mesh's angle to the light source slowly approaches 90 degrees.

All lights within 3DS MAX respect the color laws of RGB additive illumination. The selection and assignment of light color is consistent between all forms of light. See Chapter 2, "Mixing Color and Light," in this book and Chapter 20 in Volume 2 of the *3D Studio MAX User's Guide* for more information on color, illumination, and color mixing theory and their application within 3DS MAX.

Lights and Their Illumination

The many built-in light types of 3DS MAX can emulate nearly every light in nature, as well as add possibilities that can exist only in the virtual realm of computer graphics. 3DS MAX contains several types of light objects—the targeted and free spotlights, the omni light, and the directional light. These are physical lights that can be placed and moved around in the 3D scene. These lights contain common light controls that describe how a light behaves in the environment. There is also an ambient light, which is actually a lighting level because it affects the entire scene uniformly. As such, it is found in the environmental controls because it does not have any physical properties to adjust.

Types of Lights

3DS MAX includes four different light objects: omni light, directional light, targeted spotlight, and free spotlight. Ambient light, which is not a physical light object, is important to factor in an overall lighting design.

All light within 3DS MAX respects the color laws of RGB additive illumination. The selection and assignment of light color is consistent with all forms of light. These colors can be mixed using any combination of Red, Green, Blue (RGB) and Hue, Luminance, Saturation (HLS) channels and values. See Chapter 2 for more information on color.

Omni Lights

Omni lights are point light sources very similar to a naked bulb hanging on a wire or a star in a solar system. An omni light traces its illumination from its position to all faces that are oriented toward it. Because omni lights are not designed to cast shadows, their rays cannot be blocked by any mesh and, therefore, decrease the darkness of any shadows on which they cast light.

NOTE

The primary purpose of omni lights is to act as fill lights. It is quite common to have numerous omni lights at great distances, in varying colors, and with low levels to cast shades of light and mix them on the model. This technique is borrowed from theatrical lighting but is quite applicable to 3DS MAX.

In being omni-directional, omni lights are quite predictable in their resulting illumination. These lights have a variety of secondary uses as well. Placing omni lights close to meshes creates bright specular highlights; placing omni lights at strategic angles behind or below meshes can create subtle glows and give the effect of bounced color. Omni lights given negative multipliers are often placed in areas of the scene to create pools of shade.

A common mistake is to believe that "hanging" an omni light in a room creates a glow in the air about it as it would in real life. This cannot happen. Lights in 3DS MAX can cast light only upon the faces that they strike, and this actually is correct. A light placed in outer space does not emit a glow because there is nothing to illuminate. The streaks of laser light so common in the movies are actually a fallacy; in reality, nothing is seen. The street lamp outside your house creates a glow, or halo, because it strikes millions of airborne particles floating about it.

Directional Light

A directional light is best thought of as being the sun. As a light casts shadows, the angle of the shadow is the line traced from the light source to the subject. This effect is most visible when you have closely spaced objects with parallel surfaces—a picket-fence for example. Placing a spotlight close to the fence produces highly flared shadows as each picket traces its own shadow line to the light source. As you move the light away from the fence, the angle between each picket's shadow becomes shallower and shallower. When the light source is placed a considerable distance away, the angle between each shadow is so minimal that the shadows cast are effectively parallel to one another. This is what occurs with sunlight and in computer graphics is termed parallel or directional light. This is the illumination produced by the 3DS MAX Directional Light object.

The Directional Light object in 3DS MAX is somewhat of a hybrid between a traditional parallel light and a spotlight. The Directional Light is similar to a spotlight in having a hotspot and falloff. These serve to control the extents to which shadows are calculated in the scene and the extent of falloff. When the hotspot is minimized, the Directional Light is somewhat similar to a photographer's box light by casting a soft, area light. When the overshoot option is enabled, the hotspot and falloff are ignored, and the illumination is similar to the sun. Attenuation should be used for soft area lights and should be off when simulating sunlight.

A Directional Light is similar to a Free Spot or Free camera in not having a target and being controlled entirely by its rotation. When overshoot is active, the distance a Directional Light is from the subject is of minimal importance. Unlike other light objects, it does not matter how far to one side the Directional Light is placed—only the angle it is to the subject.

Targeted Spotlight

The targeted spotlight is a directional light that casts light toward its target, which can be moved independently. A targeted spotlight is similar to tying a rope to the front of a spotlight, similar to those often used in concerts. Wherever the rope is pulled, the spot turns to aim in that direction.

NOTE

The target is used only as an aid in aiming the spotlight. The distance of the target from the light has no influence on its brightness, or attenuation.

The many capabilities of targeted and free spotlights make them the primary lighting tool within the 3DS MAX environment. Unlike omni lights, the direction of their light can be controlled. Targeted and free spotlights can cast shadows, can be rectangular or circular in shape, and can even project a bitmap image.

Free Spotlight

A *Free Spot* contains all the capabilities of a Target Spot but without a target object. Instead of positioning a target to position the spotlight's cone, you rotate the Free Spot to aim its beam. The reason to choose a Free Spot over a Target Spot may be personal preference or the need to animate the light in conjunction with other geometries.

When animating lights, there are times when they need to stay in relation to another object. Car headlights, spotlights, and a miner's cap are typical examples. These are situations for which a Free Spot is intended because they can be simply linked to the object and will continue to aim their light as the object moves in the scene. This is especially important when the spotlight is rectangular and/or projecting an image. In such cases, the light needs to bank or roll with the parent object to produce the correct effect. Rotating the light and its resulting projection can only occur reliably with a Free Spot.

Ambient Light

If you were to eliminate all light objects in a scene, you would be left with *ambient light*. This is the ever present light that seems to exist in the world when you cannot identify a specific light source. In actuality, light is bouncing off of surfaces to illuminate those that are not directly illuminated. Ambient light is a method to approximate this reflected light in 3D Studio MAX.

The color of the ambient light is applied to every surface in the scene before any other lighting is applied. The ambient light serves as the starting point from which all other lights add or subtract. Because ambient light is universally applied, increasing its level will reduce contrast and "flatten" the scene. A scene illuminated solely by ambient light has no contrast or shading, with every side and facet being rendered with the same intensity. Only geometric silhouettes and material properties will be definable.

Ambient light is not an object, but rather is part of the Environment system and is adjusted in the Environment dialog accessed form the Rendering/ Environment pull-down. Because ambient light is always present, its light and color are what you see in cast shadows. If you want to make the colors of your scene look especially deep, you should tint the ambient light's color slightly to be the complement of the dominant shadow-casting lights. If the light is the yellowish cast of the moon, an ambient light level of deep purple would intensify the moonlight's effect.

At times, a pure white ambient light is useful for rendering "flat" art such as text, logos, and illustrative designs where you do not want any shading to occur. Because the scene's total light level is white, no effects from any other light sources exist *if* the materials used have identical Ambient and Diffuse base colors (as in locked Diffuse and Ambient maps). If differences exist between the Ambient and Diffuse colors, the materials will shift toward their diffuse values as illumination increases across their surfaces. Rather than adjusting material definitions, you can simply eliminate the other light sources. If you have no light objects in the scene, you will actually need to create one and turn it off to eliminate the influence of the default lighting setup.

NOTE

When only ambient light is used to illuminate the scene, the ambient base color of the assigned material is used. Illuminating a scene with pure white ambient light will render all materials according to their ambient color values. This may seem surprisingly dark given the common technique of making the ambient color a darker version of the diffuse.

In practice, many artists prefer to use a dim ambient light or none at all. This provides better control over shadows and the resulting contrast in the final images. A common mistake is to increase the ambient light considerably in an effort to reduce the need for other light sources. Rather than make things easier, this approach usually results in a dull scene without much contrast or mood.

Common Light Controls

All the different light objects share a common set of controls—they control a light's basic features, such as brightness and color. Clicking on a light's color swatch brings up these controls in the command panel (see fig. 19.5).

The On/Off check box controls whether a light affects the scene. The choice is explicit for the scene and cannot be animated. If you wish to animate a light going on and off you need to adjust its color and/or multiplier value over time instead. Note that to keep the light on at a constant rate and then turn it off you will need to either assign a Linear controller, adjust the Continuity of a TCB controller to 0, or flatten the curve of a Bézier controller.

Clicking the Exclude button brings up a list box, enabling you to choose specific objects for the light to illuminate (see fig. 19.6). You can choose either the objects to illuminate or to exclude for illumination, with the "correct" choice simply being the smaller of the two selection sets. Light exclusion does not impact rendering calculations and actually optimizes your scene—especially when used to limit what shadow casting lights need to illuminate. The exclusion/inclusion lists enable you to place accent lights wherever is necessary in the scene without worrying about how they may over-illuminate or cause undesirable highlights.

The RGB, HSV, and Color Swatch control the color and illumination of the light. While the color can be animated by adjusting any of the values, the color is always animated according to RGB values and will interpolate across RGB color space. The color of the light is significant, even at low levels. The amount a surface is illuminated is controlled by the total RGB value as modulated by the multiplier value.

FIGURE 19.5

General light controls.

FIGURE 19.6

Objects may be excluded from a light's illumination, shadow casting, or both.

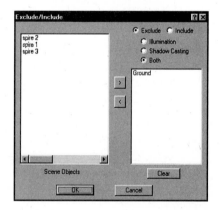

Multipliers

The multiplier is similar to dimmer switch for lights. The multiplier value is multiplied against the color swatch's RGB values to define the light's actual output color. A value of less than one reduces the illumination whereas values greater than one increase it. When the multiplier is given a negative value, the light actually removes illumination from the scene. These "negative lights" are useful for simulating radiosity effects and otherwise perfecting interior lighting setups. A common use for a negative omni, for example, is to place them at interior corners to darken them in a way that is difficult to achieve with the positive lights in the scene.

Although the multiplier has many uses, a common one is to ensure the same color is being used across a series of lights. Each light is given the same color, and the intensity is controlled with their multipliers. It becomes obvious that the same base color is being used by glancing at the color swatch. Similarly, small multipliers allow the color swatch to read as a distinguishable color while making the light's color quite dark. For example, rather than creating a dim red light with a color of 10,0,0 and a near black color swatch, give it a recognizable red of 200,0,0 and uses a 0.05 multiplier to dim it to the lower value.

As multipliers are increased, each channel caps at 255. This means a red light that began as 255,10,10 would be rose-pink with a multiplier of 10, very light pink with a multiplier of 20, and pure white with a multiplier of 26. When multipliers are this intense, the fact that the light is "red" is seen only at the falloff or with attenuation. Then the light progresses from white to bright red across the falloff halo. This characteristic is often useful for special effect lighting.

Attentuation

Attenuation controls a light's falloff over distance. Without attenuation, lights illuminate according to their orientation to the surface. If the surface is at 90 degrees, the light gives its full effect. This means that the farther you place a light from a surface, the shallower the angle of incidence becomes and the brighter the surface is illuminated. But in real life, light diminishes over distance. If you hold a flashlight directly over a table, it's quite bright. Aim it across the room and its illumination is much dimmer. Point it across the street and it barely has an influence on the neighboring home. This diminishing, decay, or watering down of light is termed *attenuation* and is a simple result of physics.

NOTE

Interiors tend to require numerous lights and if these are not attenuated, the scene rapidly becomes over-illuminated. When illuminating interiors, attenuation should be used on all lights except for the dimmest of fill lights.

In the world around us, light attenuates at an inverse square ratio. For example, if a lamp had X illumination at 10 feet, it would have $\frac{1}{4}$X at 20 feet. Although physically correct, this amount of decay is usually considered too high for computer graphics. The reason is that light bounces off surfaces and illuminates the world from all angles, even though it is attenuating. Only radiosity rendering programs have the capability to reproduce this inherited light, and they are usually the only ones that adhere to the inverse square ratio. Most computer programs that include light attenuation, therefore, do so in a linear fashion—the same lamp that had X illumination at 10 feet would now have $^1/_2$ X at 20 feet. 3DS MAX provides a hybrid method of zero and linear falloff.

NOTE

Attenuation is shown in the interactive viewports only if you enable the Attenuate Lights option in Viewport Preferences. Although useful, it does have a considerable impact on shaded view redraw times.

The Attenuation Use check box indicates whether the selected light is currently using its assigned ranges. When activated, range circles appear around the lights indicating the extents of their Start and End ranges (see fig. 19.7). These circles define the inner and outer extents for the light's illumination. The Start range (shown by the inner circle) is similar to a hotspot and defines a region where attenuation does not occur. The End range (the outer circle) is similar to a falloff and defines the distance at which the light stops illuminating. Light that falls between the Start and End range receives linear attenuation. If you want a light to always attenuate, you need to reduce the Start range to zero.

TIP

When lighting interiors pay special attention to the lights' ranges, all lights of an equal "wattage" placed in an area should have the same ranges. If ranges are different between lights, their perceived brightness is different because illumination distances will vary. This is especially noticeable in arrays of lights, where it's obvious that they should be the same. In such cases, it is usually best to make the lights instances of one another so adjusting one affects them all.

Hotspot and Falloff

The hotspot and falloff are the most commonly adjusted aspects of spot-lights and directional lights. The difference between the hotspot and falloff controls the crispness of the resulting light pool edge. The hotspot and falloff values have an effect similar to the inner and outer ranges of an attenuated omni light. The *hotspot* defines the extents of the light's full illumination—it does not increase illumination as the name might imply. Illumination within the hotspot is the light at full effect. The *falloff* defines the range at which the light ends its illumination. This fade, or *decay*, is not linear as with omni ranges but actually is a cubic spline interpolation—most of the transition occurs close to the falloff's outer edge. The size difference between the hotspot and fall off define the softness or fuzziness of the light pool's edge. A narrow hotspot and broad falloff create a very soft edge, whereas a hotspot close to the same size as the falloff makes the light pool's edge very crisp.

When overshoot is active, the falloff still defines the range within which shadows are cast and images are projected. The falloff becomes an important mechanism to control the extent to which the light's shadow map is stretched. Larger falloffs will require larger, and more memory intensive, shadow maps to produce quality shadows. You can improve the quality of your shadows and reduce the RAM requirements by restricting the falloffs of shadow casting lights to their minimum size.

FIGURE 19.7

Circles in the different viewports represent the lighting attenuation spheres.

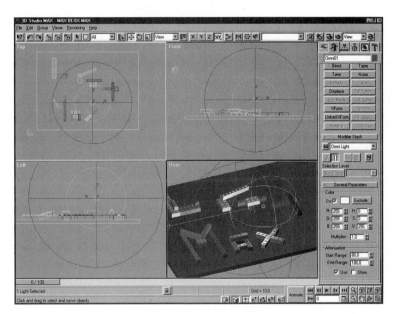

TIP

If a broad gradation over a spotlight's pool is needed, you can use attenuation to create the effect by setting the spotlight's inner range circle so that it just intersects the mesh's surface.

Overshoot

You can eliminate a directional or spotlight's light pool by activating the light's Overshoot option. This eliminates the constraints and produces the illumination equivalent to what would have been produced only within the hotspot. This option basically turns a spotlight into an "aimed omni light," yet retains the rest of the light's capabilities. Because of these qualities, this capability is sometimes referred to as *infinite overshoot*. The important thing to realize is that overshot spotlights are no longer restricted to a cone of light, illuminating in all directions similar to an omni light, and that a directional light casts light infinitely from side to side (see fig. 19.8). While ignoring hotspot constraints, lights using overshoot still respect their attenuation settings.

FIGURE 19.8

A directional light is placed between the two teapots. The one in front of the light casts a shadow, but the one behind the directional light does not.

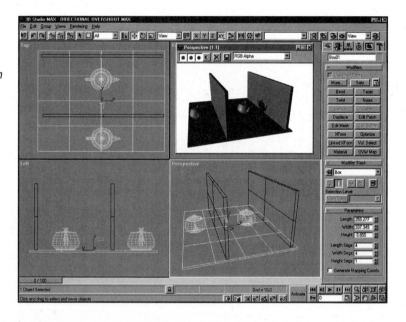

Overshoot is useful when general illumination is needed, but you still need the spotlight's shadow and/or projector capabilities. These properties still observe the spotlight's falloff cone. A spotlight with overshoot should be thought of as an omni light that has shadow casting and projector capabilities constrained to its falloff (see fig. 19.9).

Using Overshoot with a directional light creates a strong, somewhat unusual light source. For example, an overshot directional light will illuminate all surfaces it strikes at a given angle evenly, but will have no impact on surfaces that are co-linear with the light's direction (see fig. 19.10).

FIGURE 19.9

An overshot, shadow casting spotlight creates shadows in its normal hotspot and falloff ranges and acts like an omni outside them.

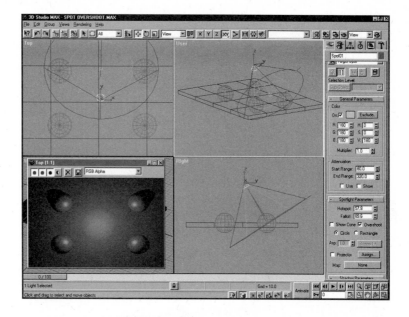

FIGURE 19.10

This overshot directional light illuminates all the planes that the light shines upon, except for the faces at right angles to it.

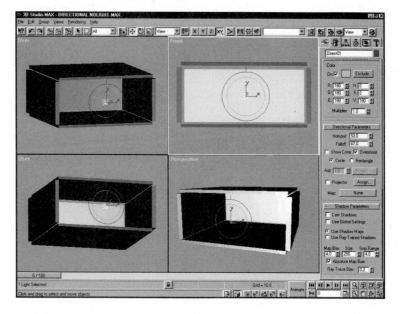

Transforming Lights

Light objects are positioned like any other object in the scene with the Move and Rotate transforms. Unlike other objects, the Scale transform only scales ranges and does not affect other attributes. Transform controls are often used to give finer control over the light's position and orientation. Path, Look At, and Expression controllers are often used to track a light on a path, follow key objects, or have them react to other events in the scene.

Spotlights, like cameras, can be used to define a viewport. Spotlight viewports allow you to see where the light is aimed and are useful tools for locating shadows and projector maps. Spotlight viewports replace the navigation icons with those that relate specifically to spotlights. These controls correspond to their camera equivalents, with falloff equaling FOV. The hotspot control has no effect on the view unless it bumps into the falloff and forces the falloff to increase.

TIP

To create a viewport that corresponds to a directional light by creating a grid object, center the grid on the light (with the Align function), and link it to the directional light. When you activate the grid and make a grid viewport, the view shown will correspond to the directional light's view. As you rotate the light, the view continues to show the directional light's view.

Lighting methods also rely on shadows and how to best use them in an overall lighting design. Specific control of shadows is of key importance when using lights. With too many or not enough shadows, a scene isn't as realistic and convincing.

Working with Shadows

In the world of 3DS MAX, light objects illuminate every face that is oriented toward them—that is, presents a normal to them—until they are stopped by their respective ranges or falloffs. This light transmits through the surfaces and is not blocked unless the light is told to cast shadows. Lights that do not cast shadows, and thus all omni lights, continue to penetrate the scene and devalue the darkness of any cast shadows.

Creating lighting effects can be somewhat difficult if you don't use shadows. The light coming from the left blends with that of the right and with the fill lights. It can be very difficult to create contrasts and drama in a model without employing shadows. Casting shadows is an expensive option, but one that adds tremendous realism to the finished scene. Ray-traced shadows consume rendering time, whereas Shadow Maps require memory resources in addition to some rendering time. Limiting the spotlight's falloff to just the area that requires shadows saves rendering time for both types. Excluding objects from shadows, either within the light or through the object's attribute, also aids in reducing rendering overhead.

Each light's shadow can be set individually or globally. Because each light affects a different area of the scene and has different requirements, you more than likely will be adjusting the shadow parameters of each light. Each directional and spotlight contains a Local Shadow Control dialog that can be accessed with the light's parameters.

The global shadow values control the parameters of all shadow-casting lights that have the Use Global Settings check box turned on. The effects of these parameters are the same, but they are not tailored to each light's needs. Newly created lights are created with Use Global Settings turned off and use built-in system default values for the shadow parameters. If you turn on Use Global settings, the parameters are changed to the global settings if any other light has Use Global Setting on. If no other light has Use Global Settings on, the current values are used as the global setting values.

3DS MAX supplies two forms of shadows with very different properties. The choice of which to use comes down to the basic questions of "Should the shadow edge be crisp or soft?" and "Does the shadow need to respect the object's transparency?"

Using Ray-Traced Shadows

Ray-traced shadows are accurate, have crisp edges, and nearly always engage the object that casts them (an annoying trait that shadow maps must fight to overcome). Any time a crisp edge is needed and an object's transparency values must be calculated, ray-traced shadows are necessary.

Ray-traced shadows also take into account a material's opacity and filter color. These shadows take into account any opacity information contained within a material. This can come in the form of an opacity map and its mask, the material's Transparency parameter sliders, and In/Out options. These are the only aspects that define transparency. Additional maps defining textures or bumps have no effect on the cast shadow. Simulation of these surface markings requires you to copy the appropriate bitmap to be an opacity map or mask for the material.

Spotlights that use ray-traced shadows treat all opacity in terms of luminance or intensity. Material cutouts can be extremely convincing when illuminated by these lights. These materials have matching texture and opacity maps and often are used for entourage objects, such as trees, people, and cars, but also can be the individual leaves of a tree or the mullion bar pattern in a window.

NOTE

Ray-traced shadows are ideal for simulating bright light sources, especially sunlight. The only drawback is that these shadows require extensive calculations during a rendering. Because the area calculated for each spotlight is based on its falloff, constraining their radii to smaller, specific areas can save considerable rendering time.

Ray Trace Bias

The only parameter that controls the effects of ray-traced shadows is the Ray Trace Bias setting. This is not immediately obvious within the light's Shadow Parameters rollout because the three shadow map parameters remain editable when the Ray-Traced Shadows option is selected.

Unlike shadow map parameters, this value rarely needs to be adjusted. A value of 1.0 forms no bias, whereas large values begin to pull the shadow away from the casting object and lower values try to pull it closer. This value needs to be adjusted if the object's casting shadows contain self-intersecting elements. Ray-traced shadows that contain holes when they should be solid or do not engage the shadow-casting mesh have bias values that are too high and need to be reduced.

Using Shadow Maps

The primary capability of a shadow map is to create soft shadows. This is a more realistic effect than ray-traced shadows but can be difficult to achieve because its control is a critical balance of its map parameters. Casting shadows with shadow maps requires memory but renders faster than ray-traced shadows, especially within a complex model. The trade-off, however, is that shadow maps take preparation time and constant testing to ensure their accuracy and appropriateness.

In real life, the crispness of a shadow is a product of the object's proximity to the surface on which it is casting a shadow. A window that casts a shadow of its mullions across the room is very soft, whereas the chair that sits in the same light casts a very crisp shadow. Because of this duality, you might consider using multiple shadow-casting lights having different shadow effects for scenes that require extreme realism.

You may find that the realistic effect of soft shadows is lost on many people who view your work. To the majority of lay people, the definition of a shadow is a crisp, definite shape cast from the object. If you do not have the opportunity to examine the shadow, such as in an animation, the sophisticated effects gained from soft shadows are nearly always lost.

Shadow Map Size and Shadow Quality

The shadow map's size is the most critical and expensive factor in getting a shadow "right." The Renderer creates a square bitmap to the size specified in the Map Size parameter. The memory cost for this map is four bytes per map pixel, so a 500-line shadow map costs 500×500×4 = 1 MB of RAM. This map is then stretched to the size of all shadow-casting objects with the light's falloff cone and projected back onto the receiving surfaces.

Because the shadow map is actually a bitmap, the shadow begins to pixelate and form jagged edges if it is not at least the size of the rendered area. The larger the shadow casting object's extents, the more the shadow map is stretched and the higher its resolution needs to be to maintain an unaliased edge. You can limit the mapped areas size, and thus the size of the required shadow map, by constraining the spotlight's falloff. You can also decrease the shadow map's extents by turning off the cast shadows attribute of distant objects.

NOTE

Overshoot is extremely useful with shadow maps because their effect can be localized without creating distinct pools of light.

Map Bias and Engagement Accuracy

The Map Bias value is basically used to fix the inherent inaccuracy shadow maps have in engaging the objects that cast them. The lower the bias value, the more the shadow is pulled to the object.

Map Bias values of 1.0 for architectural models and 3.0 for broadcast-design work are generally recommended. It is very important not to use these values without first experimenting with them in your scene. Each model's, and possibly each spotlight's, needs vary according to the light's angle and distance and the final output resolution. In addition, the size of the scene casting shadows plays an important factor in the engagement accuracy of shadow maps.

Map Sample Range and Edge Softness

The Map Sample Range value controls the softness of the shadow's edge—the higher the value, the softer the shadow edge. The key word in this parameter is "sample" because the program actually samples more of the surrounding edge to blur the result together to create the soft edge. The quality and accuracy of this edge is, as always, a balance of the shadow map bias, size, and sample range.

As the sample values increase, so does the shadow's softness. The time it takes to render these soft shadows increases as well because the program is averaging more samples over a larger area of the shadow bitmap. Note that these values are specific to the given resolution, bias map size, spotlight distance, and size of the scene; differing values vary proportionately.

Some observers might be disturbed because the shadow does not get softer as it falls away from the object. In real life, the shadow is sharpest where the object touches the shadow-receiving surface and softest at its far tip. 3DS MAX, however, does not do this naturally. When your result calls for high resolution images that have time to be scrutinized, you may have a problem and should consider carefully when choosing between ray-traced and shadow-map shadows.

Each object has shadow exclusion capabilities built into its attribute definitions. When these attributes are combined with the exclusion capabilities of lights, the capability to create special lighting effects is considerable.

As you can see from figure 19.5 shown earlier in the chapter, you can control whether objects cast or receive shadows, on a per light basis. The use of these attributes is unique for every model, but remember that using them does save in rendering time. This is especially true for objects that take up a great deal of the scene, such as ground planes, walls, and ceilings. Most of the time, these objects do not need to cast shadows, and ceilings do not need to receive them. Turning off the appropriate attributes saves considerable rendering time and makes shadow maps much more accurate.

Shadows are very important, but too many shadows may be unnecessary or distracting. In this regard, careful selection of where shadows are cast both speeds up rendering time, as well as realism in a scene. In addition to casting shadows, lights have another useful function, and that is to project an image.

Projecting Images

Spot and Directional lights can project images and animated materials in a slide/film projector fashion and, in doing so, open up many special-effect possibilities. The colors of the projected image blend with the light's and reduce the amount of light according to the bitmap colors' luminance values. Black completely blocks light, whereas white does not stop any light.

Projector lights actually have a strong tradition of use in the theater and interior/lighting design. One of the most traditional effects is when the image is opaque (black on white) and casts a shadow rather than an image. When used in this manner, a projector light is often called a *gobo light*. Implying cast shadows with this technique can create dramatic and memory efficient effects within 3DS MAX, as shown in figures 19.11 and 19.12.

FIGURE 19.11
A gobo cutout for a projector's bitmap.

Projected Lights

Spot and directional lights have the capability to project an image when their Projector option is activated. Clicking the Assign button brings up the Material Editor's Material/Map Browser (see fig. 19.13). From here, you can choose an existing map channel that is defined in the Material Editor, the scene, a library, or define a new one. Once you have chosen a map channel, its name is labeled on the light's Map button. Clicking this button allows you to assign the map channel to a particular slot in Material Editor slot for adjustment. You can also retrieve projected maps used in the scene from the Material Editor by browsing from the scene.

NOTE

If an animated map type is chosen as the projector image each frame is shown in sequence when a range of frames is rendered. The slide projector is thus turned into a movie projector. The animation may be an animated file type such as AVI, a sequence of files in a gobo, or the result of animated parameters in the chosen map channel.

The projected bitmap is stretched to fit the limits of the spotlight's falloff. For a circular spotlight, the bitmap is stretched to the boundary square that encloses the circle, and the image is clipped by the circle. You can match the aspect ratio of rectangular lights to that of the projected image with the Bitmap Fit option.

FIGURE 19.13

*The Material/Map
Browser.*

NOTE

When the Projector option is used in conjunction with Overshoot, the image is still constrained to the size of the falloff. This edge, however, is aliased if the projected image's edge color (that is, background) blocks the spotlight's color. Because white never mixes additively, it should be the first choice for an image's background as long as the light has a positive multiplier.

TIP

Including a one-pixel-wide white perimeter on projected bitmaps eliminates the harsh aliasing that occurs when the projecting spotlight is employing overshoot.

Adjusting Light Projections

A projector light's falloff border should really be thought of as a Planar Projection icon because it acts in exactly the same way. The proportions and rotation of the bitmap are dictated by the placement of the border. The border has a small vertical line to indicate the top of a projection.

The proportions of a circular spotlight are obviously fixed, but those of a rectangular one can be adjusted with either the light's Aspect or the Bitmap Fit commands.

When projecting an image, the Bitmap Fit option should be your first choice because it is easiest, most accurate, and most relevant (see fig. 19.14). Select a rectangular spotlight and access the Bitmap Fit command. After selecting the desired bitmap, which more than likely is the projected image, the light's rectangular height and width is changed to match the image.

FIGURE 19.14
Bitmap Fit sizes a projection spotlight to fit the relative height and width of a bitmap.

NOTE

The projected image can be rotated, and its rotation can even be animated. This is done in the projector map's material settings, in the Material Editor.

Setting Up the Environment

This section describes the many capabilities of 3DS MAX's Environment. Using the Environment enables you to create effects and moods that heighten a scene's realism by adding volume lighting, standard, layered, and volume fog, as well as combustion. These atmospheric controls offer a wide variety of effects, including fog, haze, fire, smoke, and dusty light rays.

NOTE

Note that all atmospheric effects work only in Perspective and Camera views, and some work only with Cameras.

Setting Up Backgrounds

A background can include either a solid color or a material. Choosing the color swatch in the Rendering/Environment dialog brings up the 3DS MAX color selector, allowing precise control of the background color. Choosing a new color does not remove the possibility of saving the alpha channel information.

TIP

For times when you do not desire the rendered image to be aliased with the background, add the line *DontAntialiasAgainstBackground=1* below the [Renderer] section of the 3dsmax.ini to remove aliasing against the background. Removing aliasing is useful for rendering sprites against a solid background, or for creating borderless graphics for the Web, cutting out the extraneous background. If a [Renderer] section does not exist, you need to add one.

Selecting a background image is similar to using a projector map for lights. Select the Environment Map Assign button to bring up the 3DS MAX Material/Map browser. From there, a custom map can be made or an existing map can be applied.

Using Volume Lights

Volume lights provide the ability to fill a light cone with particles so the beam or halo becomes evident in the rendering. In computer graphics this is commonly known as volumetric lighting, and when shadows interrupt the cone, volumetric shadows. This effect is applied to existing light objects in the scene through the Atmosphere section of the Environment controls. A Volume light atmosphere can be assigned to numerous lights, and several Volume lights can be used throughout the scene to give local control. Volume lights have a wide variety of parameters that can alter the light's look considerably. A light's color, density, volume brightness and darkness, attenuation, and noise attributes are all easily controlled within 3DS MAX's Environment dialog.

In order to use Volume lights, a light object must first exist. Then, after adding the Volume light to the Environment dialog, a light or series of lights can be assigned to the Volume light's settings. Although many lights can be assigned to one Volume light configuration, optimal results sometimes occur when all the lights don't have the same parameters.

It is important to note that the order in which Volume light effects are layered in the Environment dialog has an effect on how they are rendered (see fig. 9.15). Their order is controlled by the Move Up and Move Down buttons. Effects near the bottom of the list are layered in front of effects near the top of the list. Careful placement of atmospheric effects layers will help avoid any odd layering situations, where a Volume light in the background appears to be in front of another in the foreground.

FIGURE 19.15

Volume light parameters are accessed in the Environment dialog.

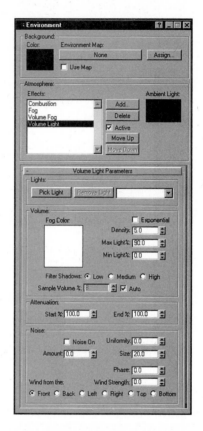

Several important parameters control the light's general look. Certainly, the Volume light's color affects everything else about the light. White is the default but is not always the most appropriate. A Volume light's color should be considered as a part of an overall lighting design. Careful use of volumetric light color can add a tremendous effect to the scene's feel. Keep in mind that Volume light is additive and that the color of the light's glow changes an object's original color according to the intensity of the glow.

Aside from its color, the Density, Max Light, and Min Light parameters are important in controlling the look of a Volume light. Density controls the light's volumetric density. The greater the value, the more opaque the entire light becomes. Looking around in nature, a really dense light is found only in dense atmospheric conditions, such as in fog. Unless you are creating a very dense atmosphere, therefore, keep the light density fairly low. The default value is 5, and a value between 2 and 6 is recommended.

After Density, the Max Light and Min Light parameters are used to control how the light dissipates. The Max Light controls the "whitest" glow of the light, and the Min Light controls the minimum glow. Note that the Min Light, if set greater than 0 creates a glow to the entire scene, similar to how Ambient light controls the entire scene. Also, a Max Light value of 100 is only as bright as is allowed by the Density parameter. To increase the brightness of the glow, increase the density.

Noise can also be added to the volumetric light, which gives the impression of a dustier environment. When the Noise parameter is enabled, additional parameters become available, including Amount, Uniformity, Size, Phase, Wind Strength, and Wind Direction. The Amount and Size parameters control the amount and size of the noise added. Uniformity controls whether the noise is an even haze or a spotty turbulence. The remaining parameters, Phase, Wind Strength, and Wind Direction all control the look of the volumetric light as it is animated. Wind Direction is rather self-explanatory, but it is important to note that Phase and Wind Strength affect each other. Phase is the value that is to be animated, but the noise's movement is affected by Wind Strength. If there is no Wind Strength, Phase makes only the noise churn, but it does appear to go anywhere. With Wind Strength, a volumetric light appears to have particles that move through the scene following its Wind Direction.

NOTE

A good example of animated noise in a volumetric light is envlite2.max (see fig. 19.16) in 3D Studio MAX's SCENES directory. All the scenes beginning with ENV are good files to explore for feature environment controls.

Using Fog and Volume Fog

3DS MAX has several types of fog; all have similar but unique uses (see fig. 19.17):

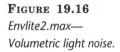

FIGURE 19.16
Envlite2.max—
Volumetric light noise.

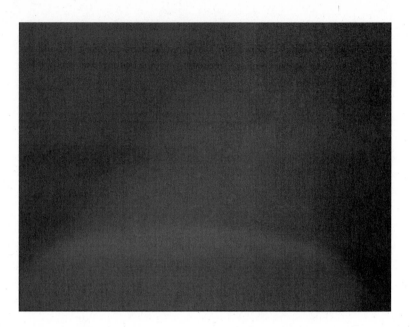

- **Standard Fog**   3DS MAX's standard fog is probably the simplest to set up and gives a general atmospheric wash to the scene. Requiring a camera, Standard Fog's depth is controlled by the camera's environment ranges. Standard Fog can use a material for the fog's color allowing a wide range of colored and textured fog. An opacity map can also be applied, giving an uneven density across the view.

NOTE

The Near and Far % values affect the fog in an inverse manner of Volume Lights. With Fog, nothing is visible past 100%. This also means that, without any background geometry, the fog is rendered at 100% and comes out as a solid color. When Exponential is checked, the rate at which it goes from 0% to 100% is exponential, dramatically changing the look of the fog.

- **Layered Fog**   A layered fog atmosphere enables you to define a floating slab of fog that is fixed in place, independent of your camera placement. The slab is always parallel to your Top viewport, but you have complete control over its vertical start and stop points with the Top and Bottom parameters. These values refer to unit distances along the vertical axis and position and are fixed for the scene.

  The layered fog's position is not fixed. You can animate the effect of lifting fog by animating its Top and Bottom parameters. All other parameters are animatable as well, by using the Animate button.

FIGURE 19.17

Standard/Layered Fog settings.

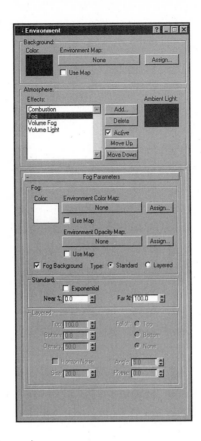

Varying a fog's density allows for a wide variety of fog, from a light mist to a fully opaque wall of fog. Layered fog has a uniform density of 50% of the object color, and uneven density is achievable with the use of an opacity map.

TIP

Layered fog has a clear, straight horizon. This effect is useful when the horizon is far away, but sometimes looks unnatural. Noise can be added, blending the horizon, which is often useful with scenes that do not offer a clear, distant horizon.

■ **Volume Fog** This type of fog is useful in creating animated clouds that can blow or be flown through (see fig. 19.18). The effect is a true 3D effect, and varies within space and time. Volume Fog is controlled similarly to other fog types, as well as volumetric noise. Wind Strength controls the speed of the wind and is used in conjunction with an animated phase parameter to create moving fog.

FIGURE 19.18
Volume Fog settings.

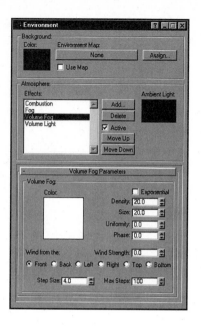

Using Combustion

Combustion, which was originally a plug-in available for download, is now included in 1.1 of 3DS MAX. This atmospheric effect is great for creating animated fire, smoke, and explosions. Because it is not a particle effect and does not generate geometry, it renders and uses less memory than other types of effects.

Combustion uses an atmospheric apparatus that can be a sphere or hemisphere. The apparatus contains the combustion effect, and its size and height can be animated over time, allowing a flame to flare up or die down, as well as move around the scene. Multiple apparatus can use the same combustion effect, as well as different combust configurations. Combust uses a random number generator at each apparatus to create its randomness, but can also be reproduced exactly by using the same seed value.

An atmospheric apparatus is a physical object and is found in the Create/ Helpers command panel Atmosphere Apparatus sub-category (see fig. 19.19). The apparatus can be either a sphere or a hemisphere, depending on the desired effect. These apparatus can be nonuniformly scaled in dimension, and can even be animated, allowing flames to "grow," and rocket jets to increase in power.

FIGURE 19.19

Creating an Atmospheric Apparatus.

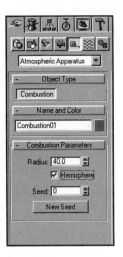

Like other atmospheric effects, it is easily animated by animating the phase value over time. Combust contains a specific order in which its effects happen. The effect of the phase values differ, depending on whether Explosion is enabled. When enabled, phase values 0–100 are the start-up values of the effect, growing to full intensity when reaching 100. Phase 100–200 is when the explosion burns off and the fire turns into smoke. Phase 200–300 is when the smoke dissipates and Combust is completed. When Explosion is not enabled, the phase controls the speed at which the flame churns. See figure 19.20.

Animating a flame's phase values should be linear, meaning they do not accelerate over time but keep a steady rate. Explosions, however, should quickly rise to 100 and then gradually taper off until 300 is reached. Specific information on Combustion's many features can be found in the 3D Studio MAX 1.1 online help.

Combust can either be set to be a Fire Ball, with no discernible top or bottom, or Tendril, which emulates a common flame. Fire Ball is a good choice for explosions and looks good joined with other hemisphere apparatus in a clump.

NOTE

Envxplod.max (see fig. 19.21) is a good example of an animated combust explosion. This file, as well as env_burn.max and env_fire.max, which are both good examples of animated fire, are found in 3DS MAX's scenes directory or on its CD.

FIGURE 19.20

Combustion settings.

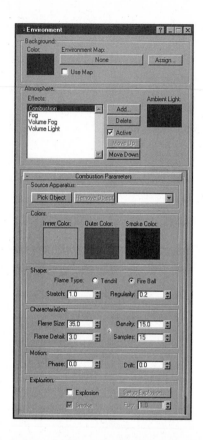

FIGURE 19.21

Env_fire.max is an example of flaming combustion.

NOTE

Note that Combust is not a light source and does not emit flickering light that would normally be seen in a real fire. Animated light sources are still needed to complete the effect.

Establishing Moods

Moods are challenging to create. Often, a moody environment is not registered and remembered for its specifics but rather registers as a feeling. This makes creating a mood even more difficult because it requires a considerable amount of deliberate observation to notice all the elements that make up a moody atmosphere.

Light Beams and Glow Lights

Beams of sunlight through a window and the hazy glow around a street light are just two examples of how a light's atmosphere affects the world. Without atmosphere, light would merely illuminate objects because there would be no atmosphere to reflect the light to begin with. For instance, in an atmospherically controlled room, light would be flat because of the lack of dust and humidity in the air. These things, although rather subtle, are important in creating a realistic, dusty world.

With 3DS MAX's volumetric lighting, light beams and glowing lights are quite simple to add to a scene. By turning down the density and keeping a wide attenuation span, a nice glowing street light can be created. Similarly, a spotlight or directional light can add a nice shaft of light, from which shadows can be cast.

Smoke, Haze, and Mist

Careful use of fog can add subtle touches of atmosphere that are otherwise difficult to achieve with lights and textures. Smoke, haze, and mist all soften the scene and tend to join the different elements. Animated volumetric fog can create realistic fog and clouds that can be used to give a scene depth and a sense of belonging to a larger world. Certainly, fog can overwhelm the scene, covering everything with a white blanket, washing out all color and detail, as well as taking away any compositional strengths. But with some attention and time, fog can add a moody, natural feel to an animation.

Radiosity Effects

When omni lights are used with exclusion and ranges, they are ideal sources for simulating radiosity and inherited color. This approach slows the rendering process more than adjusting the material's ambient color value but creates a very realistic effect.

Implementing this technique takes some careful observation of a lit environment. Naturally, light often falls off in areas, such as under tables and chairs, as well as in corners of dimly lit rooms. Use of a negative multiplier and an attenuated omni light enables these areas to be carved out while retaining a brighter value and extended attenuation ranges to light brighter areas of a room.

Lighting with Fixtures

When you try to approximate real-life lighting situations, you should pay careful attention to how lamps actually cast light. Overdramatizing a lighting effect and casting harsh-edged light is a common mistake. Most light does not occur in this fashion and is much more diffused, soft, and without definite light pools. Lighting designers and architects go to great lengths to place and space fixtures so that they do not create hotspots, scallops, or solitary pools. Lighting manufacturers try to manufacture lights that distribute light evenly and without pattern. Both of these practices are difficult in the real world, and you may find them equally difficult to simulate in 3DS MAX.

Interior Light Fixtures

There are often times, especially in architectural renderings, when simulation of interior lighting is essential. Although this may take additional time to ensure a realistic look, nice effects are certainly achievable.

Most lighting designers strive for even illumination in most areas and reserve dramatic lighting to call attention to architectural details or artwork or to act as a patterned light design on its own. Overemphasizing light sources and their impact is unfortunately all too common in computer renderings. Just because a light source is present does not mean that its effect is blatantly obvious.

Can lights are a typical example of this tendency. Many modelers feel that they must show the effects of each light; after all, they are there and they have been positioned and possibly even modeled. To make their presence clear, their light is often strong and their hotspots sharp. The result is *pools of light*—a characteristic that has its uses for highlighting certain objects—but that is generally considered poor lighting design. The correct way to illuminate the scene is to use broad soft lights that gently overlap and whose light pools are not particularly discernible.

Sconces and Light Scallops

Wall sconces are elements of lighting design that require emphasis of their effects. These indirect lights are often used to create scalloped light pools on the wall as they illuminate the ceiling—the intent being to light that area of the room indirectly by bouncing light off of the ceiling. Because 3DS MAX's lights do not do this automatically (only a radiosity renderer can), their effect must be simulated, as shown in figure 19.22.

FIGURE 19.22
Light scallops from spotlights with varying hotspots.

The quality of the light scallop is controlled by the hotspot's size, not the spotlight's intensity. These effects did not require the use of shadows or even attenuation. A common misconception is that to get these effects requires the falloff to exceed the size of the fixture and cast a shadow to form the cutoff, producing a crisp edge and taking considerably longer to render. In actuality, you need to do this only when the lighting fixtures are transparent or translucent, and you need to cast the shadows of their enclosure. Because light cannot be reflected in 3DS MAX, simulating bounced light (radiosity) requires an additional light source.

Linear Light Sources

Rectangular spot and directional lights provide a method to simulate the illumination of linear light sources such as fluorescent lights. When made rectangular and carefully controlled with attenuation and falloff, these lights can simulate linear lights quite well. The directional light's illumination will be quite strong as compared to the spotlight's, which is further adjusted by the fact that it is a point light source. The choice of which to use is dependent on the desired effect. For the most even light, the directional light is often the best choice.

Simulating Signage Illumination

Glowing signs are objects that users often need to simulate. But before modeling the mesh and placing the lights, take a good look at how the sign is really supposed to illuminate the scene.

Most signage is meant to be read, and the primary characteristic of making a sign readable is contrast. Contrast is created from color and illumination, which is why most signs do not illuminate the wall on which they are placed, but rather cast light forward. The edges or side walls of most signs are opaque and the backside of neon is painted black, preventing them from casting light onto their field and lowering, if not eliminating, their contrast.

Considering its needs, the self-illuminated material type works fairly well for signage. The object appears to glow because it has no ambient shading and does not cast light onto its surrounding area. For an added touch, the Glow filter included in Video Post adds a nice aura around a light source, revealing a slightly richer atmosphere. If the sign is freestanding or isolated on a wall's face, it is complete; there is no need for it to actually cast light if there is nothing to receive it. If the sign is close to another plane, it requires the creation of additional light sources to complete the illusion of self-illumination.

Self-Illuminated Signage

The most common form of lit signage is the *self-illuminated sign*. The self-illuminated sign usually takes the form of isolated letters with translucent faces that project colored light (see fig. 19.23). This type of sign is straight-forward.

FIGURE 19.23

A simulation of self-illuminated signage.

Starting with the desired text, use of self-illuminated materials (85% illuminated is a good starting point) and, possibly Glow, enables a simple self-illumination without special lighting.

Backlit Signage

One form of signage that illuminates its mounting plane is *backlit signage*. Backlit signage casts light from the back of the letters onto a plane, putting the text in a bright silhouette. Actually, you can easily create this effect by using the spotlight's exclude option, excluding the text, and illuminating the wall. Figure 19.24 shows such an effect.

FIGURE 19.24

The simulation of a backlit sign.

Simulating Neon Signage

One of the most interesting lighting forms is neon. The curves and shapes that are possible and the intense colors that are emitted, make it a popular effect to simulate. It also is one that puzzles many modelers. Look closely at a neon sign and you notice that it casts little illumination of its own. The letters themselves are quite bright, but the light given off can only be described as a saturated glow, actually making it easier to simulate (see fig. 19.25).

The previous figure illustrates a technique that is adequate for closely spaced neon signage, but not very good for neon that is diverse in its form. Strip and free-form artistic neon are now simple tasks with the use of Glow. Figure 19.26 is an example of Glow used in free-form neon. By using a material effects channel and a lofted shape, creating free-form neon is a simple task.

FIGURE 19.25
The simulation of neon signage.

FIGURE 19.26
Free-form neon signage, using Glow.

In Practice: Utilizing Lighting and Atmosphere

- **Triangle lighting**   For many scenes, this lighting style may be the ticket to a well lit scene. For larger scenes, move the lights out away from the objects—this will help to dissipate a light's intensity across the scene and help remove hotspots.

- **Attenuation**   This is a good place to start when lighting a scene. Very few lights illuminate objects far away, and the use of attenuation is essential in simulating this.

- **Shadows: raytraced versus shadow maps**   Both types of shadows have their strengths and limitations, and their use should be determined by assessing these factors. Raytraced shadows are easier to set up, and cast the most accurate shadow—but take longer to render—and always have a crisp edge to them. Shadow maps offer a soft edged shadow, and require less rendering time—but take up more memory, and have several settings that must be monitored in order to look realistic.

- **Projecting images**   Spotlights and directional lights have the capability to project images, which is useful for a variety of things, such as simulating a movie projector and projecting complex shadows.

- **Volume lights**   These lights are good for creating atmosphere in a scene and offer a wide array of features. Foggy, dusty, and misty lights are all possible, which can be used to remove the sterile edge of a 3D rendered scene.

- **Lighting with fixtures**   For realistic worlds, fixtures should be used to physically place the lights in 3D space. Without such physical fixtures, light in a scene seems to come from out of nowhere, and oftentimes, the viewer is subtly aware that something is not quite right. Careful attention to realistic light fixtures aids in reproducing such fixtures.

Image created by Peter Noldt
Arch Image
Houston, TX

Chapter 20

CAMERAS AND SETTING THE SHOT

The camera is the backbone of animation. Without a camera you could still animate the objects within a scene, but you would have to render your animation from a flat left, right, front, top viewport. Boring. With cameras an entire world of cinematography opens up to the animator and provides the capability to experiment with focal lengths, camera movement, and other effects — all of which will be described in this chapter.

3D Studio MAX offers some of the best tools to work with cameras that enable animators to create incredible animation to rival what comes from Hollywood. With 3DS MAX, animators have control over every aspect of the camera, from creation to output resolution.

This chapter explores the following topics:

- Creating a camera object
- The importance of naming cameras
- Placing the camera
- Moving the camera
- Using clipping panes
- Simulating camera techniques

Before becoming Steven Spielberg or Orson Welles, however, you need to know and understand the fundamentals of creating and placing a camera in 3DS MAX.

Setting up Cameras

Creating a camera is a simple process. You click the Camera category button (identified by the camera icon) in the Create panel, click the type of camera desired from the Object Type rollout, and then click (for a Free Camera) or drag (for a Target camera) in any viewport. The camera is located at the point where you clicked or began dragging.

After you create a camera, it can be adjusted in two ways: by using the standard transforms of Move and Rotate on the camera and by using the camera navigation buttons with the camera viewport.

Creating Camera Objects

Two types of cameras are available in 3D Studio MAX: Target cameras and Free cameras. Each has its own strengths and weaknesses.

Target cameras comprise two objects: the camera and the camera target. The camera represents your eyepoint, and the target indicates the point you are looking at. You can transform the camera and its target independently, but the camera is constrained to always look at its target. To create a Target camera complete the following steps:

1. Click the Camera category in the Create panel.

2. Click Target in the Object Type rollout.

3. In a Top view, click the mouse where you want the camera placed and then drag and release where you want the target located.

By design, Target cameras try to keep their up vector (the camera's local Y axis) aligned with the world Z axis. Creating Target cameras in a top view sets the camera with the correct initial alignment and provides the most predictable results. Creating a Target camera in other views—where it is easy to set the camera to look straight up or down—can cause unpredictable camera rotations.

Target cameras are your best choice for general purpose camera work. The capability to transform both the camera and camera target provide you with the greatest flexibility for setting up and animating camera views. The Target camera's designed tendency to orient itself with the world Z axis also matches our natural expectations of real-world cameras.

Free cameras are a single object, the camera. Because Free cameras have no target, they define their look-at point as being an arbitrary distance along their negative local Z axis. To create a Free camera, complete the following steps:

1. Click the Camera category in the Create panel.

2. Click Free in the Object Type rollout.

3. Click in any viewport to create the Free camera.

The Free camera is placed in the scene with it's Local coordinate system aligned with the coordinate system of the current construction plane. Because the Free camera's line of sight is along its negative local Z axis, the camera's default view is always looking into the construction plane. For example, a Free camera created in a top view is looking down, and a Free camera created in a left view is looking to the right.

Because Free cameras have no target to look at, they are more difficult to set up and aim than a Target camera; Free cameras have absolutely no sense of which direction is up. The issue of not knowing which way is up is the Free camera's advantage. Free cameras are not limited by the rotational constraints caused by trying to maintain an up-vector as with Target cameras. Free cameras are best suited for complex animation where the camera is used to fly through a scene with many banks and vertical orientations, such as when a camera is mounted on a roller coaster or a fighter plane.

You define the area viewed by the camera by setting two interdependent camera parameters: field of view (FOV) and lens focal length. These two parameters describe a single camera property so changing the FOV parameter also changes the Lens parameter and vice-versa. Use FOV framing the camera view and for cinematic effect.

Setting Field of View

Field of view (FOV) describes the area of the scene that the camera sees. The value of the FOV parameter is the horizontal angle of the camera's view cone.

3DS MAX uses an FOV definition that is different from a real-world camera FOV. 3DS MAX cameras use a horizontal FOV defined as the angle between the left and right sides of the camera view cone. Real-world cameras use a diagonal FOV defined as the angle between the lower-left corner and the upper-right corner of the camera view cone.

This difference between 3DS MAX FOV and real-world FOV is of consequence only if you are trying to match a shot taken by a real 35 mm camera. Fortunately, 3DS MAX compensates for this difference when calculating lens length and FOV angle. To correctly match a 35 mm camera view, always specify the lens length by using the Lens parameter and let 3DS MAX calculate the horizontal FOV.

Setting Focal Lengths or the Lens Parameter

Focal length, which describes the size of a lens, is always measured in millimeters. The smaller the Lens parameter, the wider the FOV and farther away from the object the camera appears to be. The larger the Lens parameter, or longer as it is most often referred, the narrower the FOV and closer to the object the camera appears to be. Lenses shorter than 50 mm are referred to as *wide-angle lenses,* whereas those longer than 50 mm are called *telephoto lenses.*

Wide-angle lenses are used for establishing shots or setting the scene in the first few frames of an animation, whereas telephoto lenses place the viewer directly in the picture. Because the wide-angle lens has a shorter focal length than the telephoto lens, it can include more information in the picture. As well, a telephoto lens may include fewer objects that compose the entire scene.

Figures 20.1 through 20.7 show how different lenses affect the look of a scene. The scene is exactly the same in each image, and the camera has not been moved—only the focal length of the camera lens has been changed.

FIGURE 20.1

15 mm lens.

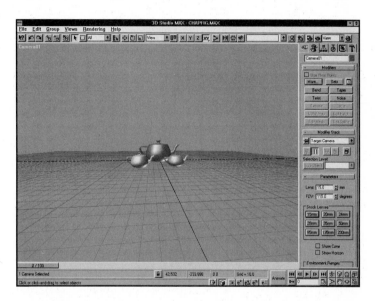

FIGURE 20.2

20 mm lens.

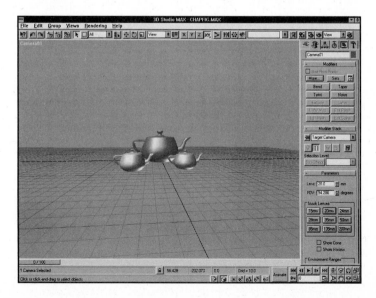

FIGURE 20.3

35 mm lens.

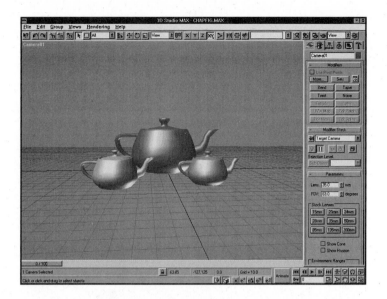

FIGURE 20.4

50 mm lens.

FIGURE 20.5
85 mm lens.

FIGURE 20.6
135 mm lens.

FIGURE 20.7

200 mm lens.

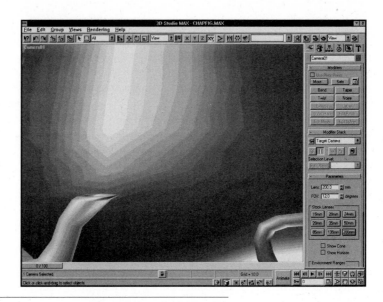

The Importance of Naming Cameras

Many times with a complex model or animation sequence, you want to create numerous cameras to view the scene from different angles. When you have numerous cameras within a scene, it is important to give each camera a unique name that describes its role in the scene. The default name for a camera is—creatively—camera01. All subsequent cameras created in a scene are called—equally creatively—camera02, camera03, and so on.

To alleviate confusion when choosing which camera you want to view or when selecting cameras by name, change the name of the camera to groundcam or closeupcam or dollycam or carcam. Use names that either describe the camera's location/angle, action, or the object on which the camera focuses.

Placing the Camera

After creating a camera, usually you need to move the camera or its target into a final position.

You can use transforms to position the camera, but in many cases it is easier to adjust the camera from within a Camera view. The following sections describe how to use the camera view navigation controls and how to transform cameras. However, you should be familiar with a couple of issues.

First, it is sometimes difficult to select the camera target because of its placement over an object within a scene. In this case, select the camera object, right-click and then choose Select Target from the pop-up menu. You can also select a camera target by choosing Cameras from the Selection Filters list on the toolbar and then clicking the target. If you expect to adjust the target repeatedly, it is wise to lock the selection by clicking on the Lock icon in the toolbar or pressing the spacebar.

Second, when you activate the camera viewport, the camera object is not automatically selected. Any previously selected object in the scene remains selected.

Using Camera View Navigation Buttons

The navigation controls for use within a camera view give you a great deal of control and flexibility. In other views, cameras and their targets are selected and transformed as you would transform any other object.

To set up a camera view, complete the following steps:

1. Create cameras.

2. Activate a viewport.

3. Press C and choose the camera you want to use for the camera view from the Select Camera dialog.

   If you have only one camera in the scene, that camera is automatically selected and the Select Camera dialog does not appear.

   You could also right-click a viewport label and choose a camera from the Views item of the viewport properties pop-up menu.

The view navigation buttons for a camera view transform the active camera and change the camera parameters as follows:

- **Dolly**   Moves the camera away from or toward its target along the line of sight. Dolly is the same as moving a camera on its local Z axis. Dragging down dollies out away from the target; dragging up dollies in toward the target.

- **Perspective**   Dollies the camera, as described previously, and also changes the FOV. The result is that you maintain the same general view composition and either flatten or exaggerate the amount of perspective in the view. Dragging down dollies away from the target and narrows FOV; dragging up dollies in toward the target and widens the FOV.

- **Roll**   Rotates the camera about its own line of sight. Roll is the same as rotating a camera about its local Z axis. Drag left or right to change the roll angle.

- **FOV**   Changes the FOV for the camera. Drag down to widen the FOV increasing the area viewed by the camera; drag up to narrow the FOV decreasing the area viewed.

- **Truck**   Moves the camera and its target perpendicular to the line of sight. Truck is the same as moving the camera and it target on the camera's local XY plane.

- **Pan and Orbit**   These flyout buttons affect how the camera rotates around the scene. Pan rotates the target around the camera, much like swiveling the camera on a tripod. Orbit rotates the camera around the target, similar to a circular trucking shot. For Free cameras, the Target Distance sets the point about which the camera orbits. The Target Distance is in the Free camera's Parameters rollout.

TIP

By holding down the Ctrl button while dragging in the viewport, you can constrain the pan and orbit to the vertical or horizontal axis, which is determined by the first direction you drag.

The use of the camera view navigation commands is essential in positioning the camera in the desired location in the scene and for setting up the type of angles and effects you want for your animation. Many times it may be necessary to move the camera in a viewport other than the camera viewport, but detail and fine adjusts are best left to the transforms that are performed in the camera viewport.

Transforming Cameras

Cameras and targets can be transformed much like any other object in your scene. As mentioned in the previous section, many of the camera view navigation commands can be duplicated by transforming a camera on its local axes.

Keep the following issues in mind when transforming camera objects:

- Do not scale cameras. The scale transforms cause the camera base parameters to display false values.

- Target cameras can rotate only about their local Z axis. Attempting to rotate Target cameras about their X or Y local axis has no effect.

- A useful technique is to rotate Target cameras using the Pick coordinate system and picking the camera target. This produces results similar to Orbit.

- Free cameras have none of the rotation restrictions of Target cameras.

Safe Frame

Safe Frame is an invaluable feature that shows how the final image will be cropped in your rendering. Three rectangles make up the Safe Frame: the Live Area (outermost rectangle), Action Safe (middle), and Title Safe (inner). The Live Area shows the area that will actually be rendered, regardless of the size or aspect ratio of the viewport. Action Safe shows the area in which it is safe to include your rendered action (the area not overshot or clipped on most TV screens). Title Safe shows the area in which it is safe to include titles or other information (low distortion in this area on most TVs). Because the Safe Frame rectangle is proportional, the output sizes of 600×400 and 3000×2000, for example, will have the same Safe Frame. See figures 20.8 and 20.9.

FIGURE 20.8

You can see the Safe Frame in the Perspective and Camera views. Safe Frame can be used in any viewport and can illustrate the areas where clipping may occur and where titles can be placed safely.

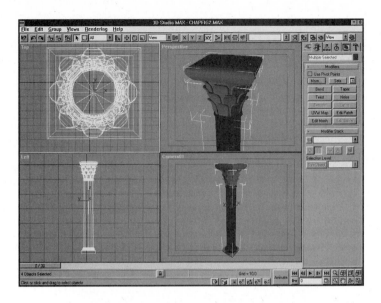

FIGURE 20.9

Users can adjust the three Safe Frame rectangles. This dialog can be found by choosing Views, Viewport Configuration, Safe Frames.

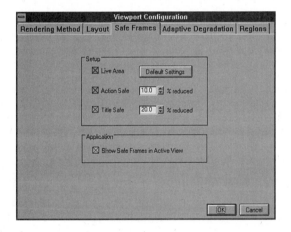

You can tailor the size of the inner border to your system's needs with the Safe Frame value located within Views/Viewport Configuration. Within this dialog you can turn on Safe Frames, set which areas you want shown, and reduce the percentage of both the Action Safe and Title Safe areas.

Using Safe Frames is very important when preparing for final render. If you do not use Safe Frames in your camera viewports, you may be cropping important elements that you wish the audience to see, or you might find that elements fly into or out of the scene more quickly or slowly than you had planned. Using Safe Frame should become second nature during any animation project so that there will be no surprises after a 24-hour rendering spree.

Moving the Camera

In the next section you will read about the theory behind camera movement during an animation, but first it is important to understand the basics of camera movement within a scene so that you can set up the shots you want to animate.

With Target cameras, the target is an aid for positioning your line of sight. The target's distance from the camera has no effect on the composition. The line connecting the camera and target visually shows the center line of sight.

When cameras and their targets are moved, they keep a constant field of view. As you move the target away from the camera, the displayed field of view cone grows, but keeps the same angle. This is equivalent to moving about the scene with a fixed 35 mm lens—the composition is constantly changing, but the lens size and field of view are not. To change the field of view, and switch lenses, you can either change the camera's FOV or Lens parameters, or click the FOV view navigation button in a camera view.

Cameras are different from other objects in that their movements always define time and speed from the audience's point of view. Although object motion may sometimes go unnoticed, camera motion rarely does. Moving cameras is usually a study in fluid motions. The camera represents the audience and the camera target represents the audience's point of interest. It is important, therefore, to make movements and pans at natural speeds, with comfortable and fluid transitions.

Careful pans require many frames so that the motion is not jerky and unsettling to the viewer. If the observer is looking up, down, and around during the pan—that is, the target is scanning while the camera is moving and rotating)—even more frames are required for the animation to smoothly convey all the motion. If you want to indicate action, startlement, or sudden change in direction, reduce the number of frames for the pan.

A common mistake is to insert too many animation keys in an effort to adjust the camera's view at specific frames. Although those frames display what you want, the transitions between frames tend to be choppy, jerky, or mechanical. This common animation error often results in what is called the *bob*, where the camera moves from what was a smooth path. For fluid movement, you should specify the minimum number of keys and let 3DS MAX create smooth transitions between the keys.

In addition to animated pans, you can animate rolls and dollies. *Rolling* gives viewers the sense of tilting their head or spinning. You can use this device effectively if you are using a subjective viewpoint for your camera, for instance, in the nose of a fighter jet. A camera roll animation usually is combined with a twisting or swerving path to give the feeling of a banking movement.

The effects of a dolly motion, or zooming, are discussed in-depth in the section "Theory of Moving the Camera," but it should be noted that a dolly path that is not smooth creates an effect that is similar to moving your head in and out. Although you cannot see the path of a dolly, or FOV change, directly, you can get a feel for its smoothness by using the Play button and examining a shaded viewport.

Viewing paths after you make your camera adjustments is a wise and beneficial step so that finer adjustments can be made in reference to the path. You can view these paths by opening the Motion command panel, clicking Trajectories, and selecting the camera object. You can also click on the camera target to view the target's path. The desired path for most camera movements is smooth, with adjacent portions of the path being tangent to one another. On paths that are kinked or sharply angled, overshoot should be avoided.

You can use Bézier position controllers to make fine adjustments to an animated camera path. (For more details on controllers, see Chapter 24, "Using Controllers and Expressions.")

Creating Paths

In addition to the paths generated for cameras via transforms, you can create paths through a scene with shape objects and then assign the shape to the Camera, Target, or a Dummy object. This alternative is sometimes easier and more controllable than using the transforms, resulting in cleaner and smoother animation.

These paths can be drawn using any shape object but the most common technique is creating a line through the scene along which you want the camera to move. The advantage of this technique is that you have complete control over path curvature and do not have to rely on the key settings to adjust the spline.

To create a path for an office walk-through, complete the following steps:

1. Open the scene with your office model.

2. Maximize the Top viewport so that it is the only viewport visible.

3. Click Shapes in the Create panel and then click Line.

4. Begin drawing straight lines to create the rough path you wish the camera to travel through the scene. By holding down the button with each click to set the next vertex, you can adjust the Bézier controls to create smooth curves. Right-click to complete the line.

   You may find it helpful to freeze the objects in the scene so that you do not inadvertently select and move something when drawing the line.

5. If you created all straight lines, click the Edit Spline modifier in the Modify panel and make sure Vertex is selected in sub-object. Right-click on each vertex, check Bézier, and adjust the handles as you wish.

6. Your path is now ready to use with any camera. Free cameras are best used with complex paths, but Target cameras can be used as well when the target is linked to the camera or both the camera and target are linked to a Dummy object, as described next (see fig. 20.10).

7. Assign the path controller to the camera and assign the spline as a path.

After you create the path for your camera, you should also create a Dummy object that acts as an intermediary for the camera, the camera target, and the path. Although camera paths can be assigned directly to cameras, substantial limitations can occur. The camera, and possibly the target, are rigidly assigned to the path, and you have little room for adjustment without disturbing the fluidity of the movement. Even with the new Free camera, assigning a path directly does not result in the best possible motion. You have more opportunities for realistic motion if you link the camera or target to a moving object or Dummy object. (Dummy objects are discussed in greater detail in the section "Using Dummy objects to Build a Virtual Studio" later in this chapter.)

FIGURE 20.10
The easiest way to move a camera through a series of complex turns and movement is to draw a path and assign the path to the camera (and target if necessary) or to a Dummy object which the camera is linked to.

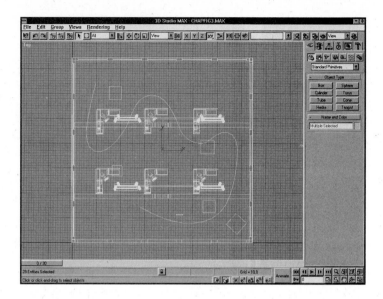

Using paths is a quick and efficient way of moving a camera through a series of complex movements within a scene. The Paths can be drawn in the exact position that you wish the camera to travel; by linking the camera and target to a Dummy object—much like a real-world camera dolly—you can achieve smooth animation.

Theory of Moving the Camera

You should not move the camera in an animation just for the sake of moving the camera. When computer animation first became popular, it seemed that every animator was swinging the camera in every direction and in all sorts of ways that are not possible in the real world. That may work for some types of animation, but with the maturation of the art, it is time to look at the movement of computer cameras and realize that they should be treated in much the same way as real-world cameras.

You can greatly affect the meaning of an animation by the way in which you move the camera. Does it dolly in or out? Does it pan with a particular object or character, or does it leave objects behind?

Dollying

As described earlier, you can move and animate the camera object in a number of ways. To dolly into a shot draws viewer's focus to the central object of the scene—in essence, telling the viewer that this object is important. Soap operas always seem to dolly, or zoom, toward a character's face at the end of every scene to add drama to what was just revealed through the dialogue. This technique, if used too often (as with soap operas), can become obvious, over dramatic, and gimmicky.

But a dolly can achieve other effects as well. For instance, when Steven Spielberg dollied his camera into the mouth of the shark in *Jaws*, most viewers experienced a sensation of dread.

A dolly can also take the viewer deeper into areas he may or may not wish to explore. When the camera dollies out of a tunnel and into the great expanse of a cave filled with riches, it is a good thing. When the camera dollies into Norman Bates' house, and the audience finds Norman's mother in the basement, it is a bad thing.

Dolly shots do not always have to be toward the main subject of the scene. Just as effective is the dolly away from the character or object of a scene, telling the viewer the character is becoming less significant to the scene or that there is separation between the viewer and the subject.

There are two ways to dolly a camera, and each creates a different feel and effect within a scene: the gradual dolly and the quick dolly. With the *gradual dolly* technique, the viewer may not even be aware that he is moving toward or away from the central subject of the scene. Use this technique when you want to create a subtle but definite effect of drawing closer to an object and establishing its importance to the viewer.

The other way to dolly a camera, a *quick dolly* or *quick zoom*, can be jarring for the viewer but effective for dramatic purposes. Quick zooms are also good in comedic situations. For example, something funny has just happened in a scene shot with a medium shot. You want to focus on the character's reaction to that something. A quick zoom into an extreme close-up as the character reacts could play very humorously.

In fact, the camera can take on a very large role in comedy, adding to the humor of a scene. Quick pans away and back from action as if the camera overshot the scene can be funny. A quick zoom in, as discussed, and then a quick zoom out—especially if the character burps—can be an effective use of camera movement to accentuate a scene.

Panning

Another camera movement is the pan. As discussed earlier, a pan generally occurs when the camera is locked-off and becomes the center of the world. The camera can pan in a 360-degree arc. After the camera begins to move sideways, the movement is no longer called a pan, but instead becomes another form of tracking shot.

A 360-degree pan or the opposite 360-degree orbit (where an object is the center of the world and the camera moves around it) are good techniques used to give the viewer a sense of omniscience. This technique reveals nearly everything about the subject and can be a very impressive camera technique.

Pans can be smooth and graceful or jerky and quick (referred to as *quick*, or *flash, pans*). Examples of quick pans can be seen in television shows such as *NYPD Blue* and *Homicide*. Quick pans can be effective when used with the subjective viewport, or first-person point of view (described in greater detail in "Theory of Frame Composition" later in this chapter). A succession of quick pans can give the viewer the sense that the character is drunk or disoriented.

Freezing

Sometimes you'll find it more effective to have no motion whatsoever—a *freeze frame*. This method can be effective to show death or conclusion in a scene. If the scene is animated and full of life and then suddenly the frame freezes, a strong message is sent to the viewer.

To Move or Not to Move

Some film directors do not like moving the camera, believing it draws attention away from the actors and action. Others believe the opposite and believe the camera can become a character in its own right. As animators it is important to find your own voice in regards to your preference of camera movement. In any event, it is important to not treat camera movement lightly. The movement of the camera in a scene fortifies the viewer's sense of the three-dimensional quality of the scene, or the actuality of the scene. But keep in mind that although it was impressive for Orson Welles in *Touch of Evil* to have a two-and-a-half minute tracking shot with no cuts, the reason it was so impressive was because it took place in the real world and was technically challenging. In the world of bits and bytes, creating camera movement is as simple as creating a mirrored sphere, and as with the mirrored sphere, it should be used in moderation.

Learning the mechanics of making good animation is a relatively simple matter, but it takes understanding and knowledge of the emotional effects camera movement and placement can have on a viewer to truly be able to create quality animation. Quality animation can perhaps best be defined as the type of cinematic masterpieces that linger in the audience's mind well after the lights have come up and everyone has left the theater.

Using Dummy Objects to Build a Virtual Studio

If you have ever been on the set of a film of a real-world motion picture, you may remember being surrounded by all sorts of camera tripods, cranes, dolly tracks, Stedicams, and more. The director of photography uses all these mechanical devices to move the camera smoothly or keep it perfectly still. Unfortunately, in computer animation these types of devices do not exist. Or do they?

You can use Dummy objects to build some of the same camera equipment and make the process of animating a scene easier, giving yourself the ability to create smoother motion paths.

The simplest use of Dummy objects is to create a tripod for the camera.

1. Create a Target camera.

2. Create a Dummy object directly beneath the camera object.

3. Link both the camera and camera target to the dummy, with the dummy as the parent to both (see fig. 20.11).

By creating this simple hierarchy you are able to move the dummy through complex motions and have the camera follow in a smooth manner.

More complex use of Dummy objects can be created to produce cranes. The following was developed by Angelo Guarino and posted to the 3D Studio forum of CompuServe (GO KINETIX):

FIGURE 20.11

By linking both the camera and target to a Dummy object, you can create a tripod which can make camera movements quick and simple.

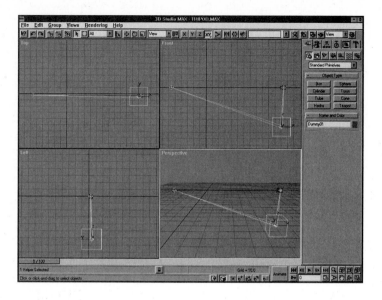

1. Create a Target camera.

2. Create two Dummy objects at the camera position. You can call these cam-elevation and cam-azimuth.

3. Create three dummies at the camera target. You can call these trgt-elevation, trgt-azimuth, and cam-position.

4. Link all the dummies, the camera, and camera target in the following order:

   cam-position

   trgt-azimuth

   trgt-elevat

   cam-azimuth

   cam-elevat

   cam1

   cam1.target

By constructing this "crane" (see fig. 20.12), you should be able to achieve many complex motions by using only "endpoint" keyframes in any one object's degree of freedom. Experiment with moving each of the Dummy objects separately, and then with combinations, to achieve the desired effects.

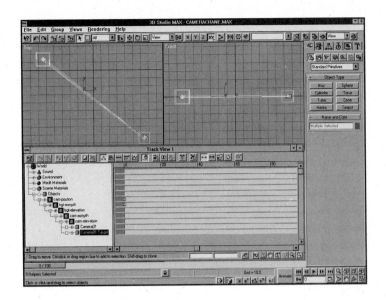

Figure 20.12

A more complex linking of the camera and target to multiple Dummy objects can create a camera crane. Saving this camera equipment for future use creates a virtual film studio for the animator.

For example, if you want to move into an object and then circle around it, move the cam-position dummy toward the desired object. When you have framed the object the way you wish, rotate the trgt-azimuth dummy the desired amount. Concentrate on defining the motions by using endpoint keyframes on each of the dummies, and you should find a greater amount of control in your camera movement.

Essentially you are creating—because many of the factors of moving real-world cameras do not affect computer cameras—a logistical way of producing smooth camera motion. If you lock off certain axes of motion on each Dummy object so that it can move only in the direction that its name represents and use these objects for all camera movement, it is easier to chart and correct unwanted jerkiness and jiggle. You know exactly how the camera has been moved and by what transform.

If you create a number of camera rigs, save them as separate 3DS MAX files and import them into scenes as needed. Now you have created a virtual studio facility in your computer.

Looking at the Look At Controller

The Look At controller is the default controller for targeted cameras, and points the negative local Z axis of the camera at the pivot of the Target object. This is helpful when you want your camera to track a specific object throughout the course of an animation. For instance, a spaceship is the central focus of the scene, and the spaceship is moving through the animation. Assign the spaceship as the target for the camera in the Look At parameters rollout. Now you need only to animate the spaceship, and the camera will keep the spaceship in view. The camera target has been replaced by the spaceship, saving you from having to animate both the camera target and the spaceship. The result is a cleaner, smoother animation.

FIGURE 20.13

The Look At rollout is found by selecting an object, clicking the Motion parameters rollouts, and then clicking Transform under Assign Controller.

Using Clipping Planes

Cameras also have parameters to control the *clipping plane*, which enables you to exclude certain sections of the scene's geometry to view the inside of the geometry. The clipping plane is a handy tool when you want to create a cross-section, or cut-away view, of a building, vehicle, person, and so on. Using clipping planes is an easy way to create architectural cross-sections or create cool animated cut-away effects. Also, the use of clipping planes can be effective as a purely logistical tool when rendering portions of a scene with a large amount of complex geometry.

Each camera has a near and a far clipping plane, which you can adjust and animate. The parameters for clipping planes are found in the creation parameters of the camera object. Both the near plane and the far plane are measured along the camera's local Z axis in current scene units.

In figure 20.14, you see a scene as normally rendered with the clipping plane turned off. In figure 20.15, you see how a clipping plane setting of 9750.0 and 20000.0 changes the scene. The clipping plane setting varies depending on the size of your models and the scene.

FIGURE 20.14

The clipping plane is a tool that cuts away from the model that the camera is focused on based on the settings in the Near and Far Clip spinners found under the Modify parameters rollout.

FIGURE 20.15

Using clipping planes is a quick and simple way to create great-looking cross-section view of architectural models.

Just placing a camera in a scene can sometimes be enough if the action in the scene is sufficiently compelling. Other times you may want to use the camera in such a way as to manipulate the viewer's emotions without them consciously knowing it. All feature films employ these methods, which animators can learn from.

Simulating Camera Techniques

Because cameras represent the observer's eye, it is extremely important to relate what the camera sees to how the observer would perceive it in the scene. People have a strong sense of what speed looks like and will interpret your animation by relating what they see to their own experience. Additionally, people can be emotionally affected by certain camera angles and focal lengths.

As a director of animation, when you set the camera into a scene you are deciding what the audience members can and cannot see. You are editorializing what is happening in the scene and manipulating the viewer to see and feel only those things you want him to see and feel. By learning and applying the following techniques, your animation will become stronger and more interesting to the viewer.

NOTE

To become a great animator, you must learn and study the art of motion picture cinematography. Animation is not simply moving characters or spaceships around on a screen; it is composing scenes and using camera angles that elicit a visceral response from the audience. Too many animators plop a camera into a scene as the last step when, in fact, it should be one of the first elements considered when setting up an animation.

Camera angles alone can set the tone for a scene for suspense, comedy, or danger. Study the films of the masters such as Welles, Hitchcock, Scorsese, De Palma, Spielberg, and Altman to name just a few. Study how these directors use the camera to tell their story. In some cases, they even use the camera as a character in the film.

The first rule of good camera placement is composition. *Composition* is the art of filling the film frame with the characters and objects that make up your scene. Whether your camera is locked-off (still) or animated, the frame can be filled in many different ways, each affecting how the viewer feels about your characters and the situation.

The two types of basic scene composition are symmetrical and random. By using symmetrical composition, the camera's relation to the characters and objects in the scene is organized and symmetrical, giving your scene an artificial feel and leading viewers to believe they are not watching real life. Random composition places characters and objects throughout the scene, giving the scene a more realistic feel and enabling viewers to forget they are watching a film.

The style of composition depends on the tone of the script and the type of animation you are producing. Is it to be stylized and artistic? If so, the symmetrical approach may work best. Is the style to be dramatic and draw the viewer into the story? Then a random style is preferable.

Theory of Frame Composition

You can frame the characters and objects within a frame in many ways to elicit different emotional responses from the viewer. The choice of frame composition is based on the type of film genre you are attempting to emulate, the mood of the film, and the messages and feelings you want viewers to experience while watching your film.

By setting up the camera with foreground objects predominately placed between the main action and character, you are dislocating the viewer from the scene. The viewer may feel a lack of connection and a physical separation. This technique works well if your character is in trouble or feeling a sense of separation within the context of the film. Maybe your character is losing a love in his life. By placing an object, say a column, between two characters, you are suggesting a physical separation to accentuate the emotional separation that is taking place in the story. If the character has committed a crime, you could separate him from the camera by placing vertical objects or fencing between the character and the camera. The placement of such objects will create not only a separation, but will also symbolically fore-shadow the character's ultimate fate if caught and sentenced to jail.

Another technique is the long shot. John Ford, the famous director of classic western films, always used long, establishing shots throughout his films to set the tone of the grand spaciousness of the wild west that the tiny, almost inconsequential, characters were up against. Setting this type of tone may tell the audience how fragile the character's existence is in the film.

Long shots can also establish the character's relation to the location. Does the character become lost in the background of a war-torn village in Vietnam? Maybe the larger story is the war, but the focus is on one story out of many.

Conversely, lack of space, or close-ups, draw the viewer into the scene and closer to the character, somewhat dislocating the character from the scene because the surroundings are unseen. Imagine an establishing shot of a location—it can be anything you want; it's your imagination—that cuts to a close-up of the lead character's face. The viewer assumes the character is at the location previously seen, but there is no direct connection because the character has yet to be seen actually in the location.

In addition to causing the viewer to feel closer to a character, this technique can also be used to jar the viewer and cause discomfort. A close-up of an alien that has just destroyed a small town might be a little disconcerting (for some). Likewise, constant close-ups—whether of the characters or objects in the scene—can cause claustrophobia and be psychologically disorienting because the viewer never actually sees anything beyond the close-up views.

Close-ups also guide the viewer to see the things the director wants seen. Hitchcock was a master of showing the audience clues and revealing things through camera set-up. In his film *The Lady Vanishes*, Hitchcock created a close-up within a medium shot by placing a glass near the camera with the character in the middle ground. By keeping both the glass and character in focus, the viewer's attention is drawn to both equally. One is not more important than the other. What makes the scene work is that the audience knows, from an earlier shot, that the glass is filled with poison, but the prospective victim does not. This scene composition creates suspense for the viewer and is great filmmaking.

Every object within the camera view is part of the film composition and should be considered as important. Is it important to have many detail objects in a scene, or do they just clutter the frame and distract the viewer from what is really important? What you want to accomplish determines what you want in the scene.

In comedy, scene composition can be cluttered, and characters or objects that are in the background or to the side of the scene may be where the humor is derived. The *Airplane* films and *Naked Gun* films are perfect examples. In how many scenes is Leslie Nielsen acting in the foreground—our central focus—but something completely ludicrous is going on behind him that he is unaware of? There lies the humor. The fact that the viewer first had to find the comedic element combined with the fact that Nielsen's character is oblivious to what is going on is what makes the scene funny. Again, this humor is achieved through frame composition. If the scene had been shot so that the audience saw only the slapstick actions, the audience may have laughed, but the scene would be nowhere near as funny as when the viewers know other characters are ignorant of what is going on. Ultimately, the spatial relationship of the characters and objects to the camera lend to the wit and humor of the scene. The establishing shots are an important type of frame composition. An establishing shot, or long shot, sets the location for the animation. Where does the animation take place? What time of day? Or year? A long shot tells the viewer almost everything he needs to know in a quick, simple shot. In *Waterworld*, for example, the opening shots of a vast ocean set the tone for a world with little or no land masses. Establishing shots are generally the first scene in an animation and are used to quickly "establish" the time and location of the film.

Composition with Lenses

Another technique, in addition to camera placement and character and object placement within a scene, is the use of different lenses to achieve certain emotional responses and effects.

Long lenses, or telephoto lenses, change the perspective of the scene and create dramatic effects. During the climatic moments of *An Occurrence at Owl Creek Bridge*, a telephoto lens was employed that compressed the scene and made the main character appear closer then he actually was. By doing this, the director achieved an effect that made it appear that although the character was running full speed toward the viewer, the character was making no progress. This shot emphasized the intense and futile effort of the character.

Conversely, the use of short lenses, or wide-angle lenses, can also produce incredible results. A case in point is the use of wide-angle lenses in *Citizen Kane*, a masterpiece of cinematography. Orson Welles used wide-angle lenses in many scenes to add to the mystique, power, and domination of the main character, Kane.

The use of wide-angle lenses makes the background planes appear farther away from the camera than they really are. As the Kane character moves toward the camera, he appears to cover a vast amount of ground in just a few short steps. Thus, a character can move from the back of the room to the front in two strides, becoming much larger and quicker and appearing powerful. The character's performance is enhanced by this type of lens and scene composition.

Another lens composition technique is the "deep focus." Luckily (or by default, as the case may be), 3DS MAX has yet to perfect the science of depth of field. You can actually use this "fault" to your advantage. In another scene from *Citizen Kane*, for example, the fact that the characters in the foreground, middle ground, and far background can all be seen equally well, adds to the importance of a scene where a young, innocent Kane is playing in the background while his mother is signing over guardianship of her son. In the middle-ground, Kane's father stands by helplessly. This composition shows the viewer the boy's innocence, while enabling the viewer to also witness the events which will forever deprive the boy of his childhood and freedom. By using this technique, the scene is more effective than if Welles had shot separate shots of each element.

NOTE

There are two all-time classic films of cinematography that should be in the collection of any animator who desires to make "films" as opposed to animation. These are *An Occurrence at Owl Creek Bridge* (Robert Enrico, 1961) and *Citizen Kane* (Orson Welles, 1941). *An Occurrence at Owl Creek Bridge* was actually shown as a *Twilight Zone* episode. Both films can be purchased on video tape.

Composition with Angles

A third way to use cameras to dramatically compose a scene is through the angle with which the camera is set up. There are four basic types of camera angles, each with its own variations:

- Eye-level
- High-angle
- Low-angle
- Subjective viewpoint

The eye-level camera setup is the standard setup for cameras. The view is basically neutral and objective to the scene. This shot is comfortable and can be seen in most mainstream films or love stories.

High-angle is when the camera is pointed down toward the object or characters. Using this angle diminishes the character or object to the viewer because it is literally "being looked down on." This can make the character look small and vulnerable.

In *An Occurrence at Owl Creek Bridge,* the main character falls into a quick moving stream and is carried away in the rapids. The scene is shot from a high-angle and the character appears small in the frame. This high-angle composition reinforces the fact that the character is vulnerable.

On the other hand, a low-angle shot makes a character or an object appear more powerful and have a greater stature. If you want a character to appear more heroic—a caricature of heroism—place your camera at his hip, looking up. This camera placement will give the character an appearance of confidence and strength. The low-angle shot will make objects appear more robust and monumental.

Low-angle set-ups can be used to achieve other types of effects as well. Steven Spielberg used a low-angle camera setup in *E.T.: The Extra-Terrestrial* to convey a child's point of view in many scenes. The camera was placed at a child's height, giving the audience a view from the child's perspective of the world, causing adults in the movie to seem more threatening.

With each of the previously mentioned angles, it is possible to mix and match them for even greater effect. For instance, composing a scene from a low-angle with a slight roll in the FOV can achieve a disorienting effect or a heightened sense of drama. This technique is useful when filming the villain of an animation to make the character more ominous. This effect can also make the viewer feel off balance and vulnerable.

Citizen Kane used both high and low angles in numerous shots to give the Kane character a grander stature and to diminish the stature of Kane's wife in the film. This use of camera angles tells us something about each character without it having to be said. It can show the audience how one character is perceived by another.

In every scene that Kane and his wife are in together, Kane is invariably shot from below waist level, or low-angle, as if from the wife's perspective, thereby making him seem more dominating. In contrast, the wife is always shot from a high-angle, thereby revealing her weakness and subservience to Kane.

Using certain camera angles every time a character is on the screen, establishes in the viewer's mind a strong feeling about that character. Later, when the character is shot from a neutral, eye-level angle, the feelings that were established earlier will still be felt subconsciously.

The fourth type of camera angle is the subjective viewpoint. This angle attempts to give the audience a first-person point of view of the scene. This effect can be useful as long as it is not overdone. When overdone, the effect becomes gimmicky and draws the viewer out of the story.

Examples of subjective viewpoint can be seen in any horror film where the camera takes on the role of the killer stalking the terrified victim. Other examples can be more benign such as in *Downhill Racer*, where the camera takes on the role of the title character, a downhill skier.

To create subjective viewpoint cameras in 3DS MAX, it is best to use the Free camera because this camera is better set up for animating with banks, swoops, and skids. Refer to the section "Moving the Camera" earlier in this chapter.

Subjective viewpoint can also give the animator an opportunity for creative scene creation. From our earlier example of aliens, you may want a scene showing how the alien sees the world. A shot from a subjective viewpoint would be a perfect opportunity to show the world through the alien's eyes (or whatever your aliens see through) in some creative way. Films such as *Predator*, *Wolfen*, and other creature-oriented horror films do this to great effect. Maybe the alien only sees the world in shades of green.

The use of subjective viewpoints can add excitement and tension to an animation. If an audience member sees what the alien sees, then for that moment the audience is the alien (which is rather disconcerting considering the alien just destroyed a town). Or perhaps the audience is looking through the eyes of a psychotic killer stalking his next victim. You can see how a visceral effect can be achieved on your audience.

WARNING

These types of dramatic camera angles should be used wisely and sparingly. An animation that uses every trick in the book may be difficult to watch and enjoy.

Remember that too many tricks draw the viewer out of the story and into the art of filmmaking—not an animator's job. Instead, these techniques should be used to further the story and better enhance the art of story telling. As a rule of thumb, if the technique does not somehow advance the story, don't use it.

Animation is not just the art of moving a character in a realistic manner. Certainly, realistic motion of characters and objects is important, but no less important is the use of the camera in a scene. Think of the camera as another character. If you are attempting to create award-winning animations that are powerful and meaningful, learning the art of cinematography is essential.

In Practice: Cameras and Setting the Shot

- **Camera Types**   3D Studio MAX offers two camera types: Target cameras and Free cameras.

- **Real-world representation**   A new equation used to calculate the field of view gives you a more accurate representation of real-world 35 mm cameras if you specify cameras by lens length.

- **Camera adjustments**   Cameras can be adjusted in multiple ways, and many adjustments can be animated. This animation of the camera can be done in ways that enhance the animation and strengthen the story-telling process. With a good script, an animator will know when moving the camera is a good idea and when it will be overbearing for the scene.

- **Camera angles**   Camera angles enhance the story-telling process as well. Choosing certain angles can tell the audience much about a character or location without having to actually verbalize this information through the dialogue.

- **Clipping planes**   Use clipping planes to create great-looking, architectural, cut-away animation.

"Doofan's Swamp"
Created by Jeremy Hubbel and Stacie Dong
San Francisco, CA
Image created and rendered in 3DS MAX V1.1 for Siggraph '96
All textures were hand-drawn using Fractal Painter 4.0
Crocodile and grass models are compliments of Viewpoint Datalabs, Inc.
Jeremy Hubbell 74521.2244@compuserve.com
Stacie Dong 104655.624@compuserve.com

Chapter 21

MATERIALS AND TEXTURES

*Materials in 3D Studio MAX are limited only by your imagina-
tion. You can take a particular material to essentially any limit
to achieve the desired surface or effect. Knowing what is possible
and how requires an understanding of the way the Material
Editor enables you to branch and make decisions in a very
general, nonrestrictive way.*

Defining a material is nearly always an exploration with much experimentation. A common technique is to copy stages of your material into the adjacent sample slots so you can compare alternate approaches. Saving materials to the private experimentation libraries is also quite common (and highly advised).

Materials can be an end to themselves, and many hours can be spent in perfecting a scene's palette of textures. You will also nearly always be coordinating your efforts with a traditional paint package (such as Photoshop, Animator Studio, Fractal Design Painter, Ron Scott QFX, and so on) and possibly a 3D paint package as well (Positron's MeshPaint and 4D Vision's 4D Paint already ship as 3DS MAX plug-ins). Often these are run concurrently with 3DS MAX, with artists switching between the two by the Windows Alt+Tab key combination. Other studios prefer to have dedicated systems for paint and 3D, connecting their output through a network.

This chapter covers the use of the Material Editor and how to apply material to the scene and presents techniques for using materials effectively in 3D Studio MAX. In particular, you'll learn about the following:

- The Material Editor interface

- Material assignments and libraries

- Using 3DS MAX's standard material

- Standard material color components and map channels

- Automatically calculated reflections

- Map types for images, compositing, and color modification

- Animating maps and their parameters

- Additional material types

Paramount to digesting this information is a thorough understanding of how materials can branch to form hierarchies or material trees.

Material Tree Concepts

It's easy to think of materials in 3DS MAX as almost being "living" things. Each material is individual, with incredible personality, that can evolve over time. Materials begin with a somewhat simple base that can then be made more intricate by branching (see fig. 21.1). In this way, the Material Editor becomes a "tree," or an extremely visual version of the Windows File Manager, with the base material being the "tree trunk" or "root directory." Every long, thin button allowing a choice is a *map channel*, acting as a "branch" or "subdirectory" that is initially bare or empty. Clicking on a map channel button enables you to choose a map type, and thus "add leaves" or fill the "directory." Most map types then contain additional channels for yet deeper branches and more "branches" or "sub-directories." The material shown in the sample window is the end result, as seen from the base of the tree. Often, the farther you branch, the more subtle the final result will be.

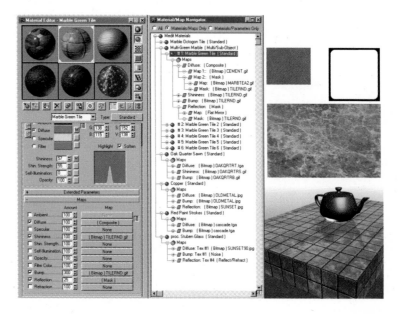

At the deepest level is the *material type*. The material type contains all the initial map channels that can be branched from—a somewhat confusing concept because most programs (such as 3D Studio DOS) have the equivalent of just one material "type." To use 3D Studio DOS as the example, its entire Materials Editor module was actually manipulating the equivalent of *one* material type. This one type has evolved into the Standard material type in 3DS MAX.

Whenever you see a selection button titled "Map," you're seeing a *map channel*. A map channel is essentially an input point, or socket, for which you can choose a map type, and so continue the material tree by adding branches. Map channels can exist within material or map types. The Standard material, for example, contains eleven map channels for selecting up to eleven map types. A *map type* often feels like an entire material in itself, when actually it's just a branch from the parent material type or map type. Bitmaps are an example of a map type, where a single bitmap is used as primary input along with all of its parameters and options. Other map types, such as Checker, contain additional map channels so the branching can continue by selecting yet more map types.

Choices and controls that are not map channels (that is, they aren't a selection button) are either *parameters* or *options*. Parameters usually have ranges and edit fields with typical material parameters including color, values, angles, and distances. Nearly every parameter has a track in Track View and can thus be animated. The remaining material and map controls are termed material or map *options*. These dictate how parameters are evaluated and are usually check boxes or radio buttons. Examples of options include Soften, 2-Sided, and Bitmap Invert. Material options can rarely be animated and thus do not usually appear in Track View.

When a material or map type has parameters only and no map channels, such as the Bitmap map type, then that branch of the tree essentially stops. Of course, you can branch at that point by changing the map type to one that has channels and choosing to keep the current map type as a sub-map of the newly chosen map type, as shown in figure 21.2.

FIGURE 21.2

Making a Bitmap map type a Sub-map by choosing another map type.

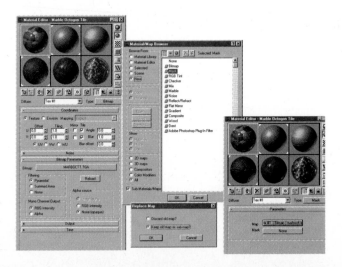

Some material types (such as Multi/Sub-Object, Top/Bottom, Double Sided, and Blend) contain *material channels* rather than map channels. The status of being a Map or Material channel is signified by how the selection button is titled. When working at the base level of such materials, you are actually choosing other material types to branch to and not map types. While the Standard material has the most map channels, it has no material channels. The Matte/Shadow material is the only real "dead end" by not providing any channels for branching. The next section describes numerous ways for selecting, navigating, and coordinating this tree of materials.

As with most things in 3DS MAX, materials and maps are actually objects and thus can be instanced. Whenever you choose an existing map or material for a channel you have the option to make it an instance of the original meaning that any future edits you do to one will also be made to the other. It is very common for a material to use the same map at numerous locations. The same map might be used for the Opacity, Shininess Strength, Bump, and Reflection Mask, for example. By making these instances, you need to adjust only one to adjust them all.

N OTE

Although you cannot instance parameters in the Material Editor, you instance them in Track View. These instanced controllers act as such only when manipulated in Track View. If you make adjustments in the Material Editor, the instanced parameters will behave uniquely. If you return to Track View and make an adjustment, the new value will be copied to the instance.

The Material Editor Interface

The Material Editor is your alchemy lab for creating nearly any surface appearance you might imagine. As with other parts of 3DS MAX, the Material Editor is an extensible environment where all materials, maps, and bitmap types are actually plug-in components. The familiar rollup buttons for accessing areas are an indication that this framework contains plug-ins and as such, its capabilities and interface change as different materials and maps are used.

One portion of the Material Editor interface never changes regardless of what type of material you're using or what kind of map type you're working with. As seen in figure 21.3, the area above the scrollable area in the interface is fixed. These functions are used commonly by all map and material types and grayed out when not applicable. The following section describes how to navigate and use the Material Editor to its fullest.

FIGURE 21.3

The fixed portion of the Material Editor interface.

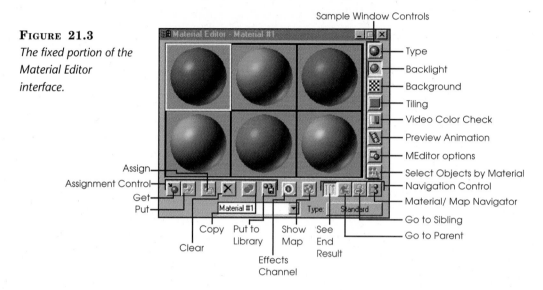

Material Sample Slots

When activating the Material Editor, whether by its toolbar button, the pull-down, or a keyboard alternate, the Material Editor is presented according to its last state. The MAX scene file maintains the materials last edited in the scene as well as the Editor's options. When working in a new scene, the default set of six material samples in figure 21.3 are shown. These six material windows, or slots, behave much like viewports. Clicking on one activates it, makes it current within the Editor, and changes the window border to white similar to the way viewports behave. If a sample window contains a material used in the scene, white triangles are placed at the corners. Your position in a material's tree is remembered as you switch between sample windows.

Materials are said to have three "temperatures" (hot, warm, or cold) based upon their scene assignment. If the material is used in the scene, it's considered hot, if it's a copy of a material used in the scene, it's warm, and if it's not used at all, it's cold. Hot materials are indicated in the material sample windows by the four white corner triangles shown in figure 21.4.

Hot materials are dynamic to their assignment in the scene. When you adjust any parameter within a hot material you are affecting the scene's material definition at the same time—*not* just the definition in the Editor. As updates are made to the material sample, they are also updated in all shaded viewports. While it's common to work this way, it can cause delays because shaded viewports are attempting to keep up with your edits.

FIGURE 21.4

The three material "temperatures."

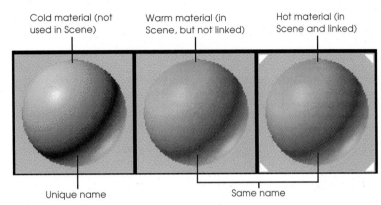

Cold material (not used in Scene)

Warm material (in Scene, but not linked)

Hot material (in Scene and linked)

Unique name

Same name

TIP

For the fastest editing of hot (assigned) materials, it's best to make a copy of the material, make all changes to this warm version, and then put it back to the scene as the new hot material.

Warm materials are formed when you copy a material by either using the Make Material Copy button or dragging a sample window onto another slot. The copied, warm material has the same name as the original but does not have the direct connection to the scene. Editing it will not impact what's currently in the scene. If you assign this copied, warm material to an object, you will be prompted to either rename the material or replace the like-named material's definition. Agreeing to replace the material is the same as using the Put function. Giving a warm material a unique name makes it cold.

Cold materials differ from warm materials only in that they do not share a name with a material that already exists in the current scene. Cold materials can be freely assigned without concern for them affecting any previous definitions. Because of this, replacing a currently assigned material definition with a cold material takes two steps. A cold material will become warm if you change its name to one already in the scene.

Material Editor Display Controls

 The Material Editor contains several controls for viewing your material samples and altering such qualities as shape, lighting, background, pattern, and tiling. The intent is to enable you to make the Material Editor environment as close as possible to qualities of the scene you will be assigning them in. These controls are located along the right-hand side of the material sample windows (see fig. 21.3).

The Sample Type button enables you to choose the geometry shown in the material sample slot. Choices are spheres, boxes, and cylinders. Choosing the one that most closely represents your object's geometry allows you to better predict rendering qualities (see fig. 21.5).

FIGURE 21.5
Using primitives that most closely match scene objects.

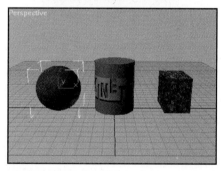

 The Backlight button places a secondary light source below and behind the material sample to alert you of material properties that can cause harsh highlights. While this option slows the rendering slightly, the information is critical when using Phong materials without the Soften option.

 The Background button changes the sample window background from a solid shade of gray to a checker pattern containing the RGB primaries, black, and white. This somewhat garish pattern is necessary to see the results of opacity controls, especially those involving colored transparencies.

The Sample UV Tiling button enables you to change the tiling repeat in the sample slot, as shown in figure 21.6. This is convenient when you need to see how patterns repeat, but adjusting map tiling parameters just for that purpose is not practical. Changing the tiling display has no impact on the material itself.

FIGURE 21.6
The result of viewing with different tiling rates.

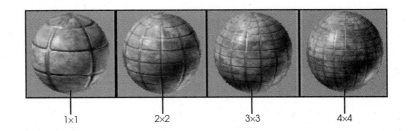

1×1   2×2   3×3   4×4

The Video Color Check button has the Editor check for colors that are "illegal" when put to video tape for display on NTSC or PAL monitors. Illegal colors (most notably bright reds) output very badly and catching such colors as early as material definition is often helpful. Figure 21.7 shows the Material Editor displaying illegal colors in a material. Note, however, that the colors are illegal only in respect to the sample's lighting and that your scene lighting will differ.

FIGURE 21.7
A material showing illegal video colors.

Illegal area

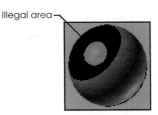

The Make Preview button enables you to create an animated preview of the active sample sphere with control for size, timing, and duration. This is a quick alternative to rendering the scene for seeing the animated effects contained within material trees.

The Material Editor Options button accesses a dialog that contains the global options for the Material Editor. Here is where the background intensity, lighting, and map scale are defined. The Anti-alias option only affects the sample's edge and does impact speed. The Progressive Refinement option is useful for slower machines with complex materials. Finally, control is given over the actual Renderer used on the material samples. The Scanline Renderer is the same as the 3DS MAX production renderer. The

Quick Renderer is a faster alternative, but cannot display wire materials and face maps. In practice, you will probably become comfortable with certain settings and rarely change them. The one parameter you are likely to change is 3D Map Sample Scale. These map types can produce an effect in real-world scale. This parameter gives you control over how large the generic sample is. Making this the equivalent size of your scene object allows you to better see the 3D map's result.

The Select by Material button brings up the Select By Name dialog and identifies which objects are assigned the current material. You can use this to select those objects, invert and select everything else, or create other selections. In practice, this is a very convenient method for selecting objects for many purposes and not just for assigning materials to.

Material Controls for Active Materials

The buttons located horizontally below the material sample windows provide functions that relate to the active material sample and not the Material Editor as a whole. Functions on the left enable you to replace the current material in the Editor or the scene, assign the material, reset, copy, or put to the library. Buttons on the right control material effects channels, texture display, result viewing, navigation, and browsing.

Creating New Materials and Maps

The Get Material button places you into the Material/Map Browser for the selection of a new material that will replace the *entire* active material. It's important to realize that the Get Material function is to replace the current material and *not* to select a sub-material or map. To select maps or materials for use within the current material, you must access the Browser from the Type button. If you use Get Material and are not at the active material's root level, a confirmation dialog will appear informing you that the entire material is about to be replaced. The assumption is that because you are not at the root level, you may have used Get instead of Type. If you are at the root level, no confirmation is requested and the material is replaced. The Get action needs to be used with the knowledge that the active material will be discarded and if its definition does not exist within the scene, a library, or another slot, it is lost.

Replacing Materials with Put and Assign

The Put Material to Scene button is only available when you are editing a warm material. The Put function will replace the like-named material definition in the scene with the one you're editing. The previously hot material reverts to being warm. This is the same as performing a Replace when assigning a warm material to the scene, except there is no warning message to delay your update.

The Assign Material to Selection button assigns the current material to the selection of objects in the scene. This option is only active when you have a selection. Together, the Put and Assign functions supply the tools for changing material assignments, giving you the following options for changing an assigned material definition:

- Edit a hot material in the Material Editor and its definition is automatically updated in the scene.

- Assign a new material to the selected objects.

- Edit a warm material, assign it to any object in the scene, and choose to replace the like-named material.

- Edit a warm material and use the Put option to replace the scene definition.

The Make Material Copy button is only available when editing a hot material. Using this function changes the material from hot to warm. The newly warm material maintains the same definition and name but no longer has a direct link to the scene. If you plan on experimenting with a material, it's good practice to use Copy to change a hot material to warm so you do not immediately impact the scene's definition. Once satisfied with the material, use Put to redefine the scene's material. In the meantime, the scene's material definition acts as a backup that can be retrieved if needed.

Saving Materials in Libraries

Materials definitions are saved in the MAX scene file along with any object that is assigned to them. When you open or merge a scene, the materials assigned within can be retrieved from the Browser using the Browse From Scene or Selected option. In contrast, you can save just the material definitions themselves in a *material library*.

A material definition is actually no more than a "recipe" containing a list of ingredients and parameters for creating the material. The library is then analogous to a "recipe box" because it holds collections of material definitions. In practice, it is often very convenient to store your favorite materials in assorted libraries. Many artists find having separate libraries for specific needs (Brick, Stone, Marble, Flesh, Grit, Atmosphere, Backgrounds, and so on) speeds searching considerably and makes the materials more accessible to other artists.

The Put to Library button sends the active material definition to the currently loaded library. While a hot material is automatically updated in your scene, it is *not* updated in the library from which it came. To add or update a material in a library, you must first use the Put to Library button. This updates the library entry in the currently loaded material library. Even though the button image shows a diskette, the library is not saved to disk unless you specifically do so. To save a library, you must choose Save or Save As from within the Browser. As materials get perfected, their definitions become quite valuable. This two-step process ensures that you will not accidentally overwrite libraries and their contents.

Material Effects Channels

Every material in 3DS MAX can include a *materials effects channel* that is used by Video Post filters to control the location of their post process effects. Video Post can access the material effects channel when you are rendering a scene event or are using an RLA file that contains the material effects channel. Figure 21.8 shows a rendering with material channels being displayed as color codes rather than the typical rendered scene. This output is intended for use in post processes and is not meant as an end in itself. The colors displayed are intended to be informational and not a finished result.

The most common use for material effects channels is in conjunction with a Video Post image filter. Filter events such as Glow enable you to assign the glow to a material rather than an object (by using an RLA object channel) or just a key-color (when scene data is not used at all). In practice, object channels are used when affecting small numbers of objects and material channels are used when you need to affect many objects with Video Post effects.

FIGURE 21.8

Displaying the Material Effects Channels contained within a rendered RLA file.

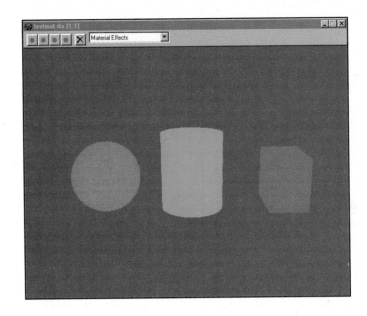

Displaying Textures

One of 3DS MAX's most useful features is the capability to display textures in the interactive viewports. Figure 21.9 shows a scene where textures exist throughout the viewports, and their display is critical for proper mapping alignment. One map can be shown in the viewports per material. The choice to do this is within all the 2D Map types with the Show Map in Viewport button.

FIGURE 21.9

A scene with numerous textures displayed.

NOTE

Only the map itself will be displayed in the viewports. Changes made to the image with parameters or other maps are not shown.

Because displaying maps requires additional RAM, 3DS MAX defaults to all maps not being shown. If you want to display a map in a viewport, you need to activate it yourself. This should be done with the knowledge that each displayed map requires RAM (although this is not a problem when using graphic accelerator boards with texture memory support). To aid in this RAM requirement, only a proxy image is actually displayed in the viewports. This allows even very large images to be displayed for the cost of much smaller ones.

Using Show End Result

By default, the Material Editor shows the entire material tree's result, regardless of which branch you are editing at. Disabling the Show End Result option will show only the result at the current level in the material. As figure 21.10 shows, disabling this option has a profound effect on Multi/Sub-Object materials.

FIGURE 21.10

The effect of Show End Result being on and off for a Multi/Sub-Object material.

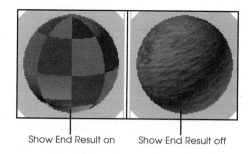

Show End Result on   Show End Result off

This is often used when you want to see the local effect, and is especially useful when used to see the full material effect within Multi/Sub-Object materials. A disabled Show End Result state reports the material only from the last branch to your current position on the tree. This is similar to the Modifier Stack using its own Show End Result function for modifiers. If, for example, you're editing material #4 on a Multi/Sub-Object material, turning off Show End Result will display only material #4 in the sample slot. If you are editing the Diffuse map of a standard material, turning off Show End Result will display the bitmap without shading.

Navigating the Material Editor

The Material Editor can appear quite complex, but with some practice it can prove to be a creative environment that is easily navigated. Figure 21.11 shows how the tree metaphor is used in understanding how a material starts at a root level and branches to contain multiple maps and even other materials. Navigating this tree can be accomplished by marching up the branches within the Editor or by selecting key levels with the Material/Map Navigator. The Material Editor interface is designed to show the current map level at any one time. Figure 21.12 shows a Standard material's Diffuse map channel information using a Bitmap map type.

FIGURE 21.11

Materials start with a root definition and branch with possibilities.

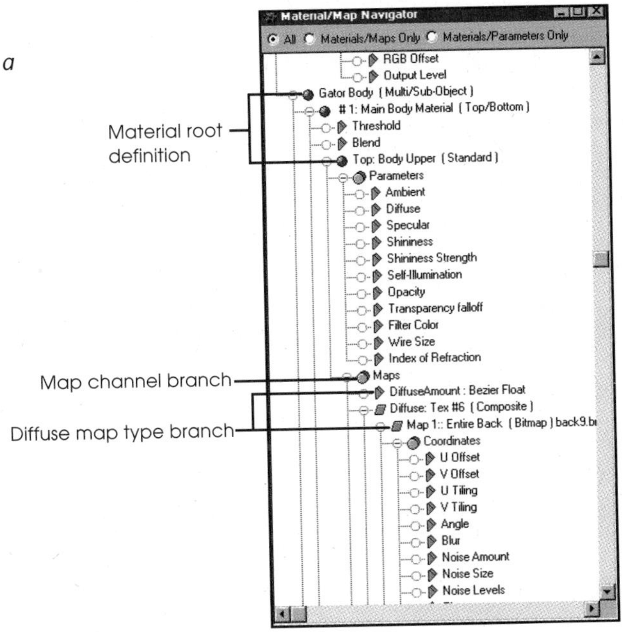

After you've added or jumped to a new branch, you have a few options to get back down.

The Need for Names

When browsing for Maps, usually as part of Standard material's map channel, the material trees can become deep. As numerous figures of the Browser have shown, the materials and map definitions types are displayed differently, with materials being listed "Material Name [Material type]" and maps as "[Map type name] File Name." While the Navigator and Track View provide map and material channel names, the Browser does not. The sole method for identifying maps and materials when choosing them in the Browser is by their name.

FIGURE 21.12

The Material Editor displays a single branch in the material's tree.

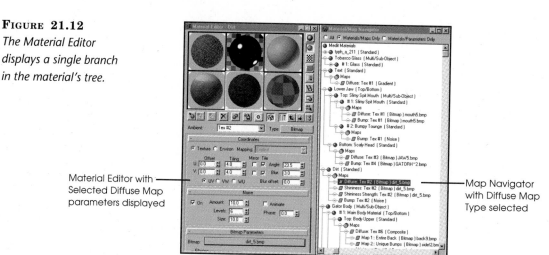

Material Editor with Selected Diffuse Map parameters displayed

Map Navigator with Diffuse Map Type selected

By default, maps are assigned the name Tex#X, where X is an arbitrary number. It is *always* good practice to customize map and sub-material names immediately after they are selected for use in a channel. When maps are logically named, you can use the Browser to its fullest and it is much easier to understand your intentions when you, or a fellow artist, return to the project at a later date. If you lapse into the habit of accepting default names, you will probably have a difficult time locating what you need in a detailed scene or a stored library.

Using the Material/Map Navigator

The Material/Map Navigator button provides a comprehensive overview of the six materials currently within the Material Editor. This interface is accessed from the Material Editor's Material/Map Navigator button, whose icon is an abstract of the hierarchy tree.

TIP

While the Navigator enables you to traverse the material tree similar to Track View, you cannot copy maps and their parameters as you can in Track View.

The Navigator is essentially a subset of Track View that is provided for examining the six material trees in the Editor and traversing them. Like Track View, the icons of blue spheres symbolize materials, and the green trapezoids are maps. Clicking on either symbol will change the Material Editor to that material or map and at that level. This is a *very* useful technique for quickly navigating within or between complex materials. While providing several filter options, the most useful for navigation is Material/Maps Only. Displaying parameters is a somewhat dubious option because they are not a tool for traversing the tree and their values can not be adjusted.

Note

When displaying both the Browser and Navigator, be sure that they do not overlap. Selecting a material in Track View will update the Navigator and place its dialog on top.

Traversing Branches within the Material Editor

The Go to Parent and Go to Sibling buttons are your primary navigation tools for traversing material trees from within the Editor itself. The Return to Parent button moves you up one branch in the tree, while Go to Sibling moves you across branches stemming from the same parent. Go to Sibling is often used when editing Multi/Sub-Object materials or Mask and Composite maps. These one-level steps can be used repeatedly to traverse the entire material tree. The Name pull-down provides a listing of all parents from the current branch. When deep in a material tree, you can move several levels up at once by choosing an earlier parent. Note that if the material or map has not been named that the field is blank—yet another reason to develop a habit of naming materials and their maps.

Browsing Materials and Maps

The Material/Map Browser (see fig. 21.13) is used in four situations: when you get a material to replace the current sample slot; when you first access a map channel for selecting a map; when you first access a material channel for selecting a sub-material; or when you use the Type button to replace the current sub-material or map. Once within the Browser, you can choose a material that is stored in a material library, is present in the scene, is currently within the Material Editor, or define your own from a new definition. The Browse From options control where your list of choices are presented from.

FIGURE 21.13

The Material/Map Browser showing Both materials and maps versus just showing materials.

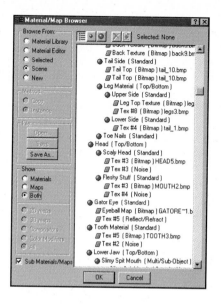

The default material library presented for browsing is the 3dsmax.mat file (see fig. 21.14) that shipped with the product and is located in the \3dsmax\maps sub-directory. You can, of course, select any library you might have to browse from. Unfortunately, the choice of what library is loaded is not stored in the MAX scene file. The Material Editor will thus always search for 3dsmax.mat when the program begins. If the file is not found, the listing will be blank and you will need to specify another library to browse from.

FIGURE 21.14

The Material/Map Browser and the default 3dsmax.mat library.

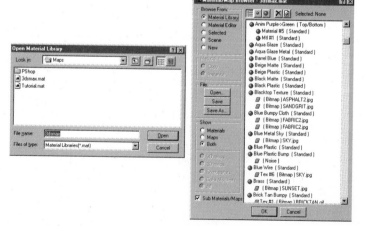

The Show options filter indicates whether materials, maps, or both are displayed for selection. By default, the Both option is active—a possibly confusing situation for material selection because choosing a map will deliver a branch that has no parent. The Show Materials choice is best for browsing materials, while the Show Maps or Show Both options are best for browsing maps.

The buttons at the top of the Browser allow you to change the display from the Track View-like entries to small or large sample spheres. While attractive in principle, this option can be slow for complex materials and uses RAM for all the bitmaps being processed. The reason is that the proxies are being generated at that moment and nothing is cached for future sessions. So while the sample spheres are useful for small libraries, it's not practical for large libraries.

When browsing materials by the named-list method, materials are listed alphabetically and by case. Indented materials indicate they are children of one of the compound materials (Blend, Multi/Sub-Object, Top/Bottom, or Double Sided). These sub-materials are perfectly valid for selection as stand-alone materials. If you want, you can filter out sub-materials by disabling the Sub Materials/Maps option at the bottom of the Browser.

Replacing Maps and Sub-Materials

You often have the need to replace a map that is currently assigned within a material. Adjusting the current map is not sufficient because you might need a different map type or the exact parameters currently used in another material. When you are at the map's root level, clicking the Type button places you in the Material/Map Browser. From here you can choose a map from a library, the scene, the Material Editor or start from scratch with New. Entering the Browser with the Type button is the same as the first time a map channel button is chosen except you are replacing an existing map.

When a material is a used within another material, replacing it is very similar to replacing maps. While it might make sense to use the Get Material function, doing so replaces the entire material definition and not just the sub-material at the current level. When you are at the sub-material's root level, clicking the Type button places you in the Material/Map Browser. From here you can select a material to replace the current sub-material.

Creating with the Standard Material

The Standard material has a modest name for all its capabilities. In practice, it usually is at least the starting point, and thus the "standard" material used for most creations. As described previously, the Standard material is essentially the evolution of everything contained within the 3DS DOS Materials Editor. As figure 21.15 shows, the Standard material type contains 11 map channels as the starting point for creating an extensive map tree.

FIGURE 21.15

The interface for the Standard material.

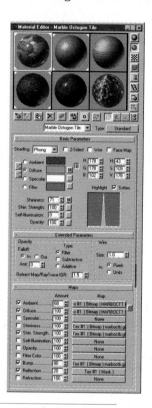

Standard Material Color Components

The Standard material's shading characteristics are broken into the three qualities: Ambient (the color shown in shade), Diffuse (the color shown in light), and the color of highlights (see fig. 21.16). Choosing the correct colors for realistic effect can take a little practice. Begin by looking at real-world objects that share your material's qualities. Look deep into their color, shade, and highlights. Is the highlight's color similar to the light source's or is it tinting it? How is the shaded color affected by what it is placed on? Do the colors change as the light moves about them?

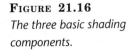

FIGURE 21.16

The three basic shading components.

Specular highlights are seen on surfaces that have at least some shine and occurs when light striking the surface is angled back to your viewing position. The surface displays the material's diffuse color when it is fully illuminated and is either dull or not within specular highlights. As illumination decreases, the diffuse color mixes with that of the ambient. Where no light occurs, only the ambient color is rendered (and then only by the scene's ambient light).

Most materials relate their colors to one another, often being shades within the same color family. The Material Editor makes this easy by enabling you to copy color swatches by dragging them from one to another. You can then adjust the color properties, such as whiteness, blackness, or value, without disturbing the basic color relationships.

Diffuse Color Component

Of the three base color qualities, Diffuse has the most impact on the material's appearance and is the easiest to determine. The diffuse color is the one you refer to when you describe a material in real life. Refer as often as possible to the world around you and analyze its colors. You will probably notice that very few objects have fully saturated hues. Some objects tend to be signs (signage, packaging, advertisements), toys, and cartoons. Others tend to have much more complex blends. The Diffuse color is often replaced by or mixed with a bitmap, with the small button next to its color swatch giving you quick access to the Diffuse map channel.

TI P

When you analyze real-world colors, you need to flood at least an area of it with white light, eliminating any surface shading. This light is ideally quartz or xenon (the highest temperature lamps readily available), but halogen works well enough. You can isolate the diffuse color by holding a pocket halogen flashlight close to the surface and then viewing it so you do not see a highlight.

Specular Color Component

The specular color mixes with the illuminating light's color. This mix varies between materials but is usually tinted to the diffuse color or has no color (zero saturation). A good starting point for materials is to copy the diffuse color to the specular color and increase the Whiteness control toward white.

The influence that the specular component has on a material is directly related to its shininess and shininess strength values. Materials that have no shine cannot form a specular highlight. If the material has shine and a highlight is formed on a material, the material's diffuse color mixes with the specular in an additive, or light-like, manner.

A material's specular color is not rendered unless a highlight is formed from a light source striking a surface and being reflected back to your viewing position. The angle from your viewing position to the surface needs to equal the angle of incidence back to a given light for that light to create a highlight on the surface (see fig. 21.17). Note that angular relationship is being adjusted by the Place Highlight function.

Ambient Color Component

Although the ambient value represents a material's shaded portion, it affects a great deal of a surface because only a small portion of an object is usually in direct light at a given time. Most or at least parts of objects are illuminated with glancing light that is shaded across their surfaces. As surfaces are shaded, the ambient color mixes with the diffuse in a *subtractive*, or pigment-like, manner. Once in complete shadow, the ambient color is used exclusively. The resulting ambient color seen without light is usually still quite dark because its only illumination is from your ambient light value.

FIGURE 21.17
Specular highlight locations being dictated by viewing and lighting angles.

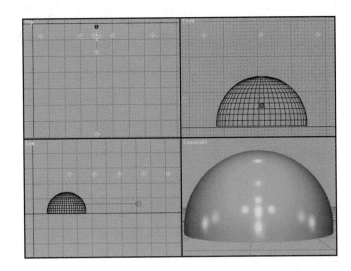

TIP

Darkening the ambient value is often beneficial to achieve deep, rich material colors. You can do this easily by copying the diffuse color swatch to the ambient color swatch and lowering its value.

Theoretically, few materials have different ambient and diffuse values. (Some that do are those materials that glow or are naturally iridescent.) The shading that occurs across most surfaces is the simple reduction of illumination, which is why it is often suggested that you start by keeping the ambient and diffuse values constant. In practice most computer artists do *not* do this.

Making the Ambient color *darker* than the Diffuse deepens the shading and tends to create richer renderings. This technique intensifies the shading and enables you to use less, more general lighting in your scene. Most artists make it standard practice to copy the Diffuse color swatch to the Ambient and then reduce the color's value by at least 50 percent. If you examine the material libraries that ship with 3DS MAX, you will notice that nearly every material uses this technique.

TIP

You can simulate materials that have a very rich quality to them, such as lacquered woods, by bringing their ambient color to full saturation and value. A chestnut brown diffuse material given a bright red ambient value forms a very warm, rich brown.

When a scene is illuminated solely with ambient light, a surface's rendered appearance is controlled entirely by its material's ambient color. This effect of color "switching" is important to realize when using a pure white ambient light to illuminate the scene (a common situation when creating flat work for two-dimensional prints). When using white ambient light, your interest focuses entirely on the diffuse color component and no other.

Locking Colors

To the left of the colors are lock buttons that lock the colors so they become the same, and then adjusting one adjusts them both. The use for locking is limited, considering the ease with which you can copy color swatches. In general, locking is not encouraged unless you want an absolutely pure color. Materials that do benefit from locked color are those intended to look like bright plastic and for advertising art where you are creating two-dimensional objects for flat illumination.

The lock to the right of the color swatches controls the locking of the Diffuse and Ambient map channels. By default, it is always locked so that when a Diffuse map is chosen, it's used for both the ambient and diffuse colors. If you disable the lock, the Ambient channel is ungrayed and a button appears next to the Diffuse color swatch—enabling you to tint a texture map in the same way you darken or saturate the base color swatches.

Standard Material Base Parameters

After defining the base color components for a material, there are several other controls that complete the Base Parameters section of the Standard material. These control the rendering mode, shininess, self-illumination, opacity values and wire, 2-Sided, and Face Map options. These base parameters are used as a starting point for these critical qualities. Most of these have corresponding map channels that influence or replace the parameters.

Shading Modes

The most dominant option in the Standard material is the shading mode. This option controls what rendering method (algorithm) will be used to evaluate and shade the base colors and shine. The three shading modes (Phong, Metal, and Constant) take the same rendering time but change the overall characteristic of the material when rendered by the production renderer, as shown in figure 21.18. The appearance of surfaces in the viewports is unchanged because the interactive renderer considers all materials to be Phong. Map channel capabilities, shadows, reflections, and atmospherics treat all shading modes the same.

FIGURE 21.18

The Constant, Phong, and Metal shading modes.

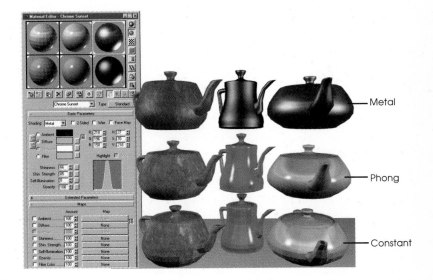

Metal

Phong

Constant

The Phong and Constant shading modes use all the same material properties but treat shading and smoothing entirely differently. The Constant shading mode ignores smoothing groups and instead looks for coplanar surfaces. Each coplanar surface, or facet, will be rendered with the same constant color with edges along facets being anti-aliased. This mode is of primary use for those who create games and flat art work.

TIP

When using Constant shading, you often want to ensure that your rendered output has pure colors per facet. To do so, you must uncheck Output Dithering for True Color in the Rendering Preference Settings. 3DS MAX dithers 32-bit, too, from its internal super-high color rendering of 64-bit color.

The Phong and Constant shading modes include a Soften option to reduce the striking highlight glare of glancing light, as shown in figure 21.19. This option should be ON for all but the glossiest of materials—glass, lacquers, gloss paint, or shiny plastic (it should definitely be on for any mapped materials). The only reason it is not the default is that the interactive renderer cannot reproduce the Soften effect.

FIGURE 21.19
The impact of Soften on materials.

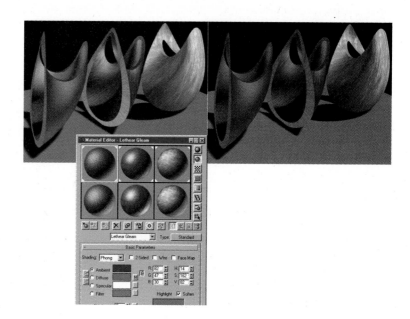

The Metal shading mode (based upon the Cook/Torrance algorithm) does away with the Specular color swatch and value. Metal materials derive their highlight color directly from their Diffuse color component and the shape of their highlight curve. The shape of the highlight curve and the resulting shine across the surface is very different between Phong and Metal shading modes, even though the shine values stay the same.

2-Sided Option

The 2-Sided option tells the renderer to ignore face normals for the surface and render both sides regardless of which way it is facing. This option is intended to be used for geometry or surfaces that you can see through such as glass and wire frames (see fig. 21.20) and modeling both sides of the object is not needed for realism. This is also used for opaque objects that are very thin and need to show both sides, such as playing cards or paper money.

Using 2-Sided materials on more substantial models can make them appear odd because their edges will appear paper thin (which they really are). This option is also used when imported models have troublesome normals that may seem too time consuming to fix. In the last case, the option should be weighed against correcting the normals because this is a somewhat expensive option that causes the program to render many more faces than usual.

FIGURE 21.20

Single-sided versus the 2-Sided material option.

NOTE

If a Refraction Map is in use, the 2-Sided option does not affect opacity or refraction and will have an impact only if the material is also a Wire material.

Wire Option

The Wire option eliminates the surface and replaces each visible mesh or patch edge with a line, or wire. This situation is one of the few where a surface's edge visibility impacts its rendered appearance. The rendered characteristic of wires is actually closer to being pieces of paper. The wire's surface is flat along the face whose edge it borders. If the edge is shared between faces, the wire appears like a creased piece of paper, as shown in figure 21.21.

The size of the wire is controlled in the Extended Parameters rollout. The size can be controlled here by two methods: Pixels makes all edges the same width in the rendered image; Units gives real-world size unit widths to the wires. In either case, all wires have the same radius. The impact of your choice of how to define the wire width comes when you view the surface in perspective. If defined in pixels, the wires do not diminish in perspective, much as if you trace a photograph with a single-width pen. If defined in units, they are essentially treated as geometry and diminish in perspective accordingly. When rendered in an orthogonal or User view, the two methods will produce the same effect, with all wires rendering with a constant width.

FIGURE 21.21
The rendered effect of Wire materials.

NOTE

Wire materials will render as solid surfaces if anti-aliasing is not on. While you are in the Material Editor, the inside of the sample is always anti-aliased and you have no need to change the Material Editor option to anti-alias.

When defining Wire size in units, it's often worth the time to set the 3D Map Sample Scale parameter in the Material Editor Options dialog to a size that represents a typical scale for your scene. This will give you a better feel for the look of your material in relation to the surfaces that will receive it. Your alternative is to make numerous test renderings.

TIP

The Renderer provides a Force Wireframe option that renders all surfaces in the scene as if they were Wire materials of one pixel width—more convenient than switching material properties for quick effects.

Shininess Parameters

The amount of polish, gleam, or gloss a material has is determined by its Shininess and Shininess Strength values. These values combine to create the material's overall specular character, with the effect graphically shown in the Highlight curve (see fig. 21.22.)

FIGURE 21.22
Shine values, the resulting Highlight curves, and their effects.

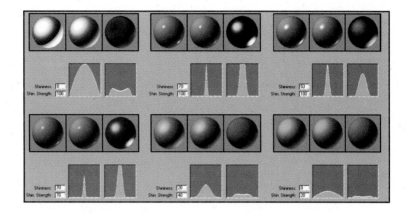

The Highlight curve, and not the numeric values, is your best gauge for what the specular highlight will be. The width of the curve dictates the width of the resulting highlight, with narrow curves being very small and wide ones very broad. The height of the curve controls the color of the highlight. When the curve touches the top, the highlight color matches the Specular color, and, as it lowers it mixes proportionally with the Diffuse color. A tall, sharp curve creates a narrow point of specular color while a low, broad curve creates a large, soft highlight that does not depart too much from the diffuse. Many real-world materials (such as leather, oiled wood, or a matte balloon) have an even, low sheen that you can simulate by using zero shininess and increasing shininess strength levels.

As the area of the highlight curve increases, so does the angle from which a specular highlight can be viewed. The higher the highlight curve, the more the highlight is composed of the specular base color. The lower the curve, the more it mixes with that of the diffuse base color.

The resulting Highlight curve varies greatly when you switch from Phong to Metal shading. The meaning of the curve is the same, but the result is far different (see fig. 21.23). The Highlight curve has the greatest effect on Metal materials because their mixture determines the specular color. The

Highlight curve display reacts differently with metal, creating a two-peaked curve at low settings and a tall, thick vertical line when high—the shinier a Metal material, the greater its contrast. It is in these dark areas that reflections are seen the most.

FIGURE 21.23

The difference in shine between Phong and Metal shading.

Opacity Parameters

By default, all materials begin 100 percent opaque. This percentage changes when you begin to adjust the various opacity controls of Opacity, Opacity Falloff, and possibly Opacity Maps. The characteristics of the opacity are further controlled by the Opacity Type and possibly the Filter Color. The basic effects of these controls are shown in figure 21.24. The Refract Map/ Ray Trace IOR parameter is for use with refraction maps and possibly ray-traced renderers. For the 3DS MAX production renderer, the option impacts opacity only when a refraction map is in use.

N O T E

When a Refraction Map is used at 100 percent strength, all Opacity controls are ignored except for the Opacity Type. If the Refraction Map is lower than 100, the Opacity percentage (defined by either the Opacity map or Opacity parameter) effectively "tints" the Refraction map with the opaque surface color. When active, the Refraction map settings have complete control over what can be seen through the object.

FIGURE 21.24
The three types of Opacity.

Filter

Additive

Subtractive

Three different types of transparency are in the Standard material: Filter, Subtractive, and Additive. The (default) Filter Opacity type is the only one that also uses the Filter color (otherwise the color swatch name is grayed-out). The filter color becomes the color in the transparent areas of the surface when the scene viewed through the material is bright. When 50 percent opacity is viewed against a white background, the Diffuse color is completely replaced by the Filter color. If between 50 and 100, the Diffuse and Filter colors mix; lower than 50 makes lighter shades of the Filter color. This description changes when the background is non-white. If the Background is black with a 50 percent opacity, the surface is the diffuse color, while a gray background will mix the Filter and Diffuse. In practice, the Filter color acts as an extra gauge whose color value influences the overall opacity of the surface. If you do not want the Filter color to affect the transparency at all, leave the color at its default 128 gray value.

NOTE

For 3D Studio DOS veterans, the only real change to transparency is the new Filter color, which replaces the default method. The Additive type is the same, and the Subtractive method is similar to the "New Subtractive Transparency" option available in the 3ds.set file. When importing 3DS files with transparency, the Diffuse color is copied as the Filter color, whose result comes close to the older method.

The Subtractive opacity type is simpler but different. As the material becomes transparent, it subtracts the diffuse color from the background. This has the effect of removing color seen through the material inversely of the opacity. A magenta material of 0 opacity, for example, will subtract the blue and red channels of everything seen through it. The Subtractive material can produce deep, rich semi-transparencies but does become unnatural when used with low or zero opacities.

The Additive opacity type will add the diffuse color to what's seen through the surface, brightening it and making the surface look self-illuminated. Additive opacity is brightest when the least opaque, with moving from 100 to 99 being a huge jump. In reality, Additive opacity of 50 or less is the same as Filter opacity using a white Filter color. In practice, Additive opacity is often used for light bulbs, light beams, ghosts, and the like.

Learning that the Opacity Falloff value always affects the material's opacity, regardless of whether the Opacity is less than 100 or if an Opacity map is being used, may be surprising (see fig. 21.25). The Falloff value dictates the transparency of the surface's center with the In option or its edge's with the Out option. When a material is transparent, you can see through to its inside. Because of this, enabling the 2-Sided option is very common if the object was not modeled with an interior as well as an exterior.

FIGURE 21.25
The impact of Opacity Falloff values.

The apparent density of the material is the next transparent quality to consider. Most physical objects will appear less transparent along their edges because more material is there to filter light. The edges of most transparent materials seem denser to your eye as you look through more material along the edges. If your model has an inside and an outside, you should try a zero Falloff value first and then adjust Inside Falloff upward until the desired effect is achieved. If your model only has an outside, then it will need Inside Falloff to not appear as an infinitely thin vessel (which it really is). The use of Outside Falloff is not as common because few surfaces are denser in their center than at their ends (examples include translucent solids, light beams, and ghosts).

You also can define the overall transparency of a material by using an assigned opacity map. Whenever an opacity map is active, it overrides the Opacity parameter because the map defines the strength and location of the material's opacity. Opacity falloff and type are still respected as before and work in conjunction with the opacity map definition, settings, and amount slider.

Self-Illumination Parameters

The Self-Illumination property produces the illusion of being self-illuminated by eliminating the Ambient shading component of the material. Increasing the value decreases the effect of the ambient calculation until shading is no longer occurring. If a material is fully self-illuminated with a value of 100, no shade is given to the surface and the diffuse color is used everywhere but at the highlights. Figure 21.26 shows how the ambient quality is replaced as self-illumination is increased.

FIGURE 21.26
The effect of Self-Illumination on the Ambient component.

NOTE ───

Because a fully self-illuminated material cannot be shaded, it will appear to not receive a cast shadow.

A self-illuminated material does not cast any light of its own, giving the appearance that it is lit internally and refuses to be affected by shade and shadow—meaning that it has uses other than simulating a glowing object. Times will occur when you might want an object to appear cartoon-like bold in color and unshaded (this works best if the object is coplanar). Objects that are being used as background "billboards" are often assigned a self-illuminated material so that their image remains consistent throughout the scene. Other objects are self-illuminated, such as televisions, projection screens, signs, and lamps. Don't worry if a material is not casting light on its own because you can simulate and control this effect. Self-illumination is often combined with additive opacity for creating convincing lamps and light beams.

Standard Material Map Channels

The 11 map channels at the bottom of the Standard Material are the starting points for perfecting your material's illusion. You can manipulate, combine, and branch maps in numerous ways to make even the simplest surface appear rich and complex. Careful use can make models extremely realistic yet efficient. Because of their impact, having a strong working knowledge of their makeup and use is important.

While a map channel can branch deeply, the way its result is interpreted varies according to the various channels. A channel's result is evaluated either in RGB *color* or as a grayscale *intensity* (see fig. 21.27). The Ambient, Diffuse, Specular, Filter Color, Reflection, and Refraction map channels all work with color. The Shininess, Shininess Strength, Self-Illumination, Opacity, and Bump map channels only consider intensity, treating the ending colors as if they were grayscale. Using color maps for these channels can be confusing because the visual contrast between colors might correspond to the contrast in luminance (pure Red, Green, and Blue will read as the same intensity values, for example).

FIGURE 21.27

The Standard material map channels and their color usage.

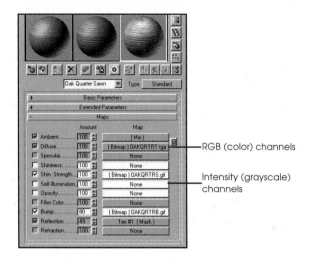

RGB (color) channels

Intensity (grayscale) channels

Bitmaps are extremely common to use with all channels but can be costly in regards to RAM. You use 1 byte of RAM for every byte deep a map definition is. A 24-bit color map will thus require 3 bytes per pixel, while a 256 indexed color or grayscale bitmap will require only 1 byte per pixel. If your bitmap uses filtering (which nearly all should), there will be an additional cost of 1 byte per pixel if Pyramidal and a whopping 12 bytes per pixel if Summed Area. Once a bitmap is referenced by a material or background, it can be used as often as you like without using additional RAM. Many artists devise several general use, tiling, random bitmaps as the starting point for nearly every material they create. These bitmaps give their materials some initial grit, spots, streaks, or texture that is essentially free of extra RAM consumption.

TIP

Using grayscale bitmaps for channels that read only intensity is very prudent. Not only do their shades relate directly to the map channel's effect, they use one-third the RAM of a 24-bit image.

When you define and use bitmaps, your goal should be to create and use the smallest image that does the job properly. The "right size" will depend on your output image's size, the prominence of the object displaying, and the speed at which it may be in motion. An often-used technique is to maintain several resolutions of the same image so the most appropriately sized one can be used for a given situation. A source image might begin from a Kodak CD-ROM with a resolution of 3072×2048 and using 25 MB. A series of smaller sized maps thus makes considerable sense, with 1200×800 using 3.8 MB, 600×400 using 1 MB, and 300×200 only 240 K. Remember that reducing resolution is acceptable, but enlarging a bitmap merely blurs it.

TIP

A good rule for ensuring high-quality images is to not allow a bitmap pixel to be as large as a rendered pixel. Thus, all rendered bitmap pixels will be sampled and the dreaded pixelated effect will not occur.

Diffuse and Ambient Texture Maps

Of all the map channels, Diffuse is probably the easiest to relate to. It applies the channel's result to the material surface much like paint or wall paper. Because of this function, Diffuse maps are often called "texture" maps by many other programs. When active at full strength, the Diffuse channel replaces the base diffuse color. The Amount slider indicates the amount of the map channel to be used. Levels between 0–100 mix with the Diffuse color component proportionally.

The Diffuse channel is unique in having a lock icon to its right. When active (the default), the Ambient map is locked to the diffuse. When locked, the Ambient map channel is grayed-out and the Diffuse map is used for both the diffuse and ambient shading components. Unlocking this option enables you to specify a different source for the ambient component, as shown in figure 21.28. Separate Ambient and Diffuse maps are used primarily to intensify a map's effect in the same way the ambient base color is often a darker or more saturated version of the diffuse base color. Copying the Diffuse map as an Ambient map enables you to control the intensity of the shade.

TIP

A saturated texture map can be made by adjusting an Ambient map copy's output. Increasing the RGB Level while lowering the RGB Offset will intensify the colors of the light to mid ranges while deepening the dark areas. For example, the result can turn a flat wood grain into a lacquered one.

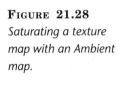

FIGURE 21.28
Saturating a texture map with an Ambient map.

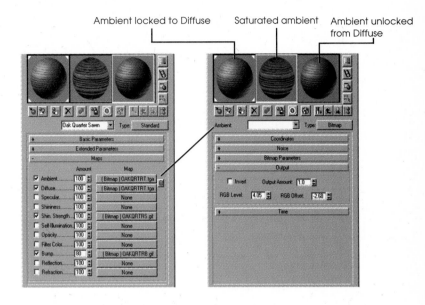

Using an unlocked Ambient map without a Diffuse map will create a subtle pattern on the surface that disappears in full illumination. This effect can be used for patterns on metallic surfaces that represent etches, anodizing, or panels. Random patterns can give a subtle texture to a surface, making solid colors much more believable.

Specular Highlight Maps

The Specular channel is for the special purpose case when you want to control what is seen in the material's specular highlight. This effect may be a subtle reflection or just a variation that is seen as a light's highlight passes over the surface. When active at full strength, the Specular channel replaces the base specular color. The Amount slider indicates the amount of the map channel to be used. Levels between 0–100 mix with the Specular color component proportionally. This map channel is the only one that impacts the color of the specular component. Metal shading does not have a specular component so the Specular channel is grayed out.

TIP

A light that has the object as its sole inclusion list entry can be very useful for controlling the placement and intensity of a highlight and thus the Specular map image.

Specular maps depend on several other variables within the material and the scene for their effect. While mapping coordinates dictate where the map will be placed on the surface, the scene's lighting setup and your viewing position to the surface determine where a highlight will occur. The material's shine properties then dictate how large and pure in color the highlight will be. As the specular color blends with the diffuse, so does the specular map. Remember that the height of the Highlight curve indicates color purity, while its width indicates the highlight's size. Because you can always mix at least the edges, the diffuse color or map has a significant impact on the coloring of specular image.

A common use for Specular maps is to place an image of the scene's light source on the object. Because this image is simulating a reflection, the bitmap should be representative of what you want the area around the highlight-causing light source to be. A bare bulb, a patterned window with curtains, an ornate street lamp, or a blazing sun are just a few examples. This addition can add considerable realism and is often seen on curved, shiny objects in daily life. When you see the shape of a window in the highlight of a balloon, you are seeing the equivalent of a Specular map. Specular maps are especially convincing when used in conjunction with Reflection maps. The reflection enforces the illusion that the material is shiny. Seeing the Specular Reflection of a nearby neon sign, for example, in the reflection bitmap's highlight can be a very realistic touch. Another common use for Specular maps is to place a texture that can only be seen when a highlight catches the surface. Water spots and stains (see fig. 21.29) are typical examples of this technique.

FIGURE 21.29

Using a Specular map to show water spots and simulate a sunset reflection.

The effect of the Specular channel closely resembles that of the Shininess and Shininess Strength channels. This resembling effect is because the color of the Specular channel is combined with the diffuse in an additive, or light-based, manner. If the Specular map is grayscale and has no saturation, the impact on the material's highlight is nearly identical to that of the shine maps. In practice, the Specular channel is primarily for introducing color.

Bump Maps

Bump maps give a simulated texture to a surface by indicating areas to pull out, project, or "bump" out. The Renderer creates this illusion by altering the light values across the mapped surface in the way that edges or "bumps" could cast shadows and receive highlights. Bump maps do not affect geometry. What seem to be raised edges are just an illusion—it's a rendering effect that only simulates the effect of highlight and shade. The ability to actually deform a surface is often termed displacement mapping (in other programs) and is done in 3DS MAX with a Displacement modifier. If you need to change a surface's profile, use a Displacement modifier. Bumps are for more subtle illusions that occur across a surface and not its profile.

The Bump map reads the intensity of the channel and treats black as having no effect, white full effect, and shades of gray proportional effect. The Amount slider controls the strength or apparent "height" of the bump rather than the percentage of the channel. Bump maps tend to be most effective when they begin at the lowest black values and work forward. In practice, you will usually get a more controllable result if you have a black field and work toward mid-gray than if you start with mid-gray and work to white.

TIP

The Output Amount parameter is a valuable aid in making fine-tuned adjustments to your bitmap's effect or increasing the Bump effect far beyond what is capable with the map's Amount slider.

Because a Bump map's effect is so prominent, it's worth examining exactly what it is doing. Each pixel on a Bump map projects forward in a square-like manner. Pixels that are of a different intensity project out from their neighbors like a terrace and do not slope toward one another. A good visualization for how Bump maps work is to take a framed grid's square pegs (or pins) and push them against the surface you want to approximate. The elevations of the resulting pegs relate to the shades of gray that would be required to approximate the same surface with a Bump map.

While the preceding analogy is easy to relate to, it does lead you to believe that the bump is projecting or recessing the various areas. In actuality, the bump illusion is done by simulating the ridges and valleys. The prominence of the edge is derived from the difference in color between adjacent pixels. Bump maps do not affect the shading properties of the different "terraces," "levels," or "steps" that appear to be formed across the surface. These areas all are rendered as if they were one smooth surface—it's their bumped edges that give the illusion of depth. This illusion is shown most clearly when you use Mask maps with bitmaps, as shown in figure 21.30.

FIGURE 21.30
Rendered edges being the secret to the Bump map illusion.

Creating the correct bitmap for a bump effect can be somewhat of an art. As with all mono-channel maps, you are always best off working in grayscale so you can easily determine contrast (and 8-bit bitmaps take one-third the RAM of 24-bit images). To simulate a dent, groove, or something else going into the surface, you might start by making the entire surface white, thus "out." The gray-to-black portions of the bitmap are then less projected, thus "in." To create a groove, you make the field white, the bottom line of the groove black, and the walls shades of gray. The "recipes" for common bump map types are listed as follows and are shown in figure 21.31.

- Grooves for grout lines, ridges, and panels are all based on simple line work, where the contrast between the line and field determines the depth. Note that an additional adjacent line of gray gives a subtle bevel and reduces the possible scintillation common with thin lines.

- Slopes for siding, ramps, v-channels, and pyramids are defined by even, linear gradations. Slopes can be done with a Gradient map type or with a bitmap given a gradient fill in a paint program.

- Cones for sharp points are actually a variation of slopes, except the even gradation happens radially. Creating cones can be done with the Gradient map type using a Radial Gradient Type or with a bitmap given a radial gradient fill in a paint program.

- Hemispheres for domes, rivets, and round groves are formed by charting the sphere's shading. This process is a "weighted" gradation where it is whiter for a greater distance toward the center and falls away rapidly to black at the end. Reversing the coloration changes a dome into an ice cream scoop dent. Complicated gradations such as these are often most easily done by modeling the geometry and rendering them.

FIGURE 21.31
Common Bump map effects and their bitmaps.

A convenient method for creating evenly shaded bump maps with anti-aliased edges is to model their basic geometry in 3DS MAX and use the rendered images as the basis for bitmaps (see fig. 21.32). A spherical bump map can be made by creating a sphere, assigning it a matte white material, and placing one spotlight dead center to it. Render the Spotlight viewport and you have a perfectly shaded and dithered image that is perfect for a bump map. If you use this technique, saving the alpha channel with the TGA file is very useful. This technique gives you a matching mask for the bump effect and doubles the usefulness of your bitmap.

FIGURE 21.32
Using rendered geometry as a source for Bump maps.

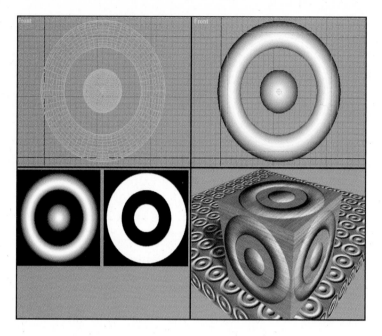

As with most maps in the Standard material, Bump maps are most convincing when they coordinate with other map channels having appropriate maps. Figure 21.33 shows how separate Diffuse, Bump, and Shininess Strength maps combine to form a realistic surface. You will find that when Bump maps are used, they should often be copied as Shininess Strength maps and possibly used as masks for other map channels.

FIGURE 21.33
Coordinating Bump, Texture, and Shininess Strength maps.

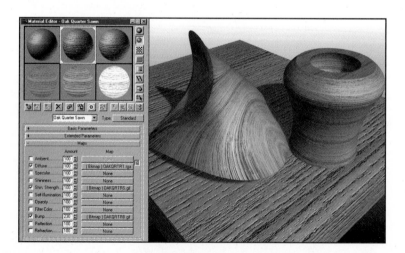

NOTE

A Bump map's projection is unidirectional—it does not matter from what angle the mapping is projected. This is different from other programs (such as 3DS DOS) where the mapping projection pushes the bump in on one side and out on the other. In 3DS MAX, the material parameters control the bump's direction.

You can reverse the direction of a Bump map three ways: by reversing the sign of the Amount slider, reversing the sign of the Output Amount, or with the Invert option. Each has its advantages, although the first two can be animated while the Invert option cannot be. There may be times when you need the bump to change direction on the same material. A bulge on one side of a surface might need to be a dent on the other side, for example. To accomplish this, you need to select the back side faces and assign them a duplicate material with a reversed bump setting.

Bump maps are valuable because they can simulate far more geometry than is actually present. They are more susceptible to render with scintillation or "jaggies" if you are not careful. The following is an approximate order of steps to take in quest of making the best possible Bump effect.

1. Avoid using bitmaps with angled lines if the same result can be achieved by drawing rectilinear lines and adjusting the Angle parameter and/or rotating the mapping projection. An angled line has an inherent, fixed amount of anti-aliasing whereas a rotated straight line is nearly resolution independent.

2. Ensure Filtering is being used in the Map type and Filter Maps is active in the Render Scene options. Bump maps will render properly only if filtering is occurring.

3. Increase the Blur Offset parameter, with a value of 0.01 being a good starting point. Large values will cause considerable blurring, so be careful with this setting.

4. Increase the Blur parameter. Balance this value with the Blur Offset to achieve the right effect.

5. Switch to Summed Area filtering if the Blur settings dull the effect too much. Remember that this option increases the overall RAM from four to 15 bytes per pixel. Note that less blur is usually required with Summed Area for a clean result.

6. Enlarge the size of the bitmap. Ensure no single-pixel-wide details occur. Remember the basic rule that no part of a bitmap should be rendered larger than it bitmap itself.

7. Add an intermediate gray border to edge details with sharp contrasts. A gray edge at a black to white transition will ease the otherwise sharp transition considerably.

TIP

When you have an often used bump effect (a square tile for example), maintaining a suite of similar maps that are identical in proportion but vary in resolution is often prudent. This maintenance enables you to choose the most suitable bitmap for the surface's prominence in the scene and conserve RAM when large maps are not needed. In the case of a tile bump map, the lowest resolution might have the grout lines one pixel wide, the next three to five pixels, and the largest seven to perhaps 15 pixels.

Creating bumps within bumps is an often needed effect. The Ceiling Tile Square material in the standard 3DS MAX library does this through the use of a Composite map that uses a Mask map (see fig. 21.34). The Output Amount parameter enables you to control the effect of each bitmap's bump strength independently.

FIGURE 21.34
Creating composite bump materials.

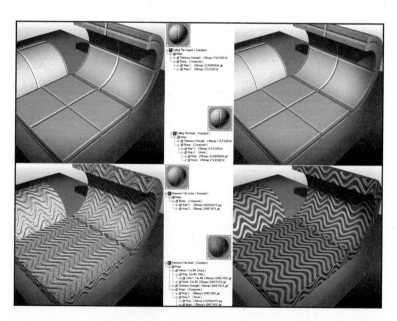

Shininess and Shininess Strength Maps

The Shininess and Shininess Strength channels (collectively referred to as "shine" maps) influence the impact of the existing Highlight curve. Unlike the other maps that have correlating base properties (Ambient, Diffuse, Specular, Opacity, Self-Illumination, and Filter Color) the shine maps work hand-in-hand with their base parameters. The base Shininess and Shininess Strength parameters control how broad and pure of color the resulting highlight is. The Shininess and Shininess Strength channels define patterns that influence the shape and percentage of the highlight (see fig. 21.35).

FIGURE 21.35

Patterns formed from using Shininess and Shininess Strength channels.

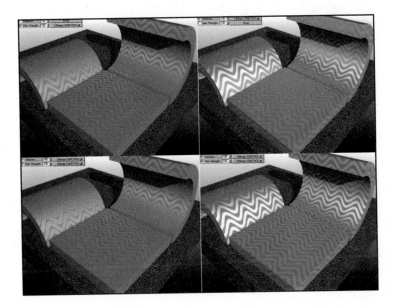

Adding shine maps does not make the material any more shiny than it already is—they define where that shine will be, or rather, will not be. Thus, a material must already be producing a highlight for the map to have a visible effect. If the shininess curve is dead flat or a vertical line or if the specular color is black, no or very little highlight exists for the shine maps to block.

The Shininess and Shininess Strength channels affect the Shininess and Shininess Strength parameters independently—that is, the Shininess channel controls the size of the highlight while the Shininess Strength channel controls the amount the specular color is mixed with the diffuse. You can control the purity of the highlight while maintaining its size, or you can define its extents while preserving the intensity. The shine maps are mono-channel in nature, working only with the intensity of the RGB color or the alpha channel (which by definition is grayscale).

WARNING

You should not use the Bitmap Output parameters or an RGB Tint map to increase the intensity of a Shininess or Shininess Strength map because it adversely affects the resulting Specular component. You can decrease it only by these methods. If you need to increase the intensity, and thus the highlight, you should use a Mix map type or adjust the bitmap in a paint program instead.

The Shininess Strength channel is your primary control for texturing the highlight because it throttles the value of the Shininess Strength parameter. Without strength no shine occurs. So black values make the surface matte by lowering the strength to zero, gray values allow a percentage of the strength value through, and white allows the full value through. You cannot increase the resulting highlight with the Shininess Strength channel—you can only "mask" out areas where the shine is reduced. The Amount slider simply allows a percentage of the channel through. Three variables serve to control the same effect: the Shininess Strength parameter, the color of the Shininess Strength channel, and the channel's Amount slider. For example, the following would all produce the same 50 percent strength shine:

- Shininess Strength 50, white Shininess Strength channel at 100 percent

- Shininess Strength 100, white Shininess Strength channel at 50 percent

- Shininess Strength 100, mid-gray Shininess Strength channel at 100 percent

NOTE

For 3D Studio DOS veterans, using the 3DS MAX Shininess Strength channel (without a Shininess map) is closest in behavior to the 3D Studio R3 and R4 shininess maps.

While similar in principle, the Shininess channel effect works very differently than the Shininess Strength channel does. Both channels reduce the corresponding base parameters, but reducing Shininess does not "dim" the highlight as lowering Shininess Strength does. Instead, the highlight becomes broader. Black values from the channel will bring the shininess for those areas to zero, while white will send no value at all. After the map channel has been modified by its Amount slider, the value is subtracted from the Shininess value that already exists. If the Shininess is zero, and thus produces a maximum sized highlight, nothing can be modulated. A Shininess channel will have the greatest effect when the base Shininess parameter is at 100, so values can still be subtracted from.

Contrary to the documentation, you should be cautious about using the two shine channels in conjunction with one another because they control very different effects. The Shininess Strength channel controls the brightness of the highlight, dimming the highlight from full to none, and does not affect the highlight's size. In contrast, the Shininess channel grows the highlight size and does not directly affect the highlight's brightness. If you were to animate the strengths of matching Shininess and Shininess Strength channels and the corresponding parameters were 100, the highlight would be brightest at the beginning but largest during the end of the animation.

NOTE

Shine channels have a much greater impact on metal shaded materials because the material's color is calculated from the shininess properties. Because of this effect, metal materials show the effects of a shininess map across their entire surface and not just in their highlights.

When used without any other map channels, the shine map textures the highlights across the surface and you are defining shine patterns for a perfectly smooth and consistently colored material. Situations that call for this include scraped, scratched, stained, and dusty areas on an otherwise shiny material, or burnished, polished, gilded, and wet areas on an otherwise matte surface.

NOTE

Be careful when you use Shininess Strength maps without tiling. In such a case, only the area defined by single bitmap decal will receive any highlight, and the rest will be matte.

The shininess channels are most often used in conjunction with other map channel types to add critical realism to materials. As a material simulates different effects across its surface, you usually need to vary the highlights for the various regions. During the life of a surface, high spots are subject to daily abrasion. Surface roughness has different effects on different types of materials. Through age, the higher areas of polished surfaces grow duller, whereas those on rough surfaces start to wear smooth and become more polished. Rivets on rough metal, raised areas of old wood, and high points on a sculpture become shinier, whereas the treads of a tire, grips on a racquet, and ridges on glass become duller.

When combined with bump maps, the shine channels can make raised areas more or less polished and recessed areas matte (see fig. 21.36). The shininess qualities of a material most often relate its recesses and projections. The grooves between metal panels, joints between glazed brick, and cracks in a pot all are matte in comparison to the rest of the material. A shimmer across these areas would spoil the illusion, and reusing the bump to control the highlight prevents this from happening. This is a common need so you should consider copying the Bump channel as a Shininess Strength channel (most often as an instance) as being standard procedure.

FIGURE 21.36

Bumped materials with and without Shininess Strength maps.

When using opacity to represent true holes, the Opacity channel needs to be copied (usually as an instance) to the Shininess Strength channel to prevent highlights where voids are supposed to be (see fig. 21.37). Otherwise, the 0 percent opaque areas are treated as if they were actually clear glass and highlights will occur in "space"—ruining the effect.

FIGURE 21.37

Transparent materials with and without a Shininess Strength maps.

When combined with Diffuse maps, the shininess maps make different areas of the "painted" surfaces more or less shiny and can differentiate areas that are actually smooth to the touch. The gloss paint on a wall, brass dividers in a wood parquet, gold leaf in a logo decal, burnished rivets on finished metal, polished dots on a watch face, or glass within a frame are all shinier than the rest of the material and would benefit from a Shininess Strength map. Shininess maps can make reflective materials look especially real when combined with a reflection map. Varying shininess values can cause reflections to "dance" across the surface as the object is rotated. When representing materials in which everything is not perfectly smooth, such as with metal plating, shininess maps can be used to chart the course of the irregularity and give play to a subtle, low-strength reflection.

Self-Illumination Maps

The Self-Illumination channel enables you to isolate the simulation of light emission in the same way as the base Self-Illumination parameter. The channel reads intensity and converts that to the equivalent of the base Self-Illumination parameter, with black equaling zero, white equaling 100, and shades of gray having proportional effect (see fig. 21.38). When this channel is active, the corresponding base parameter is ignored. When you decrease the Amount slider, the result of the Self-Illumination is decreased but it is not mixed with the base Self-Illumination parameter.

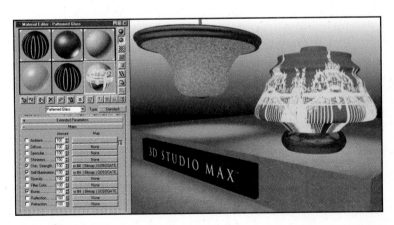

FIGURE 21.38

The effects of using Self-Illumination maps.

Remember that self-illumination is simulated in 3DS MAX by removing the ambient shading. Full strength (white) areas of a Self-Illumination channel will thus show the material's diffuse component without any shade. A map that matches the Self-Illumination channel but contains a contrasting color is often used in the Diffuse channel to intensify the break between the field and the self-illuminated portions.

When used without tiling, Self-Illuminated channels provide an excellent method for simulating signage, glow-in-the-dark paint, and etched patterns in a bright lamp. Self-Illuminated maps also prove quite useful in tailoring the effects of illuminated signage. Commonly, signs are painted on glass or pressed from plastic. The opacity of the paint and thickness of the plastic affects the amount of light emitted. You can reinforce this effect by using the material's texture or bump bitmap as a self-illuminated map and adjust its effects accordingly. Neon can be approximated with matching Bump and Shininess Strength channels and carefully placed omni lights (if not viewed too closely).

Opacity Maps

The Opacity map channel is for defining patterns in your surface that can be seen through such things as holes, patterned glass, or translucent panels, as shown in figure 21.39. The Opacity channel replaces the base Opacity parameter and uses the intensity of the channel to determine opacity. Pure white is opaque, while absolute black is fully transparent, with shades of gray delivering proportional levels of opacity. The Opacity Falloff and Type, found in the Extended Parameters rollout, are still observed when an Opacity map is active.

FIGURE 21.39
Using Opacity maps to define transparency and simulate holes.

Realizing that once an Opacity map is activated, the material is considered to have 0 percent opacity everywhere except for the areas that are non-black in the Opacity map's bitmap is important. This idea matches the concept of an alpha channel exactly. The accompanying Amount slider essentially "darkens" the result by adding a percentage of "black." A white map with an amount of 50 percent is the same as a mid-gray map with an amount of 100 percent. While the slider can make the map more transparent, the slider can not make the map any more opaque. If you need areas to be more opaque then they are, your only recourse is to adjust the color values that produced the result in the Opacity channel.

Warning

You should not use the Bitmap Output parameters or an RGB Tint map to increase the intensity of an Opacity map because it adversely affects the resulting Diffuse component. You can decrease it only by these methods. If you need to increase the intensity, and thus the opacity, you should use a Mix map type or adjust the bitmap in a paint program instead.

Opacity maps make a surface transparent only—they do not eliminate the surface from being there, meaning that the transparent areas are more like clear glass or plastic rather than holes. As with glass in real life, those transparent areas will display highlights if the Shininess Strength is present. To realistically simulate voids with a material that has shine, you must copy the Opacity map (usually as an instance) to be a Shininess Strength map as well.

Shadows will only respect the transparency defined by Opacity maps if they are casting ray-traced shadows. If you are using the default Filter Opacity type, the color of the shadow will be tinted by the base filter color, or Filter map if one is defined. Lights using shadow maps for their shadows will cast solid shadows, regardless of how the opacity is defined.

Filter Color Maps

Filter Color maps usually work hand-in-hand with Opacity. When the Opacity type is Filter, a Filter map will tint the transparent areas of the surface with its map (note that other programs may call this transmissive color). If ray-traced shadows are used, the tinted areas will also be transmitted into the resulting shadow (see fig. 21.40).

In practice, Filter Color maps are almost always color copies of a matching Opacity map. This match is required to paint the correct color onto the cast shadow. Some opacity needs to be there for a Filter map to have effect. Completely transparent surfaces are just that, so they can not display or transmit any color. If the Opacity type is Subtractive or Additive, the Filter map is ignored.

Reflection Maps

While everything in a material is an illusion in the quest of simulation, nothing may seem more so than reflections. While a ray-trace render will trace reflections throughout the scene for accurate (and extremely time-consuming) reflections, the 3DS MAX production renderer is a scan-line renderer and offers numerous alternatives to produce convincing results quickly. If objects are in motion, telling whether the reflections are accurate or not is extremely difficult. Note that these techniques are the same in which Renderman generates reflections, and they are extremely convincing in Pixar's *Toy Story* film.

Reflections are fundamentally different from every other map type because they are (or pretend to be) a result of the world around them. Because of this, they do not use and do not require mapping coordinates. Whereas other maps are fixed to a surface, reflections are dependent on your viewing position to the object. If you were to rotate a reflective object about its centroid, the reflection would stay consistent. A chrome propeller blade hub is a perfect example—as the prop rotates, the reflection remains perfectly still.

Reflections can be used as an end in themselves, such as a mirror, or as a subtle touch to make a shiny or reflective object appear more realistic. Reflections can either use a reference image (bitmap or otherwise) or generate their own through the Reflect/Refract or Flat Mirror map types. When using the latter, the reflections can be quite realistic and accurate. When using the former, the reflection is usually intended as an illusion to reinforce the concept that a surface is shiny and reflective.

Textures are fixed in location whereas reflections move across a stationary object as you move around it or stay constant as the object is revolved and your eye is stationary. The effect of reflections depends on your angle of view to them, and so are calculated properly only when viewed in camera viewports. Remember this when you make quick previews of your scene for material judgments.

Several rules govern the rendered appearance of a reflection, regardless of the reflected image's source. A reflection's color is primarily affected by the material's Diffuse component and to a smaller extent, its Ambient component. The Specular component remains unaffected by a reflection (remember that it's affected only by a Specular map). Because of this effect, reflections cannot be seen in highlights. When you want to maximize a reflection and make it mirror-like, try the following steps (or do the reverse to minimize reflections):

■ To minimize the impact of the Specular component, make the highlight curve as thin as possible (increase the Shininess property).

■ Untinted reflections require gray Ambient and Diffuse components. Making these reflections black will allow the reflection to be seen at full effect.

■ The Reflection map's Amount slider dictates the percentage the reflection mixes with the Diffuse. Making this 100 replaces the Diffuse completely.

When using bitmaps as reflections, distorting or blurring the image to at least some degree is common. Often this step is done because the "reflected" image has nothing to do with the actual environment, and you only want to give the impression of being reflective. Other times the reflected image may not be large enough and the geometry not curvilinear enough to be convincing. Many materials are not mirror like in appearance, but only have a gleam, and a crisp reflection is not appropriate.

NOTE

When using maps to represent a reflection, the result may at times appear to be "self-illuminated." This occurs because the reflection map replaces the material's diffuse and ambient components and thus reacts minimally to shade—meaning the reflection can be seen independent of a light source.

The premise is that the Reflection map represents a reflection and so there must be something in the scene that is illuminated and being reflected back to the surface. Because you are defining what this surface is "seeing" in the its reflection, you're responsible for adjusting this effect. This effect can be disturbing if the reflection's brightness is far different from the scene's light level. When the reflection is too bright, you have the following options:

- Decrease the Reflection map's Amount slider
- Increase the intensity of the Diffuse component
- Decrease the Reflection map's Output Amount
- Adjust the source image being used for the reflection
- Switch to using a Reflect/Refract or Flat Mirror map type to create the Reflection map

To prevent a reflection from occurring at specific areas on a surface, you need to use a Mask map type. When doing so, the surface will require mapping coordinates to locate the mask. Figure 21.41 shows an example of using a Reflection map with a mask. Using masks is very important when the material has areas that are shiny and dull. If you have defined a Shininess Strength or Shininess map, you should probably reuse it as a Reflection mask as well. You can then modulate the amount of reflection that occurs in that area as well.

FIGURE 21.41

Using a Mask map type as a Reflection map.

Reflection masks also are good tools for blocking areas of a flat mirror. Reflection masks enable you to create a pattern on the surface of your mirror and alleviate some restrictions of not being able to extend a flat mirror beyond an element's extents. Some examples are picture frames, tiles, and etched mirror glass. reusing the mirror mask as bump, texture, and shininess masks and maps is natural.

Refraction Maps

When you look through a thick vase, a magnifying glass, or even a glass of water, the scene beyond the material looks bent, distorted, or warped. This effect is due to the light being bent, or refracted, through the surface. In computer graphics, this distortion is termed *refraction* and it is simulated with a Refraction map. A Refraction map is actually a variation on an opacity map. With it you are simulating the bending of light through a transparent, but thick, material, as shown in figure 21.42.

FIGURE 21.42

Using Refraction mapping for transparent distortion.

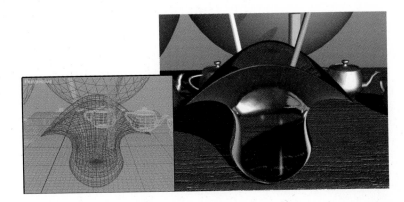

When you specify a Refraction map, you are completely changing the method in which opacity is defined. As a result, the Opacity parameter, Opacity Falloff, and Opacity map (if defined) is ignored whenever a Refraction map is active. As with Opacity maps, a Refraction map with an Amount of 100 is fully transparent. So at full strength, Diffuse, Ambient, and Opacity maps are ignored. The only Opacity parameter that is still respected is Opacity Type, which acts as it does with standard opacity.

The new parameter that suddenly becomes of use is the Refract Map/ RayTrace IOR setting (or just IOR for short). This setting indicates the Index Of Refraction for the substance. The gesture toward ray-tracing in its title is if a plug-in renderer should choose to use the setting for its own analytical uses. The IOR value has no effect at 1.0, where it is the equivalent of air. The default IOR value is 1.5 (the equivalent of glass). The higher the value, the more like a solid glass sphere the object is (with very few "real" materials exceeding 2.0). Values below 1.0 cause the distortion to be from a concave lens instead of a convex one.

What may be difficult to grasp is that when you specify a Refraction map, you cannot see through the object because the simulation of refraction makes the assumption that everything seen through it is bent. This difficulty occurs even if you lower the Refraction Amount to one and have the Opacity at zero. (All the Refraction Amount slider does is control the blend between it and the Diffuse component.)

While you can define any map type for a Refraction map, it is meant to be used with the Refract/Reflect map type. If you do choose to use a bitmap, you will have the greatest success using a cylindrical projection and then using the tiling and offset parameters to line up the map at a convincing location.

Automatically Calculated Reflections

The Reflection map can be calculated for you by using either a Refract/Reflect or Flat Mirror map type. The choice depends entirely on the geometry that is reflecting it. If the surface is curvilinear, such as a sphere, Refract/Reflect is the correct choice. If the surface is coplanar, like a wall mirror, the Flat Mirror map type should be used. If the object contains both conditions, such as chrome text, both map types need to be used for a convincing reflection.

NOTE

Because automatic reflection maps are not created until rendering time, you cannot see their effects while within the Material Editor—you must render the scene.

Figure 21.43 shows the controls for the two automatic Reflection map types. The Blur parameters enable you to blur or smudge the resulting reflection (with Reflect/Refract also providing Blur Offset because heavier blurring is often required for that map type). This effect is important for reflective surfaces that are not polished to a perfect mirror-like quality (such as stainless steel). The Render parameters for frames give you control of how often the Reflection maps are created during an animation. If your viewing position is not changing and the reflective objects are not moving, you may not need render the mirrors very often. The Use Environment Map option controls whether the background map is included in the rendering of the Reflection map. If you are using a basic Screen projection, the background may be reflected in an undesirable way (especially during animations) and you can now disable it.

FIGURE 21.43

The rollouts for the two automatic reflection map types.

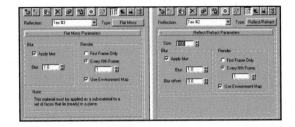

Although automatic reflections portray much of the scene, the object creating them cannot see itself because the object's bounding box determines the mirror's clipping plane and its extents obviously lay within it. This occurs even if other elements within the object have different materials and can lead to unrealistic situations when an object is composed of separate elements that would normally be able to see one another (a text string being a classic example). The only way around this situation is to detach the distinct elements as separate objects so they are no longer clipped (see fig. 21.44).

FIGURE 21.44

A string of text made into separate objects so they can be seen in reflections.

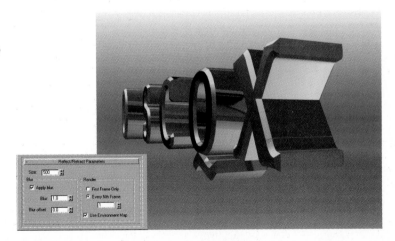

Automatic reflections are generated only for positive face normals (this occurs even if the material is 2-Sided or the Renderer is set to Force 2-Sided). This situation is not normally a problem, but may be if you are animating playing card-like mirrors. To render both sides of the same surface, you will need to use a two-sided material with an automatic material on both sides. An often forgotten fact regarding automatic reflections is that to be convincing, there must be *something* from them to reflect. While this statement may seem obvious, many modelers forget that their isolated object has nothing to reflect and at first wonder why the surface is "black" rather than reflective. Reflections also base much of their effect on your angle of view and are calculated properly only when viewed in perspective viewports—something important to remember when making previews of your scene for material adjustments.

Refract/Reflect Maps

The Refract/Reflect map type generates six maps at render time that enclose the object and are projected back on to the surface in a manner that is somewhat similar to box mapping. In concept, the renderer stands at the object's pivot point and takes a "snapshot" of the scene in each cardinal direction and assembles the six images into a reflection cube. These size images are then projected back onto the object. In computer graphic terms, this case is either termed a *cubic environment map* or a *T-map* (because the six images unfold from the box to form a "T").

T I P

You can control the placement of the cubic reflection by adjusting the location of the object's pivot point.

As the cubic reflection maps are projected back onto the reflective surface, each plane of the surface receives a specific portion. This occurrence explains why surfaces with curvilinear surfaces work best because the broad, flat sides of rectilinear objects have problems capturing enough of the projected scene to read as a reflection (see fig. 21.45). The reflected scene is far more believable on a curved surface because every facet is catching its own portion of the scene and the scene wraps around the surface. A cube that sits on a textured floor reflects only a blurred portion because its face "sees" only a small piece of the reflection cube's image.

Refract/Reflect is different from Flat Mirror in having a Size parameter to control the size of its calculated bitmaps. You are given control of this setting because it can become expensive with it costing Size×Size×4-bytes×6-maps or the Size²×24-bytes. If the rendered reflection is too blurred, rough, or pixelated, you will need to increase this value. This cost is imposed for *every* object that uses the material because a new set must be made for every unique location. A good rule of thumb is that for an object that comprises half the rendered scene, the map size should be as large as the rendering output. Be careful assigning large values used by numerous objects because even a 500-line map will use 6 MB per instance. If you have several objects sharing the same material but of different prominence in the scene, you will conserve the most RAM by creating duplicate materials with varying Size parameters and assigning them accordingly.

FIGURE 21.45
Reflect/Refract reflections on curvilinear and rectilinear surfaces.

Flat Mirror Maps

The Flat Mirror map type also generates a reflection at render time, but the application and the result are much different than with Refract/Reflect. A flat mirror is just that—a single image of the scene is projected back onto the surface as it would see it. This effect is the one that most often comes to mind when people are asked to define a reflection. The operative word in this map type's title is *flat* because this mapping type works properly only with coplanar surfaces.

When the renderer analyzes an object that uses a Flat Mirror map, it looks for the first face in the object definition that has the material ID# for that material. The first face found "wins" and defines the plane for the resulting reflection. Because you rarely know which is the first face, always assigning Flat Mirrors to a face selection at the Sub-Object level or to perfectly coplanar surfaces is good practice. Assigning is *not* required at the Sub-Object level—you are just assured of what is defining the mirrored plane. If more than one plane is defined, the reflection may appear more like a spotlight projection because it does not turn at the edges (see fig. 21.46).

FIGURE 21.46
Flat Mirror reflections defined by single and several planes.

TIP

The Box object is actually ideally designed for Flat Mirrors. The top face of a Box contains the first face and is given Material ID #1. You can reliably assign them a Standard Material using a Flat Mirror Reflection map and always know the top will reflect correctly. This works best if their height is zero because otherwise the sides will not correctly reflect.

Unlike Reflect/Refract maps, Flat Mirrors are always calculated with the appropriate resolution and do not have a map size parameter. Flat mirrors that cannot be seen from the rendered view are not calculated. This attribute does not cause additional problems because Flat Mirrors cannot be seen in reflections under any condition. The RAM required for a Flat Mirror varies with its size in the scene because only the slice of the scene that the surface can actually see is rendered.

Multiple Mirrors

Many surfaces contain more than one mirror condition. The text shown in figure 21.47 is a typical example of this condition. The front faces are coplanar and have been assigned a Flat Mirror, whereas the bevel and sides share a common Refract/Reflect map. Making this distinction is straightforward but does require some planning. When the same automatically mapped material is applied to different objects, separate reflection maps are generated. To create multiple mirrors within the same object, each occurrence must have a different, automatically mapped material. So for multiple reflections within the same object, you must use a Multi/Sub-Object material with different material definitions for the different areas.

FIGURE 21.47

Mirrored text using both Refract/Reflect and Flat Mirror reflections.

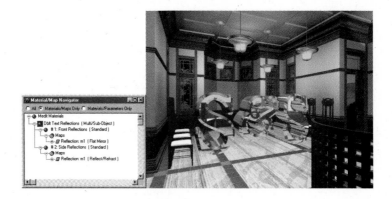

NOTE

Mirrored text is a good example of when the front faces should be detached as an object with a Flat Mirror map, and the remaining object assigned an automatic reflection.

When positioned appropriately, mirrored surfaces see each other's reflection and can bounce their reflections back and forth (an infinite number of times if they are actually perpendicular to one another). Because each iteration requires another rendering pass, the time can be excessive, and you are given control over the number of bounces that occur. For Reflect/Refract maps, the number of times reflections are bounced is controlled by the *Rendering Iterations* parameter (under Auto Reflect/Refract Maps) in the Render Scene dialog. In practice, you will rarely need to increase this number beyond three unless the reflections are actually the focus of your composition.

NOTE

Only Refract/Reflect maps can see each other's reflection. Flat Mirror reflections cannot be seen within either reflection type (although Reflect/Refract can be seen by Flat Mirrors). During rendering, all Reflect/Refract materials are rendered first, followed by all Flat Mirror materials.

The noted problem can be solved by using a cubic environment map that uses assigned images, rather than generating its own. Unfortunately, this capability is not currently present in 3DS MAX R1.1, but could be provided through a new material type (as always, check the CompuServe Kinetix forum and http:\\www.ktx.com for any news of such additions).

Using Map Types

When you click on a map channel button, you are automatically thrown into the Material/Map Browser shown in figure 21.48. The *Browse From* options enable you to choose from a previously defined map from the currently loaded material library, what is currently active in the six sample slots of the Material Editor, what has been assigned to the objects currently selected, from anything assigned in the scene, or define a map from scratch by choosing the generic types.

FIGURE 21.48

Map type choices after clicking on a map channel button.

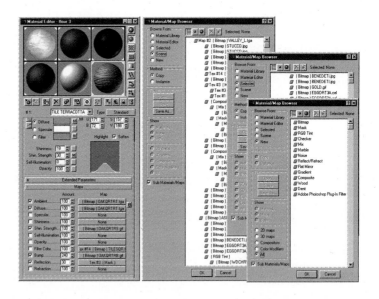

This process starts the layering of maps within a material tree. Figure 21.49 demonstrates this process by layering several different map types within a single Standard material. Here, four maps use a Composite map type to combine two bitmaps, while the Reflection map uses a Mask map type to perfect the illusion. The Starry Nebula material in the 3dsmax.mat library is an example of layering numerous Noise maps to produce a starry space scene.

FIGURE 21.49

The bottle contains several maps including a composite map in the Diffuse channel for the large label and the label around the neck.

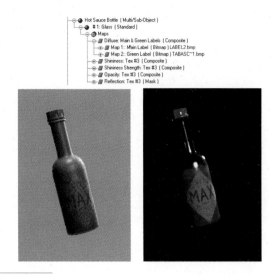

Maps Types for Images

The most commonly used maps are those that define an image. This may be procedural, being defined and calculated by the map type itself, or a reference to a physically existing one, such as a bitmap. Often, image maps enable you to define yet others to create combinations and overlay of patterns. Regardless of the options they present to you, each defines a bitmap that has passed the map channel to be interpreted by the parent material. Image maps are organized into 2D and 3D categories because some work like a bitmap in 2D, UV mapping space and the others like a solid surface in 3D, UVW mapping, or XYZ world space.

2D Maps Types

The 2D Map category is what most people think of when one speaks of "maps." Even the word "map" implies that it is flat. It also implies that it relates to something in a very specific manner, which is where mapping UV coordinates come into play. Of all the 2D maps, the Bitmap map type is the easiest to relate to because it is a simple representation of a physical bitmap that could have come from a sample disk, paint program, or even a rendering in 3DS MAX. If someone is generically talking about a "map," they are most likely referring to a Bitmap map type.

The Reflect/Refract and Flat Mirror map types generate reflection maps automatically when rendering, based on the object's location and your viewing angle to it. These map types are designed specifically for use as either Reflection or Refraction maps (and are covered in this chapter with those map channel descriptions). While nothing is stopping you from using these with any map channel, the results may be difficult to predict. Experiment, and you may find situations when an automatic reflection map can be perfect for a special effect. All 2D maps (except for the automatic reflection maps) use the same Coordinate and Noise rollouts to control the offset, tiling, repeat, angle, blur, and distortion of the map (see fig. 21.50). The Output and Time rollouts are also common to several map types. The most commonly adjusted parameters tend to be in the Coordinates rollout because this controls the size, placement, and rotation of the map. This rollout also contains the "fuzziness" of the map with the Blur and Blur Offset parameters.

FIGURE 21.50

*Rollouts common to the
2D Map types.*

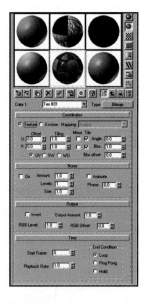

In general, common parameters affect the entire map whereas unique parameters affect the inner characteristics of the map. The Gradient map type, for example, has its own noise parameters in addition to the common Noise rollout. The unique parameters create noise within the gradient itself whereas the common ones affect the gradient as if it were one map.

Smoothing a 2D Map with Blur

By their very nature, bitmaps are not perfect. No matter how evenly shaded or complex in color depth, bitmaps are just an arrangement of colored squares, which we term pixels. These square pixels are fine when viewed straight on in 2D space, but begin to be a liability as they are placed in perspective in 3D space. Contrasting pixels become more pronounced and visible aliasing, scintillation, stair stepping, or the "jaggies" sets in. This is also where Filter maps and blur come into play. Filter maps do for 2D maps what anti-aliasing does for geometry, with blur settings controlling their effect. Figure 21.51 shows the effects of no filtering, while figure 21.52 shows the same scene with filtering enabled. Although it uses a bit more RAM, it's obvious to see why it's the default option.

FIGURE 21.51
A tile floor material rendered without Filter maps.

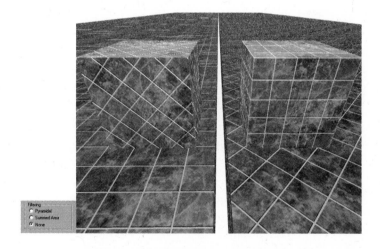

FIGURE 21.52
The same scene rendered with Filter maps.

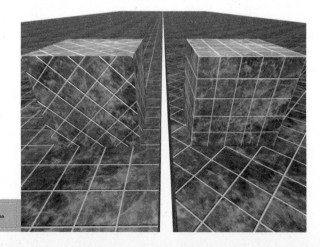

The preceding figures point out how blur's primary effect is to eliminate scintillation—those extremely annoying lines of "dancing" pixels and moiré patterns. Scintillation is especially noticeable as fine lines begin to converge in perspective (as in the distance) or come close together (as in the sides of the cubes). Examine the left cube within both figures, and you can also see how the diagonal lines appear "jagged" without blur, but render smooth with it. Also notice that the appearance of the marble texture is nearly identical in both figures. In actuality, a slight but subtle difference is there, as the filtered marble is a bit "softer" in appearance. Of all the map types, blur has the most profound effect on bump maps, with bumps not rendering correctly at all unless Filter maps are enabled.

Filter map is a computer graphics term that may use various techniques. 3DS MAX provides two types of filtering for bitmaps: Pyramidal (also known as mip mapping) and Summed Area (also known as summed area table). For other 2D maps, the default Pyramidal method is used. The Bitmap map type enables you to choose which filtering type to use or to disable it completely.

Note

Blur cannot occur unless Filter maps are enabled. When you disable filtering by either choosing None for a bitmap's filtering or turning off the Renderer's Filter maps option, blur settings for that bitmap or the entire scene are ignored.

The difference between the two filtering options is anti-aliasing quality and RAM requirements. Pyramidal filtering uses an extra byte per pixel, but the cost is minimal compared to its effectiveness. Summed Area filtering uses a superior, but more expensive technique, and uses an additional 12 bytes per pixel. Because of its cost, you may wish to remember it as "$ummed Area" instead and choose it only when your bitmaps require it. For some bitmaps, the switch to Summed Area filtering is critical while for others it's barely noticeable. Summed Area filtering has the greatest effect on materials having closely spaced lines that diminish into perspective or those that use a heavy blur setting to gain a "fuzzy" effect. Figure 21.53 illustrates the difference between the two filtering types.

As figure 21.53 shows, pyramidal filtering averages less of the image and causes moiré patterns to form in the distance. Summed Area does a larger averaging and avoids this condition. Up close, pyramidal filtering tends to look fuzzier whereas pyramidal reads crisp. If you can afford the RAM, Summed Area will provide a better result for your bitmaps.

Moiré patterns and scintillation

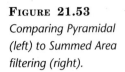

FIGURE 21.53
*Comparing Pyramidal
(left) to Summed Area
filtering (right).*

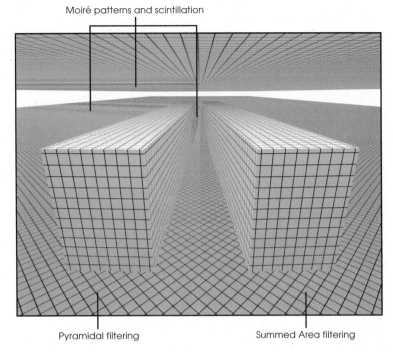

Pyramidal filtering   Summed Area filtering

The Blur parameter can then be thought of as strength setting for the filter maps. It provides its most basic effect at its default setting of 1.0, and a minimal effect at its 0.1 lower limit. Higher blur settings will predictably increase the blur, which can be very desirable for subdued reflection maps. The Blur Offset parameter is fundamentally different from Blur by filtering the 2D map before it is applied in perspective. The term "offset" is just like the Offset parameter—it shifts the bitmap by that amount, with 1.0 being a full bitmap offset. This explains why Blur Offset values as small as 0.01 have a significant effect because 0.01 means the source bitmap has been shifted by 1 percent. In most cases, use Blur Offset to adjust the softness or fuzz of the 2D map and Blur to control its anti-aliasing in perspective.

The common Noise rollout sends a distortion "wave" through the 2D map, as shown in figure 21.54, when you enable the parameters by checking its On option. The Amount parameter controls the wave's height, Level controls the number of iterations, Size controls the distance of a phase repeat, and Phase controls the position of the repeat. The Phase parameter is not respected unless the Animate option is enabled. The other parameters animate with the Animate button as normal and do not require this option to be checked.

FIGURE 21.54

Noise parameters being applied to 2D maps.

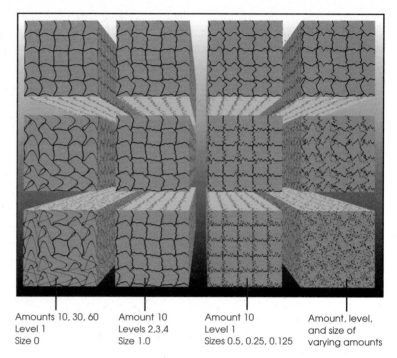

Amounts 10, 30, 60	Amount 10	Amount 10	Amount, level,
Level 1	Levels 2,3,4	Level 1	and size of
Size 0	Size 1.0	Sizes 0.5, 0.25, 0.125	varying amounts

Unique 2D Map Controls

After you realize that these controls are common, those that are unique to the particular map types aren't nearly as intimidating (see fig. 21.55). The use of the individual controls are described in depth in the standard 3DS MAX documentation, and in the case of Photoshop filters, the help file and associated Photoshop compatible plug-ins. While the Bitmap and Photoshop map types do not allow expansion, the Checker and Gradient map types both provide Color swatches that can be substituted for map channels, and so continue the material tree even deeper.

NOTE

The Photoshop Plug-In Filter map type can load only Photoshop compatible, 32-bit plug-ins. These plug-ins come from such third parties as Metatools. The filters that ship with Photoshop are prevented from working in anything but the parent program.

FIGURE 21.55

Controls unique to the various 2D map types.

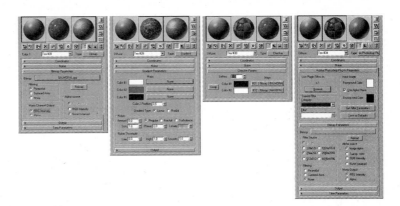

3D Map Types

The 3D type is what most people in computer graphics think of when the term procedural materials (or shaders) is used. Because these maps are applied in three dimensions, they course though an object and do not normally streak the way a 2D map does when the projection becomes colinear, as shown in figure 21.56. Of the four provided—Marble, Wood, Dents, and Noise—Noise is by far the most commonly used because it provides three variations that can be used to modulate many other map types and give realistic surface distortion, grit, and grime.

FIGURE 21.56

Using 3D procedural maps to uniformly cover a surface.

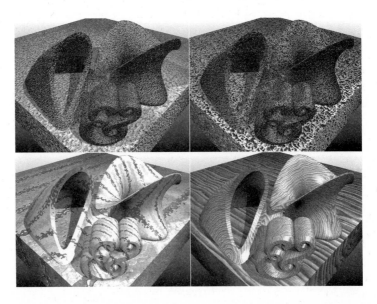

The four 3D maps share a common set of parameters for locating their effects on the surface (see fig. 21.57). If XYZ is chosen, the tiling is made according to the object's real-world size and no mapping coordinates are required. The location of the map relates to the object's creation matrix, which cannot easily be changed. The Offset, Tiling, and Angle parameters are thus provided to give you control of the map, and can be thought of as being analogous to position, scale, and rotation transforms. This form of real-world, XYZ scaling is the traditional method in computer graphics and works well as long as you only animate your objects with transforms. If, however, you animate the Modifier Stack, the mapping coordinates are still applied according to the original projection and the object will move through the mapping coordinates. Because this effect is not usually desirable, the UVW coordinate option is provided so you can use the assigned UVW mapping coordinates that translate with the vertices as the surfaces deform.

FIGURE 21.57

The common Coordinate rollout of XYZ and UVW coordinates for 3D maps.

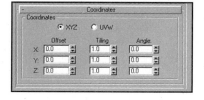

In practice, XYZ coordinates are best for static models. This statement is especially true when the same material is used between different objects because it ensures identical results. The result of these identical coordinates does make it appear as if the objects were punched or carved from the same solid block of material. When this effect is not desirable and you want the mapping to follow the lines of the object (or you are animating the object's Modifier Stack), UVW coordinates are the correct choice. When using UVW coordinates, you will most likely need to increase the Tiling considerably because a single repeat of a 3D map is usually intended to be quite small. This procedure is most easily done with the 3D map's Tiling parameter, rather than the UVW Mapping modifier tiling, because the latter would have to be quite large and might be difficult to relate to other, non-3D map types. After the common Coordinate rollout, each 3D map type has its own characteristics, as shown in figure 21.58. Coincidentally, each contains two color swatches to control the contrast and color of the particular effect. Each of these colors can be replaced by another map type in the accompanying map channel (and so continue the material tree). The parameters for the different types each control the individual effects.

FIGURE 21.58

The individual controls for the four 3D maps.

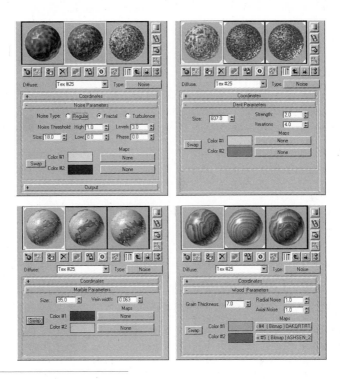

Map Types for Compositing

The Compositors category maximizes your options and enables you to combine your library of material bitmaps in limitless ways. If you are joining the effects for two or more sources, you are doing a composite. In practice, using these map types appropriately is critical to complex, realistic materials.

Mask, Composite, and Mix Map Types

For 3D Studio veterans, the Mask and Composite map types will seem very familiar, while the Mix map is an easy but very useful option. As figure 21.59 shows, each map type contains two or more channels for selecting yet other map types. Most often, these additional choices are bitmaps.

FIGURE 21.59
*The Mask, Composite,
and Mix map type
rollouts.*

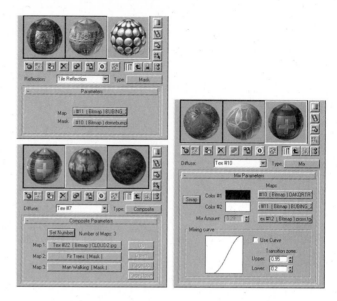

The Mask map type contains a Map channel for supplying the source image, and a Mask channel for suppressing the source map. The mask can be thought of as a stencil, airbrush friskette, cookie pattern cutout, or patterned glass through which the source image is seen. The white areas of the mask map allow the source image to show through, black areas block the source, and gray areas allow proportional amounts through.

NOTE

The eight mask file slots from 3DS DOS were all equivalent of this single map type. When you import a 3DS file that uses a mask slot, it is translated into a Mask map type.

The Composite map type combines any number of maps and defaults to a very manageable quantity of two. The maps are overlaid according to their number with Map 1 being the primary map and applied first. Map 2 is applied second, over Map 1; Map 3 is applied third, over Map 2; and so on. In order to see the primary map, Map 2 must have at least some transparency. This could be by means of an alpha channel or using a Mask map. As you layer more and more maps, the higher maps tend to need increasing amounts of transparency if the lower maps are going to be seen. This situation is similar to the way Video Post composites successive images with numerous Alpha Compositor events.

NOTE

The Texture 1 and Texture 2 map types from 3D Studio DOS are the equivalent of a Composite map having two maps. When you import a 3DS file with materials using two textures, they are translated into a Composite map type with Texture 1 & 2 becoming Map 1 & 2 respectively.

The Mix map type blends two map types and gives control over how the mixing occurs. The Mix Amount parameter indicates the percentage of Color 2 that is added to Color 1. Because the default Mix Amount is zero, you will not see Color 2's effect until you increase it. By default, this is a linear mixing. If you activate the Mixing Curve with the Use Curve option, you can weight the interpolation as shown in the accompanying Mixing Curve.

TIP

Mix maps are ideal for brightening or tinting other maps. You will usually get far better, more predictable results using a Mix map to adjust another map's effect, rather than using the map's own Output controls.

You can also specify a map type for the Mix Amount. When you do so, the Mix Amount percentage is ignored, although the Mixing Curve works as before. Use the intensity of the map to control the mix, with black being the same as a Mix Amount of zero and White a Mix Amount of 100. The Mix Amount map thus becomes similar to a Mask map type. An important thing to note is that the Mixing Curve only modulates the Mix Amount. If the Mix Amount is 0 or 100 (black or white), you will not see any effect when adjusting the transition zone because there is nothing being mixed. To use the Mix Amount percentage after specifying a map, you need to choose a "None" map to clear the channel and reactivate the Mix Amount parameter.

Map Types for Color Modification

The Color Modifying category is intended for map types that adjust the image qualities of other map types. Possible for this category is everything you might go to a paint program for (brightness, contrast, gamma, color balance, posterization, and so on). While this category shows much promise, it currently contains only the RGB Tint map type. When compared to common paint program methods, RGB Tint is fairly unconventional and is included primarily for compatibility with imported 3DS files (which contained this capability as a map setting for Texture and Specular maps).

Animating Maps and Their Parameters

As with most elements in 3DS MAX, maps properties can be animated. As a general rule, if a parameter uses an edit field for a value, then it is usually animatable. To confirm exactly what map parameters can be animated, examine the map Track View. Every animatable parameter is displayed with an animation track, while non-animatable options are left out.

The most basic way to animate a bitmap is to specify an animated bitmap type. With 3DS MAX R1.1, the FLC, FLI, CEL, and AVI files can all contain animations that will "play" across the material as the scene is rendered. When the end of the animation is reached, the animation loops. While easy to choose, it does lack control because it can be difficult to determine on what frame in the scene a given animation frame is presented.

For better control, you can specify a number of files that are either sequentially numbered or specifically listed in an IFL (image file list) file. For sequences, you specify the file name prefix that is common to the string of maps. For example, to use the 690 files in the blow0000.tga–blow0689.tga file sequence, you'd specify "blow*.tga" as the bitmap file name. When you do this, 3DS MAX automatically creates an IFL file with 690 file references. This IFL file resides in the directory that contained the file sequence and does not list any explicit path information.

After you get used to the idea of using an IFL file, you can expand on the concept and use more of its capabilities. An IFL file simply lists the files, in sequence, to be used. The bitmap references can contain explicit path names to any valid directory. Placing a number after the image name repeats the use of the image for that many frames. If the bitmap is an animated file, only the *first* frame will be used. To use additional frames of an animated file you will need to split the animation to individual images and list them in the IFL file. In practice, most professional animators prefer using IFLs to other methods of animating bitmaps because of the control they afford.

Using Compound Material Types

While the Standard material is unquestionably the most often used, several others are included with 3DS MAX that provide unique capabilities or ways of manipulating other material types as well.

Because of this initial branching into other materials, these materials are sometimes termed *compound* materials and often begin elaborate material trees. The most common situation is for compound materials to branch to Standard materials, although they could be other compound materials as well. In this way, you can continue to branch material definitions as you do with maps. Standard is the popular next step because these materials are primarily meant for combining the effects of other materials and have very few rendering properties of their own.

NOTE

Materials that rely on combining the effects of sub-materials (Top/Bottom, Blend, and Double Sided) need to maintain global characteristics. If the Face Map or Wire option is chosen within any sub-material, the others will match that choice in the compound material's result.

The Top/Bottom Material

The Top/Bottom material type enables you to assign two different materials to the top and bottom areas of an object. Which part of the object is considered "top" or "bottom" is dependent on its orientation to the World's Z axis. If a surface falls within the positive Z axis, it's assigned the Top material and if in the negative Z, the Bottom material (see fig. 21.60). This means if the object assigned a Top/Bottom material changes its orientation relative to the World Z axis, the material assignments will shift across the surface. Remember this situation when you're using Top/Bottom materials in an animation. If the object rotates, the location of the Top and Bottom assignments could shift across the object's surface.

The definition of the top-to-bottom transition is further adjusted with the material's Position parameter. Position can be thought of as weight that pulls the definition down when set low and up when set high. In reality, the angle at which a face qualifies as facing up or down is being adjusted. The transition between top and bottom materials can appear harsh because the assignment of materials is done on two faces. The Blend parameter allows you to soften this transition so break lines where faces change angle are not disturbingly obvious.

FIGURE 21.60

How the Top/Bottom material works. Based on the angle of the normal to the world Z, the face can receive either the top or bottom material.

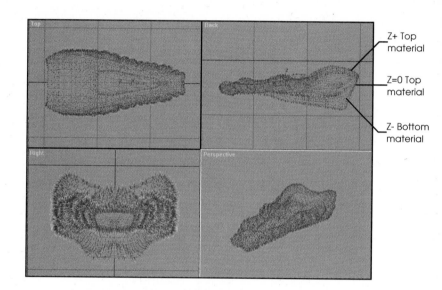

Z+ Top material

Z=0 Top material

Z- Bottom material

FIGURE 21.61

A usage of the Top/ Bottom material type. Notice how the two materials blend to produce a nice gum line transition.

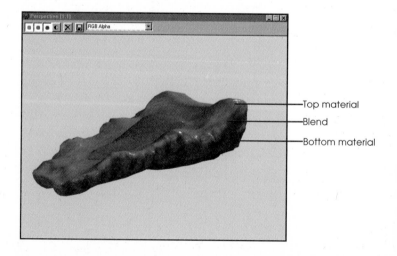

Top material

Blend

Bottom material

The crocodile's mouth in figure 21.61 is an example of where a Top/Bottom material works well. Normally, a mesh as complicated as the crocodile's mouth would be difficult to select the separate areas within for separate Material IDs. Moreover, an obvious seam would occur between separate materials. With the Top/Bottom material, the top faces receive the inner flesh material and the lower faces get the scaly surface material. The transition between the materials is adjusted with a Blend value.

The Double Sided Material

A Double Sided material addresses the problem of wanting to assign a different material to either side of a surface. Normally, when you assign a material to an object, the material is applied to both sides of a surface. 3DS MAX renders the side with a positive face normal and ignores the backface unless 2-Sided is enabled. The Double Sided material enables you to assign one material to the surface having a positive face normal, and another material to the backface of the same surface. The material labels these directions as *Facing* and *Back* respectively. The Facing and Back materials channels can then branch to any other material type you want.

The Translucency value is used to blend the Facing and Back materials. If you have a Translucency setting of 0, the Double Sided material works as you might expect—one material on one side and the second material on the other side. Values between 0 and 50 mix one side with the other until they are the same at 50. Values greater than 50 mix the opposite side more and the effect is as if you switched the material assignments. This impression increases until a Translucency of 100 effectively flips the assignments.

Figure 21.62 demonstrates where you might find yourself using a Double Sided material. The exploding object is using two different materials. The outside is cool metallic while the inside is hot and glowing. Another common use for Double Sided materials is for models that use single face thick walls where one side might require brick and the other side wallpaper.

The Blend Material

As its name implies, the Blend material allows you to blend two separate materials by a certain percentage. It also includes the capability to use a mask to control where the blend occurs and thus becomes a composite. The Blend material controls closely resemble those of the Mix map type, and you should review that map type's earlier description for more insight into Blend.

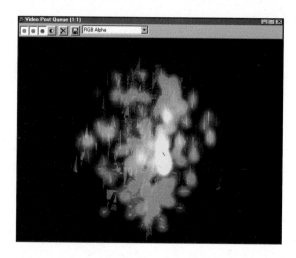

The Mix Amount value controls the percentage the two materials are blended. If a mask is referenced, the Mix Amount is grayed out and the blend is calculated by using the mask's intensity (as a mono-channel). When a mask is in use, the Mixing Curve can be used to modulate the transition between the two materials (see the Mix map type for more examples of these controls). The crocodile's skin in figure 21.63 uses a Blend material to achieve its effect. The primary difference between the Blend material and the Mix map is that Blend materials mix entire material definitions and not just map types. The Blend material mixes every parameter in the two material definitions whereas Mix affects only one channel within a material.

FIGURE 21.63

The crocodile's skin with two material types blended by a Noise map type.

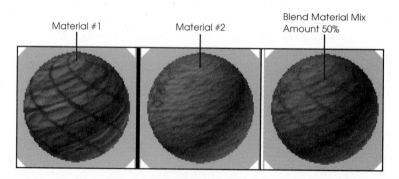

Material #1   Material #2   Blend Material Mix Amount 50%

The Matte/Shadow Material

The Matte/Shadow material is 3DS MAX's most ironic and intriguing material type. The irony is that the material doesn't render as a material; it essentially "cloaks" the surface it is assigned to. As the interface shows, there are no materials or maps to branch from. The Matte/Shadow material's sole purpose is its own special effect and is the only material from which you cannot branch. Within the Matte/Shadow is the capability to have the surface receive shadows and block other objects in the scene that might be behind it. The Matte/Shadow material becomes an essential technique for post processing or compositing background images with scene objects.

An object assigned a Matte/Shadow material becomes a "hole" in your scene that cuts out any geometry behind it and exposes the background beyond. This trait allows objects to be matched with elements of the background image.

The Opaque Alpha option controls whether the geometry assigned the Matte/Shadow material is included in the Renderer's alpha channel output. Leaving this box unchecked makes the objects invisible to the alpha channel, while enabling it includes the geometry's extents as being fully opaque. This option affects only the alpha channel—it has no impact on the rendered image itself.

The Atmosphere options integrate the matte object into atmospheric effects. If there is no atmosphere in the scene, these options have no effect. The At Background Depth option is used when rendering against background images and At Object Depth is used when rendering to files for future compositing.

The Matte/Shadow material gives considerable control for compositing, because shadows can be rendered without including the geometry that receives them. The Receive Shadows option enables this capability, and the accompanying Shadow Brightness controls the darkness of the cast shadow. Remember that control for casting shadows is an object property, and if you do not want your matte object to cast shadows, you must disable it from its Object Properties control.

The Multi/Sub-Object Material

The Multi/Sub-Object material type enables you to assign more than one material to the same object at the face level. In practice, a Multi/Sub-Object material is usually assigned to an entire object and contains as many materials as the object requires. The Multi/Sub-Object materials thus become fairly custom and are often unique for every object that requires them. Importing meshes from 3DS DOS that have face-level material assignments will automatically combine the previously separate materials into one Multi/Sub-Object, per object, upon import. Figure 21.64 demonstrates how a Multi/Sub-Object material works. Each part of the crocodile that required a separate material was given a separate ID that corresponded to a separate sub-material.

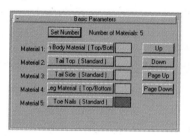

EditMesh or EditableMesh is commonly used to assign materials at the Sub-Object level, by selecting faces and assigning Material ID#s. The ID# corresponds to the Material # within the Multi/Sub-Object material. The multimaterial begins with a default number of six materials but can be any number you want. An alternative method for assigning Material ID#s is to use a Volume Select modifier to select the faces and a Material modifier to assign the desired Material ID# to the selection. Because these are independent modifiers, the selection and even the assignment can be animated while the EditMesh method is static.

Navigating a Multi/Sub-Object material can be challenging. To help in this regard, you are heavily encouraged to name every material so you know where you are in the material tree. Because the small squares on the Material Editor samples are of little value in visualizing a given material's effect, turning off Show End Result is also recommended. This allows you to see the full material at each level. Keeping the number of materials to a minimum makes navigation faster. If you only need two materials, use Set Number to change from the default number of six materials to two so you can make best use of the Go to Sibling option.

Examining Material Pitfalls

Surfaces can be built correctly, illuminated well, follow all the rules of perspective, be rendered smoothly and flawlessly by 3DS MAX, and still look incorrect. You might see the effect yourself or it might be pointed out by a colleague—or worse—by a client. You can possibly work so much with a model and see its materials rendered so often that you become anesthetized to the effect the materials actually have. The reasons for a flawed effect are many; this section covers the most common and influential of them.

TIP

Artists often examine a work in progress by looking at it in a mirror (often a hand mirror over the shoulder). This trick of flipping the image can shock your visual senses and make you analyze the image with less bias.

Wrong Size—the Need for Scale

A very annoying effect is to have the incorrect scaling for a material that has a real-world size and proportion. Brick is a common example of this. Architects and builders know these proportions intuitively and base the size of details on the number of bricks required. If these sizes and proportions are off or are different for various areas of the model, the believability of the image or animation is shattered.

Wallpaper—the Need for Randomness

Because materials are used repeatedly throughout a model, their effects can be taken for granted and become ineffective. This result is the wallpaper effect, in which the same pattern is repeated so often and so regularly that it reads as a tone instead of a texture. Most real-world materials that have a repeat to them do not do so with such regularity. Materials such as stone, tile, and brick have variation, and seeing a defined pattern destroys their believability. Applying them as basic tiled textures creates the effect of wallpaper and not, for example, brick.

To overcome the wallpaper effect, materials need variation and require a bit of randomness. Traditionally, this has been done by using increasingly larger bitmaps. So the repeat isn't as often or not at all. The drawback for large bitmaps is the time taken to produce them and the RAM needed to use them. The capability to overlay maps to any depth, combine them at varying scales, and give them individual blur and (especially) noise is invaluable to giving surfaces the look of being individual and of having life. This can often be done with a small collection of good, tileable bitmaps.

Looking "Too" Good—the Need for Grime

If one quality appears in an image or animation that signals its computer-generated origins, it is that things tend to look too good to be real. Although somewhat humorous and possibly meant as a back-handed compliment, this criticism is very valid. Real-world objects have a life to them. They become scratched and stained, wear unevenly, or are not constructed perfectly to begin with. When materials meet, they tend to have a seam or gap and are rarely perfectly flush. Objects are rarely arranged in perfect order and doing so is viewed by many as obsessive. Yet these qualities are common to computer models and mapping.

If you are striving for true realism, you will need to take the extra time to vary and give life to the materials. This extra effort is usually essential for high-resolution stills to be convincing. If you are rendering animations, you will often need to exaggerate these characteristics to make the same impact—just as they are exaggerated on stage and in film.

The key to simulating real-world materials is to represent their inconsistencies and faults. Objects are not perfectly smooth and completely clean in daily life. The best method for adding these elements of grit to your materials is to create a collection of tileable, random bitmaps that represent smears, streaks, dust, cracks, droplets, and stains. After these are created, use the same bitmaps throughout your "real-world" material library. By designing effective maps, you can reuse them repeatedly in subtle ways without them seeming overused. When the same collection of randomizing maps is used for materials, the memory costs are not overly prohibitive because you pay in RAM for them only once. These random maps can be used to modulate nearly every map type but are especially effective with Mask, Mix, and Composite map types for textures, shine, bump, opacity, and reflection. Creating truly realistic materials is not easy, but then again, neither is painting them.

Jaggies—the Need for Blur

When does a material's bitmap need more blur? This call is subjective and needs to be made by seeing the material's effect within the scene. If the bitmap is scintillating or showing irregular edges, increase its Blur. If it needs less definition, increase its Blur Offset. If it is creating moiré patterns, switch to summed area filtering. Blur is not magical and cannot make an aliased source image anti-aliased. Blur can correct only the aliasing of the bitmap as it converges in perspective. If the bitmap is inherently jaggy, you need to smooth it with a paint program before assigning it. The quality of your map's effect improves as the bitmap's scale of detail, in pixel width, increases. Details that are six pixels wide will create a much crisper edge, and especially bump, effect than that created by one pixel-wide lines.

Material Notes for 3D Studio DOS Veterans

For veterans of earlier 3D Studio versions, the 3DS MAX Material Editor is a considerable departure due to the generality of the approach and the vast scope of possibilities. While contrasting the two programs is not the primary focus of this book, it's felt that most 3DS MAX users have this basic knowledge so that many readers could benefit from the analogy. If you were comfortable creating materials in 3DS DOS, knowing a few of these correlations should speed the process of becoming as competent with the new Material Editor as you were with the old one.

- A single object can be assigned only one material. If you want to assign different materials to selections of faces (in the 3DS DOS tradition), you need to use a Multi/Sub-Object material and assign the faces according to Material ID#s. Previous 3DS models with face level material assignments will automatically have Multi/Sub-Object materials generated for them on import.

- The Flat and Gouraud shading modes for materials are gone, with a new Constant shading mode being somewhat close to Flat. The Renderer no longer has separate shading levels and always respects the material's shading designation.

- The concept of a Map Masks is now done with a Mask map type and can be used whenever a map type is requested. The map on top is the map, and the one below it is the mask.

- The concept of layering maps introduced with Texture 1 and Texture 2 maps is now done with a Composite map type, with Maps 1 and 2 being equivalent to Texture 1 & 2.

- Texture maps have been divided into Ambient and Diffuse maps. The Diffuse map provides a lock that copies its result to the Ambient and makes it the equivalent of a 3DS DOS Texture map. When unlocked, you can tint the Ambient map separately from the Diffuse as is common practice when using just base colors.

- The two shininess parameters each have maps, with the new Shininess Strength map being the equivalent of the old Shininess map.

- The term "Transparency" has been retired and replaced with "Opacity" in all situations. The new Filter Opacity type is closest to the previous, standard transparency. The new Subtractive Opacity type is similar to the "New-Subtractive-Transparency" option in the old 3ds.set file.

- "Tile" mode is the default when the U & V tiling is on. "Decal" is now done by turning off U & V Tiling. "Both" is done by using an Alpha source and leaving Tiling active. The sprite format of "upper-left hand pixel for key-color transparency" method is no longer supported.

- Alpha transparency is now additive, so black alpha areas must be matched with black RGB data or the composite will become brighter. To achieve the same alpha compositing of R3 and R4 with nonblack backgrounds, you must use a Mask map type and reference the bitmap's alpha channel.

- U & V Scale is now controlled by U & V Tiling parameters. This concept is the inverse of the way Scale previously worked but the same as the way Map Tiling did in the 3D Editor. Tiling values are now consistent between mapping and materials.

- For Mapping Parameters: Negative is now done with the Output/Invert option, RGB tint is now done with an RGB Tint map type, and Luma tint is now done with Output parameters or a Mix map type.

- Dragging color swatches and "map file slots" works like 3DS DOS in the Standard Material, except there is no method for dragging them between materials. The equivalent can be done by selecting them from the Material/Map Browser or Cut and Paste in Track View.

- Bump maps are now universal in their direction and do not project through an object. The control of a bump's direction is now solely controlled by the material's parameters.

- Multiple automatic reflections can be assigned to the same object but require separate materials (defined within a Multi/Sub-Object material) for each mirror.

While learning to create 3DS MAX materials, you are encouraged to import as many of your favorite 3DS DOS materials as possible and examine their resulting conversions. With the exception of some decal usage and CUB file references, they should convert to their very near equivalents in 3DS MAX. If you know of a way that worked in 3DS DOS, then by all means define the material there, assign it to an object, import the file, and learn how the equivalent effect is done with the new material definitions. While doing so may take some time, you will be set for exploiting all the new possibilities within 3DS MAX.

In Practice: Materials and Textures

Whenever you begin to define a material, you should pause and think about what you are trying to accomplish—what would the ideal surface look like if you had it in front of you? Some basic questions should be asked about every material, no matter how complex or mundane the material might seem to be. The following is an approximate order of questions to ask yourself when you define a Standard material:

- What is the material to represent?

  Should be reflected in material name.

- What is the material's overall color? What color do you see in its highlights and shadows?

  Choices affecting Diffuse, Specular, and Ambient colors.

- Does it resemble a plastic or metallic surface?

  Choice of Phong or Metal shading.

- How shiny is it? How strong is the highlight?

  Choice affecting Shininess, Shininess Strength, and Soften.

- Is the shine evenly cast across the surface or patterned?

  Choice affecting Shininess and Shininess Strength map channels.

- Is the material transparent? If so, how much? Is the edge thicker than the middle? Is the color weak or deep? Does it glow?

  Choices affecting Opacity parameter, Opacity falloff, and Type.

- Can you just see through parts of the material? How much can you see through? What's the pattern?

  Choices affecting Opacity map channel.

- If transparent, are things seen through it distorted?

  Choice affecting Refraction map channel and its parameters.

- If transparent, do you want to affect the color of light shining through the object?

  Choice affecting Filter color and Filter Color map channel.

- Does it cast a light or glow? If so, how much?

  Choice affecting Self-Illumination parameter and perhaps Self-Illumination map channel.

- Is it a wire frame? If so, how big are the wires?

  Choice affecting Wire option and Wire extended parameters.

- Is there an applied texture? If so, which one? How prominent? How should it be manipulated? Does it happen once or repeat?

  Choices affecting Diffuse map channel.

- If there is a texture, does it have a different quality in its shadows?

  Choice affecting Ambient map channel.

- Are the surfaces smooth? If not, what is the pattern and how bumpy is it?

  Choice affecting Bump map channel and its parameters.

- Does the surface reflect an image? If so, which one? How strong is it? How should it be manipulated? Does it happen once or repeat?

  Choices affecting Reflection map channel and its parameters.

- Do you need to see both sides of the mesh?

  Choice affecting 2-Sided option or switching to Double-Sided material.

- Can you see an image in the highlight?

  Choice affecting Specular map channel and its parameters.

All these questions are answered by the choices you make for every Standard material you define. You can always skip those that don't apply. If, for example, the object is opaque, you just eliminated at least four decisions. You "answer" these questions by adjusting parameters, choosing options, and selecting strengths and contents for map types. Your decisions shape the material. Each material is analogous to a recipe of steps and ingredients that makes up a material definition. The definition is what gets assigned to the surfaces in the scene. Material libraries then become analogous to a "recipe box" that contain the definitions you accumulate and organize.

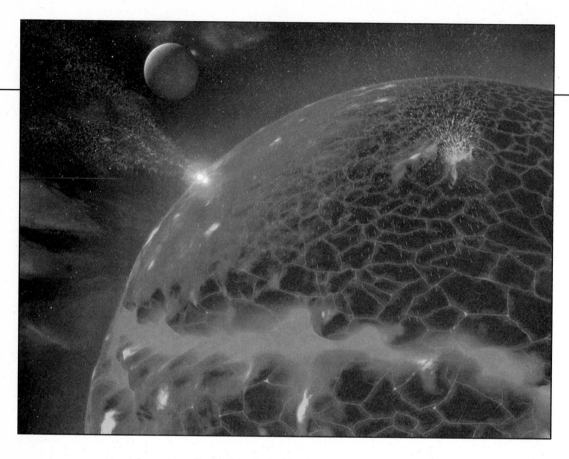

Created by Andy Murdock
Mechadeus
San Francisco, CA
Provided courtesy of Kinetix™

Chapter 22

MAPPING FOR MATERIALS

The final effect of all mapped materials is dependent on the mapping coordinates assigned to the surface. Mapping coordinates can be assigned in a number of ways, through numerous projections, with the optimal choice depending on the object's geometry and desired surface effect. This chapter will cover the following topics related to mapping:

- *UVW Mapping coordinate space and how it relates to maps*

- *Using the UVW Mapping modifier and material parameters to control mapping*

- *Techniques for planar, cylindrical, spherical, shrink wrap, and box mapping*

- *Defining accurate mapping that is free of distortion and relates to real world scale*

- *Mapping strategies for geometry*

Mapping Coordinates

The challenge of predicting the placement and result of mapping coordinates essentially has been eliminated in 3D Studio MAX because you can view the resulting bitmap in the interactive viewport.

When adjusting an assigned material that uses a bitmap or 2D procedural texture, you can display it within smooth shaded viewports by clicking the Show Map in Viewport button when in the map type's controls. You are able to show one bitmap per material. If you already are displaying a material and choose to view another, the first one is disabled to make room for your new choice. By showing the map in the viewport, you can accurately position exactly where your mapping will occur. This chapter assumes you will be using this extremely valuable feature whenever you are adjusting mapping.

A few corners are cut to achieve the interactive speed of viewport mapping adjustment. When you view bitmaps in perspective viewports, the tiling of the map is distorted as shown in figure 22.1 because bitmap sampling and correction do not occur as they do with the production renderer. If viewing your textures in perspective is important, you can enable the viewport's Texture Correction option and take a decrease in performance. In practice, you may want to toggle this option on and off for a check because leaving it on slows down the viewport considerably.

FIGURE 22.1

The same scene with and without Texture Correction enabled.

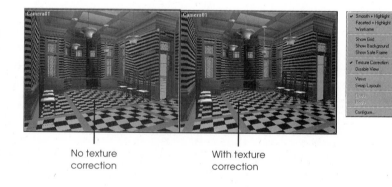

No texture correction   With texture correction

NOTE

Texture correction is not an issue when using Glint-based graphics cards or other hardware accelerators that support texture correction in their HEIDI drivers. For these cards, texture correction is a property of the chip set and is provided without penalty at all times. Texture correction is not an option when using these HEIDI drivers; it's always active.

TIP

If you prefer to work with displayed textures, you will have the best performance using an accelerator board with texture support. Boards based on the new family of 3D-Labs Glint-TX and Permedia chips have proven to give extremely good performance value.

UVW Coordinate Space

While the world and the objects within it are described in X, Y, and Z coordinates, bitmaps and mapping are described in U, V, and W coordinates to differentiate bitmap from geometric space, because the two are often very different. Geometric XYZ coordinates refer to exact locations in world or object space. Bitmap UVW coordinates represent proportions of the referenced bitmap. With UVW, you are always counting in increments of the bitmap, not referring to explicit sizes. Although the labeling may be a bit foreign, the concepts are simple (see fig. 22.2).

FIGURE 22.2
UV coordinate system for 2D bitmaps.

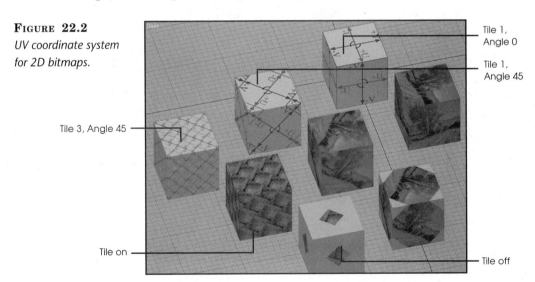

Tile 1, Angle 0

Tile 1, Angle 45

Tile 3, Angle 45

Tile on

Tile off

As figure 22.2 shows, U and V represent a width or height unit in relation to the bitmap. The U and V axes cross in the bitmap's center to define the UV origin for the map. The origin is the point about which the map rotates when the Angle value of the Bitmap map type is adjusted.

The W-space changes the mapping projection 90 degrees to the side. As it switches, the side may be rotated 90 degrees from where you might expect it. The W-space direction is used only if the material's map type actually calls for it. Although intended primarily for the 3D parametric maps (such as wood and marble), the W-space can also affect the Bitmap map type if you switch from UV projection (see fig. 22.3).

FIGURE 22.3
The effects of changing from UV mapping to UW and WU.

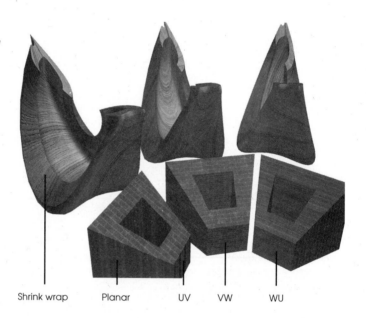

Shrink wrap   Planar   UV   VW   WU

Parametric Mapping

Mapping coordinates can be applied either parametrically or in the edit history pipeline with a UVW Mapping modifier. Parametric mapping is assigned as part of the object's creation parameters or the modifier that generated the faces, and is usually enabled by a Generate Mapping Coordinates check box within the object definition or modifier. Parametric mapping can be found in the 3D primitives, loft objects, and with the Extrude, Lathe, and Bevel modifiers. None of these methods, except lofting, give direct control over the resulting repeat of the rendered map (a characteristic known as *tiling*). Instead, the mapping usually has a tile of 1.0 in both directions.

NOTE

Mapping coordinates are not applied by default because they use extra RAM. Each face uses at least 12 bytes when it is mapped. Considering the fact that you can return in the edit history and turn mapping on at a later date, you should leave it off unless you know the object is going to receive custom mapping coordinates. You should also consider whether you want the parametric mapping when collapsing a stack.

Because most parametric mapping is applied with a 1×1 tile, you need to adjust the tiling for most materials you assign. Because you cannot adjust the parametric coordinates (except for loft objects) you need to do this with the tiling controls present in the material. Figure 22.4 shows the result of parametric mapping before and after the tiling was adjusted within the material parameters.

FIGURE 22.4

Adjusting the tiling of parametric mapping with material parameters.

When mapping is generated parametrically, you can adjust tiling and orientation only through the parameters of the material assigned to the surface. Alternatively, when you apply mapping with the UVW Mapping modifier, you have independent control over the mapping's projection, placement, orientation, and tiling. Mapping via a modifier, however, may not be as convenient as the parametric mapping applied at creation.

The UVW Mapping Modifier

When parametric mapping is not appropriate or no longer available, you need to assign mapping coordinates manually, with the UVW Mapping modifier (see fig. 22.5). The UVW mapping modifiers can be placed at any point in the stack, so the point in modeling time you apply the coordinates can be carefully controlled.

FIGURE 22.5

The UVW Mapping modifier rollout.

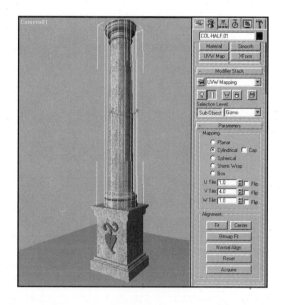

Like most 3DS MAX modifiers, the UVW Mapping modifier affects whatever is passed to it in the edit history stack. If the active selection is sub-object faces or patches, mapping is assigned to only the sub-object selection of faces or patches. If the active selection is sub-object vertices or edges, the selection is ignored and the entire object is mapped instead.

This capability to map independent sub-object selections enables you to mix mapping projection types and place mapping at numerous places within the same object, as shown in figure 22.6. The staging for applying mapping coordinates, however, is often at the end of modeling. If you model an object after applying mapping, the coordinates move with the vertices, stretch, and no longer produce even bitmaps. Mapping, therefore, is often one of the last things you do to a model.

FIGURE 22.6

Sub-object selections defining local mapping coordinates.

1 cylindrical UV projection   5 cylindrical UV projections

When modeling is finished, you often want to collapse the Modifier Stack (unless you intend to animate the modeling operations, of course). The assignment of numerous sub-object mapping coordinates usually works in conjunction with an equal number of EditMesh or EditPatch modifiers. These Edit modifiers define the face or patch selection that is being mapped by the subsequent UVW Map. Because of the expense associated with Edit modifiers, you may want to collapse the stack after applying several UVW modifiers as a way to eliminate their overhead. Replacing EditMesh selections with Volume selections is an alternative that requires very little overhead. Combining Volume Select modifiers with UVW Mapping provides an efficient mapping assignment that enables you to edit the selection and change what is mapped quite easily.

The capability to assign mapping at the sub-object level is very important in maintaining the surface properties of the object. Smoothing on faces and continuity on patches cannot occur if the surfaces are not part of the same, welded surface. Sub-object selection mapping enables you to place mapping exactly where it needs to be without affecting the topology.

Adjusting Bitmap Size and Placement

The placement of a material's map is dependent on the surface's mapping coordinates and the material's mapping parameters. As it turns out, nearly everything you can adjust within the material can also be controlled within the UVW modifier. These general methods of adjustment, therefore, are discussed together. In short, you usually have the following four options when changing the way a mapped material appears on a surface:

- Adjust the Map Type's material parameters. (This chapter always assumes you are using the Bitmap map type.)

- Adjust the UVW modifier's project type and parameters.

- Adjust the UVW modifier gizmo's position, orientation, and scale.

- Adjust creation parameters for parametric mapping that allows for adjustment (currently available only for loft objects).

The Bitmap map type is the most commonly used of all map types. It includes a wide range of options that most of the other map types (such as Checker) implement as well. Bitmap is the map type this chapter uses as the example map type for explaining mapping in general because it is so common and is easy to relate to. For the sake of discussion, we will also use Planar mapping as the example UVW modifier method for comparison to Bitmap map type parameters (see fig. 22.7). When using Planar mapping and a tiling of 1, the mapping gizmo essentially is your bitmap.

Gizmo Scale and Material Tiling Parameters

The mapping gizmo for the UVW modifier defines the extents to which a material's bitmap reaches. As you scale the gizmo, the rendered bitmap uses those coordinates scales as well. As an alternative to scaling the gizmo, you can control repeats through material *tiling* parameters. The default tiling is one, which leaves the bitmap matching the extents of the planar gizmo. A tile means a single repeat, so increasing the value to three would repeat the bitmap three times within the planar mapping gizmo.

NOTE

3D Studio DOS veterans may be confused initially because material tiling is the inverse of material map scale in Release 3 and 4. It is the same as the map tiling available in the 3D Editor, however. For 3DS MAX the concept is consistent between mapping and materials.

FIGURE 22.7

The mapping controls present in the Material Editor's Bitmap map type.

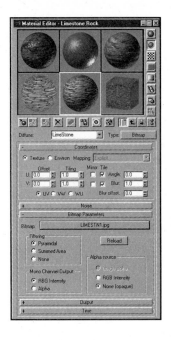

The tiling values are analogous, in effect, to X and Y scale parameters for a Planar mapping gizmo because a tiling of 2 is the same as scaling the gizmo by ½.

NOTE

To truly mirror a bitmap about either of its axes, enter a negative scale factor. For example, a V scale factor of −1.0 mirrors the map upside down.

When a material's Tile parameter is not checked, the bitmap does not tile along the given axis. Turning Tile off for both axes leaves a single imprint of the bitmap—what other programs, such as 3D Studio DOS, refer to as a "decal." The location of the tile depends on where it was defined. As figure 22.8 shows, materials always measure from the center of the bitmap, whereas the UVW Mapping modifier measures from the lower left corner.

With Tile off, and tiling greater than one, the resulting bitmap "shrinks" from the gizmo's edges. If the tile is defined in the bitmap, it gets smaller about the gizmo's center, with the bitmap's center always coincident with the gizmo's center. If the tiling is defined by the UVW Mapping modifier, the bitmap gets smaller about the lower left-hand corner, with the bitmap's corner always matching the gizmo's corner. Mixing the two methods produces a multiplied effect on the size, with the bitmap positioned closest to the origin giving the greatest tiling value.

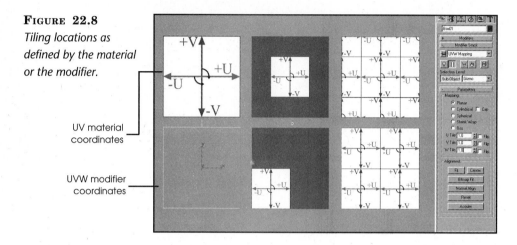

FIGURE 22.8

Tiling locations as defined by the material or the modifier.

UV material coordinates

UVW modifier coordinates

Gizmo Position and Material Offset Parameters

The position of your material's bitmap is dictated primarily by the location of the UVW Map modifier's mapping gizmo. As an alternative to moving the gizmo, the U and V Offset parameters of the material "move" the bitmap along the respective X and Y axes of the gizmo (see fig. 22.9). Keep in mind that Offset is *not* expressed in distance, but rather in units of the bitmap. The Offset value corresponds to the *original* bitmap size. When Tiling is 1.0, an Offset of 1.0 moves the bitmap 1 bitmap length to the side. When Tiling is 4.0 and the Offset is 1.0, the center of the moved bitmap remains where it was previously, but because the bitmap is smaller the map appears to have moved four times farther than when the Tiling was one. While this offset appears to be four times farther in relation to the current map size, in actuality, the offset is the same distance as measured before the map was scaled down with the Tiling parameter.

Offset parameters are primarily used when you need to position the bitmap but either do not want to move the mapping gizmo or do not have a gizmo to move because the mapping is procedural. You may also find that you have far finer control in adjusting Offset parameters than you do in moving the mapping gizmo.

FIGURE 22.9
Placing bitmaps with Offset.

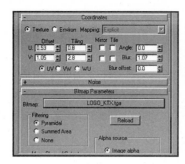 

Gizmo Rotation and Material Angle Parameters

The angle of your material's bitmap is initially controlled by the angle of the mapping gizmo to the surface. The Angle parameter of the Bitmap map type can also be used to rotate the mapping without affecting the gizmo. Figure 22.10 shows how using the Rotation parameters can be very important for projection methods where rotating the gizmo dramatically changes the project type and/or exposes points of singularity and swirling (such as cylindrical or spherical).

FIGURE 22.10
Rotating mapping projections with the Angle parameter.

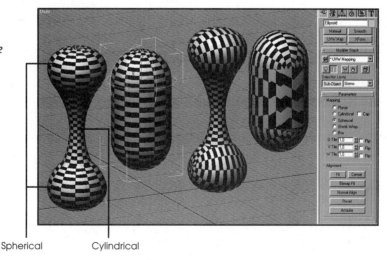

Spherical   Cylindrical

The Angle parameter rotates the bitmap about its center, with positive values rotating clockwise and negative values counterclockwise. The Angle parameter has limits at 360 degrees or –360 degrees, so animating beyond those limits must be done in coordination with the gizmo.

Mirror and Flip Options

Mirror and Flip are scaling methods in the material parameters and UVW modifier, respectively.

The Mirror option found in material map types does not do what a mirror transform does. For materials, mirroring is a combination of tiling and rotation. When mirroring is chosen, the map is scaled down by 50 percent and mirrored about the axes so that there are two bitmaps where there used to be one. If both the U and W axes are mirrored, there will be four bitmaps. The mirrored bitmap is scaled downward so that it fits the same mapping gizmo extents as a material not using the Mirror option. After being reduced in size, the bitmap tiles with this new bitmap image (see fig. 22.11).

FIGURE 22.11

Using Mirror to tile bitmaps.

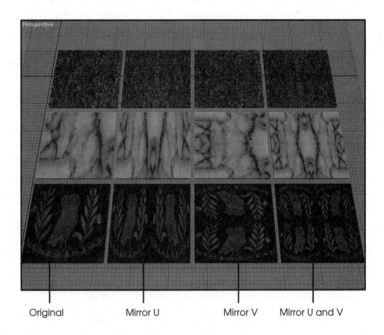

Original   Mirror U   Mirror V   Mirror U and V

If you want the material bitmap to mirror along only one axis, you will most likely want to double the tiling of the non-mirroring axis to compensate for the halved size. Mirroring is a method to make bitmaps *appear* to tile seamlessly when they do not. Some applications, such as floor tile, marble panels, and wood veneer, make good use of a seamed, mirrored pattern.

The UVW modifier's Flip option is actually a negative scale in disguise and is somewhat similar to the material Mirror option. Performing a negative tile within the UVW Mapping modifier moves the resulting bitmap location because the origin for the modifier is in the corner. The Flip option performs a negative tile about the bitmap's center so the result is not displaced. Materials do not have a Flip option because the bitmap's center is the origin for materials, and a negative scale does not move the bitmap. For a material, a –1.0 Tile parameter is the equivalent to using the Flip option in the UVW Mapping modifier.

To summarize, the following table relates the options available with the UVW Mapping modifier and their equivalents as material parameters:

Mapping Gizmo	Material Parameters
Move transform	Offset parameters
Rotation transform	Angle parameter
Scale transform	Tiling parameters
Tiling parameters (about lower left gizmo corner)	Tiling parameters (about gizmo center)
Not applicable	Mirror option
Flip option	Tiling value of –1.0

Aligning Mapping Gizmos

The UVW Mapping modifier includes several functions to aid in aligning the gizmo to the object quickly. These are all grouped in the Alignment section of the modifier, as shown in figure 22.12.

FIGURE 22.12
The Alignment options for UVW Mapping.

The Fit function centers the gizmo at the center of the active selection and scales the gizmo to match the selection's extents. The gizmo is scaled to the extents seen by its Local coordinate system. You can orient your gizmo as you wish, and the Fit function scales the gizmo appropriately. Fit should not be used when you have established a relationship to a bitmap's proportion (whether through gizmo scale or tiling) because this action changes the tiling proportions. The Fit function can be undone, so you can experiment with the results.

The Center function preserves the gizmo's orientation and scale and moves its center to that of the active selection. The Center function is safe to use with precisely scaled gizmos because it does not affect the resulting tiling.

The Bitmap Fit function examines the proportions of a chosen bitmap and scales the gizmo's horizontal dimension to match the bitmap's height-to-width ratio. The Bitmap Fit function works on Planar, Cylindrical, and Box mapping but has no effect on Spherical or Shrink Wrap.

The Normal Align function is extremely useful for aligning the gizmo so that its Z axis is perpendicular to a selected face. The face or patch must be part of an object that is currently selected, although the specific face or patch does not need to be selected. The Normal Align function positions the gizmo without affecting its scale, so it is safe to use with a gizmo that matches a given bitmap's proportion. Given that there is no direct way to align the mapping gizmo to a view, the following is the fastest method to do so, assuming that there is a face perpendicular to the view:

1. Click on Normal Align to place it in its (green) selection state.

2. Left-click and hold on the desired face or patch within the object.

3. While pressing the left mouse button, drag to move the gizmo and align to other faces until the correct one is selected.

The Reset function is the same as deleting and reapplying the modifier. It centers the gizmo on the selection with the default orientation and scale. The Reset function should be used only if you want to start from scratch.

Acquiring Mapping Coordinates

The UVW modifier's Acquire function enables you to copy the mapping from an object that has already been assigned a UVW Map modifier or even a

Displace modifier. The Acquire function works by taking the last UVW Mapping or Displace modifier it finds in the selected object's stack. You are then presented with the dialog shown in figure 22.13. You can choose whether you want the mapping to be acquired absolutely or relatively.

FIGURE 22.13

The Acquire UVW Mapping dialog.

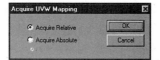

Both options duplicate the mapping type, tiling and flip options, and gizmo scale. Choosing Absolute moves the mapping gizmo to the exact same location and orientation as the target object, which is required when you need to match mapping between objects. Absolute should be chosen even if you intend to rotate the mapping gizmo because it ensures the alignment of the nonrotated axis. Choosing Relative keeps the target gizmo exactly where it is, while copying the mapping gizmo's orientation, scale, and offset. In reality, the transform from the chosen object's gizmo is being copied to the selected object.

WARNING

Acquiring a mapping gizmo *cannot* be undone. It is prudent to save your file, perform a Hold, or clone the object as a backup before using the Acquire function.

Often you need to acquire the mapping from another UVW modifier applied within the same object. To do so, a few extra steps are needed because this operation is not directly possible with the Acquire function. The most straightforward method is to clone the object to the side and ensure the desired UVW Mapping modifier is the last UVW Map in the stack. You can then use Acquire to match the gizmos. This method may not be practical if your object is extremely large because of the time it may take to perform the clone. As an alternative, enter Track View and copy the Position, Rotation, and Scale values from the desired gizmo's tracks to the new gizmo's tracks. This action is what happens when you acquire mapping absolutely (except Acquire copies all the parameters of the modifier and not just the transform).

TIP

A useful method for keeping mapping information in conjunction with the material is to assign the material and mapping to an object (for example, a Box) and name it the material's name. Save the box in a separate file and merge it in when you want the particular material. The material can be taken from the scene by the Material Editor, and the mapping can be acquired by the UVW modifier. Other boxes representing other materials can be created and saved as well—you are on your way to creating an "acquirable material library," objects from which can be merged into any model when needed.

Mapping Projection Types

The UVW modifier provides several methods to project mapping coordinates onto the surface of your object. The best projection method and technique depend on both the object's geometry and tiling characteristics of the bitmaps. The five methods available for manually assigning the mapping projection are Planar, Cylindrical, Spherical, Shrink Wrap, and Box.

The important concept to understand is that the mapping gizmo *is* the exact size and placement of your bitmap, regardless of its size or proportions. This is always the situation when both the UVW Map modifier and the assigned material and have 1.0 Tiling and 0.0 Offset settings. Different settings for tiling and offset change this initial placement as described previously. Figure 22.14 shows how each of the different projection gizmos contain visual cues to indicate which way is up and facing you.

FIGURE 22.14

The gizmo representations of the five projections.

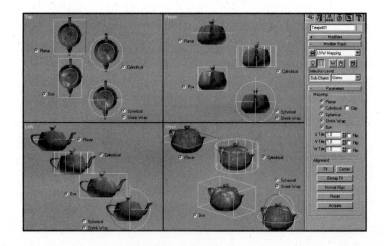

The gizmo's small vertical line, or tick mark, indicates which way is up. The Planar gizmo's green line is always the bitmap's right-hand side. The Cylindrical gizmo's green vertical line indicates the seam at which the right and left sides of the bitmap label meet. Similarly, the Spherical gizmo has a green arc that indicates the bitmap's seam edge. The Shrink Wrap gizmo is identical to the Spherical gizmo, but the green arc does not indicate a seam because the only seam is on the bottom, opposite the vertical line. The Box gizmo has no indications because it is actually based on face normals that produce a seam at every abrupt surface transition.

Mapping coordinates project onto a surface as directed by their mapping gizmo. Mapping coordinates that strike the surface at 90 degrees produce bitmaps that are undistorted. As the angle of approach changes, the pixels become stretched. When this angle reaches 180 or 0 degrees, the surface is on edge to the projection and results in pixels streaking across the surface. To correct the streaking, the gizmo must be oriented so it strikes the surface at an angle that is greater than zero degrees.

The UVW modifier is infinite in its mapping projections, with mapping coordinates being applied through whatever faces are currently selected in the stack.

WARNING

Changing your Mapping type *cannot* be undone. This is important to realize because switching mapping types usually changes the scale of your mapping gizmo; switching back will not restore the previous gizmo proportions.

Planar Mapping

Mapping is most easily understood with the Planar projection—usually the most commonly used projection method. With Planar projection, the rectangular gizmo represents the exact extents of your bitmap. As you change the shape of the gizmo, you stretch the picture. Planar mapping is projected infinitely through the object, as shown in figure 22.15. No matter how close the icon is to the mesh, only the icon's size and angle to the mesh matter.

FIGURE 22.15

Planar mapping projection.

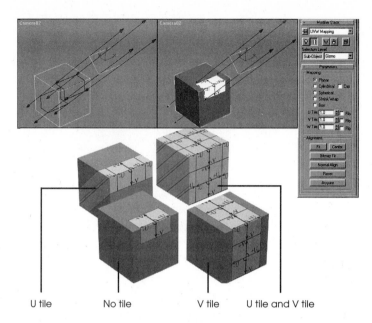

U tile   No tile   V tile   U tile and V tile

Because the bitmap stretches to fit the mapping coordinates, the gizmo needs to be the same proportions as your bitmap if you want the result to be undistorted. The Bitmap Fit function shown in figure 22.16 makes this task easy. Clicking Bitmap Fit enables you to select a bitmap to establish a new gizmo width. The existing gizmo height remains constant regardless of the bitmap's proportion.

FIGURE 22.16

Using Bitmap Fit to scale the gizmo's proportions to match a selected bitmap.

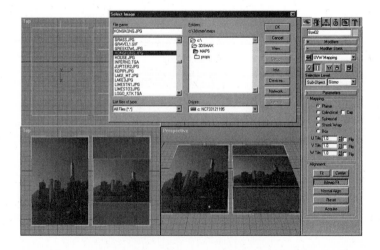

Often you know the exact size your bitmap represents and need to match the mapping gizmo's size to it. The 6×12 sequence of bricks used in figure 22.20, for example, should always be 48"×32", unless the bricks are not conventionally sized. Unfortunately, there is no clean way to make this match. You can match this size by creating a temporary object of that exact size first, as shown in the following procedure:

1. Establish the real-world size the bitmap represents.

2. Create a Rectangle spline of that size.

    Remember that keyboard entry can be fast if you don't mind the object appearing at the origin.

3. Assign the Rectangle a UVW modifier.

    The spline is automatically meshed by the applying the modifier.

4. Click Fit.

    The UVW Mapping gizmo snaps to the rectangle's extents.

5. Return to the primary object having a UVW Map modifier and use the Acquire function to retrieve the properly scaled gizmo.

    With the gizmo properly scaled, you can position and rotate it as needed and even use the Center or Normal Align functions.

For the most accurate adjustment of mapping coordinates, you need to use Track View because Transform Type-In reports only relative scale information, and when you are matching sizes, you need to control exact sizes. After adding a key for the UVW Mapping Gizmo Scale, you can right-click on the key to produce the Key Info, giving you an accurate report of the current gizmo scale, with 100 percent equaling 2". You can adjust the scale value, divide by 50, and know the exact size (in inches) of your mapping gizmo.

Warning

After you have properly scaled a gizmo to match a particular bitmap, doing *anything* to affect its scale will ruin this relationship. Do not change the mapping projection type, but do use the Fit or Reset functions within the modifier.

When your object is based on a spline that is the result of an Extrude, Bevel, or Lathe, determining the correct scale becomes a bit trickier. All these creation methods establish mapping, but do so as a 1×1 repeat across the entire length and height. To be accurate in real-world units, you need to increase the material's tiling to be in accordance with the defining spline's perimeter. Unfortunately, a direct method does not exist to determine the perimeter length of a spline. You can perform the following workaround to get this information:

1. With the perimeter object selected, turn off the Extrude, Bevel, or Lathe and subsequent modifiers leaving only the defining spline visible.

2. Create a loft from another spline shape.

3. With the Instance option active, click Get Path, and select the perimeter object.

   You now have a loft object using the perimeter object as its path.

4. Type **100** for the Path percent and then switch from Percentage to Distance.

The perimeter distance of the path is given in the Path field. If you wish, you can delete this temporary loft object or use it to trace where points lie on the path in distance or percentage of length. You can also modify the path spline and see the resulting length update. With the spline's perimeter distance known, you can divide this distance by the U axis length of the real-world bitmap to discover the Tiling required, as shown in figure 22.17.

FIGURE 22.17
Using Map Tiling to correct for an extruded length.

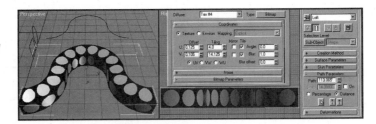

Techniques for Planar Mapping

It is common to think of Planar mapping being applied square, or normal, to a surface. Although this application produces undistorted mapping, it is not often the most convenient approach. Few objects are coplanar, and most turn corners that require matching coordinates on adjacent sides as well. For example, a brick wall that turns a corner needs perfectly aligned grout lines. For rectilinear geometry, which includes most structures, a few options exist:

- Select the faces with EditMesh and assign them their own UVW Mapping modifier. Match the original mapping gizmo's position, size, and orientation and then rotate it 90 degrees.

- Select the faces with EditMesh or EditableMesh and assign them separate Material IDs. Make the current material a multi-material, change the mapping from UV to VW and the angle to 90.

- Rotate the mapping gizmo 45 degrees.

The problem with the first option is that keeping the different gizmos in alignment with each other through future adjustments can be troublesome. You may, in fact, want to use expressions for such control. The second option is elegant, but works only if the object is truly rectilinear. The last option is fast, has no overhead, and is applicable to the majority of situations. All three options assume that the gizmo is of the correct proportions for the desired bitmap (that is, a Bitmap Fit operation has been performed).

The key to correctly angled planar mapping is to ensure an equal angle of the mapping icon to each side of the mesh. If the object has inconsistent corners, such as a hexagon or octagon, you need to apply separate coordinates to adjacent pairs of faces. In this case, you need to make sub-object face selections and apply separate UVW Mapping modifiers. A hexagon or octagon can be correctly mapped with two projections, while a 10- or 12-sided polygon would require three.

When applying mapping at an angle, you want the mapping projection to be even to each side receiving the mapping; the gizmo's angle of approach must be similar to all faces. As the mapping gizmo's angle alters from being 90 degrees, however, the projected image begins to stretch. The stretching can be corrected by adjusting the mapping along the stretched axis in one of three ways: scaling the mapping gizmo, adjusting the UVW Mapping's tiling, or adjusting the materials' bitmap tiling. Whichever method you choose, you should use it consistently to make future editing an easier and more clear process. Of all the methods, scaling the gizmo is the least accurate and most difficult to adjust. The Material tiling is a good choice only if the material is always being applied at the angle it is being scaled to correct for. In most cases, working with the UVW modifier's tiling makes the most sense because the modifier is relevant to the projection and can be acquired by other mapping modifiers needing similar values. Figure 22.18 shows how this is accomplished with tiling values.

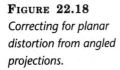

FIGURE 22.18
Correcting for planar distortion from angled projections.

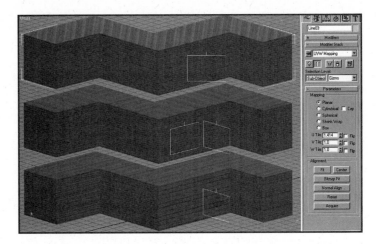

To correct for stretched mapping, you need to increase the map tiling. The amount of the increase depends on the angle of the surface to the mapping gizmo. For 90 degree (right) angles, the correction is a tiling of 1.414—the square root of two and a very good number to remember because correcting for square corners is so common. The correcting ratio can be gathered from either the approach or included angle:

Tiling Ratio = 1 / Sine (gizmo's angle of approach)

Or

Tiling Ratio = 1 / Cosine (gizmo's included angle of approach)

Figure 22.20 shows calculating this ratio in practice. Note that the gizmo's angle of approach is one-half of the corner's angle. If your gizmo is at an even angle to the corner, the correcting ratio can be derived from the corner's angle.

Tiling Ratio = 1 / Sine (0.5 × corner angle)

Don't be scared by these formulas—they're *all* the same. It's just easier for some people to relate to one method over another. A little math goes a long way, and the correcting ratio of 1.414 can be memorized to work for all rectilinear mappings.

Although an oblique planar projection can be corrected once for any surface, it cannot be corrected a second time. Figure 22.19 shows how rotating the mapping gizmo a second time produces angled mapping on all surfaces. This application may be suitable if your bitmap is quite random and tileable, also shown in figure 22.19. If you are after the latter effect, you may be better off with Box mapping.

FIGURE 22.19
Rotating Planar mapping about two axes.

Cylindrical

Cylindrical mapping projects its coordinate from the gizmo center outward to infinity, much like the ripples in a pond, as shown in figure 22.20. The height of the gizmo cylinder dictates the size of the bitmap's height or, rather, V dimension. Because of this situation, the gizmo's radius is not important—only the location of its center. You can think of the cylinder as being a visual aid for determining the height, center, top, seam, and whether it has been nonuniformly scaled.

FIGURE 22.20
Cylindrical mapping projection.

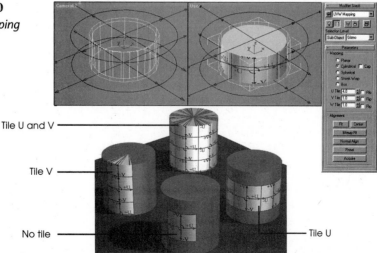

Tile U and V

Tile V

No tile

Tile U

The icon's back, green edge indicates where the bitmap's edges meet; a seam appears when rendering if the material's bitmap is not tileable in its U direction. The back seam is also the initial tiling location. When working with tiled decals, the seam becomes the bitmap's left-hand side.

Traditionally, surfaces that are parallel to a cylindrical projection experience swirls or streaks, as shown in figure 22.21. Because such streaks and swirls are rarely desirable, the production renderer treats such a situation as a special case and takes the first pixel found for the top as the cap's entire color. Because this correction is not shown in the interactive renderer, it can be confusing. Instead of accepting the correction, if you want to retain the spiraling effects shown in the viewport, you can either move one of the defining vertices a small increment or rotate the mapping gizmo bay a small amount (0.03 degrees or more should do it).

Impact of geometry

FIGURE 22.21

Cap conditions of Cylindrical mapping.

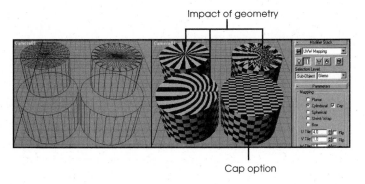

Cap option

The Cylindrical Mapping Cap option applies planar mapping to the top and bottom of the cylindrical projection. This application is similar to what Box Mapping does. The qualifying angle for being a "cap," however, is much shallower than the qualifying angle for being a box mapping's side, with faces becoming planar mapped as they approach 20–25 degrees from the horizontal plane.

An interesting trait of the cylindrical gizmo is that you can nonuniformly scale it so that you have an "elliptical" projection. Performing a nonuniform scale about the gizmo's X,Y axis has no effect on the mapping, but scaling the X and Y axes nonuniformly from each other creates an ellipse. Figure 22.22 shows when such mapping may be appropriate.

FIGURE 22.22

A nonuniformly scaled cylindrical gizmo creating elliptical mapping.

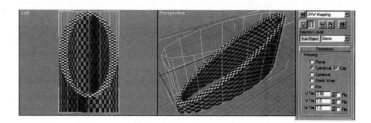

TIP

Cylinder mapping takes its proportional clue from the planar mapping. If you want a fit elliptical shape, fit the Planar mapping first and then switch to Cylindrical. If you want to reset the mapping, switch to Spherical and back again.

Techniques for Cylindrical Mapping

You often need a cylindrical projection to render the bitmap completely undistorted. This is especially true for items where distortion is easy to identify, such as text, labels, logos, portraits, or geometric patterns. Consider the classic wine label as an analogy for discussion. There are several factors to determine: the radius of the bottle, the height of the label, the percentage of the bottle that is wrapped, and the proportions of the label. If you know three of these variables, you can reliably calculate the fourth. Thus, if you know the size of bottle and the label's proportion and height, you can determine how much it will wrap.

One method to ensure an undistorted map is to balance the bitmap's ratio with the model's radius to arrive at the required gizmo height. Another approach is to use the geometric size and exact label placement to determine the proportions the material's bitmap needs to be. The fact is that for a given bitmap proportion, there is only *one* corresponding gizmo height that works for a specific object's radius.

The material's bitmap is commonly the first thing to consider, with its width to height ratio determining the gizmo's size. As the map wraps around the cylinder, its width is stretched to the length of the circumference. Multiplying this distance by the bitmap's ratio produces the required height of the gizmo cylinder:

Gizmo Height = (Bitmap V / Bitmap U) × Object's Diameter × Π

If you are creating a special bitmap for a specifically sized and proportioned object—for example, a can—you must proportion the bitmap to match the required label size:

$$(\text{Bitmap V} / \text{Bitmap U}) = \text{Can's Diameter} \times \Pi / \text{Can's Height}$$

Often your label is intended to wrap only a portion of the cylinder's circumference. Although you can establish the formulas, the easiest route is to define the gizmo as if the label were to wrap the entire cylinder and then change the tiling to control its proportions. If the resulting label is too short or wraps the incorrect distance, your only recourse is to change the proportions of the label's bitmap.

When using the Bitmap Fit function, the gizmo's height is maintained while the gizmo's radius is scaled so that the bitmap wraps cleanly around the cylinder like a "soup can" label, producing a perfectly proportioned cylinder for that one bitmap. Once matched, you need to either *uniformly* scale the gizmo to match the geometry's radius or scale the geometry so its radius matches the gizmo's; the former approach is far more common.

Spherical

Spherical mapping projects its coordinates from a center point outward to infinity in all directions, much like an omni light's illumination, as shown in figure 22.23. The size of the icon has absolutely no effect on the resulting mapping coordinates. If the icon is nonuniformly scaled, however, the spherical mapping becomes ellipsoidal mapping—perfect for elongated, lozenge-shaped objects. Even in the case of nonuniform scaling, it is not the scale itself which affects the mapping, but rather the location of the gizmo's center in relation to the object. The spherical gizmo's primary purpose is to aid you in locating the center and indicating up, back, and uneven scaling.

The Spherical Mapping option can also be thought of as a "reset" for the other map types. Switching to Spherical from another type always resets the gizmo to a pure sphere. Switching back to another type then sets them to their defaults (a square for Planar and a cylinder with the sphere's height for Cylindrical).

The orientation of the gizmo has the greatest effect on spherical projections. The icon's poles are points of convergence for the bitmap and can cause pinching and swirls (also known as polar singularity). Much of the swirling has to do with the density of the mesh at that critical point—the denser the mesh, the cleaner the resulting map. The gizmo's green arc indicates the seam at which a single tiling bitmap has its U axis edges meet. The seam can be very apparent if the bitmap is not tileable along this edge and can ruin many effects. Rotating the seam to the side where it cannot be readily seen is usually a good idea.

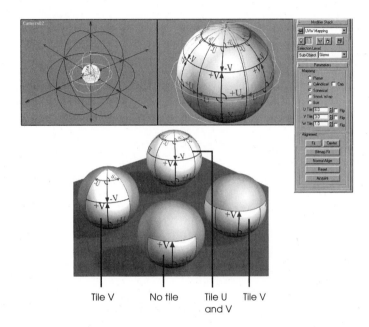

Tile V   No tile   Tile U   Tile V
                    and V

Techniques for Spherical Mapping

Spherical mapping begins by stretching the bitmap vertically from pole to pole and then wrapping it horizontally starting at the back meridian all the way around. The map is then projected back onto the surface. As any cartographer knows, there is no way to make a rectangular map fit on a sphere without distortion. The only area for which you do have some control of the distortion is the mapping coordinate's equator as shown in figure 22.24. Here the bitmap has been wrapped the full circumference, whereas the height has been wrapped around only one-half of the circumference. A bitmap, then, should have a width to height ratio of 2:1 for it to appear undistorted at the equator. Bitmaps that do not have an original 2:1 ratio should have their U or V tiling scaled to produce the same ratio.

FIGURE 22.24
Correcting for scale distortion at the equator.

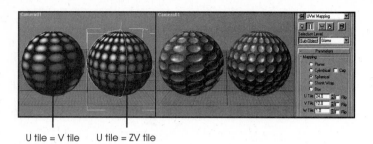

U tile = V tile   U tile = ZV tile

You can choose which axis to scale, although most bitmaps tend to be too narrow for their height. A square bitmap, for example, should have its U axis tile increased to 2 while the V axis remains the same. If the vertical dimension is to be full height, then the U tiling must be increased. A 640×480 bitmap requires its U value to be scaled by 640/(2×480)=0.6667. If the horizontal dimension must be constant, the V value would need to be scaled up by 480/(640/2)=1.5.

Shrink Wrap

Shrink Wrap mapping is an interesting alternative to spherical mapping and is ideal for many applications. Whereas Spherical has singularity at both poles, Shrink Wrap has singularity only at its base—an area that is often easily hidden—making it ideal for heads, skies, trees, and spheres on a base such as a finial.

Shrink Wrap works by considering only the central area of your bitmap. Shrink Wrap essentially treats the bitmap as a circular sheet of rubber, wrapping it around the object and tying the trimmed map up on the bottom, resulting in a nearly undistorted top half and fairly good sides. Figure 22.25 shows this treatment by wrapping a bitmap of a circle. Because Shrink Wrap trims away the corners, it appears as if only a white map was applied, rather that a white circle on a black field.

The Shrink Wrap gizmo reacts in the same way as the Spherical gizmo. Selecting it always results in a reset. The scale of the gizmo does not matter, only its center does. Like Spherical, you can scale it nonuniformly to cover ellipsoidal shapes.

FIGURE 22.25
FIGURE 22.25

The circular trimming performed by Shrink Wrap mapping.

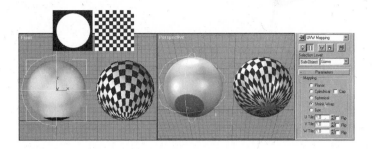

Techniques for Shrink Wrap Mapping

Shrink Wrap mapping is best used with bitmaps that can tile in both the U and V axes or with very high-resolution images. Shrink wrap trimming leaves less of the image to project, and smaller bitmaps may seem pixelated because they are viewed beyond their range. Those bitmaps that can tile are ideal for shrink wrapping. Tiling ranges of 3 or 4 in both the U and V directions produce amazingly convincing results as shown in figure 22.26.

FIGURE 22.26

Using Shrink Wrap with tiling bitmaps.

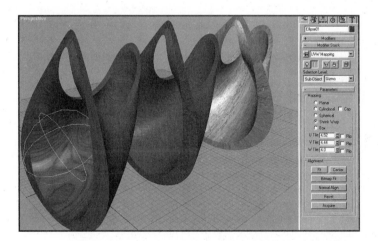

The next thing to consider with Shrink Wrap is that it often works well with VW and WU bitmap projections. When adjusting the gizmo, especially those at angles and for organic models, the different projection axes can deliver surprisingly good results when using tiling maps as described previously.

Box Mapping

Box mapping should be thought of as Planar mapping applied from six directions because that is exactly what it is. The proportions projected by each side correspond to the proportions of the referenced bitmap. Scaling the gizmo scales the resulting mapping, just as it does with Planar mapping. Nonuniformly scaling the gizmo means that sides will have different mapping proportions from one another.

NOTE

3D Studio veterans should not confuse 3DS MAX Box Mapping with the 3DS DOS Box Material. The latter stretched assigned bitmaps across each dimension of the assigned object and tended to be of little practical use. Box Mapping is very controllable and *extremely* useful by comparison.

Bitmap maintains the height of the gizmo and scales the X axis to match the bitmap's proportion. The Front, Back, Top, and Bottom projections have been fit, leaving a square Left and Right side. You can now rotate the Box Mapping gizmo as needed, if a different facing is required. The reason it chooses the sides it does is inherent to the way it maps. The left and right sides (the gizmo's X axis) are always considered "sides" whereas the others wrap around the Y axis, as shown in figure 22.27.

FIGURE 22.27
Box mapping projection.

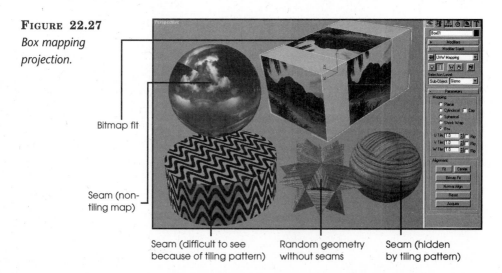

Bitmap fit

Seam (non-tiling map)

Seam (difficult to see because of tiling pattern)

Random geometry without seams

Seam (hidden by tiling pattern)

Box mapping assigns mapping according to the surface normal's orientation to the gizmo. After a face crosses the 45-degree-angle threshold between projected planes of the mapping gizmo, it receives mapping from the other side. Box mapping is thus a very fast way to assign mapping to otherwise difficult geometry.

Techniques for Box Mapping

More often than not, you want the mapping produced by box mapping to be even for all sides of its projections. This occurs only when the Box Mapping gizmo is a perfect cube. A perfectly cubical mapping gizmo works fine for materials using square bitmaps, but it stretches or squashes bitmaps of different proportions. The Bitmap Fit function scales the gizmo to match the bitmap but leaves two ends square and out of proportion with the other four. If you need all six sides to be in proportion with each other *and* the referenced bitmap, you need to adjust the map tiling instead, as shown in figure 22.28 and using the following steps:

1. Ensure the mapping gizmo is a cube by switching to Spherical or Shrink Wrap and then back to Box.

2. Use the Info option in View File to identify the Resolution.

FIGURE 22.28
Adjusting tiling to make even Box Map tiling.

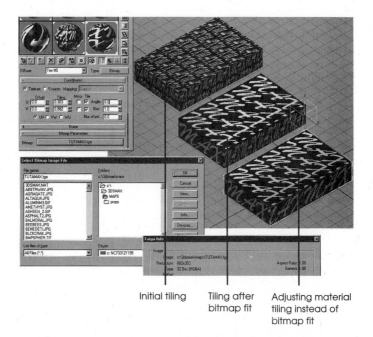

Initial tiling   Tiling after bitmap fit   Adjusting material tiling instead of bitmap fit

3. The bitmap's height-to-width ratio becomes the UTile to VTile ratio. This adjustment can be made either in the material or UVW Mapping modifier settings.

Note that the U and V tiling is the *reverse* of the Height and Width.

4. The U/V ratio must now be maintained for all future adjustments. You can adjust the tiling size by either uniformly scaling the mapping gizmo or adjusting the tiling values.

One convenient method is to set the bitmap adjustment in the material— which is linked to the particular bitmap—and use the modifier tiling to control the repeat. Either way, you have three methods to change the tiling that can be used individually or in conjunction with one another to produce the final tiling. For the sake of sanity, it is best to use only one method to adjust the bitmap's ratio and the others for overall tiling size.

When properly adjusted for bitmap size, Box Mapping can be ideal for rectilinear geometry. Planar mapping may be preferable when you need localized control over specific areas to ensure critical alignments.

Mapping Strategies

Controlling how a material should traverse a surface depends on appropriately applied mapping. Deciding how to apply the mapping to gain the desired result becomes a planning issue—where to apply it, with what projection, at what orientation, and with what tiling. You must address these questions as you finalize your surfaces.

Although nearly every model requires slightly different techniques, the following strategies are useful guidelines to determine what mapping is best suited to your model's geometry:

- **Flat surface (paper)**   Consider Planar mapping applied normal to the surface.

- **Rectilinear without caps (walls)**   Consider Planar mapping applied at an angle that wraps around the corners.

- **Rectilinear with caps (boxes)**   Consider Box mapping, adjusting the ratio of the tiling or gizmo to match the bitmap's proportion.

- **Symmetrical (a duck)** Consider Planar mapping a specially created bitmap that is allowed to project through the object and map both sides with the same image.

- **Cylindrical (a bottle)** Consider Cylindrical mapping, compensating for the bitmap's proportions with the gizmo's height or tiling.

- **Spherical (a ball)** Consider Spherical or Shrink Wrap mapping, depending on the nature of the bitmap and how prominent the poles will be in the final renderings.

- **Irregular (a plant)** Ideally you want to assign the mapping at creation (loft, extrude, bevel, lathe). Alternatively, Shrink Wrap mapping can work with smooth-edged geometry, whereas Box mapping can work for sharp-edged geometry.

Another key with mapping is to assign it while the object presents its most geometrically pure form. Before collapsing the modeling stack, analyze the progressing forms and identify points at which mapping is easiest. A leaf, for example, is best mapped when it is first extruded and is flat, rather than later when it has been curled and bent. It is not uncommon to deform an object to a more convenient shape for the sake of applying mapping and then reversing the deformation.

The last thing to consider is the UVW modifier's placement in the stack, especially when the modeling is being animated. If deformations happen *after* the UVW modifier, the mapping coordinates "stick," and mapping stretches with the object's vertices. If the deformations happen *before* the UVW modifier, the object appears to move through the coordinates because that is exactly what is happening.

In Practice: Mapping for Materials

- **Applying mapping** Mapping is usually applied at the end of the modeling sequence because further modeling threatens to distort previously defined mapping coordinates. The Modifier Stack allows you to traverse the modeling history and place the mapping when the object's form best conforms to the mapping projection's shape.

- **VolumeSelect modifiers** These modifiers are superior to EditMesh modifiers in defining sub-object selections for mapping assignments because they use a minimum of RAM.

■ **Unique mapping**   Each face on an object can have unique mapping, but only the last UVW Mapping applied to a face will be respected.

■ **Infinite mapping**   Mapping projects infinitely through an object as determined by the projection method (planar, cylindrical, spherical, shrink wrap, or box).

■ **Rectilinear geometry**   Rectilinear geometry can often be mapped with one planar projection applied at a 45-degree angle. The distortion of the angular projection is easily corrected with a 1.414x tiling or gizmo scale along the angled axis.

■ **UVW mapping gizmo**   The UVW Mapping gizmo *is* your bitmap (when Tiling is 1.0 and Offset is zero). Bitmaps within materials are stretched to meet the corners of the gizmo, so the gizmo should have the same height to width proportion as the material bitmap to avoid distortion.

■ **Real-world scale**   Many bitmaps relate to real-world scale. The size of such bitmaps should be determined and the mapping gizmo should be made to match these dimensions so the rendered material will be in scale with the bitmap representation.

Part III

ANIMATING YOUR SCENES

Image by Westwood Studios
Provided courtesy of Kinetix™

Chapter 23

ANIMATION CONTROL TOOLS

3D Studio MAX enables artists to animate virtually anything—from object transformations and modifications to material property changes. By activating the Animate button, 3DS MAX records all changes you make to your animations. Each change creates a key that stores the value to use for the modified parameter at the specified time.

No artist is satisfied with the initial animation he has applied to a scene. 3DS MAX provides a robust set of animation control tools that enables the artist to edit the animation keys and manipulate the keys in time. This chapter is an overview of the various animation controls available in 3DS MAX and how to use them. The topics covered in this chapter are

- Configuring and moving through time
- Understanding 3DS MAX's Track View
- Creating and editing keys
- Working with ranges
- Working with time
- Working with function curves
- Working with trajectories

When you animate a scene, you are adding a fourth dimension—time. In previous versions of 3D Studio, the unit used to measure time was the frame. The concept of a frame is still present in 3DS MAX, however, this concept has been dramatically expanded. 3DS MAX provides the tools necessary to define and display time in a manner consistent with your output format and to easily convert between output formats without adversely affecting the timing of your animation.

Understanding Your Animation Environment

As you've seen in previous chapters, 3DS MAX has a wide range of object modifiers with animatable parameters. This enables you to create animations in a more intuitive fashion versus using old morphing techniques to create those same animations. For example, if you wanted to create a pipe bending in the wind, what used to take several morph targets can now be done in 3DS MAX by applying a Bend modifier and animating its bend angle value. Animating object material characteristics can now be performed by simply changing parameter values at the material level versus using morph targets. These are just a few of the items that can be animated in 3DS MAX.

Although the standard views of your scene will show you the results of your animation, you will frequently want to look at the animation data itself. For example, you may want to see at what times keys were created for a parameter and either change the time associated with a key or edit the data stored in a key. 3DS MAX provides a view of the animation data called Track View (see fig. 23.1). Track View shows a hierarchy list of all the animatable items in the scene—objects, object modifiers, lights, cameras, environmental effects, and materials. For each of these items, the animatable parameters for that item are shown, along with any associated keys. Keys can be moved in time or copied to other times, or the values associated with a key can be changed.

FIGURE 23.1
Track View displays the data associated with your animation and enables you to edit it.

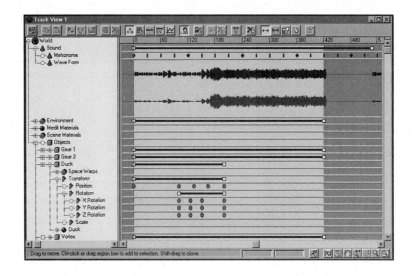

TIP

If you're using the Track View to edit your animation, you can even edit your animation while it's playing. For example, you can adjust the time or values associated with a specific key while the object is moving around on your screen to see the changes interactively.

The use of keys to specify animation data at specific times reflects the practice of traditional cel animators. The master animators create *keyframes* showing the scene at critical points in the animation. Assistant animators then create the *tween* frames between these keyframes, determining how the objects in the scene should change to reflect their start and end positions and appearances. With 3DS MAX, you specify the keys for your objects at specific frames, and 3DS MAX will create the tween positions or appearances of the objects.

Configuring Time

Because of the variety of possible output formats of your animation (film, video, and so on), 3DS MAX provides several options for choosing your frame rate and how time is displayed. The configuration of time is specified in the Time Configuration dialog (see fig 23.2). This dialog is accessed by clicking Time Configuration or by right-clicking any of the playback buttons.

FIGURE 23.2

The Time Configuration dialog is used to control how time is used and displayed.

Click to access the Time Configuration dialog

3DS MAX enables you to specify the frame rate based on your output format. The default frame rate is NTSC video at 30 frames per second (fps); however, you can choose PAL at 25 fps, film at 24 fps, or even define your own custom frame rate. The display of time itself can be in standard Frames or other displays such as SMPTE time code, Frames and Ticks, or Minutes, Seconds and Ticks—ticks being 1/4800 of a second. The Time Slider and current frame field at the bottom of the 3DS MAX display show your animation in whatever time display format you choose.

NOTE

If any of the Ticks choices are selected, 3DS MAX gives you the added option of using subframe animation, letting you set keyframes between rendered frames. This is useful for cases where exact timing of keys is required, such as accident reconstructions.

3DS MAX enables you to change both your frame rate and time display anytime you wish without altering your animation. This is convenient because you may be creating your animation for a 30 fps frame rate, but you may need to look at your animation at Film speed and in another time code to compare how your animation will fit with certain post processing modifications. For example, if you created a one-minute animation for video that uses a 30 fps speed and were then informed that the animation would be processed on film (24 fps) instead, all you have to do in 3DS MAX is change your frame rate—3DS MAX automatically rescales time without altering your given keys. In other programs you would have to scale time, thus altering and possibly reducing your given keys.

TIP

Whenever you change your frame rate in the Time Configuration dialog, 3DS MAX does not initially inform you what the fps rate is. However, if you re-invoke the Time Configuration dialog after saving the change, 3DS MAX will display the new fps value in the Custom FPS edit box.

The start and end time of an animation is specified in the Time Configuration dialog. These times actually specify only the active time segment. Setting an active time segment gives you the ability to view only a portion of time in your animation, enabling you to play back a specific portion of your animation and limit the range of on screen keyframing within the defined time. Changing the start or end time has no effect on the time or values of previously created keys.

NOTE

Although you are restricted to editing your animation within a specific time range, you can still create, delete, and edit keys outside the active time segment by using Track View.

By selecting the Re-scale Time button in the Time Configuration dialog, you can actually rescale the time associated with keys in your active time segment. In the Re-scale Time dialog (see fig. 23.3), you can change the start time, end time, and length of the new active time segment. The time of any keys located within the original active time segment are scaled to the new active time segment. If the start frame is changed, any keys occurring before the start frame are moved in time by the same amount that the start frame is changed. If the end frame is changed, any keys occurring after the end frame are moved in time by the same amount that the end frame is changed.

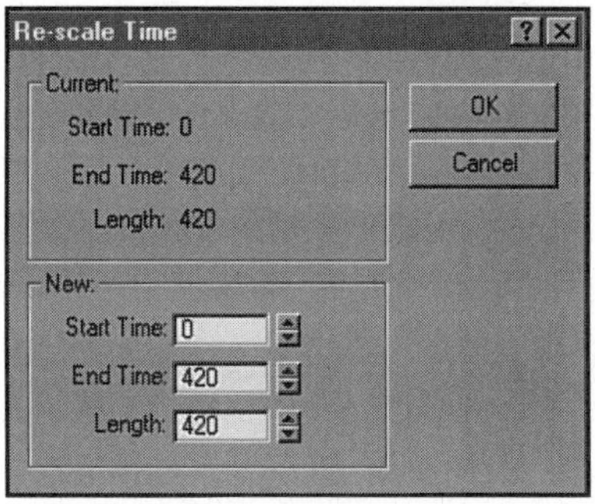

FIGURE 23.3

The Re-scale Time dialog is used for adjusting the length of a time segment, adjusting the time of the keys.

Moving Through Time

3DS MAX offers several methods of moving through time and viewing your animation. Notably, you can play back your animations in one or more of 3DS MAX's viewports in Real Time, thereby reducing the necessity for creating preview AVI files to get a quick check on the progress of your work. You will probably develop a personal preference of playback, but be aware that there are great advantages to using all of 3DS MAX's playback methods.

The Time Configuration dialog enables you to specify whether your playback is going to be in Real Time and whether only the Active Viewport will play. 3DS MAX also enables you to play selections of multiple Viewports, such as only the Camera and Top, by allowing you to disable certain viewports. You can disable a Viewport by right-clicking the viewport title and selecting Disable View from the pop-up menu or by using the keyboard shortcut D. Inactive viewports do not play animations during scene playback.

NOTE

You can still see the animation playback in an Inactive Viewport by simply selecting it. 3DS MAX temporarily reactivates the Viewport until another one is selected.

Besides being able to play the animation of all objects within your scene, 3DS MAX will allow only selected objects to play. You can select this playback method by clicking and holding on Play Animation and then selecting the Play Selected icon from the drop-down list. This feature is extremely efficient when you are working with a lot of geometry and your display speed is being affected. For example, if you are working on a scene that has characters, buildings, and vehicles, you can create a selection set of the animated objects you wish to preview and leave all others on the screen. During playback, 3DS MAX will temporally hide all non-selected animated objects in playing viewports while leaving your selected objects and all non-animated objects on-screen. You can think of this as a dynamic hide function for individual viewports.

3DS MAX also has several options for stepping through time. By using the frame indexing buttons from the Play Control area, you can index to the Beginning or End of the Active Segment, or index backward and forward one frame at a time. A much more powerful feature is the capability to index through time keyframe by keyframe, analyzing animation specified by transform keys. To activate the Key Step index, select the Key Mode Toggle button. Notice that when this mode is selected, the graphics for the Previous and Next Frame button change. Clicking on these keys will jump you to the previous or next transform key. By selecting among the various Key Steps options in the Time Configuration dialog, you can control which transform keys are to be used for stepping through your animation. These options enable you to specify whether only transform keys for the selected objects are to be used or whether the transform keys for all objects are to be used. In addition, the transform types to be used can be specified in this dialog.

Using Track View

As described earlier, Track View shows the animatable parameters associated with each object and the keys created for each of these parameters. Track View is launched under the Edit pull-down or from the toolbar with the icon with the yellow boxes hanging off a stem. Figure 23.4 shows a typical Track View. In Track View, the hierarchy list of animatable items and their parameters are shown on the left. On the right, keys are shown in the parameters' tracks as dots, and range bars are shown in the items' tracks. The range bars extend across the range of time for which keys are present on parameters subordinate to that item. We can tell by looking at figure 23.4 that item Box01 has at least one parameter that has a key at frame 0 and a parameter that has a key at frame 100. Likewise, we can tell that at least one parameter subordinate to item Sphere01 has keys present on frames 0 and 23. The transform for Box01 has been expanded, and we can see that keys are present on the position track at frames 0 and 100.

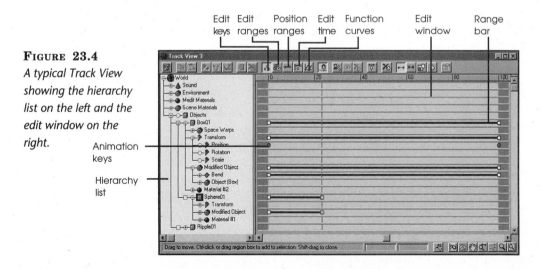

FIGURE 23.4

A typical Track View showing the hierarchy list on the left and the edit window on the right.

Track View has five different animation edit modes:

- Edit keys
- Edit ranges
- Position ranges
- Edit time
- Function curves

The Track View shown in figure 23.4 is in the Edit Keys mode. Each of these modes will be discussed in subsequent sections. But first, we discuss the structure of the hierarchy list and the controls common to each of the edit modes.

The Hierarchy List

The hierarchy list presents a structured view of the elements in your scene. The highest levels of the hierarchy represent the main groupings in 3DS MAX of sound, environment, materials, and objects. Lower levels of the hierarchy progress through the details of your scene, such as individual objects, base objects and the modifiers applied to a base object, and the parameters associated with a base object and its modifiers. The lowest level of the hierarchy contains the animatable parameters associated with your scene.

Each level of the hierarchy can be expanded or collapsed to show more or less detail. To edit a parameter's animation keys, you expand the branches of the tree to display that parameter.

The root of the hierarchy list is World. The subordinate items to World are Sound, Environment, MEdit Materials, Scene Materials, and Objects (see fig 23.5). The range bar for World reflects the animated range for all its subordinate items except Objects.

The Sound Branch

The Sound branch stores data related to sound. Two types of sound are available: the metronome and an audio sound file. You access the sound options by clicking any item in the sound branch to select it and then either right-click on that item and select Properties from the pop-up menu or click Properties in the toolbar. Or you can simply right-click in the track for one of these items. Any of these actions displays the Sound Options dialog (see fig. 23.6).

FIGURE 23.5

The Track View hierarchy list for World.

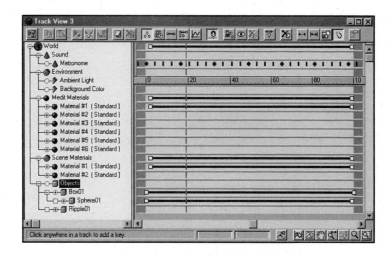

FIGURE 23.6

The Sound Options dialog is used to load sound files and specify the Metronome parameters.

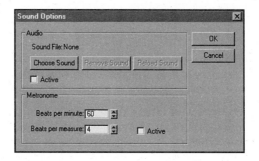

3DS MAX supports WAV files as the standard sound file type. When rendering occurs to AVI file format, the WAV sound is embedded into the AVI file. All sounds must be added in Track View. If a background is chosen that is an AVI file with sound, that sound will be ignored.

To select a sound file, click Choose Sound and select a sound file from the file browser that is presented. Set the Active option. To delete an active sound, click Remove Sound. To reload a sound after editing the sound in an external application, for example, click Reload Sound. To maintain the link to a sound file but not play it during playback, turn off the Active option. You can hear the sound file when playing back an AVI file created with the sound file active, during playback in a viewport with Real Time on, and when dragging the time slider forward. A sampling of the sound file volume is shown in Track View in the sound track (see fig 23.7). A sound card is required to hear the sound playback.

FIGURE 23.7

*The sound track with a
sound file loaded.*

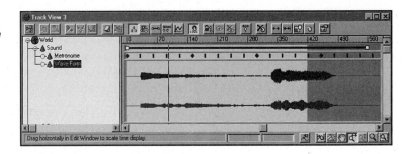

The Metronome produces a steady beat that uses two tones. The frequency of the beat is specified by the Beats per minute field. The second tone is heard every Nth beat as specified in the Beats per measure field. To maintain the Metronome setting but not hear it, turn off the Active option. You can hear the metronome during playback in a viewport with Real Time on. The metronome uses your computer's speaker.

The Environment Branch

The Environment branch shows the animatable items associated with the environment. This includes ambient light, the background color, and any environmental effects specified in the Rendering Environment dialog.

The MEdit Materials and Scene Materials Branches

The MEdit branch shows the animatable parameters associated with materials currently defined in one of the six material slots in Material Editor. The Scene Materials branch shows the same for all materials currently assigned to objects in the scene. A single material can occur several times in the hierarchy—as an MEdit material, as a Scene material, and under the objects the material is assigned to.

The Objects Branch

The Objects branch shows the animatable parameters associated with the objects defined in the scene. The hierarchy of objects shown is defined by which objects are linked to others and is similar to what you see in Select by Name with the Display Subtree option on.

An expansion of an object's branch is shown in figure 23.8. If no modifiers have been placed on the object, the Modified Object branch is replaced with the Object branch.

FIGURE 23.8

The expanded Track View hierarchy of an object.

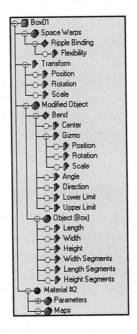

Hierarchy List Commands

Several of the Track View commands are used to control the hierarchy list display or are applied to items in the hierarchy list. These commands, shown in figure 23.9, are

- Filters
- Copy/Paste
- Assign Controller
- Make Unique
- Parameter Curve Out-of-Range Type
- Add/Delete Note Track
- Add/Delete Visibility Track

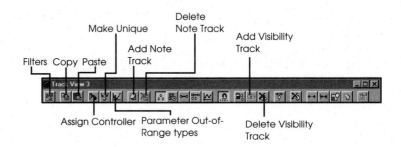

The Assign Controller command is used to assign a new controller to an item. Controllers, and the use of this command, are described in Chapter 24, "Controllers and Expressions."

The Parameter Curve Out-of-Range Type command controls how a controller outputs values for time outside of its defined range. The effect of this command's options is best seen while in Function Curve mode. This command is described in the section "Working with Function Curves" later in this chapter.

The remaining commands are described in the following sections.

Filtering the Hierarchy List

As you can see in figure 23.8, the fully expanded hierarchy list for a scene can be quite large. 3DS MAX provides a set of selectable filters to help you control the size of the display. To set these filters, click Filters to access the Filters dialog (see fig. 23.10). In the Show section of this dialog, you can select whether specific types of tracks are shown. This list is self-evident, with the exceptions of the Controller Types, Note Tracks, and Visibility Tracks options.

Controllers are used to store the animation data (key data) for each track and to interpolate values based on that data between keys. A variety of different controllers are available in 3DS MAX, some of which aren't even key-based. A full description of these controllers is provided in Chapter 24, "Controllers and Expressions." If this option is on, the controller type associated with each parameter is shown next to the parameter name.

Note Tracks and Visibility Tracks are tracks that can be added to each object and are discussed in the sections "Note Tracks" and "Visibility Tracks" later in this chapter.

The Show Only section of the Filters dialog contains three options. If the Animated Tracks option is selected, only the hierarchy of those parameters that are animated is shown. Figure 23.11 shows the same hierarchy list as figure 23.8, but with the Animated Tracks option selected. As you can see in this figure, the length of the list is significantly reduced, but it is clear which parameters are animated and how those parameters are related to the object. If you are in Track View to adjust previously defined animation, be sure to select this option to simplify the hierarchy list.

Figure 23.11

The Track View hierarchy of an object filtered to show only animated tracks.

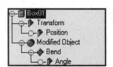

If the Selected Objects option is selected, only the parameters of the objects selected in the scene are shown. This option can be used along with the Animated Tracks option to show only animated tracks of the selected objects.

The Selected Tracks option hides all tracks that were not selected before this option was turned on. The name of all the tracks are left justified in the hierarchy list, so it is not always evident what a parameter is used for. To change the selection of tracks shown, you must turn off this option, select the new tracks, and turn this option back on.

The Function Curve Display section of the Filters dialog is used to control the color of the function curves shown in Function Curve mode and is described in the section "Working with Function Curves" later in this chapter.

Copying and Pasting Objects

By using the Copy and Paste buttons in the Track View toolbar, you can copy an item in the hierarchy list to one or more items of the same type. Although not all items in the hierarchy can be copied, a majority of them can. See Chapter 29 of the *3D Studio MAX User's Guide* for a description of the item types that can be copied. The easiest way to tell whether an item can be copied is to select it and see whether the Copy button is grayed out. If it's not, the item can be copied. Click the Copy button, and the selected item is copied into a buffer.

To paste an item from the buffer, select one or more items of the same type and click Paste. If one or more of the items selected are not of the same type, the Paste button will be grayed out.

When you click Paste, the Paste dialog is displayed (see fig 23.12). An item can be pasted as a copy or as an instance. Just as with cloning objects in the viewport, a copy is independent of the original. If you make a change to one, the other is not affected. An instance is dependent on the original, that is, if you make a change to one, the other is similarly affected. The Replace All Instances option tells 3DS MAX what to do if the item being pasted to is already an instance. If this option is selected, all the items that shared this instance will continue to share the instance and all will reference what is being pasted. If this option is not selected, the item(s) selected will be made unique (made independent) before the paste occurs.

T I P

Copy and Paste are useful for retrieving the operands of a Boolean object. Simply create a new object of any type, select the operand you want to retrieve in Track View, make a copy of it, and paste it to the object you just created.

Copy and Paste are also extremely handy ways to do things that cannot otherwise be accomplished in 3DS MAX. To make a gizmo follow a path, copy the path controller from a bonafide object onto the gizmo sub-object. Chapter 24, "Controllers and Expressions," describes this process in more detail.

FIGURE 23.12

*The Paste dialog is
used for controlling
how an item is pasted
to the selected items.*

Making an Item Unique

Use the Make Unique button to convert one or more instanced items into unique items. These items can be instanced controllers, instanced objects, or referenced objects. To make a set of items unique, select those items and click Make Unique. All instanced items in the set are made independent of all items. Any unique items in the set are not affected.

Note Tracks

3D Studio MAX enables you to store notes for each track in Track View. To create a note track, select an item and click Add Note Track. A note track is created as a branch of the selected item. If more than one item is selected, an individual note track will be created subordinate to those items. If a branch already exists for an item, the note track is added to that branch.

To create a note, you must be in the Edit Key mode. Click Add Keys and click in a note track at the time desired. This creates a Note key. Right-click on the Note key to bring up the Notes dialog (see fig. 23.13).

FIGURE 23.13

*The Notes dialog is
used for storing notes
for each item.*

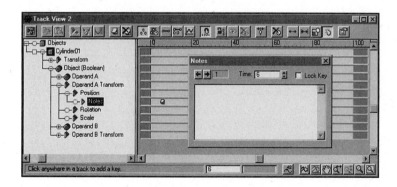

The note number is shown in the top-left of the dialog. By clicking the arrows, you can move between notes on that track. In the top-middle, the time associated with this note is shown. This time can be adjusted by the user. On the top-right is the Lock Key option. If this option is set, the note is fixed at the specified time and will not be moved by the various move, slide, and scale commands in Track View. Finally, the note text is typed into the text box. All the standard Microsoft Windows' cut and paste operations are available in this box. The first line of text in this box is shown next to the Note key in Track View.

To delete a Note track, select the Note track and click Delete Note Track. To delete a single Note, select the Note key and click Delete Keys.

WARNING

All notes stored in a track are deleted when you delete the note track. If you accidentally delete a Note track, click Undo in the main 3DS MAX toolbar to restore the track and its notes.

Visibility Tracks

Visibility tracks, similar to the Hide track in 3D Studio R4, can be applied to individual objects. To create a Visibility track, you must be in the Edit Key mode. Select the object(s) you want to add Visibility tracks to and click Add Visibility Track. A Visibility track is created as a branch of the selected item(s).

TIP

The effect of Visibility Tracks are not gradual, but instead are on or off. For objects that fade away gradually, animate the opacity of the objects' materials.

Unfortunately there is not a controller specific to Visibility tracks. The only way to specify that an object is visible or invisible at a specific time is to create a key at that time and edit the value for the key in Key Info. (Accessing the Key Info dialog is described in the section "Working with Keys and Ranges.") If the key's value is less than or equal to 0, the object is invisible at that time; if the key's value is greater than 0, the object is visible. Because a default Bézier spline controller is used for the Visibility parameter, the controller is interpolating values between successive keys and will cause the object to become visible or invisible prematurely. To prevent this, you need to set the In and Out tangent type for each of the keys to a Step tangent type in the Key Info dialog. Click and hold the In and Out tangent type buttons in Key Info and select the Step tangent type, as shown in figure 23.14.

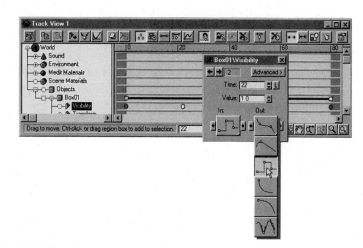

Working with Keys and Ranges

In the edit window of Track View, keys are shown in the parameters' tracks as dots, and range bars are shown in the items' tracks. The range bars extend across the range of time for which keys are present on parameters subordinate to that item. The Edit Key mode of Track View is used to create and edit keys. Both the Edit Key and the Edit Ranges modes are used to adjust the times associated with keys. The Position Ranges mode is used to adjust ranges without adjusting the keys associated with the ranges.

Two Track View commands that act on the Edit window are available in all Track View edit modes. The commands are the Snap Frame and the Lock Selection commands. Figure 23.15 shows these command buttons.

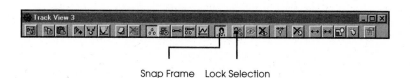

Snap Frame   Lock Selection

Normally while working with keys, you want the keys to occur exactly on a frame. If you are dealing with a detailed animation, however, you may need to place keys on subframes. If the Snap Frame is clicked, all keys created or modified are forced to occur at the nearest frame number. If Snap Frame is off, you can create or modify keys at the Tick level (remember that there are 4800 ticks to a second).

WARNING

If your time display is set to Frames or SMPTE, you cannot tell the exact time of keys created or modified with Snap Frame off. In addition, if you access the Key Info dialog when your time display is set to Frames or SMPTE, the time of the key will be moved to the displayed value.

After selecting one or more keys, it is easy to accidentally deselect the keys by clicking in the Edit window. To lock or unlock your selection of keys, click Lock Selection.

Creating Keys

To create keys in Track View, you must be in Edit Key mode. Figure 23.16 shows the command buttons for the Key Edit mode. To create a key, expand the hierarchy to display the parameter you wish to create a key for, click Add Keys, and click in the parameter's track at the time you wish.

FIGURE 23.16

The command buttons for the Edit Key mode of Track View.

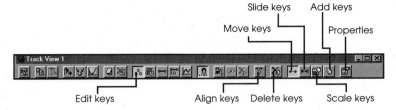

Object transformation keys (position, rotation, and scale) can also be created in the Motion, Parameters command panel (see fig. 23.17). To create a key in the Motion command panel, select the object and set Time Slider to the appropriate frame. In the PRS Parameters rollout, click the appropriate button in the Create Key section. Note that the Animate button does not need to be on to create the key.

FIGURE 23.17

Object transform keys can be added, deleted, and edited in the Parameters branch of the Motion command panel.

Deleting Keys

To delete keys in Track View, you must be in Edit Key mode. Expand the hierarchy to display the parameter you wish to delete a key from, select the key(s), and click Delete Keys.

Object transformation keys (position, rotation, and scale) can also be deleted in the Motion, Parameters command panel. To delete a key in the Motion command panel, select the object and set Time Slider to the appropriate frame. In the PRS Parameters rollout, click the appropriate button in the Delete Key section. Note that you can easily move between keys by selecting the transform type of the key you wish to delete at the bottom of the PRS Parameters rollout and clicking on the arrow buttons next to the key number at the top of the Key Info (Basic) rollout.

Editing Keys Values

To edit the values for a key in Track View, select the key and click Properties or simply right-click on the key. The Key Info dialog appears for that key. The exact format of the Key Info dialog depends on the type of controller assigned to the parameter and the number of values returned by the controller. The

two types of key-based controllers that ship with 3DS MAX are the Tension/
Continuity/Bias (TCB) controller and the Bézier controller. The difference
between these two controllers is how they interpolate values between keys.
These controllers and how to adjust their interpolation parameters are
discussed in Chapter 24, "Controllers and Expressions."

Controllers typically return one, three, or four values. Controllers that
return one value are typically used for a creation parameter of an object,
adjustment parameters for modifiers, and single field parameters for materials. Controllers that return three values are typically used for position and
scaling of objects and for colors. Controllers that return four values are
typically used for the rotation of objects. Figure 23.18 shows the Key Info
dialogs for a Bézier controller returning three values and a TCB controller
returning four values.

FIGURE 23.18

*Key Info dialogs for
Bézier and TCB
controller keys.*

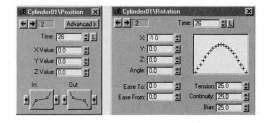

The key number is shown in the top-left of the dialog. By clicking the arrows,
you can move between keys on that track. The Time field shows the time at
which this key is placed. You can adjust the time by typing a new value or
clicking the spinner. The L button locks the key to the time specified. If this
option is set, the key is fixed at the specified time and will not be moved by
the various move, slide, and scale commands in Track View.

Next in the dialog are the values for the key, or *key values*. Again, you can
adjust the values by typing a new value or clicking the spinner. The
remainder of the fields are used to control the interpolation parameters for
that key and are described in Chapter 24.

You can also edit object transformation keys (position, rotation, and scale)
in the Motion, Parameters command panel. To edit a key in the Motion
command panel, select the object and set Time Slider to the appropriate
frame. In the PRS Parameters rollout, select the transform type of the key
you wish to edit at the bottom of the PRS Parameters rollout. The key values
can then be adjusted in the Key Info (Basics) rollout.

Adjusting Key Timing

Although you can adjust the timing of keys in Track View and in the Motion panel by editing the key's time value as described previously, you are limited to working with one key at a time. Frequently you will need to adjust the time of multiple keys or adjust the time of keys relative to other keys.

In the Edit Key mode of Track View, 3DS MAX supplies four more powerful tools for adjusting key timing. These tools are

- Align keys

- Move keys

- Slide keys

- Scale keys

TIP

After you select a set of keys, you can click Lock Selection to ensure that you do not accidentally deselect the keys.

Align Keys works on the current selection of keys when clicked. Align Keys moves those keys such that the time of the first selected key in each track is the time specified by the Time Slider (and shown in Track View by a vertical line). Any selected key that is not the first selected key in a track is moved by the same amount of time as the first selected key. The times associated with non-selected keys are not changed.

Move Keys simply moves the selected set of keys in time. Only keys that are selected are moved. The times associated with nonselected keys are not changed. You can select the keys to move before or after clicking Move Keys. You can clone and move the set of keys by shift-dragging the keys.

Slide Keys moves the selected set of keys in time but also moves the keys which occur either before or after them. If the selected keys are moved to the right (increasing time), the keys to the right of the selected keys move right by the same amount. Likewise, if the selected keys are moved to the left (decreasing time), the keys to the left of the selected keys move left by the same amount. The time relationship of keys within the selected set is not changed. You can select the keys to slide before or after clicking Slide Keys.

Scale Keys scales the time associated with the selected keys with respect to the current time. The selected keys are proportionally moved either away from or toward the current time (signified by a vertical line in the edit window) by dragging a selected key away from or toward the current time. The times associated with nonselected keys are not changed. You can select the keys to scale before or after clicking Scale Keys. You can clone and scale the set of keys by shift-dragging the keys.

Adjusting Key Timing via Range Bars

In addition to other methods of adjusting key timing, you can also adjust the key timing by adjusting the range bars. If you click and drag the range bar of an item, the range bar and the keys of all items subordinate to that item are moved. If you click and drag an endpoint of the range bar of an item, the range bar and the keys of all items subordinate to that item are scaled toward the opposite endpoint. If, for example, you drag the endpoint of the World range bar, your entire animation will be scaled.

By using the Edit Ranges mode of Track View (see fig. 23.19), you can also display the range bar for an animatable track rather than displaying keys in that track. Adjusting the animatable track's range bar as described previously will move or scale only the keys in that track.

FIGURE 23.19

The command buttons for the Edit Ranges mode of Track View.

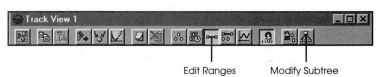

If you have objects that are linked, the Modify Subtree option is available that permits you to adjust the range of subordinate objects when you adjust the range of a parent object. This option is available in the Edit Ranges mode of Track View. If you turn on Modify Subtree by clicking it, the range bar for parent objects is extended to cover the animated region for that object and all subordinate objects. Moving or scaling the parent's range bar will affect the keys of all subordinate objects.

Working with Time

This section covers the techniques for editing blocks of time in 3DS MAX using the Edit Time mode of Track View. Figure 23.20 shows the command buttons for the Edit Time mode. Although time is manipulated independently from animation keys, Edit Time mode's primary purpose is to alter key timing. When you enter Edit Time mode, the Track View Edit window still shows keys and ranges; however, they are grayed out and for reference only.

FIGURE 23.20

The command buttons for the Edit Time mode of Track View.

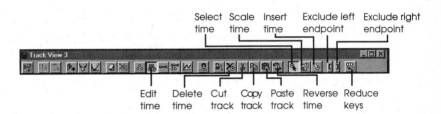

The first step when entering Edit Time is to select the tracks for which you want to edit time. Select one or more items in the hierarchy list by using the standard selection tools.

NOTE

Although you can choose nonanimatable items, Edit Time has no effect on those items.

All the tools in Edit Time—except Insert Time—require that a block of time be defined to perform the action. The time block can be specified by clicking Select Time or Scale Time and performing a drag in the Edit window. The time block is shown as a heavy black line in the selected tracks. Alternatively, you can type the begin and end times of the block in the fields at the bottom of Track View.

Inserting Time

To insert time in the selected tracks, click Insert Time, and in any track drag from the time point where you want to insert time. If you drag to the right, time will be inserted in the selected tracks. If you drag left, negative time will be inserted (that is, time will be deleted) in the selected tracks. As in figure 23.21, yellow vertical lines will be drawn showing the extents of the time being added or deleted, and the time associated with these lines are shown in fields at the bottom of Track View. In addition, heavy black lines are shown in the selected tracks showing the time being added or deleted. The keys to the right of the time associated with the initial click are moved to reflect the change in time.

FIGURE 23.21

Using Insert Time in the Edit Time mode of Track View to insert time for selected tracks.

Time Range to be inserted ——

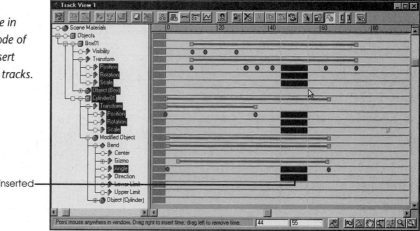

Scaling Time

To scale a block of time for the selected tracks, click Scale Time and click-drag in the marked block of time. Drag to the right to scale time up or left to scale time down. Time is scaled from the left of the block of time.

Reversing Time

Reverse Time is used to create a mirror image of the keys in the block of time. The order of the keys is reversed, as is the time between keys. Figure 23.22 shows the effect of Reverse Time on a single track.

Whether the keys at the endpoints of the range are reversed depends on the state of the Exclude Left End Point and the Exclude Right End Point buttons in the Track View toolbar. If the button is pushed in, a key occurring at the start time is not mirrored and is left in place. Likewise, Exclude Left End Point excludes a key occurring at the end time.

FIGURE 23.22

The effect of Reverse Time on an animated track.

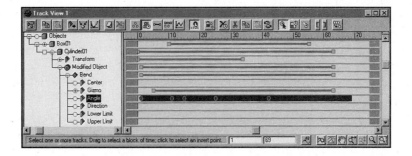

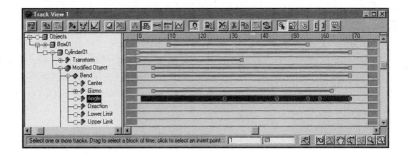

Deleting Time

Delete Time deletes the block of time and all keys in it. Keys to the right of the end time are moved to the left by the amount of time deleted. If Exclude Left End Point or Exclude Right End Point are pushed in, a key occurring at the start or end time, respectively, will not be deleted. If both Exclude Left End Point and Exclude Right End Point are on and a key exists at both the start and end time, one of the keys will be deleted. If neither key was selected in Edit Key mode, the key at the end time is deleted. If both keys were selected in Edit Key mode, the key at the start time is deleted. Otherwise, the unselected key will be deleted.

Using the Time Clipboard

The Time Clipboard is used to store a block of time and the keys associated with that block of time. The user can cut or copy blocks of time to and can paste from the Time Clipboard. Unlike copying keys in the Edit Key mode, you can paste the time block and its keys to other animatable tracks.

Unlike the other Edit Time commands, only animatable tracks can be selected in the hierarchy tree. If nonanimatable tracks are selected, the Time Clipboard commands are grayed out.

To copy a block of time to the Time Clipboard, mark the block of time and click Copy Track or Cut Track. If Copy Track is clicked, the original block of time and its keys are unaffected; if Cut Track is clicked, the block of time and its keys are deleted. The Exclude Left End Point and the Exclude Right End Point options can be selected before performing the Cut Track. The same logic used for Delete Time is used with Cut Track if keys exist at both the start and end time.

To paste from the Time Clipboard, you need to select the target tracks to receive the paste. The simplest case is when you copy from and paste to single tracks. In this case, the controller type of the target track must match the controller type of the source. (Controller types are discussed in Chapter 24.) To show the controller types, click Filters and turn on Show Controller Types. This shows the controller type next to each item in the hierarchy list. Within the object hierarchy, you can safely assume that nontransform related items can use the Bézier Float controller, even if no controller is shown for an item. Figure 23.23 shows a hierarchy list with Show Controller Types turned on. To assign a controller to an item that does not have a controller assigned, select that item, click Assign Controller, and select the controller that matches the source item's controller in the Replace Controller dialog (see fig. 23.24). If the Replace Controller dialog does not show the same controller type as the source item, you cannot paste from that source to that target.

FIGURE 23.23

A Track View hierarchy list with Show Controllers turned on.

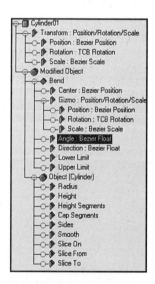

FIGURE 23.24

The Replace Controller
dialog for assigning
controllers to items.

If you paste from multiple items to multiple items or from a single item to multiple items, each target track must have the same controller type as the corresponding source track. If only the first one or more controller types match, 3DS MAX will perform the paste operation up to the first controller mismatch.

After selecting the target tracks to receive the paste, you need to specify where in time to perform the paste. You have two options: selecting a single point in time or dragging out a range of time. If you specify a single point in time, that time point is the insertion point. The block of time in the clipboard is inserted at this point, and any original keys to the right of the insertion point are moved to the right by the length of time inserted.

If you specify a range of time for the paste, that range of time is deleted before the paste occurs. Any original keys to the right of the end time are moved to the right by the length of time inserted minus the length of the range of time specified.

After you select the items to receive the paste and the time to place the paste, click Paste Track. The Paste Track dialog (see fig. 23.25) appears with an option to paste the time block absolute or relative. These options refer to the handling of the key values as opposed to time.

FIGURE 23.25

The Paste Track dialog.

If the Paste Absolute option is chosen, the values associated with the pasted keys have the exact same values as the source keys. If Path Relative is chosen, the value of the item at the paste insert time is added to key values of all keys pasted. As an example, suppose you are copying the height track of Box01 to Box02. Box01's height at the paste insert point is 100, and

Box02's height is 50. If Paste Absolute is chosen, Box02's height would be 100; if Paste Relative is chosen, Box02's height would be 150.

Reducing Keys

The Reduce Keys command acts on keys in a similar manner as the Optimize modifier acts on geometry—reducing the complexity while maintaining a specified level of detail. For each selected track, Reduce Keys analyzes the keys in the time block and creates a new, smaller, set of keys that closely matches the results of the original keys. Reduce Keys is handy for postprocessing of Inverse Kinematic motions, as well as keyframes originating with Motion Capture Systems.

To reduce the keys for a block of time for the selected tracks, click Reduce Keys. The Reduce Keys dialog appears (see fig. 23.26), enabling you to select the Threshold value. The Threshold value specifies how different from the original value at each frame the reduced set of keys is allowed to be. The unit of measure is your current unit setup for distances and degrees for angles. Each selected track is evaluated independently of all other selected tracks.

FIGURE 23.26
The Reduce Keys dialog.

Working with Function Curves

The next editing mode in Track View is the Function Curve mode. In the other Track View modes, the position of keys and ranges with respect to time is shown, but there is no indication of the actual animation values being used. Function Curve mode shows both the animation values at the keys and the interpolated values between keys for selected animated items. In Function Curve mode, as you change a key's values, the effect of that change on the controller's output over time is shown. This allows you to fine tune your animation values by adjusting the shape of function curves over time. Only animated items with key-based controllers can be displayed with Function Curves.

To display the function curve for an item, select one or more items and click Function Curves. The edit window of Track View changes to show the shape of the items' controller outputs over time (see fig 23.27) and a new set of command buttons are shown in the Track View toolbar (see fig. 23.28). To show the keys for a curve, click on the curve. The values associated with each key are shown as vertices on the curve, and the green triangle next to item in the hierarchy display generating that curve is highlighted. If that item outputs more than one value (such as a position, scale, or color), the key vertices will be displayed on all the curves associated with that item.

NOTE

The standard rotation controller outputs four values and cannot be displayed as a function curve.

In the Filters dialog described earlier, one section was devoted to function curve display options. These options control whether to show the curves associated with the X, Y, and Z outputs of the position, rotation, and scale controllers, and the R, G, and B (or H, S, and V) outputs of color controllers. Rotation is included as an option in the event that a three-component rotation controller becomes available.

FIGURE 23.27

Track View in Function Curve mode.

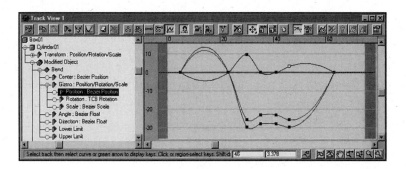

FIGURE 23.28

The command buttons for the Function Curve mode of Track View.

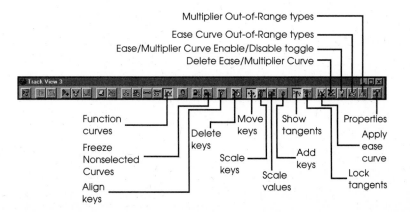

Editing Function Curves

To edit a curve, you must first select one or more of its vertices. You select vertices by using the standard 3DS MAX selection tools. To prevent the accidental deselection of a set of keys, click Lock Selection. If you are displaying curves from multiple items and only wish to select vertices from certain items, select the curves you wish to work with and click Freeze Nonselected Curves. This prevents you from accidentally selecting and modifying the curves you don't want to adjust.

You can then edit the selected vertices by moving the vertices with the Move Keys command, scaling the keys in time with respect to the current time using Scale Keys, scaling the values associated with the keys with respect to 0 using Scale Values, or deleting the keys using the Delete Keys command. When using the Move Keys or Scale Keys commands on a vertex whose associated controller outputs more that one value, the associated vertices on the controller's other output curves move in time along with the selected vertex. Note that the Move Keys command can be set to move only vertically or only horizontally by clicking and holding the Move Keys button and selecting the appropriate button from the Move Keys flyout.

The selected keys can be aligned to the current time by clicking Align Keys. If more than one key is selected for an item, the leftmost key is aligned to the current time and the remaining selected keys are moved by the same amount as the leftmost key is moved. Nonselected keys are not moved.

The values associated with individual vertices can be adjusted using Key Info by right-clicking on the vertex, by selecting the vertex and clicking Properties, or by selecting the vertex and entering values in the fields at the bottom of Track View.

TIP

The time and value for each selected vertex can be shown next to the vertex by clicking Show Selected Key Stats. Figure 23.29 shows a function curve with Show Selected Key Stats on.

Keys can be added to a curve by clicking Add Keys and clicking on the curve. A key will be added at that point with the key's value being the current value at that point.

The interpolation parameters associated with each vertex can also be adjusted in Function Curves. This will be covered in Chapter 24.

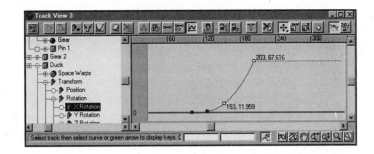

FIGURE 23.29
A function curve with Show Selected Key Stats on.

Applying Ease and Multiplier Curves

Ease and Multiplier Curves can be applied to any animatable item. An Ease Curve affects the timing of the keys for the controller it is applied to. A Multiplier Curve affects the output value of the controller it is applied to. To apply an Ease Curve, select one or more animatable items and click Apply Ease Curve. To access the Multiplier Curve command, click and hold on Apply Ease Curve and then select Apply Multiplier Curve from the flyout. Multiplier Curves are assigned to selected items in the same manner as Ease Curves.

The easiest way to understand Ease Curves is by example.

1. Load file easecurv.max from the Chapter 23 folder on the accompanying CD.

   The scene consists of two boxes moving across the top view at the same speed. Box02 (the lower box) has an Ease Curve applied to it, but it is the default Ease Curve which does not affect timing.

2. Expand the tracks for Box02 to reach the Ease Curve that has been applied to its Position track. Select Ease Curve and click Function Curves (see fig. 23.30).

   The horizontal time scale represents normal time, and the vertical time scale represents time as seen by the controller the Ease Curve is applied to. The easiest way to read the graph is to drag the horizontal time ruler down onto the Ease Curve. What now occurs at the frame number where the curve hits the ruler would have occurred at the frame number on the vertical time scale where it meets the ruler. Because the default curve is a straight line with a 1:1 slope, its input time and output time are the same.

3. Click on the Ease Curve and select the middle vertex. Change the value of the vertex to 30. Drag the time ruler down so that it meets the curve at frame 50 of the ruler (see fig. 23.31).

The horizontal time ruler meets the vertical time scale at 30. Thus, the position of the box at frame 50 is the position the box would have been in at frame 30 if there was no Ease Curve. You can observe this by moving the time slider to frame 30, noting the position of the top box, and then moving to frame 50. The lower box will have moved in 50 frames the distance the top box moved in 30.

4. Open a Track View window, select the Position track for Box02, and click Function Curves. Click on a curve to show the keys.

5. Adjust the middle vertex of the Ease Curve and observe the changes reflected in the Position track. Note how the timing of the keys in the Position track are modified by changes in the Ease Curve. If you adjust the Ease Curve such that a portion of the curve is less than 0 or greater than 100, the Position curve is clamped at the value of the first or last position key, respectively. That is because the default behavior of controllers beyond the range of their keys is to remain constant at the value used at the end of the range.

The use of a Multiplier Curve causes the value of the controller to which it is applied be multiplied by the value specified by the Multiplier Curve. The default Multiplier Curve is a horizontal line with a value of 1.0.

Ease Curves and Multiplier Curves can be deleted by selecting the curve name in the hierarchy list and clicking Delete Ease/Multiplier Curve. Ease Curves and Multiplier Curves can be disabled by selecting the curve name and clicking Ease/Multiplier Curve Enable/Disable Toggle.

FIGURE 23.30

The default Ease Curve applied to the Position track of Box02.

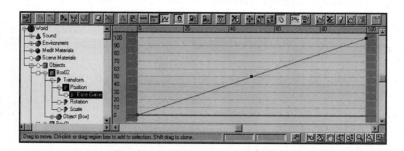

FIGURE 23.31

FIGURE 23.31

The modified Ease Curve applied to the Position track of Box02.

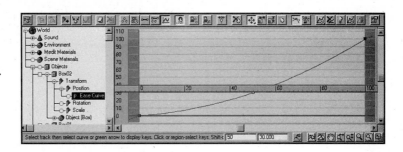

Out-of-Range Types

As stated previously, the default output of a controller outside the range of its keys is to output the value of the nearest key. This is referred to as a Constant Out-of-Range type (ORT). Six ORTs can be applied to either the left or right side of the range. In addition, the ranges themselves can be decoupled from the underlying keys, enabling you to easily create looping or repeating cycles. The six ORTs are Constant, Cycle, Loop, Ping Pong, Linear, and Relative Repeat.

To change the ORT for a animatable item, select the item in the hierarchy list and click Parameter Curve Out-of-Range Types. The Param Curve Out-of-Range Types dialog (see fig. 23.32), enables you to apply any of the six types to, before, or after the range. The solid portion of each graph line shows an example function curve over its range. The dotted portion of the line shows the effect that each ORT will have outside of the range. In the previous example used to demonstrate Ease Curves, the ORT which would most likely be applied to the boxes' motions would be the Linear ORT—the boxes would continue to move in a straight line. For a ball bouncing down a flight of stairs, you could animate the ball bouncing one step and then loop this animation to have the ball bounce down the remaining steps. In the following exercise, we will do just that.

FIGURE 23.32

The Param Curve Out-of-Range Types dialog.

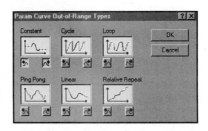

THE EFFECT OF OUT-OF-RANGE TYPES ON OBJECT MOTION

1. Load file bouncer.max from the Chapter 23 folder on the accompanying CD.

   The scene consists of a ball bouncing down a single step.

2. In Track View, expand the tracks for Ball to its Position track. Note that the range bar for Ball's Transform track is from frames 0 to 16. Select the Position track and click Function Curves.

3. Select the ball in the scene and, in the Motion command panel, click Trajectories (see fig. 23.33).

   The trajectory of the ball is shown in the viewport.

4. Play the animation and continue to play it through the rest of this exercise.

   The ball bounces from one step to the next and then sits still. The default Constant ORT is being used here, so the position of the ball after frame 16 (the end of the position range) remains constant.

5. Click Parameter Curve Out-of-Range Types and click the in and out buttons for Cycle. Click OK.

   The ball bounces from the first step to the next and then immediately returns to the first step and bounces again.

6. Click Parameter Curve Out-of-Range Types and click the in and out buttons for Loop. Click OK.

   The motion of the ball is the same as for Cycle. The Loop ORT jumps from the value of the last key to the value of the first key. The Loop ORT interpolates between these two values. In this example, the first and last keys are at the extreme edges of the range; therefore, there is no time to interpolate between the two values.

7. Click Parameter Curve Out-of-Range Types and click the in and out buttons for Ping Pong. Click OK.

   The ball bounces back and forth between the first and second steps.

8. Click Parameter Curve Out-of-Range Types and click the in and out buttons for Linear. Click OK.

The ball bounces to the second step but follows a linear path right through the step.

9. Click Parameter Curve Out-of-Range Types and click the in and out buttons for Relative Repeat. Click OK.

The ball now bounces down the flight of stairs.

FIGURE 23.33

The scene with the trajectory shown for the ball and Track View in Function Curve mode.

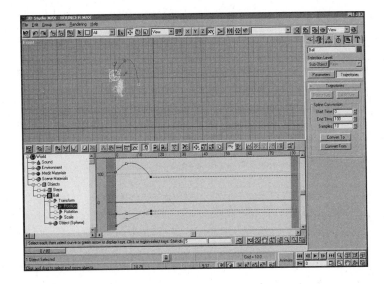

NOTE

The Out-of-Range Type for Ease and Multiplier Curves can be changed by using the Ease ORT and Multiplier ORT command buttons while in the Function Curve mode.

Position Ranges Mode

The range bars for an animated item typically start at the first key and end at the last key. 3DS MAX enables you to decouple the range for an item from its keys. This gives you added flexibility in creating loops and cycles.

To decouple a range bar for a track, select the track and click Position Ranges. A new set of command buttons are shown in the Track View toolbar (see fig. 23.34). The display of the tracks changes to show the range bar for each track laid over the track's keys. You can move the range bar by dragging the bar or adjust the length of the range bar by dragging the bar's endpoints.

Figure 23.35 shows an example of a range bar decoupled from the track's keys. The keys are located at frames 0, 20, and 80. The range bar is from frame 10 to 90. Figure 23.36 shows the function curve associated with this track. The Out-of-Range type applied to this track is the Constant ORT. From frame 10 to 20, the values used are the interpolated values from the keys at frames 0 and 20. From frames 0 to 10, the values used are the values present at the beginning of the range (due to the use of the Constant ORT). From frames 20 to 80, the values used are the interpolated values from the keys at frames 20 and 80. From frames 80 to 90, the values used are the values set by the key at frame 80. From frames 90 to 100, the values used are the values present at the end of the range (due to the use of the Constant ORT).

FIGURE 23.34

The command buttons for the Position Ranges mode of Track View.

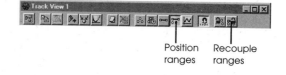

FIGURE 23.35

The Track View display of a range bar decoupled from the track's keys.

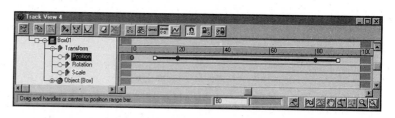

FIGURE 23.36

The Function Curve resulting from the decoupled range bar.

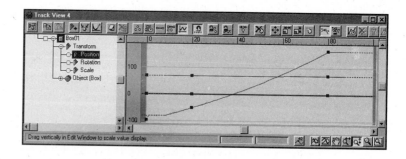

Working with Trajectories

As seen in the previous exercise, you can use the Trajectories portion of the Motion command panel to display the trajectory of selected objects in the viewports. The trajectory is shown as a blue line, with yellow dots signifying frame positions and white squares signifying key positions.

While in Trajectory, you can edit the keys of the trajectory curve, convert the trajectory to a spline, or convert from a spline to a trajectory. To edit the trajectory keys, click Sub-Object in the Motion, Trajectory command panel (see fig. 23.37). This enables you to select one or more keys and move, rotate, or scale the keys.

FIGURE 23.37

The Trajectories branch of the Motion command panel.

NOTE

When rotating or scaling keys, make sure that Use Transform Coordinate Center or Use Selection Center (located on the main 3DS MAX toolbar) is on. Otherwise, you will be trying to rotate or scale each key about itself.

While editing the trajectory keys, you may find that you need additional keys or have more keys than you need to achieve the motion desired. To add additional keys, turn on Sub-Object Keys, click Add Keys, and click on the trajectory at the locations where additional keys are needed. To delete keys, turn on Sub-Object Keys, select the keys to be deleted, and click Delete Key.

In some cases you may find it easier to convert the trajectory to a spline for editing by using the shape modifiers. The spline is created by sampling a specified region of time, where each vertex on the spline is one of the samples taken. The samples taken are evenly spaced in time, as opposed to evenly spaced along the length of the trajectory. The time region to be sampled is specified by setting the Start Time to the time you want the sampling to start and setting the End Time to the time you want the sampling to end. Samples is set to the number of samples to be taken across the time region specified. Click Convert To to convert the trajectory to a spline using these parameters.

You can use the edited spline or a new spline as the trajectory for the object. To select the spline to be used as the trajectory, click Convert From. Samples are taken from the spline and converted to position keys. The Start Time and End Time fields specify the range of time over which these position keys will be placed. Any existing keys within this time range will be deleted. Any existing keys outside the time range will not be affected. The samples are taken such that the keys representing vertices of the spline are evenly spaced in time, and keys from sampling between vertices are evenly spaced. This means that the samples taken are necessarily evenly spaced along the length of the spline. (In Chapter 24, the exercise "Creating a Burning Fuse Using an Animated Loft Scale, a Particle System, and a Path Controller" describes how to resample the spline to get an even distribution of keys over its length.)

In Practice: Animation Control Tools

- **Changing the frame rate**   The frame rate can be changed without adversely affecting your animation. 3DS MAX will automatically rescale time, without affecting your animation keys, to maintain the timing of the animation.

- **Animation keys**   The timing and values associated with all animation keys can be set, edited, and deleted in Track View. The timing and values associated with object transform animation keys can be also be set, edited, and deleted in the Motion command panel.

- **Range of time**   A range of time for your entire animation can be scaled using the Time Configuration dialog. A range of time for selected tracks can be scaled using the scaling commands in Track View.

- **Disabling viewports**   For improved interactive response in 3DS MAX, disable any viewports that do not show important information. A disabled viewport can be updated by selecting the viewport. When playing back a complex scene, use Play Selected to play only the selected objects.

- **Function Curve mode**   Use the Function Curve mode of Track View to view the interpolated animation values between keys. For certain combinations of key timing and values, the interpolated values can be much larger or smaller than the key values.

- **Copying animation keys**   Animation keys can be copied between items with the same controller type by using the Time Clipboard. This allows you to animate one object and copy the animation to another object.

- **Animated ranges**   The animated range for an object can be decoupled from the object's animation keys. This gives you extra flexibility in creating animation loops and cycles.

- **Position over time**   An object's position over time can be displayed as a spline curve using the Trajectories branch of the Motion command panel. The trajectory keys can be visually edited using the standard transform commands, and keys can be added or deleted. The trajectory can be converted to a spline for other uses, or a spline can be converted to a trajectory.

Image by Warner Interactive (Manchester)
Provided courtesy of Kinetix™

Chapter 24

Using Controllers and Expressions

Every time you animate an object in your scene, 3D Studio Max

is saving the data necessary to reproduce the animation. Because

you are not specifying how the object is to be animated on each

and every frame, 3DS MAX also needs to calculate (interpolate)

the animation data for frames where no animation data is

specified. In previous versions of 3D Studio, the way this data

was stored was not accessible to the user, and only a single type

of interpolation was available.

All animation data in 3D Studio MAX is handled by items called controllers, which store animation values and manage the interpolation from one value to the next. 3DS MAX ships with a variety of controllers. Understanding the differences between the controllers, how the controllers operate, which controller to use in which circumstances, and how to adjust controller behavior is essential for achieving the exact animation you desire.

To that end, this chapter explains the use of controllers in 3DS MAX by covering the following topics:

- Choosing controller types
- Single parameter versus compound controllers
- Parametric versus key-based controllers
- Controller data types
- Key-based controller interpolation types
- Expression controllers
- Copying and pasting controllers
- Converting parametric controller output to key-based animation

When you create an object in 3DS MAX, the core-component plug-in associated with that object specifies a list of parameters that can be animated. To conserve memory, these parameters are typically not assigned a controller. If the user animates the parameter, a default controller is then assigned to the parameter.

In addition to the parameter list returned from the object plug-in, 3DS MAX also assigns a transform controller to the object. The transform controller keeps track of where the object is located in world space, any rotation data associated with the object, and the scaling factors to be applied to the object. Default controllers are assigned to the transform controller and its input controllers when the object is created.

Figure 24.1 shows the parameters and default controllers associated with a box that has not been animated, but has had a material assigned to it. Animatable parameters are signified by a green triangle. For each parameter, the parameter name is shown, and if a controller has been assigned, the controller interpolation and data types will follow the parameter name.

FIGURE 24.1

*The parameters and
default controllers
associated with a
texture mapped box.*

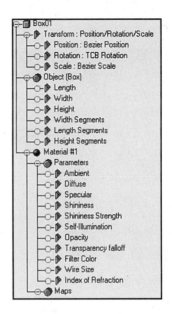

Choosing Different Controller Types

Although default controller types are assigned by 3DS MAX, you can change a parameter's controller to a different controller type. You can also change the default controller types that 3DS MAX will assign to parameters. The controller types for all parameters can be changed in Track View. Transform level controller types at the object level can also be changed in the Motion panel.

To change an object parameter's controller in Track View, complete the following steps:

1. Open Track View and expand the object's tracks to the level of the parameter.

2. Select the parameter and then click Assign Controller.

3. Select the desired controller in the Replace Position Controller dialog and then click OK (see fig. 24.2).

To change an object parameter's controller in the Motion panel, complete the following steps:

1. Select the object and open the Motion panel.

2. Click Parameters and open the Assign Controller rollout (see fig. 24.3).

3. Select the parameter and click Assign Controller.

4. Select the desired controller in the Replace Controller dialog and then click OK.

FIGURE 24.2

The Replace Position Controller dialog in Track View.

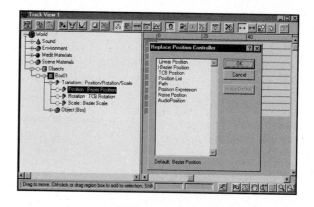

FIGURE 24.3

The Assign Controller rollout in the Motion command panel.

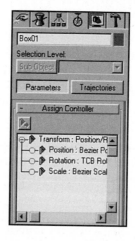

After you select a controller in the Replace Controller dialog, you may notice that the Make Default button becomes active. If you click this button, you are asked whether you are sure that you want this controller to be the default controller for all parameters with the same data type. If you answer yes, any time 3DS MAX assigns a controller to a parameter with this data type, the selected controller will be used.

If you select a parametric controller (such as the Path or Noise controller) as the default controller for a data type, you cannot interactively set or change the values for the parameters that use that data type. For example, if you set the Position Expression controller as the default position controller, all new objects are created at world origin and cannot be interactively moved.

When you change the controller type for a parameter, 3DS MAX converts any existing animation data to the format required by the new controller when possible. If you change from one key-based controller to another key-based controller, the animation data will be retained. If you convert to or from a parametric controller, however, the animation data will be lost.

3D Studio MAX does not enable you to change the controller for several parameters. These parameters are Ease Curves, Morph, loft deformation control points, and modifier Gizmo Center Positions.

Understanding Controllers

You can classify controllers in several ways: by single parameter versus compound, by parametric versus key-based, by controller data type, and by controller interpolation type. In this section, you look at the differences between controllers for each of these classification types.

Single Parameter Versus Compound Controllers

Single parameter controllers are located at the lowest level of the controller hierarchy. These controllers store the animation values specified by the user for an object's parameter and output values over time. The values returned can have either a single component (such as the height of a box) or multiple components (such as the X, Y, and Z position of the object). A single parameter controller can be either parametric or key-based.

Compound controllers take as their inputs the output of other controllers. They then combine this data with any parameter data associated with the compound controller, manipulate the data, and output the results (see fig. 24.4). The compound controllers are the Position/Rotation/Scale (PRS) and LookAt transform controllers, the Euler XYZ rotation controller, the Path position controller, and the List controller. Each of these compound controllers is described in more detail later in this chapter.

FIGURE 24.4

*An example of multiple
nested compound
controllers.*

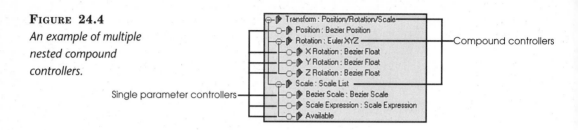

Single parameter controllers

Parametric Versus Key-Based Controllers

Single parameter controllers can be classified by whether the controller is parametric or key-based. A parametric controller takes as input user-specified data values and then provides as output values based on the equation the controller implements and the input data values. A key-based controller takes as input user-specified data values at specific time points and then provides as output interpolated values for any time point.

An example of a parametric controller is the Noise Rotation controller. The input for this controller is specified in the controller's properties dialog, and includes the frequency and strength of the noise (see fig. 24.5). This data is specified once and does not change during the length of the animation. No keys are associated with a parametric controller, and the presence of the controller is represented by a range bar in the parameter's track in Track View. The output of the controller at a given time is based on the input data, the time, and the equation implementing the noise function.

FIGURE 24.5

*The Noise Rotation
Controller Properties
dialog.*

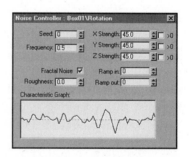

An example of a key-based controller is the Tension/Continuity/Bias (TCB) Rotation controller. The input to this controller is the rotation of the object at specific time points. This data is typically provided by setting the animation frame, turning on the Animation button, and rotating the object.

Each time you rotate an object at a different frame, a new data point is generated. These data points are referred to as *keys*, and the data specifying the amount of rotation are referred to as the *key values*. The presence of a key is represented by a dot in the parameter's track in Track View.

The output of a key-based controller is based on the key values, the time, and the equation used to interpolate between keys. For some of the controllers, the equation used to interpolate between keys can accept additional user input. With the TCB controller, for example, the user can adjust tension, continuity, and bias at each key (see fig. 24.6). Other controllers, such as the Linear controller, always interpolate the same way and cannot be adjusted.

FIGURE 24.6

The TCB Position Controller Key Info dialog.

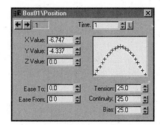

Controller Data Types

Controllers can also be classified by the data type the controller returns. The data type of the controller must match the data type of an object's parameter for the controller to be used with that parameter. A Scale data type controller, for example, cannot be used for an object's position parameter because the two are of different data types. Table 24.1 shows the available data types and examples of the parameters with which they can be used.

TABLE 24.1

Data Types Associated with Parameters

Controller Data Type	Valid Parameters
Position	Object or modifier gizmo position, gizmo center position
Scale	Object or modifier gizmo scale
Rotation	Object or modifier gizmo rotation

continues

TABLE **24.1,** CONTINUED

Data Types Associated with Parameters

Controller Data Type	Valid Parameters
Float	Any parameter with a single component value (height, number of segments, roll angle, opacity, and so on)
Point3	Any parameter with three component values other than Position and Scale (currently only used for material colors)
Color	Any material color (diffuse, ambient, and so on)
Morph	Used only for morph parameter

The Position and Scale data types are dedicated versions of the Point3 data type, and can be considered the same data type except when assigning controllers. The only apparent difference between these controllers is that a dedicated Linear interpolation type is available for the Position and Scale data types, but not for the Point3.

3DS MAX internally uses quaternion math to control rotation. *Quaternion math* (used by almost every animation system for things like camera and object rotations) is *polar-based* (using a three-component vector and an angle/scalar). This math was originally developed in the early 1800s to keep the gimbals on huge sailing ships from locking. Quaternion math results in smooth interpolated results for rotations, whereas matrix solutions (separate X, Y, and Z rotations) can result in nonsmooth results.

The Rotation data type consists of four component values required for quaternion math: the X, Y, and Z values of a unit vector, and the rotation angle about the unit vector.

T I P

Because the Rotation data type returns four values, you cannot display the function curves for a rotation controller in Track View. If you want to display the rotation function curves, use a Euler XYZ compound controller. The input to a Euler XYZ controller is three float data type controllers specifying the X, Y, and Z rotation values. You can then display the function curves for each of these float data type controllers.

The Color data type is a special case of the Point3 data type. The output from Point3 controllers can have any range of values. The output from Color controllers is limited to a range of 0–255.

Now that you're familiar with the differences between classes of controllers, the following sections explore the major controller types in more detail.

Key-Based Controllers

Key-based controllers can be classified by the type of interpolation the controller uses to determine the value(s) to return between keys. For all controllers, the function curve always passes through the key values at the time associated with the key. The different controllers only affect the interpolation of values between keys, not the keys themselves.

Table 24.2 shows the available interpolation types and the data types with which they can be used.

TABLE 24.2

Data Types Available for Each Interpolation Type

Interpolation Type	Valid Data Types
Linear	Position, Rotation, Scale, Float
Smooth	Rotation
Bézier	Position, Scale, Float, Point3, Color
TCB	Position, Rotation, Scale, Float, Point3, Morph

Each combination of interpolation type and data type is implemented by a unique controller. The method for varying the key values and interpolation parameter values for keys is the same within a group of controllers of a given interpolation type.

Controllers using the Linear interpolation type evenly divide the change in key values between one key and the next by the amount of time between the keys. The values returned from the controller follow a straight line between the keys, and the values are evenly spaced over time; that is, the values change at a constant velocity between keys. No adjustments can be made as to how the values are interpolated.

Controllers using the Smooth interpolation type adjust the tangent of the curve passing through a key value to provide a smooth interpolation through the key. No adjustments can be made as to how the values are interpolated.

Controllers using the Bézier interpolation type use an adjustable Bézier spline curve fitted through the keys to calculate values between keys. The shape of the spline curve is based on the key and tangent values at the keys. These interpolation parameters and how they affect the curve are described in the section "Bézier Controllers."

Controllers using the TCB interpolation type interpolate between keys based on five interpolation parameters: tension, continuity, bias, ease to, and ease from. The shape of the function curve is based on the key and parameter values at the keys. How the interpolation parameters affect the curve is described in the section "TCB Controllers."

For all controllers, you can set or adjust key values by turning on the Animate button, setting the appropriate time, and then setting the new value for the parameter being varied. For all controllers other than rotation controllers, you can also create keys or adjust the values associated with a key using the Function Curve tools in Track View. As described earlier, rotation keys cannot be displayed as a Function Curve; therefore, they cannot be adjusted in this manner.

For the Bézier and TCB controller types, the values of keys can also be adjusted by right-clicking on a key while in the Edit Key or Function Curve modes in Track View. This displays the Key Info dialog, where the values can be changed. Figure 24.7 shows examples of Key Info dialogs for Bézier Float, Scale, and Color controllers. Figure 24.8 shows examples of Key Info dialogs for TCB Rotation, Scale, and Float controllers. As you can see from these dialogs, within an interpolation type, the only change is the number of key value fields; the controls are otherwise the same. The exception to this is the Bézier Color controller. This controller is for use with color parameters only, and the dialog is customized to reflect this. In this controller's Key Info dialog, the user may specify colors by using either the RGB or HSV color models. A color swatch that displays the color specified by the color values is provided. If you click on the color swatch, the standard Color Selector dialog is displayed.

For transform-related controllers at the object level, the key values can also be adjusted in the Key Info rollout in the Motion command panel.

FIGURE 24.7

The Bézier Float, Scale, and Color Controller Key Info dialogs.

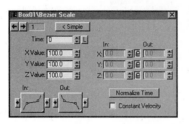

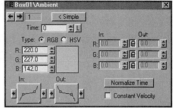

FIGURE 24.8

The TCB Rotation, Scale, and Float Controller Key Info dialogs.

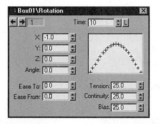

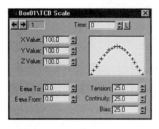

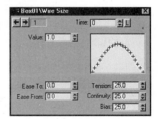

Bézier Controllers

The Bézier interpolation between two keys is based on the key and tangent values at the keys. You can adjust the tangent values by right-clicking on a key while in the Edit Key or Function Curve modes in Track View. This displays the Key Info dialog, where the values can be changed. For transform-related controllers at the object level, the tangent values can also be adjusted in the Key Info rollout in the Motion command panel.

3DS MAX provides five predefined tangent types and one custom tangent type. You select the tangent type by using the Key Tangent flyout in the Key Info dialog. Figure 24.9 shows a Key Info dialog with the Key Tangent flyout expanded.

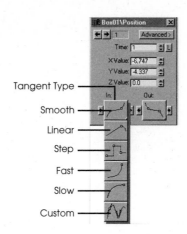

FIGURE 24.9

The expanded Key Tangent flyout in the Bézier Key Info dialog.

Tangent Type
Smooth
Linear
Step
Fast
Slow
Custom

In the following example, you look at the effect of each of the key tangent types on the motion of an object. The scene consists of a sphere that travels in a circular path. Two spline shapes show what the path would be if the path followed was circular or linear. Note that throughout this example, the location of the sphere at a key is always the location specified by the key, and that time associated with a key never changes.

THE EFFECT OF BÉZIER TANGENT TYPES ON OBJECT MOTION

1. Load file ch24_1.max from the Chapter 24 folder on the accompanying CD.

2. Select the sphere and click Trajectories in the Motion command panel.

   A blue line displays the trajectory of the sphere, with yellow dots signifying frame increments and white squares signifying keys.

3. In Track View, expand the tracks to display the position track for Sphere01. Click Function Curves. Click on a curve to display the keys.

4. Perform a region select to select all the keys. Right click on a key to display the Key Info dialog (see fig. 24.10). Reposition the Key Info dialog so that you can see the function curves in Track View and the trajectory for Sphere01 in the Top viewport.

   The Key Info dialog shows that all the keys are using the smooth tangent type. The trajectory shown in the viewport and the function curves shown in Track View are representative of smooth interpolation.

FIGURE 24.10

Accessing the Key Info dialog from Track View.

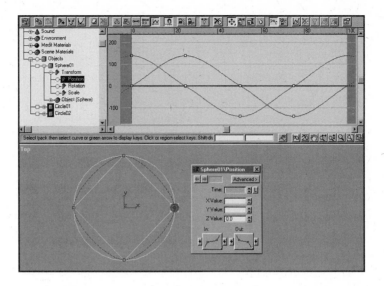

5. Click on the Y (green curve) key dot at frame 25 in Track View. The Key Info dialog now shows just the parameters for that key.

6. Click and hold the Out Key Tangent flyout, and select the Linear tangent type.

    The trajectory between the second and third key still curves, but is straighter as it exits the second key.

7. Click the right arrow next to the out tangent flyout to set thein tangent of the next key to the Linear tangent type.

    As seen in figure 24.11, the trajectory between the second and third key is straight. The interpolated value 3DS MAX calculates between two keys is based on both the out tangent of the first key and the in tangent of the second key. The effect of the tangent for a key drops off as you move closer to the other key.

8. Set the out tangent to the Step tangent type. Drag the time slider through the range of 25 to 50.

    If the out tangent for one key is a Step tangent type, the in tangent on the next key is automatically changed to a Step tangent type. The Step tangent type holds the output value constant until the time of the next key. At that time, the value jumps to that key's value.

FIGURE 24.11

*The sphere trajectory
with a Linear tangent
type.*

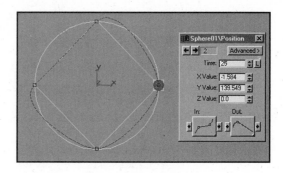

9. Set the out tangent to the Fast tangent type. Click the right arrow next to the out tangent flyout to set the in tangent of the next key to the Fast tangent type. Drag the time slider through the range of 25–50.

    As seen in figure 24.12, the sphere moves quickly as it leaves key number 2, slows down, and then speeds up again as it approaches key number 3. The frame increments on the trajectory curve are widely spaced near the two keys, and closely spaced in the middle.

FIGURE 24.12

*The sphere trajectory
with a Fast tangent
type.*

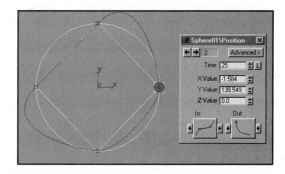

10. Set the out tangent to the Slow tangent type. Click the right arrow next to the out tangent flyout to set the in tangent of the next key to the Slow tangent type. Drag the time slider through the range of 25-50.

    As seen in figure 24.13, the sphere moves slowly as it leaves key number 2, speeds up and then slows down again as it approaches key number 3. The frame increments on the trajectory curve are closely spaced near the two keys, and widely spaced in the middle.

11. Set the out tangent to the Custom tangent type. The in tangent is automatically changed to a Custom tangent type. In Track View, select all the key dots for this key (frame 25).

FIGURE 24.13

The sphere trajectory with a Fast tangent type.

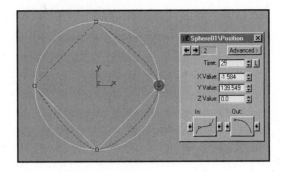

On each key dot the in and out tangent handles are shown. The tangents for this key can be adjusted by moving the tangent handles up and down, or by adjusting their values in the Advanced section of the Key Info dialog.

12. Click and drag a tangent handle.

As you move the handle, the handle on the other side of the key moves in the opposite direction. The shape of the curve through the key changes as you adjust the handle. An example of a tangent handle adjustment and the resulting trajectory is shown in figure 24.14.

FIGURE 24.14

The sphere trajectory with a Custom tangent type.

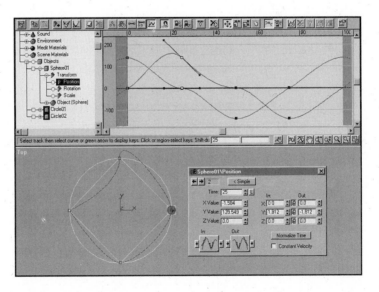

13. Click Advanced in the Key Info dialog, and adjust an in or out value. Again, both handles change.

14. Unlock the handles by clicking the lock icon between the in and out fields for a value. Adjust the in or out value. Only one handle moves.

The handles can also be unlocked by doing a Shift+click and drag on a handle. Once you unlock the handles, adjusting one handle does not cause the other to move. You can relock the handles by clicking the lock icon between the in and out fields for the value. You can also temporarily lock the handles by clicking Lock Tangents in the Track View toolbar before dragging the handles to adjust them.

TCB Controllers

Controllers using the TCB interpolation type interpolate between keys based on TCB parameters for each key. The TCB parameters can be adjusted by right-clicking on a key while in the Edit Key or Function Curve modes in Track View. This displays the Key Info dialog where the values can be changed. For transform related controllers at the object level, the TCB parameters can also be adjusted in the Key Info rollout in the Motion command panel.

In the following exercise, you look at the effect of varying each of the TCB parameters on the motion of an object. The scene consists of a sphere traveling in a circular path. Two spline shapes show what the path would be if the path followed was circular or linear. Note that throughout this example, the location of the sphere at a key is always the location specified by the key, and that time associated with a key never changes.

THE EFFECT OF TCB PARAMETER VALUE CHANGES ON OBJECT MOTION

1. Load file ch24_2.max from the Chapter 24 folder on the accompanying CD.

2. Select the sphere and click Trajectories in the Motion command panel.

3. In Track View, expand the tracks to display the position track for Sphere01. Click Function Curves. Click on a curve to display the keys.

4. Perform a region select to select all the keys. Right-click on a key to display the Key Info dialog. Reposition the Key Info dialog so that you

can see the function curves in Track View, and the trajectory for Sphere01 in the Top viewport. All keys use the default TCB parameters.

As seen in figure 24.15, the frame increments on the trajectory curve are a bit closer as you approach or leave a key than they are when you are in the middle between the keys. If you play the animation, the sphere moves more slowly around the keys.

FIGURE 24.15

The sphere trajectory with default TCB parameters.

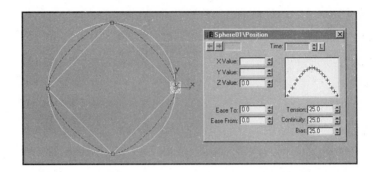

5. Gradually increase the value of Ease To.

As seen in figure 24.16, as you increase the value, the frame increments on the trajectory curve become closer as you enter a key, and further apart as you leave a key. If you play the animation, the sphere moves quickly as it leaves a key and slows down as it approaches a key.

FIGURE 24.16

The sphere trajectory with an Ease To value of 50.

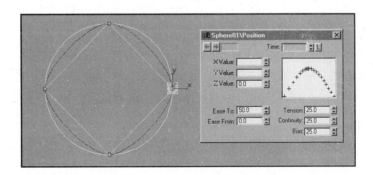

6. Set the Ease To value to 0 and gradually increase the value of Ease From. The effect is the exact opposite of increasing the Ease To value.

7. Set both Ease To and Ease From to 50.

As seen in figure 24.17, the frame increments on the trajectory curve become closer as you approach or leave a key than they are when you are in the middle between keys. If you play the animation, the sphere moves more slowly around the keys.

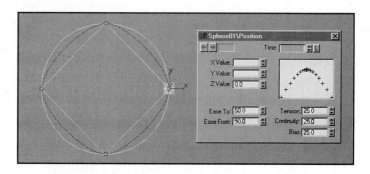

8. Set both Ease To and Ease From to 0. Gradually increase the Tension value.

As seen in figure 24.18, the curvature of the trajectory is decreased until it is a straight line between keys. The frame increments are closer around the keys and farther between them.

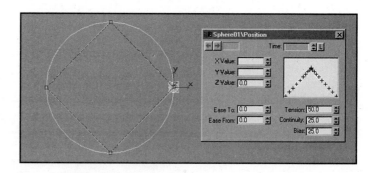

9. Gradually decrease the Tension value.

As seen in figure 24.19, the curvature of the trajectory is increased between keys. The frame increments are evenly spaced on the trajectory curve.

10. Set the Tension value to 25. Gradually increase the Continuity value.

As seen in figure 24.20, the angle between the in and out tangents of the trajectory and function curves increases, causing the interpolated values to overshoot the key values on both sides of the keys.

FIGURE 24.19

The sphere trajectory with a Tension value of 0.

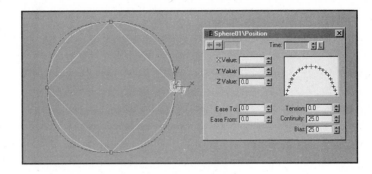

FIGURE 24.20

The sphere trajectory with a Continuity value of 50.

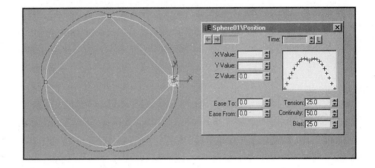

11. Gradually decrease the Continuity value.

    As seen in figure 24.21, the angle between the in and out tangents of the trajectory and function curves decreases, causing the curvature of the trajectory and function curves to approach a straight line between keys. The frame increments are evenly spaced on the trajectory curve.

FIGURE 24.21

The sphere trajectory with a Continuity value of 0.

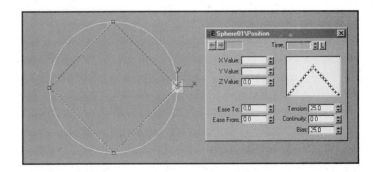

12. Set the Continuity value to 25. Gradually increase the Bias value.

    As seen in figure 24.22, the in and out tangents of the trajectory and function curves rotate, causing the interpolated values to overshoot the key values as you leave the keys.

FIGURE 24.22
The sphere trajectory
with a Bias value of 50.

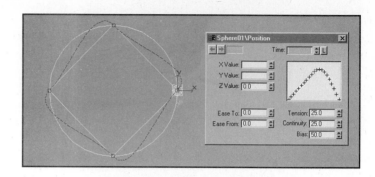

13. Gradually decrease the Bias value.

    As seen in Figure 24.23, the in and out tangents of the trajectory and function curves rotate, causing the interpolated values to overshoot the key values as you enter the keys.

FIGURE 24.23
The sphere trajectory
with a Bias value of 0.

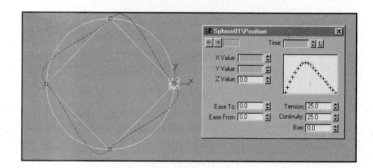

Parametric Controllers

3DS MAX ships with two parametric controller types—the Noise and Expression controllers. Table 24.3 shows the parametric controller types and the data types with which they can be used.

TABLE 24.3

Data Types Available for Each Parametric Controller Type

Parametric Controller Type	Valid Data Types
Noise	Position, Rotation, Scale, Float, Point3
Expression	Position, Scale, Float, Point3

Each combination of parametric type and data type is implemented by a unique controller. Within the group of controllers of a given parametric type, the manner in which the parameters for the controllers are specified is the same.

Noise Controllers

The parameters for a noise controller are specified by accessing the controller's Properties dialog. For all data types, you can access the Properties dialog in Track View by selecting the parameter to which the noise controller is assigned, clicking in a free area of the edit window to ensure that no keys are selected, and then right-clicking on the parameter name, right-clicking on the range bar in the parameter's track, or clicking Properties in the Track View toolbar.

For transform-related controllers at the object level, you can also adjust the controller's parameters in the Motion command panel by selecting the parameter in the Assign Controller rollout, right-clicking on the parameter, and choosing Properties from the pop-up menu.

Figure 24.24 shows examples of Property dialogs for Noise Float and Position controllers. As can be seen from these dialogs, the only change is the number of strength fields. The controls are otherwise the same.

FIGURE 24.24

The Noise Float and Position Controller Properties dialogs.

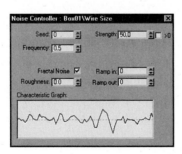

The Characteristic Graph in the Noise Properties dialog shows roughly the effect that changes in the noise parameters have on the output. In many cases it is better to see the exact effect of these changes. You can do this by clicking Function Curves in the Track View toolbar to show the function curve of the parameter. This curve changes as the noise parameters change.

TIP ───

Because rotation controllers do not display function curves, you cannot see the effect of changes in noise parameters with these controllers. Instead, use the Euler XYZ compound controller and apply a noise controller to each axis. The values in each noise controller would typically be the same except for the seed value, which should be different in each.

The Strength fields specify the range of values output from the noise controller. The range is from Strength/2 to –Strength/2 if the >0 option is off, or 0 to Strength if it is on. There are two exceptions to this. First, for the scale data type, a value of 100 is automatically added to each of the noise output values. This means that you are applying noise to a 100 percent scale factor. Second, if fractal noise is on, the output range is increased, but the center point is not. Therefore, you can have values less than 0 even if the >0 option is on. For a roughness of 0.0, the range is increased by approximately 10 percent; for a roughness of 1.0, the range is increased by approximately 100 percent.

TIP ───

You can use a List controller with a Noise controller and a key-based controller as inputs to control the center point of the result. Turn off the >0 options in Noise and then create a key for the key-based controller whose value is the desired center point.

The Ramp In and Ramp Out fields dampen the amount of noise at the start and end of the range. This dampening is not linear; it is equivalent to a Bézier curve. For a Ramp In, the curve is defined by Bézier vertices located at time 0 and at the time specified in the Ramp In field, with the vertices having zero interpolation velocity. Figure 24.25 shows the curve for a Ramp In value of 10. The shape of this curve is not adjustable.

The Ramp In and Ramp Out fields behave similarly to a Multiplier Curve applied to the Noise controller. An interesting consequence of this is that if the >0 option is on and a Ramp In value is specified, the output value of the controller goes to zero at time zero, rather than the midpoint of Strength/2.

FIGURE 24.25

The shape of a Noise Controller Ramp In Curve.

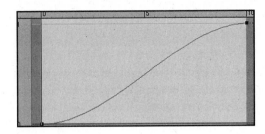

> **TIP**
>
> If you want to use Ramp In or Ramp Out and want to ramp to the midpoint value, turn off the >0 option, put the Noise controller under a List controller, and add a key-based controller to the List controller. Create a key for the key-based controller and set its value to Strength/2.

Expression Controller Basics

Expression controllers are unique in that they evaluate user-defined equations to determine their output values. Due to their relative complexity, Expression controllers are described in detail later in this chapter. To see a comparison with the other parametric controllers, look at the following basic exercise of Expression controllers.

ADJUSTING A CYLINDER'S NUMBER OF HEIGHT SEGMENTS BASED ON BEND ANGLE

1. Create a cylinder in the Top view with Radius of 50, Height of 200, five Height Segments, one Cap Segment, and 24 Sides. Make sure Smooth is on.

2. In Time Configuration, set the Animation End Time to 50.

3. Turn on Animate and apply a Bend modifier. At frame 50, set Bend Angle to 180, and set Bend Axis to Z (see fig. 24.26).

4. Turn off Animate, activate the Perspective view, click Zoom Extents, zoom out a bit to get a better view, and play the animation. (Pretty ugly.)

5. Open Track view and expand the tracks to see the controllers being input to the Bend modifier and to Object (Cylinder).

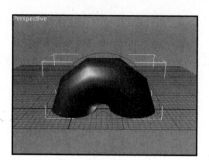

6. Click Height Segments to select it, click Replace Controller, select Float Expression, and click OK. Figure 24.27 shows the Track View hierarchy and Replace Controller dialog at this point.

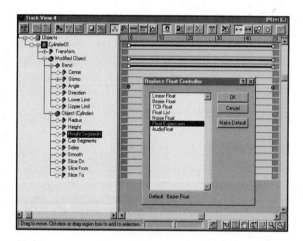

7. Right-click on Height Segments and choose Properties from the pop-up menu. You are now in the Expression Controller dialog.

8. First, you want to create a scalar variable to define the minimum number of segments you want the cylinder to have. In the Name field in the Create Variables section, type **HSMin**, make sure Scalar is selected, and click Create. Click Assign to Constant, set the value to 2, and click OK.

9. Next, you want to create a scalar variable to define the maximum number of segments you want the cylinder to have. In the Name field in the Create Variables section, type **HSMax**, make sure Scalar is selected, and click Create. Click Assign to Constant, set the value to 14, and click OK.

10. Now, you want to create a scalar variable to reference the bend angle being applied to the cylinder. In the Name field in the Create Variables section, type **BendAngle**, make sure Scalar is selected, and click Create. Click Assign to Controller, and in the Track View Pick dialog that appears, select the Angle parameter under Bend. Click OK. Figure 24.28 shows the Expression Controller dialog and the Track View Pick dialog at this time.

FIGURE 24.28

The Expression Controller and Track View Pick dialogs.

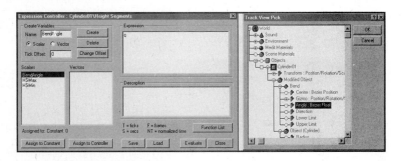

11. Finally, you need to enter the equation to evaluate. In the Expression window, type **HSMin+(BendAngle/180)* (HSMax-HSMin)**, and click Evaluate. Figure 24.29 shows the Expression controller dialog at this point.

12. Move or resize the Track View and Expression controller dialogs so that you can see the Perspective view and play the animation. The number of cylinder height segments changes as the bend angle changes.

TIP

You can go down the modifier stack to Cylinder and watch the number of Height Segments change as the animation plays. You can also change the values assigned to HSMin and HSMax in the expression and see the effects of the changes as the animation plays.

FIGURE 24.29

The Expression controller dialog with equation for adjusting cylinder segments based on bend angle.

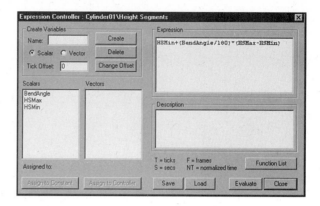

Compound Controllers

As previously described, compound controllers take as their inputs the output of subordinate controllers and then they combine this data with any parameter data associated with the controller, manipulate the data, and output the results. 3DS MAX ships with two transform level compound controllers (the Position/Rotation/Scale and LookAt controllers), a controller that combines rotations about the individual axes (the Euler XYZ rotation controller), a controller to move an object along a spline (the Path position controller), and a controller that adds the results of its input controllers (the List controller).

The way the values returned from the subordinate controllers are used by a transform level controller depends on whether the controller is assigned to an object, a modifier gizmo, or a modifier center. For a transform controller at the object level, the position value returned is the object's pivot point location relative to the world origin. The rotation and scale values returned are relative to the object's pivot point location.

For a transform controller at a modifier gizmo or center level, the position value returned is relative to the pivot point of the object; that is, a modifier center positioned at [0,0,0] is located at the pivot point of the object. If the pivot point of the object is changed after the modifier is applied, the modifier gizmo and center will remain at their original location. The rotation and scale values returned are relative to the gizmo's center point location.

Position/Rotation/Scale Controller

The Position/Rotation/Scale (PRS) transform controller combines the output from position, rotation, and scale controllers (see fig. 24.30). The output of the PRS controller is the transformation matrix used internally by 3DS MAX. The PRS controller can only be used in the transform tracks of objects and modifier gizmos.

No user-adjustable property data are associated with the PRS controller.

FIGURE 24.30

Example Position/ Rotation/Scale Transform controllers and their input controllers.

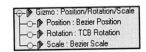

LookAt Controller

The LookAt transform controller combines the output from position, roll (a float data type), and scale controllers (see fig. 24.31). The output of the PRS controller is the transformation matrix used internally by 3DS MAX. The LookAt controller can be used only as the transform controller for objects, not modifiers.

FIGURE 24.31

A LookAt Transform controller and its input controllers.

The LookAt controller rotates an object so that the object's negative local Z axis always points at the pivot point of another object. The roll parameter specifies the roll angle of the object around its local Z axis.

The target object to be looked at is specified as a parameter of the LookAt controller. The LookAt controller's target object can be set and displayed only in the Parameters section of the Motion command panel. The LookAt Parameters rollout in the Motion command panel is shown in figure 24.32.

FIGURE 24.32

The LookAt transform controller's LookAt Parameters rollout in the Motion command panel.

USING A LOOKAT CONTROLLER ON AN OBJECT

1. Create two cones in the Top view. Drag up while specifying the cone height.

2. Choose Local from the Transform Coordinate System drop-down list in the toolbar. This shows the local axes for selected objects.

3. In Motion, Parameters assign a LookAt controller to the transform parameter for Cone02. Cone02 rotates so that its negative Z axis points at the World origin.

4. Click Pick Target and select Cone01. Cone02 rotates so that its negative Z axis points at Cone01. The pivot point for a cone is located at its bottom center; as a result, that is the point at which Cone02 points.

5. Move either cone in the Top view. As you move a cone, the base of Cone02 always points at Cone01.

   Remember to change the Transform Coordinate System or the axis constraints before trying to move a cone in another view.

6. Rotate Cone02. The cone always rotates about its local Z axis.

The LookAt controller is the controller used by Target cameras and Target Spotlights. When you create one of these objects, a LookAt controller is assigned to the object, a dummy object is created to act as the target, and the LookAt target is defined as the dummy object.

Path Controller

The Path controller positions an object so that the object's pivot point is located on a spline. A parameter subordinate to the Path controller called

Percent is also created (see fig. 24.33). The Percent parameter specifies the location on the spline to use at a particular time point. The value of Percent is automatically set to 0 at the beginning of the active time range and to 100 at the end of the active time range.

FIGURE 24.33

A Path Position controller and its input controllers.

The spline to be used as a path is specified as a parameter of the Path controller. The Path controller's path spline can only be set and displayed in the Parameters section of the Motion command panel. The Path Parameters rollout in the Motion command panel is shown in fig. 24.34. If the shape selected contains more than one spline, the first spline created in the shape is used as the path spline.

FIGURE 24.34

The Path Position controller's Path Parameters rollout in the Motion command panel.

USING A PATH CONTROLLER ON AN OBJECT

1. Create a cone in the Left view. Drag down while specifying the cone height. This creates a cone whose point faces in the positive World X axis direction. Turn on option Slice On and set the Slice To amount to 180.

2. Create an ellipse in the Top view. Figure 24.35 shows the relative sizes of the cone and the ellipse.

3. Choose Local from the Transform Coordinate System drop-down list in the toolbar. This shows the local axes for selected objects.

4. Select the cone and in Motion, Parameters assign a Path controller to the position parameter for the cone.

FIGURE 24.35

*The relative sizes of the
cone and ellipse.*

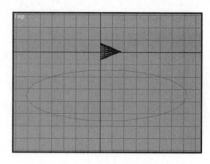

5. Ensure that Follow is off in Path Options, click Pick Path, and select the
    ellipse. The cone is repositioned so that its pivot point (located at its
    bottom center) is located at the first vertex of the ellipse. Note that the
    orientation of the cone is not changed (see fig. 24.36).

FIGURE 24.36

*The position and
orientation of the cone
on the ellipse.*

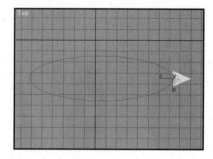

6. Move the ellipse. As the ellipse moves, so does the cone.

7. Play the animation. The cone travels the length of the ellipse over the
    active time segment.

8. Choose Edit, Hold. You continue from this point in the next exercise.

Although the Path controller is classified as a position data type, it can also
change the rotation of the object to which it is applied. The Follow and Bank
options in Path Options cause the object to rotate based on the curvature of
the path spline. The rotation applied by the Path controller is in addition to
any rotation defined by the user.

When the Follow option is off, the orientation of the object is not changed.
When the Follow option is on, the object is rotated such that the "front" of the
object is always pointing along the forward tangent of the spline. The "front"
of the object is defined as being in the direction pointing along the positive
World X axis at the beginning of the active range. Thus, the right-hand side
of an object in the Top view is the "front" of the object.

The Bank option specifies where the top of the object points ("top" being defined as the direction pointing along the positive World Z axis). If Bank is off or if the Bank Amount is zero, the top of the object tries to point in the direction of the positive World Z axis. (Two degrees of freedom are used by the Follow option, so only one degree of freedom is left for the Bank option. Therefore, the top only points in the direction of the positive World Z axis as much as it can.)

If Bank is on, the object will be rotated based on the local curvature of the spline. Bank Amount specifies by how much the direction of the top of the object is to be affected by the curvature. For low and moderate values, the top of the object tends to point toward the inside of the spline. For high values, the top of the object rotates wildly about the spline.

Smoothness specifies how fast the rotation resulting from banking is allowed to change. Higher values dampen the resulting rotation. The effects of the Bank Amount and Smoothness parameters interact with each other, so some interactive tweaking of values is usually required to achieve the motion you desire. Typically, you want to use the lowest values possible for these parameters to achieve smooth motion.

THE EFFECT OF BANK AMOUNT AND SMOOTHNESS VALUES WITH PATH CONTROLLERS

1. Choose Edit, Fetch to retrieve the scene from the previous exercise.

2. Select the cone.

3. Right-click in the Perspective viewport, click Play Animation, and continue playing the animation through the rest of this exercise.

4. In Motion, Parameters turn on Follow. The cone rotates so that its top points forward on the spline (see fig. 24.37).

5. Turn on Bank. The cone banks as it moves along the ellipse. The amount of banking varies with the curvature of the spline.

6. Set Smoothness to 2. The cone banks less at the ends of ellipse, but more on the sides.

7. Set Smoothness to 0.5 and Bank Amount to 0. Gradually increase the Bank Amount value. Figure 24.38 shows the cone with a bank value of 1.5.

FIGURE 24.37
The position and orientation of the cone with Follow on, Bank off.

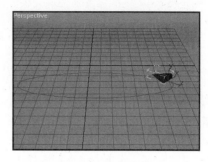

As the value increases, the degree of banking increases to the point where the cone rotates wildly as it follows the path.

FIGURE 24.38
The position and orientation of the cone with Follow on, Bank on.

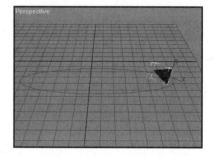

As you played the previous animation, you may have noticed that the cone moved faster at the ends of the ellipse than it did on the sides. An important consideration when using the Path controller is the relationship between the location of vertices in the spline used as the path and time. 3DS MAX positions the object on the spline over time based on the number of spline vertices—not on the length of the spline or on the distance between the vertices. Each vertex is converted to a position key evenly spaced over time. For example, if a line with 11 vertices is used as an object path, 11 position keys are created. If the active time range is 0 to 100 frames, the object is located at vertex 0 at frame 0, vertex 1 at frame 10, and vertex 2 at frame 20. Depending on the distance between these vertices, the velocity of the object can change greatly over time.

In some situations, a constant velocity over the path is required. 3DS MAX provides the capability to modify a Bézier path so that a constant velocity is maintained over the object trajectory. Modifying a Bézier path to maintain a constant velocity is performed in the Advanced Key Info dialog.

In the following exercise, the trajectory of a particle system emitter is adjusted to track an animated loft object deformation. In this scene, the lofted object (Fuse) uses an animated scale deformation to simulate the reduced length of the fuse over time. The scale deformation was defined so that the length of the fuse is reduced at a constant rate over time. The particle system emitter (Sparks) is assigned a path controller where the path is the same spline as the loft path (FusePath). Because the vertices for FusePath are not evenly spaced, Sparks precedes the scale deformation.

CREATING A BURNING FUSE USING AN ANIMATED LOFT SCALE, A PARTICLE SYSTEM, AND A PATH CONTROLLER

1. Load file ch24_3.max from the Chapter 24 folder on the accompanying CD and play the animation.

2. Select object Dummy.

3. Choose Motion, Trajectories, Convert From, set Samples to 11, and select FusePath as the spline.

4. Select the position controller for Dummy in Track View, click Function Curves, and click on one of the function curves shown in Track View for Dummy's position.

   Figure 24.39 shows the Top viewport and Dummy's position function curves in Track View. The trajectory for Dummy is shown as blue in Top view, with 11 position keys, located 10 frames from each other. The dots on the trajectory show frame increments. The number of frame increments between each position key is constant, and the frame increments are not evenly distributed between position keys. Although this isn't the path that you want Sparks to follow, you can use it to show the effect of modifying the trajectory for a constant velocity.

5. In the Motion command panel, click Sub-Object and select all trajectory position keys in the Top viewport.

6. Right-click any of the position keys, choose Key Info, and click Advanced (see fig. 24.40).

7. Turn on Constant Velocity.

FIGURE 24.39

The trajectory and position function curves for object Dummy.

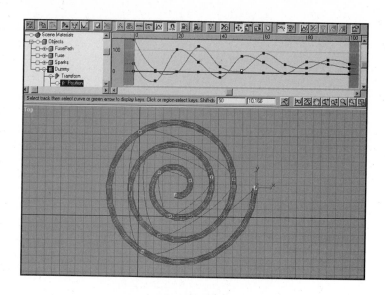

FIGURE 24.40

The Advanced Key Info dialog.

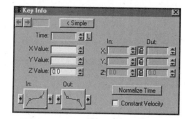

The frame increments between one position key and the next are evenly spaced. The position keys are still located every 10 frames and still reference the same location. As can be seen in Track View, only the curvature between keys has changed.

8. Turn off Constant Velocity, and click on Normalize Time.

   The position keys still reference the same location, but the time associated with each position key is changed based on the distance between position keys. There are more frame increments in larger segments than in shorter segments. The velocity is not constant between position keys.

9. Turn on Constant Velocity.

   The frame increments are evenly spaced across the entire trajectory. Now that you have seen the effects of Constant Velocity and Normalize time on a trajectory, you can complete the animation.

10. In Motion, Trajectories, increase Samples to 101, choose Convert From, and select FusePath as the spline.

11. Select all position keys in the trajectory, and in Key Info, ensure Constant Velocity is checked. Click on Normalize Time. Figure 24.41 shows Dummy's trajectory and position function curves with 101 samples.

FIGURE 24.41

The trajectory and position function curves with 101 samples.

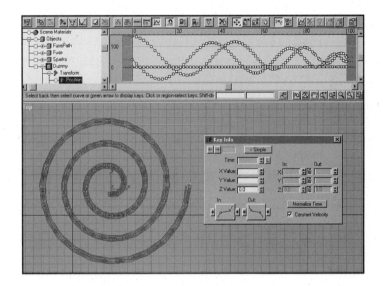

12. Close Key Info, and click Convert To. Convert To generates a shape from the trajectory called Shape01.

13. Select Sparks, and in Motion, Parameters click Pick Path and select Shape01 as the path.

14. Play the animation.

    Sparks is now located at the same location as the scale deformation across the entire animation.

Euler XYZ Controller

The TCB Rotation controller is the default controller used for rotation tracks. Although this controller provides smooth rotation, the function curves associated with this controller are not available in Track View because the TCB controller uses quaternion math to control the rotation. Quaternion math has four values—the X, Y, and Z values of a unit vector, and the rotation angle about the unit vector (see the section "Controller Data Types" earlier in this chapter for more information on quaternion math). Additional rotation controllers that use quaternion math are the Linear and Smooth controllers.

Besides being unable to display the rotation function curves for these controllers, more control over rotation is sometimes desired than can be provided with these controllers. 3DS MAX provides an additional rotation controller, the Euler XYZ controller, for which you can display function curves and individually control the rotation about each of the object's local axes.

Consider a case where you are rotating an object about its X and Y axes, and you want to adjust the interpolation at one of the keys for the X-axis rotation. You can adjust the TCB controller values for that key in either the Motion panel or in Track View, but you are also adjusting the interpolation of the Y axis rotation at that key. When using the TCB controller, you cannot adjust interpolation values for one axis without also adjusting them for all axes. If a Euler XYZ controller is used, the interpolation for keys associated with the X-axis rotation can be adjusted without affecting the Y-axis rotation.

Additional benefits of using the Euler XYZ rotation controller for an object are that expression controllers can be used for each rotation axis and other expression controllers can reference the rotation of the object.

USING THE EULER XYZ CONTROLLER TO ADJUST THE INTERPOLATION PARAMETERS FOR INDIVIDUAL ROTATION AXES

1. Load file ch24_4.max from the Chapter 24 folder on the accompanying CD and play the animation.

   The box is animated to rotate 180 degrees about its local Z axis over frames 0 to 100. The box is also animated to rotate 45 degrees about its Y axis over frames 25 to 75. As can be seen in the viewports, there is rotation about the Y axis prior to frame 25 and after frame 75. You could try adjusting the TCB parameters for the keys at frames 25 and 75, but that would also affect the rotation of the box about its Z axis at these frames.

2. Open Track View and expand the tracks to display the rotation parameter for Box01.

3. Select the rotation parameter and assign a Euler XYZ controller to the parameter.

4. Expand the tracks for the rotation parameter.

5. Select the Y Rotation parameter and click Function Curves. Click on the curve to display the keys.

   The function curves are shown in figure 24.42. The function curves show that the Y rotation value varies between the first and second keys, and between the third and fourth keys.

FIGURE 24.42

The position function curves for object Box01.

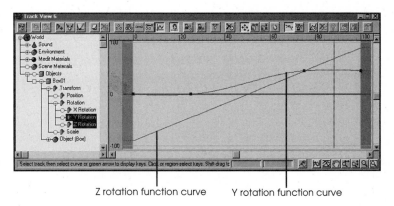

Z rotation function curve   Y rotation function curve

6. Right-click the first key to display the Key Info dialog.

7. Set the out tangent to a Step tangent type for the first key.

8. Set the in tangent to a Step tangent type for the fourth key.

9. Play the animation.

   There is no rotation about the Y axis prior to frame 25 or after frame 75. The rotation about the Z axis is still smooth.

List Controllers

List controllers are used to combine the results of multiple controllers. For example, you can add noise to a predefined motion by assigning a List controller to the desired parameter, and adding a Noise controller as an input to the List controller. The List controller also enables you to interactively add additional motion to a parameter controlled by a parametric controller, such as the Path controller.

In the following exercise, you use a Path controller for a portion of the animation and then switch over to a Bézier curve controller to complete the animation. The scene consists of a ball whose motion is controlled by a path controller. The path being followed is a circle. What you want to do in this animation is have the ball motionless at the beginning of the animation, have the ball accelerate three times around the circle, and then have it fly off to the location shown by the dummy object.

COMBINING PATH, BÉZIER, AND LIST CONTROLLERS TO RESTRICT THE PATH CONTROLLER TO A TIME RANGE

1. Load file ch24_5.max from the Chapter 24 folder on the accompanying CD.

2. Open Track View, click Filters, and turn on Show Controller Types.

3. Expand the tracks for Sphere01 to show the Percent controller under the Position:Path controller.

4. Right-click the position key at frame 100 to bring up the Key Info dialog.

5. Change the value for the key frame to 300 and exit the dialog.

6. Play the animation. The ball moves at a constant velocity three times around the circle.

7. In Track View, click Function Curves and then click Add Keys.

8. Add three keys to the Path Percent function curve and then click Move Keys.

9. Adjust the three keys to obtain a curve similar to the one shown in Figure 24.43.

   Note that you can play the animation as you are adjusting the curves and see the corresponding motion in real time. The ball now starts from a rest position and accelerates three times around the circle over 100 frames.

   Now you want to perform this motion over 80 frames and then fly off to the position of the dummy object.

10. Click Edit Keys and select the Position:Path controller.

11. Click and drag the end of range marker for the position controller to frame 80.

12. Click Assign Controller and choose Position List.

13. Expand the tracks for Position List, select Available, and assign a Bézier Position controller to the track.

14. Click Add Keys, click at frame 80 in the Bézier Position track to create a key, and click Move Keys.

15. Click in a free area of Track View to deselect the key you just created.

16. Click on the Position List controller to select it, right-click on it, and choose Properties from the pop-up dialog. The List Controller dialog that appears shows the Path controller as the active controller. You want the Bézier Position controller to be active so that you can interactively adjust the position of the ball.

17. Select Bézier Position, click Set Active, and exit the List Controller dialog.

18. Turn on Animate and move to frame 100.

19. In the Top view, move Sphere01 to the location of the dummy object.

20. Turn off Animate and play the animation.

    The ball now accelerates around the circle three times over 80 frames and then flies off to a new position. Note that there is a small variation in the velocity of the ball as it passes through frame 80.

21. Select all the keys for the Percent controller and the key at frame 80 for the Bézier Position controllers. Click Scale Keys and adjust these keys by dragging the key at frame 80 for the Bézier Position to get a smooth transition of velocity.

FIGURE 24.43

The location of keys on the Path Percent Function Curve.

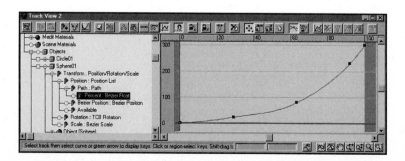

The List controller can be used to combine a Path controller and a Bézier and also be used to cause a camera to follow an object along a path. One restriction to keep in mind is that if a Path controller is a subordinate controller to a List controller, it must be the first controller in the list; if it is not, any values from controllers prior to it in the list are ignored.

In the following exercise, the scene consists of a torus rolling through an obstacle course. In this scene you want to have the camera always looking at the torus, and have the camera follow behind the torus.

CREATING A CAMERA FOLLOWING—BUT OFFSET FROM— AN OBJECT USING A PATH CONTROLLER

1. Load file ch24_6.max from the Chapter 24 folder of the accompanying CD.

2. Select the camera and open the Motion command panel. Open the Assign Controller rollout and click on Transform:Position/Rotation/Scale. Click Assign Controller, select LookAt from the Replace Transform Controller dialog, and click OK.

3. In the LookAt Target section of the LookAt Parameters rollout, click Pick Target and select Dummy01 as the target.

4. In the Assign Controller rollout, click on Position:Bézier Float. Click Assign Controller, select Path from the Replace Position Controller dialog, and click OK.

5. In the Current Path Object section of the Path Parameters rollout, click Pick Path and select TorusPath as the path. Turn on the Follow path option.

6. In the Assign Controller rollout, click on Position:Path. Click Assign Controller, select Position List from the Replace Position Controller dialog, and click OK.

7. Expand the position list, select Available, and assign it a Bézier Position controller.

8. In the Position List rollout, select Bézier Position and click on Set Active.

9. In the Front view, move the camera up about 200 units.

10. Open Track View and expand the transform tracks for the camera.

11. Select the Percent track under the Path controller.

12. Click Function Curves and click on the curve.

13. Click and hold on the Move Keys button, and choose the bottom icon from the flyout. This will restrict movement of key dots to the vertical direction.

14. Select both key dots and move the keys down about 5 units.

15. Close Track View and play the animation.

For an interesting variation in the camera movement, select the Path controller in the Position List rollout in the Motion command panel and click on Set Active. In the Path Parameters rollout, turn on the Bank path option and set Bank Amount to –0.5. The camera now "swings out" from the path in the curved sections.

FIGURE 24.44
Track View and two views of the scene.

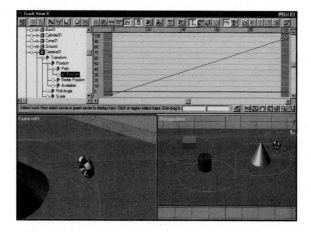

Expression Controllers

Expression controllers evaluate user-defined mathematical expressions to determine their output values. Expression controllers can be applied to nearly all animatable parameters in 3DS MAX. An Expression controller can access the outputs of other controllers, and those values can be used in the expression. The time point for which the expression is to be evaluated is also available in several forms. A variety of intrinsic functions are provided for use in expressions.

The parameters for an Expression controller are specified by accessing the controller's Properties dialog. For all data types, you can access the Properties dialog in Track View by selecting the parameter to which the Expression controller is assigned, clicking in a free area of the edit window to ensure that no keys are selected, and then doing one of the following: right-clicking on the parameter name, right-clicking on the range bar in the parameter's track, or clicking Properties in Track Views toolbar.

For transform-related controllers at the object level, the controller's parameters can also be adjusted in the Motion command panel by selecting the parameter in the Assign Controller rollout, right-clicking on the parameter, and choosing Properties from the pop-up menu.

Expression Controller Data Types

Figure 24.45 shows a sample Expression controller dialog. When you first assign an Expression controller to a parameter that already has a controller, the equation box shows the value for that parameter at frame 0. If the parameter does not have a controller, the value will be set to 0. The value shown is in one of two formats. The first format is if the parameter to which the Expression controller is assigned has a Position, Scale, or Point3 data type. These data types require the Expression controller to return a three-component vector. The format of the expression is **[eqn1, eqn2, eqn3]**. The second format is if the parameter to which the Expression controller is assigned has a Float data type. This data type requires the Expression controller to return a floating point scalar value. The format of the expression will be **eqn1**. If the format of the expression is incorrect or if an error occurs while evaluating the expression, an error message is displayed when you evaluate the expression or close the Expression Controller dialog.

FIGURE 24.45

A sample Expression Controller dialog.

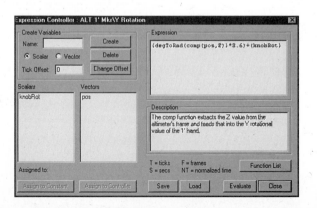

Expression Controller Variables

Two types of variables can be used in an equation. The first, Scalar, is used to reference single value float data. The second, Vector, is used to reference three-component vectors. To create a variable, you type the name of the variable into the name field in the Create Variables box, select whether the variable is to be a scalar or vector variable, and click Create. The variable is created, and its name appears in the Scalars or Vectors columns.

When a variable is created, it is assigned a constant value of 0 if it is scalar or [0,0,0] if it is vector. Variables can either be assigned a constant value over the animation or a value can be assigned as the output value of another controller. To assign a constant value to a variable, select the variable name in the Scalars or Vectors columns, click Assign to Constant, and assign the value to use.

To assign a controller output to a variable, select the variable name, click Assign to Controller, and select the controller from the Track View Pick dialog that appears (see fig. 24.46). In the Track View Pick dialog, controllers that can be chosen are displayed in boldface. A controller can be chosen if the controller data type matches the variable type and if a controller has been assigned to a parameter. In some cases 3DS MAX enables you to select a controller, and will then give you a "Can't Assign Control... Circular Dependency" error message. This error message is generated if the parameter selected and the parameter to which the expression controller is applied are both subordinate to the same controller. For example, an expression for the Length parameter of a box cannot reference the box's width parameter. It can, however, reference the box's transform parameters and the parameters for any modifiers applied to the box.

FIGURE 24.46

The Track View Pick dialog.

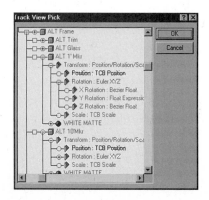

Tick Offset Values

The value returned from a controller assigned to a variable is normally the output value of the controller at the same time point that is being evaluated. In some cases the value desired is the controller's output at a different time point. 3D Studio MAX enables you to specify a fixed offset for a variable. 3DS MAX adds this offset value to the time point being evaluated, and evaluates the assigned controller at that time point. This offset value is specified in the Tick Offset field in the Create Variables box. The Tick Offset value is set when the variable is created and can be changed by selecting the variable name, setting the new Tick Offset value, and clicking Change Offset. The Tick Offset value can be either positive or negative, and remains constant over the animation. As its name implies, the Tick Offset value specifies the offset time in ticks. There are 4,800 ticks to a second. If your frame rate is 30 frames per second, then there are 160 ticks per frames.

Reserved Variable Names

There are several variable names that you cannot or should not use when creating a variable. Four of these (T, S, F, and NT) are predefined variable names with special values, and you cannot create a variable with one of these names. In addition, you should not use the names e, pi, or TPS. These variable names are also predefined with special values; however, 3DS MAX enables you to override these values. The following are the values associated with each of these variables:

T   The time point being evaluated in ticks

S   The time point being evaluated in seconds

F   The time point being evaluated in frames

NT   The normalized time. This value linearly increases from 0 at the beginning of the active time segment to 1 at the end of the segment.

e   The constant e (2.71828...)

pi   The constant pi (3.14159...)

TPS   The number of ticks per second (4800)

Data Value Ranges Associated with Parameters

As you start using Expression controllers, you begin to realize that what you see is not always what you get. Frequently, the data values you specify to 3DS MAX, and the data values shown to you by 3DS MAX, are not the actual data values stored in the controllers. An Expression controller applied to a parameter must output values in the actual range of values that the parameter expects. If it does not, the animated effect may be off by orders of magnitude.

When you create an object in 3DS MAX, the core-component plug-in associated with that object specifies a list of parameters that can be animated. In this case an object can refer to a material, a geometric object, or a modifier. For the sake of discussion, we'll call the core-component the parent. For each animatable parameter, there is a controller that is subordinate to the parent.

The parent decides how to handle the data values returned from a subordinate controller. The parent also specifies how the data values are to appear in the command panels, Track View, and other dialogs where you can view or set the data values. Frequently, the data values you see are not the true data values passed from the controller to the parent, but are data values that are "massaged" by the parent. One example of this is with parameters that deal with angles. In all cases, the data values you set and see are in degrees. Internally, most of these angles are handled in radians.

When you use Expression controllers, you are literally plugging into the middle of things. If the Expression controller is applied to a parameter dealing with angles, your output should be in radians. If your expression has a variable assigned to a controller that is dealing with angles, expect to get the results in radians.

In some cases, the way the parent handles the data from a subordinate controller varies. Although most angles are internally handled as radians, in some cases they are handled in degrees. An example of this is Bend Angle in the Bend and Twist modifiers.

The following are general rules of thumb for actual controller output values:

- If a parameter is time-based, the controller output is typically in ticks. Examples of this are the Ease Curve and particle system birth rates. The Phase parameter of the Noise modifier is also output in ticks.

- If a parameter is a percentage, or the viewable range of values is 0 to 100, the actual controller output range is typically 0 to 1. Examples of this are scale parameters and material opacity.

- If the parameter is angle-based, the controller output is typically in radians. Examples of this are camera FOV and rotation controllers subordinate to a Euler XYZ controller.

- If the parameter is a color, the controller output range is always 0 to 1.

- For parameters displayed as integers, the controller output is rounded to the nearest integer. An example of this is the Material ID parameter in the Material modifier.

- If the parameter is displayed as an option, the option is typically turned on when the controller output is greater than 0.5. Examples of this are the Fractal option in the Noise modifier and the Symmetry option in the Taper modifier.

- For other values that can be freely adjusted, the controller output is typically the value seen in the command panel and in Track View.

- As with all rules of thumb, there are always exceptions.

TIP

To determine the actual output values of a controller, animate the parameter over a range of its values. Create a Point object and assign an Expression controller to its position parameter. Use the equation **[inp,inp,inp]** as the equation, and assign the controller of interest to the scalar variable **inp**. The actual values output by the controller can then be seen via the function curve of the Point object's position.

An additional item to be aware of is that the limits 3DS MAX places on some parameters are applied only during data entry. Because Expression controllers bypass the data entry, these limits are not always enforced. An example of this is a camera's FOV. The FOV is limited to 175 degrees during data entry, but an Expression controller can supply any value it desires. Although rarely fatal, Expression controllers returning out-of-range values can result in unexpected behavior. It is best to determine the limits present on a parameter and remain within those limits.

An Expression Controller Exercise

In this exercise, you rotate a billboard so that the front of the billboard always faces the camera; however, you also want the billboard to remain perpendicular to the ground—you only want to rotate the billboard about a single axis. To accomplish this, use an expression controller that rotates Billboard about its Z axis based on the position of the camera relative to Billboard.

The scene contains the camera, a box that acts as the ground (Ground), and a texture mapped box (Billboard). The pivot point for Billboard has been adjusted so that its +Z axis is perpendicular to Ground.

The rotation expression controller to be applied to Billboard needs to access the position of Billboard. Because a rotation expression for an object is not allowed to access the same object's position controller, a dummy object is created at the same position as Billboard, and Billboard is set as a child of the dummy object.

AN EXPRESSION CONTROLLER IMPLEMENTING A LOOKAT CONTROLLER ABOUT A SINGLE AXIS

1. Load file ch24_7.max from the Chapter 24 folder on the accompanying CD.

2. Click Play Animation to view the animation.

3. Press Esc to end the playback, and click Min/Max to display all viewports.

4. Create a dummy object.

5. Choose Align and select Billboard as the Align Target Object. Choose X Position, Y Position, and Z Position, and choose Pivot Point for both Current Object and Target Object. Choose X, Y, and Z axes in Align Orientation. Click OK to exit.

6. Choose Select and Link, and link Billboard to the dummy object.

7. Open Track View and select the rotation controller for Billboard.

8. Choose Assign Controller and choose the Euler XYZ controller.

9. Expand the rotation controller track and assign a Float Expression Controller to the Z Rotation track. Figure 24.47 shows the screen at this point.

FIGURE 24.47

Track View and two views of the scene.

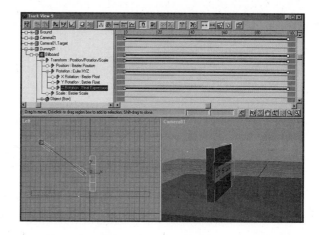

10. Right-click on the Z Rotation controller and choose Properties.

11. Click Load and load lookat_z.xpr from the Chapter 24 folder on the accompanying CD. Figure 24.48 shows the Expression controller dialog containing the Lookat_Z equation.

FIGURE 24.48

The Lookat_Z Expression controller equation.

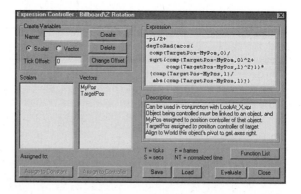

12. Select MyPos in the Vector column, click Assign to Controller, and choose the position track for the dummy object.

13. Select TargetPos in the Vector column, click Assign to Controller, and choose the position track for the camera.

14. Click Close, activate the camera view port, and play the animation.

An additional expression controller has been provided as file Lookat_x.xpr. Figure 24.49 shows the Lookat_X equation. By using this equation to control the X Rotation track of an object and the Lookat_Z equation to control the Z Rotation track, the –Z axis of the object will always point at the target object. An example scene, ch24_8.max found on the accompanying CD, shows two objects—one using the LookAt controller and the other using the above expressions.

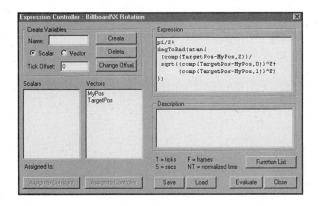

Copying and Pasting Controllers

Most controllers can be copied and pasted in Track View. With some restrictions, as long as a parameter has a controller attached to it, you can copy that controller; a controller can be pasted to a parameter as long as the parameter can accept the controller's data type.

The main restriction on cutting and pasting is that the controllers more than two levels down on an object cannot be copied from or pasted to. This restriction means that the subordinate controllers in a List controller, Ease and Multiplier controllers, and the subordinate X, Y, and Z rotation controllers in a Euler Rotation controller cannot be copied from or pasted to. Additional restrictions are that a copy/paste cannot be performed on the position track for a modifier center and cannot be performed on a PRS controller for a modifier gizmo. Copy/paste can be performed, however, on the subordinate controllers to a gizmo's PRS controller with the preceding restrictions.

A final restriction is that if a controller that uses an Ease or Multiplier controller is copied and pasted, the Ease or Multiplier channel is not retained in the copy. This is true both for controllers copied in Track View and for objects that are cloned in the main viewports.

In the following exercise you look at how instanced controllers can be used as an aid in creating geometry. For this exercise, you want to create a box that will always be square—the same value will always be used for the box's height, width, be length.

INSTANCING CONTROLLERS FOR OBJECT PARAMETERS

1. Create a box with any dimensions. The box does not need to be square.

2. Open Track View, click Filters, and turn on Show Controller Types.

3. Expand tracks for Box01.

4. Select the Height parameter and assign a Bézier Float controller to the parameter.

5. Click Copy Controller to store a copy of the Bézier Float controller.

6. Select the Width parameter and Ctrl+click the Length parameter to add it to the selection.

7. Click Paste Controller. The Paste dialog appears with an option of pasting the controller as a copy or as an instance. You want to paste as an instance so that if one value is changed the value for all three tracks is changed.

8. Choose Instance and click OK.

9. Close Track View and open the Modifier command panel.

10. Adjust the value for Length, Width, or Height.

    As the value is changed, the new value is reflected in the other fields.

TIP

In the previous LookAt expression example, the billboard was linked to a dummy object because the rotation expression controller needed the billboard's position, but was not allowed access to the object's position track. Instead of linking the objects, you could have copied the billboard's position controller to the dummy object's position controller as an instance. Then, if either object is moved, the other object is also automatically moved.

Controller types can be specified for the transform level controllers of objects in the Motion panel or in Track View. For those controller types that require the user to specify an additional object (the Path controller and the LookAt controller), that object can only be specified in the Motion panel.

Controller types can be specified for any animatable value in Track View. This includes the transform controllers for gizmos of modifiers applied to an object. Although Path controller can be specified for the position of a gizmo, there is no direct way of specifying the path to follow. This limitation can be circumvented by applying a Path controller to another object, specifying the path to follow in the Motion panel and then cutting and pasting the Path controller to the position controller of the gizmo.

The position of a modifier gizmo is specified relative to the pivot point of the object to which the modifier is applied. That is, a modifier positioned at [0,0,0] is located at the pivot point of the object. When a path controller is applied to an object or gizmo, the position values returned are relative to world center.

The following exercise uses a Position List controller and a Position Expression controller in conjunction with the Position Path controller to properly place a gizmo with respect to an object. In this exercise, a Volume Select modifier is applied to select a group of faces of an object, and a MeshSmooth modifier is applied to the selected faces to increase the density of faces in that area. An EditMesh modifier is then applied to clear the selection set, and a Displace modifier is applied to form a "dimple" in the object. In this exercise, a path controller is applied to the Volume Select and Displace modifier gizmos.

APPLYING PATH CONTROLLERS TO MODIFIER GIZMOS

1. Load file ch24_9.max from the Chapter 24 folder on the accompanying CD. Figure 24.50 shows a perspective and front view of the "dimpled" cylinder.

FIGURE 24.50
Views of the scene showing the dimpled cylinder.

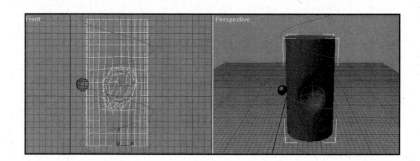

2. Open Track View, click Filters, and turn on Show Controller Types.

3. Expand the tracks, as shown in figure 24.51.

4. Select the Path position controller on Sphere and click Copy Controller.

5. Select the position controller on the Cylinder's Displace gizmo.

6. Click Paste Controller and choose Paste as Instance.

7. Select the position controller on the Displace gizmo, click Assign Controller, and choose Position List.

8. Expand the Position List controller, select Available, click Assign Controller, and choose Position Expression.

9. Right-click on Position Expression and choose Properties.

10. Create a vector variable called CylPos, click on Assign Controller, and select the position controller for Cylinder in the Track View Pick panel.

11. Enter **-1*CylPos** as the expression and close the expression controller dialog.

12. Select the Position List controller and click Copy Controller.

13. Select the Volume Select gizmo's position controller, click Paste Controller, and choose Paste as Instance.

14. Close Track View and play the animation.

FIGURE 24.51

*The expanded hierarchy
in Track View.*

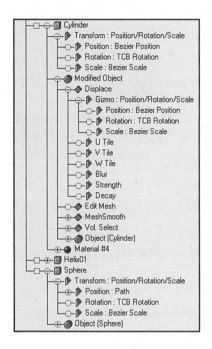

Converting Parametric Controller Output to Key-Based Animation

By using the controllers supplied with 3DS MAX, you can create complex object motions. For example, you could have an object with a path controller, list controllers, Look At controller, and parametric controllers such as the noise controller, or the object could be part of an animated hierarchy.

In some cases you may want to collapse the motion for an object to simple position, rotation, and scale keys. You may want to do this to use an expression controller that needs to reference the position or rotation tracks of such an object, or to create a path for another object to follow. You can collapse the motion to transformation keys by linking an object to the object from which you want to capture the motion and then applying Inverse Kinematics/Bind.

In the following exercise, Box01 is linked to Sphere03, which is linked to Sphere02, which in turn is linked to Sphere01. Each of the spheres is rotated 360 degrees about the Z axis over the length of the animation. The diffuse color of the material mapped to Box01 is controlled by an expression controller. This controller changes the diffuse color of the box based on the X, Y, and Z velocity of the box at the current frame. This velocity is determined by vector variables assigned to Box01's position track. As you play the animation, you see that the diffuse color never changes because there has been no motion defined for Box01 other than that provided through the hierarchy. Thus, the values returned from the position track are constant.

USING IK/BIND TO CREATE ANIMATION KEYS FROM A PROCEDURAL CONTROLLER

1. Load file ch24_10.max from the accompanying CD and play the animation.

2. Create a dummy object and open the IK portion of the Hierarchy command panel. Click Bind and bind the dummy object to Box01. Turn on Bind Position and Bind Orientation, and in Sliding Joints rollout, set the X, Y, and Z axes active. Click Apply IK.

3. Open Track View, expand the tracks and select the Diffuse parameter for Material #1 under Box01. Right-click on Diffuse and choose Properties. The expression controller dialog shown in figure 24.52 is displayed.

4. Select variable PosLast in the Vector column and click Assign to Controller. Select the position track of Dummy01 in the Track View Pick dialog that appears. Repeat for PosNow, and close the expression controller dialog.

5. Leaving Track View open, activate the camera view and play the animation. The color of the box changes as the box's velocity changes. The box's color at frame 0 is very different from the color at frame 1 and frame 100.

6. In Track View, with Diffuse still selected, click Function Curves. Note the discontinuity at frame 0. Select the position track for Dummy01.

   Also note that constant values are being used outside the active time range. Because the PosLast variable in the expression is accessing the position one tick back from the current frame; there is no change in velocity at frame 0.

7. Click Parameter Curve Out-Of-Range Types. Click on the two buttons below Cycle and exit the dialog.

8. Close Track View and play the animation. The color at frame 0 is now correct.

FIGURE 24.52

The Expression Controller dialog and equation for the box's diffuse color.

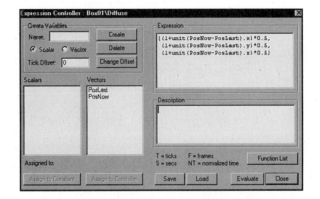

In Practice: Using Controllers and Expressions

■ **Rotation controllers** If you anticipate having to frequently modify key-framed rotations for an object, use a Euler XYZ rotation controller rather than a TCB rotation controller. The Euler XYZ controller will display function curves in Track View, and allows modifications to the rotation about each of the object's axes.

■ **List controllers** List controllers are used to combine the results of multiple controllers. Using List controllers allows you to build a hierarchy of object motions, similar to building a hierarchy of object modifiers.

■ **Expression controllers** The range of values returned from an expression must match the range expected for the parameter the controller is applied to.

■ **Instanced controllers** Instanced controllers enable you to use the output of a single controller as input to multiple parameters. Changing the value for one parameter results in the remaining parameters using the new value. By combining instanced controllers with List controllers, complex interacting controllers can be constructed.

Created by Frank DeLise

Created by Frank DeLise
Autodesk, Inc.
Provided courtesy of Kinetix™

Chapter 25

BUILDING AND ANIMATING PARTICLES

Have you ever wanted to simulate dust flying around? How about smoke or rain? In the 3D world, such conditions are produced by particle systems. A particle system is a collection of particles that when emitted can produce a variety of animated effects. In 3D Studio MAX, particle systems are objects and the particles emitted are actually sub-objects. You can animate a particle system as a whole, and you can adjust the particle system's properties to control each particle's behavior over time.

3D Studio MAX ships with two particle systems: Spray and Snow. Spray is used to simulate objects such as falling rain, whereby each particle falls in the same direction and is oriented the same way. Snow is used to animate objects that behave more like snow would—soft, falling, and usually tumbling.

Both particle systems share many of the same properties, but they also contain unique controls specific to the type of system used. In this chapter, you see how both systems behave and how to control their individual properties to get them to do more than just a spray or snow. Specifically, this chapter explores the following topics:

- Parameters for the Spray and Snow particle systems
- Render types
- Materials and types of particles
- Timing
- Emitters

As well, the latter part of this chapter covers two third-party plug-in particle systems for 3D Studio MAX—Sand Blaster from Digimation and All Purpose Particles from Sisyphus—and discusses using particles with space warps. The first topic at hand, however, is to understand how particle systems work in 3DS MAX.

Examining 3D Studio MAX's Particle Systems

Particle systems are a form of geometry. You find the particle system creation buttons in the Create panel in the geometry category. From there, you choose Particle Systems from the sub-category list. At that point, you find both Spray and Snow buttons. You may also see other third-party systems that you've installed.

When you click on the Spray or Snow button, all the editable parameters appear in the rollout (see fig. 25.1). Your cursor also changes in the viewport to reflect that you are in Create mode.

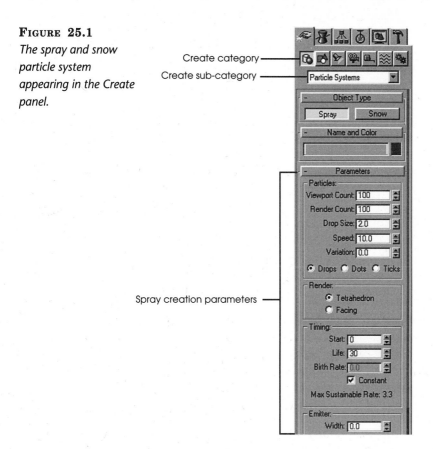

FIGURE 25.1

The spray and snow particle system appearing in the Create panel.

Create category

Create sub-category

Spray creation parameters

When you create a particle system in 3D Studio MAX, you are defining where the particles originate from as well as the initial orientation. The point of origin is called the *emitter*. The emitter is a nonrendering representation in the viewports that is used to tell you where the particles are coming from and where they are going. To create an emitter, you click in any viewport and drag out a rectangular shape. Notice that the emitter is defined by a plane with a small line perpendicular to the plane's surface intersecting it in the center. The emitter's size determines the "hole" from which the particles emanate. A small emitter produces a concentrated area from which all particles originate, and a large emitter spreads out the particle's distribution; the line indicates which direction the particles travel.

An emitter's initial orientation depends on what viewport you create it in and whether you're using the home plane or a grid object. When using the home grid as a creation plane, the emitter is always created parallel to the viewport with the emitter's particle direction pointing away from you. The exception to this rule is in perspective-type views. In this case, the emitter is created on the home grid with the direction pointing down (see fig. 25.2). The use of a grid object results in the emitter always being created on the grid's infinite plane—regardless of what is displayed. The direction of the emitter depends on the orientation of the grid object itself, but the direction is always on the grid's Z axis.

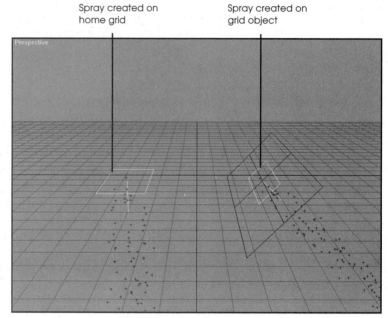

FIGURE 25.2
The emitter created on the home grid (left) and on a grid object (right).

> **TIP**
>
> When using grid objects, it is best to create objects in a viewport that is not parallel to the grid's surface. Creating in a parallel viewport results in the object being created in "infinity" and makes it very difficult to navigate your viewports.

Depending on which frame you're on, you may or may not see particles with the emitter. Because particles are time based, you see the default state of the particle system on that frame. At frame 0, you usually don't see anything.

Spray and Snow Parameters

Spray and Snow have common parameters. The settings of both Spray and Snow react the same. This section describes the common settings and explores how to use them.

Particle Counts

Both Spray and Snow provide two parameters for specifying the number of particles. One method is through the Viewport Count parameter. This value only affects the number of particles displayed in your viewports. Valid ranges are from 0 to 1,000,000,000, although the latter is an extremely unrealistic number. Use it only if you want to bring your computer to its knees.

The primary purpose of the Viewport Count parameter is to optimize how well 3DS MAX redraws your viewports. A large number of particles in your viewports can slow down viewport updates dramatically. This slowdown is especially true when you're playing back an animation in the viewport. Keep this number as low as possible, but make sure that you are still able to see an accurate representation of your particles in your viewports.

The other parameter is Render Count. This value affects only the number of particles rendered and has no effect on the number of particles in your viewports. This value is usually higher because rendering quality is the key, not interactivity.

NOTE

You cannot animate viewport or rendering count values.

Particle systems are geometric. They contain faces and vertices like any other object. Consequently, the higher that either the viewport count or render count get, the slower your scene becomes. You can often use small particle counts and still achieve outstanding results. Maintaining control over particle counts is key to having a rendering take one minute versus five.

Speed and Variation

Speed sets the initial velocity of each particle. The speed value uses its own system of units to change a particle's position over time. With a speed of 1, a particle travels roughly 10 units in 25 frames. The default value of 10 means that a particle travels 10 units in 2.5 frames. Any variation greater than 0 effectively negates this equation.

Variation controls two things: size and direction. The default value, 0, produces a steady stream of particles that go in the exact direction of the emitter's directional vector. As you increase variation, two things happen. First, the speed of the particles increases; second, the particles begin to deviate from the emitter's directional vector. Essentially, variation randomizes the direction and speed of each particle. When you increase the value, the randomization becomes more pronounced.

TIP

To have particles shoot in every direction, use variation values greater than the value specified for speed.

Viewport Representations

Particles can be displayed several ways: as Drops (with Spray) or Flakes (with Snow), as Dots, or as Ticks (see fig. 25.3). When you use Drops, particles are represented as lines that increase or decrease in size depending on the Drop Size value. When you use Flakes, particles are represented as 14-point stars that increase or decrease in size depending on the Size value. The Size settings most accurately represent the particle's rendering size.

Dots appear as a single pixel in your viewport, regardless of drop size or zoom factor. Use Dots when you don't want to clutter your viewports with unnecessary geometry.

Ticks appear as small 5-pixel-by-5-pixel crosshairs in the viewport. Like Dots, regardless of how far you're zoomed in, Ticks remain the same size. Ticks work well when you're zoomed in because you can easily see each particle. The farther you zoom out, however, the more cluttered the particles become. In that case, it is better to use Dots.

Drops   Dots   Ticks

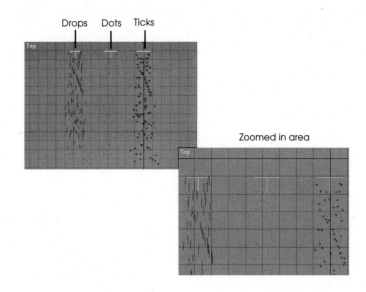

FIGURE 25.3

A view of the three particle system display methods for Snow. A zoomed in area shows detail. Note that neither the Dots nor the Ticks display method appear to change in either view.

Zoomed in area

Figure 25.4 illustrates a rendered particle with a gradient map applied.

FIGURE 25.4

A rendering of a tetrahedron particle using a gradient opacity map to give the appearance of a fading raindrop.

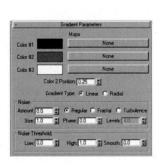

NOTE

All particle display methods redraw in the viewports at about the same rate. For faster playback
of particles, lower the Viewport Count.

Material Assignment

Because particles are objects in 3D Studio MAX, material assignment is
always at the object level. When you assign material to a particle object, all
particles use the same material. If you want a spray particle object to emit
particles with varying materials, you can use a Multi/Sub-object material.
Each particle receives a material based on its number. Particles start
counting at 0 where materials start at 1. For instance, the fifth particle to be
emitted will receive material #1 from a Multi/Sub-object material comprised
of five materials. Multi/Sub-object material assignment works great when
you're simulating things such as multicolored confetti.

NOTE

In Snow, six-point objects actually use two material IDs rather than one, which enables you
to assign different materials to each side of a six-point particle.

TIP

Particles receiving material ID assignments start counting from 0, not 1.

Controlling Particle Timing

3DS MAX gives you plenty of timing control for particles. You can simulate
a steady stream or short blasts simply by altering the timing values. The
next section explains how the values work and how to use them.

Start and Life

The Start value sets what frame the emitter begins sending out particles.
This can be any frame number, including negative frames. You use negative
frames in cases where you want the particles to be on the screen at frame 0.

The Life value sets the life, in frames, of each particle and is assigned to each particle individually. With this value, you specify the length of time before a particle is destroyed. Set this value to the last frame in your animation if you want the particle to always be present in the scene.

Adjusting Defaults

You can change the default Start and Life values to adjust a steady stream of particles emanating from the emitter. The Life value not only affects how long before a particle is destroyed, but also the distance it travels. The longer the life, the farther the particle travels from the emitter.

Constant and Varying Birth Rates

The Constant option provides a steady stream of particles at all times. By default, this option is selected. The Max Sustainable Rate right below the Constant check box displays the number of particles that can be born per frame while keeping the number of particles under the specified limit. This value changes when you alter the Life value for particles. With the default Life value of 30, you get a sustainable rate of 3.3 particles born every frame. If you double the Life to 60, the Max sustainable rate changes to nearly half, 1.7, because 3DS MAX now has more time to generate those 100 particles. Just by altering the life, you can control how many particles are present in the scene at a specific frame.

TIP

If you want the total number of particles in your count fields to be present at frame 0, set the particle start frame to a negative Life value.

By unchecking the Constant option, you can now specify the maximum number of particles born per frame in the Birth Rate field (see fig. 25.5); however, you still use the Max Sustainable Rate value as a guide. Here's how it works:

- If you want a steady stream of particles, set the Birth Rate to a value equal to or less than the Max Sustainable Rate.

- If you want short bursts, set the value higher than the Max Sustainable Rate. A value of 50, for instance, emits 100 particles in two frames.

Because you can animate the Birth Rate value, you can utilize it as a flow control value for your particles. A value of 0 emits nothing. Any Render Count value produces more and more particles.

FIGURE 25.5

The timing parameters for a particle system. Note that the current values cause the particle system to emit short bursts of particles rather than a steady stream.

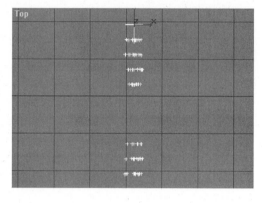

TIP

Animating the Birth Rate by using the Step In/Out option for keys in Track View produces controlled bursts versus using the default curved assignment, which produces a gradual increase/decrease in particle birth rates.

Emitter Size and Orientation

The size of the emitter controls the area from which the particles are emitted. A long thin emitter produces a narrow gap from which the particles emit. A larger area emitter spreads out the particles. Spray and Snow randomly emit particles from within the area of the emitter object. The distribution of where particles emit is controllable only through the emitter size.

Because you can animate the emitter's size, you can simulate effects such as a hose opening or sparks flying out from an increasingly growing area.

The emitter's orientation controls which direction the particles shoot. When using Spray or Snow, an emitted particle travels in a constant direction and orientation unless acted upon by another force, such as a space warp. You can use this fact to your advantage to control the direction of the spray or snow. Emitters work with normal transform commands, so you can move and rotate them. If you need to scale the size of the emitter, it is best to change the Length and Width values rather than using the scale transform.

Particles are created from the initial tip of the particle on the plane of the emitter. As a result, portions of the particle can actually exist before the emitter. This is especially visible when using large particle sizes.

Exploring the Spray Particle System

The Spray particle system is useful for simulating falling water effects. Obvious uses are for effects such as rain and other types or liquids emitting from a specific location. You can also use spray to simulate things such as sparks on a bomb's fuse or glowing cinders from a fire.

Spray particles travel with a constant orientation—that is, a drop of water falling down always points down throughout its life cycle. You can, however, change the emitter over time to simulate things such as an oscillating sprinkler system.

Using Drop Sizes

You use Drop Size to control the actual size, in units, of each particle. A Drop Size of 0 produces nothing, whereas a Drop Size of 20 produces a long streak. Depending on the effect you're looking for, the number varies.

Small sizes are useful for things such as sprinkling sugar or tiny granular-type objects. Sizes less than 1 produce extremely small particles. You usually have to set the rendering count relatively high to see small particles from a distance.

NOTE

You only see changes in the size of particles in your viewports if the particles are being displayed as drops. If you want to see the size of your particles reflected accurately in the viewports, make sure to use the Drops method of display.

Large sizes are great for creating streaks of light such as warp effects. In this case, you use smaller count values because larger particles occupy much more space than smaller ones and "clump" if there are too many. This is true for both viewport and render counts.

TIP

You can animate Drop Size to simulate the growth of streaking effects.

Spray Render Types

Render types, chosen in the spray particle's Parameter panel, enable you to specify the look of the particle when it's rendered. Spray enables you to render either tetrahedrons or square faces that can be mapped with any material. This section explores the two methods.

The tetrahedron spray particle looks much like a Hedra object using the Tetra type except that the vertex at the lower pole is pulled further "south" to look more like a polygonal drop of water. When you're trying to simulate droplets, this is the best type of particle rendering to use. Usually, tetrahedron renders faster than the facing particle.

Facing creates square faces that always face the camera, meaning that their rendering face always remains perpendicular to the camera. Their size is the Drop Size value for both width and height. Use facing render types in conjunction with a specific material to render other types of particles.

NOTE

If you don't render the camera view, the faces will point in an arbitrary direction.

You can fly through tetrahedrons and view them from different angles. Although you can also fly through facing particles, these particles are always "flat" to your point of view and can end up producing the wrong effect.

Materials and Spray Particles

Particle systems can use just about any material type. More specifically, you can use map types, such as gradient and noise, to generate special effects such as smoke. This section explains the process of using mapping and materials with particles.

Mapping

Particles are fairly easy to assign materials to. They have mapping coordinates assigned, and they work well with Multi/Sub-object material types. The following two paragraphs show how mapping breaks down.

Tetrahedrons are mapped with the cylindrical mapping type, with the V oriented along the length of the tetrahedron. The origin of the mapping begins at the origin—the flat part—of the tetrahedron. If you want to simulate a drop becoming more transparent with a gradient opacity map, the gradient would start at black for color 1 and go to white for color 3—the opposite of the default for gradient maps.

Facing maps are fitted to their extents with planar mapping. If you look at a facing particle head-on in the viewport with the emitter oriented in a top-down direction, the V would be vertical to the viewport; however, the V is actually the opposite orientation for facing rendering types. The previous example of a gradient map would have to be reversed.

Spraying Sparks

One of Spray's best features is the capability to simulate all types of flying particle droplets, including sparks. When using spray to create a spark effect, it is best to increase the Variation value. That way particles travel in several directions from the emitter, including down. The following exercise shows that using a spray system with the corresponding values produces the effect of sparks emitting along the fuse.

LIGHTING A FUSE USING SPRAY

1. Open imx25spw.max from the Chapter 25 folder on the accompanying CD.

2. Press **H** to select the Fuse object by name.

3. Go to the Modify panel and note the spray's settings.

4. Play back the animation or create a preview.

5. Close the preview or stop playback.

Notice whether the spray is acting like you would normally expect. The emitter simply sprays particles in one direction. By altering the variation to a large number, the particles shoot in many directions. You can also alter variables such as speed and particle size to create a great spark.

6. Change the variation to 5.

7. Change the speed to 1.

8. Change the drop size to 8.

9. Make a preview.

The next thing you need to do is create a nice rendering from the animation. By default, particles are little tetrahedrons. This works for sparks except for the fact that they look rather flat. You can use video post to add a glow filter to the particles. Video post is already set up to do this. If you want, you can check out the parameters of the glow filter to see what settings are used. Just double-click the glow filter in the Video Post queue, followed by the Setup button.

10. Choose Rendering/Video Post.

11. Click the Execute button.

12. Click Render.

13. When the animation is finished rendering, play back the AVI from the View File option in the File pull-down menu.

Figure 25.6 shows a still frame from the animation. Note how the sparks fly in all directions. This is a result of a large variation value.

TIP

Use the Glow filter and Volume light effects to create the glow on the sparks as well as the fuse.

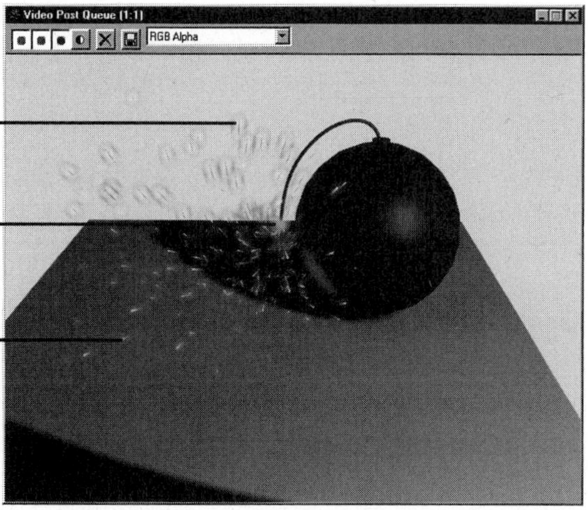

FIGURE 25.6

FIGURE 25.6

The final result using the spray particle system and the glow filter from Video Post.

Glow filter

Volumetric light

Spray particle with gradient texture map

Exploring the Snow Particle System

The other particle system that ships with 3D Studio MAX is called Snow. Like Spray, Snow emits particles from a common location. The main difference between Snow and Spray is the way in which particles behave after they have left the emitter. Unlike rain, which remains at a constant orientation and direction, snow particles can tumble through space. You can use Snow to create any type of particle effect where soft particle movement is needed.

You can use the Tumble and Tumble Rate values to control how snow particles rotate as they travel. Tumble values are valid from 0 through 1. A value of 0 produces no tumble at all, whereas a value of 1 completely tumbles the flake. The Tumble Rate specifies how much flakes actually rotate per frame. A higher tumbling rate produces wildly spinning flakes, whereas lower values produce more moderate rotation. A Tumbling Rate value of 0 effectively cancels any rotation regardless of the Tumble value set.

Using Flake Sizes

Use Flake Size to control the actual size, in units, of each particle (see fig. 25.7). A Flake Size of 0 produces nothing, whereas a size of 20 produces a large flake. Depending on the effect you're looking for, this number varies.

Small sizes are useful for effects such as tiny bubbles or dust particles. Sizes less than 1 produce extremely small particles. You usually have to set the rendering count relatively high to view particles from a distance.

FIGURE 25.7
A viewport representation and rendering of two different flake sizes for the snow particle system.

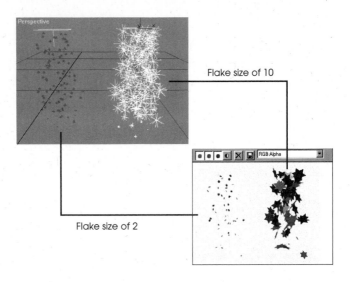

Flake size of 10

Flake size of 2

NOTE

You see changes in the size of particles in your viewports only if the particles are displayed as flakes. Both Dots and Ticks display at a fixed resolution. The Flakes display method is the only method that also displays the size.

Large sizes can be used to create real snow particles or confetti effects. In either case, you want to use smaller count values because larger particles occupy more space than smaller ones and "clump" if there are too many. This is true for both viewport and render counts.

Snow Render Types

Render types, chosen in the particle's Parameter panel, enable you to specify the look of the particle when it's rendered. You can use the render types to generate many effects from confetti to smoke. This section describes the three render types for the snow particle system.

Six-point snow flakes produce flat six-point stars that emit at varying orientations. Six-point stars can use any type of materials, including Multi/

Sub-object. Six-point flakes can also have two different materials assigned to them, one for each side. Depending on your needs, six-point stars may produce the best rendering results when used in combination with the proper materials.

Triangle produces triangular faces emitting at varying orientations. Triangular faces work much like the Six-point option with respect to materials, except that only one material can be assigned to both sides. You can randomize the material assigned to each particle by using a Multi/Sub-object material.

Facing creates square faces that always face the camera, meaning that the rendering face always remains perpendicular to the camera. Their size is the Flake Size value for both width and height. Use facing render types in conjunction with a specific material to render other types of particles.

You can fly through Six-point and Triangle and view them from different angles. Although you can also fly-through facing particles, the particles will always remain "flat" to your point of view and may end up producing the wrong effect.

Materials and Mapping

As mentioned earlier, it is easy to assign particles to materials. Particles have mapping coordinates assigned, and they work well with Multi/Sub-object material types. The following paragraphs describe how it breaks down.

Six-point particles are automatically mapped with planar mapping to the extents of the particle. The mapping is assigned as if the Six-point were actually a square with a six-point star cut out of it.

Triangle maps are also assigned planar mapping—much like Six-point— except that a triangular shape is cut out of the map rather than a six-point star.

Facing maps are fitted to their extents with planar mapping. If you look at a facing particle head-on in the viewport with the emitter oriented in a top-down direction, the V would be vertical to the viewport; however, the V is actually the opposite orientation for facing rendering types. Figure 25.8 demonstrates how mapping works on the snow particles.

FIGURE 25.8

The Snow particle system rendering types. The same map is used for all three examples, but the application is different depending on the rendered object.

Material
(Using daisy.tif)

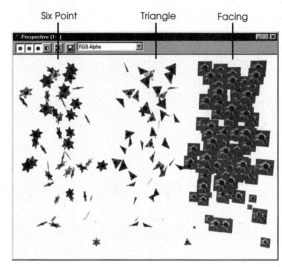

Using Snow to Generate Bubbles

The Snow particle system is well suited to create gently rolling bubbles for several reasons. The primary reason is that the particles get smaller as they get farther from the emitter. In this exercise, you see how to create bubbles just by altering a few settings in the snow particle system.

CREATING BUBBLES USING SNOW

1. Open imx25snw.max from the Chapter 25 folder found on the accompanying CD.

2. Go to the Create panel, make sure the Geometry button is selected, and click on the text "Standard Primitives."

3. Choose Particles Systems.

4. Click the Snow button.

5. Create a Snow emitter by clicking and dragging in the perspective viewport. The width and height of the emitter should each be about 20 units.

6. With the Perspective view active, click the Mirror button. Choose the Z mirror axis and then click OK.

7. Drag the frame slider to frame 100 and then click Zoom Extents All.

    Currently, 3D Studio MAX is using the Snow's default parameters. This includes the size and render type, both of which you need to alter to produce bubbles.

8. Change the Flake size to 8.

9. Change the Render Type to Facing.

    You're just about finished, except that you need to assign a material to the snow. A material called Bubble Material is already stored with this scene. You can simply choose the material from the Material Editor and apply it to the Snow.

10. Click the Material Editor button in the 3DS MAX toolbar.

11. Choose the second sample slot (top middle) and then click the Assign material to selection button.

12. Render frame 100.

If you're satisfied with the material and background, render the scene as an animation. From this point, you can add effects such as tumble and variation to randomize the bubbles a bit more. You can also clone the snow to two or more objects and vary the clone's variation and speed parameters to further add depth to the scene.

Other Particles

A true testament to 3D Studio MAX's extendibility, this section introduces two third-party plug-in particle systems for 3D Studio MAX: Sand Blaster from Digimation and All Purpose Particles from Sisyphus. Both particle system plug-ins go above and beyond what Spray and Snow can do. In fact, these plug-ins do things that many high-end particle generators have difficulty with. If you use particles often, you may want to check out these two plug-ins.

Sand Blaster

Sand Blaster is a particle system plug-in designed to literally blow apart objects into small particles. You can have these particles blow into space or even reform into other objects. Sand Blaster also gives you the option to explode an object into tiny particles that can actually be other objects. As a matter of fact, you can have up to 999 interim objects to alternate among before you reform to the target object.

Objects can blow apart in different directions, follow a path, or fly around randomly and reform the exact same way.

All Purpose Particles

All Purpose Particles provides a multitude of particle systems with which to work. You can generate effects such as bubbles and fireworks with the click of a mouse button. That's one of the best attributes of All Purpose Particles. You can work with preset particle parameters to instantly create effects. For instance, if you wanted to generate a shockwave effect much like you see in movies, just choose the Shockwave button. This option actually sets all of the editable variables for you. You don't have to change anything. However, if you want to tweak the parameters, APP gives you that option as well.

Using Particles with Space Warps

Particles have the capability to interact with certain types of space warps in 3D Studio MAX. As a matter of fact, half of the shipping space warps deal solely with particles. In this section, you learn how to use the two together. For more information on space warps, see Chapter 17, "Using Space Warps."

Creating a Fountain with Space Warps

By using Spray, you can create a great fountain effect by binding it with gravity, wind, and a deflector. In this section, you see how to use a combination of space warps to push and pull particles in various directions.

Using Gravity

The fountain object contains five iterations of spray—one main spray and four accompanying sprays. Notice how the sprays are functioning just as you would expect—no real dynamics at all. It would be more natural to have the main fountain cascade down on itself and have the other four arc downward.

This is most easily accomplished with the Gravity space warp. Gravity simulates real gravity by pushing or pulling particles to the icon. Its orientation and position in space can affect the particles significantly. To simulate gravity best for this scene, planar gravity should be used pointing downward. This is easily created by creating gravity in the Top or Perspective viewports.

USING SPACE WARPS WITH PARTICLES

1. Open imx25spw.max from the Chapter 25 folder on the accompanying CD.

2. Go to the Create panel and click the Space Warps button.

3. Choose Gravity.

4. Click and drag gravity into the Top viewport. Its size doesn't matter, only its orientation.

5. Press H to select all iterations of spray in the scene.

6. Click on the Bind button in the toolbar and press H again to select the gravity you just created.

NOTE

Because the gravity is planar, its position in space is not relevant. Its orientation—how it is rotated—is important, however. Make sure it is pointing downward. Figure 25.9 shows the result of applying gravity to the fountain's spray objects.

FIGURE 25.9

The effect of gravity on the fountain. Note how the particles arc downward as a result of the gravity binding.

No Gravity; particles continue upward

Gravity created-particles bound

Using Deflector

The Deflector space warp adds planar collision detection to particles. In the next exercise, you create a single deflector to ensure that the particles don't go through the fountain on their trip downward.

Start by creating a deflector in the Top or Perspective views. Next, bind all sprays to the deflector. Position the deflector so that it is sitting at the inside base of the fountain. Again, notice how the particles react instantly to the changing of the position of the deflector. Figure 25.10 shows the effect of deflector on the spray.

1. Click the Deflector button in the Create panel.

2. Starting at the upper lefthand corner of the fountain, click and drag a deflector into the top viewport.

3. Use the Move command to move the deflector to the level of the inner base of the fountain.

4. Use the Bind command again to bind the sprays to the deflector.

FIGURE 25.10

The Fountain with the Deflector space warp created and bound to the spray.

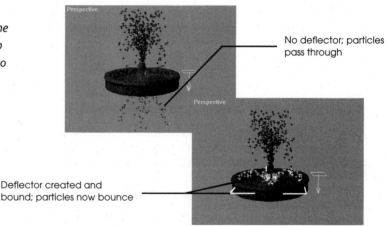

No deflector; particles pass through

Deflector created and bound; particles now bounce

Using Wind

Wind acts like gravity—it has the capability to push and pull particles to the icon, but also adds the capability to have turbulence distort the particles' travel. Have you ever noticed at the park how the wind often catches the spray of a fountain and sometimes blows it several feet in one direction (usually soaking some unsuspecting pedestrian)? To create the same effect with particles, you can use wind.

Because you want the wind to blow to the side, you need to create wind in the left viewport. Next, bind the main spray to the wind. The particles immediately start blowing to the side. If you want to build the effect of the wind blowing, you can animate the wind's strength and turbulence parameters. Figure 25.11 shows the end result of applying gravity, deflector, and wind to the fountain.

1. Click the Wind button in the Create panel.

2. Click and drag a Wind space warp starting in the center of the left viewport. (The icon's size doesn't matter.)

3. Click the Bind button and bind only the center spray to the fountain.

You can experiment with the wind values to generate different styles of wind. Try animating the wind value to gradually blow the fountain's spray.

FIGURE 25.11
The completed fountain using the gravity, wind, and deflector space warps to simulate real life dynamics.

Wind created and bound

In Practice: Building and Animating Particles

- **Similar parameters** Both of MAX's shipping particle systems have several common parameters. Remember that both particles use these parameters the exact same way. If you master one particle system, that knowledge easily transfers to the other.

- **Spray versus Snow**   Both Spray and Snow have unique characteristics that makes one more suitable for a particular effect over the other. Use Spray to create effects where the particles need to remain a constant direction and orientation. Snow works better for particles where soft and tumbling effects are required.

- **The emitter**   All particle systems must originate from one point. This point is referred to as the emitter. You can animate the emitter's orientation, position, and size to create several effects. Since the emitter is an object, you can also use MAX's animation controllers, such as noise, to affect it's behavior as well.

- **Materials and particles**   MAX enables you to assign any type of material to a particle. Remember to combine several mapping types to create the illusion of different shaped particles. For example, use facing particles with a gradient opacity map to create the effect of round objects, like bubbles, floating along.

- **Particles and post effects**   Through the usage of video post effects such as glow, you can give particles the appearance of being tiny sparks or glowing snow flakes. Any video post effect that utilizes the material or object ID parameter will work with a particle system.

- **Particles with space warps**   For more realistic particle behavior, use space warps such as gravity and wind. Combining the space warps will have an additive effect on the particle systems. For example, to create a geyser effect, use gravity to pull the water back to the ground while also using wind to blow some of the water away.

Part IV

ANIMATING YOUR SCENES

Created by James Biebl
Gaviota Graphics
Carbondale, CO

RENDERING STILL IMAGES

The realm of 3D graphics is very different from other visual arts. For camera-based imagery, the press of a button is all that is required to capture an image — just point the camera and shoot. The image is recorded instantaneously. With natural media, such as an oil painting, an image evolves from rough outlines into a finished piece through continual refinement of the image with the brush. Cartoons, such as comics found in the Sunday newspaper, are first drawn as outlines by hand, and then inked — giving the final color. Creating an image with a computer is an entirely different process. Models are created, much like objects in a woodworkers shop. Then materials are applied, allowing a simple sphere to become a glass ball, or a planet in a solar system. The object is then lit, giving illumination. Finally, the scene is rendered by the computer into an image, much like a master painter faithfully paints what he sees in front of him.

Rendering often seems simple enough at first glance, but it isn't as simple as clicking Render and hoping for the best. The type of output and its use are essential elements of a successful render. This chapter is focused on still images, and covers the following topics:

- 3D Studio MAX rendering basics
- Understanding color bit depths and their uses
- Determining output media types and their limitations
- Determining image print clarity and crispness
- Determining optimum print output resolutions
- Examining model complexity and accuracy
- Using background images with high resolutions
- Incorporating text and image overlays
- Understanding service bureaus

3D Studio MAX Rendering Basics

3D Studio MAX gives you a wide range of control over what objects and areas of the viewport are rendered, having many settings that reduce repetition usually necessary when you initiate a render.

You use the Render Scene option to set up a render. Choose the icon or select Render from the pull-down menu, which is the render command center, with all the most commonly used settings in its window (see fig. 26.1).

NOTE

3D Studio MAX includes a high-quality, fast scanline production renderer, and additional renderers are available as plug-ins. This capability adds a tremendous flexibility to the 3D Studio MAX environment, allowing unlimited different rendering types within one seamless package. Choose File, Preferences and select the Rendering tab to use plug-in renderers for raytracing or radiosity.

FIGURE 26.1

3D Studio MAX common Render parameters.

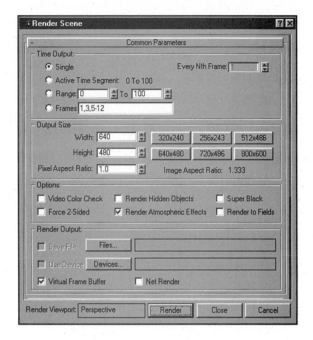

The Time Output area of the render control dialog selects the frames to render. The render could be a still frame, the active time segment, a specific range, or a string of specific frames. When using the active time segment, or a specific range, it is possible to render every Nth frame. Every tenth frame out of a specific range can be rendered, for example. This is often useful for rendering a progression of frames that represent what takes place in the animation.

A wide variety of settings also are available in the render control dialog, including Video Color Check, Super Black, Fields, and Force 2-Sided. The only one of these that is particularly useful for still images is Force 2-Sided. The others are video and animation settings, which are covered in Chapter 27, "Rendering Animation." Force 2-Sided is used to force all objects to render as two-sided objects. While this can sometimes be helpful, especially with objects that have inverted normals, or are missing back faces, it is generally not recommended for regular use because the use of two-sided materials allow specific control-saving render time.

NOTE

Anti-aliasing against the background sometimes is undesirable, especially when creating artwork to be cut out of the background. Sprite artwork for games, and buttons for multimedia projects are two such uses. You can turn off anti-aliasing by adding the line **DontAntialiasAgainstBackground=1** under the **[Renderer]** area in the 3dsmax.ini file. If **[Renderer]** is not listed, add that as well.

Rendering Control

3D Studio MAX's render controls can be broken down into two sections: initiating the render, and controlling what's being rendered. These sections work together to produce an image. 3DS MAX allows several ways to initiate the render—drawing it to the screen—as well as several ways to control exactly what is rendered by the use of render types.

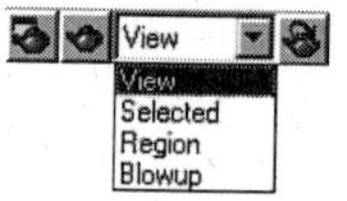

FIGURE 26.2

A view's render icons and render types.

Initiating a Render

3DS MAX can initiate a render by selecting Rendering, Render from the menu bar, or more commonly, by pressing one of three icons related to rendering: Render Scene, Quick Render, or Render Last (see fig. 26.2).

- **Render Scene** Clicking on the first, Render Scene, brings up the Render Scene dialog, enabling you to configure the resolution, output file name, and so on (refer to figure 26.1). This option is great when you need to change settings, or are ready to output to a file. For quick renders, however, the added dialog can get in the way.

- **Quick Render** For quick test renders, the second icon, Quick Render (Shift+Q) is an even more useful selection. This offers a one-click way to render any viewport, regardless of what render type you use. (See the section "Render Types" for more on this.)

■ **Render Last** The last and quickest way to render a viewport is to use Render Last (Shift+E), the icon furthest to the right. Render Last always renders the viewport and render type last rendered. Therefore, it is most useful when working in one viewport, and adjusting lighting, or textures.

Render Types

3D Studio MAX provides several options for controlling how much of a scene to render. These options are available as a cluster of render types at the top right portion of the interface. These include the capability to render View, Region, Blowup, and Selected (see fig. 26.2). In previous releases and most other programs, you are limited to being able to render only what is displayed in the active viewport.

■ **Rendering the view** Render View is the most common render type because it renders the entire viewport. For final renders, this type is the one to choose.

■ **Capturing a window with Render Region** The Render Region option enables you to render just a section of the scene. It particularly comes in handy when you fine-tune shadow map parameters, alter reflective materials, or coordinate the material and mapping placement of various objects. Objects that cast shadows or are reflected in another object's surface still are calculated, even though they might not fall within the Render Region's cropping window.

■ **Blowing up a view** 3D Studio MAX enables an area to be enlarged during the rendering process, without the necessity of zooming the viewport itself. This is accomplished with Render Blowup type. This is often useful for inspecting certain areas of a view while adjusting lights or textures in a scene.

■ **Selective rendering with Render Selected** The capability to render only selected objects is primarily an aid to see the effects of material modifications for that object. The drawback is for any material that contains a reflection or objects that have shadows cast across them. Neither of these effects can be shown using Render Selected because only the selected objects are being considered.

Color Depth

Color depth (also called bit depth) refers to the number of colors a computer-generated image contains. Nature doesn't care about the number of available colors, but computers most certainly do. Computers must convert information of any kind into numeric sequences, so naturally, they must number and store colors.

Several common bit depths are used in computer-generated imagery, including 8-bit adjustable palette, 15- and 16-bit fixed palette, 24-bit and 64-bit color depths. The more bits, the more colors. The actual mathematics of each color depth isn't as important to know for the average user as is knowing the amount of colors each color depth contains, and their strengths and weaknesses. Chapter 2, "Mixing Color and Light" has in-depth discussions about each bit depth.

- **8-bit adjustable palette** Images contain only 256 colors out of the entire spectrum. The exact colors can differ between different images as well because the palette is adjustable on an image by image basis. The low amount of colors is not sufficient to realistically display the entire color spectrum, but is quick to load, display, and has a small file size.

- **15- and 16-bit fixed palette** Images contain 32,768 and 65,536 colors respectively. These bit depths are less common than 8-bit and 24-bit bit-depths, but are a good trade-off between large file size and color realism. Containing a fixed palette also ensures that many images in either 15- or 16-bit color will not conflict in the colors they use—which is useful in games, as well as multimedia production.

- **24-bit color** Images are the most common true color image types. At 16.7 million colors, these images contain sufficient color to faithfully reproduce any image viewable to the naked eye. Animation, whether going to film or video, is almost always rendered in 24-bit color. Games, however, along with other computer graphics based works, use 24-bit color less often, due to its larger file size, and slower display times. As computer and graphics display technology advances , 24-bit will become more and more common—even for a fast-moving computer game.

- **64-bit color** Images are pretty uncommon, although this color depth is an important one for 3D Studio MAX users because 3D Studio MAX renders internally to 64-bit color, and then dithers down to lower color depths from there. While 64-bit color is not displayable on common computer screens, this color depth is used in 3D Studio MAX's superior analytical anti-aliasing. This color depth, especially when used with other render information (such as G-buffer), can be saved into the RLA file format, and used at a later time by any 3D Studio MAX Video Post plug-in or composite.

8-Bit Still Imaging

Much of the focus in magazines and in Kinetix's marketing of 3D Studio MAX is on 24-bit images and high-end output devices. Many people are intimidated by this emphasis and fail to realize that 3D Studio MAX is an excellent tool for creating 8-bit images and Animator Pro-style FLIC files.

You're not going to get your work on a major television network using 8-bit technology, but most computer games, Web sites, multimedia projects, disk-based presentations, and informational kiosks rely primarily on 8-bit technology.

Many markets exist for 8-bit images and animation. Using 8-bit color doesn't mean that your images are inferior or nonprofessional. It just means you've chosen to use this file format, for one reason or another. The 8-bit file format also has some advantages that justify its use, such as the following:

- **Small file size** Small files are a necessity for WWW-based sites or for presentations that must run on limited hardware or from a floppy disk.

- **Fast loading and display** The small file size helps speed up the time it takes to load 8-bit images into memory and display 8-bit images on-screen, essential for today's high-speed games.

- **Wide software compatibility** Many paint and presentation programs support 8-bit file formats, such as BMP, PCX, and PNG.

- **Low video hardware requirements** The low-end VGA standard that supports 8-bit color at 320×200 resolution still is used on many systems. SVGA support of 8-bit color at a resolution of 640×480 also is very popular, while higher resolutions and 24-bit color support are much less common.

If you're creating images to display on the World Wide Web, PC-based games, a client's system, portable presentations, or disk-based marketing, you may need to work with 8-bit images.

Working in 8-bit color imposes some restrictions on what you can do, but these restrictions are not as onerous as they might at first seem. The limit of 256 colors requires that you exercise care when you plan the use of color in your images. You also must compromise between minimizing file size or minimizing the side effects of the color restrictions.

Banding

Banding refers to what happens when too few colors are available to represent a smooth transition from one color to the next. These transitions are called color ramps or gradients and are used for shading geometry or when you choose a gradient background material in 3D Studio MAX. Because not enough colors exist to represent the gradient smoothly, it is divided into a few broad bands of color that approximate the gradient. Figure 26.3 shows a sphere rendered against a gradient background. Both the sphere and the background exhibit severe banding.

FIGURE 26.3
Color banding in an 8-bit image.

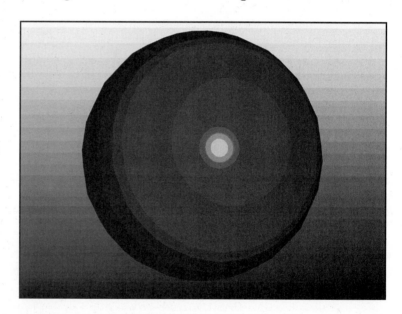

The two main techniques for avoiding banding are careful color selection and the avoidance of gradients. Color selection focuses on the fact that you have only 256 colors with which to work. If you choose colors for your scene that are widely different, such as multiple primaries or fully saturated hues, each color receives only a few palette slots for its shading colors, and banding is inevitable. If instead you choose most of your colors from one color family with a complementary color thrown in for contrast, the colors can share many of the same shades and you reduce banding.

Avoiding gradients requires breaking up the surface of your geometry. Smooth solid-color objects suffer the most from banding effects. The only way to represent shading on the surface of a smooth object is to use a gradient as the color changes from light to dark. One way to break up the surface and avoid banding is to use mapped materials. Look at the objects around you right now. How many have smooth, solid color surfaces? Painted metal usually has a smooth, solid surface but almost everything else has bumps, grooves, and patterns. Not only do bump maps, texture maps, and reflections add to the realism of your scene, but they also break up the surface to reduce banding.

Figure 26.4 shows a rendering using solid colors of widely different hues. The vase is green, the sphere is blue, the table top is brown, and the whole scene is banded. Figure 26.5 is the same scene with only the materials changed. The vase is now a tan marble, the sphere is shiny copper, and the table has a wood grain texture. Banding is hardly noticeable. The key to this rendering is that the textures break up the surfaces and the materials share a similar color range.

FIGURE 26.4
A scene with banding caused by poor material selection.

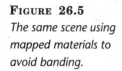

FIGURE 26.5
The same scene using mapped materials to avoid banding.

Dithering

Sometimes banding is unavoidable. You need to model smooth-painted surfaces when textures and bumps aren't acceptable. In such a case, 3D Studio MAX provides a setting in the Rendering Preferences called Dither Paletted. The default for this setting is on, but you might want to change it or at least consider whether you want to use dithering when you prepare to render. Dithering blurs the edges between bands, which helps your eye ignore the edges and accept the illusion of a smooth color gradient.

The drawback to dithering is that it can greatly increase file size. Most 8-bit image formats use a compression technique that identifies and compresses areas of contiguous color. A side effect of dithering is that it eliminates many areas of contiguous color, causing file size to increase. For example, the image in figure 26.5 increased in size by 30 percent with dithering turned on, even though dithering provided almost no improvement in the quality of the image. In general, you should try to use mapping techniques with Dither Paletted turned off to achieve your goals for image quality. You then must decide whether you need dithering for the image quality that you want and balance that decision against the need for smaller file sizes.

Understanding Model Complexity

Another issue concerning 8-bit imaging is rendering resolution and model complexity. Typically, 8-bit images are rendered for display on a standard computer screen, often at a rendering resolution of 640×480. Compare that to typical 24-bit resolutions for video at 756×512 or for film printing at 2048×1536. You quickly realize that the detail necessary for high color, high-resolution rendering is overkill for 8-bit rendering. Save yourself rendering time and build your models knowing that low color and low resolution don't require as much detail.

24-Bit High-Resolution Imaging

True color, or 24-bit rendering, might sound complicated or a little intimidating, but it's actually much easier than 8-bit color rendering. Reducing an image's color palette to 256 colors and producing a quality image isn't automatic. It takes forethought and a good deal of understanding of how color distribution, banding, and dithering work. True color, 24-bit rendering isn't nearly so demanding—it always produces the top-quality image and enables you to spend your time compositing materials and lighting the model to the highest possible degree.

Determining Output Resolution and Selecting Media

Determining the project's ultimate goals as early as possible in the modeling process is critical—preferably before you begin to model. You should ask several questions at this point, and use the answers to determine the direction to go with the modeling. These questions are important for all models and animations, but are especially important for high-resolution work because they dictate model complexity and detail, memory requirements, and file-exchange issues. Answer the following questions before you begin to model:

- What size will the printed image be?
- What media will the final image use?

- How crisp does the image need to appear?

- What resolution will be used for printing?

- Where is the visual focus within the model?

- How close will the viewer get to the various parts of the model?

You should discuss these questions during conception and planning of the project, and you should ask them even if the project is for in-house use, has no client, or is an independent venture. The answers furnish vital direction for what otherwise could end up being an overly large model that isn't accurate enough or that can't be rendered or printed.

The resolution of the output image depends on the print media, the crispness of the printed image, and the printed size. You need to make decisions on all of these issues before you can determine what you need for your final output image.

Impact of Media Selection

The most important issue when selecting the type of output media is deciding whether you want to produce a continuous tone or screened print. The choice you make has a significant impact on the required resolution. In general, a *screened print* is one produced by dithering the image, and a *continuous tone print* resembles a photograph.

Continuous Tone Prints

When you print a bitmap image, the pixels that form the composition must be translated to a format the printing device can understand. A continuous tone process places the pixels immediately next to one another without any space between them to allow the white of the paper to show through. The tones of the print are thus blended together, and no isolated dots exist, making it the easiest print type to understand because it produces an image that looks a lot like what you see on-screen. A continuous tone print also is the easiest to print because the sole determining factor of the image's quality is the resolution you supply in the image.

The most common type of continuous tone print is the standard photographic print. Outputting to photographic film involves using a film recorder to expose the image on conventional 35 mm film or 4"×5" large format film. You can use any standard 100 ASA photographic print or transparency film (although transparency is recommended to ensure proper color reproduction). Film recorders usually are capable of 4,000 to 8,000 lines of resolution.

NOTE

A film recorder's *lines of resolution* refers to the number of scanlines through which an image is interpreted. Because each pixel must have at least one scanline, a 4,000 pixel wide image is the maximum size for a 4,000 line recorder. Even though film recorders have this high capability, the image you supply doesn't have to be that large. All images are shot to fill the frame, regardless of their original resolution. Convincing images are quite possible with resolutions of 1200×800, and images with resolutions as low as 600×400 can be worth presenting.

Dye sublimation printers are another common form of continuous tone printing available for computer images. These can be desktop or E-size production printers and typically range from 100 to 400 *dots per inch* (dpi) of resolution. The look of a dye sublimation print resembles a color glossy print—both cover the entire paper and perform no dithering of their own. The dye sublimation printers deliver an explosion of molecules so that the dots run into each other, giving the appearance of continuous tone from a dot process.

The quality of the final continuous tone image is determined by the density of pixels per printed inch. This is subjective and varies from one image to the next. Images that contain text and fine detail require more pixels per printed inch, whereas abstract images can get by with fewer pixels per printed inch.

If you output to 35 mm film, you should consider the size of the prints rather than the size of the film. For photo-retouching or high-end reproduction, you should use the lowest pixel to scanline ratio possible. The standard resolution for photographic reproduction is 3072×2048 because of the introduction of Kodak's Photo CD. This translates to approximately 2,200 pixels per inch on 35 mm film. File sizes for an image of this resolution are 18.69 MB each and require large storage and transfer considerations.

Screened Prints

A *screened print* is one that takes the original image and dithers it to achieve true color. Screens are essential for many processes because the inks would bleed and blend together in pools of mottled color. The screens place the color components (cyan, yellow, magenta, and usually black) onto separate areas of the printed page. The pattern of the dispersed color dots is created by the screen. If you examine most printed material closely, you can see the individual dots that appear to be true color at a distance.

Screened images are commonly used for mass production purposes, such as magazines, marketing brochures, or advertisements. Screened images also are used with noncontinuous tone printers. The latter includes most varieties of laser, inkjet, electrostatic plotters, thermal wax, and thermal dye transfer printers. All of these devices require that you screen the image for printing.

When you print to any of these devices, the image first is dithered by a halftone screen. Screens come in many shapes and sizes, including dot, line, and diffusion. The size of the halftone screen is expressed in *lines per inch* (lpi) and often is referred to as its *screen frequency*. This is an expression of how many screen lines per printed inch are on the final document—the larger the lpi, the finer the screen. Printing houses vary their standard lpi use depending on the application. Coarse printing, such as for newspapers, might use an 85-line screen, whereas magazines typically use a 133- or 150-line screen for images. The size of the screen used determines how many pixels per printed inch are required in your images.

NOTE

It's easy to confuse the terms dots per inch (dpi) and pixels per inch (ppi). Pixels per inch refers to the number of pixels displayed per inch on your monitor, whereas dots per inch refers to the number of ink dots that the printer can print per inch. When creating computer images, you are interested in a third ratio: the number of pixels in the final printed inch. This often is termed pixels per printed inch and governs the size of your final image.

Many desktop publishing applications and some printers enable you to specify the type of screen used for printing images. (Often a default screen is applied to an image by the printer itself.) Converting images to screens takes time and can demand an enormous amount of memory for large images. It is not uncommon to wait hours for a high-resolution image to process on an average desktop printer, whereas commercial machines and film recorders can process in minutes. Image quality is determined by the sophistication and alignment of a screen. In general, the screens in desktop printers aren't as high quality as those typically found in commercial, high-quality printing.

The shape, density, and angle of screens used by commercial printers often are considered proprietary information. Because of this, each printer has individual rules of thumb for the best dpi-to-lpi ratio. You should discuss image-clarity requirements with your printer early. Most printers prefer to work with images that have between 200 and 400 pixels per printed inch. The number of pixels per printed inch makes a dramatic impact on your file sizes and memory requirements. Increasing your image from 200 to 400 pixels per printed inch requires four times more processing memory and file disk space.

Issues of Image Clarity

As images are reproduced beyond their optimum resolution, they begin to blur, fuzz, or pixelate. The extent and distraction of these effects vary according to the print media.

Pixelation

The larger an image is, the more obvious the square pixels from which it is composed are—generally known as *pixelation* and usually something you should avoid. Pixelation destroys the photorealistic illusion of computer-rendered images. Making an image pixelate is the easy part. Making it appear photorealistic takes more effort and considerably more memory. You reduce pixelation by rendering an image at a higher resolution.

N OTE

Sometimes pixelation is exactly what you want. Some dramatic images have been produced by pixelating the foreground to lead the viewer into a high-resolution center focus—actually an overlay of two or more images or an entire image created at high resolution but employing an undersized bitmap to cause the closeup pixelation. You also can use pixelation to disguise an area or reinforce the fact that the image is computer-generated.

Crispness of Screened Images

The crispness and clarity of a screened image is determined by the number of image pixels per screen line (or the pixels per printed inch to screen lines per printed inch). This is discussed in terms of the ratio of pixels per screen line and often is termed the *screen ruling* ratio. To avoid poor-quality images, never use a ratio less than 1:1. For optimum quality, use a ratio of 2:1. Increasing the number of pixels beyond 2:1 has diminishing, if not imperceptible, returns of image quality. Avoid creating images larger than 2:1 because they require substantially more memory to render, disk space to store, and time to print; all without returning a higher quality print.

If your printer uses a 150-line screen, then you provide an image that has between 150 and 300 pixels per printed inch. The needs of various screens, presses, and printers vary, so discussing this ratio with your printer before determining the final output resolution for the project is important.

Printed Size and Output Resolution

The print size of the image has the biggest impact on the required image resolution and what your model needs concerning the detail necessary to make it convincing. After selecting the media and determining the pixels per inch ratio for desired clarity, the image's resolution is simply a matter of arithmetic:

(ppi) × (Print Width) = Width Resolution

(ppi) × (Print Height) = Height Resolution

The memory required to store an image on disk and a printer to process in RAM is as follows:

(ppi)2 × (printed width in inches) × (printed height in inches) × (3 bytes per pixel) = memory required in bytes

The data size of a 24-bit color pixel (8 bits of color per channel × 3 channels) is 3 bytes. The size of the print multiplies its impact against the needs of crispness and the resulting dpi. Every printed inch requires more memory.

The media often dictates the size, or at least the maximum size, of your output. Desktop printers typically are limited to 4"×5" or 8"×10" prints, whereas dye sublimation printers are available in E-size (36"×48"). As an example, a 4"×5" print using a 150-line screen prints best if the supplied image is sized to print as follows:

(150 lpi) × (2.0 pixels per line) = 300 ppi

NOTE

E-size is a paper type, like letter or legal size. It is basically a bigger paper size, commonly used in CAD/Architectural work.

This in turn means that the image's resolution needs to be 4"×300 ppi = 1,200 × 5" × 300 ppi = 1,500 or 1,550 × 1,200. Such an image will require 1,500×1,200×3 = 5.4 MB of printer processing RAM.

Printing with Less Than True Color

You may be forced to print with equipment that can't print in 24-bit, true color. Most plotters and many desktop printers commonly have a maximum capability of 15- or 16-bit color.

When you send a 24-bit image directly to an output device, you are relying on its programming to interpolate the differences in the color depths. This usually doesn't produce the best results because most drivers rely on basic algorithms that average the differences. Typical results are banding, streaking, and moiré patterns. You can avoid much of this by having 3D Studio MAX write a 16-bit color TGA file with dither true color on.

Calculating Screens for Existing Images

Many times you will have an image that you need your printer to print the best it can. Doing so is quite easy if you know the following information:

- Resolution in pixels
- Screen lines per inch
- Printed dots per printed inch

The optimum screen size (lpi) to print an image is half the image's pixel-per-printed-inch resolution. If you have a 1024×768 image to print and the finest screen available is 150-line, the image should be printed at 300 pixels per printed inch, which results in a final image of 3.41" × 2.56". If you want to use the same image to fill a 4" × 3" space on the page, you need a 256 pixel-per-printed-inch ratio and a 128-line screen. Although coarser line screens enable you to use smaller resolutions, they also minimize the amount of detail printable in any given inch.

Examining Model Complexity and Accuracy

You need to balance the accuracy and detail of the model against the accuracy and detail of the intended final output. Determining an object's detail is twofold:

- How close will the observer get to any particular object?
- What will be the final output resolution?

NOTE

When producing animations, the speed at which an object passes across the screen creates a third accuracy factor you need to take into account.

You need this information when you build a model so that you can include the proper amount of detail at the critical locations. An object that looks acceptable at a video resolution of 512×486 could easily fall apart or look foolish when you print it as a color glossy photo with a resolution of 3072×2048.

Many times, an object created in 3D Studio MAX has parameters that can be increased and decreased at will. This is great for adding detail to objects that are being used for both print and animation because the detail can be increased for print, and then decreased, improving render times.

Model Focus Detail Hierarchy

Most scenes have a focus, be it a specific object, a group of objects, or an area. As your model begins to take shape, you should have a rough idea of the final composition and how prominent you want the focus objects to be in the final images. This object or area obviously requires the most detail and attention. For an efficient and manageable model, you should consider sketching out a list of areas as they fit into a "detail hierarchy."

Such an organization can be traced to traditional illustration as well. Architectural and design drawings often use rough sketches and loose brush or pen strokes to achieve the illusion of detail without overwhelming the rendering's focus. Artists call this *vignetting* and frequently use it on entourage, backgrounds, and even extension foreground materials.

A *detail hierarchy* clarifies which objects will be made detailed and which will be minimized. Detail comes in two forms—geometry and mapping. As the object occupies more pixels in the final output, modeling techniques that worked at one resolution might become coarse or cartoon-like at higher resolutions.

Geometry Detail

Arcs and curves need special attention as they begin to occupy more pixels in the final output. Distant arcs might be capable of getting by with as little as 15 degree arc steps, whereas objects that arc through the entire scene might require 0.1 degree steps. Seeing the segmented outlines of round and curved objects is the best way to destroy their believability. Your model is most efficient if you concentrate high arc steps at the focus of the scene and reduce them in distant or less-focused areas. Just because the foreground spheres have 80 segments doesn't mean the background spheres cannot use 10.

Maps that are convincing as modeled textures can be much less convincing if you enlarge them, especially bump maps. The dents or grooves that were once faked might now need to be modeled. Closeups, seams, and grooves are much more convincing if you take the time to model them. Taking the time often is much less trouble than making larger bitmaps and adjusting their blur until they appear acceptable. You cannot truly anti-alias bump maps, whereas you can automatically do the modeled joints using the Renderer's anti-aliasing engine—and with much less memory overhead at that.

Don't be afraid to add faces for detail when the alternative is to use larger bitmaps. Adding appropriate geometry detail requires more modeling time than it does rendering resources. You can add 8,000 faces, for example, for less than the cost of rendering one 640×480 bitmap.

Bitmap Detail

You generally need to use bitmaps in renderings. Follow these two rules of thumb:

- Use a bitmap with as high a level of color detail as possible
- Try not to exceed the original bitmap's size in the rendering

NOTE ───

Materials that use procedural textures don't need nearly as much adjustment because their effects are based on algorithms and are independent of resolution.

The size of the bitmap can become a problem as its presence in the scene increases. When you render bitmaps in excess of their original size, they begin to show signs of pixelation and square patching. The ability to notice this effect depends on the image's subject. Bitmaps that portray square, block, and rectilinear images don't show much, if any, degradation as you increase them beyond their original bitmap size. You could enlarge a bitmap of a checker pattern, for example, to 10 times its size and it would look fine as long as you didn't use it as a bump map. If the same bitmap was an image of a hummingbird, however, the pixelation would be obvious.

Background Image Issues

Unlike bitmaps, you have little leeway in the selection of a background image for high-resolution output. Background bitmaps should always be 24-bit color (without JPEG compression) and should not be stretched much beyond their original dimensions.

NOTE ───

Don't forget to set your background up in the Materials Editor and then apply it under Rendering, Environment. Seeing your background using Views, Background Image does not add that background to your rendering.

If you enlarge a background, it appears in the rendered image that the foreground has been pasted on the background. The discrepancies between the two resolutions are apparent, although a layman might not be able to identify why it looks wrong. When you enlarge images, they inevitably blur. Enlarging a black square on a white field doesn't produce just a larger black square—a soft gray gradation also forms at the square's edges.

You should always try to use images that don't need to be enlarged. Ideally, you should use images that require reducing. Images in Kodak CD-ROM format are convenient for this purpose because they have a 3072×2048 resolution.

If you must use an existing, smaller bitmap as a background image, you should bring it into a true-color paint program for conversion, which enables you to enlarge the image to exact dimensions and use soften or sharpen tools to disguise the effects of the enlargement.

Some images lend themselves to enlargement much better than others. Images of skies, smoke, water, and other free-form objects don't suffer as much as street scenes, forests, and interiors. If your smaller bitmap contains such elements, you might consider concentrating its enlargement specifically to those areas.

Using Background Objects

Several more opportunities present themselves when the background is made a backdrop object with a texture map material. Used in this way, other materials can access the bitmap without having to load it again.

The object that contains the background image acts as a billboard. With a backdrop object, you can position the image as you want and make it larger or smaller by using placement, mapping coordinates, or mapping parameters without the memory overhead of resizing a background image.

Background image objects in a scene are rendered in perspective along with everything else. Because the object is placed parallel to the viewing plane, there are no horizontal perspective effects. The elements that are vertical are affected by perspective. This can be especially important for backgrounds that contain architecture, tall straight trees, flag poles, or any objects with definite vertical lines.

The recipe for such an image is simple. You don't want lighting conditions in the scene to affect it, so it should be 100 percent self-illuminating and dead flat with a black specular color. In addition, you should have the billboard object's shadow casting and receiving attributes turned off.

Using the Show Background Image Preview

The Show Background option (accessible by right-clicking on a viewport name) can help position objects in the scene in relationship to a background image.

Background preview isn't an ideal choice for large images. As a workaround, you should reduce your background image proportionally and use it as a thumbnail of your true image. You gain no advantage by using an image that has a resolution greater than the viewable size of the viewport.

The background images can also be frames from an animation (such as an AVI, or sequence of bitmaps), or captured media from film or video. The frame number of such an animation is locked to the frame number of the scene and is extremely useful for rotoscoping and compositing. Several digital disk recorders include sophisticated plug-ins that enable direct composition of video and 3D graphics, all within 3D Studio MAX.

NOTE

Safe Frame is often used to show how the background fits within the view. It is easy to forget that a viewport is a different aspect ratio than most renderings, and reveals more than is actually rendered. Right-click on the viewport name, and select View Safe Frame from the revealed menu list to enable this feature.

Incorporating Text Overlay

A common need is to position text on top of a final image; perhaps in the form of a logo, title, signature, or diagrammatic text. All paint programs provide some capability to create text for overlay; some even have the capability to create anti-aliased text. No paint programs, however, have the anti-aliasing capability built into 3D Studio MAX. 3D Studio MAX actually is the best text compositor available on the desktop. If you want to have complete control over final text placement, you should composite it before you send it to the printer.

Issues Concerning Text Objects

Text is acutely sensitive to the effects of resolution. The resolution of the final image must be large enough to render the text sharply, with full definition and no fuzzy edges. Bold sans serif fonts are the most tolerant of lower resolutions, but might not be appropriate. Curves and fine lines of light serif fonts require the highest resolution to preserve their edges' fine detail. The text can be created quite easily using TrueType fonts. Examine these fonts carefully because large curves may require more detail given by extra steps.

After creating the text, you can compose it against the background image and render it against the background bitmap for final output. You should render in an orthogonal viewport for nondistorted text. You can render in either a Perspective or Camera viewport for three-dimensional text.

NOTE

Adjusting a views perspective is useful for controlling the perspective flare of 3D text.

The Video Post Option for Compositing Images

Video Post suite provides options for queuing bitmaps for overlay and underlay. Video Post can create multilayer effects by accessing Alpha channels and overlapping images. Video Post also provides control over a bitmap's placement, alignment, and scale. If the bitmap is smaller than the output size, it doesn't tile but rather floats against a black or colored bitmap image background.

If you need to compose the scene's geometry with more than one image, Video Post is the way to go. If you're just overlaying the geometry onto a single image, Video Post requires much more memory than the background image method. You also can't align the text with a background proxy image.

Compositing with Alpha Channels

It is common to have a "signature" credit text or logo inserted at the bottom of an image. You would do this most easily by modeling your logo text in 3D Studio MAX and rendering it to a 32-bit file. After you like the final appearance and resolution of the text or logo, you can use perfected 32-bit image to stamp or sign many images. Video Post can perform this application quite well and has no problem overlaying multiple images.

Image Output Parameters

Several factors are important to your final output decisions. The first are the size and proportions of the image. These should be the true proportions of the final print and should never need to use anything but a 1.0 Aspect Ratio. The Aspect Ratio is intended for converting images between different display devices and resolutions. Doing so for hard copy only stretches the image.

Using output gamma should be carefully considered. Many output devices, such as film recorders, don't need gamma to produce a correct image. Many of these devices work best with a gamma of 1.0 (that is, off) and deliver exactly what you see on your preview monitor. Coordinating your output with your printer's requirements is important, and you always should run a series of tests with and without gamma to ensure the proper color interpretation. If aspect ratios are in doubt, renderings of true circles provide a good test for image distortion. Run this test early in the process to avoid wasting time.

Final Image Considerations

Early on in the production process, and certainly before you make final renderings, you should consider who will use them and what is needed or preferred in the way of formats. If the printing facilities are in-house, you should know these requirements and count yourself lucky. The majority of 3D Studio MAX users require the use of service bureaus and printers. You should contact these bureaus and printers so that the correct form of data storage medium and the preferred image format (TGA/TIF/BMP/PNG, compressed/uncompressed, gamma, and so on) is used. Making incorrect assumptions can cost both time and money. These businesses also should be contacted before making substantial storage device purchases because local device compatibility is highly desirable.

Although 3D Studio MAX was designed as an animation program, it can produce superb high-resolution still images. The animation capabilities it has enable you to explore changing lighting options and capture multiple-camera compositions at the same time. Creating high-resolution images usually involves pushing your system's resources to the max and demands a full understanding of the requirements and how best to utilize available resources.

In Practice: Rendering Still Images

- **Render control** 3D Studio MAX offers a wide range of control when rendering, including resolution and file type as well as which objects and areas in the viewport are rendered.

- **Using 8-bit images** While 8-bit isn't good for print, it can be very useful when rendering still images for computer-based multimedia productions due to small file size, fast loading and display, wide software compatibility, and low graphics display requirements.

- **Dithering** Sometimes banding is unavoidable in 8-bit images, and dithering often helps blur the edges between bands. This, however, can increase file sizes. If file size is important, some experimentation might be necessary to determine if the visual improvement is worthy of the larger file.

- **Model complexity** When modeling, it is important to know how the object is going to be rendered. For print, film, or slide resolutions, careful attention to detail is important. Game production, or WWW-based graphics often require lower resolutions, lowering the necessary detail required for the object.

- **Working with a service bureau** Early on in the production process, you'll want to get with your service bureau and talk with them about file types, compression, removable storage devices, turnaround times, and other vital areas of importance for your project. Doing some test prints and working out problems ahead of time will often save you money and headaches when deadlines loom.

Image created by Peter Noldt
ArchImage
Houston, TX

Chapter 27

RENDERING ANIMATION

This chapter looks at the issues involved in rendering animation for recording and playback with digital, video tape, and film media. CD-ROM proliferation and the popularity of the Internet and the World Wide Web have created a huge demand for 3D graphic content for digital media. This chapter also discusses theories of frame-accurate animation and methods for recording single-frame animation. Some of the topics you will read about include the following:

- *Understanding digital playback restrictions*
- *Managing color palettes*
- *Digital video compression*

- Planning for timing issues
- Using animation for online content
- Real-time recording of computer-based animations
- Rendering to disk
- Rendering to film

As the basic and fundamental document of their effort, professional 3D artists and animators render an animated scene to a sequence of high resolution, deep color digital image files. Although the 3D Studio MAX platform provides very powerful processing, with snappy real-time rendering in its viewports and a useful window to the virtual frame buffer, it is still the case that in 3D work you do not always "get what you see." This same processing power, combined with graphics acceleration and digital video editing systems, now affords you the opportunity to quickly and reflexively view the rendering. Your preview and testing may in fact simultaneously provide the final product in the form of collateral material, online marketing, and interactive content. In this chapter you will examine tools and techniques for rendering 3DS MAX animation for the three basic forms of playback media: digital (disk-based and online), video tape, and film.

3D Studio MAX is a workstation-class, professional-quality modeling and animation program that internally manages 64 bits of information—that is, 16 bits per channel of RGBA. 3DS MAX can produce the highest quality digital animation for commercial motion picture production. However, it is important to realize that professional work now includes a spectrum of output, from 8-bit color to the highest resolution and color depths. Creating animation for video or film is very different from creating 3D animation intended for digital playback.

You should know both the editing and playback formats for your project long before you create your preliminary story boards because the differences among formats has a bearing on almost every decision you make during the course of your project—both creative and technical. The diverse need for 3D animation demands a playback-media-targeted approach to the rendering of your 3DS MAX scenes. You can deliver efficient multidimensional animation for the new content-hungry digital formats (CD-ROM and online) as well as rich, complex scenes and effects to be presented on video and film.

Planning for Playback

Because animation is composed of individual images, the design process is frame-centric. The playback medium's method of displaying frames dictates the approach you must take to both creating and rendering your 3D animation. Consideration for output is best made during the planning, setup, and production process. Many, if not most, aspects of 3D digital output are better managed prior to rendering and not left for medium-specific editing and post production.

3D Studio MAX's default preferences are generally set for PC display and the rendering of sequential, individual files to a bitmap format. If your animation is going to be played back exclusively as a digital video on a computer, or from video tape or film, you can plan for that eventuality by adjusting the appropriate settings in the Preferences feature. As an example, 3D Studio MAX manages Gamma correction globally (for display, input, and output), or you can override the system settings such as when you composite input images with your scenes in Video Post or render to a device such as a Digital Disk Recorder. You can implement serial numbering of files in step sequenced renderings (common for character animation in CD-ROM title development) by turning on the Output File Sequencing setting.

When rendering in consideration of your target media playback, be sure to check and record the following specific Preference settings. Carefully read the Online Help topics in these areas. Preferences are categorized in the dialog and each category is signified by a tab:

- Rendering tab

  Video Color Check   Use this tool continuously as you are creating and animating materials and when you are compositing source images that may fall out of the video spectrum for a given video signal type. Don't forget to turn it off in the Render Scene and Video Post Render Options dialog for your final render. Use the Scale Luma and Scale Saturation features to globally adjust the scene's out-of-spectrum values.

  NTSC or PAL   Configure your output for video signal formatting. Use NTSC for the U.S. and Japan, PAL for Europe. This setting will affect how the Video Color Check will find different out-of-spectrum colors.

Super Black   Set the threshold to accommodate the need to differentiate shading in your scene from black backgrounds. This is important for composite effects.

Field Order   It is important to coordinate the field order of the recording devices you will use in conjunction with playback. For example, the Accom Digital Disk Recorder expects a default ODD field order whereas the DPS Perception Video Recorder expects a default EVEN.

Pixel Size Limit   Use this setting in conjunction with the Render Scene and Video Post Render Options dialog. In the Scanline A Render, Anti-Alias section you specify the pixel size to help smooth broadcast resolution images. You would set an overall limit for this setting depending on your target playback (Beta SP, VHS, film, and so on) for the whole project and then individually adjust your renderings as needed depending on the specifics within the scene or composite.

Output File Sequencing   If you are using Step frames in your rendering, you will want to set this on to force sequential numbering of the staggered frames. This is particularly important in developing animations for interactive and online animations, where compromises are made in frame rates to accommodate performance.

Dithering, True Color, and Paletted   Pay particularly close attention to how dithering affects the creation files bound for interactive and online playback. With digital video files (AVI, FLC), you generally turn off dithering.

- Gamma

  Enable Gamma Correction   Generally turn on this feature for all rendering.

  Output Gamma   Every display has a unique gamma requirement. If you are rendering to any recording device, digital or otherwise, you will want to adjust Output gamma to accommodate devices that display gamma.

  Input Gamma   When you are compositing source images with your scene, you will want to adjust input gamma to match the scene.

- Files

  Auto Backup   Although Auto Backup is useful and important during your modeling and animation sessions, you will probably want to disable this during rendering. It introduces unnecessary processing and memory usage and increases the chances of rendering anomaly.

- Viewports (Viewport Background)

    Update background image while playing   If you are rotoscoping using animation files or sequential images you need to check this option so that the animation will play in the background of the viewport as you advance frames.

Additionally, be aware of other medium relevant settings that are saved with the each individual scene:

- Views

    Viewport Configuration/Safe Frames   Use these to ensure your animation falls within the aspect ratio of your playback display.

    Units   Use this feature to match to sound stage, film set, and general architectural blueprints to create accurate visualizations.

    Grid Objects   Use these helpful objects to match Rotoscoping perspectives. Align the grids with planes in your source image.

- Time Configuration

    Frame Rate   Set the frame rate for your target playback medium.

    Time display   Set this for keeping track of the images in your animation. Use SMTPE when you are going to match animation to sound recordings based on time.

    Set Playback/Real Time   Turn off this setting when you are rotoscoping; your playback will not skip frames to keep up with time.

Ideally, you want to create "platform independent" content; however, the timeline and specifications of a project often demand focused, media-specific output. Become intimate with 3DS MAX's preference settings. Create template MAX files and 3dsmax.ini files from your projects that correspond specifically to playback configurations.

Understand how untitled 3D Studio MAX files configure from the configuration settings in the maxstart.max file. You can save MAX files from projects to a different name, reduce or eliminate geometry, materials, and so on, and when you begin a similar project rename your project file maxstart.max and place it in the appropriate directory (default=Scenes) to load a specific set of file configurations for your new project.

Likewise, you can template overall 3D Studio MAX settings such as the viewport configuration, time configuration, and default directory locations by saving the 3dsmax.ini file as project-specific file names, renaming them to 3dsmax.ini, and loading them into your root MAX sub-directory before launching 3DS MAX.

Understanding Digital Playback

Most multimedia applications now include support for creating and playing digital 'movies' in the AVI (AVI) and FLIC (FLC or FLI) file formats. A growing number of applications, especially online browsers, also provide support for three-dimensional objects and animation. Special ASCII text files containing Virtual Reality Modeling Language (VRML) provide standardized methods for representing 3D objects and animation within a Web page. These files carry the extension WRL (for 'world').

3D Studio MAX fully supports reading and writing AVI and FLIC formats, including support for several AVI codecs (compression-decompression algorithms). Kinetix has also developed a 3D Studio MAX plug-in for exporting scenes as VRML files. To create digital video or VRML animation successfully, you must understand and manage the limitations inherent in their formats and with their playback environments.

When you create animation for digital playback, you are faced with a wide variety of constraints. Some of the issues that you must address include the following:

- Normalizing the color palette over multiple frames
- Choosing and configuring the appropriate codec
- Avoiding playback anomalies such as video tearing
- Smaller file sizes and polygon counts for efficient playback and responsive interactivity
- Optimizing your presentation to fit the chosen delivery method
- Planning break points and using transitions

Palette Control

An important problem that you must address when producing CD-ROM and some online animation is working with 256-color palettes (8-bit). Some CD-ROM titles require display in 256 colors, or they offer 8-bit and higher color depth configuration options. The typical target customer's graphics display card may only support 256 colors. In this case you must define a standard palette for the low-end option. The two most important issues to be aware of are the design of the color scheme and the avoidance of dithering.

You must plan the colors and materials selection of your 8-bit images carefully. With only 256 colors available, you need to get as much as you can out of each color selection. You do this by keeping most of your color and material selections within the same family of colors. This restriction is not as limiting as you might think, especially when you're talking in terms of warm earth tones, cool blue-greens, and subtle grays. Indeed, you might find that working with these limitations improves your eye for color. Most good color designs work with a limited palette.

Not only do you have to manage color limitations within a single image, you must also be aware of how color is expressed over time, between scenes, and in conjunction with interactive choice. What objects move in and out of view? Does the position or color of the lights change? Does your animation move to a different scene, or is it embedded within a Web page that contains its own color requirements? These questions complicate the selection of a good color palette.

You can manage color change requirements by using 3D Studio MAX to help you build a color palette. Scene and location matching is best handled by creating multiple scenes with separate palettes and designing a transition between them. Embedded animation should be coordinated with the color schemes of the Web site.

Creating an 8-Bit Color Palette

To render a custom palette from your 3DS MAX animation or from a sequential file in Video Post, choose the FLC (FLC or FLI) file format as your output file type in the Render Scene or Video Post Execute Sequence dialog, as shown in figure 27.1.

FLC output presents four palette choices: Low, Medium, Custom, and Uniform. Additionally, you have the choice to identify the number of colors that 3DS MAX will use from the designated palette choice. When you choose less than 256 colors, a Windows optimized palette is constructed, and the remaining colors are filled with black. Windows reserves 20 colors overall, therefore you should use a palette size of 236 (or less) for animations played back in Windows.

FIGURE 27.1

Using a custom palette to render a file in the FLC format. Make sure the location of this file will be available for rendering, especially when rendering over a network.

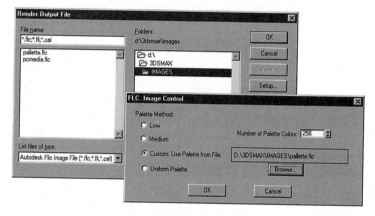

The following list describes these output options in more detail:

- **Low**   Calculates the colors for the first frame of the animation and then uses that fixed set of colors for all subsequent frames. The low setting is very fast, but leads to few problems. First and foremost, if any objects are out of the scene on the first frame, their color requirements are not taken into account. For example, imagine animating a backyard scene. You have bright green grass, dark green trees and bushes, brown tree trunks, and a blazing blue sky. After a few frames, a child's red ball bounces into view. Where do the red colors come from? If you render using the Low palette setting, you have no reds. A few warm tones may be associated with the colors for the tree trunks, but the ball will most likely be anything but red.

- **Medium**   Renders each frame with its own 256-color palette. After you finish rendering the animation, 3D Studio MAX looks at all the individual color palettes and builds a single palette to serve all frames. This option works extremely well and provides you with almost the best possible palette for the animation. The main drawback is that it's slow. After 3D Studio MAX renders the FLC file with a separate palette for each frame, it must rewrite each frame using the new color palette that it has created. This process can take a considerable amount of time.

- **Custom**   Requires that you provide 3D Studio MAX with a predefined color palette from either a GIF, FLC, or BMP file. Fortunately, 3D Studio MAX provides you with the tools to easily create this color palette. The trick involves rendering a representative sample set of frames at Medium mode and then having 3D Studio MAX render the whole animation with a custom palette taken from the sample frames. The Custom palette option is the most commonly used option.

- **Uniform**   Also renders each frame using one palette, but in this case the render uses a generic optional color cube. The palette is a system-generated, uniformly distributed table of colors. A uniform palette ensures that every frame uses the same Windows-supported colors.

You identify the sample set of frames for creating a custom palette by using the Every Nth Frame field in the Render Scene or Execute Video Post dialogs (see fig. 27.2). The value that you enter in this field should be sufficient to render anywhere from 10 percent to 25 percent of the total frames in your animation. The more frames in your animation, the larger the number you want to enter in the Every Nth Frame field.

FIGURE 27.2

Rendering a representative portion of a file using the Every Nth Frame setting.

NOTE

Be sure to save your sample FLC file to disk, and note the location. The reason for this is that when you render the final animation, you choose Custom palette and assign the sample FLIC as the custom palette files. If the FLC is not in the directory from which you loaded the MAX file or not in a Map path directory, the FLC can't be found during rendering and 3D Studio MAX displays a warning dialog, halting the rendering process.

To create an AVI file that uses the custom palette, output the scene as a FLIC file using the custom palette. Then use Video Post to convert the FLIC file to an AVI file. Make sure to uncheck the dithering options in Rendering tab of the Preferences dialog. Add the FLC file as an Image Input event and the AVI file as an Output event. Choose the Full Frame (Uncompressed) codec and Execute the sequence. You now have an AVI file with a controlled 8-bit color palette.

Using Multiple Palettes

Sometimes your animation has scenes that change drastically in both lighting and color. An example might be a walk-through animation in which you move from the warm and neutral tones of a living room to a bright and colorful patio. When this happens, you should render each part as a separate segment with its own color palette. Trying to fit the wide ranges of colors from both scenes into a single palette leaves neither scene with sufficient colors to produce acceptable results. Likewise, if your animation will occupy several environments through Web page embedding or multiple composites and rotoscoping, use custom palettes for each condition.

Avoiding Dithering

As mentioned previously, when rendering to a digital video format you are generally better off not dithering color. To prevent 3D Studio MAX from dithering, you uncheck the Paletted (256-color) check box in the Output Dithering section of the Rendering tab in the Preferences dialog. By default 3D Studio MAX dithers images bound for an 8-bit file format. This may be fine for individual bitmaps. But dithering does not translate well in a digital video file, where compression routines are searching for commonalities in files, including redundant color. Dithering reduces banding in solid color objects, but does little else to improve the realism of digital video images and it greatly increases the file size. Use various mapping techniques to add realism to the scene because maps generally prevent banding better than dithering, without creating large files.

Another reason to avoid dithering when you render digital video files is that it is very difficult to make the dither patterns stand still. As objects move around the scene and lighting patterns change, the dithering pattern also changes. Sometimes the changes in the dither pattern are harmonious with the animation and are hardly noticeable, but other times the dither patterns seem to take on a life of their own on the surface of your objects. The Custom palette technique described previously helps to minimize this effect, but does not completely eliminate it. Your best results come from using a custom palette in conjunction with using realistic mapped materials and avoiding dithering altogether.

Understanding Digital Video Compression

Compression is the process of removing or restructuring data to decrease file size. When 3DS MAX renders to an AVI file type, it will compress each frame's image information based on your selection from a list of software driven codecs.

Codecs are categorized in three fundamental ways. First, they are lossless or lossy. *Lossless compression* retains all the image data, usually employing a technique called run length encoding (RLE). RLE discards continuous regions of duplicate color, marking the file with a code that recalls the duplicate color at decompression time. RLE is very effective for computer generated graphics with large areas of like pixels, is not very effective with digitized analog video and photographs because these images usually contain few areas of continuous color.

Lossy codecs are designed to recognize and permanently remove image information that is not likely to be noticed by the viewer. The algorithm is sensitive to dithering and diffusion over a range of frames. Lossy codecs have a quality setting that controls the degree of loss (and consequently the resulting file size). These codecs are effective when compressing animated 3D geometry composited with analog video.

The second important codec category has to do with how the compression approaches the whole frame, spatially or temporally. *Spatial compression* examines one frame at a time, recognizing and removing detail within the frame. *Temporal compression* compares frames over time to strategically and gradually remove data. An important kind of temporal compression (frame differencing) stores only the changed pixel information from sequential frames.

Finally, codecs support certain pixel depths and are platform specific. Some codecs will only compress to 8 bits; others support 16-bit and 24-bit compression. Some only playback on Video for Windows. Decompression (and recompression) takes place as the movie plays back. 3D Studio MAX's View File feature launches the MS Windows (NT or WIN95) Media Player for this purpose.

Codecs are critical if your animation is to play off a CD-ROM drive or play at full size from a hard drive. The codec you choose in rendering file output from 3D Studio MAX affects the visual quality and the playback speed of your digital animation. As shown in figure 27.3, codecs are reached by entering your output file name with the AVI extension and pressing the activated Setup button in the File browsing dialog.

FIGURE 27.3

Setting up an AVI codec.

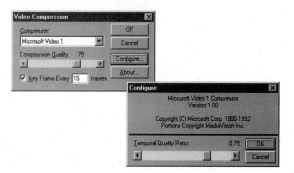

You can compress AVI files by using any of the software codecs that come with Video For Windows. At least one codec was probably installed with your operating system, and more are often installed with multimedia titles and Internet browsers. You can also add third-party codecs to your system for a variety of compression formats. Apply your understanding about how a codec works—along with a healthy amount of experimentation—to achieve the results you need for your project.

Common Codecs and 3DS MAX

The following are some codecs that are likely to be present on your system, including the codec that Kinetix ships with 3D Studio MAX:

- **Microsoft Video 1**   Use this codec to compress analog video, for example, compositing a 3DS MAX scene with uncompressed digital or frame-controlled analog video capture. Although this is not the most highly configurable codec, improved quality is available through its temporal quality slider as well as the overall compression quality adjustment in the main Video Compression dialog.

- **Radius Cinepak**   This lossy codec is used primarily for compression to 24-bit video for eventual playback from CD-ROM discs. (Sprite animation is one example.) This codec attains higher compression ratios, better image quality, and faster playback speeds than Microsoft Video 1, but you should not use it for data that contains previous lossy compressed images (such as an AVI used as a material or background). You can configure this codec to compress to black and white or color. Adjust its compression quality in the 3D Studio MAX Video Compression dialog.

- **Intel Indeo Video R3.2**   This lossy, 24-bit codec is comparable to the Radius Cinepak codec.

- **Autodesk RLE**   This Kinetix-supplied codec compresses a lossless, run length encoded, 24-bit video that can also be viewed with Autodesk's Animator Studio software. Use this codec to compress larger but higher-quality 24-bit video when you want to ensure no RGB information loss. Because this codec does not remove information, you can effectively use it for objects mapped with AVI of FLIC animation.

- **Full Frames (Uncompressed)**   This is the high-quality, universally accessible method for storing animation information in a data stream. This codec requires large amounts of disk space, but provides the convenience of a single sequential file for your animation. Because it is compatible across machine types and desktop video applications, it is quite effective for interactive multimedia production.

Video Tearing

Video tearing refers to the inability of your display hardware to keep up with the playback speed of an animation. Figure 27.4 shows a frame of an animation captured during playback that exhibits video tearing. The phenomenon occurs when your system cannot pump information through your graphics card fast enough to keep up with the motion of objects in the animation. What you see is the display of two frames at the same time. The top part of the screen shows the next incoming frame, whereas the bottom part of the screen shows the previous outgoing frame.

Hard-and-fast rules that tell you under exactly what circumstances video tearing occurs don't exist. The best you can do is plan for the lowest typical system on which your animation will be played and design according to the playback quality.

FIGURE 27.4
This animation demonstrates video tearing. Note the offset in the robot's legs and the scene's vertical posts.

A few rules of thumb exist that you can observe to help reduce the likelihood of video tearing. The degree to which the rules are effective depends highly upon understanding the hardware on which the animation is played.

- **Avoid fast-moving objects**   Video tearing is a direct result of the speed at which the computer displays a single image. The faster an object moves, the more likely it is to tear apart.

- **Avoid motion of vertical edges**   The mechanics of video information transmission (left to right, then top to bottom) means that large vertical edges that move horizontally across the screen represent the worst-case scenario for video tearing. If moving vertical edges are unavoidable, such as in architectural walk-throughs, try to detract from the area that may exhibit tearing.

- **Use the smallest acceptable screen size for the project**   The more pixels in the image, the more data to send, and thus, the more likely the system can't keep up. In other words, if 320×200 satisfies the client, don't push for 1024×768.

- **Experiment with motion blur effects**   A little bit of motion blur can enhance the realism of the motion and help mask video tearing. See Chapter 28, "Compositing Effects," for more information on motion blur.

File Size

You waste all your efforts to produce realistic images and avoid video tearing if you force the playback system to play the animation from disk rather than memory. Disk access slows everything down so much that you may as well be viewing an old-fashioned slide show. You must know the system on which you plan to play the animation, and then size your animated segments to fit within the memory limitations of that system.

If you render for playback on another system, you must decide what the minimum memory requirements are for running your presentation. The typical home and small business PC probably has no more than 8 MB of RAM, and some systems have 4 MB or less. How much memory is actually available for holding your digital video file depends on the player program and how memory is configured and managed by the playback operating system. The only way you can make an educated guess is by experimenting with a system configured the same as your target audience machine. Of course, if you are rendering for real-time playback exclusively on your own system, this task is much easier.

The goal is to design your animation so that you can break it up into segments that fit the available memory. This enables each segment to run as smooth and as fast as possible without the typical frequent pauses when you play animation from a hard drive. The key word here is design. You don't just slice up an animation to make it fit. If you want your animation to be successful, you must plan where the segment breaks occur, and then stage those breaks around a sequence in the animation where a break makes sense.

Determining Playback Speeds

Before you can plan your transitions and break points for your animation, you must determine the final playback speed. Typically, video files are not played at 30 frames per second (fps). The hardware to play digital movies that fast is not widely available yet. A more typical playback speed is 15 – 20 fps. By default 3D Studio MAX renders AVI and FLIC files at 30 fps. Use the Time Configuration feature to adjust your animation's frame rate. The dialog is reached by double-clicking the Time Configuration icon in the lower right section of the main program window. It's just to the right of the frame entry field among the VCR controls.

FIGURE 27.5

The Time Configuration dialog enables you to control frame rates for specific playback media.

NOTE

Remember that changing the frame rate does not change the overall length (in frames) of the animation. It DOES affect the amount of *time* it will take to play back the same amount of frames. So if you change the frame rate and still need the animation to occupy a certain amount of time you will also need to change the length of the animation. You may think you are accomplishing this by changing the length setting in the main Time Configuration dialog. But changing that setting will simply truncate to the start and end frame, or extend the last frame of the animation. You have to select the Re-scale Time button and change the Start, End, and Length settings to have 3DS MAX actually shrink or stretch the animation by adding or subtracting in between frames to accommodate your time length (again, NOT frame length) requirements.

Planning for Break Points

In today's fast-paced world, it is hard to hold someone's attention for more than five seconds. If you watch television, track how often a scene changes. You will notice that a change occurs every three to five seconds. If you watch music videos, the scene changes occur even faster. It's not uncommon for a music video or commercial to have a scene change every one to two seconds. Surfing the Net is much like changing television channels. At any time you can interrupt what you are viewing and introduce completely new images.

Although consideration of scene changes and the length of a shot are important for all well-designed animation, they are absolutely critical for animation you intend to use for real-time recording and playback. Every time you change a scene in your animation, you have the opportunity to break the animation into separate segments. Carefully manage these scene changes, or *transitions*, by using cuts, fades, and interactive pauses to accommodate limited playback resources.

Using Transitions

The term *transition* refers to any change from one scene to another. Many different types of transitions are common in film and video, but two are important for digital video playback: cuts and fades. *Cuts*, in the simplest sense are the abutted end frame and start frame from two animations. They may be composed of the same scene elements (including objects and materials) or completely different scenes and images. *Fades* offer a gradual image introduction (fade-in), a change from one sequence to another (cross-fade), or completion (fade-out).

Both of these techniques are useful for maintaining interest in your animation and for identifying break points to separate the digital video files into segments. Cuts are not as useful as fades, however, because the rapid change from one scene to the next defies the capabilities of most systems. In general, for a cut to work properly during video playback, both segments must be in memory and both must use the same color palette.

Cuts and fades are one way you join animated segments together. A *pause* is where you sneak the segments in and out of memory. Unless you are animating a music video or a fast-paced commercial, you need to plan for various pauses in your animation. The pause enables your viewer to read text on the screen, examine a scene more closely, or just catch up and digest the last segment of animation before moving on to the next.

The hidden benefit of a pause is that it gives you a chance to release previous animation segments from memory and load the next segments. The number of pauses required for loading and unloading animation has a direct relationship to the amount of memory available on the playback system. The less memory available, the more pauses are required to move segments in and out of RAM—which is why you need to know what type of system your animation plays on before you start keyframing and rendering the digital video.

Using 3D Animation for Online Content

One of the most exciting aspects of 3D animation today is its inclusion within Web pages. This technology is now making its way into the Kinetix core products, including 3D Studio MAX. The VRML export utility opens an entirely new and differentiating creative channel. You must engage in a specific strategy when rendering animation for this specialized digital medium. This section will cover some of the optimization techniques you can employ in this endeavor.

Several technologies are converging in the World Wide Web environment— including telephony, video-conferencing, interactive agents, vast client-server applications, and multimedia database management. From an animation perspective, producing imagery for the Web is much like production for video games. The interactive environment trades off certain imaging detail in favor of performance. As bandwidth improves, so will the content on the Web. Likewise, as the browsing applications incorporate VRML extensions, 3D content will populate Web pages, creating an expectation for the virtual experience. You can immediately use 3D Studio MAX to produce fantastic, optimized animation for this experience.

Using the 3D Studio MAX VRML Exporter

Virtual Reality Modeling Language (VRML) is a specification for including and manipulating three-dimensional objects in a program. VRML is used specifically in conjunction with Web pages, themselves specified in HyperText Markup Language (HTML). The 3D Studio MAX VRML Exporter was introduced in conjunction with the release of several World Wide Web products from Kinetix. Hyperwire, the core Web product, is a powerful object-based multimedia authoring application that creates JAVA applets— highly portable, Internet-savvy programs.

The 3D Studio MAX VRML Exporter produces files (WRL) that can be viewed in any VRML Aware application, most importantly World Wide Web browsers when they include a VRML browser. VRML browsers are generally plug-in components to Web browsers such as Netscape Navigator. The 3D Studio MAX VRML Exporter also has additional features designed to work specifically with Topper, the VRML browser from Kinetix. For example, VRML Exporter includes interactive triggers that can launch activity based on whether an object is within the line of sight.

Optimizing for 3D Worlds

The 3DS file format, originating from 3D Studio and now supported by 3D Studio MAX through import and export features is a standard for conveying 3D object information. Some virtual reality software toolkits work with raw 3DS MAX files that have been optimized for 3D world building. Due to bandwidth limitations, three-dimensional object manipulation cannot occur unless you constrain the total number of polygons (faces) in a scene. At this time that constraint is around 1,000 polygons.

Whether you export to 3DS MAX files or export VRML, you need to understand and utilize the optimization capabilities in 3D Studio MAX. This entails placing the Optimize modifier on objects in your scene and adjusting Level of Detail parameters. Figure 27.6 shows you where to add the modifier for optimization. Read and become familiar with the Optimize section of Chapter 16, "Applying Geometric Modifiers," in Volume 1 of the of the *3D Studio MAX User's Guide*.

FIGURE 27.6

Use the Level of Detail parameters in the 3D Studio MAX Optimize modifier to create optimized versions of objects for strategic placement in 3D worlds.

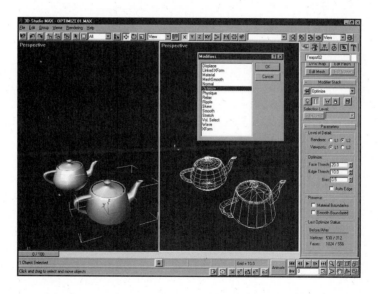

If you export to VRML, you can gain an amazing level of control over geometry simplification by using the 3D Studio MAX Optimize modifier in conjunction with the Level of Detail feature in the VRML Exporter. This Level of Detail feature substitutes cloned objects of various face counts as they are needed based on the original object's proximity to the viewer.

FIGURE 27.7

As the ship moves relative to the planet and the viewer's point of view, you can substitute more efficient geometry by using the Level of Detail parameters in the 3D Studio MAX VRML Exporter Plug-In.

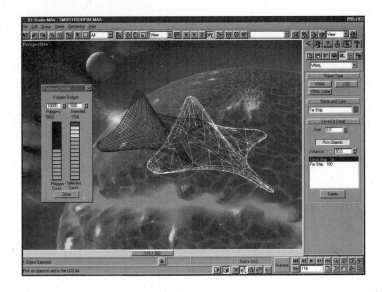

Rendering Output for Video Tape and Film Playback

Creating animation for playback from analog video tape or film is very different from creating animation intended for computer playback. As stated in the beginning of this chapter, you should know the final format for your project long before you create preliminary story boards because the differences between computer and video playback affect every aspect of 3D animation.

This section covers the details of frame-accurate animation for eventual video tape recording, and offers a brief discussion of hardware technologies in frame-accurate recording, such as digital disk recorders (DDRs).

Understanding Real-Time Recording of Computer-Based Animations

The best animation quality is achieved when high-resolution images are played back as fast as or slightly faster than your eye/brain combination can distinguish individual images in full color. When the frame rate drops below 20 frames per second the typical viewer will begin to notice "chunkyness."

Completely smooth motion is the goal, but certain physical factors make this difficult to achieve in playing back digital video from disk.

A single frame of 24-bit color (16.7 million colors) at video resolution is almost one full megabyte uncompressed. Compressed images are approximately half of one megabyte in size. Playing back these images at the speed of videotape—30 frames per second—means reading 15 MB of data from your hard disk and transferring that data onto your graphics card every second. Keeping a sustained transfer rate of that magnitude is not possible with today's standard PC technology.

First, the speed drops far below what is necessary to sustain the illusion of motion. Even more disconcerting is that the speed is constantly changing—frames that compress smaller play faster and frames that do not compress as much slow the animation by even a greater rate.

Any animation that requires extremely accurate playback speed should not depend on standard computer playback. The differences in computers, graphics boards, and even the amount of memory available affect the speed of playback.

The way to solve all these problems is through frame-by-frame recording of the animation. Each frame is stored separately on the computer hard drive or on newer specialized SCSI streaming audio video drives. All 16.7 million colors are available at high resolution. When copied to videotape one frame at a time, you can depend on your animation playing back smoothly at exactly 30 frames per second. If you are working on forensic animation for accident reconstruction or any other type of animation in which timing is an issue, plan on using frame-by-frame recording.

When rendering for playback from a video signal (broadcast or tape), you have the option of field rendering. This type of rendering, discussed later in the "Rendering Frames Versus Fields" section of this chapter, plays back on your video system at 60 fields per second, for the absolute smoothest animation possible.

Rendering to Disk

Unlike previous versions of 3D Studio, the commercially shipping 3D Studio MAX version does not offer the option to render directly to a video tape deck. Without 3D Studio MAX controller software and hardware, you must render to disk or to a Digital Disk Recorder first and then lay the images to tape from that device. Although the advantage of rendering directly to tape was that you never had to worry about running out of disk storage space, if a problem occurred, the entire project would have to be rendered again. With direct frame-by-frame taping, you also wear down the VTR recording head mechanism with repeated and frequent placement for each frame. Professional, workstation class PC-based video recorders and stand-alone Digital Disk Recorders have become the preferred method for frame accurate control and recording of digital 3D to video tape.

Professional 3D Studio MAX renderings bound for analog video will first be rendered as files on a standard hard disk, a dedicated high-speed SCSI AV drive, a RAID system, or a disk array within DDR, and then recorded to the analog video medium. The most common file format for this rendering is a compressed TARGA file. If space is at a premium, you can render to other bitmap file types—a JPEG file, for example, which has a user-definable compression ratio. As in our discussion of AVI codecs earlier in this chapter, the main difference to remember is that a compressed TARGA file uses lossless compression, meaning that what you get out is exactly what you put into the file. JPEG is a lossy compression scheme, and the results of its compression ratio can be noticeable. TARGA, therefore, is recommended for higher-quality results.

3D Studio MAX outputs files directly to devices as well as drive locations. One driver for such a device is included with the product. The Accom Work Station Disk (WSD) is a professional DDR. The WSD stores up to eight minutes of uncompressed digital video in a proprietary format. WSD offers an uncompromising, independent mechanism for storing and moving your animation to other professional media. Look for information about using the Accom WSD in your 3D Studio MAX Plug-In Help.

Advantage of Rendering to Disk

Rendering to files on disk provides much more control over the final output than rendering directly to tape. If the images are too dark or too light, you can run them through Video Post to change them. If an object has an error, you can re-render just that object and composite it back into your scene with Video Post. Also, if there is a problem while recording the animation on your VTR—such as a dropped frame, dropout, or random glitch—you need only to lay the frames to tape again, which is much faster than re-rendering the entire project.

Sequential Files

3D Studio MAX saves each frame as a consecutively numbered file. Up to four of the characters you give it are used as the first four characters of the file name, and the next four characters are numbers (for example, TEST0000.TGA, TEST0001.TGA, and so on). Be careful in naming your output because the second group of four characters of a file name are overwritten. A file name of SEASHORE.TGA, for example, overwrites SEASHELL.TGA, giving you SEAS0000.TGA in both cases.

It is also recommended that the fourth character of the file name be a letter, rather than a number. If you use the name GP14, 3D Studio MAX adds its number sequence to it. Suddenly, instead of starting at 0000, your animation numbering sequence starts at 140,000!

Disk Space Considerations

Each file can be between 500 KB and 1 MB. These file sizes can add up quickly, especially if you are rendering on a network. Rotoscoped maps and textures used in the project add further to disk space requirements.

Different file formats have different disk space requirements. BMP files have only 8 bits per pixel, or 256 colors; the file size is much smaller than a 24-bit (16.7 million color) TARGA. A compromise is to render to a 16-bit (64,000 color) TARGA file. When dithered from 24 bits to 16 bits, you may notice little or no difference in the final output, and the disk space required is reduced drastically.

NOTE

If you are rendering the alpha channel, either as Alpha-Split or as a 32-bit TARGA file (the resulting disk space is identical), remember that this takes twice as much disk space as a 16-bit TARGA.

Configuring for Frame-Accurate Recording

Whether you are recording from a DDR, a PC-based controller and drive, or if a Plug-In becomes available to record directly from 3DS MAX to a VTR, some general rules apply to any type of frame-accurate video tape recording. For more detailed information on a particular configuration, see the manuals that came with your frame controlling device and video tape recorder (VTR).

The theory of frame-accurate recording is that a device "tells" the tape deck to back up three to five seconds. This is done to make sure that the heads and tape have a chance to come up to speed before the recording actually takes place, called a *pre-roll*. Next, the deck is put into play mode, and at the exact moment the tape is on the proper frame, the Record command is given for exactly 1/30th of a second. The tape then stops after another second of forward motion. Another frame is presented for recording, and the entire process is repeated again—30 times for one second of animation or 1,800 times for a minute of animation.

Some devices use a method of recording animation to tape that is faster and causes less wear and tear on the mechanism. These devices determine how fast frames can be presented for recording, and then start a pass of numerous frames without a pre-roll. If a particular animation's frames can be loaded in two seconds, for example, the system pre-rolls and starts recording frames 0, 60, 120, 180, and so on. The system rewinds the tape and starts again, recording frames 1, 61, 121, 181, and so on until the entire animation is on tape. Depending on how many frames are to be recorded on tape, a tremendous reduction in time can occur. More time is saved for lengthier animation.

Time Code

The computer keeps track of where on tape the individual frames go through a system called *time code*. Time code (also referred to as *SMPTE time code*, for the Society of Motion Picture and Television Engineers) is a system whereby a separate track is recorded on the tape that holds the frame information in an hours:minutes:seconds:frames format—01:22:35:03, for example. The format is stored on the tape similar to the way audio information is stored on tape, and in fact, some tape decks that do not have a separate time code track work very well by storing the time code information on an audio track.

The information is stored in 80 bits per frame. The actual time code information is only 48 bits; the other 32 bits are referred to as *user bits,* which are available to the user. Information that can be stored in the user bits includes control commands, roll numbers, character information, and so on.

The two types of time codes are *Longitudinal Time Code* (LTC) and *Vertical Interval Time Code* (VITC). No practical difference exists between the two; each stores the same information, just in a different way. LTC is stored on a third audio track, whereas VITC is super-imposed onto the vertical blanking interval. With LTC the time code information is recorded along with the signal on a video or audio track. It cannot be read when the tape deck is paused. VITC stores the time code statically between frames, making it accessible regardless of the status of the tape motion. For this reason it is generally preferred over LTC.

Drop Frame Versus Non-Drop Frame Time Code

National Television Standards Committee (NTSC) video, the standard in the United States, is not exactly 30 frames per second; it is actually 29.97 frames per second due to the carrier wave frequency and field interlacing of the video signal. For very short length television segments like 15–30 second commercials, this does not present a problem. Over a longer period, however, enough of a discrepancy exists to cause a problem in a time-critical application—such as a network television broadcast show or 60 second commercial. If you lose .03 frames per second, you will lose 1.8 frames per minute.

To alleviate the timing issues, a system called *Drop Frame* (DF) time code is used. In this method, one frame for every 1,000 or so is dropped to make up for the time differential. This is not a problem in continuous video editing because the editor can factor in the dropped frame. With computerized single-frame animation however, the system cannot account for the lost frame. 3D Studio MAX cannot provide output with the correct frame number "missing." If you need your final output to be on DF time code, you must first record your animation on a *Non-Drop Frame* (NDF) tape, and then only re-record the time code track with a DF time code or dub it onto a tape with a DF time code.

NOTE

A tape must be prepared to accept data before it is first used in single frame animation. This process is analogous to formatting a floppy disk before using it in a computer and is sometimes referred to as *blacking* or *striping* a tape.

VTR Formats

Many different types of formats of frame-accurate video tape decks exist. They record one single frame in an absolutely perfect position thousands of times per day, without missing a frame or laying it down in the wrong location. How well they do this depends on the overall quality of the mechanism in the deck, which is directly related to the price. Do not expect a $3,000 SVHS deck to compare with a $15,000 BetaSP deck in mechanical quality, performance, or image quality.

The four major categories of video equipment are consumer, prosumer, industrial, and professional (sometimes referred to as broadcast). *Consumer* decks are not capable of frame-accurate work. Prosumer decks are the next level up and include both SVHS and Hi-8 decks. Prosumer decks are the least expensive decks that can be used for frame-accurate animation.

The industrial category offers better quality images, in addition to a higher-quality deck. Into this area fall the $3/4$" decks—both $3/4$" and $3/4$" SP (Superior Performance).

The professional decks include Beta and BetaSP, recordable laser disc, M-II, 1 inch, and the digital formats D1, D2, and D3. Professional-level decks keep the video signal separated into its component parts for higher-quality images. These formats can be edited numerous times without the signal degradation that accompanies copying one tape onto another. If, for example, you lay your animation onto one tape, edit it into a video, and then make dubs of the copy to distribute, you take your master down two generations. Each generation degrades the quality of the video. Professional level decks minimize or eliminate generational loss of quality.

Hardware Configuration of VTRs

Two sets of cables connect a frame-accurate deck to your DDR or computer based controller. One set carries the video signal. Depending on the deck, it can be (in order of preference) RGB, Component, SVHS, or Composite. The other set of cables is the controller cable. This can be one of three types, depending on the deck: parallel, serial RS422, or serial RS232. A considerable difference exists between the different types; although when each is set up, the user sees no practical difference.

Many older decks use a parallel interface. Although similar in concept to a computer parallel port, it is a very different interface, and must have a hardware controller to operate.

Most newer decks use a 9-pin serial RS422 interface. This is the standard Sony protocol and is emulated by almost all new decks. Serial RS422 is very different from a computer serial communications port. The cable has a 'balanced,' double-ended connections—both ends are male. RS-232 (computer serial interface cables) are unbalanced—their cable ends are of different gender. Serial RS422 is the standard control interface used between components in a video editing suite.

Some decks can now be controlled through an RS-232 serial connection, the standard computer serial interface. These decks usually are the easiest to control from a computer for that reason. For all of these devices, you must not only purchase the deck, but also a controller card or software. Specific 3D Studio MAX Plug-Ins are available from third-party developers for this purpose.

Sync Sources

The video signal coming from your computer must be synchronized with the tape deck. If it is not, you cannot place the frames in the proper location on the tape, and you might end up with half a frame. This is the equivalent of the image rolling either horizontally or vertically on your television screen.

You can choose from three methods to synchronize the computer output with the deck, and these depend on which device is used as a master sync source. You can use your controller as the master, the deck, or a separate sync generator. If both your deck and controller have a sync in and a sync out, you can use any of the three methods. If you have a device that has only a sync out or only a sync in, you are more limited in your choice.

The preferred method is an external sync generator, or *house sync*. This method synchronizes not only your computer, but also an entire edit suite. The result is that all your equipment can be perfectly synchronized, enabling you to use any piece without rewiring.

Rendering Frames Versus Fields

Knowing the difference between frame rendering and field rendering and when to use each can make the difference between a good animation and a great one. The increased smoothness of a field-rendered animation over one rendered by frames is like night and day.

If all video is shown at 30 frames per second, what can you do to make it smoother? The answer to this lies surprisingly in a technology, which the industry strives to avoid in computer monitors, called *interlacing*. This feature is used in recording to video. A computer monitor displays every scan line in succession, starting with the top one and working down in a method called *non-interlaced*, or *progressive scan*.

A television set, on the other hand, starts with the top line, but displays every other line to the bottom, and then comes back to pick up the lines it missed. This is called an *interlaced display*. Each separate set of scan lines is called a *field*. As shown in figure 27.8, a video camera records images in the same manner using two fields.

FIGURE 27.8
If you labeled frames as if they were on a film strip you would see the relationship between fields and frames.

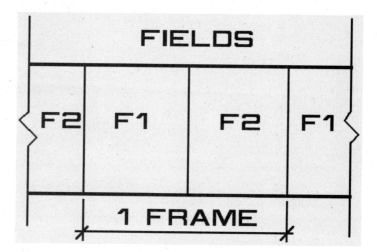

If you use a video camera to record an image of a basketball moving quickly, and then play it back and pause on a single frame with a high-quality deck, you will see that the basketball moves between the time the camera records the first field and the second one. The basketball actually appears to be in two places at once; the image appears to be jittering back and forth. This is a demonstration of *field recording*.

To demonstrate this effect in 3D Studio, create a sphere approximately one-third the size of your camera view and aim a light at it. Now, in the Time Configuration dialog, set the total number of frames to two, and place the sphere at the left edge of the camera view in frame 0 and at the right edge of the viewport in frame 2 (see fig. 27.9).

Render frame 1 and observe that the sphere is in the center of your viewport (see fig. 27.10).

FIGURE 27.9

Looking at a camera view of the image you will be rendering in fields and frames. Note the use of Safe Frames when rendering for playback on video tape.

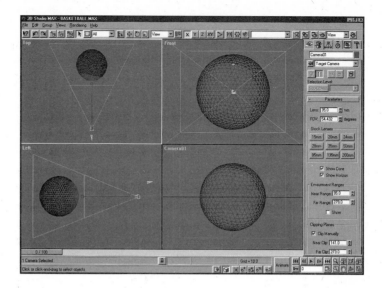

Prepare to render the same scene, but before starting the Renderer, change the Render To Fields option in the Render Scene dialog. Now render the sphere again. The Renderer now renders the scene twice, but only renders every other line each time, calculates the location of the sphere based on fields instead of frames, and renders both fields on the same file (see fig. 27.11).

FIGURE 27.10

The rendered image without fields provides a single image per frame.

FIGURE 27.11

The rendered image with fields provides sub-frame samples of the object, which smoothes the motion upon playback.

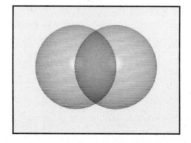

Depending on the animation, field rendering can take almost no more time than frame rendering. This is because only half the image is rendered in each pass. The time to render fields increases if shadows or automatic reflections are used. Both of these must be recalculated for each field, and this can be the most time-consuming portion of rendering.

When to Render Frames

In certain situations, frame rendering should be used. Use frame rendering, for example, when you render still images. Field rendering is not a substitute for motion blur. Never use fields if you will utilize computer playback of your animation because fields are not used in progressive scan devices. The same holds true if you are rendering to film. Film projectors play back one frame at a time.

Another use for frame rendering is when you anticipate many holds, or when your animation is to be used for slow playback, such as courtroom animations. If you want the viewer to be able to pause on any frame to review the video, render to frames.

When to Render Fields

Render to fields whenever smooth motion is required, and the project will be output to video tape or for television broadcast. If the first or last frame will be held on the tape, it is a good idea not to render these two frames with fields so that no jitter occurs during the hold.

If you hold the first or last frame when recording to video tape, it is especially important to have an ease from or an ease to on these frames for a smooth start and end to your animation. If not, your animation has a noticeable jump when the action starts or stops.

Setting Up Fields

Preparing for field rendering is a very simple procedure. Verify that your FIELD ORDER parameter in Preferences on the Rendering tab is checked ODD. Check the configuration settings for devices which will playback your animation such as Digital Disk Recorders and frame controller cards for specific field order requirements. Confirm the correct specification when working with a service bureau.

Now load your animation and access the Render Scene dialog. Check the Render to Fields option (see fig. 27.12). Any renderings you do after these preparations are properly field-rendered.

FIGURE 27.12

The Render to Fields check box is set in the Render Scene dialog. Note appropriate settings for rendering for video tape playback such as Video Color Check and Super Black.

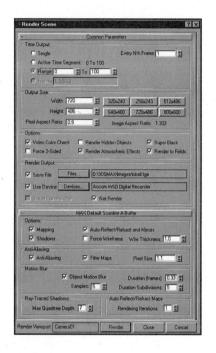

Understanding Rotoscoping

Rotoscoping, a term that comes from a traditional film technique, is applied in computer animation for the process of using video, one frame at a time, as a background or texture map. The older film definition referred to using a frame of film to trace cel animation and special effects.

3D Studio MAX provides new facility for rotoscoping. There are three main ways you can provide reference and composite images (see fig. 27.13). You can use the Views menu, Display Background feature, to build your scenes over captured or recorded video frames from a device (the Accom DDR, for example) or from audio-visual streaming, SCSI drives controlled by the Perception Video Recorder or Truevision Targa 1000 and 2000 cards. After you complete the animation you can composite it with the same background as a Layer event in Video Post. You can also use the very powerful Environment feature in conjunction with the Material Editor to map the video as a screen (traditional background), plane, sphere, or shrink wrap relative to your scene.

FIGURE 27.13

There are three methods to using your scene objects in conjunction with bitmaps and environments to produce backgrounds. The simplest method for traditional screen backgrounds is to composite using Video Post.

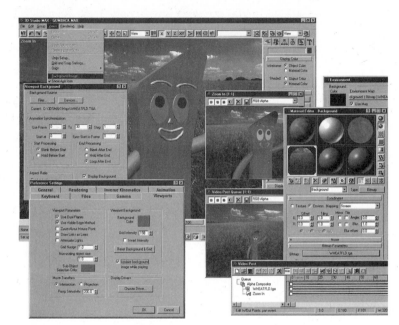

Disk Space Considerations

Files rotoscoped from tape are extremely large because they do not compress well. This is because every pixel has a different color value. Compression schemes depend on adjacent pixels being identical, and this does not happen often with live video capture.

If you are not using a specialized RAID system, a Digital Disk Recorder or a PC-based dedicated controller and drive, plan on keeping a large amount of hard disk space available for rotoscoped files. If you plan as if you had uncompressed files, you will not be very far off when predicting the amount of free disk space required to store the files. A 720×486, 24-bit file is just over 1.1 MB in size.

Capture Methods

As mentioned earlier, 3D Studio MAX includes a device controller for the Accom WSD DDR, which captures frames directly to a hard disk in its own proprietary uncompressed format. Models are available that can hold up to 8 minutes (14,400 frames) of uncompressed digital video. New Windows NT specific PC-based digital video recorders are now available from Truevision, DPS, and other companies. Some require a dedicated storage drive, whereas others can use shared drives. In any case, video is captured and subjected to very minimal compression. The result is that you can achieve high grade professional video capture (recording) and output (playback) from digital storage. Use the software that comes with the PC add-in board or stand-alone device to access frames or transfer the files to a series of standard bitmap files.

Another method of rotoscoping and outputting files quickly is the recordable laser disc or CD-ROM. The video to be rotoscoped is simply dubbed onto the disc, and each frame is brought into the computer. Like digital storage, the laser disc needs no pre-roll, and transfer occurs very quickly. Again, 3D Studio MAX does not include drivers for directly accessing these devices. Consult the latest third-party products catalog from Kinetix for driver and device availability.

When to Remove Fields

Files rotoscoped from live video are usually captured with fields. This is not a problem if the images are to be used as a background because the animation actually appears smoother due to the extra sub frame motion. If you will be mapping the images onto an object, however, the field containing images may not align correctly or could clash with other material effects. The way to solve this problem is to remove fields. This is accomplished two ways. The simplest way is to have a program copy every other scan line down one line. This removes all field effects, and is a relatively quick procedure, cutting the vertical resolution of your bitmap in half. If the object onto which the material is mapped is taking up a small portion of the screen, this may be all that is needed.

If the object is prominent in your animation, however, you might want to clean up the rotoscoped map. This can be accomplished by running the files through a program that not only copies each line of pixels down, but also interpolates between the two lines that remain to have a smooth image. When done properly, the image looks much better than if the fields are just copied down. Some of the PC-based digital recorders include utilities for this purpose.

Using Frame Control Features and IFLs

You can use the Animation Synchronization feature in the Viewport Background dialog to control when each image is presented relative to the scene's frame position. Likewise, you can use similar controls in the Material Editor Time rollout and Video Post Image Input event Options dialog to control which frame of a source digital video file or animation sequence will be in position relative to your scene animation. You can gain very precise control by creating an IFL from video frames you've captured with a device such as a DDR or a PC-based capture card. Transfer or convert the files to sequential bitmap files and let MAX generate an IFL (Image File Loader) in the directory with the files. Then load the IFL into the File section of the View Background Image dialog.

Rendering for Film

The presence of digital special effects and animation in film has now been established as a legitimate mechanism for conveying realistic effects as well as creating cinematically beautiful images. This is a function of better, cheaper, faster technology as well as a growing awareness and appreciation for the unique images that can be created with products such as 3D Studio MAX.

As stated in the very beginning of the chapter, the playback mechanism for frames determines significant elements in the 3D modeling and rendering production planning process.

Controlling Frames and Animation Length for Film Playback

Film is played back at 24 fps, so it is important to set your frame rate to that setting and rescale your animation in the Time Configuration dialog to maintain the same animation length in time. (Refer back to figure. 27.5, the

Time Configuration dialog). As more commercial films are made with consideration for collateral properties on CD-ROM, for the Web, and for the video cassette marketplace, you should become familiar with creating multiple rendering schemes for this eventuality.

Working with High Resolution Files

You may be supplied with very high-resolution sequential files from another system, such as Abekas, to rotoscope with. Be careful to match the sequential file names with your automatic numbering feature in 3D Studio MAX. Make a low-resolution copy of the files by running the files through Video Post or by using a batch file conversion utility such as Image Alchemy. Use your low-resolution copies for most of your work. Run several high-resolution output tests with single files to measure your system's current memory capabilities. You may need to reset virtual memory to accommodate disk paging.

Using Object Motion Blur for Cinematographic Effect

You can simulate film blur effects with this feature but be aware of the iterative time penalty when applying object motion blur. Experiment with applying this effect discretely in small movement circumstances to great effect. See the detailed explanations and examples regarding Motion Blur in Chapter 28, "Compositing Effects."

In Practice: Rendering Animation

- **Planning for Playback** With new forms of media distribution including the Web, CD-ROM titles, and the growth of digital editing technology, plan for rendering by strategically establishing media specific configuration settings. Create template configuration (3dsmax.ini) and startup (maxstart.max) files.

- **Digital Video Formats** When rendering Digital Video file formats, avoid dithering and optimize the geometry of your scene to create smaller file sizes. Take advantage of the new integrated VRML and Java tools available from Kinetix to explore the creation of 3D content for the Web and disc-based animation. Use the custom FLC rendering feature to control color palettes. Experiment with codec settings to achieve optimal quality versus compression in AVI files.

■ **Digital Recording**   3D Studio MAX is designed to take advantage of the power of Windows NT. New desktop video controllers and software that offer real-time playback of sequentially rendered files are available. Although you cannot render directly to tape, the quality of these devices complies with professional video signal standards. Engage the client-server network rendering capabilities within 3DS MAX in combination with NT and these devices to gain productivity and strategically target your rendering output. When video tape is the target playback medium, use Field Rendering to smooth motion. Coordinate Field Order and Gamma settings for devices with which you or your associates will be editing as well as playing back animation.

■ **Backgrounds and Rotoscoping**   For straightforward screens—that is, flat backgrounds—use the Video Post feature to composite your Scene with an Image Input event. Coordinate the output of Video Post with your Viewport Background for rotoscoping scene images with the Image Input event. For unique, procedurally controlled backgrounds (Environments), understand the relationship between the environment maps in the Material Editor and the Environmnent feature. Create template configuration and maxstart.max files to accommodate project requirements.

Created by Frank DeLise
Autdodesk, Inc.
Provided courtesy of Kinetix™

Chapter 28

COMPOSITING EFFECTS

This chapter explores methods of processing and preparing images and animation for compositional effect. Most of the effort to produce effects lies in an understanding of 3D Studio MAX's Video Post feature, which is an entire application within 3DS MAX. By combining your understanding of animated 3D scene modeling with the strategic use of source images and animation, you can produce professional 3D-enhanced graphics and motion imagery for any visual medium. Additionally, you can automate the processing of graphics files for use in other applications. The following are some of the topics that you will explore in this chapter:

- Understanding Video Post
- Preparing for image processing and post production
- Working with scene events
- Using blur to simulate speed effects
- Using image input events
- Using Video Post filters and layers to compose effects
- Understanding and using alpha
- Using loop and external events
- Controlling composite output

The arrangement of objects in an image, combined with the way those objects are viewed, describes a process and a form—referred to as *composition*. Composition is both a method and its result. A well composed three-dimensional animation, containing objects and points of view in motion, requires an aesthetic sensibility and the studied use of certain creative principles:

- **Identify the center of interest and organize around it.** This is not necessarily a spatial or temporal position, but a thematic and contextual focus that can be conveyed through the use of color contrast, masks, perspective, and so on. The center of interest of an animation can be "off screen," or it can be an environmental effect.

- **Use asymmetry to suggest movement and gain viewer interest.** Unique effects and optical illusions are achieved when asymmetrical objects travel along controlled paths.

- **Control the viewer's sense of balance.** Convey tension and relaxation by managing the visual "weight" of the compositional elements.

- **Leverage dimension for effect by overlapping objects and images.** The depth of a scene, especially when elements are moving relative to one another, is enhanced by carefully layering scene objects and two-dimensional source images.

- **Plan for the viewer's playback medium.** Use techniques of composition that will be revealed in a specific playback medium. For example, compose for the letterbox aspect ratio of feature films by creating a custom safe frame (a rectangle spline rendered to a bitmap, for example) and displaying it as a background in your viewport. You can also accurately reduce the height relative to the width of the overall 3DS MAX window by editing the 3dsmax.ini file. Change the [Window State] Size values (width and height) appropriately. Your viewports will correspondingly change their aspect ratio. Coordinating the custom background safe frame and the viewport aspect ratio will help you produce effects bound for a specific format (see fig. 28.1).

FIGURE 28.1

A letterbox composite using bitmap sized background, Render Output size, and Safe Frames.

Understanding Video Post

Video Post is derived from the term *post-production*, the final stage of filmmaking. Post-production occurs after the shooting of the film and the actual production work is complete. In this final stage, each of the elements are edited into a finished form. An editor, along with the director, decides how, when, and where transitions take place. Special effects, if any, are often inserted at this point. Usually, the transition is a *cut*, which switches to the new scene on the very next frame without any effect. In some situations, however, a more dramatic transition is called for, such as slowly fading in one image while fading out another, or revealing an image with a wipe from left to right across the screen. In the past these transitions—along with special effects—were possible only in a post-production facility that had a professional editor and paint-box artist.

3D Studio MAX's Video Post feature enables you to work with the director, editor, and artists before, during, and after production. By using Video Post, you can rapidly produce a wide variety of useful images and animation. These might include set design visualization for planning difficult and costly pyrotechnic special effects. Or you can create and deliver on-the-fly virtual backgrounds to composite with a video feed of live actors. And of course, you can create dazzling post-production special effects and transitions.

Rather than a complete desktop video editing application, Video Post is primarily a utility application used to composite 3DS MAX scenes with other animation images. Although it is educational to produce a complex layered composite still image or a complete movie sequence as in the tutorials, the typical function of Video Post will be to prepare an image or animation for a professional compositing or editing platform (digital or analog) or to visualize and prototype a larger comprehensive animation effort.

Additionally, the Video Post feature in 3DS MAX assists you in automating image processing for content inclusion in such products as video games, CD-ROM titles, and interactive online animation.

The Video Post dialog shown in figure 28.2 has two main portions, the Queue window on the left and Edit window on the right. To visualize what happens when you execute the sequence—that is, render the events listed in the Queue window—imagine the Edit window is the overhead view of a slide projector whose lens is positioned at the top left of the range bars, pointing out of the top of the window. The projector lamp is positioned at the bottom left, under the range bars for each event. The lens and lamp move from left to right, advancing through stacks of slides (frames) over time. The lamp is a sort of slide and can be inserted anywhere in the stack of slides to project those images in front of it. You can place other slides in the stack that act like masks, mirrors, prisms, and light sources.

Each of the slides has its unique way of contributing to a projection of the stack at any given moment in time. Some slides require that other slides are adjacent, grouped, behind, and so on.

Whether or not it is actually visible, if a slide participates in a view for at least one frame, it has a fixed hierarchical and relative position in the stack. This position is represented on the left side of the Video Post window by a label (icon, name, and path) and on the right by a horizontal line, the *range bar*, indicating its appearance over time.

If you change the contents of the stack of slides by adding, removing, repositioning or altering them, the projection of the stack will obviously change. The slides are individually referred to as *events* and collectively referred to as the *queue*.

In addition to its regular duty of interpreting and representing objects in view for a given Scene event, the 3DS MAX renderer knows where to position the projector lamp by reading the Event labels. As appropriate, the projected image is viewed on 3DS MAX's screen, the Virtual Frame Buffer, and can be recorded to a file or device.

FIGURE 28.2

The Video Post Queue in tut19_2.max with the actual rendering order indicated for frames 40 and 550.

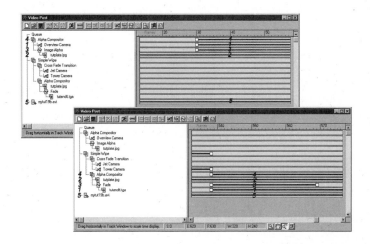

Figure 28.2 shows what would happen if you were to place an opaque slide as a third stand-alone event in the queue. The projection would be blocked— you would not be able to see the first and second slides. Obviously, the order in which you place the events in the queue is very important. While there are several tools and event types, it's helpful to consider these three general categories of events:

- Inputs—scenes and images

- Effects—filters, layers, loop and external

- Outputs—files and devices

The Renderer does not simply make its way through the queue in a top-to-bottom fashion. A given event may be stand-alone in the queue, or it may have a hierarchical relationship to another event—that is, the event may be a parent, child, or sibling to other events.

In figure 28.2, note the column of italic numbers both to the left of the Video Post queue event labels and in the Edit window over the range bars. The numbers represent the actual event rendering sequence for frames 40 and 550. By repeatedly rendering a single frame (such as 40) to the Virtual Frame buffer you can observe the Current Task section of the progress dialog and follow the actual rendering sequence in the order shown in the columns. Familiarity with the actual rendering order will help you construct queues according the renderer's logic.

The Edit Window is a timeline. Starting with zero, the timeline represents a range of frames that extend infinitely to the right in a positive direction. Each event has a corresponding range bar that enables you to manage how and when a given stack of slides appears. The "how" is accomplished by adding Scene or Image Input events and applying modifying effects such as Filters and Layers. "When" is accomplished by arranging the specific start and end parameters of range bars.

Other than its launching command in the Render menu, Video Post has no pull-down menus. The tools across the top of the Video Post window provide the method for placing new entries in the queue. Depending on the active or inactive status of events, the tools will activate themselves for application to the selection.

T IP

It is essential that you construct your Video Post sequences carefully and conservatively. You should save Video Post (VPX) files for each major stage in constructing the sequence by clicking the Save Sequence tool and confirming the overwrite of an existing file or by naming a new one. Save your 3DS MAX file regularly, too. This part of 3DS MAX contains no UNDO or REDO function, and you cannot right-click to snap your range bars back to their original positions.

Generally, you select events for editing by double-clicking their labels, *not* their range bars. By doing the latter, you can inadvertently shift the Video Post Start Time and End Time parameters. It can become tedious and cumbersome to adjust single frame mismatches between adjacent events or beginning and end points, especially when you are anxious to see your composite effects and a full render is required to preview your work.

Using Scene Events

The Scene event is a defined portion of the overall 3DS MAX scene. When you add a Scene event to the Video Post queue, you specify which view and what frames. You apply scene motion effects and coordinate the defined frame range with the overall Video Post queue.

When you add a Scene event, a viewport or camera name displays at the top of the View list in the dialog. The View list is sorted alphabetically by viewport or camera name.

You can add Scene events with different views or use the same view multiple times in the Queue to generate special effects, such as staggered motion. You can animate an ant walking across the screen, for example, by using Video Post to add several Scene entries to the queue. You then can stagger the point at which each Scene begins by adjusting the range bars to the right side of the Video Post dialog. The result is a parade of ants marching across the screen.

If you want to use different 3DS MAX files in the same Video Post queue, render one 3DS MAX file to disk and then add it to the queue as an Image Input event. If no Scene event is listed in the Queue, the current scene is ignored by Video Post, which only renders events that appear in the hierarchy window.

Managing the Scene Range Relative to the Video Post Range

By default 3DS MAX uses the full range of the Scene for the Video Post Start Time and End Time parameters. You may assume that Video Post time and 3DS MAX scene time are the same, but that is not the case. 3DS MAX scene time extends infinitely back (negative) or forward (positive) in time, whereas Video Post defines a range of positive frames. This difference becomes evident when you compare the way time is represented in the Track View and Video Post windows.

See this difference for yourself. Open the Video Post tutorial file tut19_2.max, which ships with 3D Studio MAX and is used in conjunction with Tutorial 19. Open both the Track View and Video Post windows. In the Track View, expand the Objects section so that range bars appear. Now choose the Zoom Time navigation tool, and drag it up and down in the Track View window. Notice that the range bars expand in both directions. Now select the Zoom Time navigation tool in the Video Post window. Drag the cursor in the Event Editing area. Notice how the range bars are fixed at frame zero and expand toward the right side of the window (see fig. 28.3).

FIGURE 28.3
*Zooming Time in
the Track View
and Video Post
windows.*

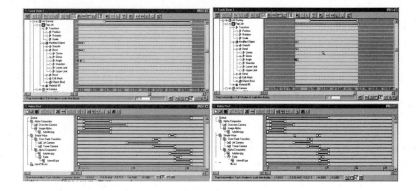

When Image Input events that contain a sequence of images or animation are added to the Video Post queue, their length and range are determined by settings in the Options sub-dialog of the Add or Edit Image Input Event dialog. Should the frame range differ from the Video Post range, Video Post will simply lock the Image Input Start frame to VP Start Time, cut off or hold the last image at the VP End Time, and loop the entire sequence depending on your settings.

The Scene Range settings in the Add and Edit Scene Event dialog enable you to separately and relatively position Scene time in the context of Video Post time. By default, the Scene Range is locked to the Video Post range. By unchecking the Lock to Video Post Range and then, if desired, the Lock Range Bar to Scene Range box in the Add or Edit Scene Event dialog, you can indicate whether the defined Video Post range will contain frames other than ones that directly correspond to the VP Start Time and End Time parameters.

Unchecking the Lock Range Bar to Scene Range box provides an interesting way to create slow and fast motion effects. If the overall range defined in the Scene Range is less than the range specified in the Video Post Start and End Time parameters, Video Post adds frames to fit the Scene range into the larger Video Post range. This process stretches the motion over playback time, creating a slow-motion effect. If the overall number of frames in the Scene range is greater than the Video Post range, Video Post skips frames to fit the overall sequence into the smaller Video Post range. More motion in less time creates a fast-motion, or sped-up, effect.

In one Scene event, for example, you could move a spaceship slowly across the screen. You could abut a second Scene event that contains the same view and Scene range, but over fewer Video Post frames. When rendered and played back, the spaceship would appear to suddenly speed up. Engage!

Render Options

The Render Scene dialog (see fig. 28.4), contains two portions separated by the characteristic 3D Studio MAX rollups: Common Parameters and the default Scanline A-Buffer. When you set up a Scene event in Video Post, you have the opportunity to change some of these settings from within the Add or Edit Scene Event dialog box. Video Post does not share the Time Output, Output Size, or Render Output settings with the 3DS MAX renderer. In Video Post these settings are in the Execute Sequence dialog because they affect all events in the queue. (See the section "Controlling Composite Output" later in this chapter for more information.)

FIGURE 28.4

Object Motion Blur settings in the Render Scene dialog.

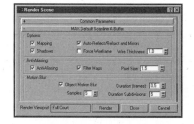

Although you can set Common Parameters and the Scanline-A buffer from Render Options in an individual Scene event, remember that these settings are *not* unique to the specific Scene event. The Render Options sub-dialog simply provides access to the global rendering settings for convenience in setting up the Scene event. If you have a Scene event in the queue and add a second, any changes you make in the Render Options dialog will affect the previously added Scene event as well. This means that you cannot separately set Anti-Aliasing, Object Motion Blur, Ray Trace Shadows, Atmospheric effects, or any other overall render setting for each Scene event in the queue. The only way to composite and edit same scene segments with different render effects settings would be to render the segment individually and add it as an Image Input event to the queue with other segments from the scene.

Examining Motion

Motion blur is an effect that exists in two variations in 3DS MAX. The first version is *object motion blur*, which is configured in the Render Scene dialog and enables you to specify a motion blur effect for the absolute change in position of individual objects. The second version is *scene motion blur* in Video Post's Scene event. Scene motion blur applies the blur effect to the entire scene, acting on the absolute and relative (camera) motion of all objects in the scene. Both blur effects work by making copies of the objects they affect, but the manner in which they calculate and distribute those copies in the frame differs. The technique that you use, or how you combine both techniques, depends on the effect you're trying to achieve.

The 3D Studio MAX User's Guide describes object motion blur as a form of smoothing an object's motion over time, and describes scene motion blur as an applied special effect. The manual indicates that you can combine the two to get the best result. This section describes both types of motion blur and how they work separately, together, and relative to field rendering, which uses a similar method to effect "smooth" lines and motion.

Motion Blur Concepts

Most people think of motion blur in conjunction with photography. If an object is moving fast enough when a picture is taken, it appears blurred on the film. What is recorded on the film is the result of the object being in one position when the camera shutter opens and in another position when the camera shutter closes. The blur effect is the result of an infinite number of copies of the object, each exposed for an infinitely small fraction of the total exposure time. The copies are exposed as the object moves from one position at the start of the exposure to a second position by the end of the exposure.

3DS MAX cannot reproduce an infinite number of images. Instead it divides time into discrete segments and renders one motion blur copy of an appropriate object for each specified time segment. Settings control the size of the time segments and the number of motion blur samples.

The technique that 3DS MAX employs is mathematically and technically correct. Unfortunately, it is visually incorrect. The top blurred ball in figure 28.5 shows the default way that 3DS MAX renders motion blur.

FIGURE 28.5
Default Motion Blur in 3DS MAX.

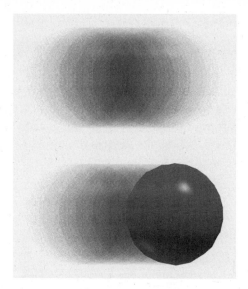

Although the render is correct technically, it does not visually convey blur. These multiple copies appear to have greater density in the middle than at the ends. Most observers would consider this to be an image of something vibrating rapidly rather than moving forward. Even if this were part of an animation, the error would be detected subconsciously. Your natural perception of moving objects sets an expectation that the leading edges of the object will be sharply focused, whereas the trailing edges blur back along the line of motion. That's why you draw "speed lines" behind objects in motion, and why traditional animators are taught to draw motion blur by blurring the trailing edges only. The bottom ball in figure 28.5 shows the result of simulating this technique in 3D Studio MAX.

Creating the effect shown for the bottom ball in figure 28.5 requires that you use Video Post to composite a non-blurred version of the object behind the blurred object. The trick involved here is to get the non-blurred object to lead the blurred object. The amount of lead required depends on the type of motion blur and the settings for each type.

Object Motion Blur

You can use object motion blur to reproduce analog-like blur and "smoothness" for moving objects and characters (machine parts or character appendages, for example). Recall the discussion in the rendering to "Frames Versus Fields" section of Chapter 27, "Rendering Animation." The Render to Fields setting is also used to enhance the smoothness of animated objects, specifically when rendering for video playback. The effect from field rendering is similar but not the same as the one employed by object motion blur.

Field rendering divides a given frame into two scanline images. Each half is combined with half of a preceding or following frame's scanlines. The resulting frames contain two half-images offset in time. When the frames are played by a field-savvy device, the animation is "smoother," resulting from the two-fields-per-second video playback, which provides more moving image representations over time.

TIP

Unlike object or scene motion blur, field rendering does have the unique capability to smooth the motion in an Environment map. Environment maps are not treated as Scene elements, so the blur does not affect them. But Rendering to Fields actually works with the buffer information, not the geometry to create its sub-frame samples, by dividing and reconstituting the scanline output over a series of frames.

Object motion blur can certainly enhance—and sometimes entirely substitute—for field rendering. Object motion blur provides discrete control over individual objects in the scene dithering between object copies and the number of sub-frame images over a range of motion. If you are rendering animation to digital video, such as AVI or FLC formats, and you want to simultaneously provide a smoother animation for playback on video tape without rendering to fields (inappropriate for digital video), it will be worth the extra planning and rendering time to employ object motion blur.

Remember that dithering is not generally recommended for digital video because the compression algorithms employed by codecs can produce color banding. So, in the preceding ball example, if you were rendering to a digital video format, you would want to carefully adjust the Samples setting, which controls dithering in object motion blur (see the "Samples" section later in this chapter). Also make sure dithering (color averaging as opposed to transparency blending) is not checked in the Rendering section of Preferences. In the Render Scene dialog set the Samples value to the highest possible setting (least amount of dither), equal to the number of Duration Subdivisions. Also remember that apparent movement caused by camera motion is not taken into account by object motion blur, although it is taken into account by scene motion blur.

To apply object motion blur to individual objects, you must select the object in the viewport and right-click to reveal the object's pull-down menu. When you select Properties, the Object Properties dialog appears. Use this dialog to enable motion blur by mouse clicking on the check box. You will specify object motion blur parameters in the Render Scene dialog (look back at figure 28.4). When you start the render, those objects that have their properties set for this effect will be blurred.

Object motion blur causes the object's modifier stack to be evaluated for each copy created for the blur. This causes animated translation, rotation, scale, and modifier parameters to be evaluated for the time point of each copy. So, for example, if you translate, rotate, and scale an animated bent cylinder, all these transformations are reflected in the object motion copies. Animated materials are not reflected in the object copies. If an animated space warp is bound to the object, the animation of the space warp is not reflected in the copies. If the binding flexibility is animated, it is reflected (because it is on the object's stack).

Duration Subdivisions

The value in the Duration Subdivisions field represents the number of copies to be rendered for each frame. The number you enter in this field is critical to the production of a successful effect. If the number is too small, the copies are completely separate—an effect called *strobing*. If the number is too large, the copies pile up on top of each other, and the result looks more like a solid smudge than a motion blur. Also, rendering motion blur copies takes time. Rendering more copies than you need can waste a considerable amount of time for a long animation.

3DS MAX imposes a maximum value of sixteen copies. You can calculate a good starting number by using the following formula:

Duration Subdivisions >= (distance/size)/overlap

The following list describes the formula's variables:

- **Distance** The distance the object travels over the Duration setting. In general, if duration is set to 1.0, distance equals the distance traveled over one frame. If duration is set to 0.5, distance equals the distance traveled over half a frame.

- **Size** The length of the object along the line of motion.

- **Overlap**   A value between 0 and 1 that controls how much the copies overlap each other. The smaller the overlap value, the more the copies overlap one another. The overlap value should usually be less than 0.5; anything greater causes the objects to appear to separate.

Figure 28.6 shows a motion-blurred ball that exhibits strobing as a result of too small a value being entered in the Duration Subdivisions field.

FIGURE 28.6

Strobing from too few Duration Subdivisions.

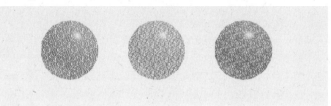

Samples

Samples controls the amount of dithering that occurs between the copies. As this value decreases, the samples are selected randomly from the Duration Subdivisions. The lower the value, the fewer samples are selected, corresponding to fewer, differentiated objects (looks grainy or dithered). The lowest valid value of 1 results in maximum dithering; the maximum valid value is equal to the Duration Subdivisions value and produces more copies that appear semi-transparent. Hence the smoothest type of blur.

Duration

Duration controls the amount of motion applied to the rendering on each frame. The 3D Studio MAX User's Guide describes this as similar to the amount of time the camera's shutter is open. Refer to the previous "Duration Subdivisions" section for the description of calculating distance traveled under the Duration Subdivision field. The number of copies specified by the Duration Subdivisions field is spread over the distance covered in the number of frames specified in the Duration field. The Duration value can be less than one, which means that the copies are compressed into a distance less than what is covered by one frame.

An interesting point about object motion blur concerns where the copies are placed. The copies are spread over the distance specified by the Duration value and then the copies are centered on the position of the object on that frame. This means that when you look at a blurred image that was produced with object motion blur, the true position of the object is in the center of the blur effect. Figure 28.7 shows a non-blurred ball composited over its motion-blurred image.

FIGURE 28.7

A non-blurred ball composited over its motion-blurred image.

Scene Motion Blur

Scene motion blur applies an effect similar to object motion blur, except that it is applied to all objects that move between frames, and it considers camera motion. Object motion blur and scene motion blur can be applied at the same time.

Scene Motion Blur Settings

Scene motion blur is applied in Video Post. You control it with entries in the Add or Edit Scene Event dialog in the Scene Options area (see fig. 28.8).

FIGURE 28.8

Entries in the Video Post Edit Scene Event dialog for applying scene motion blur.

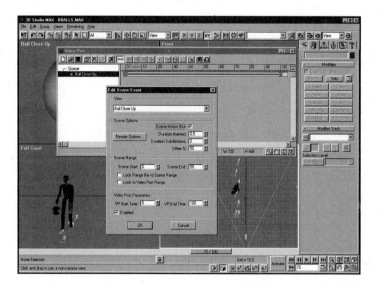

A check box enables the scene motion blur effect. When enabled, all objects in the Scene event view are subject to the blur effect—including materials, but excluding Environment maps and parent events acting on the Scene, such as layer composites or filters. The Duration Subdivisions field specifies the number of copies to render. The Duration value works the same for scene motion blur as it does for object motion blur. The default for scene motion blur duration is set at 0.5, or half the default value of Object Motion blur. This assumes that scene motion blur will be strategically employed to convey movement inclusive of apparent camera motion, which would take place within the frame's duration. (See the next section.) You have the option to dither in conjunction with applying Scene Motion blur. Dithering of this type is a method of smoothing the edges between the overlapping redundant color regions in the frame. The pixels are mixed so that the edges of objects appear to blend together. The Dither % field sets the percentage of dither applied to the copies created by scene motion blur. A value of 0 produces semi-transparent copies, whereas a value of 100 fully dithers the copies, producing distinct edges within the blur.

Scene Motion Blur Copies

Where are the copies placed? Scene Motion blur uses a technique different from Object Motion blur for deriving the effect. As with Object Motion blur, the copies are spread over the distance traveled, but they are placed starting at the current position of the object and extend forward to the position of the object on the next frame. In other words, the true position of the object is at the trailing edge of the blur effect, and the blur itself extends forward in time to the next frame. Figure 28.9 shows a non-blurred ball composited over its Scene motion-blurred image.

FIGURE 28.9
A non-blurred ball composited over an image which is blurred using Scene Motion blur.

Combining Object and Scene Motion Blur

You get the best overall results by combining Object Motion blur with scene motion blur. Use Scene Motion blur to provide the general blur effect and Object Motion blur to provide extra dithering between the Scene Motion blur copies.

Something to keep in mind when you combine Object Motion blur and Scene Motion blur is the effect it has on the Duration value. When you combine Object Motion blur with Scene Motion blur, the Duration value is applied to the distance between Scene Motion blur copies rather than the distance between frames. So when you combine the motion blur effects, the Duration Subdivisions value for Object Motion blur should be low, and its Duration value should be usually 1.0 or less.

Using Image Input Events

An Image Input event can contain any image file or device supported by 3DS MAX, including AVI, FLC files, IFL files, sequentially numbered or single-bitmap files, and files residing on devices such as a Digital Disk Recorder (DDR). The name, format settings, and location of the images are saved with the 3DS MAX file—and with the independent VPX file if appropriate.

To create one file that includes a series of numbered-image files, use global characters to identify and generate an Image File List (IFL) file. For example, enter the first few letters of the name of the file series, followed by an asterisk. 3DS MAX will create a file that begins with the designated letters, append a four-place sequence number after the letters, and add IFL as a file name extension. The IFL file is automatically placed in the same directory as the files it lists. The IFL file name is loaded into the Event dialog as your input file and the Event's label in the queue reflects its location and name too. If you have an animation or list file such as IFL, AVI, or FLC files, the number of frames in the animation appears in three places: the Video Post parameters Start Time and End Time fields, the status fields at the bottom of the Video Post window, and the range bar for that Event where they are graphically represented.

If you want to set a specific gamma value for the inbound bitmap image, choose the Gamma button in the Browse Images for Input dialog. The Preference dialog's Gamma tab enables you to globally correct Input Images. For composition with Video Post, select the Enable Gamma correction check box in 3DS MAX Preferences, set your display gamma appropriately, and plan strategically for the correction of gamma in Image Input and Output events. This is especially relevant when using images associated with devices such as a DDR.

TIP

When you edit an Image Input event by changing information in Browse Images for Input sub-dialog (location, format, or Gamma setting, for example), 3DS MAX will reset the Video Post

continues

Start and End Time parameters to default settings. You can lose some very exacting range parameters in the process because the default parameters will not only change the overall range length, they will likely remove the event from its relative location in time by placing the event at the beginning of the animation. The most conservative practice would be to separately keep a list of all parameters in the sequence, particularly the Video Post Start Time and End Time parameters. One strategy is to create an entirely new stand-alone event in the queue, referring to the parameter settings from the one you need to edit. Use the Swap tool to replace the original and the Delete tool delete it following the Swap.

You can align and resize input images during rendering. If these images are animation files or sequences, specify which frames to include. Accomplish this by entering values in the Add or Edit Image Input Event dialog, Options sub-dialog (see Volume 2 of the *User's Guide*). Composite effects such as embedded 2D offset animation in the scene, accurately placed masks, and stretch and squash techniques can all be achieved with this feature.

TIP

Be aware that Alignment offsets to Custom Sized images have one relatively obscure characteristic. This happens if the Output size in the Execute Sequence dialog is the same as your Image Input image size, or the size indicated in the Custom field is the same as the Output size. Although you choose a Preset or you enter a Coordinate offset in the Alignment area, 3DS MAX will center align the Image Inputs of the same size as the Rendered Output size. A workaround would be to increase the Rendering Output size by one pixel in each direction, or to enter a custom size of one pixel difference in the Image Input Options dialog so that your offset to the source image takes affect.

Working with Backgrounds

Video Post does not directly access the Background image, which may be positioned in the Viewport and used for Rotoscoping—constructing the scene against a background image. There are several ways to include that image in your Video Post rendering. You can use the Environment feature to map the same image to a Screen Environment map. It would then be included with the Scene event in Video Post and rendered accordingly. However, if you wanted to use that image (or animation) as a composite element in Video Post it must be added separately as an Image Input event. If it is an animation, its synchronization with the queue is managed in the Input Image Event/Options dialog.

Generally speaking, if you won't be applying an effect to the background image by using the Material Editor or Environment feature (matte/shadow materials, for example), you would simply add the background as an Image Input event in Video Post by using the Alpha Compositer in the Layer event to position the image as a background. The bitmap processing of that image as a Video Post event is very straightforward and takes less time to render. If the background is static, you can cache the image during render, and save even more rendering time. Typically, you construct a Layer event for this purpose, composed of your background Image Input event followed by a Scene event or another Input Image with an alpha channel.

Using Filter and Layer Events

As stated earlier, Filter and Layer events fall into the broader category of Effects events. These effects generally act on and behave relative to other events (Input events — Scene and Image). It is somewhat confusing as to how the queue is processing these effects, particularly the order in which they are processed and the way in which transparency is used in images that contain an alpha channel. Again, remember to render single frames of complex queues to the Virtual Frame buffer, observing the progress dialog's Current Task field. This will facilitate an understanding of the order in which filters, masks, and composites are rendered.

TIP

If you delete a child of a Filter or Layer event, the parent will also be deleted. If you have several nested events, the ancestral line all the way through the root or topmost level will be deleted. You can copy root sections of a queue by using the Ctrl key and dragging the root parent to an insertion point in the queue. Make sure that no events are highlighted before you depress the Ctrl Key. Press the key and then mouse-click on the root parent. Drag the selection to an insertion point. All children of the parent will be copied to the queue. If you just need to substitute a different child, add your new child event as a stand-alone event in the queue, then swap it (using the Swap tool) with the unwanted event. You can then delete the remaining stand-alone event without losing the hierarchy.

Strategies for Using Filter Events

Filter events are used in Video Post to produce specialized photographic effects, such as lens distortion, posterization (reducing the number of colors in an image), glows, and other overall image manipulation. Generally, and particularly with Adobe Photoshop plug-in filters, these events render the effects to a temporary image, enabling it to process each pixel according to the parameters you set.

With Photoshop plug-in filters, you have a limited opportunity to preview the effect—either with a Video Post supplied stand-in image or user-defined file. In any case, the ability to preview the exact result of the filter on the events in the queue is not available during setup. Remember to coordinate your stand-in image or user defined image with the Output Size of the Video Post queue. That value is visible in the last two Status fields at the bottom of the Video Post window.

Using Layer Events

Layer events enable you to composite two events relative to one another. For example, the Alpha Compositor Layer event recognizes the transparency values of the second child so that values from the first child show through. Because only two images can be Layered at a time, it is easy to construct a very deep nested hierarchy of Layer events. This can be a very difficult process to manage, particularly when events take place "later" in Video Post time but reside "before" other events in the queue from a hierarchical point of view. At first it would seem illogical, for example, that an event such as the Simple Wipe Layer event for the animation in Tutorial 19 is a root level parent to two other Layer events that precede it in Video Post time.

This brings us back to the slide projector metaphor described earlier in the chapter. In the preceding circumstance, the Simple Wipe Layer event acts on two child Layer events. I might have been tempted instead to place a Simple Wipe *Filter* event on the second child, the Alpha Compositor Layer event that contains the end title and plate. But the slide projector lamp would not be able to pass light through the non-transparent portion of the Simple Wipe Filter event because this filter cannot recognize any alpha or transparency in its children. The filter does not create a transparent window because it "paints" the wipe from its child image. The filter paints a combination of black pixels from the empty end title image track and the pixels from the non-transparent composite as it wipes across. When rendered, the Plate would wipe into view, but the Tower Scene would be obscured. The Simple Wipe Layer event, however, has the property of translating the empty track as transparent and "paints" the end title pixels as they wipe in. The lamp shines through to the Tower Scene until the non-transparent wipe is complete.

Managing Alpha

Color bitmap image files, such as TARGA (TGA) files, come in a variety of bit depths, such as 8, 16, 24, and 32 bits per pixel. In a 32-bit true-color file, each pixel in the image has four channels that describe it—RGBA, Red-Green-Blue-Alpha. Three of the channels—Red, Green, and Blue—comprise the source for creating the full spectrum of color hues. The Red, Green, and Blue channels use 8 bits of memory each to describe the color of every pixel in the image ($3 \times 8 = 24$ bits per pixel). A pure green pixel, for example, has RGB values of 0,255,0. Each 8-bit channel is represented by the numbers 0–255 because 256 possible combinations of zeros and ones exist in a string of eight characters, or *bits* ($2 \times 2 \times 2 \times 2 \times 2 \times 2 \times 2 \times 2$).

Alpha, in its simplest form, can be thought of as another channel. It represents the level of transparency, by using another 8 bits of memory for every pixel in the image. Suppose that you render a flat white circle over a black background by using a material on the circle that is 50 percent transparent. When the Renderer encounters a pixel that falls inside the circle, it writes the values 255,255,255,128 to a 32-bit image file for that pixel, or 8 bits for each channel. These values tell the program to display the pixel as a mixture of full-intensity red, full-intensity green, and full-intensity blue (white), and to enable any image beneath that pixel to be 50 percent visible—that is, the black background showing through the white circle, thereby producing gray. The benefit of this is that you can now composite the 50 percent transparent circle over any image in Video Post, such as a cloud-filled sky, and you see the clouds through the circle.

TIP

3D Studio MAX creates images in TGA, RLA, and PNG file formats. Whenever you output a bitmap image with 3DS MAX for the first time, the Setup dialog appears automatically. In this dialog, you have the ability to designate whether an alpha channel is included with the file. 3DS MAX remembers the last settings you entered for a particular file format.

When in the Browsing Image for Input dialog, you can select any file and choose the Info button to view details about the file. Here, you can quickly discern whether the file contains an alpha channel. By choosing View, you bring the file into a frame buffer and examine the alpha channel as well.

In Video Post you can take advantage of the alpha channel within bitmap files by specifying parameters from within the Filter and Layer events. For example, the Alpha Composite Layer event enables you to composite two currently selected events by recognizing the alpha channel of the second of the two images. If you recall the slides, think of alpha as the opacity of the images on the slide. Some images are opaque; others are translucent or transparent.

Not all images have alpha information—only 32-bit, true-color files have this capability. For this reason you are given a variety of methods to create and use alpha information for your Video Post effects. For example, the Pseudo Alpha Filter event takes the upper left-hand pixel of an RGB, non-alpha file and converts all identical pixels in the image to fully transparent alpha.

In addition to the capability of some Layer and Filter events to recognize and use the alpha channel in the files they act on directly, some also provide a Mask feature that enables you to use the alpha channel of a different file to fashion a custom area of transparency (see fig. 28.10). Here you can specify how the Mask effect is to be applied with the others in the queue. You have the ability to invert the Mask, and use other channels in the Graphics buffer (G-buffer) to control the Mask effect.

When you click in the box to the right of the Mask section in the dialog, you are presented with a list of bitmap channels, one or all of which may be contained within a source image. These are the channels that 3DS MAX currently supports for the purpose of creating the mask. 3DS MAX can output files with 16 bit RGBA channels as well as unique 3D channels like Z-buffer and object or material identification channels. The mask feature uses some of these unique channels to create its effects. The most common mask is an Alpha channel mask. It creates a mask from the alpha channel of the source bitmap image.

FIGURE 28.10

The mask settings in Video Post event dialogs.

If the Red, Green, or Blue channel is chosen as the source for the mask the binary value (0–255) of each pixel in that channel is used for the mask, with 0 being completely transparent and 255 completely opaque. You can use Z-buffer depth information or the channel identifiers of materials and objects in source RLA files to create masks as well. For example, you could output masks created with 3DS MAX to the RLA file type and implement them later in Video Post composites.

You can use 3DS MAX's unique capabilities to produce three-dimensional masks. Suppose, for example, that you have a landscape similar to the sample file wheatfld.tga You want to experiment with having a three-dimensional object appear in the sky. Using the following technique you can mix and match objects and textures without having to map materials.

First, add two Image Input events to the Video Post queue. As the first entry add the landscape image. For the second entry add a sample texture map—asphalt2.jpg, for example. The texture map has no alpha channel, but by applying an Image Alpha filter to the texture map, and identifying a filter mask composed of the Z-buffer information of a special bitmap file (RLA), you can composite the texture with the landscape using an Alpha compositor (Layer Event). In effect, you are projecting a three-dimensional texture onto the background landscape.

Using our earlier slide projector analogy, this queue creates a special slide (the texture with a mask filter). When light from the projector's lamp shines through it, the light is blocked by a three-dimensional image (the object text). The Alpha Image filter creates an alpha channel for the texture, composed of a special mask, a text object which was rendered by MAX to an RLA file. Using the Z-buffer channel of the RLA file as a mask, the Alpha Image filer paints a three-dimensional texture onto the slide. The lamp's only light projects that part of the texture masked according to the depth of the object information in the source RLA file. An Alpha Compositor Layer event applied to the two Input images uses the projection from the filtered texture (recognizing its Image alpha) to composite the mask onto the landscape bitmap. Figures 28.11 and 28.12 show the image used for the Z-buffer mask and the final composite image.

FIGURE 28.11
The RLA image with Z-depth information.

FIGURE 28.12
The 3D Studio MAX scene, Video Post Queue and composite image using a Z-buffer channel as a mask.

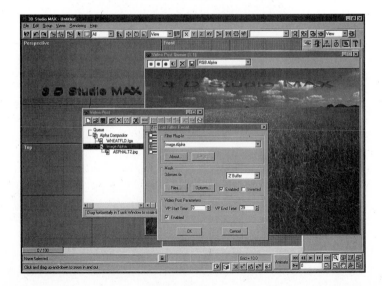

Using Loop and External Events

Loop events provide repeated frames and reverse direction (ping pong) for individual tracks and whole sequences. Although limited looping is available in Image Input events, you can use the Loop event to loop composites, thereby creating unusual images and motion.

Assume, for example, you add a Scene event to the queue, which has 100 frames, and you want the event to repeat three times. If you change the VP End Time to 299, your animation will simply stop at frame 99 and Video Post will render frame 99 for the rest of the range bar's length. Recall that when you change the Scene Range to a different value than the Video Post Start and End Times, Video Post adds or skips frames thereby creating slow- and fast-motion effects. So the only way to repeat a Scene event—other than adding the scene multiple times in the queue and abutting the Event tracks—is to use the Loop event. Use the Loop event to control the Start and End of the repeated frames by dragging the range bar relative to its child event. Experiment with this feature to achieve interesting loops and ping-pong effects.

As mentioned earlier, Input Image events will loop if the Options dialog Loop check box is selected. Otherwise, it will behave as a Scene event does, repeating the last frame for the duration of the Video Post range bar.

With the External event, you can insert other applications or your own batch files into the Video Post queue. Typically, this is how you would batch process Output events using a conversion application that can accept a command-lines parameter such as Image Alchemy or PKZIP. You can also embed processes that write out files used in subsequent events. Make sure to create PIF files for DOS applications, such as PKZIP, and use those as your External event file.

Controlling Composite Output

Output events are generally stand-alone events in the queue, and are usually the last event. Multiple output events can be used to simultaneously produce sequential files and digital animation, such as AVI files. Unlike the Input and Effects event types, which act on other events, the Output event becomes a child of the event it acts upon. As such, it will write a file composed of the information that has been processed up to the point in the queue where the parent resides, which may, for example, represent an incomplete alpha composite. Adding Output events in the Queue is like inserting the lamp in the slide projector at a point in the middle of the stack of slides. The slides (events) which fall behind it never "see the light."

In Practice: Composition for Animation and Effects

- **Creative Principles**   Basic aesthetic techniques, some unique to 3D graphics as an artistic medium, should be practiced in an effort to compose and animate the scene. Identify a center of interest. Use asymmetry to suggest movement. Control balance. Position objects strategically. Plan ahead for the playback medium.

- **Utilitarian and Collaborative use of Video Post**   Understand and use Video Post for practical workgroup purposes. Prepare images and animation for professional compositing or editing. Use it to visualize and prototype for a larger comprehensive animation effort.

- **Video Post—the Magic Lantern**   The Video Post queue is analogous to a very special slide projector. The lamp's beam navigates through transparency, opacity and other effects as it moves through time. Effects are determined by the object slid between the light source and the surface upon which the light falls, as well a by the speed and direction the light travels. Use single frame renderings to view the progress dialog's Current Task readout. This will give you a practiced understanding of the rendering process.

- **Create sequences carefully and conservatively**   Save your Video Post file (VPX) and MAX file (MAX) frequently and systematically (there is no UNDO or REDO in Video Post). Select events and highlight range bars by clicking on the Queue event label, not the range bar (to avoid moving the start and end points).

- **Video Post time versus Scene Time**   Uncheck the Lock to Video Post Range and Lock Range Bar to Scene Range boxes in the Scene event to add multiple ranges from the Scene and manipulate the direction and speed of animation. It is here that you can reverse the direction of animation without actually affecting the keyframes.

- **Blurring the lines** Use Motion and Scene blur together to create realistic animation of quick motions and smooth out jerkiness in moving objects and characters. Understand the differences between Object and Scene Motion blur as well as the smoothing effect of field rendering. Develop strategies for motion based upon playback media. For example, avoid dithering when your playback medium is digital video.

- **Smart events, effective effects** Start and end parameters are easily lost when you change settings during the event edit. Keep a record of all parameters in the sequence. Make copies or create substitute events and use the Swap tool to replace events rather than edit them.

- **Channel surfing** Much can be accomplished through the creative use of channels, especially alpha channels and masks. Use the 3D information contained in MAX output files (RLA) in conjunction with masks to produce unique effects.

"Chan Centre Concert Theatre"
Created by Eugene Radvenis
E. V. Radvenis Inc.
Vancouver BC, Canada
An interior view of the concert theatre at the University of British
Columbia's Chan Centre for the Performing Arts
Architect: Bing Thom Architects Inc., Vancouver BC
On stage quartet photograph: David Cooper Photography, Vancouver BC

Chapter 29

NETWORK RENDERING

3D Studio MAX has the capability to use the power of your network to render animations across multiple computers — network rendering. With 3DS MAX, you can use one copy to render on up to 10,000 computers with no extra software or fee. Best of all, 3DS MAX integrates with the NT networking and security systems to give you a fault tolerant solution. If the power goes down in the middle of a job, 3DS MAX can pick up rendering right where it left off as soon as power is restored.

Many companies dedicate a group of computers to only rendering purposes, known as a "rendering farm." These farms range in size from two to two hundred computers, depending on the scale of the company's rendering operation. You can also use network rendering to render to one computer for batch processing. Before you leave for the evening, you can queue multiple jobs, and 3DS MAX goes through them one by one.

Network rendering requires Windows NT with network drivers installed and a minimum installation of 3DS MAX to work properly; however, there is no need to be logged on to the computer for network rendering to take place.

In this chapter, you see how to set up network rendering for various types of network topologies and explore the various components of 3DS MAX's network rendering capabilities.

This chapter examines the following topics:

- The TCP/IP protocol

- Setting up TCP/IP on your computer

- Components of 3DS MAX's network rendering capability: Manager, Server, and Queue Manager

- Setting up 3DS MAX for network rendering

- Rendering a job

- The Job Assignment dialog

- Network rendering to FLCs and AVIs

3DS MAX utilizes a job-based network rendering system. If two rendering jobs are assigned to the same computer, using this system, the computer picks up the new job after it has completed the previous job. The entire job, which can be rendered on several computers, doesn't need to be completed first—server-based rendering—and is useful if a user sends out a one-frame job that takes several hours to render. If the other servers are sitting idle, they pick up any new jobs that come along as does the currently rendering computer when it has finished. In a job-based system, this wouldn't be possible because the first job would have to be completed before the next job would be handled by the network rendering system.

The following section covers other fundamentals you need to know before you begin working with 3DS MAX's networking features.

Networking Basics

Before you start rendering by using 3DS MAX's networking capabilities, you need to have a few basic components running in the Windows NT environment. You must have administrator privileges on the computers you're planning to use for network rendering. Without administrator privileges, you probably won't be able to install network drivers for NT, much less get them running. The following sections describe the components you'll need to install and configure in order to successfully get network rendering up and running.

The TCP/IP Protocol

TCP/IP stands for Transmission Control Protocol/Internet Protocol. A *network protocol* is a "language" that enables two or more computers to talk to each other. TCP/IP is one of many types of protocols used by networks. For instance, computers on a Novell-based network use another type of protocol called IPX. Protocols are languages that computers can use to communicate with each other. Computers can use many protocols simultaneously. For instance, an NT-based computer could access Novell NetWare, Microsoft Windows, and UNIX servers all at the same time, by using completely different protocols. This way, you have access to all types of computers from your PC, not just IBM compatible computers. You can't use multiple instances of a protocol at the same time, mainly because there is no need. After a protocol is initialized by a computer, it can communicate with as many computers as possible. You don't need the same protocol for each computer with which you communicate. Because of its universal acceptance as a networking standard, especially across the Internet, TCP/IP was chosen as the protocol for 3DS MAX's network rendering system.

TCP/IP uses an IP address to talk to any computer. An *IP address* is a series of numbers that represents a computer on a TCP/IP network. For instance, your computer's TCP/IP address might look like the following:

192.144.92.143

All TCP/IP addresses use a four-number combination to designate a computer on the network, and each computer must have a unique address to communicate correctly. Each of the four sets of numbers, when combined, represents a specific address. Think of it as a house number, city, state, and zip code for your computer. Windows NT is capable of detecting other computers on the network that use the same address and alerts you that the protocol hasn't been loaded, as a result. To remedy this, you need to get a unique address. Most networks use one of two TCP/IP address systems: DHCP (Dynamic Host Configuration Protocol) or a fixed address.

DHCP dynamically assigns a new TCP/IP address to your computer each time you log on to the network. This way, a company can have a pool of IP addresses that it can swap in and out of computer systems on the network. DHCP is useful when you have a company with multiple subnets all using the same address. A user can move to any subnet and always have a valid TCP/IP address.

When using DHCP, there is no need to configure the address manually; however, DHCP is not recommended for 3DS MAX network rendering because 3DS MAX needs to know a rendering computer's address and use that address all the time. The address cannot be changed automatically. As a matter of fact, you should avoid using DHCP at all if you want consistent performance from your network rendering setup.

Fixed addresses are the preferred method for network rendering in 3DS MAX. A *fixed address* remains assigned to that computer regardless of who is logged on or when.

Setting Up TCP/IP on Your Computer

All network settings for Windows NT 3.51 and 4.0 are located in the Network Settings dialog. You can install and configure network cards and protocols with this dialog. To access the network settings for your computer, double-click the Control Panel icon in the Main program group, and then double-click the Network icon for Windows NT 3.51; for Windows NT 4.0, click on the Start button in the Taskbar and choose Settings/Control Panel. When the Control Panel dialog appears, double-click on the Network icon. The Network Settings dialog appears (see fig. 29.1).

If your computer is not yet configured with the TCP/IP protocol, you need to add it. Windows NT ships with the Microsoft version of TCP/IP. The Microsoft TCP/IP protocol is completely compatible with 3DS MAX's network rendering system, and is the TCP/IP protocol of choice.

FIGURE 29.1

The Windows NT Network Settings dialog (click the Start button, Settings, and Control Panel). Click the Network icon, and the dialog appears.

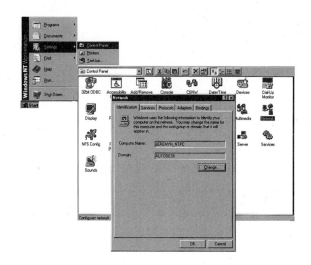

NOTE

Windows NT requires a complete installation of the TCP/IP protocol. You can install the protocol without adding an address, but this causes problems for 3DS MAX. If you don't have a TCP/IP address from your network administrator, it is best to wait to install network rendering services. Also, make sure you have the Windows NT installation CD or diskettes handy because you'll need them to install the TCP/IP.

First click on the Protocols tab. Check to see whether the TCP/IP protocol is listed. Figure 29.2 shows a computer with TCP/IP installed. If so, you don't need to install it. If TCP/IP is not listed, you can add it by clicking the Add button and choosing the TCP/IP protocol from the list. NT asks for various configuration information and then installs the protocol.

TIP

The TCP/IP is configured properly if Windows NT doesn't indicate an error upon startup.

Closed Network IP Addressing

A *closed network* is a group of computers that are not connected to a company's main network—the network where all other company business takes place. This is the ideal situation for 3DS MAX network rendering because there is less likelihood of excessive network traffic and potential IP address conflicts.

FIGURE 29.2

*The Windows NT
installed protocol
dialog. The TCP/IP
protocol is installed on
the computer.*

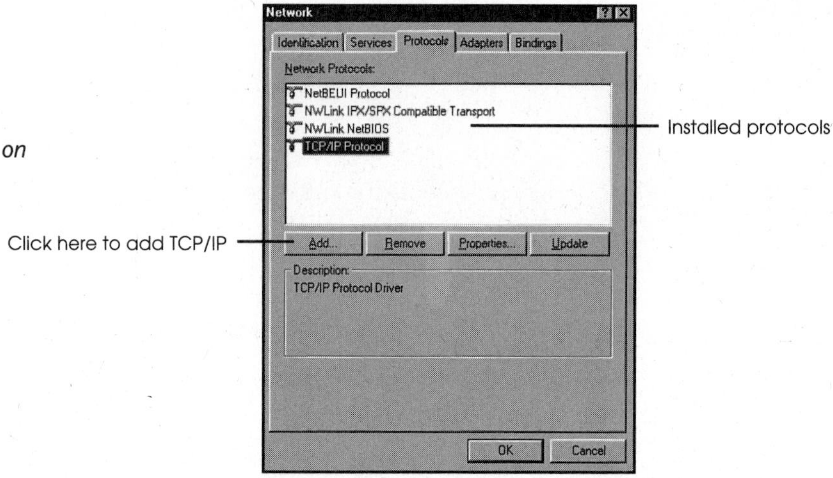

Installed protocols

Click here to add TCP/IP

If you're using the computer on a closed network, the TCP/IP address must be unique. It doesn't really matter what the numbers are; however, it is always a good idea to use a pattern of addresses that enables you to quickly identify the computer by its address. For instance, on a 10-computer network in which you're using all 10 computers for network rendering, computer number 8 may have the address 192.144.100.8, where 8 is the main designation differential. All the computers would share the same first three numbers and would only vary in the last number. 3DS MAX prefers that you use an IP address that begins with 192 and follows some common convention thereafter. Figure 29.3 shows a common TCP/IP setup.

W A R N I N G

Avoid using the number 0 or 255 in your addresses. The number 0 is reserved for computers that don't know their addresses and the number 255 is used for broadcast messages.

N O T E

Closed network addressing also applies to a single-computer setup. To run MAX net rendering on a single machine, just install the Microsoft Loopback adapter as your network adapter in the NT Network setup dialog.

Next, set up the Subnet mask. The Subnet mask value should be left at 255.255.255.0. There's no specific reason for this assignment other than your convenience. By default, if you use the 192 prefix in your IP address, NT automatically assigns 255.255.255.0 to your Subnet mask. If you need to change it for some reason, all other computers that are being used for network rendering need to be changed as well. In order for two computers to talk using network rendering, they must have the same Subnet mask value.

FIGURE 29.3

The TCP/IP settings dialog, where you can specify the TCP/IP address for the computer.

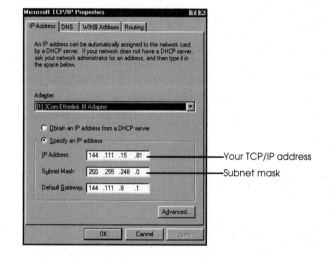

If you have no other specific network settings to configure, you're finished with installation of the TCP/IP protocol. Reboot your computer, and the process is complete.

Main Network IP Addressing

If you're planning to piggyback on the company's main network, follow the same setup process as you would for a closed network. However, you need to take a few more issues into consideration when installing the TCP/IP protocol. If your company currently uses TCP/IP (most do), you need to get unique IP addresses from the network administrator. He can provide you with valid addresses for any number of computers that you plan to use for rendering purposes.

WARNING

While setting up a network rendering farm on a company's main network, it is strongly recommended that you consult the network administrator before you change any network settings. There are often special configuration issues that are specific to your network that only your administrator knows about. Changing network settings can have an impact not only on your computer's access to your network, but everyone else connected to it.

More than likely, you have a Subnet mask value that differs from the 3DS MAX preferred 255.255.255.0. If so, make sure that all other computers being used for network rendering also have the same value.

Network rendering in 3D Studio MAX wasn't intended to run on a network using DHCP. If your network dynamically allocates IP addresses to computers, ask your administrator for a fixed range of addresses to use.

Setting up a rendering farm on a company-wide network, as you may have guessed, is a bit more challenging than a closed network solution. Besides extra configuration headaches, there is the potential for a considerable increase in network traffic, thereby slowing overall throughput. Consult with your network administrator throughout the setup process to avoid any conflicts.

The Components of 3DS MAX Network Rendering

To utilize network rendering, you need to have three major components installed from 3DS MAX. The first is obvious: a fresh installation of 3DS MAX. The other two components are the Manager and Server combination along with the Queue Manager. All of these components come with 3DS MAX.

NOTE

All computers that take part in network rendering must have 3D Studio MAX installed and authorized.

Manager and Server

In 3D Studio MAX's directory, there are two programs that are not installed as icons in your Kinetix program group: Manager and Server. Both programs are intended to be run in either an MS-DOS window or as an NT service.

The Manager program sets up a computer as the ultimate delegator and regulator of network rendering tasks. A computer running Manager has complete control over network rendering tasks. The manager's main role is to oversee the delegation of frames to each computer taking part in the network rendering job. The Manager also maintains a list of jobs submitted and pending, and acts on those jobs as current ones are completed. Manager runs only on an NT-based computer and must have a fixed TCP/IP address.

The Server program enables a computer to act as a rendering slave. The server receives frame rendering jobs from the Manager. When a job is received from the Manager, Server launches 3D Studio MAX in a special server mode. When running in this mode, the user cannot launch another session of 3DS MAX. You can specify, however, whether it is apparent to a user that 3DS MAX is currently network rendering through the services control panel.

Server can also be run on a computer running Manager. That way you can network render on one computer or use the Manager computer's resources to scale your network rendering power by one more computer.

Queue Manager

The most interactive portion of network rendering lies in the Queue Manager program. This icon is installed to the Kinetix program group along with the rest of 3DS MAX. Inside Queue Manager, you have complete control of your network rendering process—from viewing every job sent to the Manager to reordering tasks. Queue Manager doesn't have to be run on any computer taking part in network rendering; it simply needs to be on that network somehow, perhaps even a remote site. Imagine leaving the office for the evening, and being able to check up and manage your network rendering off-site. If you have a remote access account, it's possible.

Setting Up 3DS MAX for Network Rendering

After your computer is properly configured for a network, you're ready to install 3DS MAX's network rendering system. The following sections describe which files should be present in the 3DS MAX directories. You will also learn how to install network rendering while you're installing 3DS MAX, or if you've already installed 3DS MAX, how to configure network rendering after the fact.

The 3DS MAX Directory

What needs to be in your 3DS MAX directory to network render? The answer is, three directories: the main 3DS MAX directory, the Stdplugs directory, and the Network directory. The main elements you don't need are the maps that come with 3DS MAX, as well as the tutorial files.

The Main Directory

Because of 3DS MAX's component architecture, the program lies in several pieces throughout the installed directory. You can find most of the program's critical components in the main 3DS MAX directory, including the 3dsmax.exe file and its main counterpart, core.dll. Several other components are located in the Stdplugs directory.

The Stdplugs (Standard Plug-Ins) Directory

Because 3DS MAX relies on the standard plug-ins to perform specific tasks native to the software, you need to have these files around if you plan set up a network rendering station. These files include things such as the renderer and geometric primitives.

The Network Directory

The network directory contains all centrally located network rendering control files. The network directory on the manager computer keeps a list of current jobs as well as a list of servers currently registered with it. It also contains a file called manager.ini, an initialization file that the manager program uses to set itself up with the proper networking parameters, as well as any default or custom time-out settings. Manager.log contains a history of the manager's interaction with your network rendering system. You can use it to track your manager's performance and tasks assigned to it. Because it is simply an ASCII text file, you can view or print it from the Notepad utility within Windows NT.

A server's network directory mainly contains the current job assigned to it. This can be the MAX file as well as any associated maps. You also can find files called server.ini and server.log. Server.ini contains all the information specific to the server as well as what its manager is. In the installation section, there is a complete description of the options of server.ini. Server.log that is much like manager.log . It contains all the tasks sent to the server as well as Server starting and downing operations.

Third-Party Plug-Ins and Network Rendering

Because 3D Studio MAX is component oriented, there are times when you will have installed a third-party plug-in on your production computer and not on the rendering farm itself. 3DS MAX does not know which plug-ins you intend to use for network rendering; therefore, you must make sure a copy of each third-party plug-in is installed on every network rendering system. Many commercial plug-ins for 3DS MAX use an authorization protection scheme. With this setup, you must call the developer and authorize the plug-in on each machine on which you intend to use it for a fee. Most plug-in developers, however, allow you to install a copy of the plug-in on every computer. Even if the plug-in is not authorized, it can be accessed for rendering purposes—a typical situation for any rendering farm.

Installing Network Rendering with 3DS MAX

To install the network rendering features of 3DS MAX, you must choose the Custom setup option. As a rendering server, you can also choose not to install any sample or tutorial files. If you don't plan to run 3DS MAX for anything other than network rendering, there is no need to install the Sentinel Pro lock drivers. The typical network rendering computer required space is about 15 MB. Figure 29.4 shows the steps involved in setting up a computer properly.

FIGURE 29.4

The installation dialogs for 3DS MAX. Choose Custom Setup, check Manager, Server, or both, and specify a name or address for the Manager.

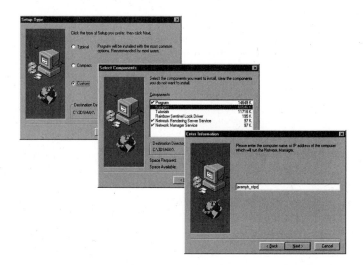

As you continue the installation process, you are prompted to enter the manager computer's name if you chose to install the Server program. At this point, type the manager's computer name or IP address.

NOTE

You cannot use dashes or spaces in computer names for 3DS MAX network rendering.

TIP

Make sure to have your 3DS MAX serialization diskette handy during the installation process. You need it to complete the installation process. Without serializing 3DS MAX, the program will not run.

After you enter the manager's name, a small confirmation of the information you entered appears and the installation process begins. At this point, 3DS MAX will install Manager and Server as NT services. When the installation process is finished, restart the computer to initialize the rendering Manager or Server programs. At this point, you're ready to begin network rendering using that computer. You can now skip to the customizing INI section.

Installing Manager and Server After 3DS MAX

Even if you didn't specify to install the network rendering components for 3DS MAX, they were copied to your hard drive. The only difference is that you must initialize Manager, Server, or both manually. The other option is to rerun the install program and install only the network components. With that method, simply complete the steps in the previous section. The following steps show how to initialize the network rendering components manually. They're also depicted in figure 29.5.

1. Start an MS-DOS session.

2. Navigate to the installed max directory.

3. For a rendering server, type **server -d**. For a rendering manager, type **manager -d**.

Both Manager and Server can run as Windows NT services. If you wish to run them as services, you must run manager and server again but with the -i option to install them to the service group. Otherwise, Manager and Server run in DOS windows, known as Desktop mode. Running in Desktop mode is acceptable and is often the preferred method for new users.

Regardless of which installation method you choose, a Network directory is created and, depending on what you installed, two files: server.ini and manager.ini. Beyond a few parameters, you won't have to edit these files except in extraordinary circumstances. The following sections, however, describe what the various parameters mean, and whether you need to edit them.

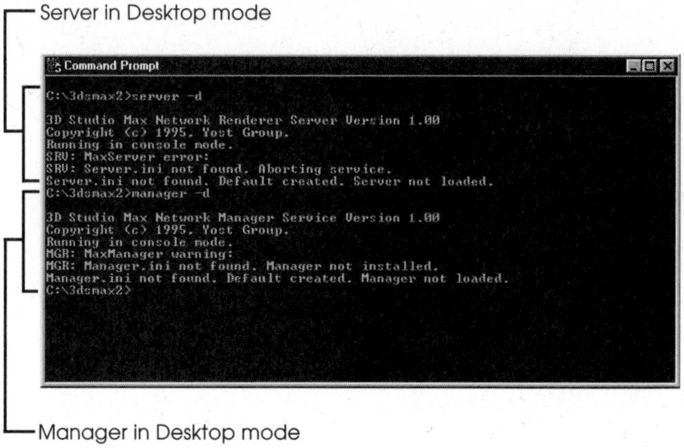

Server in Desktop mode

FIGURE 29.5

*When you run both
Manager and Server
with the -d option for
the first time,
a separate manager.ini
and server.ini are
written.*

Manager in Desktop mode

Server.ini Parameters

The server.ini file, shown in figure 29.6, is perhaps the most critical file in the network rendering process. This file tells the rendering Server computer where to look for the Manager and, most importantly, rendering jobs. The following is a discussion of the parameters contained within the sections of the server.ini file.

Network Configuration

The Manager parameter is the most critical parameter in this file. Only two values can be expressed here: a TCP/IP address or a computer name. Either value must be either the name or address of your network rendering manager. Without the proper information, the computer is not able to take part in network rendering.

The version number specifies which version of the Server program you're running. This number is expressed in hundreds; if your version is 100, it is actually version 1.0. There is no need to edit this value because it does nothing to affect net rendering.

The Port number refers to the "channel" to which the server is tuned. The port number must be the same for all servers talking to the same manager. The only reason to change this number is if you know that another program uses this port value on your network. If that is the case, sometimes it is better to change that program's usage of the port than all your servers.

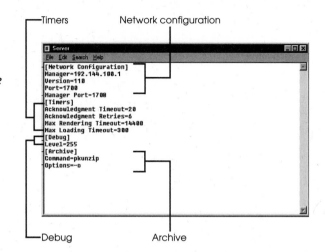

Timers   Network configuration

Debug   Archive

FIGURE 29.6

Although you can edit any of the values in the server.ini file, the most important is the Manager—it specifies the TCP/IP address of the Manager.

The Manager port is similar to the port number for the server except that it needs only to coincide with the Manager port value specified in the manager.ini file. Once again, you probably won't need to change it unless another program is using the same port value.

Timers

Acknowledgment Timeout is the time, in seconds, that the server waits after sending a message, such as a frame complete value. The default is 20 seconds.

Acknowledgment Retries is the number of times a server retries after it has timed out sending a message. If after timing out the number of times specified in this variable, the server marks the offending computer as failed and attempts no further communications with it. The default is six retries.

NOTE

These two timing variables must be the same for both server.ini and manager.ini. If not, it is unlikely that Manager and Server will communicate properly.

Max Rendering Timeout is a value, expressed in seconds of time, that a server has to complete an assigned frame. If the frame is not completed within that time, the server is marked as failed by the manager, and the frame is reassigned to another server. If you're rendering a large scene that is taking more than three hours to render on a single computer, you should probably set this value a little higher. The default is 14,400 seconds, or four hours.

WARNING

Setting the Max Rendering Timeout to any value less than one hour is typically dangerous. If a frame hasn't rendered by the timeout value, 3DS MAX automatically reassigns it to another computer—even if nothing is wrong! Keep the setting at least one hour, even if your frames are taking only 10 minutes.

Max Loading Timeout is the maximum time, expressed in seconds, that it takes 3D Studio MAX to start on a server after the server has acknowledged it has received the rendering task. If 3DS MAX doesn't start within this time, the frame is automatically reassigned to another computer. This timeout usually occurs when one of two things happen: either 3DS MAX hasn't been authorized on the server, or the video drivers haven't been configured. The default is 300 seconds, or five minutes.

Debug

The Level value specifies how much information is conveyed to the user when Server is being run in a DOS window. This value has no effect when you're running Server as an NT service. Also, the Level value doesn't affect what information is exchanged between Manager and Server. With a setting of 0, virtually no information is displayed in the DOS window, whereas a setting of 255 shows all information. Do not edit this value unless the messages coming across the screen are too annoying. The messages often provide useful information when you're trying to troubleshoot your network rendering setup. The default is 255.

Archive

The Command value is the archive program you use to decompress maps when you select the Use Maps options. This program must match the archive program selected in the 3dsmax.ini file. The default is pkunzip.

The Options value sets up any options you might run with the archive program. Remember that network rendering is largely unattended, so set up any options here that ensure that the archive program doesn't ask for user input. Otherwise, you might find every computer just hanging out waiting for you to answer yes to a simple question. You can usually see what options an archive program has by running the archive program with -? or /? after the program name.

Manager.ini Parameters

Much like server.ini, manager.ini is essential to the Manager program running properly. Although it contains many of the same or similar parameters as server.ini, more than likely you will not have to change any of these parameters. The manager.ini file, shown in figure 29.7, is generally left alone because the manager's settings remain constant. Only change the following values if you're experiencing serious problems with rendering across your network.

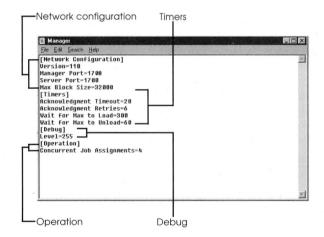

FIGURE 29.7

Notice that many of the sections in the manager.ini file are similar to the server.ini file. You should change these values only in extreme circumstances.

Network Configuration

The version number specifies which version of the Manager program you're running. This number is expressed in hundreds. So, if your version is 100, it is actually version 1.0. There is no need to edit this value because it does nothing to affect network rendering.

The Server Port number refers to the "channel" on which the Manager expects all servers to be communicating. The port number must be the same in both the manager.ini file and all server.ini files. The only reason to change this number is if you know that another program uses this port value on your network. If that is the case, it is better to change that program's usage of the port than all your servers. The default is 1,700.

The Manager port is the channel to which the Manager is tuned. Every server.ini file must have this exact value for its Manager Port entry. Otherwise, the Manager and Server won't communicate. As you can see, changing port numbers for both manager and server INI files can be an enormous task. In other words, don't do it except in extreme cases. The default is 1,708.

Max Block Size refers to the size of the data "chunks," called packets, that are exchanged between the Manager. Tweak this parameter only if you're running into problems submitting large jobs across a phone line or other slow connection. The smaller the value, the less data is included in each packet, but the modem can transmit the packets more easily and quickly. The default value is 32 KB. If you're experiencing problems, try reducing this number.

Timers

Acknowledgment Timeout is the time, in seconds, that the manager waits after sending a message, such as a frame assignment value. The default is 20 seconds.

Acknowledgment Retries is the number of times a server retries after it has timed out sending a message. After timing out the number of times specified in this variable, the manager marks the offending computer as failed and attempts no further communications with it. At that point, you need to use the queue manager client to attempt reconnection. The default is six retries.

NOTE

These two timing variables must be the same for both server.ini and manager.ini. If they're out of sync, there's a good chance that the Manager and Server programs won't communicate properly.

The Wait for 3DS MAX to load value is useful if you're looking to increase or decrease the amount of time allowed for 3DS MAX to load on a server after a job has been assigned to it. If you're submitting large projects to slower computers, you may want to increase its value. The measurement is expressed in seconds. This timeout exists because there are times when 3DS MAX fails to load on a server for one reason or another, with the most common reasons being an unauthorized version of 3DS MAX or missing maps.

Waiting for 3DS MAX to unload is much like the Wait to Load parameter. The parameter exists so that if a server fails to exit normally, it won't be assigned a new job until it is recycled somehow. The default value of 60 seconds should be sufficient for most networks.

Debug

The Level value specifies how much information is conveyed to the user when Manager is being run in a DOS window. The value has no effect when you're running Manager as an NT service. Also, the value doesn't affect what information is exchanged between Manager and Server. With a setting of 0, virtually no information is displayed in the DOS window, whereas a setting of 255 shows all information. Don't edit this value unless the messages coming across the screen are too annoying. They often provide useful information when you're trying to troubleshoot your network rendering setup. The default is 255.

Operation

Concurrent Job Assignment states the number of active jobs a manager can handle at a time. Usually you want to have this value set low. This is to enable the Manager to multitask—if two jobs are sent at different times, each one using a different server, the Manager can handle the assignment of both jobs concurrently. Because MAX files and their associated maps can get large at times, it is a good idea to limit this value unless your manager computer is a super workhorse with beefy network hardware. Most modern networks can handle approximately four to six concurrent assignments, whereas older networks should be set to around two. The reason this number is so important is that each concurrent job assignment that the Manager has to maintain eats processing time from other tasks, such as frame assignment and tracking for currently assigned jobs. The default is 4.

Rendering a Job

If you feel that you're ready to try your hand at network rendering, it is best to start off with only two computers—or one, obviously, if you're using only a one-computer setup. If you can get two computers to talk to each other, you can get a whole room talking as well, provided that the computers are configured similarly. The first section that follows describes running Server and Manager as services, as well as running them in Desktop mode. Read both and decide which one works best for you. In the next section, you see how to assign a job from the 3DS MAX rendering dialog. As well, there is a discussion on setting up maps and map paths.

Running Manager and Server

The first step to getting 3DS MAX network rendering is to initialize the Manager and Server programs on the respective computers. Both Manager and Server can be run in two different modes, as a service and in Desktop mode. Both have their advantages and disadvantages. Depending upon what your particular network setup is like, you need to decide which one best fits your needs.

As a Service

Windows NT can run programs called services to initiate certain system-critical operations. A typical service is the messenger service that enables network administrators to send messages to users on the network. The main benefit of services is that their startup and usage are totally transparent to the user. There is no need to explicitly start them or terminate them. They start when you start the computer, and they stop when you shut down the computer.

When running Server or Manager as a service, the initialization is transparent to you. The only way to determine whether they're running is to issue a network rendering task from 3DS MAX or to go to the Services icon in the Control Panel (see fig. 29.8).

Manager running as a service

FIGURE 29.8

Manager and Server running as services as shown in the Windows NT Services dialog. "Automatic" indicates both services will run when Windows NT boots.

Server running as a service

If you installed the network rendering features from the installation program, Manager and Server are already services. To get to the Control Panel in Windows NT 3.51, do the following:

1. Double-click the Control Panel icon in the main programs group.

2. Double-click the Services icon.

In NT 4.0, complete the following:

1. Click Start, Settings, Control Panel.

2. Double-click the Services icon.

You may see the 3DS MAX Rendering Manager, Server, or both as seen in figure 29.9. Notice that both are Started and set to Automatic—the default. *Started* means that the service has started and is currently running. Although some NT services can be paused, both Manager and Server run only in an On/Off state. *Automatic* means that the service starts Automatically when the computer is started. Other options include Manual or Disabled.

Who should run Manager or Server as an NT service?

- Rendering farms that are unattended 90–100 percent of the time
- Network topologies that span many offices and/or buildings
- Anyone who wants secure, unattended network rendering

The key point here is that the service method is an automatic guarantee that the Server and Manager are running. No human reliance is really necessary. Because a service runs automatically, the power can even go down and come back up. Because NT automatically boots, the service starts with NT and, consequently, the network rendering jobs pick up where they left off.

Services are also more secure. Typically, only administrators can access services. That means that a normal user can work on the computer during the day, and the administrator can take them over at night for net rendering—all remotely, completely transparent to the user at the workstation, except that the word processor may seem a bit slow! A user doesn't have to be logged on to the computer. The rendering station can be sitting at the login prompt, and the service can still be running in the background.

The main flaw of services, oddly enough, is what makes them so good—the level of control and interaction that a user has. When Manager and Server run as a service, they offer no feedback to the user except that 3D Studio MAX renders when it is supposed to. To that end, viewing what is actually going on is impossible, making it a real chore to troubleshoot network rendering. You should run Manager and Server in Desktop mode first. Make sure everything is working properly, test for every possible network rendering scenario you can think of where you're located and then install them as services.

TIP

To uninstall/install Manager or Server as services, run them from the 3DS MAX directory with the -r option.

Service Options

Both Manager and Server have standard service options that you can configure to suit your needs. To change any of the following parameters, you need to click the Startup button in the Services dialog. The Services Options dialog appears (see fig. 29.9).

FIGURE 29.9

FIGURE 29.9

In the Service Options dialog, you can specify startup and logon parameters for each service running in Windows NT.

Service startup options

Service logon options

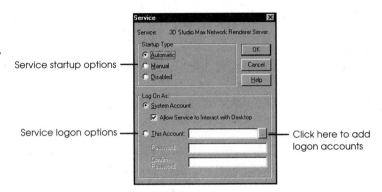

Click here to add logon accounts

The first section enables you to specify how the service starts. Typically, you want to leave this set to Automatic. That way, the Service starts every time NT boots. If you need more control over when the service starts, choose Manual. From that point on, you need to start the service from the Service dialog each time you want to use it. The last option, Disabled, deactivates the services entirely. A user cannot start the service from this panel until either Manual or Automatic is chosen again. If you begin to notice any problems in networking on that computer as a result of the services being installed, sometimes simply disabling them can be a great troubleshooting mechanism.

The next section shows you how to specify the many service logons on to the computer. Services must log on with some account because they are running even before someone is logged on to the computer. By default, the service sets itself to log on using the System Account. This account provides the least amount of access to the network and should be used only if your computer is a one-station setup or all the files are located on each computer and the output is local. If you plan to share map drives or output location on the network, you need to specify some type of account. Whichever account you choose, make sure it has sufficient rights to access network drives. To specify a user, click the More button (three dots) and then choose a user from the list. Make sure the passwords are accurate and confirmed for the user.

NOTE

After you make changes to the service account usage information, you need to stop and restart the service to initialize the new settings.

Removing

If you have already installed Manager or Server as services, you can uninstall/install them by running the executables with the -r option, for example:

c:\3dsmax\server -r

This command removes Server as an NT service, but does not delete it. The same applies for Manager. If the service is currently running, it is stopped and then removed.

In Desktop Mode

Desktop mode provides you with a window into the inner workings of the Manager and Server services. In Desktop mode, the services are run in MS-DOS windows on the desktop. These services function similarly to an installed service except that all connection information is displayed in the respective windows.

To start a service in Desktop mode do the following:

1. Go to the Main program group and double-click the MS-DOS icon.

2. Navigate to the installed max directory and type **server -d**.

Substitute Manager if you want to run the Manager in Desktop mode as well. If you want to run both at the same time, repeat the steps above. NT enables you to have multiple sessions.

NOTE

If you get an error message that states "Port is in use," you need to stop the service in the Services dialog.

Installing as a Service

After you feel comfortable running 3DS MAX in Desktop mode and want to make the transition to running it as a service, do the following:

1. Go to the Main program group and double-click the MS-DOS icon.

2. Navigate to the installed 3DS MAX directory and type **server -i**.

Substitute Manager if that is what you want to install. From that point, follow the same directions for running Manager or Server as a service outlined in the previous section. (See figure 29.10.)

FIGURE 29.10

The Manager and Server running in Desktop mode as MS-DOS sessions. Note that after both are initialized, they begin communicating with each other.

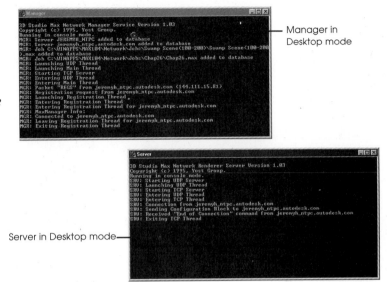

Manager in Desktop mode

Server in Desktop mode

The Job Assignment Dialog

When you're ready to Network render, check the Net Render option in the rendering dialog from within 3DS MAX. At that point, the Job Assignment dialog appears as seen in figure 29.11. The Job Assignment window enables you to specify a manager to which to send the job as well as the servers you wish to use. That and other options are discussed in the following sections.

NOTE

Both Manager and Server have to be running for any of the steps in this section to work properly.

FIGURE 29.11

The name Swamp Scene (100–200) is the job's name with the Include Maps option selected. Note that two servers are available for rendering.

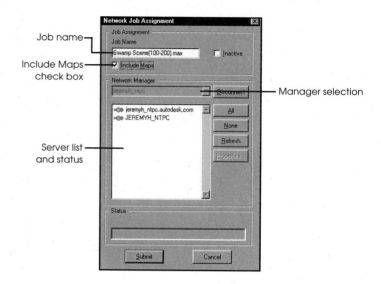

Job name

Include Maps check box

Manager selection

Server list and status

The Job Name

The Job Name field enables you to specify a name for the job that is displayed in the Queue Manager. Pick a name that is representative of what you're rendering. If you are rendering a swamp scene from frames 100–200, for instance, the name may be

Swamp Scene(100–200)

With this type of naming, anyone who looks at the job list instantly knows what the scene is and how many frames of that scene are being rendered. If a job exists with the current name you have selected, you are warned, and you have to choose another name before continuing.

WARNING

When naming jobs, note that you cannot use ";", "\", or "/" as part of the name. 3DS MAX reports an error if you try to do so.

NOTE

All current jobs are given their own directories, based on the job name in the Manager's network directory.

The Include Maps Option

The include maps feature is, by far, the best new addition to network rendering. Consequently, it is also one of the most troublesome, if you don't have it set up properly. Configuring this option incorrectly could cause your entire job to fail. So what does it do? When this box is checked, 3D Studio MAX archives the scene and all its associated maps into one file and distributes that file to each server. When the file reaches the server, it is unarchived and the rendering process begins, ensuring that every computer has exactly the same maps, and as a result, almost no rendering using this method fails. But what are the caveats?

- Each server must have the same archiving program installed as the computer issuing the rendering job using the Include Maps option.

- Each server must have access, through path settings, to the archiving program specified in the server.ini file.

- Only one archiving program can be used for a rendering farm.

- If the proper options aren't specified in the server.ini file, a server may fail. This usually happens when the archiving program requests user input, such as a confirmation.

Wᴀʀɴɪɴɢ

Both PKZIP and PKUNZIP are limited to the DOS naming convention (eight-character name and three-character extension). All operations that use the Include Maps option, (Job names, map files, and scene files) must adhere to this format.

Picking a Manager

Because it is possible to have multiple managers present on a network, you need to choose one to use for your rendering job. The manager you specify can be either by name or TCP/IP address. 3D Studio MAX remembers the last four managers entered in the Manager drop-down list.

After you choose the manager you want to use, click the Connect button. If everything is set up properly, 3DS MAX connects, and a list of the servers registered with that manager appears. If nothing appears or you receive a connection refused message, you have several problems to check out.

1. Make sure Manager is running on the computer you want to use as a manager.

2. If Manager is running, check to see whether you typed the right computer name or IP address in the Job Assignment dialog.

3. If 3DS MAX appears to connect but no servers are listed, make sure Server is running on each computer you intend to render on.

4. Last, check to see whether each computer is physically connected to the network. You can usually do this by going to the File Manager (or Network Neighborhood in NT 4.0) and trying to connect to each computer.

The colored dots that appear next to their name indicate the server's current status. See the next section to understand and manage servers and the various states in which they may be.

Server States

Servers can be in four potential states, Ready (green), Busy (yellow), Running MAX (gray), and Error (red). You typically see yellow while other jobs are currently rendering on that server. Gray displays when 3DS MAX is running on that computer in Normal (non-server) mode and cannot be used until that 3DS MAX session ends or that Server is not currently running on that machine. A Red dot signifies some kind of problem. This usually happens when a previous job failed on that server, and the server is in a holding pattern until the job is either canceled or the situation that caused the error is resolved.

No matter what state the server is in, you can assign your job to it. The only purpose of the colored dots is to make you aware of what the current status of the server is. Assigning your job to that server ensures that as soon as that server is available, it will pick up your job and begin rendering. If a computer is in an error state, however, you first have to remove it from that job using the Queue Manager. Otherwise the server can never pick up your job.

Map Paths, Shared Drives, and UNC

Perhaps the most challenging part of getting network rendering right is the use of texture maps across the network. Computers can access multiple directories on multiple computers and pull down multiple versions of the same file. This can result in mass confusion not only while working on the project, but it also can be a nightmare when it comes to rendering the scene across the network. In this section, you learn the best way to organize your network rendering farm to load maps and save files.

Map Central

In setups in which several people are working on a scene, access to maps at a central location is necessary. Everyone involved always has access to the most recent version of textures on which the 2D artists have worked. In Windows NT, this type of setup is common. Computers can mount drives on other computers, known as *shared drives*, and utilize the drives just as if they were local to their computer. Having a central location for maps is key to organizing network rendering.

WARNING

Novell-based network servers understand only the DOS naming structure—eight characters with a three-character extension (8.3).

You can use the following organizational steps to make sure your maps are loaded by every rendering server during a net render:

1. At the beginning of a project, set up a location on your network where everyone on the project has access. Then make directories for maps and scenes. Give the directories a meaningful name.

2. Next, have every person on the project connect to the central computer by using the same path and drive letter. For instance, have everyone access the maps as drive letter M. You can do this in File Manager or by using Network Neighborhood in NT 4.0. Make sure you specify to reconnect to this drive at logon. That way, the user is always connected to that drive by using the same drive letter each time they log on.

   If possible, place maps and scenes in the same directory. 3DS MAX looks for maps for a scene in the same directory where it loaded the scene the first time. From there, it looks in the map paths directories.

3. If you have a rendering farm or other computers that aren't used in the production except for rendering, set up the drive letter assignment the exact same way as the other computers. If you were using the previous example, for instance, every server would be connected to the maps directory also using the drive letter M.

4. If you cannot use the same drive letter, connect to the computer using any drive letter. The key here is to make sure the computers are connected.

When the file is sent to be network rendered, it looks first in the same directory as the MAX file, and then it searches out the maps in the directories specified in the MAX file itself. Finally, it looks in the map paths configured in the Configure Paths option in the file pull-down menu.

NOTE

Map paths are stored in the 3dsmax.ini file for a particular computer.

If you use the steps previously mentioned, all the maps should be picked up by the second step. Here's the reason.

3DS MAX uses what is known as UNC (Universal Naming Convention) for map path storage. This means that a map named weave1.tga stored on a computer named Mapserver in the Carpets directory would be stored in the .max file as

\\MAPSERVER\CARPETS\WEAVE1.TGA.

WARNING

3DS MAX will "hardwire" the directory of a locally stored map file. As a result, even if the file is available on a network somewhere, the server will attempt to find the file in the same directory on the server's hard drive. To avoid having this problem, make sure all maps are stored and accessed in the material editor from a common location on some networked map server.

Notice that no drive letter is stored in the path information. UNC doesn't rely on letters, it only relies on computer names. That's why you can be connected to the computer by using any drive letter. As long as you're connected, 3DS MAX will find the map. Note that if you want to have the UNC information for a file that is stored locally, you can connect to your computer through File Manager.

Output Paths

Much of the same information for setting up map paths for a network rendering farm applies to output directories. After the file is rendered, where does it go?

Once again, setting up a common location for output is critical for rendering farms. If 3D Studio MAX cannot write the rendered file, the rendering server fails on that particular job. You can use much of the same logic to specify where files go after they're rendered. The following organizational steps outline how to best configure paths in a net rendering setup.

1. Set up a directory on a central computer where you wish to have all the output from a rendering stored and make sure everyone has access to the directory.

2. Have all users connect to the drive. For convenience, use a drive letter that makes sense, such as O. Make sure that all other computers taking place in network rendering are also connected to that computer and directory.

3. Once a job is rendered using network rendering, instruct every user to send output in the Rendering dialog to that computer and directory.

    Because 3DS MAX uses UNC, as long as the computer's connected, it is able to output to the location specified.

Single Computers and Maps

Much of what you have read applies to a multiple computer setup. If you're using a single computer to do batch rendering, your job for setting up map paths and output directories is much simpler.

The easiest way to make sure that a job finds all maps is to use the Configure Paths option in the File pull-down menu and add as many map paths as you need. If you're loading maps from another computer somewhere on the network, you have two options. The easiest and fastest method is to copy the files local to your computer. If you can't copy the files because of space constraints, create a map path to that computer. You first have to connect to the computer, however, using File Manager or Network Neighborhood.

N OTE ───

For faster map loading, reorganize the map paths so that the directories where maps are located are toward the top of the list. 3D Studio MAX searches for maps by using this list in descending order.

Output is even easier. Specify a location on your hard drive or on the network to store the files.

The only caveat to loading maps from the network or sending output to the network is that if the network goes down for any reason, your rendering job fails. If space on your hard drive is a concern, it's best to clear off noncritical data by storing it somewhere on the network and moving the maps onto your hard drive. Remember that 3DS MAX fails if it can't find even one map, or cannot store the rendered image in the location you specified. With respect to output, there is no contingency for looking for other hard drives or directories to store images in other places as a backup.

Network Rendering to FLCs and AVIs

Network rendering is primarily intended to render out still frames, but you may want to use it to render AVI or FLC files. The problem with AVI or FLC files is that they need to be assembled linearly. Frames must be submitted one after another. With network rendering, frames can finish rendering totally out of sequence. Because of this limitation, when you choose FLC or AVI as the output file format, you are limited to network rendering on only one server. 3DS MAX does not enable you to choose more than one server. So how would you distribute a rendering across several computers using AVI or FLC as output? Easy. Use Video Post. The following sections describe how to use multiple computers to render out an AVI or FLC file, all using 3DS MAX.

Rendering from the Render Dialog

You can render AVIs or FLCs from the Rendering dialog by using network rendering as you normally would to render a sequence of still images. Then you can use Video Post to assemble them into an AVI or FLC. The following steps describe this process:

1. Choose the resolution to which you want to render. Remember that FLC and AVI files usually should be a lower resolution image than still frames.

2. Choose a still file format to which to render—TGA, TIF, JPG, and so on.

3. Next, choose the Net Render option.

4. Choose the Manager and servers as you normally would and then click Submit.

5. The frames are rendered as sequential still frames, distributed across the network.

Skip to the section "Putting It All Together" to see how to assemble all the frames into an AVI or FLC.

Rendering from Video Post

Video Post does not enable you to render FLC or AVI at all whether or not you want only to use one computer. The main reason for this is that Video Post opens each frame as a rendering session when it begins to render and closes the session when the frame is complete. Neither AVI nor FLC, when closed, cannot be reopened to add frames unless you're using a package such as Animator Pro or Animator Studio. As a result, Video Post can render only one frame from a FLC or AVI sequence—not usually the desired effect. You can render to the network, however, using Video Post via still frame output. Then you can reuse Video Post to assemble your still frames into an FLC or AVI. See the next section, "Putting It All Together," for instructions. To render out still frames from Video Post, complete the following steps:

1. Set up your Video Post queue, with all the transitions, filters, and compositing effects you need.

2. Add an Image Output event at the end of your Video Post queue and choose the output to be a still frame file format such as TGA, TIF, JPG, and so on.

3. Click the Execute Sequence button. Select the frames you want to render and the desired resolution.

4. Choose the Net Render option and then submit the job to the Manager using the servers you want.

Your animation is rendered to a sequence of still frames. From here you're ready to go on to the next section.

Putting It All Together

Now that you have the entire sequence of frames rendered, you can use Video Post to assemble them into an FLC or AVI. Video Post enables you to take sequentially numbered frames via an Image Input Event and save the result using an Image Output event to an FLC or AVI. Use the following steps to accomplish this:

1. Go to Video Post and Add an Image Input event.

2. Choose the Files button in the dialog.

3. Select the First frame from your sequence, delete the number from it, and add an asterisk in its place followed by the file extension. Click OK.

4. 3D Studio MAX automatically creates an IFL file (Image File List) that contains all the names of all of the images that are part of your sequence.

5. Add an Image Output event.

6. Choose the Files button and type a name for your file. Your file name should include an FLC or AVI extension.

7. Execute the sequence and choose Render.

3D Studio MAX and Video Post load each file from your sequential list and output it to an AVI or FLC file as seen in figure 29.12. This file must be rendered locally. Unfortunately, you cannot render this part to the network, but this method is a sufficient workaround if you need to render output from either the Rendering dialog or Video Post that used net rendering to an AVI or FLC.

FIGURE 29.12
Video Post with an IFL sequence assigned and set to render to an AVI file.

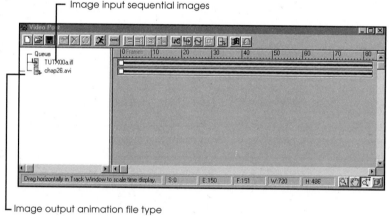

Image input sequential images

Image output animation file type

Using Queue Manager

You have your computer talking to the network and rendering away. Now how do you control this thing? All control elements for network rendering exist in the Queue Manager. The Queue Manager icon is located in the Kinetix program group with the rest of the 3DS MAX-related icons. You can use Queue Manager to control all network rendering functions—from activating jobs to specifying what times a computer is available for rendering. You can run Queue Manager on any 32-bit Windows operating system and control the queue as long as the computer is hooked to the network. See figure 29.13 for a breakdown of the Queue Manager Interface.

Current manager   Job/server status window

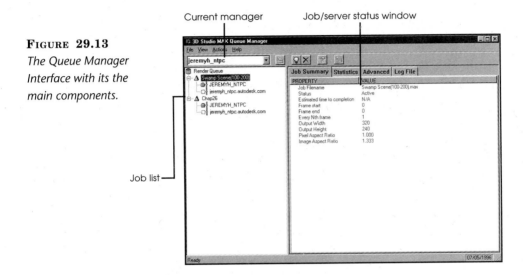

FIGURE 29.13

The Queue Manager Interface with its the main components.

Job list

Job Control

Sometimes you need to escalate a job's priority in the rendering process or delegate when a server is available for rendering. All of this functionality is available through the Queue Manager. This section outlines key components in the Queue Manager that help you control the network rendering process.

Job and Server Priority

A job's priorities are ordered in descending priority. The jobs at the top of the queue receive priority over the later jobs. A job is rendered in the order it was received. Sometimes you want to reorder a job, however, so that it is completed before current jobs. With 3D Studio MAX 1.1, reordering a job is a trivial process. Just click on the job name you want to reorder and drag it to the place you want in the queue. 3D Studio MAX will automatically stop any jobs that now appear after your newly positioned job (if they were running) and begin rendering yours.

Scheduling Servers

Rendering servers are often used during the day as workstations for other tasks. Even if a computer is being used for another task, it can be used for network rendering purposes—as long as it is not running 3DS MAX. A job could be assigned to someone's computer while they're working in, for example, a 2D paint program. Needless to say, running 3D Studio MAX's rendering system and a sophisticated 2D paint program at the same time slows the computer to a crawl and potentially makes the user irate. To avoid this, you can specify through the Queue Manager interface when rendering servers are available for network rendering (see fig. 29.14).

FIGURE 29.14

The Server scheduling dialog. Through this window, you can block off one hour increments for Server availability.

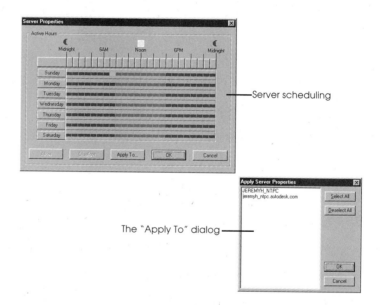

Right-click on any server and choose Properties. From there, you can select which hours the server is available or unavailable. The primary purpose of this window is to disable servers during certain times. By default, all servers are active all hours. Within this dialog, you can click and drag over the hours or a specific day(s) to disable a server. To do the same for a group of servers, use the Apply To button.

NOTE

After you set availability for a server, that availability remains in place until you change it. The only way to change the times that server can be rendered to is by creating a fake, inactive job. From there, you can go into the Queue Manager and change the scheduling of the server.

In Practice: Network Rendering

- **Server-based networking**   As a result of this new implementation in 3DStudio MAX 1.1, you can now assign multiple jobs and as servers complete one job, they'll automatically move on to the next job. This is regardless of whether another server is still working on the same job.

- **Unique TCP/IP addressing**   In order for network rendering to work properly, each computer must have a unique IP address. The best implementation is to use the 192 prefix for your address and then follow the last three number sequences with a meaningful combination that can be applied across all computers.

- **Desktop mode**   The best way to get a handle on networking is to run services in Desktop mode. That way, you'll see all communication between the manager and its servers when you need to troubleshoot your net rendering setup. Once you feel comfortable with your setup, you can run both programs as Windows NT services.

- **Map organization**   When you're working with a large network, it's always a good idea to have all users place maps at a central storage location. All rendering servers should have access to that location. With this method, you'll never have to worry about a failed rendering due to missing map files.

- **Animation file output**   Because rendering an animation file such as FLC or AVI from MAX across a network is not possible, you can use video post as a workaround. Render your animation to a sequence of still frames, much like a flip book, and use video post to compile the sequence into an animation format on one computer.

TEXTURE REFERENCE

The Texture Reference is a gallery of thumbnails of the textures found on the CD-ROM. The files are located in the NRPMAPS directory. All texture maps were created by Forcade & Associates.

ADIPOSE.TIF

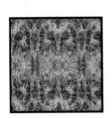

ADIPOSE2.TIF

ADIPOSE3.TIF

ALAGIEG1.TIF

ALAGIEG2.TIF

ALAGIEG3.TIF

ALAGIEG4.TIF

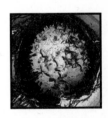

AMBER.TIF

ANNEAL.TIF

BANDOID.TIF

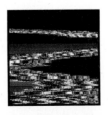

BANDOID2.TIF

BANDOID3.TIF

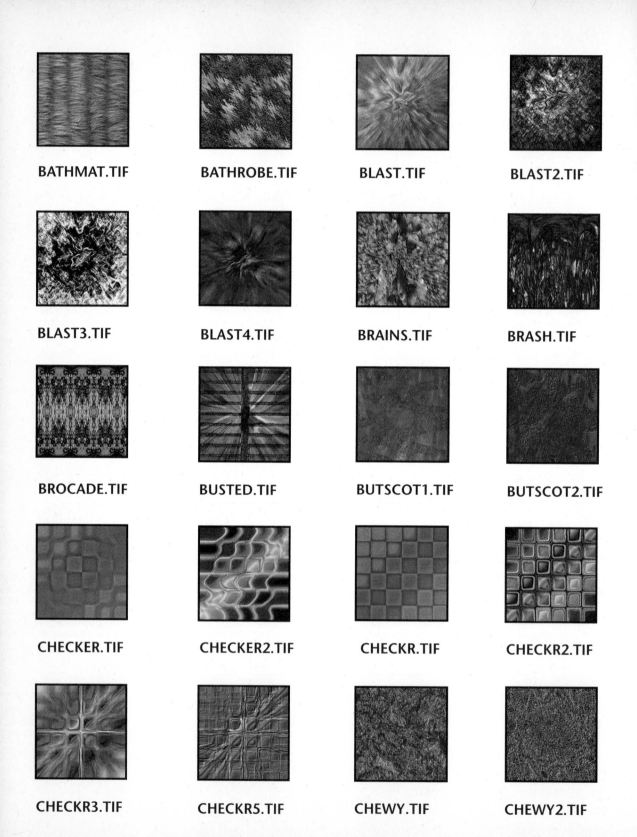

BATHMAT.TIF BATHROBE.TIF BLAST.TIF BLAST2.TIF

BLAST3.TIF BLAST4.TIF BRAINS.TIF BRASH.TIF

BROCADE.TIF BUSTED.TIF BUTSCOT1.TIF BUTSCOT2.TIF

CHECKER.TIF CHECKER2.TIF CHECKR.TIF CHECKR2.TIF

CHECKR3.TIF CHECKR5.TIF CHEWY.TIF CHEWY2.TIF

CHOPD.TIF

CIRCL01.TIF

CIRCL02.TIF

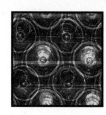

CIRCL03.TIF

CLOCK.TIF

CONDNSR1.TIF

CONDNSR2.TIF

CRINKL01.TIF

CRINKL02.TIF

CRNKCHK.TIF

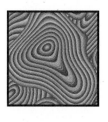

CHOPCIR2.TIF

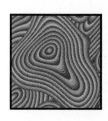

CHOPCIR3.TIF

CROPCIRC.TIF

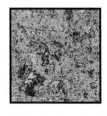

CURDSWRL.TIF

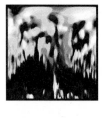

DRIP1.TIF

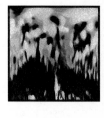

DRIP2.TIF

DRYLAVA.TIF

DRYLAVA1.TIF

EELRNCH1.TIF

EELRNCH2.TIF

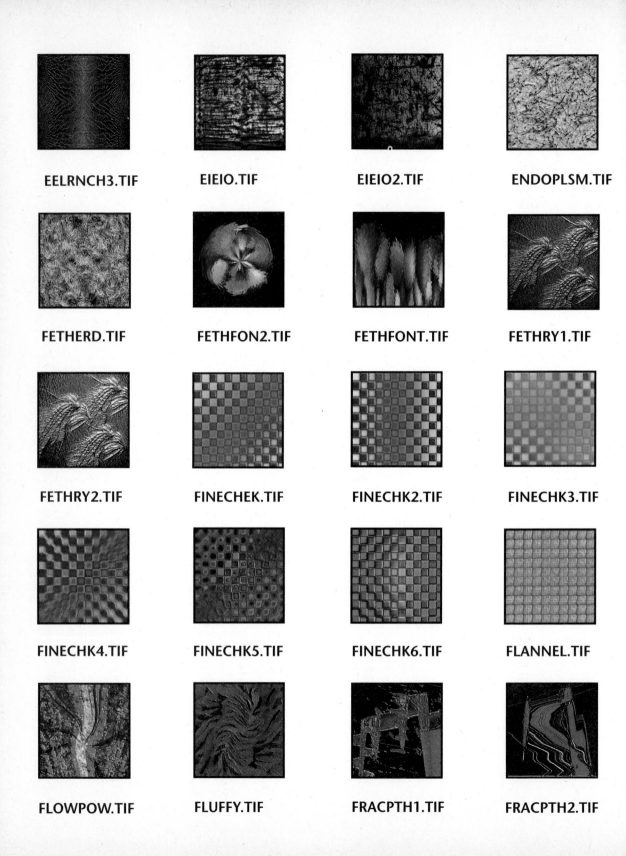

EELRNCH3.TIF

EIEIO.TIF

EIEIO2.TIF

ENDOPLSM.TIF

FETHERD.TIF

FETHFON2.TIF

FETHFONT.TIF

FETHRY1.TIF

FETHRY2.TIF

FINECHEK.TIF

FINECHK2.TIF

FINECHK3.TIF

FINECHK4.TIF

FINECHK5.TIF

FINECHK6.TIF

FLANNEL.TIF

FLOWPOW.TIF

FLUFFY.TIF

FRACPTH1.TIF

FRACPTH2.TIF

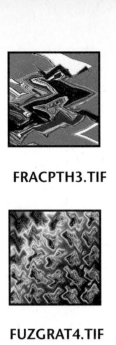

FRACPTH3.TIF

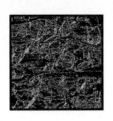

FROST.TIF

FUZGRAT2.TIF

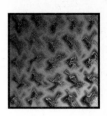

FUZGRAT3.TIF

FUZGRAT4.TIF

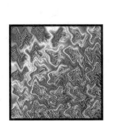

FUZGRAT5.TIF

FUZGRAT6.TIF

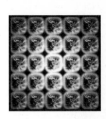

FUZGRATE.TIF

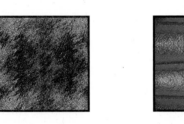

GRANWAV.TIF

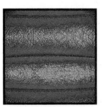

HAIRY.TIF

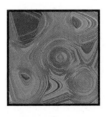

HAPPY1.TIF

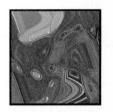

HAPPY2.TIF

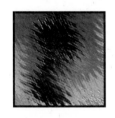

HATCH.TIF

HEMP1.TIF

HEMP2.TIF

HEMP3.TIF

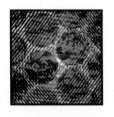

HOLES1.TIF

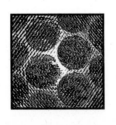

HOLES2.TIF

ICON.TIF

LEAF01.TIF

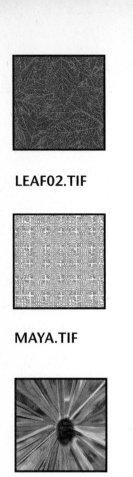 LEAF02.TIF

 LEAF03.TIF

 LEAF04.TIF

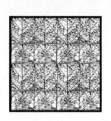 LEAF05.TIF

 MAYA.TIF

 MEATWAVE.TIF

 MELON.TIF

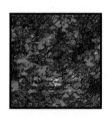 MELON02.TIF

 MELVINED.TIF

 MELTSCRN.TIF

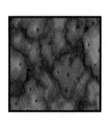 MOLD.TIF

 MUNG.TIF

 NOVA.TIF

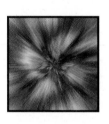 NOVA2.TIF

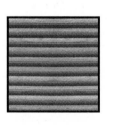 PEGSO1.TIF

 PEPPERD.TIF

 PINWHEEL.TIF

 POINT.TIF

 PULLD.TIF

 RADIAL.TIF

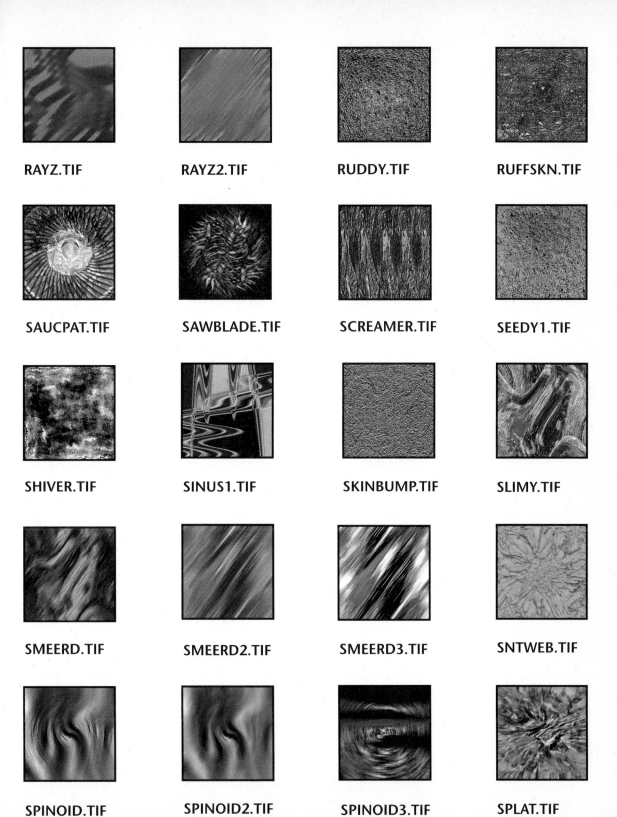

RAYZ.TIF   RAYZ2.TIF   RUDDY.TIF   RUFFSKN.TIF

SAUCPAT.TIF   SAWBLADE.TIF   SCREAMER.TIF   SEEDY1.TIF

SHIVER.TIF   SINUS1.TIF   SKINBUMP.TIF   SLIMY.TIF

SMEERD.TIF   SMEERD2.TIF   SMEERD3.TIF   SNTWEB.TIF

SPINOID.TIF   SPINOID2.TIF   SPINOID3.TIF   SPLAT.TIF

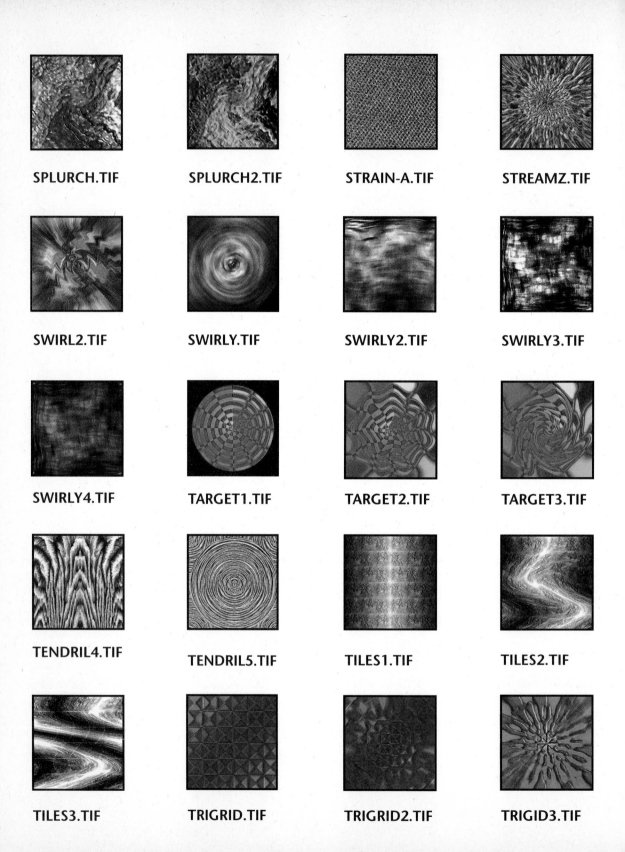

SPLURCH.TIF

SPLURCH2.TIF

STRAIN-A.TIF

STREAMZ.TIF

SWIRL2.TIF

SWIRLY.TIF

SWIRLY2.TIF

SWIRLY3.TIF

SWIRLY4.TIF

TARGET1.TIF

TARGET2.TIF

TARGET3.TIF

TENDRIL4.TIF

TENDRIL5.TIF

TILES1.TIF

TILES2.TIF

TILES3.TIF

TRIGRID.TIF

TRIGRID2.TIF

TRIGID3.TIF

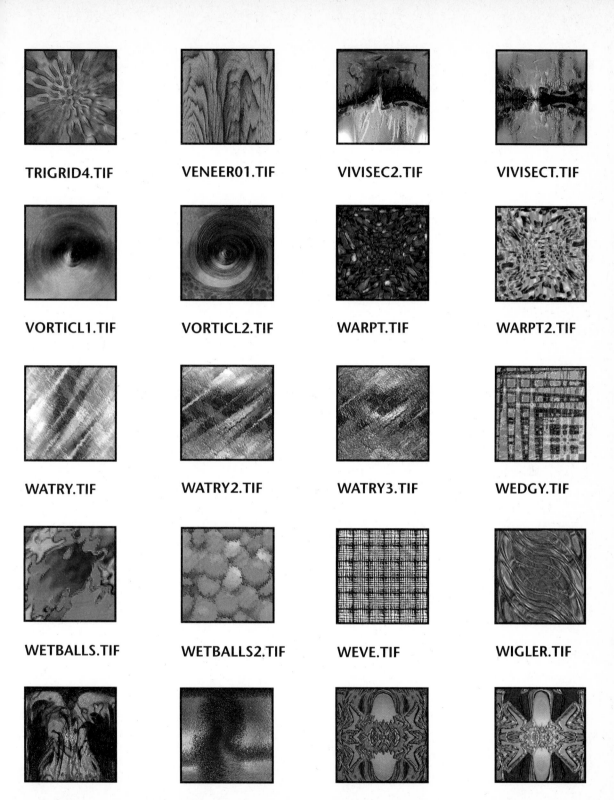

TRIGRID4.TIF VENEER01.TIF VIVISEC2.TIF VIVISECT.TIF

VORTICL1.TIF VORTICL2.TIF WARPT.TIF WARPT2.TIF

WATRY.TIF WATRY2.TIF WATRY3.TIF WEDGY.TIF

WETBALLS.TIF WETBALLS2.TIF WEVE.TIF WIGLER.TIF

WINGS.TIF WOOS4.TIF YIKES.TIF YIKE2.TIF

ZAPWART1.TIF   ZAPWART2.TIF   ZAPWART3.TIF   ZAPWART4.TIF

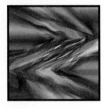 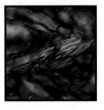  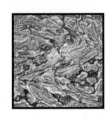

ZEED.TIF   ZEED2.TIF   ZEED3.TIF   ZEED4.TIF

Index

WANT MORE INFORMATION?

CHECK OUT THESE RELATED TOPICS OR SEE YOUR LOCAL BOOKSTORE

CAD and 3D Studio

As the number one CAD publisher in the world, and as a Registered Publisher of Autodesk, New Riders Publishing provides unequaled content on this complex topic. Industry-leading products include AutoCAD and 3D Studio.

Networking

As the leading Novell NetWare publisher, New Riders Publishing delivers cutting-edge products for network professionals. We publish books for all levels of users, from those wanting to gain NetWare Certification, to those administering or installing a network. Leading books in this category include *Inside NetWare 3.12, CNE Training Guide: Managing NetWare Systems, Inside TCP/IP,* and *NetWare: The Professional Reference.*

Graphics

New Riders provides readers with the most comprehensive product tutorials and references available for the graphics market. Best-sellers include *Inside CorelDRAW! 5, Inside Photoshop 3,* and *Adobe Photoshop NOW!*

Internet and Communications

As one of the fastest growing publishers in the communications market, New Riders provides unparalleled information and detail on this ever-changing topic area. We publish international best-sellers such as *New Riders' Official Internet Yellow Pages, 2nd Edition,* a directory of over 10,000 listings of Internet sites and resources from around the world, and *Riding the Internet Highway, Deluxe Edition.*

Operating Systems

Expanding off our expertise in technical markets, and driven by the needs of the computing and business professional, New Riders offers comprehensive references for experienced and advanced users of today's most popular operating systems, including *Understanding Windows 95, Inside Unix, Inside Windows 3.11 Platinum Edition, Inside OS/2 Warp Version 3,* and *Inside MS-DOS 6.22.*

Other Markets

Professionals looking to increase productivity and maximize the potential of their software and hardware should spend time discovering our line of products for Word, Excel, and Lotus 1-2-3. These titles include *Inside Word 6 for Windows, Inside Excel 5 for Windows, Inside 1-2-3 Release 5,* and *Inside WordPerfect for Windows.*

Orders/Customer Service **1-800-653-6156** Source Code **NRP95**

New Riders Publishing 201 West 103rd Street ◆ Indianapolis, Indiana 46290 USA

www.mcp.com/newriders/MAX

The One-Stop Resource for 3D Studio MAX Information

This site is constantly updated to bring you the most current information available. At New Riders' 3DS MAX Web site, you'll find:

- Plug-in reviews and demos
- Hardware and software reviews
- Image and animation galleries
- Tips and techniques
- Bug reports
- Shareware bank

At the 3DS MAX Web site, you can also get the latest information on our upcoming 3DS MAX titles and get updates to *Inside 3D Studio MAX Volume I.*

Reserve Your Copies Today!

Build on the knowledge you gained from *Inside 3D Studio MAX Volume I*

Inside 3D Studio MAX Volume II: Advanced Modeling & Material Editor

Go beyond the basic concepts of modeling and using the Material Editor to master the full functionality provided by 3DS MAX. Real-world examples teach you how to create top-quality models and materials that will make your images and animations stand out above the rest. Detailed coverage of:

- Patch Modeling
- Modeling for the Web
- Morphs and Booleans
- Using Multiple Maps
- Creating Animated Materials
- 3D Paint Programs

ISBN: 1-56205-679-4 $54.99 USA   CD-ROM Included
Available February 1997

Inside 3D Studio MAX Volume III: Animation & Character Studio

Learn the secrets to creating cutting-edge animations that keep you one-step ahead of the competition. High-end animation techniques are explained through hands-on tutorials that are supplemented with tips and notes from the industry's hottest animators. Also, explore Character Studio and the new world of character animation. Detailed coverage of:

- Animating Cameras and Lights
- Character Animation
- Biped and Physique
- Space Warps and Particles
- Video Post

ISBN: 1-56205-699-9 $54.99 USA   CD-ROM Included
Available February 1997

Order Now! 1-800-428-5331   **Source Code NRP96**

201 West 103rd Street, Indianapolis, Indiana 46290

Name _____ Title _____

Company _____ Type of business _____

Address _____

City/State/ZIP _____ E-mail: _____

Would you like to be on our *Inside 3D Studio MAX* e-mail update list? ☐ yes ☐ no

Which other New Riders' books have you used before? _____

_____

How many computer books do you purchase each year? ☐ 1–5 ☐ 6 or more

How did you learn about this book? _____

Where did you purchase this book? _____

What other graphics and 3D applications do you use aside from 3DS MAX? _____

_____

What other types of graphics and 3DS MAX books would you like to see? _____

_____

How do you use 3DS MAX? _____

_____

Comments: _____

_____

_____

_____

Don't forget to visit the New Riders 3D Studio MAX Web site!
http://www.mcp.com/newriders/MAX

New Riders Publishing   201 West 103rd Street ◆ Indianapolis, Indiana 46290 USA

Fax to **317-581-7448**   Orders/Customer Service **1-800-653-6156**   Source Code **NRP95**

Fold Here

NO POSTAGE
NECESSARY
IF MAILED
IN THE
UNITED STATES

BUSINESS REPLY MAIL

FIRST-CLASS MAIL PERMIT NO. 9918 INDIANAPOLIS IN

POSTAGE WILL BE PAID BY THE ADDRESSEE

**NEW RIDERS PUBLISHING
201 W 103RD ST
INDIANAPOLIS IN 46290-9058**